Encyclopedia of

World Environmental History

Encyclopedia of

World
Environmental
History

Shepard Krech III
J. R. McNeill
Carolyn Merchant
Editors

Volume 2 F–N

A Berkshire Reference Work

Routledge
New York London

Published in 2004 by

Routledge
29 West 35th Street
New York, NY 10001
www.routledge-ny.com

Published in Great Britain by
Routledge
11 New Fetter Lane
London EC4P 4EE
www.routledge.co.uk

Routledge is an imprint of the Taylor and Francis Group.
A Berkshire Reference Work
314 Main Street, Suite 12
Great Barrington, MA 01230
berkshirepublishing.com

10 9 8 7 6 5 4 3 2 1

Library of Congress Cataloging-in-Publication Data

ISBN 0-415-93732-9 (set)
ISBN 0-415-93733-7 (vol. 1)
ISBN 0-415-93734-5 (vol. 2)
ISBN 0-415-93735-3 (vol. 3)

Encyclopedia of world environmental history / Shepard Krech III, J.R. McNeill,
Carolyn Merchant, editors.
     p. cm.
Includes bibliographical references and index.
  ISBN 0-415-93732-9 (set : acid-free paper) — ISBN 0-415-93733-7 (v. 1 :
acid-free paper) — ISBN 0-415-93734-5 (v. 2 : acid-free paper) — ISBN 0-415-
93735-3 (v. 3 : acid-free paper)
  1. Human ecology—Encyclopedias. 2. Human beings—Effect of environment
on—Encyclopedias. 3. Nature—Effect of human beings on—Encyclopedias.
I. Krech, Shepard, 1944– II. McNeill, John Robert. III. Merchant, Carolyn.
  GF10.E63 2003
  304.2'03—dc21

                                              2003008288

Printed in the United States of America on acid-free paper.

CONTENTS

Famine *See* Droughts

Fascism

The history of fascism's relationship to the natural environment is complex and contradictory. Whereas some fascists have adopted a back-to-nature approach, others have been utterly indifferent to environmental concerns. When they have achieved state power, fascist regimes have displayed a markedly ambivalent environmental record. From large-scale programs of ecological restoration and nature protection to unprecedented military and industrial assaults on the landscape across several continents, fascism presents one of the most enigmatic political and economic systems to have left its mark on environmental history.

Fascism itself is notoriously difficult to define. Scholars have long disagreed over the basic contours of fascism as an ideology and as a movement. The rare moments of consensus on the question "what is fascism?" have been overshadowed by controversies about which ideologies and movements the term might apply to.

Usually regarded as a right-wing phenomenon, fascism also borrows from the left. It is both populist and elitist, combining mass mobilization with rigid hierarchies of command and obedience. Fascism is built around chauvinistic nationalism, extreme authoritarianism, and imperial ambitions for territorial expansion and conquest. It invokes a cult of the supreme leader, glorifies militarism and war, and depends on the violent repression of opposition. Fascism preaches a seductive mythology of overcoming decadence through spiritual renewal and the restoration of past glory. It promises a spurious vision of community at the expense of racial, ethnic, and political scapegoats. Dictatorship is its characteristic form, accompanied by varying degrees of state control over all aspects of culture and public life.

As an economic system, fascism occupies an ambiguous territory between traditional capitalist mechanisms and the attempt to supersede them in a totalitarian new order. The emergence of fascist movements is itself a response to the crises and contradictions endemic to capitalism. An unsteady alliance with existing elites is typically necessary for fascists to come to power, and the first priority of a new fascist regime is the destruction of working-class institutions and an onslaught against the left. Although the infrastructure of private property, production for profit, and market exchange is largely retained, effective control over major economic decisions is transferred to the organs of the fascist party, which become nearly indistinguishable from the state.

Along with its guiding vision of national regeneration, a quasi-religious sense of salvation animates the fascist worldview. Fascism's alluring promises of a healthier future represent a form of perverted utopianism. Against inauthenticity and superficiality, fascism offers an imaginary transcendence, a cathartic redemption from the corruptions of the mundane world. Rejecting the humanist ideals of the Enlightenment, fascism celebrates irrationalism and myth. Although its ideology is eclectic and ephemeral, its real-world effects are frighteningly consistent: betrayal of those it purports to save and the brutal exclusion and even extermination of those it regards as its enemies.

The history of fascism divides into two main periods: the era of classical fascism, in the first half of the twentieth century, and the era of neo-fascism, from 1945 onward. Classical fascism was primarily a European phenomenon, with indigenous fascist parties appearing in Portugal, Spain, France, Britain, Belgium, the Netherlands, Austria, Romania, Hungary, Norway, and elsewhere by the 1930s. The two countries where classical fascism had the greatest impact were Italy and Germany, but fascism also took root in Latin America and North America as well as in parts of Asia and Africa. Some scholars consider imperial Japan, the ally of fascist Italy and Nazi Germany in World War II (1939–1945), and the regime of Juan Peron (1895–1974) in Argentina, to be varieties of fascism.

Although classical fascism was militarily defeated in 1945, its successors continue to play a significant role in the politics of the twenty-first century. Although often marginalized, neo-fascism experienced a marked resurgence in the late twentieth century. Parties rooted in neo-fascism were part of the governments of India, Austria, and Italy at the beginning of the millennium, and neo-fascist movements continued to gain adherents around the world as ostensible alternatives to the dislocations of "globalization." The legacy of fascism remains a potent force to be reckoned with by all who take the history of environmental politics seriously.

Italian Fascism and the Environment

The first fascist movement to attain state power was led by Benito Mussolini (1883–1945), who ruled Italy from 1922 to 1943. Italian fascism was an unstable mix of modernizing and reactionary tendencies. It included a powerful pro-technology strand, and the fascist era coincided with a period of industrialization. An integral component of Italian fascist ideology was the notion of corporatism, an economic model that presented itself as a "third way" between capitalism and communism. In practice, corporatism failed to dislodge the structures of private enterprise, and in the wake of the 1929 worldwide depression it became increasingly irrelevant to the Italian economy. The combination of continued capitalist industrialization and a pro-technological bent did little good to the Italian environment, and when Mussolini's regime invaded Ethiopia in 1935, the ravages of war extended this bleak environmental record to Africa as well.

But Italian fascism also contained several proto-environmentalist strands. The so-called *Strapaese* tendency, for example, celebrated nature and rustic virtues as the counterpole to the corruptions of the city and of industrial society. Indeed this back-to-the-land impulse played an important role even before the fascists took power. In his 1921 article "Fascism and the Land" Mussolini declared that fascism's goal was "to reclaim the land, and with the land the men, and with the men the race" (Tassinari 1939, 14). Even the pro-environmental aspects of fascism were inextricably tied to its dubious dreams of racial and national redemption.

The ruralizing tendency was not confined to the level of ideology. The 1928 "Mussolini Act" launched a large-scale land improvement campaign that included measures to reduce urban sprawl and discourage monocropping in agriculture. Overseen by Arrigo Serpieri (1877–1960), the campaign emphasized protection of the soil and nonmechanized methods of cultivation. It was accompanied by reforestation measures and the establishment of wildlife preserves in the Alps and Apennines. Such efforts were offset, however, by other fascist projects like the "Battle of Grain," an attempt to increase wheat productivity that stimulated an increased reliance on machinery and artificial fertilizers. Perhaps the best-known instance of fascist policy toward the land was the draining of the Pontine Marshes south of Rome. The malarial fens were replaced by meadows and grasslands, as well as agricultural plots, and new villages were built as symbols of rejuvenated peasant values.

On balance, Italian fascist policy toward the land had decidedly mixed results. Whereas erosion control, water quality, and public health sometimes improved, the regime's environmentally friendly programs were curtailed or abandoned when the demands of militarization became too pressing. Much of the impetus toward ruralization gave way before the urban and industrial trends that prevailed in many countries during the fascist era. Above all, Italian fascism's ecological proclivities were subordinated to its drive toward national aggrandizement and imperial expansion. Fascist ecology remained primarily fascist and only secondarily ecological.

German National Socialism and the Environment

Undoubtedly the most notorious variant of classical fascism was German National Socialism, commonly known as Nazism. This notoriety is somewhat misleading because German fascism under the Third Reich differed from its Italian counterpart in several crucial respects. Unlike Italy, Germany was a fully industrialized country when fascism came to power in 1933. Under the leadership of Adolf Hitler (1889–1945), the Nazis implemented far-reaching programs of environmental protection while simultaneously embarking on massive industrial rearmament in preparation for an aggressive war that devastated much of Europe. While protecting flora, fauna, water, and soil, the Nazis exterminated millions of human beings.

Drawing on beliefs that were widespread in German environmentalist circles in the early twentieth century, Nazism pursued a politics of purity, tying ecological health to racial health. The foremost proponent of this "blood and soil" ideology was Nazi Minister of Agriculture Richard Walther Darré (1895–1953), a leader of the so-called green wing of the Nazi Party. Other prominent Nazi environmentalists included Walther Schoenichen (1876–1956), director of the Reich Agency for Nature Protection, and Alwin Seifert (1890–1972), Reich advocate for the landscape. The eco-fascist tendency fused love of nature with love of nation via mystical images of the sacred land as a German birthright. This fascist "religion of nature" suffused even the most practical environmental endeavors; one Nazi-era forester declared that the goal of professional forestry is to "preserve the eternal values of the German countryside and the life-renewing fountain of the German soul" (Heske 1938, 184).

Such views quickly found expression in official state policy. As soon as the Nazis took power, they initiated legislation to preserve natural areas, protect endangered species, and institute ecologically sensitive land-use planning. Laws prohibiting cruelty to animals, restricting commercial development of the countryside, and safeguarding wetlands and waterways were also passed. These measures were unprecedented at the time, and their breadth and innovation indicate the powerful influence of "green" tendencies within National Socialism.

The eco-fascist aspect of Nazism culminated in two major practical achievements: the 1935 Reich Law for the Protection of Nature and the state-sponsored campaign for organic farming. The 1935 law established wilderness reserves, conserved threatened habitats, and required that development projects be approved by the environmental protection authorities. Darré administered the organic farming initiative, promoting sustainable cultivation methods on an impressive scale even during wartime. Some historians dispute the effectiveness of these efforts, but they were extremely popular among German conservationists, who joined the Nazi Party in disproportionate numbers.

Even a number of Nazi schemes for industrial development were guided by a proto-ecological orientation. The building of the Autobahn highway system, for example, was conducted with Seifert's oversight in a relatively environmentally sensitive manner, and both watershed preservation and habitat protection were taken into consideration. As in Italy, however, the "green" strand of German fascism faced considerable internal resistance and was offset by the enormous increase in war-related industrial output.

But even while carrying out its most barbaric crimes against humanity, Nazism retained a debased kind of ecological commitment. In 1942 Heinrich Himmler (1900–1945), leader of the Nazi paramilitary organization, the Schutzstaffel (SS), decreed that respect for nature was one of the driving forces behind the removal of Jews and Slavs from territories conquered by Germany. In the midst of the war and the Holocaust, in which the Nazis annihilated millions of people they considered racially inferior, Himmler established a network of organic plantations at several of the most notorious concentration camps, including Dachau and Auschwitz. The Nazis' reverence for nature and contempt for humankind went hand in hand.

Neo-Fascist Ecological Politics

After the defeat of fascist Italy and Nazi Germany, fascist movements continued to nurture philosophies inherited from Mussolini and Hitler while isolated at the extreme right of the political spectrum. This isolation diminished as memories of the horrors perpetrated by classical fascism diminished and as mainstream political and economic systems became increasingly dissatisfying for larger numbers of people. Neo-fascist organizations and other far-right groups maintained ideological continuity with their predecessors in part through a renewed emphasis on ecological politics. From the 1970s onward, neo-fascists in Germany, France, Russia, Great Britain, the United States, and elsewhere attempted to reclaim the doctrine of natural order and respect for ecological imperatives championed by some of their fascist forebears.

In Germany the major organizational heir of the older fascist tradition, the National Democratic Party, took an early interest in environmental themes and made protection of nature a prominent part of its program in 1973. Another German group with fascist roots, the World League for the Protection of Life, opposed nuclear energy in the 1960s, when few others recognized the ecological issues involved. Led by former Nazi functionary Werner Georg Haverbeck (1909–1999), the group made significant inroads within conventional conservationist circles and helped introduce protofascist motifs into the modern environmental movement. An updated version of fascist ecological thought gradually gained currency and respectability.

Such modernized forms of eco-fascism typically drew together the natural and the national in a manner designed to appeal to nonfascists. One common strategy was to emphasize the threat that immigrants from impoverished countries supposedly pose to the environmental sustainability of wealthy nations. Similar arguments found an increasingly receptive audience among established environmentalist groups in much of the developed world throughout the 1990s. Another area of overlap between fascist and nonfascist approaches to ecological politics was the tendency to recast social issues in biological terms, thus obscuring the complex structural roots of environmental destruction. The mystical elements of eco-fascist appeals to purity occasionally resurfaced as well. These and other factors contributed to the reemergence of neo-fascist-derived themes within mainstream political discourse at the end of the twentieth century as ecological concerns gained prominence within popular consciousness.

Whether there is a distinctly fascist ecology remains a matter of dispute. Some scholars stress the manifestly antiecological elements of fascism's economic and political practice, whereas others argue that fascism's pro-nature predilections cannot be considered genuinely environmentalist. Some sympathizers of neofascism highlight the role of figures like Darré and Serpieri in order to rehabilitate the legacy of fascism, whereas antifascists point to the same figures as evidence of the potential abuse of ecological themes within an inhumane political framework. These ongoing debates indicate that the record of fascism's interaction with the natural environment will continue to generate challenging questions for students of environmental history.

Peter Staudenmaier

See also Germany; Italy

Further Reading

Berlet, C., & Lyons, M. (2000). *Right-wing populism in America.* New York: Guilford.

Biehl, J., & Staudenmaier, P. (1995). *Ecofascism: Lessons from the German experience.* Edinburgh, UK: AK.

Bramwell, A. (1985). *Blood and soil: Walther Darré and Hitler's "Green Party."* Bourne End, UK: Kensal.

Bramwell, A. (1989). *Ecology in the 20th century: A history.* New Haven, CT: Yale University Press.

Corni, G. (1988). Die Agrarpolitik des Faschismus: Ein Vergleich zwischen Deutschland und Italien [The agrarian policies of fascism: A comparison of Italy and Germany]. *Tel Aviver Jahrbuch für deutsche Geschichte* [Tel Aviv yearbook for German history], *17*, 391–423.

De Grand, A. (2000). *Italian fascism: Its origins and development.* Lincoln: University of Nebraska Press.

Dominick, R. (1992). *The environmental movement in Germany.* Bloomington: Indiana University Press.

Eatwell, R. (1995). *Fascism: A history.* New York: Penguin.

Geden, O. (1996). *Rechte Ökologie.* Berlin, Germany: Elefanten.

Gregor, A. J. (1979). *Italian fascism and developmental dictatorship.* Princeton, NJ: Princeton University Press.

Griffin, R. (1995). *Fascism.* Oxford, UK: Oxford University Press.

Griffin, R. (in press). Fascism. In B. Taylor & J. Kaplan (Eds.), *Encyclopedia of religion and nature* New York: Continuum.

Grundmann, F. (1979). *Agrarpolitik im Dritten Reich* [Agrarian policy in the Third Reich]. Hamburg, Germany: Hoffmann und Campe.

Heske, F. (1938). *German forestry.* New Haven, CT: Yale University Press.

Jahn, T., & Wehling, P. (1991). *Ökologie von rechts* [Right-wing ecology]. Frankfurt, Germany: Campus.

Lee, M. (2000). *The Beast reawakens.* New York: Routledge.

Mosse, G. (1999). *The fascist revolution.* New York: Howard Fertig.

Neocleous, M. (1997). *Fascism.* Minneapolis: University of Minnesota Press.

Nolte, E. (1969). *Three faces of fascism.* New York: Holt.

Olsen, J. (1999). *Nature and nationalism.* New York: St. Martin's Press.

Payne, S. (1995). *A history of fascism 1914–1945.* Madison: University of Wisconsin Press.

Pois, R. (1985). *National socialism and the religion of nature.* London: Croom Helm.

Proctor, R. (1999). *The Nazi war on cancer.* Princeton, NJ: Princeton University Press.

Renton, D. (1999). *Fascism: Theory and practice.* London: Pluto.

Stampacchia, M. (2000). *"Ruralizzare L'Italia!" Agricoltura e bonifiche tra Mussolini e Serpieri* ["Ruralize Italy!" Agricultural and land reclamation under Mussolini and Serpieri]. Milan: Franco Angeli.

Tassinari, G. (1939). *Ten years of integral land-reclamation under the Mussolini Act.* Faenza, Italy: Fratelli Lega.

Fertilizers

Only natural fertilization was used when primitive agriculture began about ten thousand years ago. After the early farmers planted their crops in newly opened land, they could harvest crops for only about two years until the soil nutrients were depleted. Then the farmers moved their farm plots and cut down the trees and shrubs in an adjacent plot of land, burned these trees and shrubs, and planted their crops for another two years. At the end of twenty years of fallow, often the farmers could return to the original piece of land. At this time a new crop of trees and shrubs was present, and fertilizer nutrients had accumulated during the twenty-year fallow period.

About five thousand years later farmers had tamed cattle and horses and utilized these animals for transport and plowing. These animals had an asset in addition to transport and plowing: They produced manure. The early farmers observed that plants grew larger and faster where animal and human dung was deposited. Slowly, as the livestock population increased, more dung was available for use in crop production. The use of manure as fertilizer helped the farmers increase their crop yields and reduce the fallow period that was necessary with slash-and-burn agriculture. Farmers at this early time also kept sheep, goats, and other animals.

As early as 200 BCE the Roman politician Marcus Porcius Cato (234–149 BCE) suggested that to fertilize crops, pigeon dung and other livestock dung could be saved on meadows. Collecting and transporting livestock manure to cropland for food production required significant labor. For corn producing only 1,000 kilograms per hectare, the farmers would have had to collect, transport, and apply about 3 metric tons of manure. This was a major task with the equipment available at this early period. One problem with manure is that it contains about 80 percent water, which makes it difficult to handle and transport.

Nitrogen Conservation

One large cow weighing about 800 kilograms will produce about .9 metric tons of manure per year. Collecting and storing this manure for use in crop production are difficult if the nutrients are to be conserved. Nearly 50 percent of the nitrogen in fresh cattle manure is ammonia, and most of this ammonia will volatize and escape within twenty-four hours. To conserve the ammonia, the manure must be immediately placed either underground or in anaerobic conditions in a lagoon. The liquid manure may be more difficult to handle than stored or composted manure. Composting the manure, however, results in about 75 percent of the nitrogen being lost during storage. The compost is more easily handled than manure in a lagoon.

Livestock manure continues to be a major source of nitrogen, phosphorus, and potassium fertilizers around the world, including in the United States. In the United States, livestock produce about 1.35 billion metric tons of manure. This manure is estimated to contain 6.75 million metric tons of nitrogen fertilizer. If all this manure were effectively applied to agricultural land in the United States, this would be nearly sufficient to provide the 7.2 million metric tons of nitrogen that is required for U.S. crops annually.

U.S. agriculture from 1770 to about 1940 relied primarily on livestock manure and green manures, such as sweet clover and vetch, to provide the nitrogen needed for crop production. Corn yields during this period ranged from 1,000 to 1,500 kilograms per hectare. Farmers during this period would plant one hectare to a legume, such as clover, and one hectare to corn. The following year, the hectare in the legume was plowed under and planted to corn, and the corn hectare was planted to clover or a related legume. The

Cave dwellings in the town of Göreme in Turkey. Homes are carved out of sandstone that is sculpted into towers by erosion. The inhabitants create pigeon roosts above their homes and harvest the guano for use as fertilizer. COURTESY OF NICOLE LALIBERTE.

legume that was plowed under before planting the corn provided from 50 to 100 kilograms of nitrogen per hectare. In addition, some livestock manure was applied to the corn acreage, depending on the farming system.

During World War II, when large quantities of explosives were produced, it was discovered that nitrate is one of the ingredients in explosives. Nitrate, like other nitrogen products, such as ammonia, can also be an effective fertilizer.

Commercial Fertilizers

After World War II, commercial nitrogen, phosphorus, and potassium fertilizers began to be applied to U.S. and other croplands. Initially the amounts were extremely small. In 1945, for example, only about 8 kilograms of nitrogen per hectare were applied to U.S. corn acreage. The quantity of nitrogen fertilizer applied to U.S. corn increased to about 150 kilograms per hectare by 1985 and continues near this rate as of 2000. (See table 1.) Commercial phosphorus and potassium fertilizer nutrients also increased from 6 to 8 kilograms per hectare to about 60 kilograms per hectare in 2000. (See table 1.)

The use of commercial fertilizers eliminated the need for 2 hectares to produce 1 hectare of corn. One hectare of a legume to produce nitrogen nutrients for corn production was no longer needed. Of course, large quantities of fossil energy are necessary to produce fertilizers, especially nitrogen fertilizer. For example, the production of 1 kilogram of nitrogen fertilizer requires about 18,690 kilocalories or slightly more than the energy in 2 liters of gasoline.

To illustrate how rapidly agricultural technology changed after commercial fertilizers were discovered and produced, the energy inputs just for the nitrogen fertilizer today are greater than the total fossil energy inputs in producing corn in 1945. Corn yields have increased dramatically since 1945, when corn yields were about 2,000 kilograms per hectare. Corn yields in the United States as of 2000 were 8,600 kilograms per hectare. (See Table 1.)

Worldwide, about 80 million metric tons of nitrogen are applied to crops. This nitrogen is vital to crop production. Even with all the nitrogen, phosphorus, potassium, and other nutrients applied in world agriculture, the World Health Organization reports that more than 3 billion people are malnourished in the world. In addition, the Food and Agricultural Organization of the United Nations reports that per-capita grain production has been declining for nearly two decades. Grains are estimated to provide 80 percent of the world's food. In addition to shortages of cropland and irrigation water, per-capita fertilizer use during the past decade has declined more than 20 percent.

The food shortage cannot be blamed only on lack of fertilizers. Cropland is suffering from severe erosion and degradation, and there are severe shortages of freshwater, especially freshwater for irrigation.

David Pimentel

See also Guano

Further Reading

Cato, M. P. (1998). *Cato on farming de agri cultura* (A. Dalby, Trans.). Devon, UK: Prospect Books.

Food and Agriculture Organization of the United Nations (FAO). (1961–2000). *Quarterly bulletin of statistics*. Rome: Food and Agriculture Organization of the United Nations.

Food and Agriculture Organization of the United Nations (FAO). (1999). *Agricultural statistics*. Retrieved October 17, 2000, from http://apps.fao.org/cgi-bin/nph-db.pl?subset-agriculture

Pimentel, D., Doughty, R., Carothers, C., Lamberson, S., Bora, N., & Lee, K. (2002). Energy and economic inputs

TABLE 1.
QUANTITIES OF COMMERCIAL FERTILIZERS APPLIED TO U.S. CORN LAND PER HECTARE FROM 1945 TO 2000

Fertilizers	1945	1954	1964	1975	1985	2000
Nitrogen kg	8	30	55	111	152	147
Phosphorus kg	8	13	36	56	58	63
Potassium kg	6	20	28	62	75	55
Corn Yield kg	2070	2572	4265	5143	7400	8600

Source: Pimentel et al., 1990; Pimentel et al., 2002.

in crop production: Comparison of developed and developing countries. In R. Lal, D. Hansen, N. Uphoff, & S. Slack (Eds.), *Food security & environmental quality in the developing world* (pp.129–151). Boca Raton, FL: CRC Press.

Pimentel, D., & Pimentel, M. (1996). *Food, energy and society.* Niwot: Colorado University Press.

Pimentel, D., Wen, D., & Giampietro, M. (1990). Technological changes in energy use in U.S. agricultural production. In S. R. Gliessman (Ed.), *Agroecology* (pp. 305–321). New York: Springer-Verlag.

U.S. Department of Agriculture (USDA). (2001). *Agricultural statistics.* Washington, DC: U.S. Department of Agriculture.

Fiber Crops

Fiber crops of nonwoody plants have been important in world history for the products they have provided and for their economic value. These plants have produced fiber for fabrics, cordage for rope and twine, and pulp for paper for thousands of years in many places around the world (woody fiber plants, such as papyrus and trees, also have yielded pulp for paper).

Seed-Borne Fibers

Plants that have hairs attached to their seeds or the inner walls of their fruit are valuable fiber crops. Commercially important in this category are cotton and kapok (the silky hairs around ceiba tree seeds used as filler for mattresses and life preservers). Strains of cotton, originating in Asia, Africa, and on the tropical west coast of the Americas, were domesticated four thousand years ago but came into high demand when Great Britain's textile industry boomed in the late eighteenth century. Thus European planters exploited cotton where it thrives in warm climates in India, Egypt, Brazil, Mexico, and the U.S. South, among other places.

The U.S. South became a "cotton kingdom" from South Carolina to Texas and by 1820 was producing 500 million bales a year. The cotton plantations caused severe erosion (depleting 50 percent of the region's topsoil), spawned insect infestations, and required slave labor imported from Africa. When resources were depleted in one place, the growers simply converted more land to cotton fields on a westward-moving grid across the Deep South. Today California, Texas, and Arizona are the largest U.S. cotton producers. Internationally, China, the United States, Russia, India, Pakistan, Turkey, and Egypt are the leading producers. Brazil, Mexico, and Central America also raise great quantities of the versatile fiber, which is used to make cool, comfortable clothing.

Stem and Bark (or Soft) Fibers

Some of the world's most commercially valuable plants are grown for stem and bark (or soft) fibers. An example is hemp, among the oldest cultivated plants known to humankind—cultivated as early as 2800 BCE in China. From there it spread to Europe, especially Russia, and was introduced to other temperate zones. In the United States hemp varieties grew particularly well in Kentucky and Wisconsin. Hemp fiber has been used to make paper (including that on which the Declaration of Independence was written), cloth, and most importantly for the manufacture of rope. Thus its military importance to supply rope to ships has been great. During World War II U.S. farmers raised 54,431 metric tons of hemp a year for the war effort.

The plant, growing over 3 meters in height, can drain the soil of nutrients and requires a great deal of organic matter. It also is prone to soil-borne fungi and various diseases, but crop rotation usually averts those problems. There is little evidence of hemp causing ecological degradation. On the contrary, proponents claim it is among the best crops to cultivate in temperate climates.

Hemp also grows well in the tropics, but the warmer, moister climate stimulates the plant's production of the resinous narcotic tetrahydracannibinol (THC), which produces psychoactive qualities when prepared as hashish, ganja, or marijuana (made from the dried flowering tops of the female plants). Thus raising hemp is illegal in some nations. In the United States, Congress passed the Marijuana Tax Act in 1937 to impose high taxes and strict guidelines on the crop. Some scholars argue that *New York Journal* publisher William Randolph Hearst was behind the act's passage so that hemp would not compete against his own forest and pulp interests. Today hemp is raised commercially throughout the world (except in the United States, where the tax still discourages its production). The leading hemp countries are Russia, China, Chile, Italy, Poland, Serbia and Montenegro (Yugoslavia), Hungary, and Romania. Canada legalized hemp production in 1999.

Other soft-fiber crops include jute, kenaf, ramie, and flax. After cotton, jute is the second-most economically important fiber crop in the world. It is grown primarily in its native India and Bangladesh and in China, Nepal, and Brazil. The fiber is used to make rope and coarse fabrics. Kenaf, also from India, is similar to jute and is gaining in popularity due to its resistance to drought and adaptability to diverse conditions. Its fibers are used to make paper and cordage products. Ramie—one of the oldest and strongest of all vegetable fibers and used to make cloth, paper, yarn, curtains, and tapestries—is grown primarily in China and Japan but is becoming more popular in Europe and the Americas. Flax is the world's third-most-important fiber cash crop. The plant, used by the ancient Egyptians and mentioned in the Bible, produces a fine fiber that has been used for thousands of years to make linen, lace, and apparel fabric. Over 80 percent of the world's flax supply now comes from Russia. Belgium, Germany, Canada, and the United States are other producers. (A different variety of flax produces linseed oil.)

Leaf (or Hard) Fibers

Leaf (or hard) fiber crops include sisal, henequen, and abaca (Manila hemp), whose leaves are cut and retted (soaked) primarily to make rope and twine but also for hammocks and gunny sacks. Sisal and henequen are agave plants native to Mexico's Yucatan Peninsula, but sisal has been successfully introduced in Africa, Brazil, and the Caribbean Basin. Abaca is fiber from a relative of the banana plant that is native to the Philippines but that now thrives in India, Indonesia, and the Pacific islands. Sisal and henequen were in high demand from 1890 to 1950, when the twine that their fiber produced was needed for a grain-harvesting implement called the "binder." The grain industry throughout the United States and Canada became dependent on this twine, causing an economic boom and an environmental transformation in Yucatan when hundreds of thousands of acres were converted to henequen plantations. And in North America the binder helped to expand the grain industry when demand for wheat during World War I was high. So dependent was the grain industry on sisal twine that in 1915 (a record crop year for wheat) the United States sent gunboats to Mexico to secure shipment of the fiber when, during Mexico's revolution, an export/import blockade was imposed on Yucatan. The scenario represents the degree to which a double dependency emerged between different agricultural commodities, yet it all came to a close by 1950, when North American farmers switched to combine harvesters that did not require twine. The henequen industry in Yucatan was left virtually paralyzed; attempts to find similar markets for the fiber failed, leaving the local economy in serious decline—a victim of nondiversified monocrop agriculture and dependence on foreign interests. Today there are only remnants of the former henequen boom, with a small fiber industry producing burlap, mats, and twine. In an ecological twist, however, much of the former plantation landscape is reverting to its former Yucatan vegetation with renewed habitat for local wildlife. With the world forests dwindling at the beginning of the twenty-first century, fiber from crops like those mentioned here offer viable alternatives and will be much in demand.

Sterling Evans

See also Cotton; Silk and Silkworm

Further Reading

Bosca, I., & Krus, M. (1998). *The cultivation of hemp.* White River Junction, VT: Chelsea Green Publishing.

Catling, D., & Grayson, J. (1982). *Identification of vegetable fibres.* London: Chapman and Hall.

Cowdrey, A. (1983). *This land, this South: An environmental history.* Lexington: University of Kentucky Press.

Daniel, P. (1985). *Breaking the land: The transformation of cotton, tobacco, and rice cultures since 1880.* Urbana: University of Illinois Press.

Dempsey, J. M. (1975). *Fiber crops.* Gainesville: University Press of Florida.

Herer, J. (1985). *The emperor wears no clothes: The authoritative historical record of cannabis and the conspiracy against marijuana.* Van Nuys, CA: Hemp Publishing.

Hunt, T. F. (1907). *The forage and fiber crops in America.* New York: Orange Judd.

Kirby, R. H. (1963). *Vegetable fibres: Botany, cultivation, and utilization.* London: Leonard Hill Books.

Maiti, R. K. (1997). *World fiber crops.* Enfield, NH: Science Publishers.

Pollan, M. (2001). *Botany of desire: A plant's-eye view of the world.* New York: Random House.

Wells, A. (1985). *Yucatan's gilded age: Haciendas, henequen, and International Harvester, 1860–1915.* Albuquerque: University of New Mexico Press.

Fire

Fire is a creative force of the living world. Life supplies oxygen and fuel for combustion. The chemistry behind combustion is truly elemental. When it occurs within a cell, it is called "respiration." When it occurs outside, it is called "fire."

Natural Fire Regimes

Fossil records of fire, in the form of charcoal, date to the Devonian period, roughly concurrent with the first land-colonizing plants. Natural fire occurs in patches and pulses, driven by a two-cycle climatic engine of wetting and drying, shaped by the kinds of biomass (living matter) that may or may not thrive under such a regime, waiting on lightning's lottery to kindle. A place has to be wet enough to grow fuels and dry enough to burn them. The patterns of burning result in what are known as "fire regimes." (Such regimes are a statistical concept. A fire is to a regime as a storm is to a climate. The rhythms are many but orderly.)

That fire simply happened meant that the biosphere (the part of the world in which life can exist) had to accommodate that fact. Fire became a factor in evolutionary selection and an ecological presence. It shaked and baked, a form of creative destruction in nature's economy. Plants and animals adjusted to fire's regime, as fire did to them. Even so, much of the Earth doesn't naturally burn. Much of the historical Earth so failed to combust that vast quantities of biomass were simply buried (to be exhumed and combusted over the last two centuries). Nature's economy, in brief, lacked a broker that could match flame with fuel.

Anthropogenic Fire

That changed with the later hominids (early humans). It seems that *Homo erectus* could tend fire, although probably not until *Homo sapiens* could humans start fire more or less at will. Still, it was easier to keep fire alight than to constantly rekindle it. So, likewise, people kept fire continuously in nature. The sputtering flame became constant, something that accompanied people wherever they went; and they went everywhere. What they didn't burn outright, they relied on catalytic fire to help manipulate.

Since the first tread of *Homo sapiens*, fire ecology has thus meant human ecology. The biosphere had long exercised some control over fuel and oxygen because life produced both. Now, through humans, it could in principle exert some power over ignition as well. But humans did not set fire by instinct. They set fire for their own ends. They inscribed lines of fire and fields of fire that sculpted new landscape mosaics; they kindled flame according to new rhythms. Biotas (flora and fauna) would have to adapt to this regime. In reality, anthropogenic (human-caused) fire *competed* with natural fire. Ever after, fire regimes would have to reconcile culture with climate. Flame, and the landscapes it touched, entered the moral universe of humanity.

Aboriginal Fire Practices

Human as ignitors were most effective where fire already existed or where the conditions for fire were present but lacked regular ignition. Thus people favored fire-prone places and shunned places hostile to fire. They sought out places with vigorous wet-dry cycles, receptive to a new source of ignition. They could seize control over the land by the simple practice of preemptively burning in patches before lightning arrived. The greatest shock occurred in places like Australia that had the conditions for burning but lacked a reliable source of ignition.

People could further leverage their firepower by hunting and foraging. So intensive can such human manipulation of a landscape become that anthropologist Rhys Jones, scrutinizing aboriginal Australia, coined the term *firestick farming* to describe a scene that was often as intricately manipulated as outright cultivation. Especially important was the survival or disappearance of large animals. In fire-prone areas, such beasts competed with fire for biomass. Removing these animals increased the amount of fuel available for burning. In fire-intolerant areas, however, eliminating those biotic bulldozers could allow scrub to overwhelm fire. Likely this scenario—a breakdown in the cycle of wetting and drying along with the recession of megafauna—helps account for the puzzling fact that closed forests exist anywhere on the planet, that fire-intolerant biotas could advance in the face of anthropogenic burning.

Fire has proved an eccentric, pliable technology. In some respects it behaves like a simple tool. A flame sits on a candle as an ax sits on a handle. In other respects fire behaves more like a domesticated species, a kind of pyric sheepdog or milch cow. It demands human breeding, tending, feeding, training; it takes its power from the environment, which is also domesti-

Fire's Role in Nature

No Fire

Dense evergreens rob lower plants of sunlight. Many plants die and pile up as dead wood and litter.

Natural Fire

FIRE — T I M E — 250 YEARS LATER

Fire starts again by lightning or people.

As the forest gets older, food for wildlife is reduced.

As the forest grows it provides a home and food for changing kinds of wildlife.

New growth produces a variety of food.

"When you try to change any single thing, you find it hitched to everything else in the universe." *John Muir*

Distributed by

This diagram distributed by the National Forest Service points out the benefits of natural fires.

cated and hence sustains it. In still other respects, fire more resembles a captive animal, a trained bear or elephant. The wild is redirected or conjured up and applied to landscapes in which it can free-burn but to human ends.

The reality is that limits on anthropogenic fire remained. Mostly, people could work only with what nature presented to them by way of weather and fuels. They could not often bring fire where nature would not allow it. The early keepers of the flame knew full well both their power and its limits. Although the possession of fire made them unique, distinct among creatures, their firepower itself flowed from nature, which inscrutably gave and withheld.

Agricultural Fire Practices

What people needed was a means to make fuel on demand as they could spark. From a fire-history perspective this occurs with agriculture. There are systems of agriculture for which fire is irrelevant, that use water instead of flame to disturb, destroy, and fertilize. But they are not many, and they cannot extend far from floodplains or hillside terraces. (To see how much fire matters, one can try this simple thought experiment: Remove fire completely from the web of cultivation and see how long and in what forms farming and herding can endure.)

The reason lies in basic fire ecology. Flame purges and promotes. For a time, fire's catalytic presence drives off the local biota, liberates nutrients, and rearranges microclimates. (Revealingly, almost all of agriculture's hearths occur in places characterized by wet-dry seasonality, which are thus intrinsically fire-prone.) Eventually the local biota closes in, and the process must begin anew. The fire ceremonies of agrarian societies testify to the belief that fire destroys the bad and encourages the good.

Farming thus exploits a fire-driven cycle. Either the farm moves through the landscape (as with classic slash-and-burn farming), or the landscape in effect cycles through the farm (as with spatially stable crop rotation). Either way, at some point, the system requires the push-pull of fire to turn its ecological cranks. Fire, however, demands fuel. So the cultivator must either seek out new sites or else bring new fuel to the old site. The agronomic name for that fuel is "fallow." The fallow, in short, was not burned as waste, but rather was grown in order to be burned.

Agriculture expanded enormously the realm of fire. Where fire had not previously existed, it could now thrive. Where it had previously flourished, it could change character. Aboriginal fire regimes could morph into agricultural ones. Particularly if outfitted with livestock—hoof and tooth proved as powerful as ax and harrow—people could return anthropogenic fire to regions like temperate Europe (or at a later time, Amazonia) from which they had been expelled. The flocks and herds replaced the megafauna that had earlier vanished.

The possible combinations of plants, animals, ax, plow, people, and fire are many. What matters is that all demand a controlled disturbance, and the form that best matches human desires with ecological possibilities is burning. What matters, too, is that cultivation placed fire's ecology even more strenuously into human hands. How fire would behave on Earth became more closely bonded to the will and whim of human life, to a widening gamut of politics, trade, scholarship, war, and legal conceptions of land owner-

ship, none of which had touched natural fire or shaped its regimes. Ideas and institutions would prove as significant as storms and bark thickness.

Industrial Fire

Yet, limits still remained. Anthropogenic fire was only as powerful as the fuels that fed it. The cultivator could, within bounds, make and break biomass to fashion fuel, but the cultivator could not evade the cycles of growth and decay that oversaw how much living biomass was available for converting into combustibles. Humans could hope to transcend this profound cycle only if they could tap another source of combustibles. With fossil biomass, they did precisely that. The combustion of coal, gas, and petroleum launched a new epoch in the Earth's fire history, the era of industrial fire.

Thus began the Big Burn. Combustion now extends through geologic time as well as across geographic space. The competition between lightning and torch over biomass continues, but both now face a combustion competitor for whom the source fuel is, over several centuries, unbounded. Rather, the problem is one of sinks, the capacity of the plant to absorb combustion's byproducts. Industrial fire burns without regard to ecological context. The Earth is awash in its effluent, the pollution of combusted fossil biomass. The Big Burn has inspired a Big Dump.

Steadily, and on a vast scale, industrial fire has substituted for previous pyrotechnologies. In their built environment, industrial societies have all but extinguished open flame. In fields, fossil fallow has replaced living (typically, with a subsequent loss of biodiversity). Even in wildlands, industrial societies have actively sought to suppress all expressions of open flame. This complex competition has bequeathed an Earth that is fissuring into two great combustion realms, one dominated by biomass burning, the other by industrial fire. There are few points of overlap, and these are likely transitional.

In effect, a kind of pyric version of the familiar demographic transition occurs. Fire births boom, while fire deaths slow. The old traditions of fire survive, even as new burning proliferates. The population of fires explodes, like a plague of locusts. Eventually substitutions and outright suppression quench the old or drive the flames into nature preserves. The process lingers longest in places like India and Mexico that hold rich deposits of fossil biomass and stubbornly planted rural societies. Beyond such vague observations, however, the dynamics of industrial fire and its curious ecology remain unknown.

Contemporary Fire

Today the trends in fire are these: a boom in industrial combustion, a revival of natural fire, and a collapse in anthropogenic burning. How these interact, however, is the vexing three-body problem of fire science. Overall, the Earth seems to suffer a vast maldistribution of burning. There are places, mostly in the developing world, that have too much fire; places, largely in the developed world, that have too little fire; places along exurban (beyond city suburbs) frontiers that have volatilely mixed fires. There is too much of the wrong kind of fire and too little of the right. Probably the planet has too much combustion and too little fire. The crisis over global warming is, finally, a crisis over combustion.

These are separate problems, amenable to distinctive analyses and solutions. The need to limit the Big Burn is obvious, although how to bolster carbon sinks and shrink combustion-released carbon sources is less so. It is an easy matter, technically, to keep houses from burning. It is trickier—a cultural call—to decide what to do with natural fire in wilderness preserves. In fire-prone landscapes, fire will enter, and in places long subject to burning, the abrupt removal of fire (or a sudden shift in its regime) may be as upsetting as its untoward introduction. It is as though a forest that received 90 centimeters of rain evenly distributed over the year got only 13 centimeters and that in two months. The most profoundly disrupted biotas are those that had experienced regular surface burning two or more times a decade. Paradoxically, the chief fire crisis in the nature reserves of industrial nations traces to fire's attempted abolition.

The real quagmire, however, concerns the oldest of human fire practices. What is the proper place for anthropogenic fire? Removing fires from areas that have adapted to human-tended fire regimes can be as ecologically disruptive as thrusting fires into places lacking such history. Reinstating fire that has been stripped out of biotas is not a simple process of reversal. Fire is not ecological pixie dust that, sprinkled over degraded lands, renders them hale and lovely. Fire will take its character from its context: It will synthesize its surroundings. Rather, fire's return must more resemble the reintroduction of a lost species, like a wolf. To thrive, fire must have a suitable habitat. All this is to state one of the truisms of fire history: There is no neutral position. Fire deleted may be as ecologically powerful as fire inserted.

Still, there are reasons to lump these various expressions of contemporary combustion together. They interact, they share a history, and they rely on *Homo sapiens* as a fire creature. In this sense, fire is less a tool or even an ecological process than a relationship, and less a technical problem than a cultural negotiation. One form of combustion does not exist autonomously from the others. They compete for biomass, they compete for space in the atmosphere, they shape very different, even antagonistic ecosystems. Yet, they have one common element. How they appear on Earth will depend on humans, who remain, however disdainful their sense of mission and slovenly their practice, the keepers of the planetary flame.

Stephen J. Pyne

Further Reading

Bond, W., & van Wilgen, B. W. (1996). *Fire and plants.* London: Chapman and Hall.

Cheney, P., & Sullivan, A. (1997). *Grassfires: Fuel, weather, and fire behaviour.* Collingwood, Canada: CSIRO Publishing.

Clark, J. S., H. Cachier, J. G. Goldammer, & B. J. Stocks (Eds.). (1997). *Sediment records of biomass burning and global change.* Berlin, Germany: Springer-Verlag.

Collins, S. L., & Wallace, L. L. (Eds.). (1990). *Fire in North American tallgrass prairies.* Norman: University of Oklahoma Press.

DeBano, L. F., Neary, D. G., & Ffolliott, P. F. (1998). *Fire's effects on ecosystems.* New York: John Wiley and Sons.

Gill, A. M., R. H. Groves, & I. R. Noble (Eds.). (1981). *Fire and the Australian biota.* Canberra: Australian Academy of Science.

Goldammer, J. G. (Ed.). (1990). *Fire in the tropical biota.* Berlin, Germany: Springer-Verlag.

Goldammer, J. G., & Furyaev, V. V. (Eds.). (1996). *Fire in ecosystems of boreal Eurasia.* London: Kluwere Academic Publishers.

Goudsblom, J. (1992). *Fire and civilization.* London: Penguin Press.

Johnson, E. A. (1992). *Fire and vegetation dynamics: Studies from the North American boreal forest.* Cambridge, UK: Cambridge University Press.

Levine, J. (Ed.). (1991). *Global biomass burning.* Cambridge, MA: MIT Press.

Levine, J. (1996). *Biomass burning and global change.* Cambridge, MA: MIT Press.

Pyne, S. (1995). *Fire in America: A cultural history of wildland and rural fire.* Seattle: University of Washington Press.

Pyne, S. (1997). *Vestal fire: An environmental history, told through fire, of Europe and Europe's encounter with the world.* Seattle: University of Washington Press.

Pyne, S. (1998). *Burning bush: A fire history of Australia.* Seattle: University of Washington Press.

Pyne, S. (1998). *World fire: The culture of fire on Earth.* Seattle: University of Washington Press.

Pyne, S. (2001). *Fire: A brief history.* Seattle: University of Washington Press.

Rossotti, H. (1993). *Fire.* Oxford, UK: Oxford University Press.

Wein, R. W., & MacLean, D. A. (Eds.). (1983). *The role of fire in northern circumpolar ecosystems.* New York: John Wiley and Sons.

Whelan, Robert J. (1995). *The ecology of fire.* Cambridge, UK: Cambridge University Press.

Fishing

Fishing, together with hunting and food gathering, is among the oldest means of human subsistence. Prehistoric peoples fished lakes, rivers, and shallow inshore waters. Fishing played a central role in discovery, and in the spread of humans throughout the globe. Today, commercial fisheries have depleted the resources of the oceans, and the future may see a significant change to aquaculture.

6000 BCE–500 CE

After the last Ice Age global sea temperature rose, and in the period 6000 to 2000 BCE the sea was 2°C warmer than today, making it possible to sustain fisheries throughout the year in many regions of the world. Analysis of human skeletons shows that the food composition of coastal populations of northern Europe was predominantly marine. So-called kitchen middens, made up of the faunal remains of the sea, provide a rich source of information. The food intake of these peoples was primarily seal, fish, shellfish, and seaweed. Because of the importance of fishing, archaeologists have dubbed the millennium before the advent of agriculture the fishing stone age. Settlement concentrated along the coastlines of the world, as the abundance of seafood provided a relative ad-

A father and son fishing on a lake in Alabama. COURTESY PHYLLIS COOPER/U. S. FISH AND WILDLIFE SERVICE.

vantage to marine communities over hunting forms of subsistence.

Sea hunting voyages induced widespread travels, and it is likely that fashions such as the characteristic western European megalithic tumuli were spread along the coasts in this way. In Southeast Asia settlements of the sixth millennium BCE are associated with fishing and the collection of shellfish, while the use of plant food occurred later. The historical Japanese Jōmon culture also seems associated with rising sea temperatures around 6000 BCE. Studies of fish bones from well-preserved kitchen middens show that Japanese fishermen sailed far into the Pacific by 2000 BCE. Polynesian migrations probably also were related to fishing. The Maori colonization of New Zealand was especially based on a marine food culture.

Fish as a source of food was more important than meat in the ancient Mediterranean cultures. Along the Nile, settlements with huge amounts of fish bones have been identified. Hundreds of fulltime fishers were employed by the Lagash temple in Sumer around 2400 BCE. The fish was dried, salted, and stored. Babylonian sources from around 1750 BCE show the importance of

The Presidents Bush on Fish and Fishing

The days a man spends fishing or spends hunting should not be deducted from the time that he's on earth. In other words, if I fish today, that should be added to the amount of time I get to live. That's the way I look at recreation. That's why I'll be a big conservation, environmental President, because I plan to fish and hunt as much as I possibly can.

George Bush, *Los Angeles Times*, December 30, 1988.

I know the human being and the fish can coexist peacefully.

George W. Bush. Comment made in Saginaw, Michigan, during presidential campaign, September 29, 2000.

---

fishing. Greek merchants conducted an extensive fish trade from the Black Sea and the Russian rivers to the Greek and later the Roman market.

Aquaculture developed in ancient times both in Asia and Europe. Fish ponds for herbivorous carps were developed in China, while excavations have revealed numerous fishponds by Italic villas providing fresh fish for the rich. While aquaculture remained important for local markets, the rise of an international fish market was, however, related to the development of catch operations. Contrary to terrestrial food production, the supply of fish depended on hunting rather than cultivating the resource in most parts of the world until the mid–twentieth century.

500–1850 CE

In the early middle ages, European fisheries were mainly coastal and riverine. Around 1100 the waters around Lofoten in northern Norway sustained a considerable trade in dried cod to continental Europe, and by 1200 a fully commercialized economy had developed around the herring fishery in the Danish Sound and the West Baltic based in the settlements of Skanør and Falsterbo in Scania. Around 1250, German merchants organized in the Hanseatic League gained control of the fish market, and took advantage of their access to rich salt mines in Lüneburg to market quality-controlled salted herring barrels throughout the continental market.

Between 1350 and 1500, the price of fish relative to meat and grain rose to very high levels in Europe. The causes of the price rise are not well researched but must have been linked to the rising living standards of the urban population after the Black Death and possibly

increasing patterns of preference for fish during Lent. Much improved curing practices and marketing also helped develop the market. Good prices induced European fishers to venture into the open sea, both south and north. Portuguese fishers pursued tuna along the North African coast, and turned fishing expeditions into voyages of discovery from around 1440. Flemish and later Dutch fishers conducted an extensive herring fishery in the North Sea while English fishers went cod-fishing near Iceland. In 1497 the Italian Giacomo Caboto (John Cabot, c. 1450–c. 1499) discovered a vast abundance of cod near Newfoundland. The Grand Banks became a rich source of income to English, French, and Spanish fishers who undertook annual migrations across the northwest Atlantic through the seventeenth century. The rise of the fishery was perceived by the English crown as a way to nurture a population of seamen that was necessary not only in economic terms but also and foremost to man the rapidly growing navy. As it happened, many fishermen chose to over winter and gradually a permanently resident fishing population took possession of Newfoundland from the indigenous Indian population.

After 1550 European fish prices fell relative to agricultural products, possibly as a side effect of the abolition of Lent practices after the Reformation. The decline hit Northern European coastal populations hard. In Norway, Denmark, and Iceland, many fishing villages were abandoned, large parts of the coasts were deserted, and emphasis was put on agricultural resources. The Dutch succeeded in gaining control of the fish market thanks to superior curing and marketing, but after 1650 even their fisheries were declining. The Grand Banks fisheries succeeded through the eighteenth century by drawing on the enormous resources of the sea. By the mid-eighteenth century the inshore waters of Newfoundland were already fully utilized, and the expansion of the fishery was only possible through a geographical extension of fishing grounds into the sea, and from the 1830s along the Labrador coast. The fishery was conducted by an impoverished resident population in Newfoundland and Nova Scotia, while the fish trade was controlled by European merchants.

1850–1950

Major changes in world fisheries occurred after about 1850. The first developments benefited the traditional Atlantic market for salted and dried fish. Salt-fish prices rose in real terms between 1825 and 1875 compared to general food prices of the period. The favorable conditions prompted French, American, and British deep-sea long-liners to compete with inshore Newfoundland, North Norwegian, Faeroese, and Icelandic fishermen for demersal species, mainly cod. At the end of the century, however, salt-fish prices fell relative to other food commodities, while fresh fish prices improved.

By the mid-nineteenth century, fresh fish was a low-priced commodity that often reached the consumer in decayed state and markets were nonintegrated. Global production was therefore extremely localized. Only a few large cities such as Boston, New York, London, or Copenhagen had regular fresh fish provisions from nearby inshore, riverine, or estuarial fishing grounds. However, the fresh fish industry profited greatly from the transport revolution of railways and steamships as easy transport changed the market profoundly. On the one hand, fresh fish could be sent inland and arrive at markets—which developed in the population a taste for high-quality, high-value fish. On the other hand, iced fish could be transported in bulk and be marketed for the urban population as cheap, low-quality, but nutritious food. These two markets were well defined, both in Europe and North America, by the 1890s.

Fast transport was the prerequisite for highly specialized markets and producers of fresh fish. Fast smacks and railroads facilitated fast deliveries of high-quality fresh and even live fish to consumers, and the growing urban middle classes on the European continent and in North America were willing to pay for fashionable and perishable goods as a marker of lifestyle. Generally, the inshore fisheries became characterized by self-ownership and market-orientation,

either for nearby city populations or for export. Markets could influence local fisheries over long distances. Thus, high-priced specialties such as smoked mackerel for New York's bar customers or iced whitefish for Berlin's middle classes were the foundation for the breakthrough of Scandinavian fisheries around 1900. Inshore fishermen earned enough money to buy decked motor-powered vessels and the fishing sector became an important export trade.

More significantly, a new distant-water fishery developed in Great Britain. Steam was put to the service of a quantity-oriented fishery that was defined by the invention of and spread of the steam-trawler after 1878 and the development of the fast-food market. In late-nineteenth-century Britain, many workers' homes had no kitchen or fireplace. By 1920 some twenty thousand fish-and-chips shops provided the urban masses with cheap and nourishing food. Batter proved an appetizing disguise for North Atlantic haddock and cod that had been caught two or three weeks before consumption and often was less than adequately iced. The fleet consisted of a few thousand very expensive steam trawlers. Ownership was organized in limited liability companies, which wielded much influence on political decisions on railway and port investments. The trawling industry concentrated on a narrow product segment (the whitefish industry) and soon faced a need to explore new fishing grounds. The North Sea was showing signs of depletion by the 1890s, and the fleet sought new grounds off the Faeroes and Iceland and later in the Barents Sea, which was regularly visited after World War I.

The British model for the trawling fisheries was adopted by most major European countries, which perceived high-seas fisheries not only as an economic option but as a marker of national political presence on the world scene. Germany in particular developed a state-subsidized distant-water fleet in a drive to feed the fast-growing domestic population while at the same time developing a maritime labor force. The German government nurtured hopes that the fishing fleet would be a "nursery for seamen" for the German navy as was the current belief in the U.K.

The American fisheries stagnated in the interwar period. There was not a large home market for fish, and consequently not the trade volume needed to invest in large trawlers. Many jobs were connected with the traditional pattern of fishing on the Grand Banks and supplying salt fish for the Mediterranean and the Caribbean. Canadian fisheries were still dominated by line fishing and salt fish production until World War II, but production was run at a deficit and therefore heavily dependent on state subsidies. As in Norway, the role of fishing for dispersed settlements was the key factor for political willingness to subsidize. The traditional salt-fish ports of the United States, which did not receive the same support, succumbed to international competition and declining demand for salt fish. After World War II the salt-fish market contracted, and sales are today virtually restricted to a few Mediterranean countries. In return both the U.S. East and West Coast inshore landings increased as city demand for fresh fish rose.

The biggest impact of the British steam-trawling model was in Japan. In the Pacific, the Japanese developed a deep-sea salmon fishery in order to feed a domestic market that could no longer be fed by the traditional inshore artisanal fisheries. A massive investment program brought Japan's landings on a par with the British already in 1910, and by 1938 Japan was the world's leading fishing nation with a catch of three million tons or three times the stagnant British landings.

All in all, from the late nineteenth century and especially after World War I, national fisheries were shaped with individual characteristics as regards the fishing fleet and state involvement. State subsidies played a decisive role in shaping the world market for fish when first continental European and later Japanese and Russian governments encouraged the building of distant-water fishing fleets. While there was a demand for feeding the urban masses, politicians were often more concerned with furthering the fisheries as a "nursery for seamen" for the navy and slicing out a national share of the world's marine resources. Distant-water fisheries found a secure backing in political circles, which did not necessarily reflect their true economic importance. Some fleets went farther and farther to sea to secure large enough catches to pay for even more expensive ships, while other fleets concentrated on inshore resources.

After 1950

Both the North Atlantic and North Pacific fish stocks were heavily fished by the 1930s but World War II served as a moratorium on fishing. In the 1950s the fishing fleets were rebuilt at great pace and technology changed the hunting practices from trial and error to scientifically aided mapping. Sonar—developed from the wartime asdic system—detected the shoals of fish beneath the surface and improved productivity immensely.

By 1950, the catches of the North Atlantic dominated the world's fish supplies. Soon, however, the Pacific Ocean was to be the world's most important source of fish. The Japanese fleet was rebuilt by government help, and rapid growth in the Japanese fishing fleet secured the lead for the Pacific Ocean during the 1950s and '60s. By 1959, 14 factory ships and 407 fishing vessels operated in the Bering Sea.

The Soviet Union had built a considerable steam trawler fleet in the 1930s and set up large combines to process the fish. From the early 1950s, the Soviet state launched an ambitious plan for distant-water resources. Soviet economists argued that fewer man-hours were needed to produce one unit of fish protein than one unit of meat, and a massive change from inshore artisanal fisheries to large-scale fisheries ensued. Due to large subsidies the fleet by 1975 consisted of 831 fishing vessels of over 1,000 tons and 547 floating factories in addition to transport vessels, fuel, and water carriers, operating up to 8,000 miles from home. The factory ships made six–eighteen month trips, and Russian trawlers reached both well-known banks in the North Atlantic and new-found fishing grounds off the coasts of Third World countries.

Another remarkable addition to global fisheries in the 1950s was the Peruvian anchoveta fishery. Demand for cheap protein for agricultural use, mainly in the rearing of pigs and chicken, was a driving force behind the new large-scale pelagic trawling operations. Industrial reduction of low-value fish for meal and oil was a well-known technology, but it only took on large-scale proportions with the discovery of immense pelagic resources off the South American coast. Production went from 59,000 tons in 1955 to 3 million tons in 1960 and peaked in 1970 with 13.1 million tons, making it the world's largest fishery. Three years later the fishery collapsed with only 1.7 million tons landed as the combined result of overfishing and the recurrent climatic change known as El Niño.

The postwar years were characterized by worldwide operations and ruthless exploitation of marine resources, some of which—like the North Atlantic cod—were showing clear signs of overexploitation by the end of the period. Most of the distant-water fisheries were driven by domestic demand and subsidies and little of the catch was therefore traded internationally, the most notable exception being fish meal. For the same reason the increasing political conflicts over the protection of marine resources took on a nationalist character, most notoriously in the British-Icelandic cod wars from 1960 to 1976.

Already in the 1950s, the British government, hitherto opposed to state subsidies, introduced support for medium-range trawlers fishing in the Mid-Atlantic, and later even for the largest and most modern trawlers fishing in the Barents and Greenland seas. Distant-water fisheries were simply not profitable relative to the high operation costs but were supported perhaps because government associated significant British qualities with a large fishery. Similarly the Japanese fisheries became ever more subsidized. When other coastal states began to claim nearby resources for themselves and bar foreign distant-water fishermen from access, these actions were not only a question of fish but a signal of new rules on the international scene. The keywords were territorialization and globalization.

In 1945, U.S. President Truman declared his intention to protect U.S. coastal resources, both fish and oil, not least against Japanese fishers, and in 1952 Iceland followed suit by extending its exclusive fishing zone. In a succession of declarations heavily opposed by the United Kingdom, the fishing zone around Iceland was extended to 200 nautical miles by 1976, and similar declarations of Exclusive Economic Zones (EEZs) were quickly introduced by most other coastal nations of the world. Thus, the fisheries had been territorialized and the free move of distant-water operators was severely challenged.

The effect on the distant-water operations was immediate. Total nonlocal catches by all states rose from 7.5 to 9 million tons from 1970 to 1990 but dropped as a percentage of global marine catches from 13 to 11 percent. Britain and Germany scrapped or sold the remains of their North Atlantic fishing fleets, while the European Union's own territorial waters were a poor compensation for lost resources in distant waters. By 1980, Japan was also feeling the brunt of the EEZs in the Pacific and diminished returns on fishing operations led to a real contraction of the Japanese high-seas fisheries from 2.1 million tons in 1970 to 0.9 million tons in 1993. The USSR distant-water fleet continued operations through the 1980s by obtaining fishing rights within the EEZs of Third-World countries mainly in West Africa. With the dissolution of the Soviet Union and the abrupt cut of state subsidies, the distant-water fleet was either scrapped or privatized. The fisheries of the Russian Federation declined dramatically from 10 million tons in 1989 to 4 million in 1994. Outside the major economic blocks, Norway and Iceland benefited from the collapse of the old European distant-water companies by buying up trawlers and obtaining quotas on both sides of the Atlantic and in the Arctic.

Generally, the landings of distant-water operations declined between 1980 and 1997, in particular thanks to the breakdown of the Soviet and East European fleets, and the dissolution of the Japanese fleets. West European fishing capacity was redistributed but largely maintained.

Heavy state subsidies are involved in the operation of the world's excess fishing capacity. In 1989, the United Nations Food and Agriculture Organization (FAO) estimated that total world revenues in fishing of around $70 billion were achieved at total operating costs of the world's fishing fleet of $92 billion. Including capital costs the deficit was calculated about $54 billion. The Soviet fleet alone accounted for a deficit of $5 to $8 billion. The Japan Fisheries Association at the same time estimated that the credit balance extended to fisheries from both commercial and government sectors was around $19 billion. Direct European Community support rose from $80 million in 1983 to $580 million in 1990. Indirect subsidies, including protectionist measures, and loans and payment by government for distant-water fishing licenses, continue to distort fleet size and encourage wasteful fishing practices.

Nevertheless, Extended Economic Zones have been a heavy counterweighing power to state subsidies. The main beneficiaries of the EEZs were coastal nation states close to the continental shelves. Most of these are a handful of developing countries, mainly in East and Southeast Asia and in South America. Countries such as Thailand and Indonesia obtained a leading position among the world's fishing nations by the 1990s, as they expanded their catches, especially of tuna. Biological surveys indicate that there is still some potential for increased catches. China now holds the position as the world's chief fish producer, although the statistics for this country seem much inflated. Chinese growth is mostly related to aquaculture, although a policy change in the early 1980s entailed the development of distant-water fisheries in the North Pacific and export of fish, mainly to the large Hong Kong market.

Asian aquaculture is rapidly emerging as a major source of fish. In 1994, five Asian countries accounted for 80 percent of global freshwater and saltwater aquaculture production, China alone accounting for 60.4 percent (15.4 million tons). India, Japan, Republic of Korea, and the Philippines are other main producers. Only 10 percent of aquacultured products originate from outside Asia. Unfortunately, many aquacultural enterprises are heavy polluters, and future development can only take place at the cost of a strong environmental effort.

The North American fisheries have also grown considerably in recent decades, benefiting both from the exclusion of European and Japanese fleets and rising prices on the national fresh fish market. Canadian fishermen also benefited initially, while they suffered from the collapse of the Grand Banks fisheries in the early 1990s and have little prospect of immediate improvement. In spite of growing fishing effort, North America is a net importer of fish, especially of some species of high quality. Peru and Chile have also expanded their fisheries, mainly as concerns the resurrected fish meal industry, which experienced some good years in the early 1990s, until a new collapse occurred in connection with the El Niño effect of 1997, but also as concerns aquaculture which is still growing.

While territorial control of marine resources has increased, the fish trade has become extremely globalized in recent decades. Total global landings have stabilized around 100 million tons per year because of a full utilization of the ocean's resources, but global demand for fish continues to rise. The recent rise in Western per capita demand for fish seems to be associated with the recognition of fish as a health food. On the eve of World War II fish consumption in the Western world rarely exceeded 10 kilograms per capita. In recent decades, however, fish consumption in the Western world has risen to the present level of 22 kilograms per capita. From 1948 to 1989, the share of total food dollars in the U.S. spent away from home increased from 24 to 46 percent. While most of the growth has occurred in the fast-food industry, the full-service restaurants have also expanded, not least in the market for specialized fish menus. High-income families spend more on fish than low-income families. The fish demand in Europe and Japan probably follows the same trend, albeit on a slower pace. While real prices of fish were 75 percent higher in the United States in 1988 compared to the base year of 1971, they were 20 percent higher in Japan and 35 percent higher in the United Kingdom.

As a result fish is shifted rapidly by both ship and air all around the globe to be processed in low-cost countries and marketed in high-price countries. Exclusive zones and national quotas privilege national concerns, but large fishing companies that both operate fishing vessels and trade in the fish market have bought licenses to fish in Third World countries. Big ocean-going factory trawlers operate in distant waters thousands of miles from their port of ownership, while at the same time fish-farmers in Third World countries produce fish for the world market. Vertical integration of the market has occurred at high speed, leaving just a handful of companies large enough to cater to the North American and European markets. While the fisheries even as late as around 1950 were dominated by small and medium-sized enterprises, they are today part and parcel of multinational companies that operate in many different food segments.

The luxury fish market likewise follows the globalization trend. In the past ten or fifteen years, air freight has increased the sales of desirable species such as lobster, shrimp, salmon, and tuna to European and American customers. The Norwegian farmed salmon industry is a case in point, as regards worldwide trade, state interventionism, and the rise of developing countries. While the Norwegian industry profited in the 1980s when salmon aquaculture was first introduced, it suffered a severe blow as international competition made prices fall continuously through the 1990s. State subsidies have enabled Norwegian producers to secure a worldwide market share of 54 percent by 1997. The main markets for farmed salmon are Japan, Europe, and the United States.

At the same time, East Asian aquaculture has grown rapidly, both serving the global market for luxury fish and crustaceans and the ever-larger domestic market. The future expansion of this industry, however, relies on an increased import of expensive fish-meal as feed, as the best quality feed brings the best prices and minimizes waste which has become a serious threat to the industry as large coastal stretches have become polluted. European fish-meal producers are the main suppliers of quality meal, and Asian growth therefore increases the globalization trend in both exports and imports.

The collapse of the East European distant-water fleet has meant that the West African fish market has suffered in the short run. Previously the Russians paid for the licenses with supplies of fish, while payment today is in cash. If the income from the sale of fish quotas to the European Union were invested in local shipbuilding and service industries there would be a potential for a future West African fishery, but it is doubtful if this possibility is being seized. The FAO therefore expresses concern over the lack of supplies of cheap and nourishing pelagic fish for the African market. This negative development is as much a result of local politics as of globalization itself.

Challenges

In the Western world, globalization in the fisheries has meant fewer fishermen, less catches, more state control, and more state subsidies. In a few developing countries, mainly in Asia, globalization has meant more fishermen, rapidly growing catches, and a boom in aquaculture with relatively little state control and subsidies. Markets are still ineffectual in many developing countries, but overall fishermen in the developing world and consumers in the developed world have profited from the dissolution of the old national distant-water fishing regimes. Western fish traders and Asian fishing industrialists have profited by globalization, while the losers have been distant-water fishing operators, especially in the former Soviet block and Japan. Western inshore fishermen have become exposed to global competition as markets are less protected. Most Third World countries have been little affected by the change. Immense problems of resource management of the oceans and environmental protection remain.

The consensus of the United Nations Food and Agriculture Organisation is that the majority of the world's marine resources have been used to the full—many indeed are overexploited. Apart from a few marginal resources, only the Indian Ocean has not yet been fully utilized. The growing population of the world will cause fish prices to soar and put even further stress on the limited marine resources. However, the rise of aquaculture may alleviate some of this pressure. While world fish catches increased fivefold from 17 million metric tons in 1950 to 91 million tons in 1995, aquacultural production grew tenfold from 2 million to 21 million tons in the same period. FAO forecasts that there is a potential for doubling the world's aquacultural output provided the environmental problems are solved.

Poul Holm

See also Cod; Coral Reefs; Estuaries; Lamprey; Law of the Sea; Nile Perch; Salmon; Snail Darter; Sturgeon; Tilapia; Water Pollution; Zebra Mussel

Further Reading

Bartz, F. (1964). Die grossen Fischereiräume der Welt. Wiesbaden: Steiner.

Coull, J. (1993). World fisheries resources. London: Routledge.

Holm, P., Smith, T. D., & Starkey, D. J. (Eds.). (2001). The exploited seas: New directions for marine environmental history. St. John's, Newfoundland: International Maritime Economic History Association/Census of Marine Life.

Holm, P. (1998). The global fish market: Internationalization and globalization, 1880–1997. Research in Maritime History 13 (St John's, 1998) 239–58.

Nicolson, J. (1979). Food from the sea. London: Cassel.

Starkey, D. J., Reid, C., & Ashcroft, N. R. (Eds.). (2000). England's sea fisheries: The commercial sea fisheries of England and Wales since 1300. Rochester, UK: Chatham Publishing.

United Nations, Food and Agriculture Organization. Yearbook of fishery statistics. Retrieved 20 August 2000, from: http://www.fao.org/fi/default.asp

Floods

Floods result whenever the banks of a stream or lake can no longer hold the water available to it. When this happens, water flows over the banks onto the surrounding floodplain, a lowland that is often a valley floor. In those regions of the world where snow falls, floods most likely occur in the early spring as snowmelt and spring rain combine to increase the volume of water flowing into freshwater bodies. Elsewhere, monsoons, typhoons, hurricanes, and other violent storms can contribute to flooding. Heavy downpours can cause savage flash flooding through canyons, gullies, and other locations where the floodplain is naturally narrow.

Stream channels cannot accommodate all possible sizes of flows, and it is entirely natural that flows substantially exceeding the average must overflow onto the floodplain. Significant benefits result. The water brings nutrients that fertilize the floodplain, among other things enabling agricultural development. It recharges groundwater, and it replenishes water supplies for fish and wildlife. In short, floods are part of nature's rhythm.

But floods also threaten life and property, and humans who live within a floodplain assume some risk. Flood damage can truly be awesome. Whole communities eliminated, thousands killed, economic devastation, famine, and disease may result. Historical evidence suggests that floods have far exceeded other

The Flood Motif in Creation Stories

The flood motif is a theme found in the creation stories of many peoples. The following is a selection from the creation story of the Yanomamo people of Brazil and Venezuela.

Both Omauwa and Yoawa began digging a hole to find water to quench the boy's thirst. They dug the hole so deep that when water did gush forth, it caused a large lake to form and covered the jungle. Then some of the first beings cut down trees, and floated on them to escape the flood. Because this was such a strange thing to do, they changed into foreigners and floated away. Their language also changed into the tongue of foreigners, and gradually became unintelligible to the Yanomamo. This is why foreigners have canoes and cannot be understood.

Many of the first beings were drowned in this flood. Those who managed to escape and remain Yanomamo did so by climbing mountains. They climbed Maiyo, Howashiwa, and Homahewa mountains to escape the flood, Maiyo being a peak near the area where Kaobawa's village had its origin. Then Raharariyoma, the mother of the girl whose vagina was changed into a mouth, took a piece of red pigment and painted dots all over her own body. After she was completely covered with red dots, she plunged into the lake and caused it to recede. Omauwa then caused her to be changed into a rabara, a snake-like monster that lives in large rivers. After that, she caused Yanomamo to drown when they tried to cross large rivers, either by eating them or by splashing large waves on them. Omauwa then went downstream and became an enemy to the Yanomamo. Today he sends hiccups, sickness, and epidemics to the Yanomamo.

It is because the foreigners refused to climb the mountains to escape the flood that they became enemies to the Yanomamo. The foreigners tried to make friends with the Yanomamo after the flood, but because their language was so different, the Yanomamo refused to be friends. Today, however, the Yanomamo are becoming friends with foreigners.

Source: Chagnon, Napoleon A. (1968). *Yanomamo, the Fierce People*. New York: Holt, Rinehart and Winston, p. 47.

natural disasters, including fires and earthquakes, in their impact on life and property, especially in industrialized nations.

The power of unleashed water has been extensively recorded in documents that reach back into antiquity. Indeed, archeological evidence pushes our knowledge of floods back into prehistory. The best-documented example is the Bonneville Flood, which occurred about 15,000 BCE in the western United States. Prehistoric Lake Bonneville occupied 51,800 hectares of what is now western Utah and parts of Nevada and southern Idaho. At its largest, it was about 217 kilometers wide and over 300 meters deep. Nearly seventeen thousand years ago the lake elevation rose, possibly because a tributary river above the lake captured another river and water from both rivers soon increased the lake water level above capacity. Lake water began escaping northward toward the present Snake River. Within a year, the lake elevation was lowered by 114 meters. The flood carved out much of western Washington state and left behind a variety of geological relics, including Utah Lake, Sevier Lake, the Great Salt Lake, and Bonneville Salt Flats.

Within the confines of human history, floods can be myth, reality, or somewhere in between, depending on the sources. The biblical story of Noah and the flood finds its parallels in the Babylonian epic of *Gilgamesh*, Norse mythology, and flood legends among the indigenous people of North and South America. No doubt, some of these stories at least partly emanate from fact. For example, archeologists have discovered a 2.4-meter layer of clay left by a flood of the Euphrates River around 3200 BCE. So devastating was this flood that it is easy to understand that ancient civilizations may have thought it signaled the end of the world. Many of these flood stories are didactic: They may reveal the

Flood warning sign in Colorado. COURTESY MARTIN REUSS.

floods as divine retribution for human wrongdoing or, at the very least, as an act of god(s) beyond human power and understanding.

It makes no difference whether basins are large or small, deep or shallow; floods come. In small basins, agricultural activities and urbanization affect peak discharges of water by decreasing infiltration into the ground, increasing surface runoff, and, via storm water outlets, speeding surface water downstream. In large basins, the effect of these developments is less dramatic. Instead, floods usually result from some combination of continuous and extraordinary rainfall, frozen ground, and snowmelt over a large area.

To protect themselves against floods, humans have devised dams, dikes (levees), floodwalls, and jetties. They dig deeper channels, stabilize banks, and occasionally provide outlets for excess water. All of this is both ancient technology and current practice. Changes have been only in the details. Today engineering theory, new kinds of construction material, and vastly more powerful construction technology combine to allow for stronger, safer, and more durable structures, but the basic approach remains the same. Neither better science nor improved technology ensures the success of flood projects or guarantees complete protection. In fact, history shows that success is generally only transitory and that eventual failure is more the rule than the exception.

Great River Basin Floods

For destructive power, no stream matches China's Yellow (Huang) River. Known as "the Ungovernable" and "China's Sorrow," it flows 4,631 kilometers to the sea.

Legend sets one of its first floods twenty-three centuries before the birth of Christ. A monstrous flood was reputed to have lasted for thirteen years. What is indisputable is that Chinese dynasties have attempted to control floods on the river by both building dikes along the banks and dredging to deepen the channel and keep it clear of obstructions. The Han dynasty built a unified system of dikes between 202 and 220 CE. This was the first attempt to unify all the various dike systems that had previously been built by farmers and villagers. Repeated attempts to ensure flood protection over the succeeding years proved futile. Calamitous floods occurred nearly every other year. The river's periodic changes of course—twenty-six significant ones in the last thirty-five hundred years—further challenged flood protection works. In 1855 the river overwhelmed a dike near Tungwa Hsiang, about 48 kilometers east of Kaifeng. Engineers tried to repair the dike system over the next six years but failed. Uncontrolled, the river rampaged over the countryside, finally settling into its present channel about 804 kilometers to the north of where its main channel had been nearly six hundred years before. In 1887 heavy rains in Hunan Province brought about what still ranks as the worst flood disaster in human history. The Yellow River tore through the dikes at Cheng-chou and within minutes completely inundated the city. Racing toward the east, the river demolished six hundred villages; another fifteen hundred villages in the floodplain experienced severe flooding. The river deposited so much sediment that it prevented any agricultural production. The exact number of dead will never be known, but the estimate ranges from 2 million to 4 million. Significant breaches appeared again in 1921 and 1929. A flood in 1939 destroyed crops and villages. Japanese occupation prevented the distribution of relief supplies. About 10 million persons were left homeless, and about two hundred thousand died in the ensuing famine.

Floods along China's other principal river, the Yangtze (Chang), also have caused much suffering. The Yangtze is the longest in the country at 5,471 kilometers. Nearly 18,129 square kilometers of lakes are connected to the Yangtze system, providing space for upstream floods. However, if heavy precipitation falls on downstream areas already swollen with floodwaters, disaster may result. The river's formidable discharge into the sea can double. If dikes cannot contain the floods, the water spills over into an area that may reach 181,299 square kilometers along the middle and lower reaches of the river. In 1931 weeks of constant rain led to the Yangtze cresting 29 meters above its normal stage. More than 3.7 million Chinese died, mainly from famine, and property losses reached $1.4 billion, an incredible amount for that time. Again in 1998 severe floods on the Yangtze displaced millions of people and killed more than three thousand. In all, the floods may have affected as many as 250 million people—millions directly and other millions because of health problems or the disruption of vital electrical, transportation, and water distribution systems.

In North America the Mississippi River basin gathers water from thirty-one states and two Canadian provinces. It drains 41 percent of the continental United States, excluding Alaska. From its headwaters in Minnesota to the Gulf of Mexico, the Mississippi River flows 3,778 kilometers. To this must be added the 4,092-kilometer-long Missouri River, the longest in North America, which empties into the Mississippi just north of St. Louis; the Ohio River, which joins the Mississippi at Cairo, Illinois, and actually contributes more water to the Mississippi than the Missouri does; and a number of lesser tributaries. The combined water from these rivers flows southward to the Gulf of Mexico, like water going into a funnel. Spanish explorer Hernando de Soto saw a flood on the Mississippi in 1543, perhaps the first European to do so. Since that time floods have periodically returned. Congress in 1879 established the Mississippi River Commission, a mix of civilian and military personnel to develop plans to improve flood protection and navigation along the Mississippi. The commission mainly relied on levees, a method advocated by the U.S. Army Corps of Engineers. Local levee districts followed suit, and levee construction or improvement marked much of the lower stretch of the river (beneath Cairo, Illinois). The work could not be completed fast enough. Floods occurred every year from 1881 to 1884, again in 1886, and a major one in 1890. More flood devastation came in the early twentieth century. Finally, the 1927 flood compelled a reevaluation of flood control methods. Close to five hundred people perished, over 6.4 million hectares of land were flooded, forty-one thousand buildings were destroyed, 162,000 homes were demolished, 325,000 people were cared for in temporary Red Cross camps, and another 311,000 people were temporarily put up in private homes. The flood—actually a sequence of floods beginning in January and lasting through May—clearly showed that reliance on levees was not the answer. Rather, in 1928 Congress authorized a new Corps of Engineers plan that combined bigger and stronger levees with various human-made outlets, dredging, banks, and other measures.

Of course, construction did not stop the floods nor the damage. Indeed, seventeen major floods have hit the lower Mississippi River since 1879, an average of one major flood every seven years. A particularly devastating flood struck the Ohio and Mississippi Rivers in 1937. A flood in 1973 killed twenty-seven people, inundated 4.5 million hectares, and caused $420 million in damage. It almost took out the Old River Control Structure, which regulates the amount of water that flows into Louisiana's Atchafalaya Basin, a major safety valve for floodwaters. Had the structure gone, eventually the Mississippi River would have changed course and stranded Baton Rouge and New Orleans miles from the river's main channel. The economic and public health problems would have been incalculable. The structure held, however, and the Corps of Engineers estimated that flood control measures prevented $7 billion in damages. As for the middle and upper stretches of the river, a 1993 flood that resulted from exceptionally long and heavy rainfalls inundated 2.6 million hectares, left from $12 billion to $16 billion in damages, and caused at least thirty-eight deaths. On the other hand, the Corps of Engineers estimated that flood works—principally levees—prevented more than $19 billion in flood damages.

Small River Basin Floods

The Yellow, Yangtze, and Mississippi Rivers exemplify the large river basins that periodically endure floods. In contrast, the Arno River in Italy shows that even relatively small river basins may endure devastating floods. The Arno is a short stream, running 241 kilometers from the Apennines Mountains to the Mediterranean Sea. It is not particularly beautiful; the color of its water is often brown, and it is little more than a mud flat in dry seasons. Yet, sitting astride the Arno in the shadow of the Apennines is the magnificent city of Florence. The Arno has flooded the city many times. Significant damage occurred in 1117, 1333, 1547, 1666, and 1844, but other floods were nearly as costly in lives and property. On average, floods occurred once every twenty-six years. Leonardo da Vinci (1452–1519) once proposed to divert the Arno around Florence, using a large retention basin, a canal, tunnel, and floodgates, but the city fathers ignored his plans. Although Florence lived under the constant threat of floods, the flood that hit the city in 1966 caught the city unprepared. In November of that year floodwaters from heavy rains poured down the steep ravines to the west of the city. The lower slopes of the ravines were densely populated. Two upstream dams produced hydroelectric power but had not been built for flood control (the two purposes are fundamentally in opposition: hydroelectric power requires full reservoirs to supply water to the turbines; flood control requires low water elevations to provide space for upstream floodwater). The city had made no attempt to dredge the river so that it could accommodate more water in its channel.

The flood largely resulted from extraordinary downpours. During two days at the beginning of November, the upper Arno River basin, already saturated with October rain, received 48 centimeters of rain. Yet, human error probably contributed to the tragedy. In the weeks preceding the flood, the operators of the Penna hydroelectric dam, about 48 kilometers upstream from Florence, had held water behind the dam rather than gradually releasing it over an extended period of time. During the downpour, late on 3 November, they determined that they had to release a significant amount of water, presumably to relieve pressure on the dam. The wall of water from Penna descended on the lower dam, Levane, just 6.4 kilometers above Florence. The engineers there believed that they had no choice; they, too, released water in order to accommodate the additional flow. A wall of water descended on the city of Florence. The flood overwhelmed Florence's inadequate defenses, rendered the city without power, and devastated the city's ancient churches and invaluable art collections. Water swirled around the basement stacks of the Biblioteca Nazionale Centrale, Italy's largest library, damaging or destroying over 1 million books and manuscripts. It licked the tombs of Michelangelo, Galileo, Rossini, and Machiavelli in the church of St. Croce. Five of the sculptor Ghiberti's ten bronze panels came loose from their portals. More than one hundred thousand persons sat marooned on their rooftops and on upper floors in the darkened city. Only thirty-five people lost their lives in the flood, but thousands became homeless, and hundreds were injured. As the water receded, the world came to Florence's aid. Ghiberti's doors were found in the muck; Michelangelo's statues and Donatello's sculpture of Mary Magdalene were painstakingly cleaned; the Museum of Archaeology's unsurpassed Etruscan collection was repaired, although many pieces were badly damaged; and the enormous work, still not completed more than thirty-five years later, of rescuing Florence's books and manuscripts began.

The 1966 flood of Florence was, of course, both dramatic and tragic. Yet, similar floods can be found around the world. Lynmouth, England, for example, sits at the confluence of the West and East Lyn Rivers in north Devon. The two streams plunge some 457 meters over a distance of only 6.4 kilometers before joining for a short stretch to the sea. In mid-August 1952 torrential rains blackened the skies and swelled both the East and West Lyn Rivers. After a brief lull, the rain began again. Water poured down into Lynmouth from both rivers, flooding out the city's hydroelectric plant. During the peak of the flood, about 521 metric tons of water per second formed a wall of water 9.1 meters high that all but demolished the town. Ninety-three houses were demolished, seventeen bridges destroyed, 132 vehicles washed out to sea, and at least thirty-four people lost their lives. In some places, mud and silt deposits reached a depth of 7.6 meters.

In the United States, one of the deadliest flash floods in the country's history occurred within the confines of the 40-kilometer-long Big Thompson Canyon, just east of Estes Park, Colorado. In that canyon, Big Thompson River descends 762 meters before joining the South Platte River. Thunderstorms beginning in the late afternoon of 31 July 1976, turned the usually shallow river into a torrent. Within two to three hours, a wall of water 5.7 meters high swept through the canyon, destroying motels, cars, and just about everything else in its path. Between 139 and 145 people died; 418 houses and 152 businesses were destroyed; and another 138 houses were damaged. Subsequent investigations showed that much of this tragedy was preventable. Hampered by budget restrictions, the local weather service reporting system had fallen into disarray, and the one automated rain gauge in Big Thompson Canyon malfunctioned. The result was that flash flood warnings appeared far too late; indeed, they appeared after much of the destruction had already occurred. Moreover, people caught between the canyon walls did not know what to do. Some sought shelter in their cars—precisely the wrong response—or tried to drive out of the canyon instead of climbing the canyon walls. Valuable lessons were learned but at a terrible price.

Dam Failures and Floods

Not all floods result from hydrologic circumstances. Some result from human failure. Poorly engineered dams and levees may break under the stress of enormous amounts of water, unstable foundations, poor choice of building material, earthquakes, negligent operation and maintenance, or faulty design. Probably ten dams have failed for every one thousand existing today. An estimated two thousand dams have failed since the twelfth century CE. The chief problem has been ignorance of what is now called rock and soil mechanics. Under the weight of the dam, unstable foundations can shift or slide, causing cracks in the dam itself. Moreover, mountainsides and canyon walls may collapse into dam reservoirs, pushing a torrent of water over the top of the dam. Another major problem has been inadequate spillways, which force the water over the dam crest, rather than safely conveying the water downstream.

Sometimes flooding is the result of both ignorance and hubris. The Johnstown, Pennsylvania, flood of 1889 is one example that has attained legendary proportions in American history. The number of deaths was officially estimated at twenty-one hundred, and Grandview Cemetery in Johnstown contains the graves of 777 victims who were never identified. The catastrophe resulted from the collapse of South Fork Dam, located on Little Conemaugh River, 19 kilometers upstream from Johnstown, a community of twelve thousand persons in western Pennsylvania. The dam—poorly constructed by a private fishing club, in need of repair, and with spillways blocked to prevent fish behind the dam from swimming downstream—broke on 31 May, sending a wall of water 38 meters high into the Conemaugh Valley. This was the first substantial dam disaster in the United States, caused entirely by humans, not nature.

Both inattention to geology and engineering hubris contributed to the failures of the St. Francis Dam in California and the Vaiont Dam in Italy. The St. Francis Dam, built to store water from the aqueduct that supplied Los Angeles with water, was a 62-meter arched concrete dam located in the San Francisco Canyon, about 72 kilometers from Los Angeles. On the night of 12 March 1928, it collapsed without warning. Within seventy minutes almost the entire reservoir had been spilled. The resulting flood killed 450 people. Subsequent investigation showed that the dam had been built on conglomerate along one canyon wall that could not withstand the hydrostatic pressure. The opposite wall and the canyon wall contained mica schist, interspersed with talc, almost guaranteeing foundation movement. Indeed, evidence existed that the dam was moving well before the collapse. William Mulholland (1855–1935), general manager and chief engineer for the Los Angeles Bureau of Water Works and Supply,

received much of the blame for the disaster. A man of both talent and arrogance, Mulholland never consulted professional geologists before constructing the dam.

In Italy, on the night of 9 October 1963, a tremendous rockslide fell into the reservoir behind Vaiont Dam, a thin-arched dam and one of the highest in the world (264 meters) near Belluno in Venuto Province. The rockslide occurred at a terrifying speed and caused gigantic waves that overtopped the dam. Tremors from the slide were detected on seismographs throughout Europe. Although the dam itself suffered no major damage, the resulting downstream flood killed twenty-six hundred people. Water pouring over the dam rose to a height of 100 meters above the dam's crest. In this case, engineers and geologists had underestimated the geological stresses. The steeply sloping upper reaches of Mount Toc, which looms above the dam, contains limestone and crumbly marl. The combination made for an unstable area likely to slide, but the engineers had thought that more gently sloping regions farther down the mountainside would stabilize the small slides thought most likely to occur. They had underestimated the threat. Unusually heavy rains and accumulating groundwater that exerted an upward pressure created unusual hydrostatic conditions in the summer of 1963. As the reservoir behind the dam swelled to capacity, the region above the reservoir became more and more unstable. A day or so before the disaster, engineers finally realized the danger, but it was too late.

The Teton Dam disaster on the Teton River in southeastern Idaho in 1976 led to numerous changes in engineering practice within the U.S. Bureau of Reclamation, the dam's builder. The 92-meter-high earthfill dam failed on 5 June during the initial impoundment of water within the reservoir. A tiny trickle observed in the early morning on the downstream face of the dam grew to a steady flow within a few hours. Bulldozers futilely tried to plug the leak, but just before noon water breached the dam crest. By the end of the day, eleven people had been killed, twenty-five thousand were homeless in downstream communities, and property damage amounted to $400 million. Investigators concluded that "internal erosion" deep in the foundations had initiated the dam failure. The eroded soil particles had escaped through small channels between the dam and the abutment rock; Bureau of Reclamation regulations called for a tight seal on cracks in the dam wider than 12.7 millimeters but had required no seals on smaller cracks. Once started, this internal erosion rapidly progressed. Investigators also believed that the dam design did not adequately address geological and soil conditions.

Engineers do all they can to prevent dam failure, but so many forces and circumstances are involved in the design, construction, and operation of a dam—among the bulkiest and heaviest structures ever erected—that it is virtually impossible to guarantee against failure. Vigilance and good maintenance are essential.

Nonstructural Solutions

Humans have become more modest in their attempts to control nature. In the nineteenth century a common term was *flood prevention*. *Flood control* emerged as the favored term in the early and mid-twentieth century. Today people commonly and more accurately speak of *flood reduction*. As early as the 1940s doubts emerged about the efficacy of structures such as dams and levees to control floods. In his dissertation *Human Adjustment to Floods* (1942), the American geographer Gilbert F. White (1911–) first noted that flood damages increase despite new construction to control floodwaters. He observed that new engineering structures provide people with an illusion of security. They also accelerate property development and contribute to increased property values. The result is that when floods overwhelm dams and levees, the property damage is greater than if the structures had not been there in the first place. Subsequent studies confirmed White's observations. Per-capita flood damages in the United States were nearly 2.5 times greater for the period 1951–1985 than for the period 1916–1950, after adjusting for inflation.

White completed his dissertation six years after passage of the 1936 Flood Control Act, which established that flood control is an appropriate federal responsibility in the United States. Congress charged the Army Corps of Engineers with building most of the structures authorized in the act. The effect of the act, amended and expanded in the following years, was dramatic. From 1856 to 1936 federal expenditures for control amounted to only $400 million. In the sixteen years subsequent to passage of the act, the federal government appropriated about $3.5 billion to pay for about one thousand projects, including dams, levees, floodwalls, and channel straightening. By the late 1970s the figure had climbed to about $13 billion. According to the Corps of Engineers, these structures prevented about $245 billion in damages between 1960 and 1985 (in 1985 dollars). Yet, when floods come, the

property damage remains significant, as does the toll of lives lost. The National Weather Service estimated that during that same period, 1960–1985, flood damages amounted to $62.5 billion in 1985 dollars. Nor does the number of annual flood-related deaths indicate a downward trend after it is adjusted for population changes. From 1916 to 1940 there was an annual average of 153.7 flood-related deaths; from 1941 through 1965, 86.1; from 1966 through 1985, 144.8; and from 1989 through 1998, 95.7.

White encouraged using nonstructural measures rather than relying on dams, levees, and similar bulwarks. These measures include zoning to restrict or reduce construction in flood-prone areas; flood-proofing buildings by, for instance, raising them above the floodline or moving them; improving flood forecasting; and issuing federal flood insurance (which requires community compliance with federal floodplain policies). Since the late 1960s the United States has had a national flood insurance program. Of the twenty thousand communities eligible for the program, over 90 percent participate.

There will always be floods, and there will always be flood damages despite human efforts to reduce the losses. With increased attention to restoring the ecosystem, minimizing disturbances to the environment, and reducing the potential negative effects of large structures on both the human and natural environment, it seems likely that future engineers and planners will combine both structural and nonstructural methods to fight floods.

Martin Reuss

See also Weather Events, Extreme

Further Reading

Clark, C., & Time-Life Books. (1982). *Flood*. Alexandria, VA: Time-Life Books.

Hoyt, W. G., & Langbein, W. B. (1955). *Floods*. Princeton, NJ: Princeton University Press.

Jansen, R. B. (1980). *Dams and public safety*. Washington, DC: U. S. Department of the Interior, Water and Power Resources Service [Bureau of Reclamation].

Leopold, L. B. (1997). *Water, rivers and creeks*. Sausalito, CA: University Science Books.

L. R. Johnston Associates. (1992). *Floodplain management in the United States: An assessment report*. Washington, DC: Federal Emergency Management Agency.

Rosen, H., & Reuss, M. (1988). *The flood control challenge: Past, present, and future*. Chicago: Public Works Historical Society.

White, G. F. (1945). *Human adjustment to floods: A geographical approach to the flood problem in the United States* (Research Paper No. 29). Chicago: University of Chicago Department of Geography [White's 1942 dissertation].

Fodder Crops

Many of the world's major crops are grown, at least in part, for animal feed as well as for direct human consumption: maize, wheat, barley, potatoes, soybeans, various root crops, and others. However, there is a wide range of crops cultivated specifically as animal feed. These include many species of grass and legumes to provide pasture as well as hay and silage, which is fed to housed animals. Such resources have been important since Paleolithic hunter-gatherers manipulated herds of wild animals and began to encourage appropriate browse through the use of fire. As animals were domesticated, beginning around ten thousand years ago, forage species grew in importance and in many regions the use of fire to clear natural vegetation for arable and pastoral agriculture transformed wildscapes into landscapes.

Today, forage crops are vital in the worldwide production of meat, milk, hides, and wool, for human use. They are grown in environments ranging from boreal to tropical, on nutrient-rich and poor soils, at high and low altitudes, and in water-stressed and non-stressed areas. Moreover, forage-producing agroecosystems may be characterized by low energy or high energy inputs. The more mechanization and chemicals that are employed, the greater the energy input, as these all come from fossil fuels. Pastures comprise areas of naturally occurring grassland with varying degrees of management, or may be specially planted. The species composition reflects management and environmental constraints. Some species are cosmopolitan; most species are either fast growing or exhibit high productivity.

Many grass species (family Gramineae) are encouraged or cultivated as forage. In tropical/subtropical regions, Sudan grass (*Sorghum sudanense*) is particularly important whilst in higher latitudes varieties of perennial rye grass (*Lolium perenne*) and fescue (e.g., tall fescue—*Festuca arundinacea* and red fescue—*Festuca rubra*) dominate. Similarly, many legumes are encouraged in pastures or are cultivated specifically for forage. They are important because they have a sym-biotic relationship with specific bacteria with the ability to trap nitrogen from the atmosphere and to convert it to nitrogen compounds that can be used by other organisms, including the legumes. This enrichment of soils with nitrogen encourages overall plant growth and reduces the need of artificial fertilizers. This capacity has led to the term "green manure" and to the inclusion of leguminous species as forage in many low-latitude agroecosystems that are based on agroforestry—the combination of tree and ground crops that may incorporate forage and/or arable crops. Some forage legumes dominate tropical regions and others temperate environments, but the perennial alfalfa (*Medicago sativa*), also known as lucerne, and various clovers (*Trifolium* spp.) are important worldwide. Both grasses and legumes benefit from management that may include fertilizer applications, crop protection chemicals to reduce unpalatable plant species and insect predators, water conservation in drought-prone areas, and especially the regulation of numbers of grazing animals to avoid pasture degradation and soil erosion.

Alfalfa (Lucerne)

Alfalfa is a widespread forage crop because it is highly nutritious, providing protein, vitamins, and minerals for sheep, cattle, and goats. Its history is not well established but it is likely that it was domesticated in Central Asia, possibly Iran, where its wild ancestors were used in abundance. It subsequently spread throughout Europe, and probably to the east. Eventually it was introduced to South America, probably by European colonists after 1500; it then entered North America via California in the late 1800s and subsequently spread north and east. Today, it is a major forage crop in North America, both in pastures and as a specialty crop for silage as well as the production of meal and pellets. In the latter forms it can be used to supplement silage based on maize and grass. Alfalfa's value as a forage crop has made it the subject of considerable research. It grows best in well-drained nutrient-rich soils and is most productive when rotational grazing regimes are employed; for example, three days of grazing followed by thirty days of fallow are recommended in temperate environments, though each of the many varieties of alfalfa grows best under specific microconditions. Grazing is not recommended in wet, muddy conditions as crop damage through trampling and uprooting may occur.

Alfalfa benefits from applications of phosphate (a source of available phosphorus), potash (a source of available potassium), and lime (calcium carbonate) to decrease the soil acidity. Before alfalfa is sown, its potential productivity may be enhanced by treating the seed with lime, a fungicide to reduce fungal rot, and an inoculant containing nitrogen-fixing bacteria that will promote root nodulation. A first harvest can usually be achieved between 70 and 90 days, with subsequent harvests every 30 to 38 days; in temperate regions harvests are not possible in winter.

Traditional plant breeding has given rise to numerous varieties of alfalfa but recently attention has focused on genetic modification. A major short-term objective is to produce herbicide-resistant alfalfa so that the effectiveness of weed control using herbicides can be improved without damage to the alfalfa crop; subsequent developments may include improved feed value by promoting protein production and the generation of phytase enzymes to improve phosphorus utilization by animals. Moreover, the development of aluminum tolerance would bring benefits to the environment and to productivity by curtailing the need for liming aimed at reducing soil acidity—which causes alfalfa to concentrate sufficiently high amounts of aluminum that crop damage occurs.

Prospects for Forage Crops

Competition for land will undoubtedly increase in the next twenty years; population growth and urbanization, especially in developing nations, will encroach onto arable and pastoral land at the same time as food requirements increase. In developed nations, despite land-use diversification involving the encouragement of wildlife conservation, leisure, and tourism activities, meat and animal products will remain significant. The overall need for increased productivity is an objective that forage grasses and legumes, improved by conventional plant breeding and genetic modification, will provide. Consequently, their importance in world agriculture is likely to remain undiminished.

Antoinette Mannion

Further Reading

Finch, H. J. S., Samuel, A. M., & Lane, G. (2002). *Lockhart and Wiseman's crop husbandry* (8th ed.). Cambridge, UK: Woodhead Publishing Limited.

Frame, J., Charlton, J. L. F., & Laidlaw, A. S. (1998). *Temperate forage legumes.* Wallingford, UK: CABI.

Givens, D. I., Owen, E., Axford, R. F. E., & Omed, H. M. (Eds.). (2000). *Forage evaluation in ruminant nutrition.* Wallingford, UK: CABI.

Food Chain

A food chain is an arrangement of the organisms of an ecological community according to the order of predation in which each member uses the next member as a food source. Although the term was not used until 1913 by the American ecologist Victor Shelford, the concept had already been anticipated by Charles Darwin in 1859 as "the tangled bank" metaphor and developed by the zoologist Karl Semper in 1881. Charles Elton (1927) further developed the concept and promoted food chains as one of the basic principles forming the basis of community ecology. Since the 1950s much research has been conducted on food webs (the totality of interacting food chains in an ecological community). Some ecologists—for example, G. E. Hutchinson, R. Paine, B. Menge, P. Sutherland, and G. Polis—studied the complexity of food webs and their importance to community ecology. Others, including R. Lindeman, J. Teal, and H. T. Odum, studied energy transfer through food webs and ecosystems. A detailed mathematical theory describing food-web dynamics has been developed by S. Pimm, R. May, J. Cohen, L. Oskonan, N. Martinez, and others.

Definition

Food webs describe who eats whom in a particular ecological community. In some instances, food webs

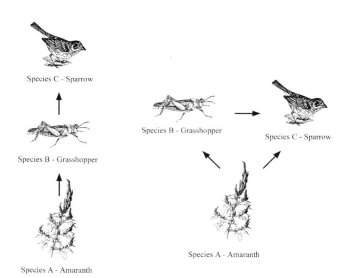

Food chain diagrams demonstrate the pathway of food through the ecosystem. Some paths are simple chains, but in most cases paths are more complex and form webs. Illustration layout by V. Medland, some images © 2003 www.clipart.com

Complexity in Food Webs: Multitrophic Species

Omnivory is one of the reasons food webs are so complex. Some species feed in many different trophic levels. This greatly increases the complexity and interactions present within the web. It was originally suggested that omnivory was rare in food webs because it led to instability. More recent research especially that on complex detritus based food webs suggests that omnivory is quite common and does not lead to instability in many cases. Detrivores are also difficult to categorize because they feed on dead organic matter accumulated from many trophic levels. Certain species feed in different trophic levels as juveniles. In some species each sex has a different trophic level. The effects of feeding on many different levels greatly increases food web complexity.

Vicki Medland

are simple chains: Species A is eaten by species B, which is eaten by species C. In most cases, species relationships are far more complex: Species A is eaten by species B and species C, which also feeds on species B. The food web of even a relatively simple community would be extremely large and complex. In order to simplify large webs, individual species are commonly placed into groups that have the same predators and prey in the food web. The trophic level of a species indicates how many links separate its prey from the original energy source, usually the sun. Primary producers or autotrophs are organisms that produce their own food (plants and in some cases autotrophic bacteria). Consumers such as herbivores, omnivores, and carnivores make up the ascending levels. Decomposers feed on a pool of decomposing organic matter that can come from many trophic levels. Because of this they are often separated into a separate food chain where detritus (loose material resulting from disintegration) makes up the primary food source of the decomposers, which are in turn eaten by carnivores. It is important to remember that a food web represents only presence or absence of predation between species. In the real world, these interactions are highly dynamic and may vary in presence or importance depending on environmental factors such as season or on biotic (relating to life) or demographic factors such as sex or developmental stage.

Complexity

Few food webs are simple chains. Most involve consumers as omnivores that feed on more than one trophic level, such as coyotes, which are predators that

sometimes feed on herbivores such as rabbits or on other predators such as lizards. Consumers can be herbivores (feeding on grasses or fruits) and are often detritivores (scavenging on dead animals). Some species feed at different trophic levels at different life stages. For example, mosquitoes are detritivores as larvae, whereas females are blood-feeding predators, and males are nectivores (feeding on nectar) or may not feed at all. A measure of complexity called "connectance" has been developed to better understand food-web dynamics. Connectance is the ratio of the number of actual feeding interactions between the members of the food web to the total possible number of interactions. A higher ratio indicates greater complexity. A second critical factor is interaction strength, which is the actual amount of influence one species has on another. By measuring connectance and interaction strength scientists are able to evaluate the stability of a food web or its ability to remain unchanged following different types of disturbance. It was originally believed that more complex food webs are less stable, but recent studies of food webs with high connectance but weak interaction strengths refute this belief.

Food-Web Theory

Charles Elton (1927) made the original observation that food chains tend to be short. The inefficiency of energy transfer between trophic levels places constraints on the number of top consumers that can be supported by the base of producer biomass (the amount of living matter). More importantly, as a food chain becomes longer, it becomes unstable. Trophic pyramids are diagrams that present the amount of energy or biomass in each successive trophic level, with producers at the bottom. Such diagrams suggest that food-web dynamics are controlled by "bottom up" processes in which the original amount of primary production controls all other interactions. The "Green World" model developed by N. Hairston, S. Smith, and S. Slobodkin in 1960 suggested there is always an excess of primary production, so each trophic level must be controlled by its consumers, reflecting "top down" control. The "Exploitation Ecosystem Hypothesis" first described by Fretwell (1977) suggested that variability in the number of trophic levels determines numbers or biomass. Food webs with even numbers result in low levels of plant biomass, whereas those with odd numbers result in excess biomass because predation is suppressed. This model also suggests that food webs are limited to only three or four trophic levels. Trophic cascade models, like those described for aquatic systems by S. Carpenter and J. Kitchell (1988) and M. Power (1990), describe systems in which primary productivity is controlled by bottom-up factors like nutrient availability, but it is the number of trophic levels and predators that then controls food-web dynamics. R. J. Williams and N. Martinez (2000) have recently introduced the "Niche Model." This model is based on the idea that each trophic species fits into a specific niche; this model seeks to predict food-web characteristics more accurately than do earlier models.

Trophic Pyramids

Karl Semper (1881) introduced the concept of energy transfer through food webs, which was later formalized into the food pyramid or "pyramid of numbers" concept by Elton in 1927. Any trophic interaction represents a transfer of energy in the form of calories from plants, detritus, or animals to other animals, so food webs can also show the movement of energy or biomass through a particular community. These are sometimes called "Eltonian" or "Lindeman" pyramids in recognition of the pioneering work done by Elton (1927) and Lindeman (1942) in formalizing the trophic pyramid concept, but again it was Semper in 1881 who first recognized that the transfer of energy is incredibly inefficient and hypothesized that only 10 percent of the energy present at the lower trophic level is assimilated and converted to growth, activity, or reproduction, the other 90 percent is lost mainly through egestion as feces or other waste products or as heat. Experts know from numerous studies on real food webs that this inefficiency varies considerably but is

generally less than 20 percent. As energy is transferred from one consumer to the next there is the same loss of energy. So, in a food chain with one producer and just three consumers, only about 0.1 to 0.2 percent of the original energy is available to the top consumer in the food chain. Consumers that feed "low on the food chain" are able to capture more of the original total energy produced and often support populations with larger total numbers or biomass than can consumers that feed at higher levels.

Keystone Species

Keystone species are unique because their effects on the dynamics of a given food web are out of proportion to their abundance or biomass and they have strong interactions with other species. Removal of a keystone species, as its name suggests, results in changes in the food web. R. Paine introduced the concept in 1969 to explain the results of a series of experiments where removal of predatory starfish from a rocky intertidal area greatly changed the rest of the food web. Other examples of keystone species are sea otters, fruit-eating bats, beavers, termites, and harvester ants.

Applications in Environmental Science

The most important uses of food-web theory in environmental science are in the biomagnification (accumulation of toxins up the food web) of toxins and in the introduction of invasive species. Toxins such as DDT and PCBs (polychlorinated biphenyls) are not typically broken down when ingested. Instead they are sequestered in fatty tissue, where they accumulate over the lifetime of the organism. When predators eat many toxin-containing organisms they sequester a higher total dose. Predators at the next level of the food web ingest the accumulated toxin of their prey, so that species at the top of the food web are, in fact, ingesting all the toxins ingested by all the individuals that fed before them. Biomagnification effects of toxins were first brought to the public's attention in 1962 in Rachel Carson's influential book, *Silent Spring*.

People have been deliberately or accidentally introducing exotic species into novel ecosystems for millennia. However, only recently have people begun to focus on the effects that those species can have on food-web dynamics. Because an exotic species is often free from the predators, diseases, or parasites of other native species feeding at its trophic level, it can exert strong interaction effects on the food web, often with catastrophic effects. For example, the continuing introduction of exotic species into the Great Lakes, which began in the 1930s, has resulted in destabilization in the lake food web as well as extinction of several species.

Vicki Medland

Further Reading

Carpenter, S. R., Kitchell, J. F., & Hodgson, J. R. (1985). Cascading trophic interactions and lake productivity. *Bioscience, 35*(10), 634–639.

Carson, R. (1962). *Silent spring.* Boston: Houghton Mifflin.

Cohen, J. E. (1978). Food webs and niche space. In J. E. Cohen & D. W. Stephens (Eds.), *Monographs in population biology* (pp.208). Princeton, NJ: Princeton University Press.

Darwin, C. (1859). *On the origin of species by means of natural selection.* London: John Murray.

Elton, C. S. (1927). *Animal ecology.* London: Sidgwich and Jackson.

Fretwell, S. D. (1977). The regulation of plant communities by food chains exploiting them. *Perspectives in Biology and Medicine, 20*, 169–185.

Hairston, N. G., Smith, F. E., & Slobodkin, L. S. (1960). Community structure, population control, and competition. *American Naturalist, 94*, 421–425.

Hutchinson, G. E. (1959). Homage to Santa Rosalia or why are there so many kinds of animals? *American Naturalist, 93*(870), 145–159.

Lindeman, R. L. (1942). The trophic-dynamic aspect of ecology. *Ecology, 23*(4), 399–418.

Martinez, N. D. (1993). Effects of scale on food web structure. *Science, 260*(5113), 242–243.

Martinez, N. D. (1991). Artifacts or attributes? Effects of resolution on the Little Rock Lake food web. *Ecological Monographs, 61*(4), 367–392.

May, R. M. (1988). How many species are there on Earth? *Science, 241*(4872), 1441–1449.

McCann, K., Hastings, A., & Huxel, G. R. (1998). Weak trophic interactions and the balance of nature. *Nature, 395*(6704), 794–813.

McIntosh, R. P. (1985). *The background of ecology: Concept and theory.* Cambridge, UK: Cambridge University Press.

Menge, B. A., & Sutherland, J. P. (1987). Community regulation: Variation in disturbance, competition, and predation in relation to environmental stress and recruitment. *American Naturalist, 130*(5), 730–757.

Odum, H. T. (1957). Trophic structure and productivity of Silver Springs. *Ecological Monographs, 27*, 55–112.

Oskanen, L. (1991). Trophic levels and trophic dynamics: A consensus emerging? *Trends in Ecology and Evolution, 6*(6), 58–60.

Paine, R. T. (1966). Food web complexity and species diversity. *American Naturalist, 100*, 65–75.

Paine, R. T. (1988). Food webs: Road maps of interactions or grist for theoretical development? *Ecology, 69*(6), 1648–1654.

Pimm, S. L. (1982). *Ecological food webs.* London: Chapman and Hall.

Polis, G. A. (1991). Complex trophic interactions in deserts: An empirical critique of food-web theory. *American Naturalist, 138*(1), 123–155.

Polis, G. A., & Strong, D. (1996). Food web complexity and community dynamics. *American Naturalist, 147*(1), 813–846.

Power, M. E. (1990). Effects of fish in river food webs. *Science, 250*(4982), 811–814.

Schoener, T. W. (1989). Food webs from the small to the large: The Robert H. MacArthur Award Lecture. *Ecology, 70*(6), 1559–1589.

Teal, J. M. (1962). Energy flow in the salt marsh ecosystem of Georgia. *Ecology, 43*, 614–624.

Williams, R. J., & Martinez, N. E. (2000). Simple rules yield complex food webs. *Nature, 404*(6774), 180–183.

Ford, Henry

(1863–1947)
U.S. automobile manufacturer

Henry Ford was the most successful of the early American automobile manufacturers and an industrial innovator whose introduction of the assembly line and mass marketing made automobile ownership possible for the majority of American families. Ford's initiatives greatly increased the use of gasoline and would eventually lead to automotive air pollution and a great increase in the consumption of natural resources; his initiatives also allowed Americans to experience the riches of their environment through national parks and automobile vacations.

Henry Ford was born in rural Michigan near Dearborn. He began work as a machinist in Detroit at the age of sixteen. Nine years later he married and was made chief engineer at the Detroit Edison Company. This job required him to be on call at all hours of the day but permitted him access to a well-equipped machine shop and plenty of time to tinker. By 1896 he had built his first gasoline-powered vehicle.

In 1899 Ford left his job at the Edison Company and established the Detroit Motor Company with the help of a number of investors. But despite bringing seven models to market, the company failed. He formed the Ford Motor Company in 1903 with only a dozen workmen and $28,000 in capital. More established automobile manufacturers accused Ford on infringing on the patents they controlled but lost their case in court in 1911. As a manufacturer, Ford was of a highly independent mind and often made decisions without informing his partners. By 1919 he was able to buy out their interests in the company.

Ford was a strong believer in the moral benefits of labor and was proud that his company had hired immigrants, ex-convicts, and racial minorities at a time when there was no legal requirement to do so. In 1914 Ford announced that he would pay workers five dollars a day, about twice the going rate, and require an eight-hour workday instead of the nine-hour workday that was standard at the time. By operating three shifts and focusing production on a single model, the Model T, Ford was able to make several reductions in cost, at one point selling Model Ts for less than $300. In response, other automakers, who could not beat Ford's prices, began selling cars on the installment plan. By 1926 two-thirds of all cars were purchased on time payments.

Ford considered World War I to be a tremendous and pointless loss of life. In 1915 he was persuaded by a number of pacifists to finance the voyage of a ship, the *Oscar II*, with himself aboard, to visit the capitals of neutral nations in Europe to encourage them to set up a process of mediation to end the war. Ford blamed the war on the manufacturers of military hardware and the bankers who financed them. Ford was prone to anti-Semitism and for a while accepted the notion that Jewish financiers were responsible for the world's problems. He allowed the publication of a number of anti-Semitic articles in the *Dearborn Independent*, which he had purchased in 1918. He publicly apologized for these articles in 1927.

Ford yielded control of the company to his son Edsel in 1917 but took over again after Edsel's death in 1943. Henry Ford died in Dearborn.

Donald R. Franceschetti

Further Reading

Flink, J. J. (1990). Henry Ford and the triumph of the automobile. In C. W. Pursell Jr. (Ed.), *Technology in America* (pp. 177–189). Cambridge, MA: MIT Press.

Hershey, B. (1967). *The odyssey of Henry Ford and the great peace ship*. New York: Taplinger.

Kraft, B. S. (1978). *The peace ship: Henry Ford's pacifist adventure in the First World War*. New York: Macmillan.

Forestry

See Agroecology and Agroforesty; Forests, Temperate; Forests, Tropical; Logging, Wood

Forests, Temperate

The term *temperate forest* is applied to heterogeneous (consisting of dissimilar components) broad-leaved deciduous (leaf-shedding) and evergreen forests that are found within the temperate zones of the Earth between the two tropics and the polar circles. On the basis of temperature variations and precipitation levels occurring within it, the temperate zone is divided into two hot-temperate zones in which the mean temperature exceeds 20° C for a few months and never falls below 5° C; two cold-temperate zones in which the temperature never exceeds 20° C at any time of the year and is less than 10° C for at least four months; and a cold zone in the Northern Hemisphere alone where the mean temperature rises above 10° C during only four months of the year.

Although there are some exceptions, the typology (classification based on types) of the temperate forests is correlated with the duration of the warm season. Where the mean temperature of 10° C lasts for more than five months there are broad-leaved deciduous forests; where it is shorter there are evergreen forests. The exceptions to this "rule" are coast redwood (*Sequoia sempervirens*) forests in the western United States and the beech forests of the European mountain plains.

Cold-Temperate Zone: Broad-Leaved Deciduous Forests

The broad-leaved deciduous forests comprise mostly trees with open leaves that fall in winter when temperatures can fall below 0° C. Leaf loss is a strategy for adapting to cold and suspends the trees' metabolic activity.

Geographically, in the Northern Hemisphere these forests extend from Europe, between the Atlantic

A virgin forest is where the hand of man has never set foot.

—Anonymous

Ocean and the Ural Mountains, the northeastern portion of the United States, and eastern Asia (Ussuri Basin, Manchuria, central-northern China, Japan, and Korea). In the Southern Hemisphere they are limited to two areas: The first straddles Chile and Argentina, and the second is Tierra del Fuego. In all these regions annual precipitation ranges from 500 to 1,500 millimeters, and winters are marked. When compared with the vegetation in tropical environments, the broad-leaved deciduous forests present a simple "architectural structure" that is stratified on two levels: a dominant layer of trees and shrubs and a dominated layer of trees that is the result of "cultivation" by humans over the course of centuries. The human effect is less evident on the herbaceous (having the characteristics of an herb) and mossy layer and part of the shrub layer, which are good indicators of soil condition and vegetation potential.

In central and western Europe the broad-leaved deciduous forests are uniform from the physiognomical (term deriving from the discipline that tries to interpret the features of an individual from his external aspect) standpoint. They are characterized by a low number of species that create extensive, relatively open stands. This floristic "poverty" is the consequence of the Quaternary glaciation (an event occurred in the Pleistocene period during the Neozoic or Quaternary geological era, between 0,01 and 2 millions years ago). Paleo-botanic studies have shown that there was a greater number of species during the Tertiary period.

A distinction must be made between mixed broad-leaved and beech forests. The species in the mixed broad-leaved forests are *Quercus robur* (common oak) and *Quercus petraea* (European oak), associated with *Fraxinus excelsior* (common ash), *Populus sp. pl.* (poplars.), *Betula sp. pl.* (birch), *Ulmus sp. pl.* (elms), *Alnus glutinosa* (common alder), and *Prunus avium* (cherry). These associations vary according to the type of soil and altitude. On the plains the dominant species are common oak and white beech, whereas ash and common alder forests prevail on the alluvial lands. The mountain zones are characterized by common beech forests *(Fagus silvatica)* that are either pure or associated with pines *(Abies alba and Picea abies)*. The chestnut forests *(Castanea sativa)* are a case unto themselves:

They are found on siliceous (relating to silica) or volcanic soils and are cultivated by humans for their fruit.

With respect to their European counterparts, the mixed forests of eastern North America are richer in tree species and comprise the genera *Quercus* (oak), *Fagus* (beech), *Betula* (birch), *Juglans* (walnut), *Acer* (maple), *Tilia* (lime), *Ulmus* (elm), *Fraxinus* (ash), *Liriodendron* (tulip-tree), *Castanea* (chestnut), and *Carpinus* (hornbeam) and are often mixed with conifers. Because they extend over a vast area that is not uniform in terms of climate, a distinction, on the basis of ground moisture, is made between mesophytic (growing under medium conditions of moisture) and xerophytic (growing under minimum conditions of moisture) forests. The mesophytic forests consist of lime, maple, and birch forests in the northwestern United States and those associated with Canadian beech *(Fagus grandiflora)*, sugar maple *(Acer saccarum)*, and Canadian hemlock *(Tsuga canadensis)* in the northeastern United States. The xerophilic forests are dominated by oak *(Quercus borealis, Quercus velutina, Quercus alba, Quercus macrocarpa)* and hickory *(Carya sp. pl.)* trees in the western area.

The temperate forests of east Asia, with a humid, continental climate and mainly summer rains, are floristically comparable to those of America. They are broken down into three sectors: Inner Mongolia and northern Manchuria dominated by birch *(Betula)* associated with poplars *(Populus)* and willows *(Salix)* in the humid environments; northeastern Manchuria and southeastern Siberia with birch *(Betula)*, oak *(Quercus)*, alder *(Alnus)*, lime *(Tilia)*, elm *(Ulmus)*, hornbeam *(Carpinus)*, beech *(Fagus)*, maple *(Acer)*, ash *(Fraxinus)*, chestnut *(Castanea)*, and hazel *(Corylus)*; and Japan, where there is a prevalence of beech *(Fagus japonica, Fagus crenata)*, oak woods, and mixed forests that often include conifers.

In the Southern Hemisphere the broad-leaved deciduous forests of the genus *Nothofagus* (Southern beech) are often associated with cypress *(Cupressaceae)*, araucaria *(Araucariaceae)*, and podocarp *(Podocarpaceae)*. In Chile they occupy two areas: one in the north on the Argentine border and one in the center, known as "Valdivian" after the city of Valdivia, that is rich in floristic terms. In this area the ocean's influence causes precipitation to range from 2,000 to 3,000 millimeters per year, and this permits the growth of epiphytes (plants that derive nutrients and moisture from the air and rain) and vines in a dense undergrowth. Here various species of Nothofagus (*Nothofagusobliqua* and *Nothofagus procera*) are associated with conifers of the genera *Fitzroya (fitzroya), Podocarpus (podocarp), Araucaria (monkey-puzzle), Libocedrus (incense cedar),* and *Magnoliacee (magnolie)*. In the southern part of this area the dominant broad-leaved species is ulmo (*Eucryphia cordifolia*), which is associated with conifers of podocarp (*Podocarpus*).

Cold-Temperate Zones: Evergreen Forests

There are large regions of the Earth with a temperate climate that host evergreen forests. In Europe, North America, and Asia these are cold-temperate conifer forests, and in the northwestern United States, more temperate forests (sequoias).

These forests are mainly characterized by conifers with small, narrow, needle- or scale-shaped leaves that can reduce transpiration (passage of watery vapor from a living body through a membrane or pores) to low levels that last through the winter and allow the tree to photosynthesize when the climate permits. The exceptions are larch that lose their leaves during autumn, and they extend to the farthest latitudes where no other species can survive. From the physiognomical standpoint, the conifer forests do not undergo obvious changes during the course of the year unless a consistent percentage of open-leaved shrub and tree species is associated with them.

The northern forests and taiga (a moist subarctic forest dominated by conifers that begins where the tundra ends) occupy the northern areas of Canada and Eurasia (Scandinavia, Russia, and eastern Siberia) between fifty-five and seventy degrees latitude. Here, in January, temperatures can fall to −70° C, and the ground is covered with frost for a long time. The summers are short but relatively warm: During the hottest month temperatures range from 10° to 20° C, and the vegetative period varies from five to seven months. Precipitation, between 250 and 750 millimeters per year, occurs mainly in summer, but the climate can, in fact, be considered constantly humid because there is no real hot season. The North American forests are colonized by conifers of the genera *Picea* (spruce), *Picea glauca* (white spruce), *Picea mariana* (black spruce), *Abies* (fir), *Abies balsamea* (balm of gilead fir), *Larix* (larch), *Larix laricina* (tamarack), *Pinus* (pine), *Pinus*

banksiana (jack pine), and *Pinus murrayana* (lodgepole pine) and farther south by *Pinus strobus* (weymouth pine) and *Pinus resinosa* (red pine), and *Tsuga* (hemlock), *Tsuga Canadensis* (eastern hemlock-spruce). This last species is not found in Europe where *Picea abies* (Norway spruce*)* alternates with *Pinus sylvestris* (Scotch pine*)*. The pines create pioneer forests on poor soil that can last for a few centuries before they are colonized by common spruce, which forms dense forests on mature soil. Farther east the common spruce is replaced by Siberian spruce (*Picea obovata*), Siberian larch *(Larix sibirica),* Siberian fir *(Abies sibirica),* and Siberian stone pine (*Pinus sibirica*). In the north where the cover is thinner, there are more lichens (*Cladonia* and *Vetraria*). The conifers are associated with broad-leaved trees of the genera *Populus* (poplar*), Alnus* (alder), *Sorbus* (whitebeam), and *Betula* (birch). The undergrowth is uniform because of the permanent forest cover and the slow decomposition of the litter and consists of species of the genera *Vaccinium* (bilberry), *Sedum* (stonecrop), *Kalmia* (sheep-laurel), and *Empetrum nigrum* (crowberry). Although the trees grow slowly and present narrow annual rings, their longevity is high.

In western North America evergreen conifer forests are associated with broad-leaved forests. Going north along the Pacific Coast one first encounters forests of Douglas fir (*Pseudotsgua menziesii*), western red cedar *(Thuja plicata),* and western hemlock (*Tsuga heterophilla),* mixed with large maples and firs; then coast redwood (*Sequoia sempervirens*), in areas with high levels of winter rainfall and summer fog. From the thermal standpoint this forest is hot-temperate, and on the south it borders on laurifilli oak woods that mark the boundary with Mediterranean chaparral.

In North America, around the Great Lakes where precipitation ranges from 600 to 1,150 millimeters per year, there is a forest dominated by Weymouth pine (*Pinus strobus*), red pine *(Pinus resinosa),* and eastern hemlock-spruce (*Tsuga Canadensis)* associated with numerous broad-leaved species, including big-toothed aspen (*Populus grandidentata*), eastern poplar (*Populus deltoides),* cherry birch (*Betula lenta),* and old field birch (*Betula populifolia*).

This type of mixed forest is also found in the Far East north of Hokkaido, Japan, where large conifers Manchurian fir (*Abies holophylla*) and Korean pine (*Pinus koraiensis*) are associated with species from the genera *Betula* (birch), *Ulmus* (elm), *Tilia* (lime), and *Juglans* (walnut).

Hot-Temperate Zones

The hot-temperate zones are characterized by 1,500 to 3,000 millimeters of annual precipitation and temperatures that drop below 0° C only accidentally. In physiognomical terms the forests in these environments are less lush than those in tropical zones; they lack buttresses and reveal visible differences during the course of the seasons because they abound in deciduous species, even though many trees of the dominant and codominant layers are conifers. The leaves are smaller than those of the tropical species and are more coriaceous (resembling leather). The undergrowth is often dense and impenetrable. These forests are found in the southern United States near the northern shores of the Caribbean Sea and to a greater extent in southern Japan, Korea, western South America, the southern tip of Africa, New Zealand, and some parts of Australia. Similar typologies can be found in the mountains of southern Asia.

The humid forest in southern Japan consists of evergreen oaks associated with bay family *Lauracee (Machillus)* and *magnolie (Magnoliace)*. The undergrowth is dense, and there is an abundance of woody vines and orchids.

The evergreen forest in the southeastern United States comprises evergreen oaks, such as live oak (*Quercus virginiana*), associated with laurel magnolia (*Magnolia grandiflora*). The undergrowth is rich and impenetrable.

The humid forest of New Zealand is characterized by a mosaic of formations, with kauri dammar-pine (*Agathis australis*) dominant in the north and podocarp (*Podocarpaceae*), celery-pine (*Phyllocladaceae*) associated with small-leaved southern beech (*Nothofagus*), or other broad-leaved evergreen species. Usually there is a second, lower tree layer. The shrub layer consists of ferns and abundant vines and epiphytes.

The humid temperate forest in southern Chile is almost impenetrable because of the lush undergrowth. It grows on the slopes of the Andes Mountains except for the northern portion near the Taitao Peninsula. The dominant species belong to the genus *Nothofagus* (southern beech), small-leaved evergreens that are associated with species typical of the Valdiviana forest. However, here there are no vines, and the epiphytes are mosses and lichens. In the undergrowth is found bamboo of the genus *Chusquea* (bambus).

Mediterranean–Climate Forests

In the hot-temperate zones, where hot, dry summers alternate with a damper cold season, vegetation consists of forests, maquis (thick, scrubby underbrush), and garigues (low, open scrublands) of evergreen broad-leaved species that may in some areas be associated with conifers. These species have small, coriaceous leaves—hence the name *sclerophyll*—that developed this mechanism for adapting to the dry summers.

Whereas the sclerophyllous forests are climax formations (equilibrium status of an organism's community which remains stable until the environmental conditions do not change remarkably), the maquis and garigue are the secondary results of repeated exploitation. The maquis typical of siliceous soil is a stand of xerophilous and sclerophyllous evergreen trees and shrubs that is sometimes so dense as to be impenetrable. It can attain heights of 3 meters and comprises species that belong to the undergrowth and the open spaces of primary forests.

The garigue (or medium or low matorral) that grows on limestone gets its name from the Castilian *garric*, which is used for the kermes oak (*Quercus coccifera*) and does not exceed 2 meters in height.

The Mediterranean sclerophylls may be associated with conifers that are generally localized. In some cases they represent a climax stage, whereas in others they were planted by humans. In Europe the sclerophyllous forests are typical of the Mediterranean coasts, Portugal, central-southern Spain, and Crimea; in the Americas they are found in California, Mexico, and central coastal Chile; in Africa in Morocco, Algeria, Tunisia, coastal Libya, and South Africa (Cape region); and in the southern part of the Australian continent.

On the best lands in the Mediterranean region, zonal vegetation has been replaced by crops, primarily olives and grapes, so it is now confined to marginal environments with almost always superficial soil. In Europe one must distinguish the coastal from the subcoastal and Mediterranean mountain forests. Along the northern shores of the Mediterranean, evergreen oak (*Quercus ilex*) formations are the most typical. These can reach heights of 15 meters, and in areas with noncalcareous substrata they are replaced by cork trees (*Quercus suber*). The species in the shrub layer (*Viburnum tinus* (laurustinus), *Phillyrea latifolia* (tree phillyrea), and *Phillyrea angustifolia* (narrow-leaved phillyrea), *Pistacia lentiscus* (mastic-tree), and *Pistacia terebinthus* (turpentine tree), *Rhamnus alaternus* (buckthorn), *Rosa sempervirens* (evergreen rose), *Buxus sempervirens* (common box), and vines such as *Smilax aspera, Clematis flammula* (plume clematis), and *Lonicera sp. pl.* (honeysuckle) grow to heights of 3–5 meters. In the warmer areas evergreen oak grows on the mountain plain, whereas along the coast it is superseded by wild olive *(Olea oleaster)*, carob *(Ceratonia siliqua)*, and dwarf fan-palm *(Chamaerops humilis)*. Nearly all the Mediterranean regions are mountainous, and, therefore, above certain altitudes typical Mediterranean vegetation is replaced by deciduous or mixed forests where pubescent oak *(Quercus pubescens)* is found.

In Africa there is a northern section where evergreen oak groves alternate with maquis and a southern section. On the Atlantic coasts typical Mediterranean vegetation is flanked with an almost aphyllous (without leaves) cypress, African thuya *(Tetraclinis articolata)*. The innermost and highest Atlantic sector along the slopes of the Haut and Moyen Atlas Mountains is colonized by evergreen oak and Spanish juniper *(Juniperus thuripherea)*; the southern mountains, between 1,300 and 2,000 meters above sea level, are characterized by open formations of *Cupressus atlantica* or Spanish fir *(Abies pinsapo)* or atlas cedar *(Cedrus atlantica)*.

Mediterranean vegetation in southern Africa is limited to the southern slopes of the Karoo mountain chain, which protect it from the effects of the continental climate. It comprises small groupings of trees or maquis and high garigues that differ floristically from those of northern Africa and present species of the genera *Olea* (olive), *Gnidia* (gnidie), *Leucadendron, Berzelia, Agathosma, Cliffortia, Cussonia*, and *Protea*—this last species is designated as "tall heather."

In California sclerophylls are limited to a narrow coastal strip that is rich in species known as "chaparral," comprising shrub species of the genera *Quercus* (oak) and *Arbutus* (strawberry-tree), *Ceanothus* (ceanothus), *Arctostaphylos* (bearberry), and a rosacea (belonging to the rose family) with needle-shaped leaves, *Adenostoma fasciculatum*. From the physiognomical standpoint chaparral corresponds to the Mediterranean maquis, but unlike its counterpart it is affected by periodic outbreaks of fires caused by lightning. It includes scattered trees such as conifers and evergreen oaks that acquire a shrublike appearance in the driest stations. Similar types of vegetation can be found along the Chilean coast.

In Asia evergreen oak is found only in some stations in northern Turkey; the coastal forests consist of wild olive (Olea oleaster) and carob trees (Ceratonia siliqua), whereas the subcoastal forests comprise kermes oak *(Quercus coccifera)* known as calabrian pine *(Pinus brutia)* and greek juniper *(Juniperus excelsa)*. Up to an altitude of 2,200 meters along the southern mountain slopes are found associations with black pine *(Pinus nigra ssp. Palladiana)*, cedar of Lebanon *(Cedrus*

libani), Cilician fir *(Abies cilicica)*, Greek juniper *(Juniperus excelsa)*, Calabrian pine *(Pinus brutia)*, yew *(Taxus baccata)*, kermes oak *(Quercus coccifera)*, aleppo oak *(Quercus infectoria)*, and Lebanon oak *(Quercus libani)* in various groupings in the single locations. Maquis of *Pistacia palestinica* and *Quercus calliprinos* dominate the Palestinian and Lebanese coasts.

In southwestern, south-central, and southeastern Australia, the sclerophyllous formations are similar to those of the Northern Hemisphere's Mediterranean forests, even though their systematic origins are different. Locally the maquis is known as "malle-scrub": It is dominated by species of *Eucalyptus* (gum) associated with *Acacia* (acacia), *Malaleuca, Pimelea* (rice-flower), *Chorizema, Baronia, Leptaspermium*, and *Pittosporum* (klebsane) with manifest blossoms. Where humidity levels are lower, vegetation takes on the form of maquis that can reach a height of 3 meters, and in areas where precipitation ranges from 750 to 1,500 millimeters, eucalyptus trees are associated with plants of casuarinas *(Casuarina)*.

On the whole, temperate forests cover 2 billion hectares distributed over the continents: 41 percent are found in Russia, 32 percent in North America, 10 percent in northern Asia, 8 percent in Europe, 2 percent in Latin America, and the remaining 7 percent in Australia, New Zealand, and South Africa. The forest cover in these countries varies considerably, and one can say that temperate forests are disappearing in the southern parts of the world due to intensified exploitation for wood harvesting and that they are extending in the North as a result of the abandonment of farmlands and reforestation programs.

M. Agnoletti and L. Lenzi

Further Reading

Aubreville, A. (1961). *Etude écologique des principales formations vegetales du Brésil* [Ecological study of the principal vegetation in Brazil]. Paris: Centre Technique Forestier Tropical.

Birot, P. (1965). *Les formations végétales du globe* [Vegetation of the world]. Paris: SEDES.

Bournerias, M. (1979). *Guide des groupements végétaux de la région parisienne* [Vegetable groupings of the Parisian region] (2nd ed.). Paris: SEDES.

Braque R. (1987). *Biogéographie des continents* [Biogeography of the continents]. Paris: Masson.

Braun, E. L. (1950). *Deciduous forests of eastern North America*. Philadelphia: Blakston.

Budyko, M. I. (1974). *Climate and life*. New York: Academic Press.

Campbell, D. H. (1926). *An outline of plant geography*. London: Macmillan.

Cronquist, A. (1981). *An integrated system of classification of flowering plants*. New York: Columbia University Press.

Dajoz, R. (1971). *Précis d'Ecologie* (2nd ed.). Paris : Dunod.

Dansereau, P. (1957). *Biogeography: An ecological perspective*. New York: Ronald Press.

Hardy, M. E. (1913). *A junior plant geography*. Oxford, UK: Clarendon Press.

Hardy, M. E. (1920). *The geography of plants*. Oxford, UK: Clarendon Press.

Kuchler, A. W. (1967). *Vegetation mapping*. New York: Ronald Press.

Miles, J. (1979). *Vegetation dynamics*. London: Chapman and Hall.

Nimis, P. L., & Crovello, T. J. (1991). *Quantitative approaches to phytogeography*. Dordrecht, Netherlands: Kluwer Academic Publishers.

Schimper, A. F. W. (1903). *Plant-geography upon a physiological basis* (Rev. ed.). Oxford, UK: Clarendon Press.

Shelford, R. (1963). *The ecology of North America*. Urbana: University of Illinois Press.

Simmons, I. G. (1979). *Biogeography: Natural and cultural*. London: Edward Arnold.

Sulov, S. P. (1960). *Physical geography of Asiatic Russia*. San Francisco: Freeman.

Tansley, A. G., & Chipp, T. F. (1926). *Aims and methods in the study of vegetation*. London: Crown Agents for the Colonies.

Walter, H. (1973). *Vegetation of the Earth in relation to climate and eco-physiological conditions*. New York: English University Press.

Walter, H. (1984). *Vegetation of the Earth and ecological systems of the geo-biosphere*. Berlin: Springer.

Forests, Tropical

With boreal (northern) and temperate forests, tropical forests are one of the three major forest types in the world. But tropical forests are by no means uniform. The upper latitudes of the tropics, which are arid or semiarid, are covered by savanna woodland, in which trees are widely spread over grassy plains. Tropical forests are particularly prevalent in Africa, Australia, northwest India, and northeastern Brazil. They are the result of low and erratic rainfall but also probably of centuries of rapacious cutting by humans. It is not until zones of high temperatures and high humidity are reached on either side of the equator that "tropical" forests appear, variously described as "dense," "lush," "luxuriant," "prolific," "multispecied," "impenetrable jungles" dominated by hardwoods, heavy with insect and wildlife, and consequently rich in biodiversity (biological diversity as indicated by numbers of species of animals and plants). Yet, even these forests are of two kinds: the evergreen broad-leaved forests that constitute the cores of Amazonia, Zaire, and southeast Asia (often called "equatorial forests") and the surrounding tropical, moist, deciduous forests (also called "monsoon forests") that lose their leaves in the dry season.

The exact mapping—and hence known area—of forests is still largely guesswork because most comprehensive surveys are based on satellite images that distinguish mainly closed forest (i.e., a minimum of 20 percent forest crown cover of the land surface, which could be tropical, boreal, or temperate) and open or woodland areas. Nonetheless, a reasonable estimate would be that closed forests cover about 2.8 billion hectares, or 21 percent of the Earth's land surface, and woodlands about 1.7 billion hectares. Of the closed forest, just over 1.2 billion hectares are tropical forests, the overwhelming bulk (90 percent) being tropical moist forests. Of these, about half are in the Amazon River basin, with the other half shared about equally by Africa and southeast Asia.

Characteristics of Tropical Forests

Tropical forests are qualitatively different from other forests, particularly temperate forests, to which they are sometimes compared. Temperate forests have been altered by millennia of clearing and manipulation to create productive farming lands, without any apparent detrimental effect. In fact, their clearing has seemed to be the first step to economic development and advancement and a model of how to develop the tropical forests.

However, the tropical forest is different. First, its variety and density of life and species are astounding, and elimination of the forest leads to unknown loss. Estimates vary widely, but it is thought that tropical forests contain between 5 and 30 million animal species—ranging from vertebrates to insects—and an untold variety of plant life. It may be more because many plants have still not been identified, and the tropics

Firing the Gardens in Tropical Africa

In slash-and-burn horticulture, the subsistence system found most commonly in tropical regions, the burning of the garden plots is the crucial element in the process, Burning clears the garden, pushes back the margins of the encroaching forest, and fertilizes the soil. The following text describes burning as carried out by the Bemba of Zimbabwe.

Sometimes a woman works side by side with her husband, piling up branches as he cuts them from the tree. Both may move out into temporary shelters (*imitanda*) built near their gardens, and live there for some weeks together. But the branches are harder to carry when they are heavy with leaves and green sap, and the Bemba reckon that any but a woman who 'loves her husband', i.e. a specially devoted or newly married wife, would prefer to wait till the boughs have dried! The important thing is to finish the work before the end of the hot weather, when the parched bush often bursts into flame, and fires sweep across the gardens before the *ifibula* have been properly stacked. If the work has been delayed into September the man hurries to help his wife, and both carry in the last branches, stacking together in haste. Laggards are sometimes reduced to making several small gardens (*akakumba*, plur. *utukumba*), instead of one or more large ones, piling the boughs where they have fallen from the trees. With the last branch stacked, the family rest. The women begin to enjoy themselves, and go on a round of visits to friends. The country is covered with circular heaps of dried wood waiting through long sultry days for the firing of the bush.

Firing the gardens (*ukuoce fibula*). The firing of the *icitemene* is an exciting and important event in the agricultural year. No one may set light to his branches until a special signal has been given by the chief, otherwise one blazing garden might set the whole bush alight and possibly destroy in a day the unstacked branches of countless gardeners. Heavy damages are claimed by a man whose *ifibula* have been burnt before they were ready. In the old days a native who set fire to the bush, whether accidentally or on purpose, had to give up his own *icitemene* in compensation, and if he had destroyed too much property to be able to make the damage good, he became the chief's slave. If the chief's own gardens were burnt, some say the culprit would have been mutilated or beaten; others that he would have been made to work for the chief. Nowadays financial compensation is asked for, and I have records of cases in which sums from 10s. to 3 pounds. 10s. were demanded as a return for what is, after all, the loss of the whole prospect of harvest for the year.

The chief must give the signal for the firing of the branches as late as possible in the dry season to give the people time to finish the work, but he must not wait till the rains have fallen . . .

Source: Richards, Audrey I. (1939). *Land, Labour, and Diet in Northern Rhodesia: An Economic Study of the Bemba Tribe.* Oxford, UK: Published for the International Institute of African Languages and Cultures by the Oxford University Press, p. 294.

may contain more than 90 percent of all known species. Moreover, this rich diversity is the theater for much ingenious adaptation and innovation that may be central to human understanding of the fundamental problems of evolution and ecology. At a more utilitarian level the genetic diversity has been likened to a "source-book of potential foods, drinks, medicines, contraceptives, abortificents, gums, resins, scents, colorants, specific pesticides, and so on, of which we have scarcely turned the pages" (Poore 1976, 138).

Secondly, for all their variety and robust vegetative exuberance, tropical forests and their soils are inherently infertile, deficient in soil nutrients, poor in structure, and if cleared are liable to severe erosion and leaching with the subsequent formation of a subsoil, hard iron-pan layer. Unlike in temperate areas, only small patches of forest are suitable for agriculture. Rain in the tropics does not fall as a gentle drizzle but rather as short, sharp downpours that leach and erode the exposed soil when the forest and its binding roots are

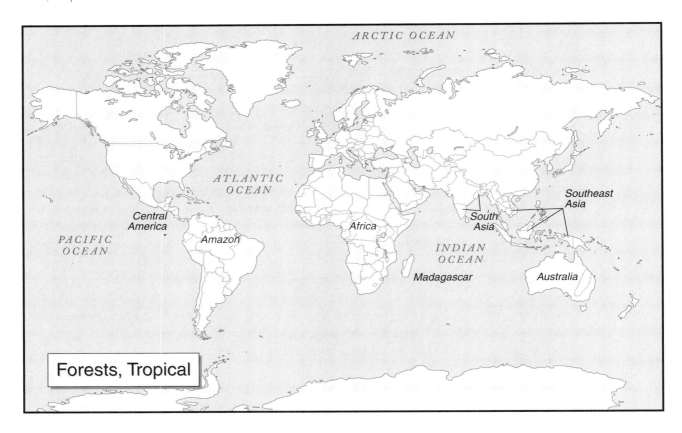

Forests, Tropical

removed. After the soil is denuded, the rapid runoff of rainwater not absorbed in the soil has a knock-on effect downstream in areas well outside the forests in the form of unregulated and erratic water supply and excessive sedimentation that clogs reservoirs.

Although it is a scientifically contentious issue, there is some evidence that large expanses of forest have local and even global effects on rainfall and climate. Certainly their clearing and burning put enormous amounts of carbon into the atmosphere.

Finally, tropical forest are not uninhabited. They are home to many millions of tribes people who have adapted to this habitat by hunting, collecting, and practicing swidden (rotational, slash-and-burn) agriculture. Again, only estimates can be made, varying from 50 to 250 million people. In addition, the bounty of the forest in providing game, fodder, fuel, and forage is essential to the livelihood of farming communities on its edges.

Diminishing Extent: Before 1945

The crucial interest of environmental historians in the tropical forests is their diminishing extent. The word *deforestation* has become almost synonymous in people's minds with *tropical forests*. Tropical deforestation is commonly thought to be a modern phenomenon, occurring largely after World War II. But nothing could be further from the truth. Long before the supposed Eden was spoiled by the exploitative European, American, and Japanese invaders, shifting cultivators and peasant agriculturalists were chopping, cropping, burning, and grazing their forests.

Indigenous impacts on the forests came mainly through the widespread use of fire to create cultivable patches. However, erosion, weed infestation, and formation of a subsoil layer of a hard "pan" of iron-rich soil as a consequence of excessive rainfall and leaching all took their toll on soil fertility, and cultivators typically shifted from place to place. In Malaysia and Indonesia, shifting cultivation was called *ladang*, in Central America, *milpa*, in parts of Africa, *chitemene*, in India, *kumri*, and in Sri Lanka, *chena*. Only the crops were different—maize and beans in central and northern Latin America, manioc in Brazil, small grains, usually called "millet" or sorghum, in Africa, and upland rice in southeast Asia. All but the largest trees were felled or deadened, and during the dry season the debris was set ablaze, and then the ground was opened up and planted with the onset of wet weather. If burning was too frequent, especially in climatically marginal zones, the land was quickly overgrown by tough perennial grass that prevented further cultivation.

The extent of indigenous clearing and alteration to the forest was rarely appreciated by early Western observers, but one writer in the 1920s, Orator Fuller, was convinced that the forests of Central and Latin America, "far from [being in] a virgin state," bore the marks of "many stages of reforestation" (Cook 1909, 21). Generally, the system was perceived as inefficient and wasteful as magnificent trees were sacrificed for small plots of ground soon to be abandoned.

Despite the inherent difficulties of the soils, considerable areas were cleared by peasant agriculturalists who cultivated irrigated land and created gardens for vegetables and spices. For thousands of years Sumatra (Aceh Province) supplied the Chinese, Indian, and Muslim worlds with cinnamon, mace, cloves, nutmeg, and pepper, and after about 1600 it supplied Europe in vast quantities. Nutrient levels were maintained with animal and human excreta and the plowing-in of vegetable "waste" and green leaves from the forest. Irrigation required an elaborate system of water impoundment, and it supported dense populations.

Traditional societies exploited their forests commercially in a manner no more egalitarian or caring than that of their later European overlords. In pre-British southwest India, permanent agricultural settlement existed side by side with shifting cultivation, and village councils regulated how much forest exploitation could be undertaken by agriculturalists. The forest was not regarded as a community resource; larger landowners dominated forest use in their local areas. Scarce commodities such as sandalwood, ebony, cinnamon, and pepper were under state and/or royal monopolies. With variations the same was true, from the sixteenth century onward, of Hunan Province in south-central China, where a highly centralized administration encouraged land clearance in order to enhance local state revenues, increase the tax base, and support a bigger bureaucracy and militia.

Most of the forest destruction went undetected, but by 1700 the tropical world as popularly conceived (although excluding China, which is dominantly temperate) had 355 million people and 128 million hectares of cultivated land. By 1850 it had 485 million people and 180 million hectares of cultivated land, the bulk of that new cropland coming out of the forest edges. From 1850 to 1920 cropland rose to 295 million hect-

ares, of which 75 percent came out of the forest, almost all the rest degenerating into unusable grassland.

One example of the change must suffice. Looking from the summit of the Dempo volcano in the Pelambang region of south Sumatra in 1885, the botanist and traveller Henry Forbes was amazed at the vast extent of the land that was treeless. The forests were rapidly disappearing as each year immense tracts were felled for rice fields and as gardens were consumed by fires. Trees of the rarest and finest timber were hewn, half burned, and then left to rot, only to be replaced by worthless secondary forest and grasses. He lamented that "our children's children will search in vain in their travels for the old forest trees of which they have read in the books of their grandfathers" (Forbes 1885, 214).

With a few exceptions (for example, growing sugar in the Caribbean and northwest Brazil from the early seventeenth century onward, growing cotton in the southern United States, cutting exotic woods like ebony and mahogany for furniture, and trading in spices), the main European impact came after the mid-nineteenth century. It was of two kinds: plantations and the facilitation of peasant agriculture.

Plantations were the industrialization of tropical agriculture to produce goods en masse to service the increasing needs and nutrition of an ever-more-affluent population, served by efficient shipping and a reliable financial infrastructure. Tropical forests were cleared to produce great quantities of sugar, coffee, tea, chocolate, and tobacco, all part of the West's "soft drug culture" (which, incidentally, also changed the distribution of the world's population through slavery and indentured labor). To these can be added cotton, sisal, quinine, rice, and rubber.

Peasant agriculturalists were drawn into this new global economic connection and made cash to pay for taxes and other goods. Nowhere was this more so than in India, where additionally the spread of the railways increased accessibility and created cheap and efficient transport links to the wider world. ·

By 1920 clearing in the forests of the temperate world was all but over, but knowledge of what happened to the tropical forests is tantalizingly slight. There was little hard fact, but contemporary observers had a suspicion that great activity was occurring and that enormous inroads were being made into the forests. All the forces that drove change during the nineteenth century continued and accelerated. Peasant agriculture intensified as population in the tropical world rose from 1.1 to 1.76 billion from 1900 to 1950, and in addition to feeding themselves, peasants produced cash crops that were caught up in the expanding world economy. Commercial agriculture and plantations expanded enormously to feed the demands of an ever-more-affluent North Atlantic population. Tropical cropland grew from 295 million hectares to 460 million hectares between 1920 and 1950, the bulk of those extra 165 million hectares coming out of the forest. The amount cleared was probably even greater as another 69 million hectares went into grassland, which was probably abandoned or degraded cleared forest. The annual rate of clearing during these years was 11.5 million hectares, which rivals the post-World War II totals.

Zon and Sparhawk's survey in *The Forest Resources of the World* (1923) and Tom Gill's *Tropical Forests of the Caribbean* (1931) are peppered with qualitative phrases referring to clearing going on "steadily" although slowly in response to expanding populations, so that "a great deal of the original forest . . . has been cleared away" and replaced by plantations and expanded peasant agriculture (Zon & Sparhawk 1923, 568, 594). The greatest intensity of change was in Brazil, Central America, and the Caribbean fringe, where once extensive forests were "only a memory" (Gill 1931, 66).

Diminishing Extent: After 1950

After 1950 forest clearing had almost totally ceased in the temperate world (in fact, much cultivated land reverted to forest) and was concentrated wholly in the tropical world. Improved health led to declining mortality and a massive population explosion that nearly doubled world population in thirty-five years, most of that in the tropical world, where growth rates of 2–3 percent raged across Africa, Latin America, and south and southeast Asia. New land was brought into cultivation everywhere, often with government subsidies, as in Brazil, Indonesia, and Malaysia. Newly independent countries mined their forest resources mercilessly as a means of generating hard cash and often to avoid tackling more contentious issues such as land reform, rural development, and poverty and inequality. Western countries (now joined by Japan) devoured great quantities of wood and wood fiber.

In retrospect, it is amazing how long it took the world to realize what was happening. The true magnitude of population increase was not fully appreciated until the late 1960s; those who warned about tropical forest decline, such as the tropical botanist Paul Richards and the environmental writer Norman Myers, were virtually ignored; and not until the early 1980s

did global concern emerge in a well-defined form. It is instructive to realize that the word *biodiversity* (biological diversity as indicated by numbers of species of animals and plants) was not coined until 1986, although the concept of biological diversity had been around for at least a decade before.

Outlook for the Twenty-First Century

Current estimates suggest that 318 million hectares of tropical forest disappeared between 1950 and 1980 and at least another 220 million hectares since. The annual rate of destruction is variously estimated as being between 11.5 and 15 million hectares, the bulk being caused by agricultural/pastoral clearing and perhaps 20 percent by logging and harvesting timber for fuel.

Whatever the true extent of destruction—and experts are uncertain due to inaccurate data and surveillance—the total forest area is going down. The lone voice of Eldred Corner, a mycologist (a biologist who studies fungi) in the Singapore Botanical Gardens who in 1946 deplored what was happening, is coming all too true as this century unfolds: "I fear lest all the virgin lowland forest of the tropics may be destroyed before botany awakes; even our children may never see the objects of our delight which we have not cared for in their vanishing" (Corner 1946, 186).

Michael Williams

Further Reading

Brown, K., & Pearce, D. W. (Eds.). (1994). *The causes of tropical deforestation*. London: University College Press.

Cook, O. F. (1909). Vegetation affected by agriculture in Central America. *U.S. Dept. of Agriculture; Bureau of Plant Industry* (Bulletin No. 145). Washington, DC: Government Printing Office.

Cook, O. F. (1921). *Milpa agriculture, a primitive tropical system: Annual report of the Smithsonian Institution for 1919*. Washington, DC: Government Printing Office.

Corner, E. J. H. (1946). Suggestions for botanical progress. *New Phytologist, 45*, 185–192.

Forbes, H. O. (1885). *A naturalist's wandering in the eastern archipelago: A narrative of travel and exploration from 1878 to 1883*. London: Mason, Low, Marston, Searle and Rivington.

Gill, T. H. (1931). *The tropical forests of the Caribbean*. Baltimore: Read Taylor.

Grainger, A. (1993). *Controlling tropical deforestation*. London: Earthscan Publications.

Myers, N. (1979). *The sinking ark: A new look at the problem of disappearing species*. Oxford, UK: Pergamon Press.

Nadkarni, M. V., Pasha, S. A., & Prabhakar, L. S. (1989). *The political economy of forest use and management*. New Delhi, India: Sage Publications.

Perdue, P. C. (1987). *Exhausting the Earth: State and peasant in Hunan, 1500–1850*. Cambridge, MA: Harvard University Press.

Poore, M. E. D. (1976). The values of tropical moist forest ecosystems. *Unasylva, 28*, 127–143.

Richards, J. F. (1990). Land transformation. In B. L. Turner II, W. C. Clark, R. W. Kates, J. F. Richards, J. T. Mathews, & W. B. Meyer (Eds.), *The Earth as transformed by human action: Global and regional changes in the biosphere over the last 300 years* (pp. 163–178). New York: Cambridge University Press.

Richards, P. W. (1973, December). The tropical rain forest. *Scientific American, 229*, 58–67.

Williams, M. (2002). *Deforesting the Earth: From prehistoric to present global crisis*. Chicago: University of Chicago Press.

Zon, R., & Sparhawk, W. N. (1923). *Forest resources of the world*. New York: McGraw-Hill.

France

(2001 est. pop. 59 million)

Ecosystems and societies have interacted in France, a historic nation bridging the Mediterranean Sea and northern Europe in the western part of the continent, for at least fourteen millennia. Changing relationships between ecosystems and societies over time in France can best be examined through the lens of four crucial resources—agricultural land, water, forests, and coal.

Agricultural Land

People of the Mesolithic period (beginning 12,000 BCE) began to reshape the dense deciduous forests through burning and sheepherding. Areas thus stripped of their heavy vegetation were likely the favored sites of France's first agrarian society, the Chassean civilization of the late fifth millennium BCE. The Neolithic (beginning c. 7000 BCE) way of life combined grain cultivation with small livestock raising and hunting and gathering; large and continuously cultivated open fields became a feature of ancient Gaul long before Romans arrived. Bronze and Iron Age (3500–500 BCE) migrations of Celts brought an extension in the cultivated area and eventually iron plows to the heavier soils of the North. Nine-tenths Celticized by the time of Roman conquest in 58–51 BCE, Gaul contained 10 million people, although estimates have ranged up to 30 million. The dense population of Gaul, well known in the ancient world, would lessen only temporarily in the early Middle Ages and favored the creation of an agrarian landscape.

Romans inaugurated a slave-based agricultural system, organized around villas (estates). They maintained the open fields and the old grains—soft wheat, barley, and millet—and introduced new crops, namely olives, vines, cherries, and peaches. Spreading gradually, vine cultivation led to the export of wines from present-day Bordeaux to Roman Britain by the first century CE. Much later, a feudal system again reshaped the agrarian landscape: During the ninth and tenth centuries, concentrated villages began to organize the strip farming of open, regular fields in much of the north of France, whereas in the south and west, larger, frequently enclosed fields were farmed under fewer collective obligations. Of arguably greater ecological importance were the crop rotation systems, which were established after about 1250 in order to boost lords' incomes by better reconciling farming with grazing. Despite exceptions, a three-field, triennial system dominated in the north, a two-field, biennial system in the south. The heavier soils and greater precipitation in northern France allowed for fallowing (leaving unsown) only one year in three, yet the fallow periods provided by each system helped regenerate soil impoverished by the truncated ecosystem of the fields. Only when nitrogen-fixing fodder crops became widespread in the eighteenth and nineteenth centuries was fallowing gradually abolished.

Long-term demographic pressure made land the most contested resource in France, yet "wastes" (uncultivated land), forests, fallow land, and harvested land could be as fiercely defended or coveted as cultivated land. Collective rights—to glean; to graze on unenclosed fields, stubble, or fallow land; to access meadows after haymaking; to cut wood—might guarantee survival for the rural poor or help the better off to turn a profit. The maintenance of collective rights generally hindered increases in productivity, but clearing land for agricultural reduced wastes and forests from the eleventh century, and sixteenth-century lords actively usurped common property, hoping to partition it among new tenants. The French Revolution's Rural Code of 1791 maintained key collective rights, and although partition of the commons was authorized in 1793, little partition occurred. On balance, however, revolutionary policies promoted agrarian individualism by vindicating private property but *not* redistributing land, thus setting the legal and social basis for agrarian capitalism.

Both public and private efforts have promoted greater agricultural productivity and regional specialization in modern times. State-backed marsh drainage resulted in a 10 percent increase in pasture by 1860. The massive planting of vineyards in the nineteenth-century Midi region best exemplifies the trend toward monoculture spurred by the demands of national and international markets. The vast vineyards of the south became prey a to louse that attacks root stock called phylloxera, which was first detected in 1863. An environmental catastrophe for winegrowers, phylloxera spread from south to north, ultimately destroying 30 percent of the surface area of French vineyards. Ultimately, the crisis was resolved through grafting resistant American root stock to French plants. France did, however, remain a mosaic of small and large properties. The post-World War II era saw increasing mechanization, chemical outputs, and plot consolidation. Since the mid–1950s, the Common Market's Common Agricultural Policy has guaranteed a market for surpluses at higher than world prices. The largest growers benefited most from these policies, and polluted water, soils laden with heavy metals, destroyed hedge rows, and erosion have been their ecological legacy. Meanwhile, smaller growers were abandoning approximately 72,000 hectares per year by the late 1990s. Roughly half of this land ultimately comes back into cultivation or pasturage, whereas the rest becomes part of the built environment—buildings, streetscapes, and related structures—or a wild ecosystem. Agribusiness, subsidized by France and the European Union, is presently contested by the Confédération Paysanne (a union supporting the interest of independent small farmers) under the leadership of José Bové and François Dufour.

Water

Agriculture depended on freshwater resources, but just as consequential was France's exposure to two seas. No point in France is more than 400 kilometers from a sea, and extensive Atlantic *and* Mediterranean coastlines go far to explain the country's historic orientation to both northern and southern Europe. Efforts to connect the two coastal areas helped forge the political entity of France, as did the presence of an impressive network of rivers. The Loire and Seine Rivers cut through the old provinces, whereas the Rhone and Saône functioned as barriers, and the Rhine often marked part of the northeastern border. Historian Fernand Braudel called the Rhone River corridor the "French isthmus", for it formed part of the great commercial artery that connected northern Italy to the Low Countries, reaching into the French interior by tributaries of the Loire and Seine (Braudel 1988, 265).

Water directly influenced urban development by allowing for both commerce and early manufacturing. In the well-watered north, canal building in the eleventh century followed by marsh draining in the twelfth reshaped Caen, Rouen, Amiens, Beauvais, Troyes, and Reims, into "mini-Venices" (Guillerme 1988, 51). The constant flow of diverted water and a benign textile industry kept these northern cities relatively clean. For their part, waterwheels represented a stable energy potential until the early nineteenth century.

The association between urban waters and disease originated in the fourteenth century, when warfare prompted the building of large moats that filled with stagnant water. Moats and ramparts cut cities off from the countryside and its flowing waters. Incidences of fevers and pulmonary diseases were worsened by the greater humidity caused by a lowering of temperature from the early fourteenth to the late nineteenth centuries. This Little Ice Age saw an annual dip of 1.5° C during its coldest periods, which also led to a number of grain crises and a decline in freshwater fishing. Eighteenth-century concern over stagnant water and noxious vapors helped create the Pasteurian mentality of the nineteenth, which sought to analyze the bacterial content of water and to purify it. Providing clean water to cities and eliminating foul water characterized much nineteenth- and twentieth-century urban improvement, starting with the renovation of Paris's infrastructure during the Second Empire (1851–1870). The Public Hygiene Act of 1902 promised significant state involvement in the provision of pure water throughout France. Ironically, the dismantling of walls, ramparts, and moats made French cities vulnerable to free-flowing water in the form of floods.

Free-flowing water has been subject to greater control during the past two centuries in the interests of irrigation and a well-maintained canal network. France has led in the commodification of water through the marketing of mineral water, and modern industry has been fed by water as well, especially the Rhone, site of numerous hydroelectric and nuclear power plants.

Regarding the latter, water functions to cool spent fuel rods for two to three years in the initial stage of treating nuclear waste. Spent fuel is then shipped from French as well as foreign reactors to the controversial facility run by Cogema at Cap de la Hague in Normandy. There, untreated waste cools for another six to seven years before chemical treatment separates unburned uranium from plutonium and fission byproducts. These highly radioactive materials are then vitrified—turned into glass—prior to permanent storage in canisters underground.

Tourism, secondary residences, port development, and pleasure boats have compromised France's coastal ecology, yet the proportion of French beaches and lakeside swimming areas meeting the European Union's water purity criteria increased to 91 percent by the late 1990s. Through land purchases, the national Conservatoire du Littoral assured the conservation of 13 percent of France's coastline between 1975 and 2000. France's freshwater ecosystems have perhaps fared worse, with eutrophication (the process by which water becomes enriched with nutrients) from agricultural runoff threatening lakes and rivers in the north and west. The provision of pure water to many rural communes has remained an elusive goal.

Forests

The deciduous forest is the fundamental biome of France, a forest typically harboring a multilayered understory of shrubs, ferns, grasses, mosses, and mushrooms. Pine, spruce, and larch reign in the upper elevations of the Alps and Pyrenees, and thinner oak forests dominate in the highly eroded soils of the Mediterranean region. The composition of France's deciduous forests has been anything but stable over time due to changes in soil and climate and, more recently, to human action. Since the Middle Ages, pressures to cultivate land have steadily relegated forests to marginal, often acidic, soils; forest clearance reached its peak during the twelfth century. Only in the mid-nineteenth century did forest begin to replace inland waters as state foresters carried out a massive reforestation of the extensive Sologne and Landes wetlands. Using trees to control water also justified the ambitious project, begun in 1860, to reforest the Alps, Pyrenees, and Massif Central: Blanketed with evergreens, the mountains would retain their waters and soils and not threaten lowlands with flooding and debris flows. These two modern examples illustrate a long historical association between forest management and state power.

An even longer history points to the fundamental role of forests in the peasant economies of France. Use rights to the forest included gathering firewood, construction wood, plants for barn litter, and human food such as berries, mushrooms, and honey. Rights to graze livestock in forests stemmed from the structural shortage of meadows and fallow land. The peasants' forest, marked by the presence of livestock and people, contrasted greatly with royal and aristocratic forests, kept off limits to all but elite hunters and their game. The common tendency to sacrifice forest for more arable land threatened the equilibrium of forest-field-pasture. From the passage of the landmark Forest Ordinance of 1669 to the tightening of official control over forests in the nineteenth century, the state limited and even eradicated use rights. France's first national forestry school (1824) deepened the state's imprint on forests by teaching even-aged, single-species management. Rural communities vigorously contested both the state's jurisdiction and methods of management, especially during the revolutions of 1830 and 1848.

Many other factors tolled heavily on French forests. Cities required wood for building and, especially, heating and cooking after other European urban populations had turned to coal for domestic needs. Charcoal-powered iron forges consumed vast quantities of wood. The state demanded thousands of oaks to build naval ships until the later nineteenth century. During the Old Regime (France's period of absolute monarchy, approximately 1600–1789), the state routinely sold forests on the royal domains to shore up finances. Approximately 200,000 hectares of forest in northern France suffered damage ranging from degradation to obliteration during World War I, and the military effort itself devoured wood.

In all, though, during the twentieth century there was a significant, spontaneous return of forest to previously cultivated land in areas of severe depopulation. Land abandonment alone presently increases forest cover by about 1 percent every two years; over one-quarter of the surface area of metropolitan France is now covered with forest, giving France the third largest forested area in Europe, following Sweden and Finland. Voluntary reforestation has also continued; since the 1950s foresters have begun favoring mixed plantations over single-species coniferous forests due to alarm over soil acidification and the lack of resistance exhibited by single-species forests to wind, fire, and pathogens. The capacity of a diverse forest to resist high winds was, in a negative sense, brought home in December 1999 when Hurricane Lothar swept across

France, felling the equivalent of three years' wood production; it was cited by historians of climate as the most destructive storm in France since 1739. Recent concern has also focused on the pine forests of Provence—dense, low forests with a heavy understory that are highly susceptible to fire. Finally, the popularity of forests for outdoor recreation has created new imperatives for management and exposed more vulnerabilities.

Coal

Energy supplied by waterwheels and charcoal forges remained sufficient into the early nineteenth century. The chief disincentive to fully harness coal for industry was its poor distribution across a relatively large national territory. Eventually, heavily exploited forests drove up the price of charcoal, and the introduction of the steam engine resulted in a new use for coal: France's cotton industry was the nation's first industry to mechanize using coal-fired steam engines after 1811.

Traditionally, manufacturing had been highly dispersed throughout the French countryside. Industry based on coal led to distinct industrial regions because transportation cost more in France than in smaller England or Belgium. Mechanized metallurgy lagged behind textiles: Coal deposits, concentrated in the North (Pas-de-Calais) and the center (St.-Etienne/Le Creusot), occurred far from iron deposits, concentrated in Lorraine. Moreover, the high phosphorous content of Lorraine iron limited its appeal to steel manufacturers. Two developments made French coal and iron compatible: railroads, which linked them profitably to each other, and the Thomas converter (1878), which purified iron sufficiently for steel production. The mass production of steel in Lorraine exemplifies the regionalization of industry based on coal, as does the cotton industry around Mulhouse, fed by coal brought from Le Creusot by canal. However, the largest industrial belts ultimately depended more on cities than on the location of natural resources: Paris, with its intellectual and material resources and huge market; Lyon, the hub along the French isthmus; and Marseille, with its port-based trade, all spawned industrial complexes.

Railroads spurred coal production and industrialization in general. France's first rail line (1827) extended from St.-Etienne to Andrézieux, connecting the coal basin to the Loire River. Had mining engineers prevailed, France's rail system would have continued to link manufacturing and resource extraction, but such was not the case: Mimicking the royal highways of the mid-eighteenth century, the main lines of France's railway system radiated from the capital and famously defied natural landforms and property boundaries. The railroads helped create a national market in the years from 1850 to 1900, furthering the specialization of agriculture.

Coal indisputably helped create a modernized, industrialized France: Growing from 880,000 tons of coal mined in 1815 to 13 million tons in 1869, France resembled its western European neighbors in the relative increase in coal production. But compared to England and Germany, France was notoriously deficient in this fossil fuel. As global power became evermore a function of industrial capacity in the nineteenth century, French leaders had yet more reason to worry in the twentieth, which brought the full industrialization of warfare on the European continent. Hostilities on the western front during World War I engulfed the Pas-de-Calais coalfields; France's insistence on working the coal seams of Germany's Saarland, allowed for fifteen years by the Treaty of Versailles, responded to the wartime loss as well as to traditional shortages. Imported petroleum became cheaper for industry than domestic coal shortly after World War II, and France's turn to nuclear power in the postwar era represents a quest for renewed geopolitical power in light of pressing needs for energy.

Industry based on fossil fuels has brought degradation but also popular consciousness of environmental risks. Early efforts at regulation—a Paris ordinance of 1898 prohibiting prolonged emissions of black smoke over the capital and a national law of 1917 instituting inspections of polluting businesses—are more noteworthy for their dates than their real effects. After the 1860s French industrialists constructed tall brick smokestacks to disperse emissions and resisted regulation until recent decades. Even hydroelectricity, nicknamed "white coal" in the 1870s, compromised the aesthetic value of the mountains and reduced the alluvial deposits of alpine rivers. Daily emissions from aluminum and electrochemical plants in the Maurienne Valley in the northern Alps equaled those produced by a large city such as Lyon by the 1970s. Since the 1960s, though, overall emissions of the major polluting gases—hydrocarbons, sulfur dioxide, nitrous oxides— have declined as France has imposed tighter regulations and heeded those of the European Union. As elsewhere, greenhouse gases remain largely uncontrolled, and ozone levels in major cities have forced the occasional restriction of automobile traffic. Washed by oceanic winds, France will continue to benefit from its location at the western end of the European continent; acid rain, for example, has been detected only in the northeast portion of the country.

The French have reacted to ongoing threats to flora, fauna, air, and water in ways that parallel developments in other western countries. The Ministry of the Environment, created in 1971, has spawned legislation on a wide range of issues including air pollution, species conservation, and water conservation. Between 1960 and 2000, a variety of natural areas—from pristine alpine habitats to natural regional parks embracing farms and villages—acquired varying degrees of legal protection. Now 8 percent of the French territory is covered by protective statutes, the same percentage as in the United States. The French government responded with enthusiasm to the European Union's "Natura 2000" initiative of 1992, an ambitious project to create a network of parks and nature reserves across the fifteen member states. France continues to lead in the negotiation and support of international environmental treaties. At home, vibrant local and regional associations advocate for specific causes, and two green parties were gaining an increasing share of the vote in local, regional, national, and European elections up to the legislative elections of 2002.

Tamara L. Whited

Further Reading

Bess, M. (2003). *The light-green society: Ecology and technological modernity in France, 1960–2000.* Chicago: University of Chicago Press.

Braudel, F. (1972). *The Mediterranean and the Mediterranean world in the age of Philip II.* (S. Reynolds, Trans.). New York: HarperCollins.

Braudel, F. (1988). *The identity of France* (Vol. 1). (S.Reynolds, Trans.). New York: Harper & Row.

Clout, H. D. (1977). *Themes in the historical geography of France.* London: Academic Press.

Clout, H. D. (1996). *After the ruins: Restoring the countryside of northern France after the Great War.* Exeter, UK: University of Exeter Press.

Corvol, A. (1987). *L'Homme aux bois: Histoire des relations de l'homme et de la forêt, XVIIIe-XXe siècles* [Man in the woods: A history of human-forest relations, eighteenth to the twentieth centuries]. Paris: Fayard.

Delort, R., & Walter, F. (2001). *Histoire de l'environnement européen* [History of the European environment]. Paris: Presses Universitaires de France.

Duby, G., & Wallon, A. (Eds.). (1976). *Histoire de la France rurale* [History of rural France]. Paris: Seuil.

Goubert, J. (1989). *The conquest of water: The advent of health in the industrial age.* (A.Wilson, Trans.). Cambridge, UK: Polity Press.

Green, N. (1990). *The spectacle of nature: Landscape and bourgeois culture in nineteenth-century France.* New York: Manchester University Press.

Guillerme, A. E. (1988). *The age of water: The urban environment in the north of France, A.D. 300–1800.* College Station: Texas A&M University Press.

Harrison, R. P. (1992). *Forests: The shadow of civilization.* Chicago: University of Chicago Press.

Hecht, G. (1998). *The radiance of France: Nuclear power and national identity after World War II.* Cambridge, MA: MIT Press.

Landes, D. S. (1969). *The unbound Prometheus: Technological change and industrial development in western Europe from 1750 to the present.* Cambridge, UK: Cambridge University Press.

McPhee, P. (1999). *Revolution and environment in southern France: Peasants, lords, and murder in the Corbières, 1780–1830.* Oxford, UK: Oxford University Press.

Neboit-Guilhot, R., & Davy, L. (1996). *Les Français dans leur environnement* [The Frech and their environment]. Paris: Nathan.

Osborne, M. A. (1994). *Nature, the exotic, and the science of French colonialism.* Bloomington: Indiana University Press.

Planhol, X., & Claval, P. (1994). *An historical geography of France.* (J. Lloyd, Trans.). Cambridge, UK: Cambridge University Press.

Pritchard, S. B. (2001). *Recreating the Rhone: Nature and technology in France since World War II.* (Doctoral dissertation, Stanford University).

Whited, T. L. (2000). *Forests and peasant politics in modern France.* New Haven, CT: Yale University Press.

Free Trade

For generations the fault line in debates over trade was between proponents of free trade (trade between countries that is exempt from duties, customs, or tariffs) and champions of protectionism (a mechanism used by some countries to protect its industries by imposing high tariffs on imported goods). Following the ideas of Adam Smith, whose influential work *The Wealth of Nations* was published in 1776, free traders built their case for unfettered trade, in which markets would act as the famous "invisible hand," creating maximal wealth. In fact the rationale for free trade is over two centuries old: Free trade encourages specialization, market-based prices guide resource allocation, and the end result is that free trade leads to greater good. The case for protectionism, as expressed in certain French and German ideas, has lost ground in recent years. Nineteenth-century protectionists maintained that markets should be managed by the guiding hand of the state. The French term is *dirigisme* (government control or intervention, especially in business activity or economy). Marxists welcomed the strong state, which was theoretically the prelude to an era of voluntary communitarianism, but in practice the heavy-handed state in Communist regimes ushered in the gulag. But now central planning has for the most part been abandoned. The upshot is that this earlier debate is largely over: The free traders have won; open markets are the key to economic growth.

The New Debate over Free Trade

Now free traders find that the wealth-creating engine of free trade is being asked to accommodate newer issues, such as labor and environmental standards, and socioeconomic equity, so that those who have been left out can become part of the system. The emergence of these so-called social issues pits free traders in the classic mould against those who seek something called "free but fair trade"—a halfway house combining liberalization with certain market interventions—and others who reject free trade altogether as a force that threatens and degrades labor and the environment while widening the gap between the ever-richer haves and the legions of have-nots. These rejectionists often use the attack on free trade as an attack on the market economy.

Environmental historians can hardly avoid being pulled into this new debate, which links trade and social issues. Although protectionism is now passé, these newer forms of market intervention have emerged with great speed and have wide appeal. This troubles free traders, who smell protectionism, but this new perspective—with its explicit reliance on a greater role for government—is gaining ground. With these new issues in mind it is well to consider how free trade came to be adopted.

The Rise of Free Trade

Adam Smith maintained that free trade was the most efficient and effective way to create more wealth for more people. In Great Britain, nineteenth-century liberals put their belief in laissez-faire and individualism into practice with the Corn Law reforms of the 1840s. Letting markets set the prices for commodities such as wheat and ending the quotas on sugar resulted in lower prices and a surge of mass consumption. It was then that the British as a nation became addicted to sugar and sweets with their afternoon tea. However, it happened that the repeal of the Corn Laws is one of the few examples of pure liberal economics in action.

France and Germany, for their part, followed more directed forms of capitalism in their pursuit of economic growth and national interest, while Japan (after it embarked upon modernization in the late nineteenth century), especially, and even the United States, deviated from classic economic liberalism in forging their own pathways to growth. All in their ways pursued empires, projections of state power that had little to do with the dictates of classic free-trade theory. (Whether imperialism paid is debatable; only in the case of impoverished Portugal living off its overseas possessions is the answer an unambiguous yes.) Meanwhile, the Latin American model of mixed economies (state-run industries with a macroeconomic model of import substitution with little emphasis on exports) as developed in Brazil and Mexico proved less efficient than the export-based model of the so-called Asian Tigers (Singapore, Korea, Taiwan, and Malaysia), who raced from behind to overtake Latin America in productivity and national wealth.

To be sure, by the end of the nineteenth century laissez-faire liberalism in the Western world was already being modified as governments intervened in markets with regulations to protect and advance the public interest. In the United States this took the form of mandating such things as food and product safety standards, the eight-hour day, and breaking up monopolies such as Standard Oil to promote competition and hinder price fixing. Meanwhile, Great Britain enacted the first urban air pollution abatement regulations in the 1870s. Thanks to Otto von Bismarck, the first chancellor of the German empire, Germans reaching age sixty-five could retire on the country's new and first-of-its-kind state pension plan. This was the high road of interventionist public policy. Less compatible with free-trade theory was (and is) the tendency of governments to use trade protection selectively to shield specific sectors from imports or to promote domestic employment and output. It is in that arena that free-trade policy meets politics in the real world.

Free Trade and Politics

Proponents of globalization argue that trade is necessary to maintain the peace in an interconnected world. Unfortunately, trade alone is not always enough to maintain the peace; witness the speed with which the era of global trade (which began in the late 1880s) unraveled. Starting with the Balkan wars of 1912, the rapidly integrating world economy first contracted and then received the coup de grace in Sarajevo, when the shot that killed an Austrian Archduke unleashed the guns of August and the huge disaster of the Great War. With all their power to create wealth, free trade and open markets are highly susceptible to contingent events. It remains to be seen whether the present global obsession with security will disrupt the second global era, with its promise of seamless cross-border connectivity.

The intertwining of politics with free trade, up to and including the denial of trade benefits for political ends, should come as no surprise. For years, trade sanctions have been used as a form of coercion short of war, with mixed results at best. A famous case in point is the League of Nations' retaliatory oil boycott against Italy in the 1930s for the invasion of Ethiopia, an economic sanction that was widely evaded by the signatories and, ultimately, ineffectual. The United States' denial of petroleum to the Empire of Japan backfired when it became a justification for Japan to widen the Pacific War. On the other hand is the U.S. economic embargo imposed against Libya for supporting terrorism (most specifically for its failure to accept responsibility for its involvement in blowing up Pan Am Flight 103 over Lockerbie, Scotland, in 1988). The U.S. embargo appears to have worked, since as of late 2002 Libya had offered a $2.7 billion settlement to the families of the people killed on the Pan Am flight. Certain schemes of market invention have worked for awhile, such as the Brazilian coffee valorization plan of 1907 (a state policy of minimum price supports for coffee based upon varying coffee bean qualities, or valorizations). In the 1970s, the Organization of Petroleum Exporting Countries (OPEC) succeeded in wresting control of oil pricing away from private companies, but like the Brazilian scheme, this policy of market intervention backfired because it stimulated alternative sources of supply.

It remains to be seen whether green boycotts such as the protest over Mexican tuna fishers' netting practices (which capture dolphins as well), or the campaign to compel higher labor and environmental standards in Nike plants in Southeast Asia will become a standard weapon in the arsenal of environmental activists. Boycotts carefully targeted to achieve specific ends can be highly effective. For their part, Third World governments tend to see green boycotts as a new form of trade protectionism. Perhaps more effective in the long run will be the pressure of consumers demanding products with green labels, which certify environmentally sound production practices and high labor standards. Recently, even that most hidebound of banana producers, Chiquita brands (the successor to notorious United Fruit) has responded to market forces by implementing a green label certification program that assures consumers that Chiquita makes only limited use of pesticides, trains its workers in proper use of those chemicals it does use, and has instituted a plastics recycling program.

The fact that market interventions by groups seeking specific social ends have proliferated in recent years is the result of deep changes in civil society. No longer do trade professionals set the rules behind the scenes in concert with a limited range of traditional actors. The burgeoning of nongovernmental organizations and other "nonelected groups" (as their critics call them) signifies a much broader constituency for trade issues. In fact, the clash of cultures between experts used to negotiating complex trade deals among themselves and their usual constituencies, and these newly emergent and often rambunctious groups seeking access and action on complex issues is a feature of our times. Arguably, free traders hold the intellectual high ground, but the fact that more and more policy makers feel the need to accommodate this wider range of concerns and actors in trade discussions, under pressure from activist groups and their own constituencies, is something really new.

Regionalism and the timing of market openings are also issues of concern to free traders. For example, opinion is divided over the wisdom of regional trade agreements such as the North American Free Trade Agreement, or NAFTA (a first-order trade pact), Mercosur (a common-market agreement among the nations in the southern part of South America), and the projected Free Trade Agreement of the Americas, which is slated to come into effect by 2005. Those in favor of regional trade pacts hail the potential of "open regionalism" to increase the flow of goods and services. Those opposed point to the risk of "trade diversion" from the global trading system to a few privileged partners. Due to increased trade among regional groupings, the open regionalists, to date, appear to have the better argument.

Another issue is the timing of market opening. However desirable lowering tariffs and other forms of protectionism is in theory, some nations, such as Brazil, have been slow to open for fear of losing their industrial base. Mexico has chosen to risk the "creative destruction" of old industries for the benefits of a more rapid transition to free trade. And for their part, the celebrated Asian Tigers coupled their export-led growth policies with interventionist policies at home to promote and protect certain industries. What, then, of the emerging environmental issues which many free traders dislike but with which they now must deal?

Free Trade and the Environment

Since the 1992 landmark United Nations Conference on Environment and Development (UNCED) held in Rio de Janeiro, trade and the environment have been linked together as two factors critical to a lesser-developed nation's formula for achieving modernization and development. The challenge now is how to express this trade-environment linkage in public policy. Should it be in separate agreements (such as the Montreal Protocol to ban the production and use of ozone-depleting chlorofluorocarbons, or CFCs)? Should it be in parallel, coordinated agreements that liberalize trade while protecting the environment, or perhaps in side agreements (such as the Commission for Environmental Cooperation under the main NAFTA treaty)? Or should it be in comprehensive trade agreements that, in addition to addressing environmental issues, may also address labor rights and the equity question—that is, raising the standard of living of the poorer nation in the trade agreement to the level that is comparable with that of the richer nation? Free markets are efficient, but unregulated free markets do not sufficiently advance the public interest, as the late-nineteenth-century reformers understood. Taking a leaf from their book, one could argue that free trade in the current era of globalization requires more than simply cutting all forms of protectionism, setting up rule-based systems to protect and encourage investment flows, and creating a dispute settlement mechanism. Those goals are encompassed in the new World Trade Organization (WTO). Necessary, but not sufficient, the critics say.

To be sure, the goals of free trade and environmental protection do mesh nicely in the new pollution trading schemes based on market mechanisms. In the United States, the establishment of a market in 1990 to trade pollution credits has worked well to reduce emissions of sulfur dioxide and acid rain from coal-fired power plants. Combining mandatory emissions reduction targets with emissions trading, this "cap and trade" program enables large polluters to buy credits from companies that are far below their pollution limits. This market rewards clean producers; less controlled plants must pay for the privilege to pollute. Tradables (as they are called) are incorporated in the Kyoto treaty on global warming, and may become the market instrument of choice to control regional cross-border air pollution, as for example in North America.

With respect to the environmental history of free trade, it is abundantly clear that the long-running debate between free traders and protectionists was until recently little concerned with the environmental consequence of creating wealth through market integration. The quantifiable benefits of goods produced, of markets opened, and of people moving freely, rarely, if at all, factored in the full costs of this increased production and exchange. All too often the natural world was accepted as a given—a storehouse of resources to be used, used up, and replaced with new sources, little concern being given to the destruction of habitat and the loss of biodiversity, forests, croplands, and wetlands, let alone the rising tide of pollution. Nor were the losers in this grand exchange given much heed—witness the displacement of native peoples and the replacement of customary systems of resource allocation and communal rights by individual property rights. Only recently, with the rise of environmentalism and environmental consciousness in the 1970s, has the possibility (and the promise) of achieving a balance between market integration and environmental protection been a viable option. The bar is raised higher still when sustainability is made the goal.

No one denies that since the 1870s and the first age of liberal internationalism, free trade has been a driver in accelerating the pressure on nature. But it is difficult to untangle free trade from other factors, such as the role of new technologies, changing energy sources, and the enhanced ability of capital and people to flow freely across international borders, all in the general march toward market integration. The conservationists who made their entrance at the end of the nineteenth century grappled with this problem. In our day, in the second age of market integration that began after 1945 and accelerated in the late 1980s, environmentalists seeking out the links between trade and the environment are very much engaged with the same problem.

Achieving clarity and specificity is important if sound policy choices are to be made, including the choice to adopt market mechanisms to abate pollution.

When all is said and done, what has been the outcome of the accelerating use and abuse of nature? Historians with a "declentionist" bent—focusing on the negative impact that free trade has on the environment—point to the heedless destruction of tropical forests in order to produce such mass consumption goods as coffee (in Brazil) and bananas (in the Caribbean basin), reckless overfishing, and unreclaimed mine sites, among other things. Other historians see the emergence of small farmers, cooperatives, and labor unions in the wake of this commodity exchange; the recovery of fisheries through regulation and finding alternative sources of income, and the move (still in early days) to socially responsible production methods in mining and minerals. All along, voices were raised against the destruction of resources, some even couching it as an attack on nature, though until recently few were listening. Did free trade bring unidirectional catastrophe to various world areas? In policy terms, a somewhat more generous view of the history and process of exchange may provide new insights into how the benefits of free trade were actually distributed.

In light of the brief history traced above, the conclusion must be that free trade has been and is today a powerful engine for creating wealth. How that wealth was created in the past, for whose benefit, and at what price to the environment are very modern questions, questions that belong, rightly and inescapably, to the debate over free trade today.

John D. Wirth

Further Reading

Audley, J. J. (1997). *Green politics and global trade: NAFTA and the future of environmental politics.* Washington, DC: Georgetown University Press.

Barry, D., & Klein, R. C. (Eds.). (1999). *Regionalism, multilateralism, and the politics of global trade.* Vancouver and Toronto: UBC Press.

Bhagwati, J. (2002). *Free trade today.* Princeton, NJ: Princeton University Press.

Irwin, D. A. (2002). *Free trade under fire.* Princeton, NJ: Princeton University Press.

McNeil, J. R. (2000). *Something new under the sun: An environmental history of the twentieth century.* New York: Norton.

Mander, J., & Goldsmith, E. (Eds.). (1996). *The case against the global economy and for a turn toward the local.* San Francisco: Sierra Club Books.

Oxfam International. (2002). *Make trade fair.* London: Oxfam International.

Roett, R. (Ed.). (1999). *Mercosur: Regional integration, world markets.* Boulder, CO: Lynne Rienner Publishers.

Yergin, D., & Stanislaw, J. (1998). *The commanding heights: The battle between government and the marketplace that is remaking the modern world.* New York: Simon and Schuster.

Fresh Air Fund

The roots of the Fresh Air Fund can be found in the philanthropic activities of such people and organizations as Reverend William Muhlenberg, who took poor people from New York City on excursions to the countryside in the 1840s, and St. John's Guild (a charitable organization working to help the urban poor), which worked with the *New York Times* to arrange for city children to visit with country families in the 1860s. By the late nineteenth century, a fresh-air movement, intended to improve public health, was under way.

It was in this context that, in 1877, Reverend Willard Parsons, formerly of Brooklyn, New York, established the Mountain Air Fund in Wayne County, Pennsylvania. In 1878, the *New York Evening Post* became the official sponsor and renamed it the Fresh Air Fund. In 1888, the *New York Herald Tribune* became the sponsor and established group homes in "friendly towns." In these towns, services for the visiting children were provided by a coordinated effort among community members. In 1897, there were at least sixty-two Fresh Air Societies in New York City. These societies provided poor, mainly immigrant, inner-city children with day, weekend, or weeklong trips to the countryside. Since tenements used coal stoves and had no indoor plumbing or trash removal, clean air and hot baths were rare. In order to participate children underwent a medical examination to determine if they had a contagious disease or head lice. Children who participated in the program enjoyed the benefits of exposure to clean air, regular baths, healthy food, exercise, a change of scenery, and rest. Advocates asserted that exposure to nature and to the lifestyles of people who lived in rural areas would encourage the children to be good citizens and productive members of society. Throughout the twentieth century camps and land were donated. The Fresh Air Fund became the largest, and most lasting, fresh-air charity in the country. In 1967, the *New York Times* assumed newspaper sponsorship of the Fresh Air Fund.

Today the Fresh Air Fund, a not-for-profit agency, provides free vacations each summer to approximately seven thousand inner-city children from New York City through its Friendly Town program. There are currently three hundred participating Friendly Towns in the northeast, from Virginia to Canada. Volunteer host families live on farms, in suburbs, and in small towns. Approximately three thousand children from New York City attend five summer camps in upstate New York each summer. Year-round camping trips are available for approximately a thousand teenage participants. The Fund also operates a year-round career awareness program for twelve- to fourteen-year-olds.

The children who participate in the Fresh Air Fund are enrolled by social-service agencies and community organizations. All of the children are from low-income families; the majority are African-American and Latino, from single-parent households that receive some public assistance. First-time participants range from six to twelve years old and stay for two weeks. They may continue to participate until they are eighteen years old. The Fresh Air Fund reports that over 65 percent of host families invite their Fresh Air guests to return year after year.

Kirby Randolph

Further Reading

Cronin, W. (1996). *Uncommon ground: Rethinking the human place in nature.* New York: W. W. Norton.

Nash, R. (1967). *Wilderness and the American mind.* New Haven, CT: Yale University Press.

Tolman, W. H. (1895, September). Fresh Air work in New York City. *Chautauquan 21*(6), 713–721.

Ufford, W. S. (1897). *Fresh Air charity in the United States* (Doctoral dissertation, Columbia University).

Friends of the Earth

Friends of the Earth (FoE) is one of the three major international nongovernmental organizations (along with Greenpeace and the World Wildlife Fund, or WWF) that have helped define the international environmental agenda over the last thirty years. It was founded in September 1969 in the United States, and there are now FoE organizations in sixty-six countries around the world, linked through Friends of the Earth International, which claims to be the world's largest federation of environmental groups.

Each national body has a high degree of autonomy, subject to specific membership criteria, in choosing its priorities for work, while sharing an underlying approach. This approach is very different from that of Greenpeace and WWF, which have international boards that oversee their operation. FoE is also less media-focused than Greenpeace, preferring to focus on scientific research and political lobbying.

David Brower, an environmentalist and former director of the Sierra Club, founded FoE in San Francisco. His key reason for leaving the Sierra Club was its refusal to oppose the expansion of nuclear power in the United States, and this move from conservation-focused work to more assertive political action set the tone for contemporary environmentalism.

The FoE movement quickly spread; in 1971 four organizations from France, Sweden, the United Kingdom, and the United States met to form FoE International. Key campaigns in the early days varied from nation to nation but opposition to nuclear energy, examination of resource use, and opposition to whaling were central to the work. In some nations, notably the United Kingdom, local action linked to national issues became an important part of the operations, and this made it clear to the public that FoE could work at every level.

In the early 1980s the organization hit problems, with internal conflicts and declining revenues in some nations. In the United States David Brower departed to establish Earth Island Institute, and FoE moved to Washington and became increasingly focused on lobbying and international processes. In the United Kingdom FoE restructured under an influential new director, Jonathon Porritt. Staff numbers grew from thirteen in 1984 to over a hundred by 1990, fueled by issues such as the Chernobyl disaster, climate change, the deteriorating ozone layer, and destruction of tropical forests.

In the 1990s FoE grew rapidly as environmental politics went global around the 1992 United Nations Earth summit. FoE stressed the impact of Northern Hemisphere consumption patterns on the global environment and developed the influential idea of so-called environmental space, where each nation would have equitable access to resources. Quoting from a

Netherlands FoE Action Plan, environmental space is described as "the overall quantity of environmental resources available to the world at large on a sustainable basis. In other words, the rates at which the planet's energy, fresh water, land, fisheries, forestry, pollution rights, and waste disposal, and other resources can be used without decreasing their availability to future generations" (van Brakel and Buitenkamp 1993, 38).

In 1994 FoE International, with more new members coming in from eastern European and Southern Hemisphere nations, developed closer cooperation to play a leading role in lobbying on international processes developing out of the Earth Summit, such as the Kyoto climate change process and the broader sustainable-development agenda.

FoE's key campaigns now focus on such issues as climate change, desertification, and biodiversity, along with a special emphasis on resisting economic globalization from corporations, mining, and international financial institutions—showing clearly the long-held FoE belief that the solutions to environmental problems come from economic and social action.

Chris Church

Further Reading

Friends of the Earth International (2003). Campaigns. Retrieved January 24, 2003, from http://www.foei.org/campaigns/index.html

van Brakel, M., & Buitenkamp, M. (1993, Fall). Our fair share: Getting specific about "environmental space." *In Context*, *36*, 38. Retrieved January 24, 2003, from http://www.context.org/ICLIB/IC35/FOENL.htm

Gaia Theory

In 1969 the British scientist James Lovelock postulated that life on Earth regulates the composition of the atmosphere to keep the planet habitable. The novelist William Golding, Lovelock's friend and neighbor, suggested Lovelock call the hypothesis *Gaia*, after the Greek Earth goddess. Although in its early exposition and in the popular press the Gaia hypothesis was understood as saying Earth itself was a living organism, the theory as Lovelock came to articulate it said rather that Earth *acts* like a living organism, with its living and nonliving components acting in concert to create an environment that continues to be suitable for life.

Development of the Gaia Hypothesis

The idea that life is more than a passenger on Earth dates back to the work of the Scottish geologist James Hutton (1726–1797) and was held by T. H. Huxley, the animal physiologist Alfred Redfield, the aquatic ecologist G. Evelyn Hutchinson, and the geologist Vladimir Vernadsky. The radical notion that life and the material environment evolved together as a system was first proposed by Alfred Lotka in 1924 but few took him seriously.

In the late 1960s, as part of its search for life on Mars, the National Aeronautics and Space Administration (NASA) gathered information on the composition of planetary atmospheres. Lovelock, then a NASA consultant, noted that Venus and Mars both had atmospheres dominated by carbon dioxide and close to chemical equilibrium. In contrast, gases made by living organisms dominate the Earth's atmosphere, which, despite being far from chemical equilibrium, is stable in the long term. Lovelock realized that such stability required a regulator and, since the atmosphere was mainly a biological product, proposed that Earth's collective life forms played this role.

In 1971 he began collaboration with the eminent biologist Lynn Margulis. Margulis brought her extensive knowledge of Earth's microorganisms and added flesh to what was otherwise a chemical hypothesis based on atmospheric evidence.

Criticism and Refinement of the Gaia Hypothesis

Lovelock and Margulis's joint work brought strong criticism, mainly from other biologists. W. Ford Doolittle and Richard Dawkins, two vocal critics, stated that there was no way for living organisms to regulate anything beyond their individual selves. Their criticism was in the best traditions of science and required a proper answer. In 1981 Lovelock answered the critics by creating the numerical model Daisyworld. Daisyworld was an imaginary planet on which there were two species of plant, one light colored and the other dark colored. The planet was warmed by a star that, like Earth's sun, grew hotter as time passed. When the star was cooler, each dark-colored daisy warmed itself by absorbing sunlight, until dark daisies predominated and warmed the planet; as the star grew hotter, each pale-colored daisy, by reflecting sunlight, kept itself and the planet cooler. The competition for space by the two daisy species kept the planet's temperature constant, thus sustaining a habitable condition despite changes in the heat output of the star. The model showed that even without regulating anything other than themselves, organisms and their environment evolve together as a powerful self-regulating system. This demonstration, along with successful predictions of mechanisms for the regulation of the Earth's climate and chemistry, put Gaia on a firm theoretical basis, which was strengthened by a further suite of models from the ecologists Tim Lenton (in 1998) and Stephan Harding (in 1999).

The Heart of Gaia

Gaia views Earth's surface environment as a self-regulating system composed of all organisms, the atmosphere, oceans, and crustal rocks, which sustains conditions favorable for life. It sees the evolution of life and the evolution of Earth's surface and atmosphere as a single process, not separate processes, as taught in biology and geology. Organisms evolve by a process of natural selection, but in Gaia, they do not merely adapt to the environment, they change it. Humans, clearly, are changing the atmosphere, the climate, and the land surfaces, but other organisms, mostly microscopic, have in the past made changes that were even more drastic. The appearance of oxygen in the air two billion years ago is but one of them. Gaia stands to Darwinism somewhat as relativity theory stands to Newtonian physics. It is no contradiction of Darwin's great vision but an extension of it.

What use is Gaia? It has been a fruitful source of new research and an inspiration for environmentalists. It led to the discovery of the natural compounds dimethyl sulfide and methyl iodide, which transfer the essential elements sulfur and iodine from the oceans to the land. It showed how life in the soil and on the rocks increases the rate of removal of carbon dioxide from the air and so regulates both the levels of carbon dioxide and, consequently, climate. Its most daring prediction stated in 1987 by Robert Charlson, Lovelock, Meinrat Andreae, and Stephen Warren, was that the microscopic algae of the oceans are linked by their emission of a gas, dimethyl sulfide, with the clouds and with the climate. As Earth gets hotter, the theory says, these algae release more dimethyl sulfide into the atmosphere, which increases Earth's cloud cover, which in turn cools the earth: Without clouds, the Earth would be hotter by 10 to 20° C. This idea is crucial to the proper understanding of climate change. The authors received the Norbert Gerbier Prize and a medal from The World Meteorological Office for this theory in 1988. Ten years later hundreds of scientists worldwide were studying the links between ocean algae, atmospheric chemistry, clouds, and climate. Climatologists and even physiologists have used Daisyworld in their research. Over the years, Gaia has changed the way scientists think. There is no better example of this change than the Amsterdam Declaration of 2001. A conference of environmental scientists in 2001 issued the declaration, which had as its first bullet point: "The Earth System behaves as a single, self-regulating system comprised of physical, chemical, biological and human components" (Open Science Conference 2001). Although not yet a full statement of Gaia theory, it a substantial advance on the separated view of earth and life sciences that went before.

James Lovelock

Further Reading

Charlson, R. J., Lovelock, J. E., Andreae, M. O., & Warren, S. G. (1987). Oceanic phytoplankton, atmospheric sulphur, cloud albedo and climate. *Nature, 326*(6114), 655–661.

Harding, S. P. (1999). Food web complexity enhances community stability and climate regulation in a geophysiological model. *Tellus, 51*(B), 815–829.

Lenton, T. (1998). Gaia and natural selection. *Nature, 394,* 439–447.

Lotka, A. (1956). *Elements of mathematical biology.* New York: Dover. (Original work published 1924)

Lovelock, J. E. (1988). *The ages of Gaia: A biography of our living earth.* New York: W.W. Norton.

Lovelock, J. E. (1979). *Gaia: A new look at life on earth.* Oxford, UK: Oxford University Press.

Lovelock, J. E. (1969). Planetary atmospheres: Compositional and other changes associated with the presence of life. In O. L. Tiffany & E. Zaitzeff (Eds.). *Advances in the astronautical sciences* (Vol. 25, pp. 179–193). Tarzana, CA: American Astronautical Society.

Lovelock, J. E. (1991). *The practical science of planetary medicine.* London: Gaia Books.

Lovelock, J. E., & Margulis, M. (1973). Atmospheric homeostasis by and for the biosphere: The Gaia hypothesis. *Tellus, 26,* 2–10.

Lovelock, J. E., & Watson, A. J. (1982). The regulation of carbon dioxide and climate: Gaia or geochemistry. *Planet. Space Science, 30*(8), 795–802.

Open Science Conference (2001, July 10–13). *The Amsterdam declaration on global change.* Retrieved September 5, 2002, from http://www.sciconf.igbp.kva.se/Amsterdam_Declaration.html

Watson, A. J., & Lovelock, J. E. (l983). Biological homeostasis of the global environment: The parable of Daisyworld. *Tellus*, 35(B), 284 –289.

Gandhi, Mohandas K.
(1869–1948)
Indian political leader

Mohandas Karamchand Gandhi is best known around the world as the leader of India's independence movement—which led to the establishment of the nations of India and Pakistan in 1948—and for his groundbreaking use of nonviolent civil disobedience to achieve political goals. Gandhi's significance within environmental history and the environmental movement comes from his questioning and ultimate rejection of the Western models of economic development, technology, and unrestricted exploitation of natural resources.

Gandhi grew up in Porbandar, Gujarat. His father was a minister and judge in the princely state government. His father was also a skilled mediator and his mother a devout Hindu; both parents had an enormous influence on his own values and his involvement in the independence movement.

After earning a law degree in London, Gandhi returned to India and then traveled to South Africa to mediate a legal dispute among Indian Muslims residing there. He then became in involved in defending the rights of the Indian minority in white South Africa. Appalled and shocked by white treatment of the Zulu, Gandhi decided to devote his life to work for political and social justice, developing *satyagraha* ("holding on to the truth"), a philosophy and political method espousing nonviolent resistance to unjust laws. He quickly expanded his activities to advocate for Indian independence from British rule and in 1909 wrote the influential *Hind swaraj* ("Freedom of India").

Gandhi returned to India in 1915 and from then on was actively involved in ending British rule. From the early 1920s on, the Indian National Congress political party was a major mechanism for independence, and although Gandhi held no official position, he was the most influential member. In 1948 independence was finally achieved, although Gandhi had to accept the partition of India into two nations, India and Pakistan.

Although he did not live long enough after independence to put his ideas concerning development and the environment into practice, Gandhi has nonetheless has become an inspirational force in the environmental movement. His opposition to Western-style economic development were first set forth in the *Hind swaraj* and his simple—some would say austere—lifestyle was adopted also while he was in South Africa. Gandhi argued that the Western model of economic development, based on massive consumption of resources and acquisition of much material wealth, would destroy the environment and could not be sustained by available natural resources. He labeled the Western model of modernity as *Bhasmasur*, meaning destructive monster. He advocated instead an approach more in harmony with nature that distinguished between human needs and human wants and argued that there were adequate resources to meet all human needs, if those resources were allocated fairly. These ideas are reflected in the "Agenda 21" of the 1992 Rio de Janeiro Earth Summit. Gandhi also extended his strong belief in nonviolence to the nature-human relationship. He believed that nature was to be revered, and humans should exploit nature only in ways that maintain an ecological balance.

Gandhi was assassinated in 1948—five months after India achieved independence—by a Hindu nationalist who objected to Gandhi's support of Pakistan. Revered in India and by people around the world, he has become known as the Mahatma, or Great Soul.

Further Reading

Brown, J. (1989). *Prisoner of hope*. New Haven, CT: Yale University Press.

There is a sufficiency in the world for man's need but not for man's greed.

—Mohandas K. Gandhi

Gandhi, M. (1997). *"Hind Swaraj" and other writings* (A. J. Parel, Ed.). Cambridge, UK: Cambridge University Press.

Prasad, N. (Ed.). (1985). *Hind Swaraj: A fresh look*. New Delhi, India: Gandhi Peace Foundation.

Rothermund, D. (1992). *Mahatma Gandhi: An essay in political biography*. New Delhi, India: Manohar.

Ganges River

The Ganges (Ganga) River originates 3,959 meters above sea level in the Himalaya Mountains of India, flowing from the Gangotri glacier, which bears ice that is four thousand years old. The Ganges flows through many important Indian cities such as Kanpur, Allahabad, Varanasi, Patna, and Calcutta before reaching the Bay of Bengal. Around 40 percent of the Indian population lives in the Ganges watershed; as of 2003, about 400 million people live along the banks of Ganges River. At 2,525 kilometers, the Ganges River basin ranks among the largest in the world in drainage area and length. The Ganges brings sustenance to the alluvial Indo-Gangetic Plain, which is one of the world's most bountiful food-growing areas. Having a rich biodiversity (biological diversity as indicated by numbers of species of animals and plants), with fifteen species of mollusks, fifty-one species of insects, four species of freshwater prawns, eighty-three species of fish, twelve species of freshwater turtle, and three species of river dolphins, the river is a lifeline for many aquatic creatures. It has many tributaries, and the largest is the Ghaghara River, which meets the Ganges before Patna. Two major dams on the Ganges, one at Hardwar and the other at Farakka, have a crucial impact on the flow of the river. The Hardwar dam diverts much of the Himalayan snowmelt into the Upper Ganges Canal, built by the British in 1854 to irrigate the surrounding land. Experts contend that this has caused severe deterioration to the flow in the river and is also a major cause for the decay of the Ganges as an inland waterway.

Although the Ganges is associated with myth, and its water is considered to be holy and to have healing properties, rampant pollution has marred its water quality. Among the most polluting industries on the Ganges are tanneries, especially near Kanpur, which empty toxic chrome into the river. The river basin also has sugar and paper mills, cloth, woolen, cotton, and rayon mills, battery industries, ordnance factories, thermal powerhouses, distilleries, and fertilizer corporations. Heavy metals such as cadmium, zinc, nickel, lead, chromium, and copper are concentrated in the river water and the sediments. In 1995 the Central Pollution Control Board (CPCB) listed 191 polluting industries in the state of Uttar Pradesh, 6 in the state of Bihar, and 67 in West Bengal. These industries were found to be discharging toxic substances into effluent flows with BOD (biological oxygen demand) concentrations of more than 100 milligrams per liter. However, industry is not the only source of pollution. Around 1 billion liters of untreated municipal waste also flow into the river. In addition, inadequate cremation procedures and surface runoff from farmlands where chemical fertilizers and pesticides are applied contribute to pollution of the Ganges. Dr. D. S. Bhargava, an environmental engineer at the University of Roorkee, suggests that while the Ganges decomposes organic waste fifteen to twenty-five times faster than other rivers, no feat of organic decomposition can match mass quantity of organic waste is poured into its waters from the cities along its banks. In Varanasi, for example, fecal coliform levels have been recorded as high as 100,000 colonies per 100 ml. Another threat looming over the Ganges is silt deposited in its higher reaches in the Himalayas. Taking stock of the situation, the Uttar Pradesh Forest Department is planting trees in the catchment areas (areas where water gathers) to prevent soil erosion. However, at the current rate of 3,000 hectares of forest a year, it will take 150 years to arrest siltation fully. In response, the Chipko movement was launched in the Raghwal hills of India in the 1970s. Chipko movement activists, who are mostly local villagers, are demanding a stop to tree felling in the Himalayas so that floods in the Ganges basin can be checked.

To combat pollution, the $270 million Ganges Action Plan (GAP) was started in 1986. GAP Phase I aimed at building waste-treatment facilities with Dutch and British support. Rakesh Jaiswal, executive secretary of a Kanpur-based nongovernmental organization, EcoFriends, said nearly $150 million pumped into Phase I was misspent mainly due to bureaucratic delays and indifference. In fact, sewage treatment plants under the plan have not been completed. Electric crematoria are standing like white elephants, entirely unfunctional. The plan has not worked satisfactorily, largely because of the lack of participation by people along the river. Activist Supreme Court lawyer M. C. Mehta said GAP has failed because politicians have sided with industrialists. Recently GAP Phase II was approved by the Supreme Court. GAP Phase II is designed to clean the tributaries of the Ganges—the Yamuna River, which flows past New Delhi and the Taj Mahal, and the Gomti River, which flows through the historical city of Lucknow. Proponents hope that GAP Phase II works better than GAP Phase I.

Tirtho Banerjee

See also Rivers; Water Pollution

Further Reading

Krishna Murti, C. R., Das, T. M., Bilgrami, K. S. , & Mathur, R. P. (Eds.). (1996). *The Ganga: A scientific study.* New Delhi, India: Northern Book Centre.

Monte, D. D. (1996). Filthy flows the Ganga. *People and the Planet, 5*(3), 20–22.

Rao, R. T., Sahu, S. K., & Pandit, R. K. (1995). *Studies on biological restoration of Ganga in Uttar Pradesh: An indicator species approach. Final technical report, 1995.* Gwalior, India: School of Studies in Zoology, Jiwaji University.

Sampat, P. (1996, July–August). The river Ganges' long decline. *World Watch, 9*(4), 24–32.

Shukla, A. C., & Vandana, A. (1995). *Ganga: A water marvel.* New Delhi, India: APH Publishing Corporation.

Gardens and Gardening

The efforts of people to create and use gardens operate at the connection of human relationships and the environment. Gardens for enjoyment come out of efforts of humans living within highly developed landscapes to connect with a more pastoral landscape and to extend the comfort and security of the home into the open air. Gardens for food provide a ground for subsistence or enrichment but also provide a place where people can focus on a basic human activity, on coaxing edible foods from the environment. In some gardens the two purposes—enjoyment and food—are mixed, and aesthetic values are interwoven with utilitarian ones in the design and maintenance of these gardens.

Although scholars differ in their recognition of the universality of gardens and gardening, they view gardens as markers of culture. In different places and at different times people have had different opinions on just what a "garden" is, how and by whom it is organized, what plants are valued and grown in it, how it is tended and who does the tending, and what general

Maintenance workers in Seoul, Korea in 2002 tend to a roadside lawn and flower beds. COURTESY KAREN CHRISTENSEN.

value it has for larger groups of people. However, whether the owner of a garden does the gardening himself or herself or hires professional gardeners or laborers to do it instead, gardening requires both plan and execution and blends understandings that are aesthetic, utilitarian, and scientific—and that derive from the cultural system of which the garden is an expression.

The garden as an idea is also important in some cultures. The idea of an idealized Edenic garden as a place of sanctity and retreat is deeply embedded in Judeo-Christian cultures. When this idea has been combined with ideas about how mixed small-scale farming and certain kinds of land-owning patterns create a hearth for public virtue, as in the Jeffersonian agrarian ideal in the United States, it has played an important role in the political life of a nation. Looking closely at the gardens of a culture, both real and idealized, reveals a great deal about what is important to that culture.

Origins and History

In general, gardening as a kind of intensive attention to the growing of plants for food, flavoring, and medicine followed agriculture as a mode of human manipulation of the environment. Growing a few plants in a garden for food and often at the same time for enjoyment has been traditionally a part of household production. A culture had to be relatively affluent to support the leisure and expense that the planning, installing, and tending of formal pleasure gardens required. In less-affluent cultures that have had little time for garden dreams or pleasure, more utilitarian gardens and gardening have sometimes provided a

Flowers are the beautiful words and hieroglyphs of Nature with which she tells us how much she loves us.

—Johann Wolfgang von Goethe

crucial margin of food supply and nutrition that has assured survival. At the same time, even the less affluent blended considerations of beauty with those of subsistence in dooryard gardens.

Although the origins of garden making and gardening as human activities are obscure, evidence of early formal gardens is clear in the archeological record. Evidence of gardens in Egypt dates back to 1400 BCE, and the wealthy and powerful in early Assyrian, Babylonian, and Persian cultures created pleasure gardens that were sometimes quite elaborate in their designs and game parks that provided an additional increment of managed pleasure for the wealthy. The roots of the modern garden in the West can be found more directly in Renaissance Italy, where the makers of extensive gardens for the aristocracy developed a model that regarded the garden as an extension of the built environment. In these gardens an architecture of straight lines and sharp corners was reinforced by well-trimmed plantings—all opened up to the air. This model of design was refined by the French and Dutch, who added to it several features, including well-developed smaller gardens off the main garden axis and an emphasis on topiary and plantings of yew and boxwood.

In the eighteenth century a new interest in pastoral landscapes by artists and a general growth in interest in the "natural" contributed to a design revolution in England, especially in the hands of the painter and architect William Kent. Kent, who believed that nature abhors a straight line, designed gardens with meandering paths, undulating reliefs, and clumps of untrimmed trees. Sometimes a view of the sky was blocked by a canopy in these gardens. In the hands of a new generation of English landscape designers, gardens began to look more like parks.

In the eighteenth and nineteenth centuries garden design in Europe was also influenced by the flow of plants from lands explored or colonized by Europeans. One of the purposes of the medieval herb garden and the specialized botanical garden—to preserve specimens of valuable plants for study and use—was introduced into garden design, and many nineteenth-century gardens became not just works of art but also museums of plants. This purpose was apparent in a new emphasis on beds of flowers in large formal gardens and in the increasing influence of horticulturalists in garden design and development. Romantic reinterpretations of "nature" produced yet more abhorrence for the straight line, and gardens in England—and in some cases on the Continent and in the United States—acquired a studied informality that emphasized organic flow. As "wilderness" shrunk all over the world, and especially in their own backyards, people in Europe and the United States sought to re-create some measure of wildness in their gardens.

Garden design has had a rich history in Asia as well, producing stunning expressions of human relationships with nature of a less-domineering sort. Instead of structures that exalted an architecture of physical control of the environment by humans, Chinese gardens sought to accentuate certain qualities of nature that contributed to moral and civic harmony. Chinese gardens were meant as places for meditation and as places for the owners and their friends to cultivate—and quietly display—a calm moderation in their relations with nature. Makers of Chinese gardens studiously avoided symmetry and created a landscape of winding paths and exchanges of human-made hills, meanders and cascades of water, carefully placed rocks, and islands and bridges that were designed to evoke sets of linked aesthetic sensations, which, in turn, were inspired by spiritual and moral ideals.

Chinese garden design infiltrated Japan by 1000 CE, but the Japanese impressed upon the Chinese model a penchant for ritual and organization that gave gardens a formality that they often lacked in China. Two good examples of this tendency were the abstract garden of stones placed in an elegant relationship to each other in a bed of raked sand and the tea garden, which was created according to a set of clearly defined rules as a site for the tea ceremonies that were important among the Japanese elite in the fourteenth through the sixteenth centuries. Some Japanese gardens also sought to represent valued landscapes, such as that around Mount Fuji, through highly stylized assem-

Sir Francis Bacon's Garden Design

For *Gardens*, (Speaking of those, which are indeed *Prince-like*, as we have done of *Buildings*) the Contents, ought not well to be, under *Thirty Acres of Ground*; And to be divided into three Parts: A *Greene* in the Entrance; A *Heath* or *Desart* in the Going forth; And the *Maine Garden* in the midst; Besides *Alleys*, on both Sides. And I like well, that Foure Acres of Ground, be assigned to the *Greene*; Six to the *Heath*; Foure and Foure to either *Side*; And Twelve to the *Maine Garden*. The Greene hath two pleasures; The one, because nothing is more Pleasant to the Eye, then Greene Grasse kept finely shorne; The other, because it will give you a faire Alley in the midst, by which you may go in front upon a *Stately Hedge*, which is to inclose the *Garden*. But, because the Alley will be long, and in great Heat of the Yeare, or Day, you ought not to buy the shade in the *Garden*, by Going in the Sunne thorow the *Greene*, therefore you are, of either *Side* the *Greene*, the Plant a *Covert Alley*, upon Carpenters Worke, about Twelve Foot in Height, by which you may goe in Shade, into the *Garden*. As for the Making of *Knots*, or *Figures*, with *Divers Coloured Earths*, that they may lie under the Windowes of the House, on that Side, which the *Garden* stands, they be but Toyes: You may see as good Sights, many times, in Tarts. The *Garden* is best to be Square; Incompassed, on all the Foure Sidres, with a *Stately Arched Hedge*. The *Arches* to be upon *Pillars*, of Carpenters Worke, of some Ten Foot high, and Six Foot broad: And the *Spaces* between, of the same Dimension, with the *Breadth* of the *Arch*. Over the *Arches*, let there bee an *Entire Hedge*, of some Foure Foot High, framed also upon Carpenters Worke: And upon the *Upper Hedge*, over every *Arch*, a little *Turret*, with a *Belly*, enough to receive a *Cage of Birds*: And over every *Space*, betweene the *Arches*, some other little *Figure*, with Broad Plates of *Round Coloured Glasse*, gilt, for the *Sunne*, to Play upon. But this *Hedge* I entend to be, raised upon a *Bancke*, not Steepe, but gently Slope, of some Six Foot, set all with *Flowers*. Also I understand, that this *Square* of the *Garden*, should not be the whole Breadth of the Ground, but to leave, on either Side, Ground enough, for diversity of *Side Alleys*: Unto which, the Two *Covert Alleys* of the *Greene*, may deliver you. But there must be, no *Alleys* with *Hedges*, at either *End*, of this great *Inclosure*: Not at the *Hither End*, for letting your Prospect upon this Faire Hedge from the *Greene*; Nor at the *Further End*, for letting your Prospect from the Hedge, through the Arches, upon the *Heath*.

Source: Bacon, Francis. (1907). "Of Gardens." In W. Aldiss Wright (Ed.), *Bacon's Essays*. London: Macmillan and Co., p. 189.

blages of hills and ponds. These were scaled down to garden size, which could vary greatly as long as the essential elements were preserved. Gardens with lakes, streams, islands, hills, bridges, and real trees were created in spaces as small as a foot square. Different elements of Japanese gardens symbolized different spiritual and moral qualities and were arranged to express valued relationships—to be aesthetically pleasing but also "natural."

Gardens in India were also designed to express religious values and had within them plants and artifices of special importance within the religious traditions of Indian culture. Trees, for example, were venerated by the Hindus. It was in a garden of lotus-covered pools, flowers, and trees that Buddha was reputed to have been born. After invading Mughals (members of a Muslim dynasty) introduced Islam garden ideas, Indian formal gardens acquired more in the way of flowing water, coming from all corners like the four rivers of Eden. Similar to European styles of gardens previous to the nineteenth century, Indian gardens also expressed an architectural approach to garden design, which saw the garden as an extension of the building or buildings to which it was attached.

Garden design in the twentieth century borrowed from traditions from around the globe. The easy flow of both garden materials and garden ideas from one part of the world to another and an openness to endlessly recombinant possibilities have meant that garden designers have combined elements of design from whatever suits them and have created gardens that are highly inventive expressions, elegant restatements, restorations of classical designs, or fusion failures. More common, in the United States at least, is the vaguely formal design of parks around public buildings, which are meant to open up spaces around office buildings, communal dwellings, and arterial roads—and not much more. The distinction between garden and park, always not very clear, has been further blurred in urban community vegetable gardens that have also become social gathering places or in greenways that have been carefully cultivated and managed to produce an urban "wild" place for recreation.

Informal Gardens

The emphasis on highly designed gardens whose development has been executed from specific principles and a careful plan ignores the wide array of meaningful gardens that has not followed these practices and has acquired a design through improvisation and inventive responses to necessity. An emphasis on formal gardens in garden history also ignores the important role that gardens play in cultures that have not often produced museum-quality formal gardens. Again, gardening defined broadly appears to have been a universal human activity, and historians must look to the dooryards, back patches, courtyards, rooftops, porches, and sills if they want a comprehensive view of the subject.

Historians, for example, have recently revealed a hitherto largely invisible history of gardening among African Americans in the U.S. South that derives from long traditions of African-American and African gardening, which does not proceed from a formal design (although design is expressed by these gardens), and which reinforces both individual and community values. These vernacular gardens are middle grounds not between nature unmodified and nature erased, but rather between cultivated fields and places of abode in the rural South. The sites of these gardens have traditionally been the swept yards of rural African-American southerners—which themselves have been both practical responses to the environment (they provide an area around the house that can be easily kept free of vermin and also an outdoor place where food can be processed and washed) and a continuation of an African practice. An array of ornamental plants was planted in the yards or in pots that could be moved around, and most of the gardens included highly valued shade trees. Adjacent to or interlocked with the yard were kitchen gardens that were sometimes large enough to qualify as "fields"

where large quantities of beans, sweet potatoes, or other crops were grown for family consumption. Sometimes animals were kept in pens or ranged freely in these yards. Although slaves often kept small gardens adjacent to their cabins, the informal gardens of African Americans came into their own after emancipation, when freed slaves had more—albeit still severely restricted—control over both their time and the resources in the environs of their homes. In all, the yards and gardens of rural African Americans were important informal landscapes that extended the living and working space of the cabin or house, linked fields and large food gardens directly with the household, re-created notions of beauty and the use of space that had deep roots in this group of people, and provided a preserve for both work and socializing.

How a group of people makes gardens provides a window into what those people hold dear—both for subsistence and for beauty. Gardens are places where people take their leisure and in doing so express the values with which they are most comfortable. A close look at who decides what a garden will be and how it will be made, as well as at who does the work of making and maintaining the garden, is revealing of the social relations of a society. Comparing gardens of different groups of people can explain other differences between those groups and how they think about themselves—especially if gardens beyond those celebrated in garden guidebooks or displayed in highbrow garden tours are experienced.

Mart Stewart

Further Reading

Berrall, J. S. (1978). *The garden: An illustrated history.* New York: Penguin Books.

Brookes, J. (1987). *Gardens of paradise: The history and design of the great Islamic gardens.* New York: New Amsterdam.

Brown, J. (1999). *The pursuit of paradise: A social history of gardens and gardening.* London: Harper & Collins.

Langenheim, J. H., & Thimann, K. V. (1982). *Botany—plant biology and its relation to human affairs.* New York: John Wiley and Sons.

Leighton, A. (1983). *American gardens in the eighteenth century: For use or for delight.* Amherst: University of Massachusetts Press.

Leighton, A. (1986). *Early American gardens: For meat or medicine.* Amherst: University of Massachusetts Press.

Leighton, A. (1987). *American gardens in the nineteenth century: For comfort and affluence.* Amherst: University of Massachusetts Press.

Marx, L. (1964). *The machine in the garden: Technology and the pastoral ideal in America.* New York: Oxford University Press.

Morris, E. T. (1983). *The gardens of China: History, art, and meanings.* New York: Charles Scribner's Sons.

Pollan, M. (1991). *Second nature: A gardener's education.* New York: Atlantic Monthly Press.

Pollan, M. (2001). *The botany of desire: A plant's eye view of the world.* New York: Random House.

Simpson, B., & Conner-Ogorzaly, M. (1986). *Economic botany: Plants in our world.* New York: McGraw Hill.

Thacker, C. (1979). *The history of gardens.* Berkeley and Los Angeles: University of California Press.

Vaughan, J. G., & Geissler, C. A. (1997). *The new Oxford book of food plants: A guide to the fruit, vegetables, herbs and spices of the world.* Oxford, UK: Oxford University Press.

Westmacott, R. (1992). *African-American gardens and yards in the rural South.* Knoxville: University of Tennessee Press.

Gas *See* Natural Gas

Genetically Modified Foods

Genetically modified (GM) foods are foods that are, or are made from, organisms that have been modified using biotechnology. Such genetically modified organisms (GMOs) contain alien genes, also called "transgenes," that are taken from plants, animals bacteria, or viruses, or that were created synthetically in a laboratory. Genetic engineers have harnessed the mechanisms adapted by bacteria and viruses to overcome the defenses that nature designed to protect individual genomes (an organism's genetic material) from invasion by foreign DNA. This allows engineers to insert novel genes that confer a commercial advantage for agricultural production. These genes include those for traits such as herbicide tolerance, pest resistance, ability to grow faster and bigger, delayed ripening, longer shelf life, and higher oil content. Biotechnology is also being used to convert plants and animals into factories for producing drugs and other products. This is referred to as "biopharming." Although there are alternate methods of achieving the same food produc-

tion goals, methods that pose none of the same risks to human health and the environment that GMOs do, bioengineers producing GM foods claim that such foods offer a safe alternative to agricultural chemicals and are necessary to feed the world's expanding human population. GM foods raise a myriad of issues related to the safety of human health and the environment, as well as to economics, politics, public policy, and international trade relations. They are highly controversial and have been dubbed with contrasting labels from "Frankenfoods" by anti-GM groups to "super crops" by pro-GM groups. Consumers get mixed messages about GM foods, and nations are polarized in their acceptance or rejection of GMOs.

Creating a GMO

In genetically engineered foods, a gene from a foreign species (virus, bacterium, animal, or plant) or a synthesized gene (one that is constructed or modified in a laboratory and does not occur in nature) is linked to a reporter gene (often for antibiotic resistance) that signals successful insertion of the alien DNA, and to other viral or bacterial DNA sequences necessary for insertion and expression of the gene in the host genome. The resultant cassette of chimeric DNA is spliced into a bacterial plasmid, which is used to create multiple copies of the transgenic construct. Then the cassette is inserted into a viral or bacterial carrier that is introduced into the host plant or animal. Other methods for introducing the foreign DNA include, for animals, injection directly into an egg, or, for plants, either the use of a gene gun to shoot the DNA into a group of plant cells or electroporation, which uses electric shock to trick the host into allowing passage of the alien DNA through the cell wall. Transformed cells are then grown into organisms by cloning or tissue culture. The term for a successful transformation is an "event." The only GM animal product currently approved for the U.S. market is recombinant bovine growth hormone (rBGH), which is injected into cows to stimulate milk production. A number of GM crop plants, however, are being grown in the United States and other countries. Consequently, over 60 percent of food products on American grocery store shelves contain genetically modified material. Unless it is either produced from organically grown crops or imported from a country where GM foods are either labeled or banned, almost every processed food product in the United States contains some ingredient derived from GM corn, soybeans, or canola. Corn and soybeans, which are the most widely grown economic crops in the United States, are incorporated almost universally as ingredients of processed foods. Most consumers in the United States are consequently not aware of the extent to which they are consuming GM foods.

Advocates of GM foods claim that genetic modification of plants and animals is not new because humans have been artificially selecting desirable traits in plants and animals for thousands of years. Humans saved the seed of the most productive and delicious plants and used prime animals for breeding. Genetic engineering, however, is vastly different from conventional plant and animal breeding methods because it allows scientists to insert a gene or genes from virtually any organism into any other organism. A description of how a type of GM corn is developed illustrates the difference between conventional methods that select traits for improving crops through natural recombination in sexual reproduction and genetic engineering that transfers one or more alien DNA sequences using the tools of biotechnology.

GM Corn Example

The worst insect pest of corn in the United States is rootworm, the larval stage of a beetle. The underground larvae feed on the roots of developing corn plants and can cause up to 50 percent reduction in grain yield. The total costs to growers are over $1 billion a year in crop losses and insecticide costs. Biotechnology companies have developed a genetically engineered rootworm-resistant corn by inserting a gene from the bacterium *Bacillus thuringiensis* (*B.t.*). This *B.t.* gene, referred to as *cryBb1*, codes for a potent enzyme that breaks down the insect digestive system. Approval for commercial use of Monsanto's GM rootworm-resistant corn, referred to as "MON 863," is pending. MON 863 contains various DNA sequences from three types of bacteria, as well as from a virus, wheat, and rice. The DNA sequences are spliced together, cloned in a bacterial plasmid that was then cut with a restriction enzyme (molecular scissors), coated to form metal beads, and shot into corn cells with a gene gun. The cells are then placed in an antibiotic-containing medium because only cells that have successfully received the gene to make them resistant to antibiotics can grow there. Those transgenic cells grow into rootworm-resistant corn plants. The MON 863 plants are then cross-pollinated with inbred lines to incorporate the GM trait into the commercial production pipeline. Analysis of this GM corn reveals changes

in its nutritional composition when compared to conventionally bred corn. There is an increase in levels of the essential amino acids cysteine, aspartic acid, and glycine; there is a decrease in the amino acids leucine, phenylalanine, and glutamic acid; and there is also a decrease in the other important nutrients phosphorous, magnesium, zinc, manganese, vitamin E, and phytic acid. This illustrates how, along with the introduction of novel DNA sequences, GM crops have altered compositions from their original, non-GM counterparts.

Benefits and Risks

Beneficial traits derived from GMO technology include resistance to insects or pathogens (agents of disease), herbicide tolerance, longer shelf life in the supermarket, drought resistance, ability to fix nitrogen, ability to manufacture under drugs or vaccines, and so forth. However, because this technology recombines DNA from widely disparate organisms and overcomes natural boundaries of evolutionary genetics that have evolved to protect and ensure the integrity and stability of an organism's genomes, GMOs may pose significant risks to human health and the environment. For instance, in insect-resistant genetically engineered plants, the pesticidal toxin is produced throughout the plant, including the parts eaten for food. Individuals may have allergic reactions to the GM protein product in a plant. Furthermore, transgenes can be transferred by wind, insect, or animal pollinators into non-GM and organic crops, as well as wild plants in the natural environment. Insecticidal proteins that kill target insects may also be harmful to beneficial insects in the environment, as demonstrated by the mortality decline of monarch butterfly larvae fed *Bt* corn pollen. Another concern is that target insects develop resistance to transgenic toxins just as they do to agricultural pesticides.

Regulations and Safety

No laws have been passed in the United States to specifically regulate the safety of GM plants and animals. If a product is not regulated under current laws, the government has limited authority. The Food and Drug Administration (FDA) oversees food and feed safety following the principle of substantial equivalence, which means that newly introduced substances must be functionally similar to other proteins, fats, and carbohydrates commonly and safely consumed in the diet. The FDA does not conduct independent testing or make judgments about the safety of any GM product. Determination of safety for any food or feed product is the full, voluntary responsibility of the company producing the product. Because GM foods contain novel proteins not previously in the human diet, and because a single amino acid change can mean the difference between a nutritious food and a poison, the question of whether the concept of substantial equivalence is adequate to ensure safety has been raised. The United States Department of Agriculture (USDA) issues permits for companies to conduct field tests of GM crops. The Environmental Protection Agency (EPA) regulates plant protection trials and labeling of plants engineered to kill insects or tolerate weed-killing chemicals. EPA safety guidelines for GMOs are based on the regulations for agricultural pesticides to prevent humans from consuming excessive amounts of a harmful toxin in food and to restrict release of harmful chemicals into the environment. There is a crucial distinction between a transgenic product manufactured within the plant and chemical pesticides that are externally applied.

An important consideration is the opportunity for transgenes to recombine with the DNA of other organisms in nature after a GM plant or animal is released into the environment. Escaped transgenes crossing with wild relatives of plants and animals could result in genetic swamping if the genes are rapidly incorporated into the wild populations. This would lead to greatly accelerated loss of natural biodiversity (biological diversity as indicated by numbers of species of animals and plants). How rapidly and how far transgenes can move were graphically illustrated by the discovery of *Bt* insect-resistant genes in native varieties of cultivated corn in remote areas of southern Mexico, the heartland of corn biodiversity. This is alarming because it is against the law to plant GM seed in Mexico where it could lead to contamination and loss of native genetic resources that plant breeders traditionally use in corn improvement. This international incident has demonstrated that issues of GMOs crossing restricted political boundaries, liability, clean-up of contaminated seed supplies, and biodiversity loss are not just theoretical concepts. There is an urgent need to address these issues in an international legal framework.

Genetic Changes

Although some bioengineers claim that GMOs are no different from plants and animals derived from tradi-

tional breeding, genetic engineering is revolutionary and provides unprecedented power to alter and accelerate evolution. GMOs are radically different from anything produced before. Unanticipated incidents signal how unprepared science and society may be for unanticipated consequences of widespread utilization of this technology in food production. The DNA insertion sequences from viruses and bacteria that allow these pathogens to infect their host organisms also permit movement of transgenes to new positions within an organism's genome. GM soybeans exemplify how this instability of transgenes can lead to new mutations. Roundup Ready brand soybeans were engineered to survive applications of the herbicide glyphosate. The molecular marker that tracks the Roundup-resistant transgene has detected a new molecular signature in Roundup Ready seed now on the market that is distinctly different from the approved transgenic event. This confirms that a genetic change has occurred and illustrates the inherent genomic instability of GM products. In addition to movement within genomes, transgenes may move from the host organism into the DNA of other organisms, a phenomenon referred as "horizontal gene transfer." For example, a synthetic transgene for herbicide resistance in oilseed rape has been detected in bacteria that live in the gut of honey bees. Although horizontal transmission of transgenes to close relatives of crop plants was expected, movement of transgenes into organisms other than closely related wild species was not anticipated. Because of this instability and movement of transgenes it is impossible to predict where and when genetic changes may occur, what effect they might have on gene expression in host or other organisms, and what the environmental and human health effects might be. The application of transgenic technologies in agriculture extends beyond basic science into public policy and regulatory affairs where consumer safety and environmental protection are paramount.

Allergenicity

One of the health risks posed by GM foods is the possibility that eating proteins to which the human body has never been exposed may cause allergic reactions. An allergic reaction is a complex immune system response to a foreign substance. Typical symptoms include skin rashes, headaches, asthma, nausea, colic, and diarrhea. More serious reactions include difficult breathing, anaphylactic shock (a reaction to exposure to an antigen), and even death. Allergic reactions can be worsened by other molecular conditions in a person's body or the environment. The only treatment for food allergies is dietary avoidance. Critical to avoidance is the ability to identify the source of exposure. Because GM products are not labeled in the United States, it is virtually impossible for consumers and clinicians to determine when symptoms that may be caused by an allergic reaction to food are caused by a GM ingredient.

Two criteria are currently used to gauge whether a transgenic protein is safe for human consumption. One compares the amino acid sequences of the transgenic products to the amino acid sequences of food proteins known to elicit allergic reactions. However, the critical criterion for predicting allergenicity involves subtle differences between similar proteins that are not picked up by computer programs and search engines currently available. Another problem that cannot be detected by comparison of primary amino acid structure to proteins in databases is that allergic reactions are often caused by modifications to proteins after they are produced in the cell to accommodate their functional role in the body.

The second criterion for predicting allergenicity is the test tube assay, which measures stability of the transgenic protein to digestive enzymes. This assumes that food allergens exhibit more stability to digestion than other foods. However, such digestion assays are not reliable for determining food allergenicity because some major food allergens are broken down by gastric enzymes. These cannot be detected in the digestion stability assays. Another flaw in the assay for assessing safety is these in-vitro (outside the body) tests use enzyme concentrations that are much higher than occur in the human digestive tract. Therefore, they do not adequately simulate how GM proteins will perform in the human gastro-intestinal tract. Furthermore, there is considerable variability in results from different laboratories because of lack of standardization.

People develop sensitivity to allergens depending on exposure, their developmental stage, and individual sensitivity. Babies and children up to age three are more sensitive to allergens because of their immature immune systems. Immune systems of the elderly are also more vulnerable because of age-related conditions. In the United States about 7 million people have documented food allergies. A severe allergic reaction can cause anaphylactic shock, the most feared form of hypersensitivity, which can be fatal unless the person receives immediate emergency treatment. With 150–175 deaths per year from allergic reactions in the

United States alone, there is a clear need for better understanding of the genetics and physiology of allergenicity and the molecular modulators that regulate the complex, enigmatic reactions to food allergens. Although a possible benefit of biotechnology in the future could be to reduce the amount of allergic substances in foods, there are significant loopholes in current methods for assessing GM foods for possible adverse reactions in humans.

A dramatic incident illustrates that failing to have a comprehensive regulatory scheme to address the complex dimensions of genetics, toxicology, ecology, and evolutionary biology can have serious consequences. In October 2000 it was discovered that taco shells sold at a fast food chain tested positive for a GM corn approved only for animal feed. StarLink was not approved for human consumption because of the possibility that it could cause allergic reactions. Since the revelation of the presence of StarLink corn in taco shells, it was found that millions of bushels of StarLink had gone to food processors and that the product was widely distributed in processed foods from corn chips and corn flakes to a wide array of products that contain a corn ingredient. There were massive recalls, and EPA withdrew the manufacturer's permit to sell StarLink. A number of allergic reactions to the *cry* protein in StarLink were reported, and some were life threatening. This incident documented that widespread contamination of food by transgenic products that are unapproved for human consumption—but that are approved for other uses—is virtually unavoidable because of multiple opportunities and sources for human error in addition to natural cross-contamination in the fields. The inadequacies of regulatory laws to ensure human health and environmental safety are beginning to be more widely recognized. Several bills were introduced in 2001 in the 106th session of the U.S. Congress to address these concerns.

Global Perceptions of GMOs

Biotechnology was put on the development fast track in the United States when the administration of President George H. W. Bush lowered the regulatory hurdles in 1992. In 2001, 52.6 million hectares were planted in GM crops in thirteen countries. With 68 percent of the world total, the United States is the clear global leader in GM crop production, followed by Argentina, Canada, China, South Africa, Germany, and Spain, respectively, in area planted. The number of GM hectares in the United States has risen from 1.4 million in 1996, when the first GM seed was sold, to 35.6 million in 2001. Although this technology has been fast-tracked in the United States, most countries have adopted the European Union (EU) policy of the precautionary principle in regard to GM crops. The basic premise is that safety of new technologies must be vouchsafed before the technologies are introduced into consumer markets. The majority of people living in the fifteen countries of the European Union (Austria, Belgium, Denmark, Finland, France, Germany, Greece, Ireland, Italy, Luxembourg, Netherlands, Portugal, Spain, Sweden, and the United Kingdom) are concerned about potential harmful effects of GMOs on human health and the environment. There has been considerable public opposition to GM foods in the European Union, led by consumer organizations and environmental groups. The greatest opposition has come from the United Kingdom, France, Germany, Austria, Italy, Greece, Belgium, and Denmark. In 1998 the EU stopped approving any new GM crops and removed many genetically engineered foods from the market. Mandatory labeling is required for any foods that contain more than 1 percent GM product. Many food producers and supermarket chains claim to sell only GM-free products. Rabobank, a leading European financial institution, refuses to finance certain forms of biotechnology related to GMOs. Countries with bans or moratoriums on GMOs include Algeria, Austria, Brazil, France, Germany, Italy, Japan, Korea, Greece, Mexico, Norway, Philippines, Portugal, Russia, Spain, Thailand, Saudi Arabia, Sri Lanka, and the United Kingdom. An increasing number of countries, including Australia (1 percent GMO content), China, EU (.5 percent), Japan (.1 percent), Korea, Mexico, New Zealand, Paraguay, South Africa, Thailand, United Kingdom, and Vietnam, are legislating mandatory labeling. The African continent is divided over GM foods. Whereas South Africa, Kenya, and Egypt have approved some GM crops, countries such as Ethiopia, Zambia, and Zimbabwe are so strongly opposed that they have refused U.S. shipments of GM grain, even when people are starving. Developing countries are deeply concerned about issues of food safety, contamination of biodiversity, ownership issues related to intellectual property, loss of free markets, and economic control by multinational corporations that own and tie the technology to their chemical products. In addition to the uncertainties and discord in regard to biotechnology, it raises many issues in regard to globalization, free trade, international governance, and countries' rights to implement and enforce what they believe is safe and prudent policy to protect their citizens.

In summary, GM foods are produced by a revolutionary technology that recombines the DNA of vastly different organisms by bypassing natural mechanisms that protect genomic integrity. This technology is so new that it presents many unknowns, particularly in regard to genetics. Current guidelines to monitor the safety of GM foods do not adequately address issues of human health or environmental impact. Sound principles of toxicology, ecology, and evolutionary genetics that are necessary to accurately assess the impact of releasing transgenes into the human food supply and the environment have not been incorporated into the regulatory structure. In light of the unknowns and potential risks posed by GM foods, until the risks of using genetically engineered crops are better understood and regulatory protocols are in place, some experts think it would be wise to slow development of GMOs and in the interim promote safer food-production methods already available.

Mary W. Eubanks

Further Reading

Ackerman, J. (2002, May). Food. *National Geographic, 201*(5), 2–51.

Charles, D. (2001). *Lords of the harvest: Biotech, big money, and the future of food.* Cambridge, MA: Perseus Publishing.

The Economist. (1999, June 19). Who's afraid of genetically modified foods? *The Economist, 351,* 19–21.

Eubanks, M. (2002). Allergies à la carte: Is there a problem with genetically modified foods? *Environmental Health Perspectives, 110*(3), A130–A131.

Eubanks, M. (2002). Tapping ancestral genes in plant breeding: An alternative to GMO crops. In J. R. Stepp, F. S. Wyndham, & R. K. Zarger (Eds.), *Ethnobiology and biocultural diversity* (pp. 225–238). Athens: University of Georgia Press.

Goldburg, R. J. (1992). Environmental concerns with the development of herbicide-tolerant crops. *Weed Technology, 6*(3), 647–652.

Hart, K. (2002). *Eating in the dark.* New York: Pantheon Books.

Huang, F. L., Buschman, L., Higgins, R. A., & McGaughey, W. H. (1999). Inheritance of resistance to *Bacillus thuringiensis* toxin (dipel ES) in the European corn borer. *Science, 284*(5416), 965–967.

Letourneau, D. K., & Burrows, B. E. (2002). *Genetically engineered organisms: Assessing environmental and human health effects.* Boca Raton, FL: CRC Press.

Lewis, R., & Palevitz, B. A. (1999). GM crops face heat of debate. *The Scientist, 13*(20), 8–9.

Lindsey, K. (Ed.). (1998). *Transgenic plant research*. Amsterdam, Netherlands: Harwood Academic Publishers.

Losey, J. E., Rayor, L. S., & Carter, M. E. (1999). Transgenic pollen harms monarch larvae. *Nature, 399*(214), 214.

Lurquin, P. F. (2001). *The green phoenix*. New York: Columbia University Press.

Mann, C. (2002, March 1). Has GM corn "invaded" Mexico? *Science, 295*(5560), 1617–1619.

Mikklesen, T. R., Andersen, B., & Jørgensen, R. B. (1996). The risk of crop transgene spread. *Nature, 380*(6569), 31.

National Agricultural Biotechnology Council. (1989). *Biotechnology and sustainable agriculture: Policy alternatives* (Report No. 1). Ithaca, NY: National Agricultural Biotechnology Council.

National Agricultural Biotechnology Council. (1991). *Agricultural biotechnology at the crossroads: Biological, social and institutional concerns* (Report No. 3). Ithaca, NY: National Agricultural Biotechnology Council.

National Research Council. (2000). *Genetically modified pest-protected plants: Science and regulation*. Washington, DC: National Academy Press.

Nelson, G. C. (Ed.). (2001). *Genetically modified organisms in agriculture: Economics and politics*. New York: Academic Press.

Nordlee, J. A., Taylor, S. L., Townsend, J. A., Thomas, L. A., & Bush, R. K. (1996). Identification of a Brazil-nut allergen in transgenic soybeans. *New England Journal of Medicine, 334*(11), 688–692.

Palumbi, S. R. (2001). *The evolution explosion: How humans cause rapid evolutionary change*. New York: W. W. Norton.

Raybould, A. F., & Gray, A. J. (1994). Will hybrids of genetically modified crops invade natural ecosystems? *Trends in Ecology and Evolution, 9*, 85–89.

Williams, N. (1998). Agricultural biotech faces backlash in Europe. *Science, 281*(5378), 768–771.

Geothermal Energy

Earth's heat is the only major nonsolar energy flux on our planet. Three distinct sources heat the Earth's surface from below: heat conducted through the lithosphere from the underlying hot mantle (its temperatures, at the core-mantle boundary, are as high as 4000° K); radiogenic decay of long-lived ^{40}K, ^{232}Th, and ^{235}U and ^{238}U isotopes in the crust, and heat transported convectively by magmas and fluids. We are still uncertain about the shares of the total geothermal flux originating in these processes, but numerous measurements of heat flows have made it possible to map their continental and oceanic patterns. As expected, average flows peak along mid-ocean ridges where new oceanic lithosphere is continually created by hot magma that rises from the mantle.

Heat Flows and Geothermal Potential

Heat flux associated with this process includes the latent heat of crystallization of newly formed and cooling basaltic ocean crust, and the heat of cooling from magmatic temperatures (around 1200° C) to hydrothermal temperatures (around 350° C). Total hydrothermal flux of 7–11 terawatts is about a third of the global oceanic heat flow of 32 terawatts; this, in turn, equals roughly 70 percent of the global heat flux of 44 terawatts. Almost a third of the total oceanic heat loss takes place in the South Pacific and its rates decline with the age of ocean floor, from as much as 250 megawatts per square meter in the youngest crust to less than 50 through the sea floor older than 100 million years. Planetary heat flux of 44 terawatts prorates to about 85 megawatts per square meter (equal to a mere 0.05 percent of solar radiation reaching the Earth's surface), with the means of almost 100 megawatts per square meter for the oceans and only about half as much for the continents. Continental heat flows range from 41 megawatts per square meter in Archean rocks to 49–55 in Phanerozoic formations. But unlike with solar radiation, this flux is available everywhere all the time. As a result of plate tectonics and hot spot phenomena, many places around the Earth have a much more intensive heat flow through the crust, often delivered by hot water or steam and suitable for commercial extraction of geothermal energy.

Total geothermal energy stored within the crust is at least five orders of magnitude larger than the annual heat flux, but estimates of its extractable potential depend on the category of the considered resources and on temperature and depth limits. Hot magma that intrudes into the top 10 kilometers of the crust in many regions around the world contains an order of magnitude more of heat than do hydrothermal flows, and hot dry rocks within the same depth have an order of magnitude more heat than does the near-surface magma. However, these resources could be tapped only through drilling and injections of liquids to recover the heat. But while drilling to depths of more than 7 kilometers to reach rock temperatures in excess of 200° C (average thermal gradient is 25° C per kilometer) is now possible it would be economically prohibitive to do so in order to inject water for steam generation.

Consequently, only those geothermal resources that are dominated by vapors and liquids can be used directly for electricity generation, but these flows reach the Earth's surface, or are accessible through relatively shallow drilling, at only a limited number of locations. Hydrothermal resources with temperatures below 100° C can supply hot water for various industrial processes or for household heating. Reykjavik, Iceland is the best example of such application of hydrothermal resources; nearly all of its houses are heated by hot water, which is also used in many outdoor swimming pools, greenhouses, aquaculture, electricity generation, and for melting snow and de-icing sidewalks. Accessible flows of pressurized water and water vapor with temperatures above 100° C add up to only tiny fractions of the enormous global geothermal potential. A recent estimate puts their total at about 72 gigawatts of electricity-generating capacity, and enhanced recovery and drilling improvements could raise this to 138 gigawatts. The largest shares of this accessible geothermal potential are along the tectonically active Pacific margins of the North, Central and South America and Asia but significant geothermal sites are found also in interiors of most continents (United States (Wyoming), Czech Republic, Hungary, Tibet).

Geothermal Electricity Generation

The world's first geothermal electricity generation began at Italy's Larderello (in Toscana) field in 1902. New Zealand's Wairakei was added in 1958. Geysers in the northern California came on line in 1960, and Mexico's Cerro Prieto in 1970. All of these fields tapped high-temperature vapor that could be used directly for electricity generation. Post–1970 diffusion of geothermal generation resulted in construction of new capacities in about a dozen countries. At the beginning of the twenty-first century the United States had the highest installed capacity (nearly 2.9 gigawatts), followed by the Philippines (1.8), Italy (768 megawatts), Mexico, and Indonesia.

Global geothermal total of 8.2 gigawatts is no more than 0.25 percent of the world's installed capacity (dominated by fossil-fueled power plants) and it is equal to only about 11 percent of the geothermal energy that could be harnessed with existing techniques. Even if we were to develop the prospective potential of 138 gigawatts, geothermal electricity would represent less than 5 percent of the world's total generating capacity. This means that while the geothermal energy has a considerable scope for expansion, it cannot supply a significant share of the world's energy generation during the coming decades. But geothermal electricity can supply nationally and locally important shares and geothermal heat can make an even greater contribution in distributed supply to industries and households. Iceland's reliance on geothermal heat is the best-known example of these uses but even the U.S. geothermal heating capacity is already more than twice as large as is the installed capacity in geothermal electricity generation.

Geothermally assisted household heat pumps, preferably closed-loop systems storing summer heat and releasing it in winter, are a particularly efficient option. If they were used in all U.S. households with no access to natural gas they would have saved nearly 100 gigawatts of peak winter electric capacity during the late 1990s. Geothermal heat should be also used more widely by industries, greenhouses, and in aquaculture. Combination of electricity-generating and heating applications could make the greatest difference in about forty low-income countries (many of them islands) with large geothermal potential and shortages, or outright absence, of other energy resources.

Vaclav Smil

Further Reading

Elderfield, H., & Schultz, A. (1996). Mid-ocean ridge hydrothermal fluxes and the chemical composition of the ocean. *Annual Review of Earth and Planetary Sciences, 24,* 191–224.

Gavell, K., Reed, M., & Wright, P. M. (1999). *Geothermal energy, the potential for clean power from the Earth.* Washington, DC: Geothermal Energy Association.

International Geothermal Association. (1998). Geothermal power plants on-line in 1998. Pisa: IGA. Retrieved 27 August 2002 from http://iga.igg.cnr.it/index.php

Mock, J. E., Tester, J. W., & Wright, P. M. (1997). Geothermal energy from the Earth: Its potential impact as an environmentally sustainable resource. *Annual Review of Energy and the Environment, 22,* 305–356.

Rudnick, R. L., et al. (1998). Thermal structure, thickness and composition of continental lithosphere. *Chemical Geology, 145,* 395–411.

Sclater, J. G., et al. (1980). The heat flow through oceanic and continental crust and the heat loss of the Earth. *Reviews of Geophysics and Space Physics*, 18, 269–311.

Smil, V. (2003). *Energy at the crossroads.* Cambridge, MA: The MIT Press.

Vitorello, I., & Pollack, H. N. (1980). On the variation of continental heat flow with age and the thermal evolution of the continents. *Journal of Geophysical Research*, 85, 983–995.

The main street and old gate house of the nucleated farm town of Uehlfeld in Bavaria in 1992. The gate house is all that remains of the wall that protected the town in the Middle Ages. COURTESY DAVID LEVINSON.

Germany

(2001 est. pop. 83 million)

The Federal Republic of Germany occupies an area of 357,000 square kilometers in central Europe. It is bounded by nine countries and two bodies of water: by Poland and the Czech Republic in the east, by Austria and Switzerland in the south, by France, Luxembourg, Belgium, and the Netherlands in the west, and by Denmark, the North Sea, and the Baltic Sea in the north. The official language is High (or Standard) German, but regional variations and dialects are widespread.

Germany is Europe's second-most populated country behind Russia. Its population density, almost 235 per square kilometer, is among the highest in Europe. Germany has only three cities with more than 1 million inhabitants: Berlin (3.5 million), the nation's capital and largest city; Hamburg (1.65 million), a major port city on the mouth of the Elbe River; and Munich (1.2 million), the fast-growing capital of Bavaria, Germany's largest state. Most Germans live in small- (100,000 to 500,000) and medium-sized (500,000 to 1 million) cities situated close to each other. The Ruhr region, in the state of North Rhine-Westphalia, is a network of cities that includes Cologne, Düsseldorf, Duisburg, Essen, and Dortmund, with a combined population of over 8 million. Other important networks include Frankfurt-Mainz-Wiesbaden and Mannheim-Ludwigshafen. Bremen, Hannover, Stuttgart, Leipzig, and Dresden are also important urban-industrial centers.

The birthplace of Martin Luther (1483–1546), Germany remains a religiously divided country, with around 40 percent professing Protestantism and 35 percent Catholicism. Most Protestants live north of the Main River, most Catholics south of it. Before Adolf Hitler (1889–1945) seized power in 1933, Germany had a vibrant Jewish community of around 600,000, about 1 percent of the country's population. Today that population stands at around sixty thousand. Germany has a fast-growing Muslim population; many are of Turkish descent (2.4 percent of the population), who came to the country as part of the guest worker (*Gastarbeiter*) program.

History, Politics, and Economy

The terms *German* and *Germany* are of Latin derivation. Germans use the terms *Deutsch* and *Deutschland*. Historically, Germans lacked political unity and well-defined borders; language and ethnicity ("blood lines") functioned as the main cultural unifiers. Before the nineteenth century Germany was essentially the same as the Holy Roman Empire of the German nation (962–1806), which was under the tutelage of the Vienna-based Habsburg dynasty for over four hundred years. Thereafter, it became essentially the German empire (1871–1945), ruled from Berlin by Prussia's Hohenzollern dynasty.

The German empire (or "Second Reich" to distinguish it from the Holy Roman Empire) was characterized by rapid industrial growth, socialist-led labor unrest, and rabid militarism, especially after William II (1859–1941) assumed the emperor's throne in 1888. Germany's defeat in World War I (1914–1918) was followed by a brief period of extreme political and economic instability under the Weimar Republic (1919–1933), then the establishment of Hitler's Third Reich

(1933–1945). The Nazi goal of conquering Europe and exterminating its Jewish population came close to success during World War II (1939–1945) until thwarted by a combination of Soviet, American, and British forces.

The Cold War politics of the post–1945 period led to the division of Germany into two states: the Federal Republic of Germany (1949–), also known as West Germany, and the German Democratic Republic (1949–1990), also known as East Germany. A satellite state of the Soviet Union, East Germany collapsed in the wake of Soviet Premier Mikhail Gorbachev's reforms and was absorbed by West Germany in 1990.

Today Germany is a federal republic consisting of sixteen *länder* (thirteen states and three city-states) with a parliamentary form of government and a bicameral legislature. The powerful Bundestag (federal diet) consists of around 670 delegates (the number varies) elected to four-year terms. The Bundestag selects the chancellor, the country's most powerful political figure, and passes all legislation. The less-powerful Bundesrat (federal council), composed of around sixty-eight delegates elected by the states, has veto power only over legislation that relates to education, culture, law enforcement, and other state prerogatives. Germany also has a largely ceremonial president, elected to a five-year term by the Bundestag and representatives of the state governments. The Federal Constitutional Court, composed of sixteen justices elected to twelve-year terms, has the power to declare legislation unconstitutional.

Germany's two largest political parties—the conservative Christian Democratic Union/Christian Social Union (CDU/CSU) and the left-leaning Sozialdemokratische Partei Duetschlands (Social Democratic Party or SPD) —have dominated national, state, and local politics since 1949. The liberal Free Democratic Party (FDP) has frequently been part of the governing coalition, more often with the CDU/CSU than with the SPD. Founded in 1979, the environmentalist alliance '90/Greens (Green Party) has been represented in the Bundestag since 1983. The Party of Democratic Socialism (PDS), successor to the Socialist Unity Party (Communist Party) of the former East Germany, has also enjoyed a modicum of electoral success since 1990. Parties that receive less than 5 percent of the vote are not represented in the Bundestag.

Germany's economy is the strongest in Europe and the third strongest in the world behind those of the United States and Japan. The country generally lacks natural resources, although it does possess extensive deposits of coal and lignite as well as modest deposits of iron ore, natural gas, timber, uranium, copper, potash, and nickel. Its export-driven economy depends on the production of high-quality manufactured goods, including motor vehicles (DaimlerChrysler, BMW, Audi, Volkswagen, Opel), chemicals (Bayer, BASF, Aventis, Agfa), and machine tools and electronics (Bosch, Siemens). It also possesses an extensive transportation network that includes an efficient railway, high-speed autobahns, navigable rivers (Rhine, Elbe), and large seaports (Hamburg, Bremen, Bremerhaven). Germany has an abundance of arable land, but agriculture accounts for just over 1 percent of its gross national product. Crops include barley, oats, wheat, sugar beets, vegetables, fruits, and wine grapes. Cattle, pigs, sheep, and poultry are the principal livestock.

Geographical and Environmental Features

Geographically, Germany consists of three zones: the north lowland plain, the central uplands, and the southern alpine foreland. The north lowland plain, which covers about one-third of German territory, is part of the broad plain that stretches from the Netherlands to Russia. The central uplands is a hilly and forested area that includes the Harz and Thüringer Mountains in the north, the Erzgebirge Mountains and the Bohemian Forest in the east, the Swabian and Franconian Jura Mountains in the south, and the Eifel Mountain and Hardt and Black Forests in the west. The southern alpine foreland is situated in the southern tip of Germany just north of the Alps. It contains Germany's highest peak, the Zugspitze (2,964 meters), and largest lake, the Bodensee (Lake Constance).

Germany's principal rivers cut across these geographical zones. They include the Rhine in the west, the Danube in the south, the Weser in the center, and the Elbe and Oder in the east. All flow northwesterly from the Alps or central uplands to the North or Baltic Seas except the Danube, which flows easterly from the Alps to the Black Sea. The German government reengineered most German rivers in the nineteenth and twentieth centuries to promote land reclamation, flood control, and navigation. Nearly all also became polluted with industrial effluents, urban sewage, and agrochemicals. Government-mandated cleanup efforts have greatly improved water quality over the past thirty years.

Germany was blanketed in old-growth forest two millennia ago, but the spread of agriculture, towns, wood-based industries, and roads over the centuries has expunged all but around one-quarter of its forest cover today. Since the eighteenth century Germans have been in the forefront of scientific forest management, establishing some of the world's first forestry schools and promoting the practice of sustainability (*Nachhaltigkeit*) long before it became a watchword of modern conservationism. Although oak, birch, beech, chestnut, oak, and walnut trees are still found in Germany, the foresters' preference for fast-growing commercial timber has tipped the balance in favor of conifers (principally pine and fir), which now account for about two-thirds of remaining forest cover. In the 1980s there was widespread concern that acid rain was causing *Waldsterben* (forest death), especially in the fabled Black Forest. Closer inspection, however, revealed that monocultural practices, exotic species introductions, underbrush removal, and soil exhaustion also explain why so many of Germany's forests are disease ridden.

Before the Industrial Revolution, natural resource utilization—land reclamation, forest management, and similar activities—was known as *Naturpflege* (the cultivation of nature). In the late nineteenth century, as Germany began experiencing unprecedented air, water, and soil pollution from coal-fired industries, the botanist Hugo Conwentz (1855–1922) popularized an alternate term, *Naturschutz* (nature protection), and lobbied in favor of state-sponsored conservation of the country's resources. Derivative coinages include *Tierschutz* (animal protection), *Landschaftschutz* (landscape protection), *Denkmalschutz* (monument protection), and even *Naturdenkmalschutz* (natural monument protection). About the same time, the early Darwinist Ernst Haeckel (1834–1919) coined the term *Ökologie* (ecology) to highlight the relationship between an organism and its environment.

For the past two centuries most German conservationists have championed the establishment of nature reserves, monument landmarks, and national parks (an idea borrowed from the United States), with the goal of protecting certain important bioregions and historical sites from the impact of industrial and urban growth. It is largely through their efforts that Germany now has an extensive network of protected areas throughout the country. Some conservationists, however, took a more antitechnological and pronationalist stance, notably the musician Ernst Rudorff (1840–1916), founder of the *Heimatschutz* (homeland protection) movement; the ethnographer Wilhelm Heinrich Riehl (1823–1897), advocate of a folk-based (*vvölkisch*) nationalism that links nature with Germandom; and the geographer Friedrich Ratzel (1844–1904), popular-

izer of the term *Lebensraum* (living space). From there it was a short step to the race-based "blood and soil" (*Blut und Boden*) brand of conservationism that Walter Darré (1895–1953) and other prominent Nazi leaders used to justify the extermination of Jews and the appropriation of agricultural land in eastern Europe.

The Nazi government did pass one significant piece of nature-protection legislation—the Reich Conservation Law of 1935, which standardized conservation practices among the states and established bureaucratic oversight by a reich forest chief (one of Hermann Göring's many positions). In reality, however, the Nazis were committed to breakneck economic recovery and military expansion, not nature protection, and their twelve-year reign of terror left a legacy of air and water pollution of breathtaking proportions.

Postwar Economic Policies

The economic policies of the immediate post-World War II era served only to exacerbate the problems inherited from the Nazi era. In West Germany the "economic miracle" of the 1950s resulted in the utter befoulment of the Ruhr region. When the Christian Democratic government under Chancellor Konrad Adenauer (ruled 1949–1963) failed to address this issue, the Social Democrats launched their "Blue Skies over the Ruhr" campaign, which helped bring Chancellor Willy Brandt (ruled 1969–1974) to power. Meanwhile, the Green Party emerged over issues such as nuclear-reactor safety, river pollution, urban congestion, airport runway expansion, and nuclear-weapons modernization by the North Atlantic Treaty Organization (NATO). In 1983 the Greens won 5.6 percent of the national vote and joined the Bundestag for the first time. Since 1998 the party has been in coalition with the SPD-led government of Chancellor Gerhard Schröder (b. 1944). Foreign Minister Joschka Fischer (b. 1948) and Environmental Minister Jürgen Trittin (b. 1954) are both members of the Green Party. In June 2000 the Greens secured an agreement that foresees the total phaseout of Germany's nineteen nuclear power plants as early as 2021 (thirty-two years after the last plant became operational in 1989).

In East Germany, Soviet-style economic practices entailed a concentration on heavy industry—coal, lignite, steel, chemicals—especially in the urban centers of East Berlin, Leipzig, Dresden, and Chemnitz (Karl-Marx-Stadt). The country's communist system stifled any significant civic and political discourse, so government leaders were free to pollute with little fear of public backlash. As a consequence, East Germany's land, air, and water continued to deteriorate for the duration of the country's existence. The two most visible symbols of the country's environmental mismanagement were the once-ubiquitous Trabant, a small car made mostly of plastic and equipped with a two-stroke engine that spews a trail of toxins from its tailpipe; and Bitterfeld, nicknamed "the filthiest city of Europe," which lies close to some of Europe's largest lignite strip mines. Fortunately, air and water quality improved tremendously in the former East Germany after 1990 as the Trabants were gradually phased out and the worst-polluting mines, factories, and power plants shut down. Paradoxically, the buffer zone that once separated East and West Germany (and the wall that once divided Berlin) functioned as an unofficial nature refuge; industrial and agricultural development now threatens this open space.

Within Europe, West Germany has been in the forefront of antipollution legislation for many decades. Notable laws include the 1957 Federal Wastewater Act, the 1974 Federal Air Pollution (Emissions) Act, the 1976 Hazardous Waste Disposal Act, and the 1991 Packaging Disposal Act. Chancellor Helmut Kohl (ruled 1982–1998) was also instrumental in forcing other European governments to ban the use of leaded gasoline in automobiles. Internationally, Germany has participated in forums such as the 1972 Stockholm Conference on the Human Environment and the 1992 Rio Conference on Environment and Development. It is party to most major international treaties, including the 1973 Convention on International Trade in Endangered Species (CITES), the 1979 convention on Long-Range Transboundary Air Pollution (LRTAP), and the 1992 Framework Convention on Climate Change (as well as the 1997 Kyoto protocols).

Severe environmental problems nonetheless continue to plague Germany. Its economy is highly dependent on oil (imported from Russia, Norway, United Kingdom, and Libya), coal, and lignite, which generate large quantities of carbon dioxide, sulfur, and ozone. This dependency on fossil fuels will undoubtedly grow, at least in the short term, as the country's nuclear plants are shut down. Air pollution is especially problematic in the densely populated Ruhr region and in the vicinity of the German-Czech-Polish border (the "Yellow Triangle"). Water pollution remains a problem as well, especially along the heavily industrialized stretches of the Rhine, Main, Emscher, Erft, and Elbe Rivers. It may take decades to develop more-benign energy sources, clean up the country's industrial re-

gions, and mitigate the damage caused by East German authorities.

Mark Cioc

Further Reading

Ardagh, J. (1988). *Germany and the Germans*. London: Penguin.

Berghahn, V. (1982). *Modern Germany: Society, economy, and politics in the twentieth century*. Cambridge, UK: Cambridge University Press.

Carr, W. (1969) *A history of Germany 1815–1990*. London: Edward Arnold.

Craig, G. (1980). *Germany: 1866–1945*. New York: Oxford University Press.

Detwiler, D. (1989). *Germany: A short history*. Carbondale: Southern Illinois University Press.

Dominick, R. H. (1992). *The environmental movement in Germany: Prophets and pioneers, 1871–1971*. Bloomington: Indiana University Press.

Fischer, K. P. (1996). *Nazi Germany: A new history*. New York: Continuum.

Lees, C. (2000). *The Red-Green coalition in Germany: Politics, personalities, and power*. Manchester, UK: Manchester University Press.

Mayer, M., & Ely, J. (Eds.). (1998). *The German Greens: Paradox between movement and party*. Philadelphia: Temple University Press.

Papadakis, E. (1984). *The Green movement in West Germany*. New York: St. Martin's Press.

Rollins, W. (1997). *A greener vision of home: Cultural politics and environmental reform in the German Heimatschutz movement, 1904–1918*. Ann Arbor: University of Michigan Press.

Glaciers

Glaciers are masses of ice that flow downhill. They form when snow remains on the ground through summers so that, over time, the weight of successive snow layers compacts the snow and eventually turns it to ice. Ice becomes a glacier after it begins to move internally (deform) and slide downhill, which generally requires an ice thickness of at least 35 meters. Glaciers cover approximately 10 percent of the Earth's land surface, and glacial ice represents 80 percent of the world's freshwater. Antarctica contains 90 percent of the world's glacial ice, and Greenland contains 9 percent, leaving just 1 percent in all the world's other glaciers. Of course, glacial coverage changes through time: At the height of the last ice age twenty thousand years ago, glaciers covered as much as 30 percent of the Earth.

Glaciers as Natural Resources

Glaciers offer many benefits to people, including practical or economic resources. Glaciers are ideal for water storage: The ice melts when summer temperatures rise and people most need the water, whereas ice (and thus water) accumulates during cold, wet winters. People use glacial water to drink, to irrigate, and to provide hydroelectric power. Glacial ice has also been used to cool drinks and to refrigerate foods. The use of mountain snow and glacial ice dates back thousands of years in China, the Middle East, north Africa, and Europe. By the sixteenth century Europeans used ice consistently, and major markets developed in London, Paris, Granada, and Florence. In the 1600s Spanish colonizers in the Andes Mountains of South America imposed an ice *mita*, a system of forced labor that sent indigenous people to collect glacial ice for wealthy Spaniards living on South America's coast. In Europe, Norway was a leading exporter of glacial ice before the late 1800s, when mechanical refrigeration took over. Some Japanese still use Alaskan glacial ice to cool their drinks.

Glaciers and People

Glaciers have shaped cultures and guided people's spirituality. For at least two thousand years peoples of South America have venerated the life-giving glaciated peaks of the Andes. Today religious pilgrims annually climb to the glaciers of Mount Ausangate in Peru, where they collect sacred, healing, and purifying glacial ice. Glaciers have also played a prominent role in the culture of Tlingit and Athapaskan peoples in northwestern Canada. Oral histories reveal that glaciers not only affected hunting patterns and trade routes for these people, but also influenced social behavior, language development, place naming, and spirituality.

Glaciers also lure recreationists. Since the late 1700s mountaineers have climbed glaciers to reach the world's highest peaks. The link between glacier study (glaciology) and mountaineering has deep roots: Early mountaineers carried scientific instruments and made geological investigations during their climbs. For example, Scottish physicist James Forbes—who in 1843 made the first attempts to explain physical dynamics

of glacial ice motion—found that studying glaciers quenched his intellectual thirst and that hiking on glaciers fulfilled his emotional passions. The appeal of glaciers has also driven people to the Earth's poles. Curious explorers have visited the Arctic since a Greek sailor, Pytheas, attempted a voyage there twenty-five hundred years ago. The first landing in Antarctica was in 1895, and the first visit to the South Pole (by Norwegians) was in 1911. Recreationists' interest in Antarctica increased after 1958, when New Zealander Sir Edmund Hillary made the first traverse of Antarctica by land.

Glacial Hazards

Glaciers can pose serious threats to people. During the Little Ice Age (c. 1350–1850) global temperatures fell by 1–2° C. In response, glaciers generally advanced worldwide, occasionally creating problems for nearby inhabitants when glaciers overtook their pastures, fields, irrigation systems, bridges, homes, and even entire villages. In 1663 Alps residents below the Aletsch glaciers pleaded with nearby Jesuit priests to perform ceremonies that would turn back the wicked glaciers. When the Black Rapids glacier in Alaska surged in 1936–1937, a wall of ice began racing at 66 meters per day toward local residents; today a surge in this glacier could break the Alaskan Pipeline.

Catastrophes also occur when glaciers generate outburst floods. Advancing glaciers from side valleys often dammed main valleys during the Little Ice Age. In 1595 the Giétroz glacier dammed the Val de Bagnes in Switzerland; when the ice dam burst, it killed five hundred people. In Argentina's Mendoza region advancing glaciers have produced ice-dammed lakes and catastrophic floods since 1788, and a 1934 flood killed many people, destroyed bridges, and wrecked 13 kilometers of railway. Retreating glaciers can also trigger outburst floods. A deadly example occurred in Huaraz, Peru, when a melting glacier formed a lake that, in 1941, burst its moraine dam and killed six thousand people. Efforts were made to drain these glacial lakes and prevent catastrophic flooding in the Alps during the Little Ice Age, the Andes from the 1940s to the present, and the Himalayas since the 1980s.

Ice avalanches pose additional threats. In 1970 fifteen thousand people perished when an earthquake triggered an avalanche in Peru's Cordillera Blanca. When glacier-covered volcanoes erupt, glacial ice melts quickly and creates mudflows called "lahars" (avalanches consisting of ice, mud, water, and other debris). One of the worst cases occurred in 1986 when Colombia's Nevado del Ruiz erupted and produced a lahar that killed thirty thousand residents.

Glaciers and Climate Change

Because temperature and precipitation determine their size, glaciers make excellent climatic indicators. Glacier advances in Europe around 1600–1610, 1690–1700, 1770s, 1820, and 1850 reveal the coolest periods of the Little Ice Age, whereas glacier retreats during the Medieval Warm Period (c. 800–1200) and during much of the twentieth century demonstrate warmer periods. To understand climate history, glaciologists have drilled ice cores in glaciers, which store data about precipitation, temperature, atmospheric conditions, volcanic eruptions, and winds. Scientists have drilled cores worldwide—from Kilimanjaro in Tanzania to Huascarán in Peru to Everest on the Tibetan Plateau to Vostok in Antarctica. But results from Greenland, where drilling began in 1958, offer the most accurate and longest records, which extend back 110,000 years. These records have become particularly important in recent debates about global warming. Glaciers that store climatic history may also hold the key to understanding global climate in the future.

Mark Carey

See also Antarctica; Circumpolar Regions

Further Reading

Alley, R. (2000). *The two mile time machine: Ice cores, abrupt climate change, and our future*. Princeton, NJ: Princeton University Press.

Cruikshank, J. (2001). Glaciers and climate change: Perspectives from oral tradition. *Arctic, 54*(4), 377–393.

David, E. (1994). *Harvest of the cold months: The social history of ice and ices*. London: Michael Joseph.

Fagan, B. (2000). *The Little Ice Age: How climate made history, 1300–1850*. New York: Basic Books.

Grove, J. M. (1988). *The Little Ice Age*. New York: Routledge.

Hambrey, M., & Alean, J. (1992). *Glaciers*. New York: Cambridge University Press.

Le Roy Ladurie, E. (1971). *Times of feast, times of famine: A history of climate change since the year 1000*. New York: Doubleday.

Mayewski, P. A., & White, F. (2002). *The ice chronicles: The quest to understand global climate change*. Hanover, NH: University Press of New England.

Mulvaney, K. (2001). *At the ends of the Earth: A history of polar regions*. Washington, DC: Island Press/Shearwater Books.

Oliver-Smith, A. (1986). *The martyred city: Death and rebirth in the Andes*. Albuquerque: University of New Mexico Press.

Glen Canyon

The Glen Canyon region lies within the Colorado Plateau Province, an area of some 337,000 square kilometers drained by the Colorado River system. Glen Canyon proper is a sinuous chasm more than 480 kilometers long, variable in depth and width, through which the Colorado River once flowed. The riverbed gradient was shallow, about 1,000 meters in elevation. It is now inundated by Lake Powell. Physiographically the canyon extends from the Dirty Devil River at the upstream end to the Paria River at the downstream end. Two other rivers, the San Juan and the Escalante, empty into Glen Canyon at about its midpoint. Some thirty smaller tributaries enter the main stem from both banks.

The walls of the Glen Canyon chasm are composed primarily of massive Jurassic-period sandstones of the Wingate, Kayenta, and Navajo type, 300–350 meters in thickness. Overlying this group in places are other Jurassic sedimentary rocks, up to 780 meters in thickness, forming the Kaiparowits, Red Rock, and Rainbow plateaus adjacent to Glen Canyon. Two laccolithic (igneous) extrusions, the Henry Mountains (2,700–3,000 meters in elevation) and Navajo Mountain (3,050 meters in elevation), rise through the sedimentary formations. The high mountains, the deeply dissected canyons, and such erosional features as the 88-meter-high Rainbow Bridge form one of the most spectacular scenic ensembles in North America.

The region was sporadically occupied by Indian hunter-gatherers from about 6000 BCE. At around 300 CE and again from 900 to 1300 CE, Ancestral Puebloan (formerly called "Anasazi") farmers occupied the tributary canyons and adjacent uplands. The region was first explored by Spanish missionaries in 1776. American exploration began in the 1850s, most notably the famous river expeditions of John Wesley Powell in 1869 and 1871–72. Gold prospectors arrived in the early 1870s. There is extremely fine "flour gold" in the river gravels, but its fineness made all attempts at large-scale mining by dredges or other mechanical means unprofitable.

Tourists began boating through Glen Canyon as early as 1900. Only a few dozen trips were made until after World War II, when "river running" became increasingly popular. In the last years (about 1952 until 1963) before the Glen Canyon Dam was completed, hundreds of people made trips through Glen Canyon.

The 216-meter-high Glen Canyon Dam was constructed between 1957 and 1963. The dam has an installed hydroelectric capacity of 1,288,000 kilowatts. Lake Powell is 480 kilometers long, with over 5,076 kilometers of shoreline. The lake has a maximum surface area of 65,320 hectares, a maximum depth of 173 meters, and a full-pool elevation of 1,100 meters. The Glen Canyon National Recreation Area, managed by the National Park Service, received over 4 million visitors in 2001. An emerging environmental problem is gasoline and hydrocarbons in the lake water from boat motors.

Environmentalists lament the loss of Glen Canyon, recalled as one of the great scenic wonders of North America, although from the time of Powell's exploration, only several hundred people ever saw it. To others, Lake Powell and its setting comprise a scenic wonder of another sort, enjoyed by millions yearly.

Don D. Fowler

Further Reading

Fowler, D. D. (2003). *Glen Canyon: a personal history*. Salt Lake City: University of Utah Press.

Geib, P. R. (1996). *Glen Canyon revisited*. (University of Utah Anthropological Papers No. 119). Salt Lake City: University of Utah, Department of Anthropology.

Martin, R. (1989). *A story that stands like a dam: Glen Canyon and the struggle for the soul of the West*. New York: Henry Holt Co.

National Research Council. (1987). *River and dam management. A review of the Bureau of Reclamation's Glen Canyon environmental studies*. Washington, DC: National Academy Press.

Global Warming

Global warming, also referred to as *global change* or *climate change*, is a topic frequently in the news. With reports of extreme weather events such as flooding, severe droughts, and storms, people have become more aware of the potential risks of global warming. Governments of the world have been under increased pressure to take action to reduce these risks. However, it seems that little progress has been made, despite scientific predictions, international protocols, and the desires of some decision makers and organizations to act.

Ecosystems, including humans, have always had to adapt to climate change as a natural phenomenon. The use of technologies and unsustainable practices such as a heavy reliance on fossil fuels, increased human consumption, and a growing world population have led to a crisis in terms of the influence of human activities on world climate. Production of greenhouse gases, especially carbon dioxide (CO_2) and methane (CH_4), has reached levels never recorded before in the past 160,000 years. Most (76 percent) of this additional production comes from human use of fossil fuels in industrialized countries.

History and Causes of Global Warming

The connection between global warming and greenhouse gases, especially CO_2, is not a new concept. In fact, Jean Baptiste Joseph Fourier in 1824 was the first to suggest that the gases in the atmosphere serve as barriers for solar radiation escaping from the Earth and thus influence temperatures at the surface of the planet. In 1896 Svante Arrhenius formulated a theoretical model with CO_2 as the main greenhouse gas. The principle is simple: The gas layered atmosphere serves as a barrier for solar radiation, keeping it trapped at the surface of the planet. The principle is referred to as the *greenhouse effect*. But only in the past thirty years have models been sophisticated enough to correctly link recent human activities and the use of fossil fuels to increased greenhouse gases and global warming.

Examining records from monitoring stations around the world, scientists from the Goddard Institute for Space Studies in the United States were able to demonstrate that the global temperature of the Earth has steadily increased over time. The global mean temperature was 0.6° C warmer in the 1990s than in the 1890s. At the same time, they reported that not only was CO_2 increasing in the atmosphere but so were other greenhouse gases such as methane (CH_4), nitrous oxide (N_2O), chlorofluorocarbons (CFCs) and their substitutes, hydrofluorocarbons (HFCs) and hydrochlorofluorocarbons (HCFCs). For example, CH_4 has increased by more than 145 percent in the atmosphere since the beginning of the industrial era.

Natural variation in greenhouse gases is common, and climate records, through analysis of ice cores, clearly show that mean temperatures and CO_2 levels in the atmosphere have been naturally varying over the past 400,000 years. These variations are normal and related to the changes in the inclination of the Earth and its orbit around the sun. Recent data showed that for ten thousand years the concentration of CO_2 in the atmosphere was about 280 ppmv (parts per million in volume). The concern comes from the rapid changes that have occurred over the past 120 years. Since the 1800s, with the use of coal and other fossil-fuel sources, the concentration had increased to about 368 ppmv by 2000. Whereas under natural conditions the atmosphere would contain approximately 750 billion metric tons of gaseous carbon, the current increase in CO_2 of about 0.4 percent per year can be translated into an additional input of 3 billion metric tons of CO_2 gas into the atmosphere per year. Normally, under natural conditions, there would be a balance in the global carbon cycle. But deforestation, land degradation, and habitat loss have reduced the capacity of some ecosystems to absorb carbon. With greater gas emissions from anthropogenic activities, the short-term exchanges and reservoirs are unbalanced, leading to more input of greenhouse gases than sinks (a loss or a permanent reservoir such as trees). The increase of CO_2 in the atmosphere is obviously caused by fossil-fuel consumption. Fossil fuel as a source of energy is readily available for most populations, and current technology makes it cheap. Although it is nonrenewable, its availability and the current reserve suggest that humans will rely on it for many more years. Greenhouse emissions can be associated with many human activities; humans cause emission of CO_2 mainly by combustion of fossil fuels and deforestation. Fossil fuels include coal, petroleum, and natural gas and are mostly used for energy generation. In the United States, for example, the energy sector is one of the largest consumers of fossil fuels, producing 35 percent of all CO_2 emissions as well as 25 percent of all NO_x (nitrogen oxides) emissions and almost 70 percent of SO_2 (sulphur dioxide) emissions. Cement manufacturing is also a huge contributor of greenhouse gas emissions at 3 percent. The production of greenhouse gases from human activities is not similar among all countries. As would be expected, industrialized countries contribute at a greater rate than do developing countries. For example, in 1991 countries such as the United States and Australia emitted on average 4.7 metric tons of CO^2-carbon per person per year, whereas countries such as Cambodia and Rwanda emitted 0.02 metric tons of CO^2-carbon per person per year.

Deforestation, the other major cause of an increase in human-created greenhouse gas emissions, is a global phenomenon in which wood is harvested for various uses, such as fuel, construction material, or paper production. In developing countries, where the population is increasing rapidly, land is deforested for agricultural use. In many ways, carbon storage is positive as it helps reduce the amount of GHG in the atmosphere. However it can take the planting of 140 trees to compensate the emissions of only one car. So yes, it is important, but we shouldn't, think that just by planting trees, we will reduce GHG emissions. The reason is that forests are part of the large sink for carbon accumulation. Ninety percent of the carbon stored on land is located in forests. Half of this amount is stored in tropical forests. In the past 130 years, deforestation has caused a decrease in carbon storage in forests by 38 percent. Most of this decrease has come in tropical forests. But contrary to what is commonly believed, in the past fifty years northern regions of Europe and America have been able to increase their carbon storage by the regeneration of forests and the abandonment of agriculture.

Current data show the important role that industrialized countries can play in reducing greenhouse gas emissions through changes in technology, energy sources, and socioeconomic behaviors. Their levels of emissions are such that without changes, it is difficult to see long-term reduction of greenhouse gases. With the accelerated economic growth of several developing countries it is predicted that the global levels of greenhouse gases will substantially increase. Unless these countries implement important socioeconomic strategies, they will experience situations similar to those in industrialized counties. Because these data can be controversial and can have incredible impacts on most countries, the challenge has been to have adequate and credible data and assessment to convince decision makers of the threat of global warming.

Global Warming Models and Predictions

The concept of global warming does not imply that the temperature is getting warmer at the same rate all over the surface of the Earth. Although it is on average warmer over time, some regions can experience cooling, whereas other regions can experience warming.

Land surfaces, for example, warm at a faster rate than do oceans because oceans can store more heat and can assimilate it better than land surfaces. Variation will also occur across a continent due to air current patterns, latitude, and distance from large bodies of water. In higher latitudes changes may be more severe in the winter than in the summer or vice versa. Inland ecosystems may experience severe drought, whereas coastal ecosystems may experience flooding more often.

With the discoveries of rapid changes in greenhouse gases and temperatures and the need to better understand how global temperatures and ecosystems would be affected by global warming, in 1988 the Intergovernmental Panel on Climate Change (IPCC) was formed. All countries were invited to participate in the IPCC's efforts with the World Meteorological Organization (WMO) and the U.N. Environment Programme (UNEP). The IPCC has its secretariat in Geneva, Switzerland, and includes biologists, geologists, glaciologists, health scientists, sociologists, and oceanographers. The mission of the IPCC is to support comprehensive assessment of global warming in order to develop policies, technologies, adaptation and mitigation strategies, and methodologies for emission inventories. The panel is composed of three groups: WG (Working Group) I (climate science), WG II (impact, adaptation, and mitigation), and WG III (economic and social dimensions). Its third assessment report was published in 2001. This report tends to confirm the previous assessment and strongly recommends actions and policy changes in industrialized countries to reduce gas emissions.

Predicting global warming is not a simple task because many factors have to be considered, from air and ocean movements to land cover and human activities. Since the 1950s scientists have developed models to simulate variation and changes in climate and atmosphere. These models have become very sophisticated in recent years and help determine various scenarios expected across the world. There are still limitations, but improvements of resolution and inclusion of more physical parameters are continuous. These global climate models (GCMs) examine changes in terrestrial vegetation, land masses, oceans and sea ice movements, and atmospheric components and simulate what the climate could be under different scenarios of greenhouse gas emissions. The main challenge is predicting the levels of gas emissions in the future. These levels can also reflect different conditions in terms of population or economic growth, technological change, energy use, and so forth. Because experts do not accurately know how policies and other factors are going to vary in the future, all of these human parameters are assumptions. GCMs can be very sensitive to rapid variations in the parameters, but it is not always clear whether the slow changes in oceans will bring slow or rapid climate response. Although GCMs can greatly vary in projections, they predict an increase of global temperature of 1–3.5° C in the next century.

Possible Impacts on Ecosystems and Extreme Events

The complexity of the climatic system makes any prediction difficult, and there is room for uncertainty. However, recent changes can already be attributed to global warming, and scientists can predict for some regions what types of impacts are more likely to happen over time. In recent years temperature and precipitation patterns have been commonly reported in the news. The IPCC has already predicted that floods, fires, and heat waves can be more frequent. Regions such as sub-Saharan Africa, South America, and Southeast Asia can experience increased heat and thus a decline in subsistence agriculture, leading to desertification. Grasslands of North America and Africa may initially have positive impacts from global warming as the photosynthetic rate increases. But unpredictable climatic conditions can reduce crop production in important agricultural regions. Forests of northern latitudes seem to have already benefited from global warming. Warmer temperatures may extend the optimal growing conditions of North American forests farther north. A shorter ice period and the decay of permafrost may drastically change the lives of migrating animals and nomadic human populations of the Arctic.

With longer growing seasons and increased temperatures, several species of animals and plants will be forced to migrate or respond through adaptations to new conditions. For some species, such as birds, migration is a highly probable response, whereas the migration rate for most plants may be too slow, and adaptive responses are the only means of survival to new environmental conditions. For several species, with habitat loss and the existence of human settlements, migration will not be an option. In the oceans, changes in temperatures can bring variations in sea current patterns and a change in the distribution of many species of fish. In both aquatic and terrestrial ecosystems, these potential changes in species can have huge impacts on global biodiversity and rate of extinction.

Another major change may be a rise in ocean levels. Estimates of the increase in sea level range from 1 to 10 centimeters per decade during the next century as polar ice continues to melt in the warmer climate. Experts do not know if these rates are real, but the rates may have disastrous consequences. Because a large number of people live along the world's coastlines, the number of environmental refugees could reach millions of people per year during the next century. It is unclear where all these refugees will go. This is a major concern for the Caribbean islands. Trinidad and Tobago, for example, have already examined the possibilities and have started developing strategies for possible environmental refugees.

Similarly, impacts on human health can be severe. With habitat loss, deaths, starvation, and infectious diseases have been predicted, especially in developing countries, where mitigation and adaptation measures have not yet been developed. Displacement of refugees can degenerate into conflicts for new arable lands. Under such degraded conditions, as is the case in several countries, cases of infectious diseases (such as cholera, typhoid, and malaria) can explode due to lack of hygiene and poor living conditions. Northward spread of many infectious diseases currently limited to subtropical and tropical regions can occur under higher temperatures. In recent years diseases such as dengue fever have been reported in northern areas where they had never been or had been previously eliminated. This is also the case for malaria, which reappeared north and south of the tropics.

In urban areas, human health can be of greater concern. Heat strokes have been more frequently reported in the past few years. For example, in 1995 Chicago experienced a heat wave so severe that more than seven hundred heat-related deaths were reported in the metropolitan area alone. Although it is unclear if that heat wave was related directly to global warming, similar scenarios can be more frequently predicted around the world. In urban centers, with increased temperatures, additional problems such as intensification of ground-level ozone smog will arise, leading to more asthma and other respiratory problems.

Extreme weather events (e.g., hurricanes, storms, droughts, etc.) associated with global warming can harm human health directly and indirectly. A recent report on the state of the environment suggested that with climate change, the coasts of the Gulf of Maine could be more prone to extreme weather events, especially hurricanes and storms. The number of deaths can increase during such events in areas where ecosystems

have been so degraded that they are vulnerable to any type of disturbance. Hurricane Mitch in Central America in 1998 is a good example of an extreme event that had a huge impact on regions with degraded ecosystems. In that case, more than ten thousand people were killed due to mudslides on deforested hillsides. Under such conditions, the impact can be amplified.

Solutions?

Due to uncertainty and the complexity of the processes behind global warming, international policy actions to redirect current levels of fossil-fuel consumption and socioeconomic behaviors have been futile. In 1992 the Framework Convention on Climate Change (FCCC) was ratified, and the Kyoto protocol was developed from it in 1997. In 2000, 186 countries had signed the agreement and therefore had agreed to voluntarily reduce or stabilize their greenhouse gas emissions to their 1990 levels by the year 2000. Most countries, however, were unable to reach this target. As of 2001 eighty-three countries and the European Union had signed the Kyoto protocol. The United States decided in 2001 not to sign the protocol, and other countries such as Canada, although they have committed themselves, have yet to sign it. Among the challenges that industrialized countries face in order to meet this commitment are an advanced economy, the level of economic activities, heavy reliance on fossil fuels, great distances between urban centers, and, in some cases, cold climate. Industry lobbyists have tried to avoid changes in policies because they are well aware that this might cause loss of revenues for their industries. With globalization and market competition, politicians are sensitive to any policy that could decrease economic growth. Therefore, other solutions must be found to reduce greenhouse gas emissions while maintaining economic growth at an optimal level. To do so, some industrialized countries are concentrating on two approaches: reducing greenhouse gas emissions or taking greater quantities of greenhouse gases from the atmosphere through carbon sequestration (actions that reduce [trap] the atmospheric CO^2, such as planting trees or fossil-fuel conservation).

Under the FCCC, the industrialized signatory countries must develop a full inventory of the sources of emissions of greenhouse gases and from it a national plan to reduce these emissions. National plans greatly vary between countries and include measures to promote energy efficiencies and new technologies as well as increased taxes on fossil fuels and limitations for certain polluting industries.

Most plans to reduce greenhouse gas emissions will cost countries in various ways, from insurance or tax hikes to financial support for new clean energy and technologies. The major problem with fossil fuels is that they are nonrenewable. The obvious solution is therefore to produce fuels from renewable or recyclable sources, such as vegetation. Two forms of such fuels have been marketed but on a very small scale: ethanol and methanol. A few countries have already implemented limited use of these fuels. For example, Brazil uses ethanol produced from sugarcane for local transportation. With this fuel, the net emission of greenhouse gases can be reduced, but this would mean conversion of agricultural lands from food production to energy production. In the end, the balance may not be met. Other alternative sources of energy are being introduced in a greater rate across the world. The most important are wind and solar energy. Systems using these sources can be built on a small scale in many regions and thus reduce the cost related to the transportation of energy. In California windmills have been in operation for many years and have supplied energy to several local communities. The drawback to this technology is the harm caused to birds.

Other sources of renewable energy are geothermal facilities, hydroelectric power plants, nuclear power plants, and tidal dams. Although all of these are considered in some ways to be renewable sources, they have received a bad public image because of their dangers to human health or their risks to ecosystems.

The second approach to reduction of greenhouse gas emissions is to add carbon sinks. The main strategy is reforestation. Mainly industrialized countries are planning to use this approach. They believe that if they were capable of helping their own industries or the governments of developing countries to plant trees, the global amount of CO_2 would be reduced through carbon sequestration. The main question related to reforestation is "How many trees are needed to counter the impact of global warming?" Although this is a complex question, the current 6 billion metric tons of carbon emitted into the atmosphere would require about 1 million square kilometers of forests to balance the system.

Industrialized countries are in a better position in most cases to respond, adapt, or mitigate in the face of global warming. Excellent health-care systems, effective prevention measures, and advanced technologies are present, and thus the introduction of new diseases can be mitigated. However, due to lack of resources, developing countries face problems in the near future. Due to lack of sanitation and degraded environmental conditions, infectious diseases are already daily concerns for medical practitioners in those countries. With greater uncertainty about climatic conditions and lack of hygiene, food, potable water, and shelter, people will be even more vulnerable in the future.

The coming decades may be the most crucial ones in the history of humankind. With the world population possibly increasing to 8–10 billion within the next three decades, with economic activities tripling, and with the desire of developing countries to reach standards of living similar to those of industrialized countries, slowing global warming might not be an achievable goal for many more decades. However, how much longer does the Earth have before irreversible damage to key ecosystems occurs? Global warming is a global issue that can be tackled at the local level. The driving force is local nongovernmental organizations (NGOs), which have the most at stake in a region. It is now believed that most remedies to global warming will occur at this level. Only through education and community actions can greenhouse gas emissions be reduced. Although new technologies can help, without community acceptance most of these solutions will never be implemented. The future of humanity depends on the will of citizens to change their behaviors and to push others to do the same. In the long term, international policies might be useful but might come too late.

Liette Vasseur

See also Ozone Depletion

Further Reading

Bernstein, S., & Gore, C. (2001). Policy implications of the Kyoto protocol for Canada. *Isuma, 2*(4), 26–36.

Bruce, J. (2001). Intergovernmental panel on climate change and the role of science in policy. *Isuma, 2*(4), 11–15.

Colwell, R. R., Epstein, P. R., & Gubler, D. (1998). Climate change and human health. *Science, 279*, 968–969.

Commission for Environmental Cooperation (CEC). (2001). *State of the environment of North America report.* Montreal, Canada: CEC Secretariat.

Commission for Environmental Cooperation (CEC) Secretariat. (2001). Environmental challenges and opportunities of the evolving North American electricity market (Article 13 Initiative discussion paper). Montreal, Canada: North American Commission for Environmental Cooperation.

Draper, D. (1998). *Our environment: A Canadian perspective.* Scarborough, Canada: ITP Nelson.

Environmental Protection Agency. (2001). Global warming—health impacts. Retrieved February 13, 2003, from http://www.epa.gov/globalwarming/impacts/health/index.html

Freedman, B. (2001). *Environmental science: A Canadian perspective.* Scarborough, Canada: Prentice Hall.

Government of Canada. (1996). *The state of Canada's environment 1996: Supply and services.* Ottawa, Canada: Government of Canada.

Hengeveld, H. G. (2000). *Projections for Canada's climate future.* Downsview, Canada: Meteorological Service of Canada.

Lindgren, E. (1998). Climate change, tick-borne encephalitis and vaccination needs in Sweden—a prediction model. *Ecol. Modelling, 110*(1), 55–63.

McBean, G., Weaver, A., & Roulet, N. (2001). The science of climate change. What do we know? *Isuma, 2*(4), 16–25.

Serreze, M. C., Walsh, J. E., Chapin, F. S., III, Osterkamp, T., Dyurgerov, M., Romanovsky, V., Oechel, W. C., Morison, J., Zhang, T., & Barry, R. G. (2000). Observational evidence of recent change in the northern high-latitude environment. *Clim. Change, 46*(1–2), 159–207.

Turco, R. P. (1997). *Earth under siege: From air pollution to global change.* New York: Oxford University Press.

U.N. Development Programme, U.N. Environment Programme, World Bank, & World Resources Institute. (2000). *World resources 2000–2001: People and ecosystems: The fraying web of life.* Amsterdam: Elsevier.

Vasseur, L., Rapport, D., & Hounsell, J. (2002). Linking ecosystem health to human health: A challenge for this new century. In B. Costanza & S. Jorgensen (Eds.), *Understanding and solving environmental problems in the 21st* century (pp. 167–192). New York: Elsevier.

Woodward, A., Hales, S., & Weinstein, P. (1998). Climate change and human health in the Asia Pacific region: Who will be most vulnerable? *Climate Research, 11*(1), 31–38.

Globalization *See* Colonialism and Imperialism, Ecological Imperialism

Goats

With an evolutionary history dating back 20 million years, goats (genus *Capra*) are even-toed, hoofed ruminants adapted to the harsh conditions of rocky, mountainous terrain. Goats, although closely related to sheep, can be distinguished by their backward-arching horns, erect tails, and beards on most males. As herbivorous mammals, goats prefer to browse on leafy plants, although they also eat grasses and occasionally climb trees to eat leaves off of branches. Generally traveling in groups, goats form rigid hierarchical formations, and "males and females will establish social dominance in their respective groups through head to head fighting" (Smith & Sherman 1994, 2). The goat was one of the first animals that humans domesticated and has been used primarily as a source of meat and milk but also, to a lesser extent, for its skin and hair.

Domestication and Geographical Diffusion

Of the wild goat species currently living, the bezoar goat *(Capra aegagrus)* is likely the chief progenitor of the domestic breeds *(Capra hircus).* Archeological evidence suggests that goats were domesticated between 7000 and 8000 BCE in the Zagros Mountains close to the border between Iran and Iraq. Researchers have suggested various routes that domestic goats took to diffuse from this point of origin to southern and eastern Asia. Two possible continental routes—one through Afghanistan to northern China and the other across the Indian subcontinent to southeastern Asia—are likely candidates, although the diffusion may have resulted from trade routes across the Indian Ocean as well.

Goats spread throughout much of Africa via Egypt. Because there is little evidence of wild goat species inhabiting continental Europe, with the exception of the ibex *(Capra ibex),* it is believed that domestic goats were brought from southwestern Asia, although the

Members of the Samburu in Kenya tending to their goat herd.
COURTESY D. BRUCE DICKSON.

details of this process are not fully understood. Goats are a fairly recent arrival to the Americas, having first come with Spanish settlers during the early sixteenth century.

During the period of European expansion and colonialism, explorers brought goats to various Pacific islands and left them "as a source of food for later sailors" (Mason 1984, 97). British explorer Captain James Cook's expedition, for example, brought goats to New Zealand in 1777 and to Hawaii the following year. The goat was just one of a number of domestic animals that Europeans introduced into the various places that they colonized. The introduction of Old World plants and animals into such colonial territories—as well as the transfer of different species back to Europe via imperial networks of exchange—was a crucial element of such colonization projects and had lasting consequences for the environmental history of many regions of the world.

Geographical Distribution of Domesticated Goats

At the end of the twentieth century there were an estimated 710 million goats worldwide. Of these, the majority were in Asia (63 percent) and Africa (29 percent). The accuracy of such estimates, however, is far from certain because many countries with large goat populations do not have adequate resources to conduct proper census counts. Goats are often used for subsistence purposes in many Asian and African countries, where they can be relied on for meat and milk when crops fail. In addition to rural areas, goats can often be found in urban areas in many tropical regions, where they tend to be "more convenient than cattle in providing members of the urban population with a source of milk, meat, and cash" (Peacock 1996, 19–20).

In countries such as France and Norway dairy goat production has become a large-scale industry. Although dairy goat production is still a relatively marginal industry in the United States, the consumption of goat products is on the rise, and Texas is becoming a center for mohair production. Of the main milk-producing goats currently in use in many regions around the world—Saanen, Toggenburg, Nubian, and French-Alpine—many descend from Swiss breeds. The introduction of Swiss milk-producing breeds has had a major impact on goat milk production in Australia, Europe, New Zealand, North America, and other regions.

Throughout much of Africa various goat species serve as a source of meat. For instance, the west African dwarf and the small east African goat are used primarily to produce meat for subsistence consumption and are rarely milked. Other goat species, such as the Angora, are exploited for the production of fiber in various north African countries and Asia. Angora populations also exist in Argentina, Australia, Lesotho, South Africa, and the United States (mainly Texas).

Future Prospects

Since the 1960s environmental issues have come to the forefront of political debate, and goats have often been condemned as a cause of desertification. This view of the goat as environmental villain, however, has been challenged by numerous development workers and veterinarians. Goats, they argue, are no more to blame than other domestic animals for the denudation of vegetation and the resulting soil erosion. Because goats can survive in harsher conditions than sheep or cattle, "goats are left surviving when vegetation is almost gone" (Smith & Sherman 1994, 3), even if they were not the main culprits of environmental degradation. Commentators who defend the reputation of the goat, however, recognize that there are certain cases in which goats have outstripped the capacity for vegetation to regenerate. The problem arises from the fact that goats often graze close to the ground, thereby killing the roots of grasses in some instances. Goats have been particularly destructive when introduced on tropical islands, yet they are also partially responsible for intensifying desertification in numerous continental regions, from central Chile to western Australia. Balancing the goal of environmental conservation with the needs of local populations that rely on goats, and other domestic animals, for subsistence is a major challenge to policymakers around the world.

This issue is part of the larger political debate about sustainable development that emerged during the 1990s and will likely continue throughout the twenty-first century. A considerable literature has emerged on the significance of goats in many rural areas of Africa and Asia, and as the debates rage on, goats will continue to play a major role in the livelihood of millions.

Reuben Skye Rose-Redwood

Further Reading

Clutton-Brock, J. (1999). *A natural history of domesticated mammals.* Cambridge, UK: Cambridge University Press.

Gall, C. (1996). *Goat breeds of the world*. Würzburg, Germany: Margraf Verlag.

Haenlein, G. F. W., & Ace, D. L. (1984). *Extension goat handbook*. Washington, DC: U.S. Department of Agriculture.

Mason, I. L. (1984). *Evolution of domesticated animals*. New York: Longman Group.

Matthews, J. G. (1999). *Diseases of the goat*. Oxford, UK: Blackwell Science.

Peacock, C. (1996). *Improving goat production in the tropics: A manual for development workers*. Oxford, UK: Oxfam.

Smith, M. C., & Sherman, D. M. (1994). *Goat medicine*. Philadelphia: Lea & Febiger.

Taylor, R. E. (1992). *Scientific farm animal production: An introduction to animal science*. New York: Macmillan.

United Nations Food and Agricultural Organization. (1999). *FAO production yearbook: Vol. 53*. Rome: United Nations Food and Agricultural Organization.

Valdez, R. (1985). *Lords of the pinnacles: Wild goats of the world*. Mesilla, NM: Wild Sheep and Goat International.

Zeuner, F. E. (1963). *A history of domesticated animals*. New York: Harper & Row.

Gold

Gold was probably the first metal of any kind to be explored for or mined by humans, and its exploration began in Mesopotamia around 4000 BCE. Gold is mostly found pure in nature, but for industrial use it can be joined with other metals, such as copper, nickel, or zinc. The color of gold varies from white to yellow. It is a soft metal, good for heat and electrical conduction, with a high point of fusion and ebullience and flexibility, that is, 1 gram of gold could produce 2.5 kilometers of wire. It also can be transformed in plates so thin that 150,000 of them would be only 1 centimeter thick. These qualities and its rarity, durability, malleability, and resistance to corrosion give gold a stable and high value. It is commonly used as an investment, as a material to make coins and jewelry, as an electronic compound (because it is a good conductor), and as a reserve for currency.

Gold is used in such products as computers, communications equipment, spacecraft, and jet aircraft engines. It is important to art, jewelry, and industry, but most of all it has a unique status as a long-term store of value. Most of the gold produced every year in the world is stored in the vaults of government treasuries or in central banks, in part to give credibility to currency.

Gold is found on the surface of the Earth, in rivers, and in mines. It is formed in the inner parts of the Earth and brought to the surface by water action and carried to rivers as grains. The simplest way to explore for gold is to mine the land surface or explore a riverbed, washing the river sediment in a pan to separate the gold, which remains in the pan because it is heavier. That simple way was used for many years to explore for the more external deposits of gold. But as external deposits of gold are removed, more sophisticated methods of exploration, such as hydraulic mining, are required. The deepest deposits can be explored in open or subterranean mines, where gold is found in the rock.

From Mesopotamia the exploration for gold spread across Asia and Mediterranean societies, especially Egypt, where gold was used for adornment. Gold is easy to melt, and because its characteristics are immutable it can be melted several times with no loss of quality. The tale of King Midas illustrates how gold was considered a precious metal in antiquity. Midas was a king in Asia Minor who loved gold above all else. When God decided to grant one of Midas's wishes, Midas asked that everything that he touched would turn to gold. Soon his wish became a nightmare because he could not even feed himself. So Midas begged God to free him from his wish. God told Midas to bathe in the Pactolus River, and he obeyed immediately. The

This drawing shows miners in the American west using a "Long Tom" sluice box to separate gold from gravel.

ancient Greeks used the tale of King Midas to explain why gold was mixed in the sand of the Pactolus River.

During the Middle Ages gold was considered by alchemists to be a perfect element because it defies the decay that characterizes life and also because fire purifies it instead of destroying it. Alchemists called gold the "fifth element" because they believed that every life or thing is made of four essential elements—earth, fire, wind, and water. The search for the philosophers' stone—an imaginary stone, substance, or chemical preparation believed to have the power of transmuting baser metals into gold—was important to the development of medicine, chemistry, and metallurgy.

In the fourteenth century gold was sought because it was used as currency in Europe. The great voyages of discovery allowed the gold of the New World to be brought to the European market. When Europeans reached the New World the Mayas, Aztecs, and Incas already had discovered gold and considered it a precious metal. The desire of the Spanish for gold was so intense that when Spanish explorer Francisco Pizarro conquered Peru, he arrested the Inca emperor Atahualpa and promised to free him if he could provide enough gold to fill an entire room as tall as the emperor. As soon as the Incas filled the room, Pizarro killed Atahualpa and took the gold.

In Brazil gold was discovered in the eighteenth century in riverbeds in Minas Gerais State. This discovery made Portuguese monarchs, especially King John V, rich. In Minas Gerais a large civilization arose, and many cities, such as Ouro Preto, were built, and many churches were covered with gold.

In the nineteenth century there were gold rushes in Australia and in California in the United States, where in the 1840s John Sutter—a Swiss immigrant—was determined to exploit cattle and agriculture. In 1847 Sutter sent James Marshall and about twenty men to the American River to build a sawmill to provide lumber for his ranch. There Marshall and the other men found gold. News of the discovery spread, and thousands of immigrants rushed to the region to prospect. That gold rush was immortalized in 1925 in English actor Charlie Chaplin's film *The Gold Rush.*

Today gold is mined mainly in South Africa, Russia, and Canada. In Brazil in 1980 gold was discovered in Serra Pelada in Para State, which now has the largest open mine in the world.

Junia F. Furtado

Further Reading

Agricola. (1950). *De re Metallica* (About the Metals). New York: Dover.

American Geological Institute. (1962). *Dictionary of geological terms.* New York: Dolphin Books.

Dorr, A. (1984). *Minerals: Foundations of society.* Montgomery, AL: Montgomery Memorial Library Fund.

Scliar, C. (1996). *Geopolmítica das Minas do Brasil* (Geopolitics of Brazilian mines). Rio de Janeiro, Brazil: Revan.

Grains

Grains are a human creation because they are simply those grasses (members of the botanical family *Gramineae Juss* [alternatively, *Poaceae Nash]*) whose seeds have been selected by humans as staple foodstuffs. The interaction between cereal grains and humans has been fundamental to both in their rise to dominance in their environments. Without cereal grains the human population would likely have remained small—it is estimated to have been less than 4 million in 10,000 BCE—just one species in a widely varied global fauna, instead of becoming the 6 billion who today pervade the environment of the Earth. More than three-quarters of human food today comes from cereal grains, either directly or indirectly as animal feed (one-third of the world's output of cereal grains is used as animal feed).

Equally, without humans the great cereal grains—wheat, barley, rice, maize—would have remained limited in range and distribution, just grasses among the roughly seven thousand species in the family *Gramineae.* Perhaps the greatest environmental shift brought about by grains is the shift of the dominant form of vegetation on the planet from trees to grasses.

Grains and Humans

The advantages of grains as foodstuffs have profoundly altered human culture. Grains, although not perfect foods, do contain large amounts of carbohydrates and small but important amounts of proteins (although certain proteins such as lysine are not available in the major grains and must be obtained from other sources). Historically, grains provided large quantities of foodstuffs in a small area—either in the dense wild stands in favorable locations or in the new fields of agriculture—which allowed a much denser

An Iroquois (New York State) Prayer Offered at the Time of the Planting of the Corn

She is planting corn, ey'ntwas.

The corn is sprouting, odiag'io'n.

The ears are forming, ohw'da'o'n, or

onogw'yuwan's (sing.).

Corn silk, ogee'da'.

The silk is forming, ogee'da'o'n.

The tassel, ogw'da'haa', or ogw'da'haa'o'n.

Pollen, aw'ha'.

The pollen is being shed, aw'ha' wa'

s's.

The corn is in the milk, ha'sa" deyuisate'k a'ni'yut.

The green corn is ready for use (for boiling),

ha'degaiye'i'o'n

ayeno'gwa'yo'. The corn is getting ripe,

deyonoyane'dao'n (husk is getting yellow now).

Corn leaves, odjiowa'so'wan's.

Root (of corn), uhe' ukde'ha'.

Germ or heart of a grain of corn, aweya'sa' on'ha'.

Hull or skin, on'ha', ogeegwa'.

Corn-cob, ono'gwaya'.

The butt of a cob, u'ni'sda'.

The nose or end of a cob, o'niu''sa'.

The corn is hung over a pole, gast' sa'nio'da' o'a'na'g'.

Source: F. W. Waugh, "Iroquois Foods and Food Preparation." *Canada Department of Mines, Geological Survey*, Memoir 86, No. 12. Ottawa: Government Printing Bureau, 1916 22.

human population to be supported in a limited area. This allowed permanent settlements of a size that hunting and gathering had not.

An essential part of the importance of grain is that it can be stored for lengthy periods (rice has been stored over one hundred years), thus providing nutrition throughout the year, compared to the practice of hunting and gathering, which must be carried on continually. Historically, because the labor of agriculture, although intense, was limited to certain seasons of the year, farmers could devote other portions of the year to increasingly sophisticated and specialized pursuits.

The storability of grain also made it a transferable basis of value. As a means of payment, grain made possible the specialization of labor because persons could develop skills and devote their entire time to the production of goods that could be traded to farmers for their surplus grain. In the earliest written record of both Egypt and Mesopotamia, grain is the prevalent standard of exchange.

The storability and transferability of grain also made possible the beginning of government because grain was a suitable means of taxation, and taxation is the essential feature of the transfer of wealth for common purposes that defines government. The earliest government processes probably developed as agriculture was carried from the open hills of Palestine, Syria, and the foothills of the Taurus and Zagros mountains down onto the floodplains of Egypt and Mesopotamia. After the few optimal natural sites had been taken, the

TABLE 1.
WORLD PRODUCTION OF CEREALS (IN METRIC TONS)

	1961	1981	2001
Cereals, Total	877,026,930	1,632,698,810	2,076,828,420
Maize	205,004,683	446,722,107	605,212,620
Rice, Paddy	215,654,697	410,029,013	592,831,326
Wheat	222,357,231	449,673,086	578,931,612
Barley	72,411,104	149,633,191	139,653,609
Sorghum	40,931,625	73,279,991	58,149,772
Millet	25,703,968	26,960,922	29,206,508
Oats	49,588,769	39,888,464	27,278,194
Rye	35,109,990	24,548,192	22,717,722
Triticale		1,405,480	11,675,341
Buckwheat	2,478,596	2,799,060	3,261,403
Fonio	178,483	167,676	265,700
Canary Seed	61,026	85,291	146,730
Quinoa	32,435	26,252	54,500
Mixed Grain	5,983,643	5,581,744	5,232,815
Other Cereals	1,349,700	1,546,069	2,210,566

Source: Food and Agriculture Organization of the United Nations Statistical Databases (2001). Retrieved February 27, 2003 from http://apps.fao.org/default.htm

scale of work to build and maintain irrigation systems would be beyond the ability of the individual or family. Collective organization would be required both to put irrigation in place and to allocate and protect possession of the irrigated fields.

From Grasses to Grains

The wild grains were not a major food of early humans because the seeds, over their desirable starch and protein, have an indigestible hull. Eating any substantial quantity of raw grains would have resulted in acute digestive discomfort (whereas natural grain eaters such as birds have digestive mechanisms to deal with the hull). Not until humans learned the use of tools and fire could they make use of grains. Bruising or grinding could loosen and remove part of the hull, but it was application of heat, in "parching" or roasting, that was most effective in removing the hull and making the nutritious kernel available. After grains were in cultivation, selection toward "naked" seeded varieties made grains more readily usable.

Some archeologists have suggested that the mortars and pestles found in sites of the Natufian culture in the Fertile Crescent (the area from the southeastern coast of the Mediterranean Sea around the Syrian Desert north of the Arabian Peninsula to the Persian Gulf) from about 10,000 BCE are evidence that people there were gathering and using wild grains. However, because mortars and pestles can be used for grinding many other things than grains, it is better to see the first definite evidence of grain use as being about 9000 BCE, the date of the first archeological discoveries of carbonized grain in human-use contexts. Because fire appears to have been the main early tool for dehulling wild grains, the lack of carbonized grains at earlier sites make earlier use questionable. Grain gathering encouraged permanent settlement rather than nomadism, so the first known villages arose in the prime grain-collecting arc of the Near East.

Reliance on a secure and concentrated food resource such as grain led the harvesters to try to protect it, driving off animals that were in competition with them for the ripe grain and clearing away plants (the first "weeds") that might compete with and slow down the growth of the grain. Just when this grain "husbandry" changed to actual agriculture, with farmers selecting and saving seed between seasons to sow in ground that they had plowed or otherwise loosened, is unknown. However, by about 8000 BCE, seeds altered from the wild strain by selection for tougher rachis, or central stem, (reducing shattering of the ear when gathering) and plumper grains, of emmer wheat (*Triticum turgidum ssp. dicoccum*), einkorn wheat (*Triticum monococcum*), and barley (*Hordeum vulgare*) turn up in early Neolithic sites such as Jericho, Tell Aswad, and Cafer Höyük. These are considered clear evidence of cultivation and selection away from the wild grain. By 7000 BCE modern bread wheat (*Triticum aestivum*) is also found.

Middle East and Europe: Wheat and Its Associates

The original food grains (emmer and einkorn wheats and barley) were initially domesticated in their natural wild range habitat—the Near Eastern arc of open hillsides with yearly rainfall of more than 250 millimeters, lying between forest to the north and arid plains to the south. All of the early agricultural settlements arose in this area, albeit relatively limited. As the success of cultivation and population grew, farmers looked to artificially expand the range suitable for grains, thus starting the process of environmental alteration to suit grains that has continued from that time on. Moving north required clearing the forest because grains do not thrive in shade. Moving south required irrigation of the arid lands to provide sufficient moisture.

The move to irrigated agriculture, by allowing denser, more concentrated, more productive plantings of grain, allowed greater population densities and eventually the first cities, in Mesopotamia and Egypt.

Mesopotamian population densities grew first in the low-lying delta area to the east, where the flat land allowed the seasonal waters to be distributed by a relatively simple system of canals. The Sumerian cities of Ur and Eridu, close to the coastline of the Persian Gulf, grew up first in the later fourth millennium BCE, then Uruk, Umma, and Larsa slightly farther inland on the delta. However, the heavy irrigation for annual grain crops caused the water table to rise, and evaporation deposited soluble salts in the soil and raised the salinity of the groundwater. These events reduced the fertility of the soil. Between 2350 and 1850 BCE crop yields declined by almost half, and seed requirements more than doubled. This was despite a shift in crop concentration from wheat to barley, which is more salt tolerant. The result was a decline of both population and political power for the delta, with the weight of both shifting westward upstream to the river plain region of Mesopotamia, where cities such as Nippur, Kish, and Babylon rose from about 1800 BCE.

This central part of Mesopotamia had greater gradient, meaning that floods had more energy and that stronger and larger-scale canals were necessary to carry the irrigation water out of the river channels. The height of the canal system was reached during Sasanian times (226–651 CE). However, salinization, although less rapid, continued to be a problem. The large irrigation works were liable to break down in times of natural or human crisis, leaving large areas of land to revert to desert. This happened in the years after the Arab conquest of Mesopotamia in 637 CE, when high floods combined with political change caused the elaborate canal system to collapse by 1000 CE, greatly reducing the cultivated area and population in Mesopotamia.

In Egypt fewer problems arose. The annual flooding of the Nile River flushed the salts from the soil, and the grain crops watered by the flooding flourished, supporting long-term production, which continued robustly enough to allow export of much of the grain that fed the urban population of imperial Rome. Failure of the Nile floods could result in famine and chaos, however. It has been suggested that the break between the Old and New Kingdoms of Egypt was caused by repeated flood failures between 2200 and 2000 BCE.

The Near Eastern system of agriculture based on barley and wheat spread through the Mediterranean, southward to the Ethiopian plateau, and eastward to India, flourishing in the areas where conditions were similar to the original Near Eastern arc or where forest clearance readily made them so.

During late antiquity and the early medieval period the introduction of the heavy moldboard plow allowed plowing and planting of the heavier and wetter northern soils of northern and western Europe. Previously the arable (suitable for cultivation) lands there tended to be confined to the uplands, where the soil was lighter and the forest thinner. Now, with the new plows available, there was a fresh assault on the forests of Britain, Germany, and central Europe as they were cut down to make plowland (such as the "assarts" of England). The net result was a loss of forest cover—England, originally a heavily forested country, gradually changed to open land—and the growth of population and shift of power moved to northern Europe. However, the more northern location meant greater emphasis on the "coarse" grains (barley, rye, and oats), which have shorter growth periods. Rye (*Secale cereale*) and oats (*Avena sativa*) had been of minor importance before but now became staples in the more northern parts of Europe. There were serious side-effects: Ergot, a common fungus attacking rye, when eaten in contaminated bread, causes ergotism, called "St. Anthony's Fire" in medieval times. The afflicted suffer convulsions and hallucinations, and many die. The modern psychoactive drug LSD was developed from one of the alkaloids in ergot.

The deforestation push continued eastward as German colonists moved into Prussia and eastern Europe during the tenth through the thirteenth centuries, converting the primitive forest to wheatland and enriching the Hanseatic League of northern European merchant towns, which prospered by selling the grain produced. Then, as the European powers expanded during the sixteenth through the nineteenth centuries, wheat conquered the world as an important part of the mechanism of colonial dominance in North and South America, southern Africa, and Australia.

Eastern Asia: Rice

Rice (Oryza sativa) is the most important of the world's grains, being the staple food of almost half of the world's population. Although rice can grow in a variety of environments, "paddy" or "wet" rice (grown in artificially flooded fields) accounts for about 75 percent of production. "Dryland" or "upland" rice accounts for 10 percent, and "deepwater" rice (grown in water depths of more than 50 centimeters) accounts for the remaining 15 percent. Wet rice cultivation has had the most visible environmental effect, with its leveled terraces and surrounding dikes rising far up the mountainsides, reshaping the landscapes of China and Indonesia.

Domesticated rice originated in the uplands region running through Assam, northern Burma (Myanmar), northern Thailand, southwestern China, and northern Vietnam. However, the earliest archeological finds of cultivated rice, dated to about 5000 BCE, are from Hemudu in the lower Yangzi region of central China. By 3000 BCE the range of rice cultivation had spread through southern China and the northern part of southeast Asia. Rice cultivation reached India by about 1500 BCE and Japan by about 300 BCE.

The extension of rice into the equatorial zone did not take place until the discovery of photo-insensitive (day-length neutral) strains whose development did not depend on seasonal triggers. The spread to the Malay Peninsula and the Indonesian Archipelago was therefore rather later, probably not until the middle of the first millennium CE. There the shift from swidden (slash-and-burn) cultivation of dryland crops such as millet to sawah (wet rice) cultivation led to greater population densities (a field of 1 hectare could support a family). This allowed surpluses necessary for urban development and trade and therefore the appearance of powerful states such as Srivijaya (southeastern Sumatra, seventh to tenth centuries) and Majapahit and its precursors (Java, eighth to fifteenth centuries).

Rice was not the first agricultural crop in its realm—proso (Panicum miliaceum) and foxtail (Setaria italica) millets preceded it in China; Job's tears (Coix lachryma-jobi), tubers, and fruits preceded it in southeastern Asia and Indonesia. However, over time rice became the preferred grain, replacing the other crops. Intensive rice cultivation, with an increase in population density and effects on social and political structures, started in China in the third century BCE, and rice as a dominant crop spread outward. As a food it was so much preferred that huge quantities were traded or transferred to nonrice-growing areas. The Grand Canal system of China, over 1,000 kilometers long, was built in the early seventh century primarily to carry tax rice from the producing areas of the south to the Sui dynasty capital in Daxingcheng in northwestern China. In 1011 the Chinese Emperor Zhenzong ordered the distribution of a new kind of rice seed imported from Champa (in modern Vietnam). It had the advantages of maturing quickly, allowing double-cropping in some areas, and also was drought resistant and thus could be planted in higher and more northerly areas.

The spread of both rice cultivation and rice consumption has continued to the present. During the colonial era cheap bulk shipping opened vast commercial markets and caused ever-increasing conversion of land to rice production. For example, between 1855 and 1905 rice area and production in the Burmese delta multiplied roughly tenfold, exporting 1.8 million metric tons annually by 1905. In the past two decades rice has overtaken wheat as the most-produced food grain.

The Americas: Maize

Maize (Zea mays) is commonly known in North America as "corn" but is more fittingly referred to as "maize" because "corn" means any cereal grain in Britain and much of the rest of the world. The great cereal staple originating in the Americas, maize is high in carbohydrates and fats but low in certain proteins and vitamins. It made a successful staple when complemented in the diet with beans and squash, as it was and is in the Americas. During the post-Columbian era, as maize has been introduced to the Old World and adopted as a staple foodstuff—but without those complementary foods—diseases such as pellagra (deficiency of vitamin C and nicotinic acid) and kwashiorkor (a protein deficiency) have been the result of heavy dependency on maize alone.

Maize is a heavy feeder, quickly depleting the soil of nutrients. Its cultivation in the Americas and later in the Old World has encouraged the type of agriculture known as "shifting cultivation" (slash and burn), where an area of forest is cleared, maize is grown for a few seasons until the fertility of the soil is exhausted, then the field is abandoned, and the farmer moves on to clear new fields.

The origin of the cultivated species of maize has been debated among scientists for over a hundred years because modern maize is so highly developed, with tight-fitting husks completely covering the grain on the ear, that maize is no longer capable of dispersing its seeds without human assistance. Botanists did not find wild maize clearly ancestral to the cultivated plant; therefore, they speculated that maize was descended through chance mutation or human selection from other related plants that do grow wild, particularly one known as "teosinte." However, the recent discovery in Mexico City of maize pollen over eighty thousand years old, dating long before human occupation of the continent, has swung the argument to the side of an original wild maize, rather than mutation or selection from teosinte.

The earliest evidence of human use of maize, either gathered from the wild or in the early stages of domestication, dates to about 5000 BCE in northern Mexico. By the third millennium BCE maize was definitely cultivated in northeastern Mexico and the southeastern United States. By about 1500 BCE the nixamalization process (soaking and cooking the grain with lime or wood ashes, which makes the grain easier to grind and enhances its protein value) had been discovered, increasing maize's desirability as a foodstuff. Whether maize was transferred to the Andean region from Central America or separately domesticated there is uncertain, but from these two areas the cultivation of maize spread through most of the Americas, being the basis of agriculture and increased population wherever it spread.

Columbus discovered maize on his first voyage to America, and the seeds taken back were soon spread through the Old World. Maize became a major crop in Italy, the Balkans, the Near East, and as far as China. In Africa, in particular, it became the staple crop of much of the continent.

Africa: Millets

Africa is different from the other continents in having not a single dominant grain, but rather a range of local-ized grains, most of which are categorized as millets. Millet is not a single grain species, but rather includes many small-grained species, from several genera, tolerant of high temperatures and low moisture. Millets are cultivated widely across Eurasia, especially in India and China, but are most prominent in sub-Saharan Africa, where the "imperial" grains are less dominant.

Domestication of grain crops appears to have occurred independently in various areas of Africa and rather later than on the other continents. Extensive gathering of wild grass seeds continued until about a hundred years ago.

The main crop of the Sahel (semidesert southern fringe of the Sahara Desert) and dry savanna is pearl millet (Pennisetum typhoides), which is most drought resistant of all millets. In the tall grass savanna, sorghum (Sorghum bicolor) is the most important food crop. Both pearl millet and sorghum were domesticated by 2000 BCE, and both were spread to India at an early date. The east African highlands have their own preferred grains: finger millet (Eleusine coracana) and teff (Eragrostis tef), the smallest seeded of all millets, which is the most popular food grain in Ethiopia but almost unknown outside that country.

Western Africa also has African rice (Oryza glaberrima), descended from wild rices that grew in water holes that dried up in the dry season. African rice is now largely replaced in cultivation by oriental rice. After 1492 maize also became an important food crop, especially in the southern half of Africa.

Imperial Grains

Three grains—wheat, maize, and rice—have most suited the conditions created by the European expansion of the sixteenth to eighteenth centuries and the Industrial Revolution of the nineteenth and twentieth centuries. Urban growth in the industrializing nations was facilitated by the new global transportation networks. A major impetus for the growth of European colonial empires was the need for cheap foodstuffs for the factory workers of the European countries that no longer grew enough for their own needs. Also, in these colonies the emphasis shifted from subsistence farming to commercial cash-crop agriculture producing for export. This encouraged monoculture, with farmers in each region concentrating on the single crop that would yield them the highest monetary return. However, monoculture, in addition to creating "best conditions" for production of high yields, establishes "best conditions" for diseases and pests that live on the grains.

North American Wheat "Imperialism"

The case of the North America prairies may be taken as typical of the environmental results of the vast expansion and intensification of grain growing in the modern era. Similar results may be seen in other cases, such as Russia's Virgin Lands development projects of the 1950s and 1960s, China's agricultural and industrial Great Leap Forward of 1958–1961, and the jungle clearing still going on in Brazil.

From the start of European settlement in North America, there was concentration on wheat growing in New England and the central U.S. colonies. After the American Revolution, agricultural settlement, accompanied by massive deforestation, expanded across the Appalachian Mountains into the interior east of the Mississippi River. After the U.S. Civil War and after Confederation in Canada in 1867, the North American frontier moved westward onto the open Great Plains, ideal for grain monoculture. However, the northern areas, especially on the Canadian prairies, were restricted by climate to mixed farming because successful harvests of the most desired grain, wheat, were unreliable. However, new strains of wheat—such as Marquis wheat introduced in 1911, which ripened eight days faster than the previously standard Red Fife strain—allowed monoculture of wheat even in the North.

Between 1860 and 1913 the Great Plains turned to grain, largely wheat. The Great Plains became the great "bread basket," supplying the hungry cities of Europe and providing capital for North American development. However, the cheap wheat from North America (and similar plantings in Argentina, Australia, and Russia) impoverished farmers in Europe and tended to drive the other traditional grains out of production in those countries.

The environmental effects of the wheat monoculture were both varied and significant. The Rocky Mountain locust (*Melanoplus spretus*) was one of the two major herbivores on the Great Plains in the 1870s (the other was the bison). By 1900 both were gone, unable to survive in the changed conditions. Not that farmers could rejoice, though, because other species of locusts and grasshoppers, previously insignificant, replaced them with equal voracity. Locusts and grasshoppers today cause losses of more than $100 million on the Canadian prairies alone and require hundreds of thousands of liters of insecticides for control.

The near-continuous planting of wheat, from northern Mexico through the prairie provinces of Canada, created ideal conditions for the rust fungus, which has established a yearly "migration" pattern of over 4,000 kilometers. Infection starts out each year in northern Mexico. Spores are blown northward through repeated generations. Rust cannot overwinter at the northern end of the wheat belt but arrives each year from the south; it cannot oversummer in the southern end, so spores must be blown southward in the fall to infect winter wheat there to start the next year's cycle. Efforts have been made to defeat this cycle by breeding new "rust-resistant" cultivars (organisms originating and persisting under cultivation) of wheat, but each new version has only a limited usefulness until the rust evolves new strains that are not protected against.

The loss of the native grass cover (the prairie sod), destroyed by the annual plowing and harrowing, meant that when drought came, especially in those drier areas marginal for agriculture, the soil had nothing to hold it and blew in millions of tons. Desertification resulted from efforts to extend grain farming into ever more marginal areas. The first bout of droughts hit the U.S. central plains in the 1870s and 1880s, resulting in a short-term exodus of population. The area was resettled after a series of wetter years. Then came the drought years of the later 1920s and 1930s, resulting in the Dust Bowl of Oklahoma and surrounding states and the exodus from the parched region. Similar conditions prevailed in the Palliser triangle of southern Saskatchewan and Alberta, Canada, where grain yields dropped by over 75 percent.

In more recent years efforts to alleviate drought risks by irrigation have led to groundwater supplies rapidly being used up because wells need to be drilled deeper and deeper.

Twentieth-Century Issues

From the late nineteenth century onward scientific breeding, based on genetic principles, superseded older methods of selection of new grain. This produced dramatic results such as Marquis wheat, which, by shortening the time required to ripen, allowed wheat monoculture on the Canadian prairies. In the 1930s the first "artificial" grain was created—triticale, a cross of wheat and rye—which was heralded as a new wonder grain because it contains more protein than either parent, but it has not lived up to the promises.

Since the 1940s selections of HYV (high-yield varieties) maize, rice, and dwarf wheat have driven what is known as the "Green Revolution," aimed at the Third World (tropical and subtropical areas of Asia, Africa, and Latin America). The Green Revolution led to great increases in production but required heavy use of machinery, fertilizer, and pesticides (leading to increased concentration of production in the hands of larger-scale and higher-capitalized farmers and to loss of strain diversity). Also, many of the new hybrids either had built-in sterility or did not breed true, so seed could not be saved but rather had to be bought.

Most recently, genetic modification (GM) techniques have allowed plant biotechnologists to create desired characteristics not available by conventional breeding by altering genes or introducing genes from other plant species. This has produced such plants as maize with built-in tolerance for herbicides, valuable for large-scale mechanized agriculture. However, problems have arisen with drift of these genes to other strains of maize and other unexpected results—maize strains with built-in defenses against harmful insects are also toxic to butterflies.

The commercialization of plant breeding has also led to issues over "ownership" of plant genetics and strains and limitations on genetic diversity as commercial operations, especially in the United States, have tried to pressure farmers around the world to use patented seed.

Although pollution from traditional agricultural activities has long existed, artificial fertilizers, synthetic pesticides, and herbicides brought into use during the twentieth century changed both the nature and the scale of the problem. Because grains are the largest agricultural crops, grains have also accounted for the largest use of these chemicals. Soils themselves may be subject to damaging buildups of these chemicals or their derivatives, but larger effects come from runoff and leaching into the water system. This is particularly the case with rice because its culture requires regular flooding and draining of the rice paddies. The "miracle rices" of the 1960s onward, which give best results only with heavy fertilization and pest control, have worsened the problem.

David Dendy

Further Reading

Coe, S. D. (1994). *America's first cuisines.* Austin: University of Texas Press.

Fowler, C., & Mooney, P. (1990). *Shattering: Food, politics, and the loss of genetic diversity.* Tucson: University of Arizona Press.

Glantz, M. H. (Ed.). (1994). *Drought follows the plow: Cultivating marginal areas.* Cambridge, UK: Cambridge University Press.

Harlan, J. R. (1995). *The living fields: Our agricultural heritage.* Cambridge, UK: Cambridge University Press.

Kahn, E. J., Jr. (1985). *The staffs of life.* Boston: Little, Brown.

Mangelsdorf, P. C. (1974). *Corn: Its origin, evolution, and improvement.* Cambridge, MA: Belknap Press.

Solbrig, O. T., & Solbrig, D. J. (1994). *So shall you reap: Farming and crops in human affairs.* Washington, DC: Island Press.

Tannahill, R. (1988). *Food in history* (2nd ed.). New York: Crown Publishers.

Toussaint-Samat, M. (1992). *A history of food.* Cambridge, MA: Blackwell.

Zohary, D., & Hopf, M. (2000). *Domestication of plants in the Old World: The origin and spread of cultivated plants in west Asia, Europe and the Nile Valley* (3rd ed.). Oxford, UK: Oxford University Press.

Grapes

Viticulture (grape growing) and the use of its products (i.e., fresh grapes, raisins, and wine) have been intricately associated with the history of humans. It is thought that the evolution of *Vitis vinifera*, often termed the "European" or "Old World" grape, occurred in Transcaucasia in Asia Minor. *Vitis vinifera* presently accounts for more than 95 percent of all grapes produced, with an estimated ten thousand cultivars (organisms originating and persisting under cultivation) of this species grown throughout the world. Well-known grape cultivars include Cabernet Sauvignon, Chardonnay, Reisling, Syrah, and Thompson Seedless.

It is thought that humans prior to the first settlements consumed wild grapes directly from the grapevine. Cultivation started when humans protected grapevines supported by trees from animals. The production of wine from grapes most likely occurred accidentally. The concentration of sugars (glucose and fructose) in grape berries can be as high as 25 percent and thus is an ideal substrate for fermentation. In addition, the skin of grape berries is a favorable habitat for yeasts. There is chemical evidence indicating that wine may have been produced as early as 5400 to 5000 BCE.

Pottery jars from a Neolithic village in the Zagros Mountains of Iran contained the calcium salt of tartaric acid. Tartaric acid is found only in grapes.

Grapevine cultivation spread to Mesopotamia and into Egypt by the fourth millennium BCE. By 1000 BCE grapevines were being cultivated around the eastern Mediterranean Sea and into Greece. During the Roman Empire grapevines spread throughout Gaul, west into Spain, and farther north into present-day Germany and eastern European countries. At this time grapes and wine had considerable significance for Middle Eastern and Mediterranean peoples. Fresh grapes had a high caloric value, 20 to 25 percent sugar, which is higher than that of most common fruits, and the caloric value of dried grapes is even higher, containing upward of 75 percent sugar. Thus grapes constituted one of the few sources of sweet material and one of the few easily stored and transported food sources of high caloric value. Monastic orders and secular nobility sustained viticulture and wine-making techniques after the fall of the Roman Empire and throughout the Middle Ages. From the sixteenth to the nineteenth centuries the European grapevine was transported around the world and vineyards planted in areas with Mediterranean-type climates (warm, dry summers and cool, wet winters).

During the middle of the nineteenth century a root-feeding aphid called Phylloxera (Daktulosphaira vitifoliae) was introduced into France from North America. Unfortunately, Vitis vinifera roots were highly susceptible to Phylloxera and were killed. The significant reduction in the production of grapes and wine led to fraud and other circumstances that affect grape production in the twenty-first century. The only viable means of overcoming Phylloxera is to graft Vitis vinifera cultivars onto North American rootstocks resistant to the insect. In addition, in many countries laws enacted during that time remain today to regulate which cultivars and production practices may be used to grow grapes for wine production.

Larry E. Williams

See also Phylloxera

Further Reading

Boulton, R. B., Singleton, V. L., Bisson, L. F., & Kunkee, R. E. (1998). *Principles and practices of winemaking.* Gaithersburg, MD: Aspen Publishers.

Mullins, M. G., Bouquet, A., & Williams, L. E. (1992). *Biology of the grapevine.* Cambridge, UK: Cambridge University Press.

Olmo, H. P. (1976). Grapes. In N. W. Simmonds (Ed.), *Evolution of crop plants* (pp. 294–298). New York: Longman.

Robinson, J. (1986). *Vines, grapes and wines.* New York: Alfred A. Knopf.

Unwin, T. (1991). *Wine and the vine: A historical geography of viticulture and the wine trade.* London: Routledge.

Grasslands

Grasslands are terrestrial plant communities dominated by nonwoody vegetation, often plants of the grass family. They can be as small as a forest opening, or as extensive as the Eurasian steppe and North American prairie. Grasslands may be the product of environmental conditions such as shallow soils, saturated soils, harsh climates with strongly seasonal rainfall, high elevations, or frequent fire. Grasses are well-adapted to defoliation by both grazing and fire. Grasslands may be to some degree anthropogenic, resulting from or maintained by frequent human-started fire, cultivation, woodcutting, heavy livestock grazing, or other activities. Grasslands are sometimes a temporal stage in vegetation development, found where cultivation has recently ceased, where wildfire has removed trees and shrubs, where soils are first developing, or after timber harvest, woodcutting, or flood.

Grasslands can be highly diverse communities including several kinds of grasses, legumes, sedges, rushes, and innumerable flowering species in a small area. Variations in soils, topography, and water availability lead to variations in the plant communities within grasslands. For example, vernal pools, pools of water supported by a clay layer that persist at the cessation of the rainy season, are often a site of concentrations of unusual species and flowers.

Terrestrial grasslands expanded about 30 million years ago, as the global climate became drier. The expansion of grassland and savanna environments supported the evolution and radiation of numerous large-bodied herbivores with specialized adaptations for open grassland environments. These adaptations include rapid locomotion, hooves, high-crowned teeth, and digestive systems for cellulose-rich fibrous plants.

In many cases the origins of a grassland are ambiguous, because they may be assumed to be a "natural" formation resulting from physical habitat characteristics, when instead humans and wildlife have played a

The Settlement of the American Plains

O. E. Rolvaag's epic novel of the settlement of the northern American Plains by Scandinavian peasants was first published in Norwegian in two volumes in 1924 and 1925. In 1927 it was translated and published in English. The following passage describes the initial effect of the open grasslands on Beret, one of the pioneer women.

The infinitude surrounding her on every hand might not have been so oppressive, might even have brought her a measure of peace, if it had not been for the deep silence, which lay heavier here than in a church. Indeed, what was there to break it? She had passed beyond the outposts of civilization; the nearest dwelling places of men were far away. Here no warbling of birds rose on the air, no buzzing of insects sounded;* even the wind had died away; the waving blades of grass that trembled to the faintest breath now stood erect and quiet, as if listening, in the great hush of the evening. . . . All along the way, coming out, she had noticed this strange thing: the stillness had grown deeper, the silence more depressing, the farther west they journeyed; it must have been over two weeks now since she had heard a bird sing! Had they traveled into some nameless, abandoned region? Could no living thing exist out here, in the empty, desolate, endless wastes of green and blue? . . . How could existence go on, she thought, desperately? If life is to thrive and endure, it must at least have something to hide to hide behind! . . .

* Original settlers are agreed that there was neither bird nor insect life on the prairie, with the exception of mosquitoes, the first year they came.

Source: Rolvaag, O. E. (1927) *Giants of the Earth; A Saga of the Prairie.* Translated by Lincoln Colcord and O. E. Rolvaag. New York: Harper & Row, p. 37.

part in creating and maintaining them. For example, it has been argued that in pre-Columbian North America the eastern portion of the Great Plains was maintained as grassland by a combination of Native American-caused and natural fire. The grassy moors of England are believed to be to some degree anthropogenic, resulting from thousands of years of woodcutting, burning, and livestock grazing. Perhaps the most ubiquitous example of the definitely anthropogenic grassland today is the golf course, where mowing, herbicide application, and weeding prevents the growth of other plants. Ecologist Frederick Clements developed his mono-climax theory of vegetation succession in part to support his argument that prairies are stable vegetation types, rather than a stage preceding the development of woody vegetation, or the result of frequent fires.

Human cultures in grassland environments often rely on herbivores for a large portion of their diet, because the environmental conditions typical of grasslands often make cultivation difficult. Toward the western extent of the North American Great Plains,

a lack of precipitation results in a dry grassland that provided the setting for the tragedies of the "sod-busting" era, as settlers attempted to grow crops and trees in areas where the environmental conditions simply could not support such growth without irrigation. Wild grasses and herbs, with high proportions of indigestible fiber and low protein quality, provide only limited direct nourishment to humans. The relationship between the North American Plains Indians and the bison is a well-known example of human use of herbivores in grassland environments. Another example is the indigenous hunters of the African savannas and grasslands. In many parts of the world, pastoralism, with or without some cultivation, is a traditional way of capturing the energy of grassland plants for human use. The yak-herders of Tibet, nomads of Mongolia, llama herders of the Andes, and reindeer herders of the taiga all make extensive use of grasslands. Both pastoralists and hunters often use fire to create, extend, and maintain the grassland environments that provide their sustenance. Grazing by livestock and herbivores can also limit the intrusion of trees and shrubs, thereby maintaining the environment on which they depend. When trees and unpalatable shrubs expand into grassland areas, forage for livestock and wild herbivores is reduced.

The more productive grasslands occurring where cultivation is possible are often the first vegetation types to be converted to crop production. Typical in arid environments is that the meadow areas along rivers and streams are converted to croplands and irrigated. Where saturated soils support a grassland, human cultivators can use ditches and levees to drain soils and provide a rich substrate for crop production. Examples include the Nile Delta, the highland lakes of Bolivia, and the much more recently developed Sacramento-San Joaquin Delta of California. The regions of the North American Great Plains where rain-fed agriculture is possible are now almost all converted to production of crops, most notably corn (maize) and soybeans. In recent decades, urban expansion has often supplanted grassland areas.

Grasses themselves are an important source of the food crops providing the majority of total human food calories. Maize, wheat, barley, and rice are all members of the grass family that humans have bred to maximize seed size. Grasses have traveled with colonists all over the globe. The grasslands of the Mediterranean regions of the world, including California, the Fertile Crescent, South Africa, and parts of Chile and Australia, today each generally include grasses from all the other regions. Tropical grasses have likewise become introduced between the new and old worlds.

Environmental historians, ecologists, land managers, and other observers have often based their interpretation of grassland landscapes on limited knowledge of their ecological history and development. The relationship between the extent, condition, and even existence of grasslands and human land use or wildlife populations is often little understood. A lack of trees may be wrongly interpreted as a symptom of some sort of environmental degradation. The exclusion of fire, and the criminalization of its use in many parts of the world, has resulted in invasion of grasslands by shrubs and trees and a resulting reduction in herbivore populations. Planting of trees in an effort to "restore" forests or to produce timber can reduce the utility of a land area for the support of local pastoralists and hunters, and cause significant change in wildlife habitat. On the other hand, overexploitation of forest resources, a high frequency of fire, and some kinds of grazing can convert a forest or shrubland to grassland.

Lynn Huntsinger and James W. Bartolome

See also Argentina; Bison; Cereals; Pastoralism; United States—Midwest

Further Reading

Clements, F. E. (1916). *Plant succession: An analysis of the development of vegetation.* Washington, DC: Carnegie Institution of Washington.

Coupland, R. T. (Ed.). (1979). *Grassland ecosystems of the world: Analysis of grasslands and their uses.* New York: Cambridge University Press, International Biological Programme.

Coupland, R. T. (Ed.). (1992). *Natural grasslands.* New York: Elsevier.

Weaver, J. E. (1956). *Grasslands of the Great Plains: Their nature and use.* Lincoln, NE: Johnsen Pub. Co.

Weaver, J. E. (1968). *Prairie plants and their environment: A fifty-year study in the Midwest.* Lincoln: University of Nebraska Press.

Great Auk

The last flightless birds of the Northern Hemisphere, great auks were often referred to as "penguins"; indeed they became the namesakes of a myriad of unrelated species in the Southern Hemisphere as Europeans applied this name to unrelated flightless birds in Antarctic regions. The great auks' extinction and their involvement with humans provide compelling lessons for conservation.

The largest known colony of great auks was on Funk Island, a rocky outcrop about 80 kilometers off the northeast coast of Newfoundland in the North Atlantic. In what may have been North America's first population estimate of marine birds, Sir Richard Whitbourne, British colonizer, (1622) wrote that the great auks on Funk Island reproduced "indefinitely . . . for the sustentation of man" (Whitbourne 1622). The species was so abundant off the coast of eastern Canada in the 1500s through the 1700s that Basque fishers and whalers used great auks as navigational indicators of the great fishing banks of Newfoundland. Charts in the *English Pilot* of 1706 had crude sketches of great auks to indicate the Grand Banks for British mariners.

For millennia before European movements into the New World, aboriginal peoples exploited great auks for food, feathers, and eggs. The maritime archaic peoples also held the species in spiritual esteem, as indicated by the many auk beaks that were included in human burials in ancient cemeteries three thousand to five thousand years ago on Newfoundland's Great Northern Peninsula. Beothuk natives navigated their canoes through the treacherous waters around Funk Island to collect great auk eggs, which they used for puddings.

In 1534 French explorer Jacques Cartier on his first exploratory voyage to North America visited Funk Island, where his crew collected fresh eggs and great auks. During a second trans-Atlantic crossing the following year, Cartier's first stop was at Funk Island to secure great auks for his crews before proceeding to Labrador. Cartier's activities and descriptions of Funk Island were soon widely known, and it became commonplace for vessels from many European origins, including France, Spain, England, and Portugal, to stop at Funk Island to gather the much-needed fresh protein for crews following month-long trans-Atlantic voyages. In essence, Funk Island, lying off of the northeast coast of the New World with its huge population of flightless and hence easily procurable "penguins," became North America's first "fast-food takeout."

Overkill

Through centuries of exploitation for food and bait, the great auks of Funk Island survived. However, circumstances changed radically in the late 1700s, and ship crews stayed on the island for extended periods, killing the auks for feathers and fat. They killed far too many. Great auks were herded into stonewalled corrals where they were killed before being parboiled to allow easy removal of down feathers. There were no trees on Funk Island, so the bodies of the fat-laden auks were also used to fuel the fires. Pieces of charcoaled great auk remains have been uncovered on Funk Island. Following defeathering, and possibly rendering for lipid-rich oils, the carcasses were discarded in mounds.

Captain George Cartwright of warned of the plight of the great auks in 1785:

> . . . it has been customary of late years for several crews of men to live all summer on that island (Funk) for the purpose of killing birds for their feathers, the destruction they have made is incredible. If a stop is not soon put to that practice, the whole breed will soon be diminished to almost nothing, particularly the penguins: for this is now the only Island they have left to breed upon. . . . (Cartwright 1792; Townsend 1911)

Some great auk carcasses were removed by ships in the 1860s and delivered for fertilizer use in the eastern United States. The remaining carcasses continued to compost and eventually created the "cemetery of the great auk" on the otherwise bald granite rock of Funk Island. Nature clearly abhors a vacuum, and a colony of Atlantic puffins (Fratercula arctica) now digs its nest burrows into the soil formed by the composted great auks.

In 1841 Peter Stuwitz from Bergen, Norway, was the first scientist to visit Funk Island and collect great auk bones just prior to extinction of the species. He described "enormous heaps" of great auk bones, many of which he collected. In 1887 Frederic Lucas visited Funk Island as part of a fisheries research cruise sponsored by the Smithsonian Institution National Museum of Natural History and the U.S. Fish and Wildlife Commission. Lucas collected bones and assembled a number of great auk skeletons, at least two of which are now housed at the Museum of Comparative Zoology at Harvard University.

Easy Prey

Many aspects of the great auks' biology and population ecology made them particularly vulnerable to overkilling by humans. The auks had a delayed sexual maturity and did not begin breeding for several years and then laid only a single egg per breeding season. The auks' flightlessness made them easy to capture in abundance, especially during times when rudimentary weaponry made such a task difficult among birds capable of flight. Great auks were large and fatty, with heavy pectoral (breast) muscles that made them nourishing food. Great auks were also highly aggressive, breeding in a few large colonies that were sources for other smaller colonies. Colonies likely retracted from numerous smaller ones. As indication, charts show a number of Penguin Islands, Penguin Heads, and Penguin Arms in Newfoundland and Labrador. All of these circumstances made the species easy to exploit to excess, that is, below minimum viable population thresholds.

The last known breeding pair of great auks was killed by fishermen on Eldey Island off the southwest coast of Iceland on 3 June 1844, for museum curators in Copenhagen. Although a few surviving individuals roamed the North Atlantic for a few more decades, the ultimate finality of the killing on Eldey Island pales in comparison to the extinction of the species, which likely was determined by the elimination of the massive colony on Funk Island about fifty years earlier.

People now know that a species's abundance bears little relationship to its perpetuity on Earth. Highly aggregative, abundant species are indeed highly vulnerable to overexploitation and extinction, as has been the case with the passenger pigeon *(Ectopistes migratorius)* and many highly aggregative fish species.

W. A. Montevecchi

Further Reading

Bucher, E. H. (1992). The causes of extinction of the passenger pigeon. *Current Ornithology, 9*, 1–36.

Burness, G. P., & Montevecchi, W. A. (1992). Oceanographic-related variation in the bone-sizes of extinct great auks. *Polar Biology, 11*, 545–551.

Cartwright, G. (1792). *A journal of the transactions and events, during a residence of nearly sixteen years on the coast of Labrador.* Newark, UK: Allen and Ridge.

Lysaght, A. M. (1971). *Joseph Banks in Newfoundland and Labrador, his diaries, manuscripts and collections.* London: Faber.

Montevecchi, W. (1994, August). The great auk cemetery. *Natural History Magazine, 45*, 6–8.

Montevecchi, W. A., & Kirk, D. A. (1996). Great auk. In A. Poole & F. Gill (Eds.), *Penguinus impennis: The birds of North America.* (pp. 20). Philadelphia and Washington, DC: Academy of Natural Sciences and American Ornithologist's Union.

Montevecchi, W. A., & Tuck, L. M. (1987). *Newfoundland birds: Exploitation, study, conservation.* Cambridge, MA: Nuttall Ornithological Club.

Pauly, D., Christensen, V., Dalsgaard, J., Froese, R., & Torres, F., Jr. (1998). Fishing down marine food webs. *Science, 279*, 860–863.

Stephens, P. A., & Sutherland, W. J. (1999). Consequences of the Allee effect for behavior, ecology and conservation. *Trends in Ecology and Conservation, 14*, 401–405.

Townsend, C. W. (1912). *Captain Cartwright and his Labrador journal.* Boston: Estes.

Tuck, J. A. (1975). *Ancient people of Port au Choix.* St. John's, Canada: Memorial University of Newfoundland.

Whitbourne, R. (1622). *A discourse and discovery of Newfoundland.* London: Kynston.

The Great Lakes and St. Lawrence River

Forming part of the U.S.-Canadian border, the Great Lakes (244,100 square kilometers) consist of Lakes Superior, Michigan, Huron, Erie, and Ontario. They contain 18 percent of the world's supply of freshwater and are the largest system of fresh surface water on Earth. Historically, these lakes have provided water for consumption, transportation, fishing, recreation, power, and industry. A dominant factor in industry and agriculture, by the 1950s the lakes were polluted and eutrophic (high nutrient concentrations) from municipal wastes, industrial pollution, and agricultural runoff, making them unfit in many areas for fish populations and human use. In an unprecedented move of international cooperation the United States and Canada are cleaning up and reviving this shared resource and cultural treasure.

Created by erosion and deposition during the glacial movements of the Pleistocene epoch (1.6 million years ago), the Great Lakes are interconnected by rivers, straits, and canals. The St. Lawrence Seaway (1959) links them with the Atlantic Ocean via the St. Lawrence River, the primary outlet of the ecosystem. Except during icy months, these passages serve as one of the world's busiest shipping areas, with over 50 million metric tons of freight each year.

The Great Lakes region was home to numerous Native American groups who fished and traded. When Europeans arrived in the 1500s, the lake waters were cool and clear. However, early settlers (1700s) deforested the basins for agriculture and timber, leading to erosion, sedimentation, and high nutrient loads. Eventually more than two-thirds of the wetlands were drained. By the late 1800s unregulated industries and municipalities were using the lakes as dumping grounds for untreated wastes. Because outflows from the Great Lakes are small, these pollutants were retained in the lakes and became more concentrated with time. Additionally, the lakes' large surface area made them vulnerable to increasing atmospheric pollutants of the 1900s.

Industrial pollutants (polychlorinated biphenyls [PCBs], and pesticides (dichlorodiphenyl-trichloroethane [DDT], added to water quality problems. Consequently, many beaches were closed, and water became nondrinkable, raising public concern. Without their natural pollution sinks (bodies that act as a storage device or disposal mechanism, such as forests and wetlands) and with increasing pollution loads, the Great Lakes became warmer and eutrophic. In the 1950s Lake Erie was declared "dead."

Fish populations also changed dramatically in the twentieth century, first through overfishing and then through the introduction of exotic species such as the parasitic sea lamprey, which virtually eliminated lake trout in Lakes Huron and Michigan. In 1986 zebra mussels, which filter and clean water by consuming algae, were introduced from Europe. However, the mussels also absorb toxic substances, causing ongoing toxic buildup higher in the food chain.

In response, the Great Lakes Water Quality Agreements of 1972 and 1978, expressing the commitment of the United States and Canada to maintain the chemical, physical, and biological integrity of the Great Lakes, replaced the original Boundary Waters Treaty of 1909. Although problems still exist, since the agreements, beaches have reopened, water is drinkable and clear, most fish are edible, Lake Erie has thriving fish populations again, and most point source (from a single place) pollution has been controlled.

Irene Dameron Hager

Further Reading

Abell, R. A., Olson, D. M., Dinerstein, E., & Hurley, P. (2000). *Freshwater ecoregions of North America: A conservation assessment.* Washington, DC: Island Press.

Ashworth, W. (1987). *The late, great lakes: An environmental history.* Detroit, MI: Wayne State University Press.

Government of Canada & United States Environmental Protection Agency. (1995). *The Great Lakes: An environmental atlas and resource book* (3rd ed.). Chicago: Great Lakes National Program Office.

Sproule-Jones, M. (2002). *Restoration of the Great Lakes: Promises, practices, and performances.* Vancouver, Canada: UBC Press.

Green Building

Green building is a way of designing and constructing to create safer, more environmentally responsible buildings. Although elements of green building go back hundreds—even thousands—of years, the modern green building movement grew out of the solar energy movement of the 1970s and 1980s. Solar buildings became popular after Earth Day in 1970. Early on in the solar energy movement, the focus was on active solar-collector systems; by the late 1970s the focus had shifted to simpler passive solar energy systems. By the 1980s superinsulation (high levels of insulation and high-performance glazings) became a key part of the

mix and was often the most cost-effective strategy for saving energy.

In the late 1980s green building took these ideas a step further with the recognition that people could do more than simply save energy. People were learning about such environmental concerns as ozone depletion, global warming, endocrine disrupters (man-made chemicals that mimic the action of natural hormones), and loss of biodiversity, and forward-thinking designers and builders recognized that many of the decisions they make in designing and constructing buildings have an impact on these concerns. Green building is a melding of many concerns into a general design ethic.

Issues Addressed

Unlike solar design or energy-efficient design, green building design addresses a wide range of issues. These include:

1. Land use and community planning. People have a growing recognition that where people build and how people design communities have tremendous impacts on sustainability. Green building seeks to lessen dependence on automobiles while fostering communities in which neighbors know each other and needs can be met locally.

2. Protection of local ecosystems. The loss of biodiversity in the world is considered by many to be the most serious environmental threat that people face. An important tenant of green building is to protect open space—often by clustering buildings so that a portion of a site can be left undeveloped. More than simply protecting natural areas, green development can also be a driver to actually restore ecosystems—whether tall-grass prairies, woodlands, desert, or wetlands.

3. Energy savings. Low energy use is a key aspect of green building design. Decisions made in the design and construction of a building that reduce energy consumption will continue benefiting the environment for decades—or even centuries—to come. Such strategies as high levels of insulation, high-performance glazings, passive solar design, cooling-load avoidance (for example, shading strategies to keep sunlight out of buildings), and natural ventilation are important components of green building design.

4. Water savings. Many experts believe that water will become a more limiting resource in the twenty-first century than will energy. Most green buildings include strategies and products to con-

serve water—from water-efficient plumbing fixtures and appliances to Xeriscaping (low water use) practices outdoors.

5. Green products and materials. Green building includes reducing the impact of the production and eventual disposal of building materials. This impact usually occurs elsewhere, and understanding it involves a process known as life-cycle assessment (LCA). Green building materials are those that have minimal environmental impacts in their raw material extraction, manufacture, use, and disposal.

6. Efficient use of materials. Green building seeks to use materials efficiently. Strategies include designing smaller buildings, using less material by optimizing structural design, building to standard dimensions to minimize cut-off waste, and combining structure and finish in the same material (finished concrete-slab floors, for example).

7. Durable, low-maintenance buildings. Significant environmental impacts occur in the maintenance of buildings (cleaning, painting, etc.) and in repairs and replacement of failed systems. Green building pays attention to these issues and seeks to maximize durability and minimize high-impact maintenance requirements.

8. Indoor air quality. It is not enough simply to create a building that is healthy for the environment; it must also be healthy for the people who live or work in it. Maintaining good indoor environmental quality is a high priority in green building.

Wide Relevance

Green building design is relevant to all types of buildings, including residential, commercial, institutional, and industrial. It is relevant to any region of the world. Depending on the location, the type of building, the specific needs of the clients, and local environmental considerations, green building priorities may differ from one project to another. For example, for an office building in the southwestern United States, saving water and protecting ecosystems may be top priorities, whereas for a day-care center in Minnesota, conserving energy and maintaining indoor air quality may be top priorities.

Good green building design involves integration and whole-systems thinking. Traditional building design generally involves an architect designing the building shell, then passing the project to a mechanical engineer who designs the heating and cooling systems, then to an interior designer who designs the building interior, then to a landscape architect who deals with the site—all with little coordination. Integrated design involves all of these disciplines working together.

Through such integration, cost savings can often be realized. For example, by upgrading the energy performance of a building envelope and incorporating passive solar energy design features, it may be possible to downsize (or even eliminate) heating and cooling equipment—thus paying for the energy-saving features. On a large commercial project it may be possible to avoid the construction of conventional storm sewers and detention ponds by providing storm water infiltration on-site with porous paving and infiltration trenches—savings hundreds of thousands of dollars (enough to pay for many higher-cost green features).

Alex Wilson

Further Reading

Earth Pledge Foundation. (2000). *White Papers*. New York: Author.

Kilbert, C. (Ed.). (1999). *Reshaping the built environment: Ecology, ethics, economics*. Washington, DC: Island Press.

Lechner, N. (2000). *Heating cooling lighting: Design methods for architects* (2nd ed.). Hoboken, NJ: John Wiley & Sons.

Mendler, S. & W. Odell. (2000). *The HOK guidebook to sustainable design*. Hoboken, NJ: John Wiley & Sons.

Wilson, A., J. L. Uncapher, L. A. McManigal, L. H. Lovins, M. Cureton, & W.D. Browning. (1998). *Green development: Integrating ecology and real estate*. Hoboken, NJ: John Wiley and Sons.

Green Consumerism *See* Consumer Movement, Commodification, Ecological Simplicity

Green Parties

Green Parties are political organizations that focus on a wide range of social and environmental issues in their party platforms. They have grown from a tiny fringe movement into a significant voting block in many parts of the world, though almost entirely in developed

From the Green Party Agenda

Key Value No. 3

Ecological Wisdom

Human societies must operate with the understanding that we are part of nature, not separate from nature. We must maintain an ecological balance and live within the ecological and resource limits of our communities and our planet. We support a sustainable society which utilizes resources in such a way that future generations will benefit and not suffer from the practices of our generation. To this end we must practice agriculture which replenishes the soil; move to an energy efficient economy; and live in ways that respect the integrity of natural systems.

Source: *Ten Key Values of the Green Party* (2002). Retrieved February 24, 2003, from http://www.greenpartyus.org/tenkey.html

countries. They achieved considerable prominence—and notoriety—during the 2000 U.S. presidential elections. Environmental issues have always been a significant concern for "Greens," and the movement developed out of the environmental and alternative political movements in the 1970s. For many supporters, however, their approach to economic and social issues has come to be a more significant factor than their position on environmental issues such as land use, global warming, and population.

Emergence and Influence of Green Parties

The first environmental party emerged in Britain in 1973, and it was known as the Ecology Party until 1986. The German Greens (*die Grünen*) were formed later but are considered the mother of all Green parties because they have had a strong national presence since 1983. Green Parties have generally been more successful in nations where there is proportional representation in parliament (thus, a party receives seats proportional to its share of the popular vote). There is a Mongolian Green Party and, according to the Global Greens website, an African Federation of Green Parties.

Germany's Foreign Minister, Joschka Fischer, came to international prominence when the German Green Party, which he led (inasmuch as any Green Party accepts the idea of having leaders), won 6 percent of the vote in the 1998 election and, consequently, was invited to join a coalition government by the Social Democrats. As Foreign Minister, he had to deal with decisions to be made after the 2001 attacks on the World

Trade Center in New York, including the war against Afghanistan and, in 2003, against Iraq. Without question the most prominent and mainstream politician ever to have come from the ranks of a Green party, Fischer had to contend with dissension in his own party, traditionally pacifist, as well as with criticism from those outside it.

In the United Kingdom, where in the 1989 European Parliamentary elections the Green Party won the highest percentage of the popular vote ever won by a Green Party—15 percent (2.5 million votes)—the organization has been plagued by internal divisions.

The U.S. Green movement began in 1984 with the formation of local groups in Maine and elsewhere. By 1989, there was a loosely formed national organization called the Green Committees of Correspondence, after the Committees of Correspondence that organized in the years before the American Revolutionary War.

The U.S. Green Party's annual convention in 2002 was held in Philadelphia and included delegates from thirty-four state Green Parties, along with the development of a system for selecting a presidential candidate for 2004. Ralph Nader's candidacy in 2000 was seen—typically for the Green Party—as both a success and a disaster for progressives, contributing, some claim, to the seizing of the White House by the Republicans. In another twist typical of the Greens, Nader was not even a member of the Green Party.

Green Party Principles

Over the years, local and national gatherings have spent a great deal of time debating the meaning of what

613

The Green Party 1989 Brochure
to encourage people in the European
Community to cast a "green" vote.

became known as the Ten Key Values, which were originally assembled at the Green's first national meeting, held in St. Paul, Minnesota, in August 1984. The Ten Key Values were originally drawn from the "Four Pillars" of the then West German Greens: ecological wisdom, social justice, grassroots democracy, and non-violence. (In 2000, equal opportunity was added to the list of pillars.) In addition there are three other sets of principles, each with two related values: respect for diversity and feminist values; decentralization and community economics; and global responsibility and sustainability (or "thinking to the Seventh Genera-

tion"—the idea, said to come from Native American tradition, that our decisions should take into account the effects on the seventh generation, that is, our descendants some two hundred years from now). The exact terminology has changed over time, no doubt after lengthy consideration, debate, and eventual consensus. It is interesting to note that in the 2003 U.S. Green Party literature, "ecological wisdom" is listed third—no longer first—appearing after "grassroots democracy" and "social justice and equal opportunity."

The debates were intense and often surprisingly acrimonious. The most drawn-out and bitter fight was between proponents of social ecology and deep ecology. The social ecologists were led by Murray Bookchin, based in Vermont, and the deep ecologists were inspired by Arne Naess, a Norwegian ecophilosopher. Social ecologists believed that it was necessary to liberate human beings—through improved welfare and opportunity—before saving the natural world. Deep ecologists, on the other hand, believed that the human exploitation of nature was a core problem, and that changing the human relationship with nature would lead to the needed improvements in human well-being.

Consensus decision-making and other organizational rules provided challenges to the growth of an effective national movement. In 1990, for example, at the Green Gathering in Boulder, Colorado, small group meetings required men and women to speak alternately. Curiously enough, it was those on the deep ecology side of the debate who took the lead, after a bitter split in 1991, in forming the Green Politics Network, which would eventually help to form the U.S. Green Party. Social ecologists tended also to be anarchists or libertarians, unwilling to participate in the political process. They did not agree with the more mainstream Greens whose slogan became, "Don't beat the government, BE the government!"

For a time in 2000, it seemed possible that Ralph Nader, the Green candidate chosen by the Greens because of his prominence as a consumer advocate since the early 1960s (not as a social reformer or environmentalist), would get at least 5 percent of the popular vote. This would have meant more than $10 million in public funding for a Green presidential campaign in 2004. In the end, after an exceptionally close race between Republican George W. Bush and Democrat Albert Gore Jr. (once known, incidentally, as a strong environmental candidate and as the author of *Earth in the Balance*), Greens claimed that many who would have voted for Nader voted for Gore instead. (Nader did, nonetheless, receive 3 percent of the popular vote.)

Critics contend that the Greens are a spoiler in close elections, throwing the vote to the more conservative party by splitting the progressive vote. There are also those who believe that it is more effective to influence parties in power than to work outside the system.

Like the environmental movement in general, Green Party membership in the United States has been mostly white and middle-class, and in early days was dominated by men, but concerted efforts to address issues of environmental justice and to attract both women and people of color have had some success.

Environmental issues continue to be important to those who are Green Party members, but it would be a mistake to see the protection of the natural world as the primary focus of this movement. Social and economic justice has come to dominate the platforms of many Green Party members and their political candidates, while organizations focused on the protection of wilderness, energy conservation and so on, largely direct their lobbying efforts towards the major political parties. Internal debates continue over whether Greens should support capitalism or socialism, reform or revolution. But the argument of the Greens is that the destruction and degradation of the environment cannot be dealt with apart from other pressing human concerns, and that long-term problems require creative, integrated solutions.

Karen Christensen

See also Ecology, Deep; Environmental Justice; Environmental Politics; Germany

Further Reading

Feinstein, M. (1992). *Sixteen weeks with the European greens.* San Pedro, CA: Distributed by R & E Miles.

Gore, A., Jr. (1992). *Earth in the balance.* New York: Plume.

Parkin, S. (1989). *Green parties: An international guide.* London: Heretic Books.

Rensenbrink, J. (1999). *Against all odds, the green transformation of American politics.* Raymond, ME: Leopold Press.

Porritt, J. (1984), *Seeing Green.* Oxford, UK: Blackwell.

Spretnak, C., & Capra, F. (1986). *Green politics.* Santa Fe, NM: Bear & Co.

Tokar, B. (1987). *The green alternative: Creating an ecological future.* San Pedro, CA: R & E Miles.

Green Revolution

In the narrowest sense, the Green Revolution has been the adoption and spread of specific agricultural technologies that allow farmers to substantially increase food production per unit of land and per unit of labor. Successful implementation depends on a series of supporting institutional and infrastructural arrangements, however, and the Green Revolution in a larger sense includes a combination of these technologies and their supporting arrangements. Finally, the Green Revolution in the largest sense includes a general view of society as well. Although Green Revolution technologies have been adopted on large-scale corporate farms in developed countries, their primary purpose has been to serve the needs and interests of small-scale independent farmers in underdeveloped countries. In this sense, the Green Revolution was not only a technological or agricultural revolution but also a full-scale social revolution, a true democratic alternative to the centralizing "Red Revolution" promoted by the Soviet Union.

The Green Revolution has assured that for the present and the immediate future, total world food production will exceed world food needs. Many countries formerly facing famine are now self-sufficient. At the same time, however, it has permanently changed the way the world's farmers relate to their social and technological contexts.

Producing the Core Technology

The core of the Green Revolution is a series of cultivars (domesticated plant variety), mainly grain crops, called "high-yielding varieties" (HYVs). HYVs differ from normal crop varieties in that they will not maintain their desirable characteristics by normal on-farm reproduction. The seeds are created under highly controlled off-farm environments. Farmers then buy them and plant them for the usable crop. Farmers may be able to gather seeds from this crop and repeat the cycle a few times, but the quality of the crop declines, and after a few cycles it is necessary to return to the off-farm seed source. High-yielding varieties are capable of giving substantially higher yields of desired crop materials than conventional varieties because they are designed to be much more responsive to increased inputs than are conventional varieties. These inputs are primarily fertilizer and water but may include insecticides.

The development of HYV food crops began in Mexico in 1943, when the Rockefeller Foundation and the government of Mexico established a cooperative research program to improve the yields of wheat and maize. Mexico was an original center in which maize had been developed, but its yields in the 1940s were among the lowest in the world. Wheat was its second-most important food crop, but it was a net importer.

The first director of the Mexican research program was Dr. George Harrar, a plant pathologist from the University of Washington. In 1944 Dr. Norman Borlaug joined him. In 1961 Dr. Harrar became president of the Rockefeller Foundation itself. Their strategy was genetically based but holistic. Borlaug's aim was to produce the most "efficient" plan possible for the production of food. One important aspect of this concept of efficiency was the ability of the plant to respond positively to high doses of fertilizer.

The method was to view the Mexican crop populations genetically and think in terms of ways to alter the balance of genes for more desirable characteristics. To do this, the program built up an extensive "gene bank" from crop varieties around the world. For wheat, one of their most important achievements was to cross wheat from Japan with genes for short stature with Mexican and Colombian wheats to obtain the first dwarf HYV wheats, released in 1961. By 1965 these were the most important wheats in Mexico, giving yields up to 400 percent of those of 1950.

The second major aim of the program was to examine the growing conditions for the various genetic strains and make institutional and infrastructural rec-

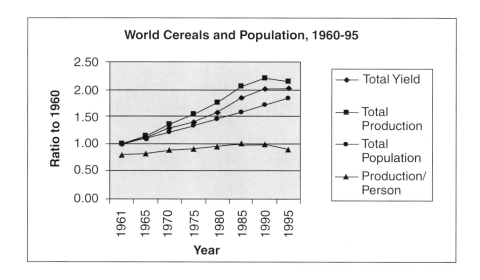

ommendations. HYV recommendations generally included provision for irrigation, improved credit, and agrochemicals.

The Mexican program succeeded. From 1945 to 1965 maize production increased fourfold, and wheat production increased sixfold. Cotton, another crop that the program focused on, increased from 107,500 metric tons to 605,000 metric tons and became Mexico's major export commodity.

The research strategy and methods of the Mexican program were replicated on an international scale in 1960 when the Rockefeller and Ford Foundations jointly established the International Rice Research Institute (IRRI) located next to the College of Agriculture of the University of the Philippines, near Manila. Dr. Robert Chandler, its first director, was responsible for its organization. This has become the pattern for a large and still-growing number of similar international institutions concerned with other crops.

The Rockefeller Foundation officially closed the original cooperative research program in Mexico in 1962, but at the request of the Mexican government the Rockefeller Foundation kept on certain of the senior scientists. In 1963 these scientists were brought under a new agreement, with limited support, under the name of the International Maize and Wheat Improvement Center (El Centro Internacional de Mejoramiento de Maíz y Trigo, or CIMMYT). In 1966 this agreement was succeeded by another agreement with the Mexican government that granted it "full international status" and expanded it into a full-scale international institute organized like IRRI, with greatly increased support from both the Rockefeller Foundation and the Ford Foundation. CIMMYT now has seventeen branches in other countries around the world. In 1967 the International Center for Tropical Agriculture (CIAT) was founded on the same pattern in Cali, Colombia, and the International Institute for Tropical Agriculture (IITA) in Nigeria.

Finally, in 1971 the Ford and Rockefeller Foundations, World Bank, Food and Agriculture Organization of the United Nations, U.N. Development Organization, and several governmental bodies agreed to establish what is now the capstone organization coordinating the funding for these and other Green Revolution research institutions: the Consultative Group on International Agricultural Research. This group brings together many additional private foundations as well as agriculture departments of sixty governments. It supports fourteen major research agencies dedicated to increasing food and other crop production around the world in addition to the four founding organizations. The Green Revolution is now formally institutionalized at the highest levels worldwide.

Adoption and Spread

Although the Mexican wheat and maize revolutions were well underway by 1950, the Green Revolution worldwide is generally considered to have occurred between about 1965 and 1978. Before the technologies could spread, national governments had to see the need and develop the means to adapt them to local conditions.

Before the end of World War II, agricultural policy in most of the world was an aspect of the trading and economic policies of colonial empires. The interests of the colonial empires were mainly focused on the crops they needed to import, and the agricultural development of their colonies was mainly focused on finding ways to get local farmers to produce those crops. Farmers who grew such crops were seen as "progressive" and favored by government action, whereas those who grew for their own and local consumption were seen as "traditional" and discouraged.

In the aftermath of World War II, the former colonies became independent nations. At the same time, however, world political debate and economic relations came to be dominated by the Cold War. The long colonial period had seen increasing economic disparities between the colonial empires and the colonized populations, and in addition many of the colonies were also theaters of combat. The consequence was that these newly independent nations faced enormous problems with little built-in capacity to deal with them and faced a sharply polarized outside world from which to seek help.

Western and communist authorities differed little in their development recommendations. Unlike the agricultural scientists quietly building the basis of the Green Revolution, Western "development economists" and communist ideologists alike saw the key to rising per-capita income only in industrialization, and they both argued for drawing resources out of agriculture—particularly "traditional" agriculture—in order to attain it. When these policies were implemented alongside policies to improve public health and sanitation, the effect was a rapid increase in population that was not accompanied by a corresponding increase in agricultural output. The result, in the late 1950s and early 1960s, was a crisis in food production. The greatest famine of the century occurred in China in 1959–

1961, although few in the outside world had more than a vague sense of it at the time. Estimates of direct and indirect mortality now run between 6 and 30 million people. The world did know that by 1965 there were serious food shortages around the developing world, including Indonesia, Egypt, Pakistan, India, and Korea. Had it not been for wheat sales from Argentina and Australia and subsidized imports from the United States financed through Public Law 480 (an act of Congress that allowed countries to buy U.S. commodities with their local currency rather than U.S. dollars), famine would have been widespread. In 1968 the trend and its probable consequences were summed up in Paul Ehrlich's much-cited book, *The Population Bomb*. It was at this point that governments recognized the need for radical improvements in agriculture and turned to the experience with HYVs to meet that need. The problem was how to do so. There were two main answers. One was to build a counterpart to the American Land Grant Universities, which were the ultimate source of most of the science and scientists that had created Green Revolution research institutions. The other was to create a partial substitute for such institutions by expanding the role of the agriculture departments that had generally been established in the colonial periods and by adding or strengthening their extension services.

In the mid–1960s the U.S. Agency for International Development, with the Ford Foundation, brought together a consortium of American universities to work out ways to transfer the land grant model to developing countries and set up initial programs in India, Pakistan, Bangladesh, and Nigeria. Almost simultaneously, the World Bank established a large-scale program to streamline and expand extension activities with the idea of "training and visitation" in these same countries and also in countries that did not adopt agricultural universities but rather stayed with tighter governmental control. Finally, most governments of underdeveloped countries loosened economic controls to allow more provision of the needed inputs and machinery through private business.

Results

Since 1960 HYV crops have been adopted in every major agricultural country, and world cereal production has outpaced population growth. However, even though this is unquestionably a result of the Green Revolution, it has not been a result solely of the use of HYVs. (See figure 1.) Figure 1 shows cereal production and yield in each year as a ratio to cereal production and yield in 1960 along with the absolute average production per person per day. The decline in per-person consumption after about 1990 probably does not indicate a reduction in total food but rather a shift in quality with more calories from noncereal sources.

Where HYVs were introduced without proper supporting inputs they commonly gave no increase at all. Where they were introduced with proper supporting inputs in a technical sense but not in a social sense, they substantially underperformed. A particularly well-analyzed example of the latter situation was the introduction of HYV rice on Bali in the early 1970s. The introduction was managed by the Indonesian central government in a way that disenfranchised traditional organizations for water management and undermined cooperative planning by farmers that had been associated with certain local "water temples"—farmers would get together at temples and agree on their water schedules. Government agricultural experts dictated the varieties to grow and the ways to grow them. This included the requirement that the farmers abandon their demand of allowing a contiguous block of about one-third of their total fields to lie fallow for one season to kill pests. The consequence was that even though yields went up, as J. Stephen Lansing describes it, "by the mid–1980s, Balinese farmers had become locked into a struggle to stay one step ahead of the next rice pest by planting the latest resistant variety of Green Revolution Rice. Despite the cash profits from the new rice, many farmers were pressing for a return to irrigation scheduling by the water temples to bring down the pest populations" (Lansing 1991, 115). Other serious problems concerned irrigation system maintenance and water sharing. Risk and farmer discontent were rising, and disaster appeared imminent. Control was returned to the temples a few years later, however, and in 1997 an Asian Development Bank reassessment concluded that pests were again under control (while retaining the HYV rice) and that the other problems should also be addressed through farmer involvement.

By contrast, where HYVs were introduced with responsive organizational support and where farmers retained organizational autonomy, higher yields from the HYV crops were often accompanied by similar increases in other crops. The Indian state of Punjab established a particularly effective agricultural university on the American Land Grant model to provide agricultural extension and research support to the farmers and to assist the state government in planning and policy formation. The state also initiated an excellent system of farmer-controlled credit cooperatives, but no one tried to control farmers' decisions on what to grow. The result was that while they adopted HYVs they also greatly intensified fodder production, and by 1988 the Green Revolution had been followed by a "White Revolution," with important nutritional and economic gains.

The contrast between cases like Bali and cases like Mexico and Punjab has moved development agencies worldwide to a greater appreciation of the need to respect local organizations and local knowledge. Before the Green Revolution, the idea that peasant farmers following traditional practices would be important partners in economic modernization was almost unthinkable. Now it is unthinkable to attempt it without them.

Present and Future

The developers of the Green Revolution technologies were limited by the requirement that the organisms in their gene pool had to be capable of interbreeding. Advances in molecular biology have led to the development of techniques for transferring specific genes from a medium into a living cell by means of bacterial and viral vectors and, most recently, by the use of a "gene gun," a device that shoots pellets coated with gene material into plant cells. Such methods have made it possible to insert into plant chromosomes genes from bacteria, insects, and animals, creating what are now called "genetically modified organisms" (GMOs). GMOs are now objects of substantial public anxiety, in part because of their inherent danger but also in part because the technology has come to be adopted and promoted by large agribusinesses in the context of secretive and sometimes threatening business practices. Although practices adverse to the public interest must be controlled, the technology cannot be rejected. The increased use of fertilizers, agrochemicals, and fuels required by the Green Revolution is adding substantially to world environmental pollution. GMO crops have already been developed to address this problem by requiring substantially less fertilizer and agrochemicals, and much more is possible. The aim of research in the institutions that grew up with the Green Revolution is no longer only increased yields but also increased yields and environmental sustainability. This aim will not be attained by setting aside the fundamental Green Revolution idea of meeting the needs of farmers and consumers with "effi-

cient" cultivars and responsible organizational support, but rather by applying it in new ways.

Murray J. Leaf

See also Agriculture; Cereals; Rice

Further Reading

Asian Development Bank. (1997). Reevaluation of the Bali Irrigation Sector Project (loan no. 522-INO) in Indonesia, December 1997. Retrieved June 1, 2002, from http://peo.asiandevbank.org/Documents/Reevaluation_Study/RE–27.doc

Chandler, R. F. (1982). An adventure in applied science: A history of the International Rice Research Institute. Retrieved May 30, 2002, from http://www.irri.org/ChandlerBook/Adventure.htm

Consultative Group on International Agricultural Research (CGIAR). (2002). Consultative Group on International Agricultural Research: Who we are. Retrieved June 1, 2002, from http://www.cgiar.org/who/wwa_ctrchronology.html

De la Riva, G., González-Cabrera, J., Vázquez Padrón, R., & Ayra Pardo, C. (1998). The *Agrobacterium tumefaciens* gene transfer to plant cell. *Electronic Journal of Biology, 1*(3), 1–14. Retrieved May 30, 2002, from http://www.ejb.org/content/vol1/issue3/abstract/1/

Lansing, J. S. (1991). *Priests and programmers: Technologies of power in the engineered landscape of Bali*. Princeton, NJ: Princeton University Press.

Leaf, M. J. (1998). *Pragmatism and development: The prospect for pluralist transformation in the Third World*. London: Bergin and Garvey.

Randhawa, M. S. (1980–1986). *A history of agriculture in India*. New Delhi, India: Indian Council of Agricultural Research.

Green Urbanism

People historically have perceived cities as destructive of nature, gray and natureless, and separate from natural systems. Green urbanism is a movement that rejects that perception and argues that cities can be environmentally beneficial and restorative, can be full of nature, and are inherently embedded in complex natural systems.

What, more precisely, does green urbanism do? Green urbanism encourages city building in harmony with nature. It minimizes the ecological footprint of population and development and seeks to live lightly on the planet, incorporating green and ecological features as central design elements and at the same time creating just and healthy places with a high quality of life. Cities incorporating green urbanism are called *ecological cities, green cities, sustainable cities*, or *sustainable communities*.

Green urbanism calls for readjusting the agenda of environmentalism to explicitly acknowledge the great environmental benefits of city life. The potential for sustainable living is great in cities, where land can be consumed sparingly, where less dependence on the automobile is possible, and where per-capita consumption of resources is low.

The design and planning of cities have tremendous implications for the global environment. Most energy is consumed within cities, and tremendous amounts of waste and pollution are produced there. London is estimated to consume 13 million metric tons of oil per year and to emit over 40 million metric tons of carbon dioxide. The ecological footprint of cities—the land area needed to support the population, lifestyles, and economic activities occurring within their boundaries—is large indeed. London's ecological footprint is estimated to be almost three hundred times the size of the city itself. As British cultural ecologist Herbert Girardet said, "The cities of the 21st Century are where human destiny will be played out, and where the future of the biosphere will be determined. There will be no sustainable world without sustainable cities" (Girardet 1999, 9).

Green urbanism argues that cities must be green both in the sense of making nature (trees, parks, green rooftops) present but also in a broader ecological or resource-conserving sense (using small amounts of energy, reducing emissions of carbon dioxide and toxic waste). The combining of the words *green* and *urban* also makes the statement that green design ideas and technology can be applied within cities. Ecological communities need not be in rural or remote places (and indeed should not be). Solar energy technology, organic food production, sustainable building design—these should be applied in cities.

Green urbanism envisions cities that function organically and embrace natural principles. Green architect William McDonough uses the metaphor of a tree to describe how ecological buildings should be designed and function. Green cities, by extension. should function as forests do—powered by the sun, recycling the Earth's nutrients and materials (there is nothing

wasted in nature), cleansing air and water, and restoring (not destroying) natural systems. Also, like forests, cities should provide beautiful shelter and habitat for humans and other species.

Although there is no consensus about what green urbanism entails or what a green city is, the following are consistently cited features.

Compact, Walkable Cities

Green urbanism seeks a compact, land-efficient urban form that is highly walkable and that mixes activities and uses to a large degree. A major goal of green urbanism is to overcome the wastefulness and environmental damage associated with urban sprawl. Compactness not only conserves precious land, but also makes possible many of the other technologies and living strategies, such as public transit and district heating (the distribution of steam or hot water to multiple buildings from one outside source), that allow cities to be more sustainable. Creating compact, walkable cities is also increasingly a matter of public health. In the United States, for instance, sedentary car-dependent lifestyles and sprawling land-use patterns have become a major health threat because walking and daily exercise are difficult (60 percent of Americans are considered to be overweight, and the rate of adult onset diabetes has risen dramatically in recent years).

Green, Organic Urban Environments

Green urbanism seeks to bring nature into cities and to restore, nurture, and celebrate urban ecology. Important green urbanism strategies include creating parks, forests, and green spaces throughout a city (and region). Significant greening can also occur at the level of the neighborhood, the block, and the individual building. A green urban neighborhood includes such elements as trees, community gardens, restored streams, and buildings with rooftop gardens, vegetated walls and facades, and other natural features. Green elements are an effective way of addressing a host of urban problems. Green rooftops, for instance, reduce energy consumption in cities, provide species habitat, sequester carbon, and control urban storm water runoff.

Circular Metabolism

Ecological cities recognize a complex flow of inputs (food, energy) and outputs (waste, pollution) associated with urban life. The city of Sydney, Australia, for example, requires 14 million metric tons of oil, coal, and gas, 3.6 million metric tons of food, and about 4 million metric tons of timber. Ecological cities aim for a balanced system of eco-cycles, or a circular metabolism, in which the flow of inputs and outputs is minimized and the outputs (wastes) become productive inputs to something else. In some green cities, such as Stockholm, biogas from wastewater is recovered and used as a fuel in the city's combined heat and power plants. In the Swedish city of Uppsala, forty municipal buses run on biogas extracted from organic household wastes.

Self-Sufficient

Few cities can be truly self-sufficient, but an important goal of a green city is to locally produce as many of its necessities as possible. Food can be grown locally, and energy can be produced locally as well. Consumption is kept close to production, minimizing the environmental costs of transporting and transmitting and encouraging more responsible, less environmentally damaging forms of production. Green design and building result in offices and homes that use small amounts of energy, are constructed with local materials, and are harmoniously sited to respect the local landscape and ecology.

Sustainable Mobility

Green cities put priority on less environmentally damaging forms of mobility—using public transit, bicycling, and walking. Land use and development decisions in green cities are coordinated with transit investments so that new residents have viable, affordable alternatives to the automobile. Green cities are bicycle-friendly, incorporating bicycles into the design of new housing areas, for instance, and generally working to make it easier and safer to ride a bicycle (e.g., bicycle lanes, bikeways, protected bicycle parking facilities). Green cities encourage walking by creating pedestrian-only areas, mixing land uses, calming traffic, and emphasizing proximity over mobility. The ecological benefits are clear: Public transit consumes, on a per-passenger-mile basis, much less energy and generates much less pollution than do automobiles. A trend in European green cities is the design and construction of car-free (or car-limited) housing districts where new residents are prohibited or economically discouraged from owning a car. Green cities seek to adjust subsidies and incentives to level the economic playing field between auto and nonauto transport (e.g., reducing costs of public transit while increasing charges for car parking).

Ecological Economies

Green cities also support more ecologically restorative forms of industry and commerce. This can take many forms but includes locally owned and managed green businesses, industry and commerce that are resource efficient and that minimize waste and pollution (e.g., by using the wastes from one industry as productive inputs for another), and industry and commerce that utilize sustainably harvested and managed resources and substitute local imports for imports (e.g., food, material, and energy) from far away. Green cities use a variety of sustainable economic development strategies, including eco-industrial parks (communities of businesses, located together on a common property, that collaborate in managing environmental and resource issues), micro-credit programs (in which people are granted small, collateral-free loans for use in income-generating activities), and programs to provide technical support for and public recognition of green businesses (e.g., the Businesses for a Sustainable Tomorrow program of Portland, Oregon).

Ecological Governance

Green urbanism calls for new ways of managing cities. The condition of urban ecosystems and the environmental impacts of decisions made by city governments become primary considerations in local decision making. Green cities take stock of their local environment and of the impacts of local actions on the global environment through a variety of tools, including state-of-environment reports, sustainability indicators, and ecological accounts. Ecological governance implies consideration of the local and global impacts on the environment of every decision, the democratic involvement of citizens and neighborhoods in decision making and governance, and an active program for educating the public about environmental issues. Although many green urban decisions are best made at the local level, green urbanism recognizes the need for governance structures at higher levels, especially at the regional level.

Challenges and Obstacles

Green urbanism faces many challenges and obstacles. Many of the technologies applied in green cities, from

621

rooftop photovoltaic systems to public transit to eco-industrial parks, can be costly in the short term and require significant public investments. Because conventional fossil-fuel and pollution-generating alternatives need not take account of their full environmental and social costs (e.g., global climate change, health costs), their price in the marketplace is unfairly low. The long-term public health, ecological, and social benefits of green urbanism techniques and technologies, moreover, are often difficult to assess and are undercounted. Many unsustainable urban development practices, such as road building and car use, have strong political constituencies and are highly subsidized (leveling the economic and political playing field is a major goal). Lack of public concern about environmental issues and a difficulty in seeing connections between local actions and global problems also are obstacles. Some elements of green urbanism also raise cultural and lifestyle questions: Are people willing, for instance, to give up or significantly reduce their dependence on automobiles and to live more compactly and more densely? Nevertheless, the potential of green urbanism is great and the impediments surmountable. Cities by necessity will remain one of the most promising areas for global sustainability.

Timothy Beatley

Further Reading

Beatley, T. (2000). *Green urbanism: Learning from European cities*. Washington, DC: Island Press.

Best Foot Forward. (2002). *City limits: A resource flow and ecological footprint analysis of greater London*. London: Best Foot Forward.

Girardet, H. (1992). *The Gaia atlas of cities*. London: Gaia Books.

Girardet, H. (1999). *Creating sustainable cities*. Devon, UK: Green Book.

Gordon, D. (Ed.). (1996). *Green cities: Ecologically sound approaches to urban space*. London: Black Rose Books.

Hough, M. (1984). *City form and natural process*. London: Croom Helm.

Newman, P. (1996). Greening the city: The ecological and human dimensions of the city can be part of town planning. *Alternatives, 22*(2), 10–17.

Newman, P., & Kenworthy, J. (1999). *Sustainability and cities: Overcoming automobile dependence*. Washington, DC: Island Press.

Platt, R. (Ed.). (1994). *The ecological city*. Amherst: University of Massachusetts Press.

Register, R. R. (2002). *Ecocities: Building cities in balance with nature*. Berkeley, CA: Berkeley Hills Books.

Roseland, M. (Ed.). (1997). *Eco-city dimensions: Healthy communities, healthy planet*. Gabriola Island, Canada: New Society Publishers.

Wilson, A., Uncapher, J. L., McManigal, L., Lovins, L. H., Cureton, M., & Browning, W. D. (1998). *Green development: Integrating ecology and real estate*. New York: John Wiley and Sons.

Greenbelt Movement

A greenbelt is an area of open and low-density land use surrounding settlements where urbanization is controlled. The concept has been used since the late nineteenth century, although the use of the term has been expanded to incorporate linear open spaces, including greenways and parkways.

The greenbelt movement originated in the garden city movement of the nineteenth century. English reformer Ebenezer Howard's garden city schemes in the United Kingdom incorporated an encircling greenbelt as protection against unconstrained urban expansion, as a source of agriculture and recreation, and as a rural counterbalance to urban living. Influenced by his American experiences, particularly in Chicago (then known as the Garden City) after the fire of 1871 and in landscape architect Frederick Law Olmsted's garden suburb of Riverside, Illinois, Howard returned to Britain with a planning vision that combined elements of Fabian (an intellectual and middle-class social democratic movement that originated in United Kingdom) socialism with a rejection of the worst elements of industrialization.

In 1892 Howard published *To-morrow: A Peaceful Path to Real Reform*, reissued in 1902 as *Garden Cities of To-morrow*. The book had enormous international impact. In Britain the first garden cities and greenbelts were developed by Raymond Unwin and Barry Parker at Letchworth and Welwyn Garden City in Hertfordshire. Land acquisition costs prohibited further British garden city development until the 1947 Town and Country Planning Act. The high point for the British greenbelt movement was architect Patrick Abercrombie's 1944 Greater London Plan, which advocated "a gigantic Green Belt about built-up London" that stressed outdoor recreational access with "lesser girdles for the separate communities, old and new" (Abercrombie 1945, 11).

In America the greenbelt movement found its greatest advocates in the Regional Planning Association of America (RPAA), founded in 1923. The RPAA adopted a fivefold program that included the creation of garden cities, development of relationships with British planners, community planning, development of the Appalachian Trail, and surveying of the Tennessee River basin. Under President Franklin Roosevelt's New Deal a greenbelt-towns program was developed by Rexford Tugwell's Resettlement Administration (1935–1938). Tugwell hoped for three thousand greenbelt-towns. However, of the initial list of twenty-five, the program was given funds to start only eight; Congress cut this to five, of which two were blocked by legal action. The eventual program consisted of the towns of Greenbelt, Maryland; Greenhills, Ohio; and Greendale, Wisconsin.

Tugwell was attacked in Congress as socialistic, and in 1938 the supervisory oversight of the greenbelt-towns were transferred to the Federal Republic Housing Agency. In quantitative terms the impact of the American greenbelt movement of the 1930s was minimal, but its legacy is substantial. In the short term the American initiative influenced the 1947 British Planning Act, which provided for compulsory purchase of land and government control over development. The British greenbelt model for London was later applied to other British cities and also adopted internationally. Just as importantly, the American greenbelt movement, influenced by diplomat and scholar George Perkins Marsh and writer Henry David Thoreau, also integrated ecological ideas into a planning movement previously more concerned with aesthetic, social, and recreational issues. Although many greenbelt areas have been lost due to urban infill, advocates for the development and retention of urban parkland, parkways, and greenways are the movement's intellectual heirs not only in terms of the desire for green space but also in the belief that such space is central to the idea of community.

C. Michael Hall

Further Reading

Abercrombie, P. (1945). *Greater London plan 1944*. London: Her Majesty's Stationery Office.

Dal Co, F. (1979). From parks to the region: Progressive ideology and the reform of the American city. In G. Ciucci, Dal Co, F., Manieri-Elia, M., & Tafuri, M. (Eds.), *The American city: From the Civil War to the New Deal* (pp. 143–291). Cambridge, MA: MIT Press.

Hall, P. (1988). *Cities of tomorrow: An intellectual history of urban planning and design in the twentieth century*. Oxford, UK: Blackwell.

Howard, E. (1898). *To-morrow: A peaceful path to real reform*. London: Swan Sonnenschein.

Munton, R. J. C. (1983). *London's green belt: Containment in practice*. London: Allen & Unwin.

Greenhouse Effect *See* Climate, Global Warming

Greenpeace

The international nonprofit organization Greenpeace promotes environmental protection and peace through nuclear disarmament. Founded in 1971 by a group of peace activists in Vancouver, Canada, Greenpeace organized its first protests to stop U.S. underground nuclear weapons tests and to alert the public to the associated environmental and human health threats. A crew of twelve sailed the eighty-foot fishing vessel *Phyllis Cormack* into the U.S. nuclear test zone in Alaska's Aleutian Islands to prevent a nuclear test dubbed "Cannikin." This confrontation between the purveyors of war and advocates of peace proved advantageous not only for inspiring widespread opposition to nuclear testing, but also for putting an end to nuclear testing in the Aleutians in 1972.

Bearing Witness and Taking Direct Action

Greenpeace's organizational mission encompasses bearing witness and taking nonviolent direct action to prevent gross assaults on the Earth. As a form of passive resistance, bearing witness "involves going to the scene of an objectionable activity and registering opposition to it simply by one's presence there" (Brown & May 1989, 8). The political power of putting this Quaker philosophy into practice became increasingly apparent in 1972 and 1973 when Greenpeace sailed its ship, *Vega*, into the South Pacific to prevent French nuclear weapons tests on the island of Moruroa. The French government postponed both tests until it could remove the protesters from the area. During the second protest, however, damning newspaper photographs and stories documenting the violence used by the government against the protesters further garnered public support and escalated the global antinuclear movement.

As Greenpeace expanded its protests beyond nuclear testing to other targets wreaking havoc on the environment, it broadened its notion of bearing witness to encompass taking nonviolent direct action. Nonviolent direct action goes beyond simply observing or witnessing to include taking steps to prevent an environmentally harmful act from occurring, even if just for a short while. During nonviolent direct actions, Greenpeace activists have stopped environmentally damaging activities by positioning their bodies between harpoons and whales, men with clubs and baby harp seals, and dumpers of nuclear waste barrels and the sea. These direct actions focus attention on previously hidden environmental assaults. They inspire public outrage and social action and often result in the withdrawal of destructive practices. As Greenpeace's direct actions are shown on televisions around the world, millions join in bearing witness and in holding the responsible parties liable for their actions.

In the early 1980s, Greenpeace extended its reach beyond the sea to encompass land-based sources of environmental problems. As Greenpeace's campaigns succeeded and whaling and sealing began to subside, the organization shifted its focus from saving charismatic mega-fauna to protesting environmentally destructive mega-projects such as the deforestation of ancient forests and the production of non-renewable, oil-based energy. Today, Greenpeace confronts environmental problems that affect the everyday lives of people and the places where they live, such as the genetic engineering of food and toxic chemical production and pollution. Having broadened its scope, Greenpeace still campaigns to "save the whales" and to protect the world's oceans.

Cultivating Change

Before resorting to direct action, Greenpeace critically investigates a source of environmental degradation and analyzes the extent of damage done to the environment and its human and nonhuman inhabitants. Greenpeace pressures the responsible parties to alter their practices and proposes practical steps for achieving positive, long-lasting change. At the grassroots level Greenpeace works with communities, schools, and civic organizations to raise environmental consciousness and to forge new generations of activists.

Greenpeace draws upon this network to pressure governments to adopt and strengthen environmental laws at the national, regional, and global levels. Thus when Greenpeace participates in political meetings of environmental importance, friendly and unfriendly governments alike feel pressured to take note because many of their constituents support the positions of Greenpeace on a range of issues.

Greenpeace seeks to transform dominant ideologies and worldviews that support the overexploitation and degradation of the environment in the name of development, economic growth, or food production. In particular, Greenpeace aims to change the ways in which people view their place in the environment and their role in its decline and protection. This goal is explicit in membership newsletters and magazines, college outreach programs, fund-raising efforts, corporate and scientific investigative reports, and public information bus and boat tours.

Accomplishments

Noteworthy Greenpeace accomplishments include securing a ban on hazardous waste trade from highly industrialized nations to less-industrialized ones; scuttling oil industry plans to bury the Brent Spar oil rig off the British coast; achieving a moratorium on the planting of genetically engineered crops in Europe; and eliminating toxic (polyvinyl chloride) plastic in baby toys manufactured by a leading toy company. At the political level Greenpeace has helped persuade national governments to adopt international agreements that curtail environmentally destructive practices worldwide. These agreements include one to establish Antarctica as a world park, a global ban on the burning of toxic waste at sea, and a global moratorium on nuclear waste dumping at sea and commercial whaling.

Based in Amsterdam, Netherlands, Greenpeace has built an international network of paid staff and volunteers located in thirty-five offices around the world. Its activists spearhead six major campaigns to (1) stop global warming, (2) save ancient forests, (3) eliminate toxic chemical production and pollution, (4) halt the genetic engineering of food, (5) achieve a nuclear-free future, and (6) protect the world's oceans. Greenpeace owns five ships, including the legendary *Rainbow Warrior II*, which replaced the original *Rainbow Warrior* after the French government bombed and sank the vessel in 1985 to prevent environmental investigations of its nuclear tests in the South Pacific. Greenpeace staffs its ships with trained activists prepared to document environmental abuses and to take direct actions to prevent such activities on land and at sea. Its high-tech communication systems allow the organization to visually document environmentally harmful behavior and transmit photographs and video images for the world to witness.

Two and one-half million members worldwide donate the majority of funds used to support Greenpeace's campaigns. These agreements include one to establish Antarctica as a natural reserve; the adoption of the Comprehensive Nuclear Test Ban Treaty; a moratorium on whaling; and a global ban on the burning of toxic waste at sea, ocean dumping of radioactive waste, and the use of large-scale driftnets in the high seas.

Role in the Environmental Movement

Greenpeace has earned a unique role in the international environmental movement due to its willingness to take direct action and its refusal to compromise on issues of critical environmental import. Greenpeace works on issues of global importance; yet, unlike more mainstream nature and wildlife conservation groups, it uses confrontational tactics to change corporate and government behavior. Greenpeace is not a local membership group, although its toxics, energy, and genetic engineering campaigns increasingly work at the grassroots level to enhance environmental activism in communities worldwide. Although Greenpeace is a self-proclaimed direct action group, its commitment to non-violence precludes the use of property damaging tactics such as those employed by decentralized and anarchistic direct action groups. Greenpeace does not participate in party politics or support political candidates; however, it does lobby governments and holds them accountable for failing to adopt stringent laws to safeguard human health and the environment.

Criticism of Greenpeace

Greenpeace has at times been criticized for pursuing an environmental issue at the expense of legitimate social or economic concerns. For example, in the mid 1980s, Greenpeace was criticized for advocating the "zero kill" of baby harp seals in Newfoundland, Canada, because the organization failed to consider the effects it would have on the indigenous people. Seal hunting not only provides a subsistence livelihood for many Newfoundlanders and Eskimos but the practice also holds important cultural meaning for hunters.

After this issue was brought to Greenpeace's attention, the organization modified its position to oppose large-scale government subsidized hunts, and to support subsistence hunts which have helped people meet their clothing and food needs for centuries.

In 1984, Greenpeace was criticized by New Jersey's Oil, Chemical, and Atomic Workers Union (OCAW) for failing to consider the economic and job loss implications of their campaign against the discharge of toxic waste into the Atlantic Ocean from Ciba Geigy's chemical plant. Although Greenpeace had networked with local environmental groups, it failed to contact the union even despite objections from some Greenpeace campaigners. The snub backfired as potential allies turned into enemies and the union launched a state-wide smear campaign against Greenpeace. It took several years of working with unions during subsequent campaigns against polluting chemical companies before Greenpeace gained the union's trust, respect, and, at times, assistance.

Connecting Social and Environmental Consequences

Greenpeace illuminates the connections between the social and environmental consequences of global industrial and agricultural production. For example, during protests against Dutch Royal Shell's oil drilling operations in Ogoniland, Nigeria, Greenpeace witnessed the company's pipelines leaking and parching the Earth in local communities. When the Nigerian government hanged nine local activists in 1995 for demanding that Dutch Royal Shell clean up its operations, Greenpeace denounced both the human and environmental abuses suffered by the Ogoni people. Similarly, in Bhopal, India, Greenpeace has participated in protests against Union Carbide (now Dow) for its failure to compensate the more than 150,000 people still suffering ill effects from the gas leak at its pesticide plant in 1984. Greenpeace has joined local groups in their demand for health care, compensation, and environmental reparations.

In 2002, when the U.S. government responded to the hunger epidemic in Zambia by offering genetically engineered (GE) corn against the will of the people, Greenpeace publicly demanded that the United States instead donate some of its vast supply of non-GE-engineered food stocks.

In the future Greenpeace will be increasingly challenged to address social issues within the context of its environmental work. Terrorist attacks such as the one that devastated New York City's World Trade Center in 2001 and the subsequent reinvigoration of armed forces around the world heighten this challenge as Greenpeace seeks to define a "green" peace within a politically sensitive climate. Thus one of the greatest challenges for Greenpeace remains how to situate its campaigns within broad global, economic, and geopolitical frameworks without losing sight of its environmental mission.

Lisa J. Bunin

Further Reading

Boettger, C., & Hamdan, F. (2001). *Greenpeace, changing the world: Die Fotodokumentation*. (The Photographic Record). Steinfurt, Germany: Edition Rasch & Röhring.

Brown, M., & May, J. (1989). *The Greenpeace story: The inside story of the world's most dynamic environmental pressure group*. London: Dorling Kindersley.

Bunin, L. J. (1997, Summer). Reconceptualizing radical environmentalism: Greenpeace's campaign against the burning of toxic waste at sea. *New Political Science, 40*, 75–88.

Dale, S. (1996). *McLuhan's children, the Greenpeace message and the media*. Toronto, Canada: Between the Lines.

Epstein, B. (1991). *Political protest and cultural revolution: Nonviolent direct action in the 1970s and 1980s*. Berkeley and Los Angeles: University of California Press.

Hunter, R. (1979). *Warriors of the rainbow, a chronicle of the Greenpeace movement*. New York: Holt, Rinehart and Winston.

King, M. (1986). *Death of the Rainbow Warrior*. New York: Penguin.

McTaggart, D. (1978). *Greenpeace III, journey into the bomb*. London: William Collins Sons.

Sachs, A. (1996, May–June). Dying for oil. *World Watch*, 10–21.

Shears, R., & Gidley, I. (1986). *The Rainbow Warrior affair*. London: Unwin.

Taylor, B. R. (1995). *Ecological resistance movements: The global emergence of radical and popular environmentalism*. Albany: State University of New York Press.

Grinnell, George Bird

(1849–1938)

U.S. conservationist

Over the course of George Bird Grinnell's long life, he developed a close association with many of the places and personalities that shaped the American conservation movement and became a popular authority on western landscapes and American Indians. Born a child of wealth and privilege in Brooklyn, New York, Grinnell benefited from unique opportunities in his youth that would shape his lifelong interests. As a boy he attended school at John James Audubon's mansion estate on the Hudson River in Upper Manhattan, New York, where he enjoyed free access to the entire grounds, including the barn that housed Audubon's huge collections of bird specimens. Grinnell later attended Yale University, where he pursued a course of study in the natural sciences. Upon graduation in 1870 he joined a fossil-collecting expedition to the American West that would cement his interest in the region for the rest of his life. Four years later Grinnell served as the naturalist on Colonel George Armstrong Custer's expedition to the Black Hills, and in 1875 he served as geologist and zoologist on a military expedition to the newly established Yellowstone National Park.

Despite his early connection to such famous people and places, Grinnell would become even better known for his efforts protect wildlife and conserve public lands. In 1886 he established the first Audubon Society. Later that same year he joined with future U.S. President Theodore Roosevelt to create the Boone and Crockett Club, an elite organization dedicated to hunting and conservation. Grinnell used his position as editor of *Forest and Stream*, which he held from 1876 to 1911, to rail against poor management of Yellowstone National Park, advocate the creation of Glacier National Park, and galvanize support for game laws and habitat conservation.

Grinnell's influence on the conservation movement is perhaps best measured by his impact on Theodore Roosevelt. An avid reader of *Forest and Stream*, Roosevelt launched his career as a conservationist by joining Grinnell's battle for Yellowstone. Grinnell also directly influenced the career of Edward S. Curtis, the famous photographer of American Indian subjects. The older Grinnell served as a mentor to Curtis and others on the 1899 Harriman expedition to Alaska, which also included such notable conservationists as John Muir, John Burroughs, and C. Hart Merriam.

By the early twentieth century Grinnell had become a widely respected commentator on a variety of issues, whose opinions frequently influenced national policy. He was most successful in his advocacy of wilderness preservation and Indian policy reform, yet his efforts in these areas were not without controversy. For example, he championed the removal of native peoples from

George Bird Grinnell on His Research with the Pawnee in the 1870s

The task that I have set for myself is that of a recorder. No attempt has been made to give a literary color to the hero stories and folk-tales here written out. I have scrupulously avoided putting into them anything of my own. The stories are told to the reader as they were told to me. They are not elaborated. I have tried to show how Indians think and speak, rather than to make their stories more entertaining by dressing them up to suit the civilized taste. My object in giving these narratives in their present shape is to make a book which shall be true to life, and shall faithfully reflect the Pawnee character, as the story tellers have themselves painted it. In a very few cases I have added some words explaining matters so well understood by those familiar with the Indians as to need no explanation. If these tales have any ethnological value, it will be enhanced by their being given in the precise form in which they were told by those to whom they have been handed down from generation to generation; but quite apart from this is another point which is entitled to consideration.

The entire ignorance concerning Indians, which prevails among the general public, can be dispelled only by letting that public understand something of the ways of life of the wild Indian, something of the subjects about which he thinks and talks, as well as of how he looks at these subjects, and what he has to say about them.

Source: Grinnell, George Bird. (1889). *Pawnee Hero Stories and Folk-Tales, with Notes on the Origin, Customs and Character of the Pawnee People*. New York: Forest and Stream Publishing Company, pp. xi–xii.

Yellowstone and Glacier National Parks. Likewise, his support for establishing forest reserves in the Adirondacks of New York often came at the expense of rural working-class communities, who lost their rights to hunt, fish, and gather timber in the mountains. Despite this mixed legacy, which tended to characterize many conservationist efforts, Grinnell's actions were largely selfless and public spirited, and continue to shape the American landscape in important and lasting ways.

Mark Spence

Further Reading

Grinnell, G. B. (1913). *Beyond the old frontier: Adventures of Indian-fighters, hunters, and fur-traders*. New York: Charles Scribner's Sons.

Parsons, C. (1993). *George Bird Grinnell: A biographical sketch*. Millbrook, NY: Grinnell and Lawson Publishing.

Reiger, J. F. (Ed.). (1972). *The passing of the great West: Selected papers of George Bird Grinnell*. New York: Winchester Press.

Roosevelt, T., & Grinnell, G. B. (Eds.). (1895). *Hunting in many lands: The book of the Boone and Crockett Club*. New York: Forest and Stream Co.

Spence, M. D. (1999). *Dispossessing the wilderness: Indian removal and the making of the national parks*. New York: Oxford University Press.

Guano

Guano is a natural fertilizer extracted from the accumulated feces of seabirds or bats. Seabird guano was first used as a fertilizer by pre-Inca civilizations of coastal Peru, such as the Mochica (500 BCE). The Inca empire continued to use guano for the cultivation of tubers and regulated its production and distribution. In Quechua, the language of the Inca empire, *wanu* means "bird manure." Although Spanish observers commented on the properties of guano and Andean farmers continued to use it to fertilize their fields throughout the colonial period, Europeans ignored guano's properties until the 1800s, when Peruvian guano triggered an agricultural revolution that preceded the Industrial Revolution. The Peruvian government nationalized its guano reserves in 1842 and embarked on what historians have called "the guano age" for the following forty years.

The fertilizing qualities of Peruvian guano are due to environmental factors. The best-quality guano was gathered in the Chincha Islands off the Peruvian coast. In this area the Humboldt sea current carries large amounts of plankton that feed huge shoals of fish that, in turn, sustain colonies of birds such as cormorants, pelicans, and gannets that nest in these and other barren islands off the South American Pacific coast. The meeting of the cold Humboldt current and warm, dry air prevents rainfall, creating the deserts of coastal Peru. The general atmospheric dryness and lack of rain prevent the evaporation of nitrates, phosphates, and ammonia from bird droppings. At the outset of the guano boom, some islands had accumulated, over thousands of years, deposits that were 30 or 45 meters deep.

Peru's guano monopoly through British merchants ensured a steady flow of cash to the Peruvian government but also led to international conflicts. Other countries, such as Bolivia and Ecuador, started to extract guano from their coasts, even though it was considered of lower quality. In 1842 the Chilean Congress claimed many guano-producing areas of its neighbor Bolivia, and in 1865 Spain occupied the Chincha Islands to exact reparations from the Peruvian government. Chile's interest in guano eventually led to the War of the Pacific (1879–1883), which ended with Bolivia's cession of its coastline to Chile and with Chile's occupation of Peru for three years. In response to the British monopoly on guano, the U.S. Congress proclaimed the Guano Act of 1856, which enabled the United States to claim any guano-producing areas if exploited by U.S. citizens. Under the authority of this act the United States acquired scores of islands in the Pacific (such as Howland, Baker, and Jarvis Islands) and in the Caribbean (such as Navassa, Petrel, and the Serranilla keys).

The large profits from guano and the nature of its extraction led to the widespread use of coercive labor practices. As early as 1842 Bolivia used convicts to work on its guano islands, and Peru complemented convicts with army deserters, indentured Chinese laborers, kidnapped Pacific islanders, and a few black slaves. Similar labor practices were practiced elsewhere: U.S. guano operations in the Pacific also employed Pacific islanders, and in the Caribbean they relied on black West Indians or on the poor black populations of the mainland. The extraction of guano was particularly harsh, with long hours and poor working conditions, and laborers were exposed to many accidents and diseases. The dust and ammonia-laden vapors that guano produced led to respiratory, skin, and gastrointestinal ailments.

Although the discovery of alternative guano sources, the depletion of Peruvian guano deposits, and the havoc of the War of the Pacific were instrumental in ending Peru's "guano age," the growth of manufactured fertilizers and superphosphates dealt it its final blow. By the beginning of the twentieth century Peru was producing minimal amounts of guano for the export market, and after that it served just its domestic market. Although the Peruvian government legislated protection of the guano islands' environment and tried to stimulate the use of guano by Peruvian farmers, guano never recovered its status as Peru's main source of revenue.

The growth of organic agriculture in the late twentieth century revived interest in guano. Bat guano and bird guano are marketed in relatively large quantities to organic farmers and gardeners. The potential of Peruvian guano as an alternative fertilizer, though, has been jeopardized by environmental factors. The warming of the Humboldt current and overfishing have reduced the once-immense shoals of fish, and, consequently, the bird populations of the Peruvian coast have been vastly reduced. This has been compounded by El Niño (an irregularly occurring flow of unusually warm surface water along the western coast of South America), which has destroyed many of the nesting areas of Peruvian birds and has disrupted weather patterns in the area. Ironically, in an era that has started to value the virtues of organic farming, one of the potential sources of organic fertilizers has been drastically reduced by environmental and human influences.

Frederic Vallvé

Further Reading

Bonilla, H. (1974). *Guano y burguesía en el Perú* [Guano and bourgeoisie in Peru]. Lima, Peru: Instituto de Estudios Peruanos.
Gootenberg, P. (1989). *Between silver and guano: Commercial*

policy and the state in postindependence Peru. Princeton, NJ: Princeton University Press.

Gootenberg, P. (1993). *Imagining development: Economic ideas in Peru's "fictitious prosperity" of guano, 1840–1880.* Berkeley and Los Angeles: University of California Press.

Hunt, S. J. (1985). Growth and guano in nineteenth-century Peru. In R. Cortés Conde & S. J. Hunt (Eds.), *The Latin American economies.* New York: Holmes and Meyer.

Mathew, V. W. (1981). *The house of Gibbs and the Peruvian guano monopoly.* London: Royal Historical Society.

Querejazu Calvo, R. (1979). *Guano, salitre, sangre, historia de la Guerra del Pacífico* [Guano, saltpetre and blood; History of the Pacific War]. La Paz, Bolivia: Los Amigos del Libro.

Scaggs, J. M. (1994). *The great guano rush: Entrepreneurs and American overseas expansion.* New York: St. Martin's Press.

Haber, Fritz

(1868–1934)
German chemist

Fritz Haber is remembered for two very different reasons: as the inventor of synthesis of ammonia from its elements, and as the mastermind of German gas warfare during World War I. The first achievement was perhaps the most important technical invention of the twentieth century, as the availability of nitrogenous fertilizers removed the key barrier to increased crop yields. About 40 percent of the world's population now derive their dietary protein via plants, from applications of synthetic nitrogenous fertilizers. In contrast, gas warfare raises many troubling issues regarding the modern scientific-military complex and ethical obligations of scientific research.

Haber was born on 9 December 1868 in Breslau in Prussia (today's Wroclaw in Poland), the only son of a non-observant, affluent Jewish family. After studying organic chemistry in Berlin and Heidelberg he got his doctorate in 1891. His first university appointment was in Jena where he converted to Protestantism in 1892. In 1894 he became an assistant at the Technische Hochschule in Karslruhe where he stayed for seventeen years, becoming a pofessor of physical chemistry and electrochemistry in 1906. In 1901 Haber married Clara Immerwahr (1870–1915), the first woman to receive a chemistry doctorate at Breslau University. Their only child, Hermann, was born in 1902. Haber's experiments with ammonia synthesis began in 1904 and soon afterwards he began cooperating with the BASF, at that time Germany's and the world's leading chemical company, to develop a commercial version of the process. Many of Haber's predecessors and contemporaries tried to synthesize ammonia from its elements, as this technique would have eliminated the limits imposed on the availability of agricultural nitrogen by organic recycling and allow for worldwide increase in crop yields. Haber was ably aided by his English assistant Robert Le Rossignol, and they finally accomplished the deceptively simple reaction ($N_2 + 3H_2 \longrightarrow 2NH_3$) by combining the gases at high temperature (> 500 °C) and high pressure (> 10 Mpa [Megapascals]) in the presence of catalysts (first osmium, then uranium) and by recirculating the unreacted gases to increase the final yield.

Successful demonstration of this process took place in Karslruhe on July 3, 1909. BASF immediately took over the challenging task of scaling the bench experiment to industrial level and thanks to the leadership and ingenuity of Carl Bosch it succeeded in producing the first commercial ammonia in 1913. This output was soon diverted to wartime production of explosives, and worldwide advances in nitrogen fertilizer use were slow until after World War II. Subsequent expansion brought the global output of nitrogenous fertilizers from just 5 million tons N in 1950 to more than 80 million tons by 2000. These compounds became an indispensable factor in the success of Green Revolution that boosted the yields of staple cereals and allowed sustained increases of grain harvests from a diminishing area.

Soon after his successful demonstration, Haber left Karlsruhe to become the director of the newly established Institute for Physical Chemistry and Electrochemistry in Berlin, and in 1914 he took over the development of Germany's gas warfare. The first chlorine attack at Ypres in April 1915 killed 5,000 French soldiers and on its eve Clara Haber committed suicide. Haber continued his military work, convinced that using the gas would lead to a decisive victory that would end the suffering of the trench warfare. Germany's defeat led to his chronic depression, which was not lifted either by a new marriage or a Nobel Prize in Chemistry awarded to him in 1919 for the synthesis of ammonia. After the Nazi rise to power in 1933 he lost the directorship of his beloved institute and died a broken man in January 1934.

Vaclav Smil

Further Reading

Haber, F. (1927). *Aus Leben und Beruf.* [From lives and occupation] Berlin: Julius Springer.

Smil, V. (2001). *Enriching the earth: Fritz Haber, Carl Bosch, and the transformation of world food production.* Cambridge, MA: The MIT Press.

Stoltzenberg, D. (1994). *Fritz Haber: Chemiker, Nobelpreistrdäger, Deutscher, Jude* [Fritz Haber: Chemist, Nobel Prize winner, German, Jew]. Weinheim, Germany: VCH.

Szöllösi-Janze, M. (1998). *Fritz Haber 1868–1934: Eine Biographie* [Fritz Haber 1868–1934: A biography]. München, Germany: Verlag C. H. Beck.

Hamilton, Alice

(1869–1970)
U.S. doctor and reformer

Alice Hamilton was a pioneering figure in the study of industrial diseases and in social and industrial reform. Born in New York City, Hamilton grew up in Fort Wayne, Indiana, the second of four daughters (she also had one much older brother). Raised in comfortable circumstances, she was first educated by her parents, but attended Miss Porter's School in Connecticut from 1886 to 1888.

Obliged to earn her own living after the wholesale grocery business in which her father was a partner failed in 1885, she chose to study medicine, believing it to be an occupation where she could make a difference. She spent several years at the Fort Wayne College of Medicine before transferring to the medical department of the University of Michigan, from which she received her M.D. in 1893. She then interned at hospitals in Minneapolis and Boston and briefly worked in a bacteriology laboratory. Following studies abroad at Leipzig and Munich universities from 1895 to 1896, she completed a final year of postgraduate study at Johns Hopkins University in Baltimore. She was appointed professor of pathology at Northwestern University's Women's Medical School in Evanston, Illinois in 1897. She simultaneously began a long association as resident, teacher, and physician at Hull House in Chicago. The Women's Medical School closed in 1902, but Hamilton remained in Chicago, where her Hull House experience introduced her to the study of industrial diseases.

Appointed to the first state occupational disease commission by Illinois governor Charles Deneen in 1908, she led an expanded study of the subject two years later. She became known as an authority on industrial health and occupational medicine. These were her professional concerns for the rest of her career. As a special investigator for the Federal Bureau (later Department) of Labor from 1911 to 1920, she emerged as the preeminent American authority on lead poisoning in the workplace, particularly as it affected poor and underprivileged women. In 1915, Hamilton and her friend and colleague Jane Addams attended the Second International Women's Congress at The Hague in the Netherlands, and later visited several European nations, advocating a women's peace proposal. Her visit to war-ravaged Belgium, then controlled by the German Army, converted her into a confirmed pacifist.

Hamilton was appointed the first woman faculty member at Harvard in 1919, where, despite discrimination because of her sex, she served as assistant professor of industrial medicine at the Harvard Medical School until forced to retire for age in 1935. She insisted on a half-time schedule so as to be able to continue her field research and other activities, but actively raised money for her department. Her *Industrial Poisons in the United States*, the first such textbook to be published in this country, appeared in 1925, and the first edition of her *Industrial Toxicology* was released in 1934. In 1924, Hamilton was appointed the first woman member of the Health Committee of the League of Nations, serving until 1930.

Her professional interests were international in scope and wide-ranging. They included family planning and public health, including challenges of poverty, malnutrition, and poor medical care. She was also active in seeking treatments for many epidemic and endemic diseases. Initially opposed to an equal rights amendment to the U.S. Constitution—on grounds that it would work against workplace safety for women—she changed her stance in 1952. From 1912 until the 1940s, Hamilton published a number of papers on industrial health and women's health issues, many of which appeared as Bulletins of the U.S. Department of Labor. In the late 1930s, Hamilton served that agency as a consultant to the Division of Labor Standards. Her last field study in 1937–1938 exposed toxic conditions in the viscose rayon industry. Long before the federal government regulated health conditions in the workplace, Hamilton did pioneering research in this field and demonstrated the need for vigorous federal intervention. She made lasting contributions in the areas of occupational medicine and a wide range of health and humanitarian initiatives.

Keir B. Sterling

Further Reading

Grant, M. P. (1967). *Alice Hamilton: Pioneer doctor in industrial medicine.* London and New York: Abelard Schuman.

Haller, R.M. (1997). Alice Hamilton (1869–1970). In Grinstein, L.S., Bierman, C.A., & Rose, K. (Eds.). *Women in the biological sciences: A biobibliographical sourcebook.* Westport, CT: Greenwood Press.

Hamilton, A. (1943). *Exploring the dangerous trades: The autobiography of Alice Hamilton, M.D.* Boston: Little Brown.

Hamilton, A. Papers, 1909–1965 (correspondence, articles, speeches, notes, clippings and awards). Schlesinger Library, Harvard University, Cambridge MA.

Sicherman, B. (1984). *Alice Hamilton: A life in letters.* Cambridge, MA: Harvard University Press.

Hardin, Garrett

(b. 1915)
U.S. ecologist

Ecologist Garrett Hardin was born in Dallas, Texas. He is known for his controversial work on population control, carrying capacity (the population that an area will support without undergoing deterioration), resource limits, ecological systems, and human values. He received his undergraduate degree at the University of Chicago and completed his doctorate at Stanford University in 1941. He then joined the Department of Biological Sciences and Environmental Studies at the University of California at Santa Barbara, where he taught from 1946 to 1978. Although he was initially interested in plant biology, Hardin soon became fascinated with genetics, evolution, and population growth. In his acclaimed book, *Nature and Man's Fate* (1959), Hardin argued that mass disease, starvation, and social disorder will result unless human population growth is curbed.

Although Hardin achieved recognition for his research on these issues, his major contribution to public policy, economics, and ecology came with the publication of his 1968 *Science* essay, "The Tragedy of the Commons." This revolutionary essay linked the problems of overpopulation and resource degradation in traditional social systems. Hardin drew a bleak picture of how people, when attempting to maximize their benefits from a shared resource, often exceed the carrying capacities of basic ecological systems. His essay portrayed a pasture open to all herders and their cattle. It is only rational for each herder, Hardin argued, to keep as many cattle as possible on the commons, even though each herder knows that additional stocking will erode the soil and plants.

The idea of the commons works if human and animal populations are kept in check by tribal wars, poaching, and disease, which keep the numbers below the land's carrying capacity. But after societies stabilize, the logic of the commons creates problems. The positive utility to the individual herder of adding an extra animal had been +1 (the herder received all the proceeds from the sale of the additional animal), and the negative utility had been less than −1 (the effects of overgrazing were shared by all herders). But when resources become scarce, the rational, benefit-maximizing action of each herder threatens the viability of the group. Hardin argued in "The Tragedy of the Commons" that

> [T]he rational herdsman concludes that the only sensible course for him to pursue is to add another animal to his herd. And another; and another . . . But this is the conclusion reached by each and every rational herdsman sharing a commons. Therein lies the tragedy. Each man is locked into a system that compels him to increase his herd without limit—in a world that is limited. Ruin is the destination toward which all men rush, each pursuing his own best interest in a society that believes in the freedom of the commons. Freedom in a commons brings ruin to all. (Hardin 1968, 1244)

> The exquisite sight, sound, and smell of wilderness is many times more powerful if it is earned through physical achievement, if it comes at the end of a long and fatiguing trip for which vigorous good health is necessary. Practically speaking, this means that no one should be able to enter a wilderness by mechanical means.
>
> Garrett Hardin, *The Ecologist*, February 1974.

Hardin's insight into the destruction caused by a common resource system has many applications for the ways societies think about animal hunting, land rights, marine resources, and energy use—any system with finite resources. Hardin applied his work to his campaign for legalized abortion during the 1960s and to his work with the Environmental Fund in the 1980s.

Jessica B. Teisch

Further Reading

Hardin, G. (1959). *Nature and man's fate.* New York: Rinehart.

Hardin, G. (1968). The tragedy of the commons. *Science, 162,* 1243–1248.

Hardin, G. (1972). *Exploring new ethics for survival: The voyage of the spaceship Beagle.* New York: Viking Press.

Hardin, G. (1999). *The ostrich factor: Our population myopia.* New York: Oxford University Press.

McCay, B. J., & Acheson, J. M. (Eds.). (1987). *The question of the commons: The culture and ecology of communal resources.* Tucson: University of Arizona Press.

Soden, D. L. (1988). *The tragedy of the commons: Twenty years of policy literature, 1968–1998.* Monticello, IL: Vance Bibliographies.

Heavy Metals

Heavy metals are those elements that have metallic properties and a relative density greater than 4.5 grams per cubic centimeter. Copper, cadmium, lead, selenium, arsenic, zinc, nickel, mercury, and chromium are all heavy metals. They occur in nature in different forms, being present in rocks, soil, and living organisms; some (such as selenium, copper, and zinc) are micronutrients necessary for plant and animal survival. The production and consumption of heavy metals has acquired a strategic importance in contemporary industrial societies, but their high toxicity makes them extremely dangerous for human health and the environment. Because they are not chemically or biologically degradable, heavy metals that are released into the environment can remain in the ecosystem for hundreds of years. They also enter the food chain with great ease and bioaccumlate, becoming increasingly concentrated (and hence dangerous) as one moves up the food chain. Humans, located at the end of many food chains, are thus exposed to high concentrations of toxic metals. Environmental and work-related illnesses, diverse types of cancer, renal pathologies, anemia, difficulties and delays in growth, and cardiovascular and neurological problems are just some of the possible consequences of exposure to heavy metals.

The cycles and the sources of emission of heavy metals to the atmosphere can be both natural and human-generated processes. The most frequent natural processes are geologic and volcanic phenomena. Those of human origin are almost always associated with mining activity, metallurgy, the chemical industry, combustion of fossil fuels, and disposal of urban and industrial waste. In general, in remote and inhabited regions, processes of natural character prevail, while in urban and industrial spaces, human processes are dominant. Once emitted, certain heavy metals can move easily through the air, water, and soil, affecting areas and ecosystems very distant from the point at which the heavy metals were initially generated.

Preindustrial Societies

Although serious environmental pollution caused by the emission of heavy metals is eminently a contemporary phenomenon, the problem has in fact existed as long as there has been mining and metallurgy. The seven basic metals of antiquity are gold, silver, iron, mercury, tin copper and lead; of those, three (copper, lead, and mercury) are heavy metals. The primitive techniques employed to obtain them caused important and unavoidable trace-metal emissions to the atmosphere.

Copper is one of the few metals that can be found in its metallic form in the nature, so it was one of the first metals recognized and used by humans (c. 4200 BCE). Its properties and characteristics (malleability, ductility, and resistance to corrosion) made it suitable for utilitarian purposes, as a substitute for stone, wood, or bone for weapons, tools, and domestic utensils.

Lead, which did not come into use until somewhat later (c. 3500 BCE), doesn't exist in a metallic state in nature, but mineral compounds containing lead as the main mineral (for example, galena, or lead sulphide) are abundant. Indeed, most silver mines are in fact galena mines, and the metallurgy of lead and silver have always been closely related. The low melting point of lead (328° C), the ease with which can be worked, and its resistance to corrosion made it especially suitable for diverse domestic uses and for water pipes. Even in ancient days, some Greek and Roman authors associated the expansion of its use with possible harmful effects on health.

As for mercury, also known from antiquity (c. 1750 BCE), it too was identified early on as a poisonous substance. Generally extracted from cinnabar (monosulfide of mercury) by distillation, it was used in Greek and Roman times for gilding and was likely used by the Egyptians in religious ceremonies. (It has been found in Egyptian tombs dating from approximately 1500 BCE). From an industrial point of view, the importance of mercury lies in its abilty to form alloys (amalgamate) with other metals.

The last of the heavy metals known prior to the industrial revolution is arsenic. Widely distributed in Earth's crust, usually in association with other metals, is highly toxic and carcinogenic, although, administered in small doses, it has been used to combat certain illnesses (for example, syphilis). It was identified as an element in the seventeenth century, but compunds of arsenic were known as early as the fourth century BCE and used in early copper smelting techniques. The Egyptians used arsenic-copper ores, natural alloys that improved the mechanical properties of copper artifacts.

Although it is difficult to track the evolution of heavy-metal pollution before the industrial revolution, it has been possible to obtain highly significant data by analyzing records coming from diverse types of natural deposits, especially bogs, aquatic sediments, and polar ice caps. In fact, this type of study has made it possible to reconstruct an accurate picture of paleo-pollution from ancient to contemporary times, with fluctuations also noted. The available data show an increase in the emission of traces metals, especially copper and lead, in the Northern Hemisphere during the Roman empire (500 BCE–300 CE). From the eleventh century, there is evidence of increased mining and metallurgic activities in Central Europe that intensified again in the sixteenth century. On the American continent, the introduction in the sixteenth century of the patio system (involving an amalgam of mercury) for the production of silver caused a spectacular increase in mercury contamination.

Industrialization and Heavy-Metal Pollution

Increased metal consumption is considered one of the best indicators of material progress. Since the industrial revolution, the production of heavy metals has increased exponentially, which has caused a constant increase in human-caused emissions of toxic metals into the atmosphere. The relative weight of the different sources of emission has varied, depending on the industrial intensity and technological trajectory. Mining, the metal industry (especially nonferrous metals), and certain branches of the chemical industry continue to be the main contemporary human sources of heavy-metal emissions.

A large portion of heavy-metal pollution comes not from production, however, but from domestic and industrial waste, especially into aquatic environments (rivers, lakes, and oceans). Incineration of urban and industrial residuals, used in numerous countries as an alternative to letting waste accumulate in dumps, is one of the main sources of dioxins and toxin heavy-metals emission. The combustion of fossil fuels (especially coal, oil, and wood) to produces electricity and heat is also a major cause of contamination. Coal burning, a major source of energy of the early industrial revolution and the most affordable for developing countries, is the major source of mercury, arsenic, chromium, and selenium pollution, while oil is the most important source of nickel and vanadium pollution

If we consider in an individualized way the problem of the main polluting metals, lead is probably the worst offender. Lead is used in the production of other commodities and also in storage batteries, additives for gasoline, pigments and paints, electric-cable coverings, glassmaking, ammunitions, roofing, and in linings for water pipes and systems for the processing and transport of corrosive chemicals. Air emissions (primarily sulfur oxides and paticulates, including lead oxides, arsenic, and other metallic compounds), and solid and liquid wastes (containing antimony, arsenic, copper, tin, and other elements depending on inputs), are the polluting substances linked to lead production. Although lead used in metallic form is easily recovered as scrap and reused for new applications, when it is in chemical compounds, it generally dissipates into the atmosphere and is not recoverable. Chemical compounds containing lead are found in certain insecticides, paint pigments, and leaded gasoline, products whose toxicity has created serious air pollution problems.

At the present time mercury is used primarily for different electrical applications, such as electrolytic processes to obtain chlorine and caustic soda, and to remove impurities from other metals, as well as in wiring devices and switches, fluorescent lamps, batteries, and measuring and control instruments. In addition to the pollution associated with the production of these devices, products containing mercury pose a hazard when they are disposed of, whether they are deposited in dumps or incinerated: the mercury ends up either in the soil or groundwater, or in the atmosphere. When mercury makes its way into aquatic ecosystems, its toxicity is increased by microbial activity, which converts it into methyl mercury, a highly toxic organic form of mercury. In these cases, bioaccumulation in the food chain can cause serious health problems, such as the famous case in Minamata, Japan, in which the ingestion of fish contaminated by effluent from Nippon Chyisso Hiryo Company (a chemical company), gave rise in 1956 to a toxic syndrome known as the Minamata disease. Mercury-contaminated water also affects the quality and fertility of soil, reducing its yield and damaging agriculture and livestock.

Copper consumption has gone down in recent decades as other materials are used in its place (aluminum for wiring, fiber-optic cables in long-distance communications, and plastics for plumbing, for example), but it continues to be in wide demand, both as a primary product and as a compound with other metals. Copper is now frequently used in electrical and electronic products; machinery and equipment; transportation, chemical, and medical processes; fungicides; wood preservatives; and pigments. Air emissions (sulfur dioxide and particulates containing copper and iron oxides, sulfates, and sulfuric acid) from the smelting process and wastewater produced in electrolytic refining procedures are the main pollution problems in the copper industry.

Zinc is the fourth most widely used metal after iron, aluminum, and copper; it is one of the most important industrial metals. It is predominatly used as an input in the production of other commodities. It is used to galvanize other metals (galvanization helps metals resist corrosion), in die casting for the automotive and construction industry, in the electrical and machinery industries, in alloys with copper (primarily to produce brass), and in chemical compounds, pharmaceuticals, and paints. Sphalerite (zinc sulfide) is the most common mineral used in zinc production, and sulfur dioxide, a by-product of the roasting process, is the biggest pollutant in the industry. The slags from zinc production also contain copper, aluminum, iron, and lead.

Arsenic is a natural element of the Earth's crust but is an environmental pollutant, especially when it enters acquifers and water supplies. The contamination can be caused either by natural deposits in the Earth or by human agency. Tin and copper mining and smelting, coal burning, and pesticides used in agriculture are the main human sources of arsenic pollution.

Nickel, although used from the antiquity in alloys with copper in the coinage of currencies, was not identified as a metal until 1751. At the moment it continues to be used as an alloying metal in the manufacture of stainless steel and other ferrous and nonferrous alloys, increasing hardness and resistance to heat and corrosion. Other heavy metals, including chromium, cadmium, and selenium, were not discovered until recently, and their industrial use has been developed

TABLE 1.
WORLD PRODUCTION OF HEAVY METALS (AVERAGE OF THE PERIODS, IN METRIC TONS)

	Chromium	Lead	Zinc	Copper	Cadmium	Arsenic
1900–1919	42,915	1,040,600	730,650	878,900	59	12,152
1920–1939	162,585	1,303,278	1,058,650	1,457,500	1,738	41,070
1940–1959	797,450	1,781,333	1,967,500	2,581,000	6,473	37,090
1960–1979	1,866,000	3,093,500	4,630,000	5,692,000	14,965	35,105
1980–1999	6,355,898	3,210,526	7,012,632	9,200,500	19,235	35,685

Source: U.S. Geological Survey. (2002). *Historical statistcs for mineral commodities in the United States: Open-file report 01-006.*

mainly during the twentieth century. Their environmental and health impacts are very different. For example, while chromium does not bioaccumulate in the food chain, cadmium is an extremely toxic metal, and selenium, although toxic above certain levels, is an essential trace mineral in the human body.

Trends

After a long period of intense and continuous increase in human sources of heavy metals, the last decades of the twentieth century demonstrated a significant new trend. The economic crisis of the seventies, the technological change and the application of more rigorous environmental policies, especially in the developed countries, have led to a desire to reduce the emissions of heavy metals. (See tables 1 and 2.) Although economic growth continues to be linked to the production and consumption of heavy metals, their emissions, especially in developed countries, are now controlled, thanks to the significant improvement in pollution control technologies and to strict public regulation and legislation. The emissions of heavy metals per unit of heavy metal processed is generally decreasing. To some degree, however, the regulation and control measures adopted in the developed countries has merely meant that polluting activities have been displaced to less restrictive and generally poorer countries. Keeping in mind that contamination can exist thousands of kilometers away from the source of pollution, it will serve the world well to adopt the most comprehensive possible international agreements and programs to control emissions.

R. Uriarte Ayo

See also Air Pollution; Copper; Mining; Water Pollution

Further Reading

Darling, A. S. (1990). Non-Ferrous Metals. In I. McNeil (Ed.), *An encyclopaedia of the history of technology* (pp. 47–145), London & New York: Routledge.

Duchin, F., & Lange, G-M. (1994). *The future of the environment: Ecological economics and technological change*, New York: Oxford University Press.

EMEP. (2001). *Anthropogenic emissions of heavy metals in the ECE region.* Retrieved December 20, 2002, from http://www.emep.int/emis_tables/tab9.html

Newell, E. (1997). Atmospheric pollution and the British copper industry, 1690–1920. *Technology and Culture, 38*(3), 655–689.

Nriagu, J. O. (1996, April 12). A history of global metal pollution. *Science, 272,* 223–224.

Smith, D. A. (1987). *Mining America: The industry and the environment, 1800–1980.* Lawrence: University Press of Kansas.

Tylecote, R. F. (1988). *A history of metallurgy.* London: Mid-County Press.

U.S. Geological Survey. (2002). *Historical statistcs for mineral commodities in the United States: Open-file report 01–006.* Retrieved January 24, 2002, from http://minerals.usgs.gov/minerals/pubs/of01–006

Herring Gull

The herring gull *(Larus argentatus),* is a large seabird of the family *Laridae* (gulls). As adults herring gulls have a white head and body, pale gray back and wings, and black wingtips. Juvenile herring gulls change from a completely grayish brown first-year plumage

TABLE 2.
ANTHROPOGENIC EMISSIONS OF HEAVY METALS ON THE EUROPEAN CONTINENT (IN METRIC TONS PER YEAR)

	Lead	Cadmium	Mercury	Arsenic	Chromium	Copper	Nickel	Selenium	Zinc
1991	2,581.00	20.82	30.62	90.86	141.80	123.30	442.40	130.60	981.90
1992	2,356.00	20.41	28.53	90.02	139.30	117.20	444.90	125.60	991.70
1993	2,121.00	19.93	22.31	86.43	130.40	110.70	432.60	11.50	988.20
1994	1,869.00	19.15	21.77	80.03	123.90	105.10	397.20	100.30	986.00
1995	1,555.00	12,33	17.27	69.54	107.30	89.13	329.30	83.47	911.20
1996	1,321.00	10.39	13.17	64.45	97.19	80.00	294.70	78.02	800.80
1997	1,170.00	8.75	11.16	56.79	86.55	65.21	219.00	63.21	731.30
1998	906.00	7.06	10.69	50.71	82.00	63.14	193.50	61.23	655.50
1999	552.70	6.47	8.53	46.79	66.73	59.06	147.30	44.22	442.00

Source: EMEP. (2001). *Anthropogenic emissions of heavy metals in the ECE region.*

through a series of plumages before achieving the adult plumage at four years of age. Herring gulls inhabit shorelines and coastal waters of large bodies of water, including oceans, seas, lakes, and large rivers. Their breeding range is circumboreal (throughout the temperate to cool areas of the Northern Hemisphere), including much of Central Asia. It may be the most common and familiar gull of northeastern North America and Western Europe. In North America, it breeds along the Atlantic Coast from Cape Hatteras, North Carolina, north to Baffin Island in northern Canada and Davis Strait between Baffin Island and Greenland, and throughout Arctic Canada into Alaska. In winter, herring gulls may be found throughout their breeding range and south into tropical waters, primarily along coastlines in California and the Gulf of Mexico.

This species has been divided into at least nine subspecies, of which only one, *L. a. smithsonianus*, breeds in North America. Several Asiatic and European subspecies have recently been accorded tentative species status. Herring gulls form hybrids in zones of sympatry (overlapping ranges) with several other large white-headed gulls, including the glaucous-winged gull and the lesser black-backed gull, and the possibility exists that new species have arisen through hybridization in this group in Asia.

The behavior and ecology of this species are very well studied, especially in Europe, Canada, and New England. Herring gulls form male-female pairs that can last for the lifetime of the individuals, which can exceed twenty years. Male gulls establish breeding territories that they share with their mates and upon which they raise their offspring. Their primary nesting habitat requirement appears to be a site that is near a body of water and safe from terrestrial predation; examples include islands, offshore rocks, abandoned piers, and so forth. Gulls have a wide variety of vocalizations that function to warn other herring gulls of dangers and as communication between neighbors, members of a pair, and parents and offspring. The herring gull typically lays three eggs in May; the offspring achieve independence by mid to late July, although parents may care for them for up to six months after fledging.

Herring gulls are opportunistic feeders that take a wide range of food types, including fish, marine invertebrates, small mammals, seabirds and eggs, and human refuse. Most birds feed primarily on natural prey, and successful breeding is related to taking of natural prey in most areas. Studies from both Europe and North America indicate that gulls show individual foraging specialization, and that diet choice influences breeding performance. Birds that feed primarily on human refuse have low breeding success, primarily because eggs do not hatch.

Herring gulls were driven to near extinction by plumage hunters and eggers in North America during the nineteenth century. Populations have recovered as a result of protection under the Migratory Bird Act. By the 1960s population sizes may have exceeded historical numbers, possibly because of feeding on fisheries waste and increased overwinter survival from feeding on human refuse. Numbers in New England stabilized during the 1970s. In recent years the species has expanded its range south into Maryland, Virginia and North Carolina, but herring gulls have also been largely displaced from some breeding habitats in New England by great black-backed gulls *(L. marinus)*.

Raymond Pierotti

Further Reading

Hunt, G. L. (1972). Influence of food distribution and human disturbance on the reproductive success of herring gulls. *Ecology, 53,* 1051–1061.

Kadlec, J. A., & Drury, W. H. (1968). Structure of the New England herring gull population. *Ecology, 49,* 222–233.

Pierotti, R. (1982). Habitat selection and its effect on reproductive output in the herring gull in Newfoundland. *Ecology, 63,* 854–868.

Pierotti, R. (1987). Behavioral consequences of habitat selection in the Herring gull. *Studies in Avian Biology, 10,* 119–128.

Pierotti, R., & Annett, C. A. (1991). Diet choice in the herring gull: Constraints imposed by reproductive and ecological factors. *Ecology, 72*(1), 319–328.

Pierotti, R., & Good, T. P. (1994). Herring gull (*Larus argentatus*). In A. Pool & G. Gill (Eds.), *The Birds of North America*. Philadelphia, PA: Philadelphia Academy of Natural Sciences; American Ornithologist's Union.

Tinbergen, N. (1960). *The herring gull's world* (2nd ed.). New York: Basic Books.

Himalayas

Himalaya means "realm of snow." The Himalayas are a vast bow of mountains reaching from the Indian state of Arunachel Pradesh, north of Burma, to Kashmir. The total length of the system is about 2,500 kilometers, the width about 250 kilometers.

Orogeny and Topography

The Himalayas arise from a collision between two continental plates. The South Asian plate, coming from the south, is driving under and lifting the Asian plate. This in turn scrapes and folds the South Asian plate surface to form the mountains. Reflecting this orogeny, the Himalayan topography from the Indo-Gangetic plain to the highlands of Tibet falls into three main bands: the foothill formations, the lesser Himalayas, and the Great Himalaya. The main foothill formations are the Siwaliks and the Terai. The Siwaliks are low hills with semiarid brush. The Terai is a zone of rough and often swampy land generally in front of the Siwaliks. The Terai is generally densely forested and was considered uncultivable until it was opened up in Uttar Pradesh and Nepal the 1950s.

Behind the foothill formations, the first ranges of the lesser Himalayas rise abruptly to 2,100 to 2,400 meters. The peaks of the spine of the Great Himalaya rise to more than 8,000 meters. After this, except in Kashmir, the elevation drops steeply to the Tibetan plateau at about 4,000 meters. In Kashmir, the Great Himalayan ranges are backed by more high valleys and a still higher range, the Karakoram. The general parallelism is interrupted by ridges that extend out laterally from the main spine and rivers that break through to the South Asian plains.

The system is divided lengthwise into the Western, Central, and Eastern Himalayas. The Western Himalayas drain into the Indus and the Central Himalayas into the Ganges. The Eastern Himalayas, beginning at about the Kali Gandaki River in central Nepal, hold many of the highest peaks in the chain, receive the greatest rainfall and snowfall, hold the largest glaciers, and on their lower elevations, are covered by the greatest extent of dense subtropical forest.

Ecologies

The topography shapes the human ecologies by shaping the human physical environment, and also through its global and local effects on the weather. Globally, interaction between the westerly jet stream and the Himalayan heights is a main cause of the monsoon pattern of climate itself. Locally, given this pattern, the mountains steer and direct its rains. The Eastern Himalayas, facing the Bay of Bengal, receive up to 11 meters

a year in the mountains, with generally over 1.25 meters on the plains below them. From here the water-bearing winds follow the mountains inland, falling most heavily on the southern slopes and in, in a narrowing plume, on the plains immediately in front of them.

The human response to the weather and topography has been to make virtually every valley the home of a relatively autonomous and self-sustaining community with a distinctive cultural character, always pluralistic but varying from a dominantly Indic style overall on the Indian side of the range to a Tibetan style on the Tibetan side. Historic political divisions follow cultural divisions.

Culture and Cultural Ecology

The self-sustaining character of local Himalayan communities reflects certain widespread adaptive strategies. As one proceeds upward in elevation from foothill formations to the highest valleys, the climate runs from tropical lowland to arctic desert, but the basic system of agriculture and allied occupations is the same throughout. At the base, the main contrast with the plains is that the fields are always terraced and irrigated, usually by diversion from small streams. There are two cropping seasons. In most places the historic summer crop has been rice, along with sugar cane, millet, pulses, and vegetables. Since the land around a mountain village is never wholly cultivable, cropping is supplemented by grazing and gathering. The winter crop is most often rice again in the southern parts of the range, or wheat in the north, again with vegetables and pulses. Important fruit trees are mango and banana.

At higher elevations the terraces and irrigation remain the same but the crops change. At about 2,600 meters, the summer becomes too cold and rice is replaced by wheat. At elevations where the winter involves freezes, mangoes and bananas are replaced by fruit trees with a chilling requirement. Other crops depend on the growing season. Still higher, above 3,000 meters, the crops may be only barley, millet, and peas in summer accompanied by fruit trees, particularly apricot. There are also local specialties. Willow and poplar are major tree crops in the vale of Kashmir (2,400 meters), used for making cricket bats. Deodar cedar is cut commercially in the Western and Central Himalayas, and deciduous hardwoods in the more humid eastern Himalayas. Fishing is important in the rivers and lakes.

Throughout the western and central sections, agriculture is complemented by transhumant herding by specialized nomadic groups. Some herd goats and sheep, others herd goats and buffaloes. Others, at the highest elevations, herd mainly yaks. Distinctive Himalayan animals include the goats that produce extraordinarily fine wool and cows and buffaloes that stand barely waist high to a man.

In the Eastern Himalayas heavy forests preclude transhumance. Social organization and social identification is often tribal and forest-based subsistence systems still include swidden agriculture.

Poverty and Development

Himalayan adaptations provide sustainable subsistence under difficult conditions, but very little cash. Wages in the region are low and there is little opportunity to break out of traditional occupations. The main development efforts have focused on industrialization, lumbering, agriculture and tourism. Benefits have accrued mainly to the governments and well-funded businessmen from outside the area. Costs have been increasing pollution and marked decreases of forest, resulting in increased runoff, siltation of rivers, and probably landslides. The main causes lie in the highly centralized and remote administrative structures of the Indian and Nepalese central governments and the lack of effective enforcement of the environmental protection laws. The main exception has been in the Indian state of Himachal Pradesh, which has made the state a major producer of temperate fruits and other cold-adapted crops. The new Indian state of Arunachel Pradesh, broken off from the much larger plains-based state of Uttar Pradesh, promises to follow Himachal's example.

The idea that successful development must incorporate local knowledge and be adapted to local institutions is now well established in programs focused on intensive agriculture elsewhere in South Asia, but in the Himalayan region it is mainly confined to the Himachal Pradesh agricultural programs and a few new programs in "community forestry. "

Murray J. Leaf

Further Reading

Johnson, B. L. C. (1971). *South Asia: Selective studies of the essential geography of India, Pakistan, and Ceylon.* London: Heinemann Educational Books.

Kohli, M. S., and Bali, Yogendra (Eds.). (2000). *Himalayas: ecology and environment studies.* New Delhi, India: Har-Anand Publications.

Warikoo, K. (Ed.). (1995). *Society and culture in the Himalayas.* New Delhi, India: Har-Anand Publications.

Hinduism

In ancient Indian literature, the word Hindu appears nowhere. When people from Persia, Arabia, and Europe crossed over the river Sindhu (in English, Indus) in the northwestern part of the Indian subcontinent, they found a vast area of rich cultures and religions, but there was no one name to describe them. Even the lands and kingdoms themselves were known by hundreds of different names. There was neither one god, nor one book that could be used to categorize the population of that area religiously. So, for the sake of convenience, it is believed that the newcomers from the West described them as "the people east of Indus," which later became shortened to Indoos and then Hindus. Now, for ease of categorization, everyone has accepted the label.

Surrounded by the snow-covered high mountains of the Himalayas to the north, the Indian Ocean to the east and south, and the Arabian Sea to the west, the land of the Hindus was well protected from outside invasion. In such relative peace and tranquillity, with land blessed by fertile soil and exuberant natural beauty, it was possible to develop an organic, inclusive, and tolerant religion. In forest hermitages Hindu scholars and sages meditated on the meaning of life and developed a nature-centered spirituality. The religion that developed out of this meditation and exploration became known as Hinduism. Hinduism stresses the interconnectedness of all life and therefore in theory (if not always in practice) is well suited to nurturing modern environmental concerns. Hindu scholars and philosophers emphasize that life is a cyclical rather than a linear process; forms are transformed and souls are reincarnated. Since we return to life again and again, it is our responsibility to keep and maintain our planet in good order. Thus, the ancient Hindu thought of reincarnation and contemporary concerns for the environment go hand in hand.

Sacred Texts

Historians have not been able to determine the exact beginnings of Hinduism, since there is no founder, no prophet and no book. The earliest Hindu texts are the four Vedas, composed in Sanskrit to be remembered and chanted. They are presumed to be around 5,000 years old. These poems and hymns are written in praise and adoration of nature as manifested in the forms of earth, air, fire, water, and space. The Vedas proclaim the divinity of the natural world and pay homage to the elements with devotion.

The forest philosophers moved on to explore a more mystical dimension of the divine, probing the soul in every being as well as ultimate cosmic divinity. These same sages and philosophers concluded that the divine was present in everything, in the entire phenomenal world. One and all are the embodiment of the sacred; even a blade of grass or a piece of rock is alive and to be revered. These explorations on the sacred nature of existence are brought together in the hundreds of texts that make up the Upanishads (c. 500 BCE). They are made up of dialogues between teachers and students. The famous book *Bhagavad Gita* ("The Song of the Lord"), which is part of the epic *Mahabharata* (c. 500 BCE–400 CE), is also considered to be an Upanishad. The *Bhagavad Gita* is both a religious text and great literature; it is considered the most beautiful poem ever written in the Sanskrit language. It is studied and commented upon by vast numbers of Hindus around the world. In form, the *Bhagavad Gita* is a poetic conversation between the enlightened charioteer (Lord Krishna, a manifestation of the god Vishnu) and the despondent warrior Arjuna, who, faced with the unpleasant task of fighting a battle, wonders whether to act or not to act. In order to resolve Arjuna's doubts, Krishna expounds the philosophy rooted in reverence for all life, which is at the heart of the Hindu religion. He tells Arjuna to act, but to act without selfish motives—neither give up action nor forsake the world, but only forsake worldly desires. The action that emerges from a pure heart that is free of cravings for selfish gains is the source of liberation. The faithful surrender their ego to God, becoming his devotee; they trust the sacred laws of the universe and do whatever comes to them naturally out of compassion for all beings. By so doing, there are no negative consequences (karma) from their actions.

The Caste System

The social structure of the Hindus is organized around the caste system, whose negative side is all too apparent nowadays, but which in ancient days, in the absence of a welfare state, fulfilled the social requirements of security, training and employment.

Society was divided into four divisions called Varnas, within which were hundreds of castes and subcastes. The Brahmans were the religious teachers, Sanskrit scholars, and keepers of philosophical texts such as Vedas and Upanishads. The Brahmans performed rituals, organized ceremonies, managed festivals, recited epic stories, and gave spiritual guidance to those in need. Next came the Kshatriyas. They were the rulers, the administrators, the warriors, and the defenders. They also owned the land, managed the animals, and maintained order. Third were the Vaisyas, who were merchants, traders, and managers of business. They kept shops, provided provisions, and ensured that everyone in the community had equal access to basic necessities of life. Fourth were the Sudras. The Sudras were the workers, the craftspeople who built the houses, made the shoes, wove the cloth, tilled the land, and offered their manual skills in every field of life. In return, they received religious teachings from the Brahmans, food and protection from the Kshatriyas, and other supplies from the Vaisyas.

Unfortunately there were those who did not fit into any of the above four categories. They became the outcasts, the untouchables, who were the curse, the shadow of Hindu society. At the beginning of twentieth century many Hindus, led by Mohandas (Mahatma) Gandhi, mounted a great campaign to bring an end to untouchability. Gandhi called untouchables harijans ("children of God"); he lived among them and worked for their betterment.

Hindu reformers tried to bring an end to caste distinction and discrimination with limited success. Although urban Hindus often no longer pay attention to their caste upbringing, rural Hindus in India still practice caste loyalty. However, with increasing awareness of the basic unity of the human family and in the wake of political independence and democracy in India, the caste system is increasingly becoming irrelevant.

Hindu Spirituality

The aims of Hindu spirituality, philosophy, and religion are to celebrate, integrate, and synthesize the rich diversity of life on earth. The Hindus look at the world and see it whole. For them, existence is infinite, eternal, interdependent, multi-dimensional, ever unfolding, all-inclusive, mysterious, and intricately interconnected. This reality is expressed and explained in imaginative and metaphorical language. Nothing in Hinduism should be taken as literal or fixed truth. That is why much of popular Hinduism is to be found in poems, pictures, temples, statues, stories, legends, and rituals. At the time of Diwali (The Festival of Lights), which is perhaps the most important day in Hindu calendar, this profound sense of interconnectedness is clearly visible. Families and friends come together to celebrate the sanctity of seeds, the fertility of the land, the abundance of the harvest, the return of the Lord Rama from his fourteen years of exile, the adoration of Laxmi (the goddess of wealth), the worship of trees, rivers, and cows, and to give thanks to life itself.

The *Trimurti*

It is believed that there are 36,000 gods and goddesses manifesting divine principles. For Hindus there are gods in rivers (such as the Ganges), gods in animals (such as the cow) and gods in mountains (such as the Himalayas). But there is also a universally recognized triad or trinity of gods *(trimurti)*: Brahma, Vishnu (with Lakshmi) and Siva (with Shakti). These three represent the three-dimensional reality of existence: creation, continuation, and diminution.

Brahma is the birth principle. Whenever and wherever there is a beginning, there is the presence of Brahma, the creator of the universe. Brahma is abstract and absolute at the same time. There are hardly any statues, temples, or images of Brahma. It is the least accessible, yet the first and foremost principle of life coming into being.

The second are Vishnu and Lakshmi. Vishnu is the male aspect and Lakshmi the female. Together they form the law of continuity and conservation. Vishnu and Lakshmi are always at hand and available at every moment of becoming. They are the symbols of prosperity, preservation, and peace. Whenever there is a crisis, a downturn, explosion, darkness, or deprivation, Vishnu and Lakshmi come into the world to help. They restore order, establish balance and create harmony. As Rama and Sita they restored harmony in the world by destroying demons. Similarly, as Krishna and Radha they came to slay the wicked.

Then there is Siva (the male aspect) with Shakti (the female aspect), who together are the laws of decay and death. Siva and Shakti in their multiple forms destroy what needs to be destroyed. There is a time for birth, time for blossoming and then a time for the end. Only through this cycle of life and death, may earth refresh itself and continue.

Truth, Consciousness, and Bliss

In parallel to the trinity of birth, life, and death there is another significant Hindu trinity—the trinity of truth, consciousness, and bliss. Every Hindu is on a quest to search out the one ultimate truth. All actions, thoughts, and words should be devoted to that search, which should be undertaken without fear, without delusion, and without compromise, and yet in humility and with a hint of uncertainty. This search for truth can be carried through only by keeping personal consciousness clear and identifying oneself with the universal consciousness. For a Hindu, consciousness is integral to material manifestation. Consciousness is at the core of creation as well as being the canvas on which material manifestation is painted. It is the consciousness which makes the material world scared and worth preserving.

While the search for truth continues and identification with the universal consciousness is pursued, the Hindus are to live their everyday life in joy and bliss. Whether in the small act of washing the dishes or in the greatest act of meditating on supreme truth, Hindus should find pleasure. Beauty, aesthetics, taste, color, smell, sound, sex, and all other sources of joyful living with restraint, proportion, balance and simplicity are wholly in order in the Hindu religious tradition. When a Hindu takes up the robe of a *sadhu* (monk) he or she is given a new name, which always ends with the word *ananda* (joy). For example, consider the name Yogananda. It is no good practicing yoga day after day without joy; yoga should be accompanied by *ananda*—joy. The same is true for the name Vivekananda. *Viveka* means wisdom; wisdom too should be accompanied by joy. Similarly for Satyananda; *satya* means truth, to be accompanied by joy, and so on. Thus, truth, consciousness, and joy are the foundation upon which the Hindu religion, as well as society, is built.

Satish Kumar

Further Reading

Bhave, V. (1970). *Talks on the Gita*. Varanasi, India: Sarva Seva Sangh Prakashan.

Radhakrishnan, S. (1999). *Indian philosophy* (Vol. 1). New Delhi, India: Oxford University Press.

Rajagopalachari, C. (1973). *Mahabharata*. Chowpatty, India: Bharatiya Vidya Bhavan.

Shastri, H. P. (Trans.). (1985). *Ramayana of Valmiki* (Vols. 1–3). London: Shantisadan.

Honeybee

For millennia honey from bees was the primary source of sweetness for humans. For this reason, as well as for its preservative and medicinal benefits, it has been highly prized. The wax that bees use to construct their honeycomb cells was also an important product, used in candles, polish, ointments, cosmetics, and inks. And from fermented honey a pale yellow wine—called "mead" in Europe, *tej* in Ethiopia—is made. It is thought to be one of the earliest alcoholic beverages ever produced.

Although all bees collect nectar and other plant secretions to feed to their young, honey in the normal sense is made by only four species in the genus *Apis*. *Apis cerana* (eastern honeybee) occurs in India, southeastern Asia, and China; *Apis dorsata* (giant or rock honeybee) occurs in the Himalayas; and *Apis florea* (little honeybee) occurs in India and southeastern Asia. The most important species, however, is *Apis mellifera*, a native of eastern Europe, Asia Minor, and Africa that has been domesticated and carried by humans all over the globe.

The social behavior of honeybees is complex and has fascinated people for as long as honey has been known. A colony revolves around the activity of a single fertile female, the queen, whose sole occupation is laying eggs. The majority of the bees, up to fifty thousand in a large colony, are nonreproductive females called "workers." The workers forage, collecting nectar (and pollen) from flowers. Unlike many other natural insect pollinators, honeybees practice "flower fidelity," tending to target the flowers of a particular plant species during each foraging trip from the hive. This fidelity makes them one of the most important pollinators and has led to the large-scale use of mobile hive transporters—truckloads of hives are strategically positioned during key flowering periods in agricultural land. Honeybees are particularly important pollinators of alfalfa, berry crops, and fruit trees.

In the bee's honey stomach the nectar is transformed by reduction of water content and by enzyme inversion of the sucrose into glucose and fructose. It is then regurgitated into beeswax storage cells, capped with wax and kept to feed to the bee maggot brood, which is usually housed in another part of the honeycomb.

Waggle Dance

Targeting of certain flowers is made possible by communication between bees. Successful scouts return to the combs and perform the "waggle dance" to their sisters. This abdomen-shaking ritual takes the form of a figure 8 performed on the comb and closely monitored by other workers being recruited. Direction to the food source (relative to the sun's position) is indicated by the orientation of the central portion of the dance on the comb, and the distance (energy required to get to the flowers) is indicated by the length of the central portion and the "tempo" of the bee's movements. Other "dances" are used to communicate daily and seasonal foraging needs and to choose new nest sites.

Workers also defend the colony using their barbed stingers to inject powerful venom. The stinger is a modified part of the egg-laying tube, hence only females (workers and queen) can sting. They also control the internal climate of the nest by bringing water, collected from puddles and ponds, onto the combs and by fanning air through with their wings.

The complex social structure of honeybee colonies derives, for the most part, from the unusual genetic system of sex determination. Most organisms have paired chromosomes in their cell nuclei, one virtually identical set from each parent. The sex chromosomes, however, are not identical (called "X" and "Y" in humans, for example, for their shape under the microscope), and they determine female (XX) or male (XY) gender. In honeybees an arrangement called "haplodiploidy" exists. This arrangement occurs through all of the insect order Hymenoptera, which includes bees, wasps, and ants. Individuals with only one set of chromosomes (the haploid condition) are males, those with paired chromosomes (diploid) are females. When a queen mates with a male (a drone), she stores the sperm in the spermatheca, a sac inside her abdomen. As each egg is laid, it can be fertilized, or not, using the sperm store. Fertilized eggs (diploid, with two sets of chromosomes) become females, unfertilized eggs (haploid with only one set) become males.

Defense of the colony against an attacker leads to the death of many workers, who effectively commit suicide when their barbed stingers are torn from their bodies. The stingers, with muscle-contracting venom sacs still attached, remain in the enemy's flesh, thus

Honey in Africa

The following ethnographic text describes the value the Mbuti of Central Africa place on honey.

Falling approximately in the middle of our calendar year, and lasting a full two months, the honey season is of vital importance to the Mbuti not only from a nutritional point of view but structurally . . .

Never is any honey wasted, never is it kept or used in the preparation of other foods; what is not consumed on the spot is eaten or drunk the moment it is brought back into camp.

There is a craving for honey during the season that never seems to be satisfied. No amount of alternative foods, even meat, can reduce this passion for honey. Each band has its own way of listening for the telltale sound of bees swarming. Among some, a leaf is rubbed between the hands, which are then rubbed across the forehead to enable the hunter to see the bees high up in their hives. I found this practice among the eastern archers. Elsewhere, throughout the net-hunting region also among the western archers, at least, the chameleon (*ameuli*) is believed to lead the Mbuti to honey by uttering a long, drawn-out throaty cry. . . . But most noticeable among a people who take the success of hunting and gathering so much for granted is the presence of honey-collecting magic, and an inordinate emphasis on song and dance, legend-telling and other recreational activities. There is no doubt that whatever else it may be, the honey season is also a festive season where celebration is the order of the day, even at the cost of a relatively empty stomach.

Source: Turnbull, Colin M. (1965). *Wayward Servants; The Two Worlds of the African Pygmies.* Garden City, NY: The Natural History Press, pp.168, 170.

---

increasing the intensity of the pain, but the bees perish. Mathematical models can explain such "altruistic" behavior because even though a worker dies, her increased level of relatedness to all other workers in the colony means that her "fitness" in the evolutionary sense of passing on genes to the next generation is increased.

Drones and Queens

Drones are produced in small numbers throughout the life of the colony and develop from unfertilized eggs. They mate with queens, but because their genitalia are ripped out during mating they do not live long.

Development of queens in the colony is under complex control of pheromones (chemical signals) and seasonal factors. Specially constructed cells containing a fertilized egg are selected, and the grub is fed a special diet of extra honey and "royal jelly," a substance rich in sugars, vitamins, and protein secretions. The extra nutritional intake allows a larger bee, with fully functional ovaries, to develop. Emergence of new queens causes the colony to divide. Some queens are killed, but eventually a new queen will take over the colony, while the old queen leaves with a cohort of workers to swarm and form a new colony elsewhere. This natural division of the colony by swarming was long the basis for beekeeping.

The origins of apiculture (beekeeping) are shrouded in prehistory. Bees appear to have been domesticated for many centuries before Roman times, after which there is good written evidence of beekeeping practices. Honey was probably first harvested, from wild colonies, during the Stone Age. Bushman cave paintings made in the last two thousand years in the Natal Drakensberg Park of South Africa show aspects of honey gathering—stick figures of men climbing ladders to a colony surrounded by a cloud of flying bees. In parts of Africa and Asia honey is still collected in this way from wild combs in trees and on rockfaces.

Honeybees were already domesticated by the time of the ancient civilizations of Egypt, Greece, and Rome, and the basic techniques of honey harvesting remained relatively simple until the nineteenth century. Colonies were housed in crude containers, usually cylinders of woven grass or domes of straw called "skeps." At the end of the foraging season the colony was destroyed and the honeycombs extracted. New colonies were either collected from wild swarms or from part of the domesticated stock during the natural process of division when part of the colony leaves to found a new colony.

Modern Beekeeping and Honey Production

The development of modern hives started with U.S. pastor L. L. Langstroth, who first made a moveable-frame hive in 1851. Stacking layers of regular hanging combs means that brood combs (those where eggs are laid and grubs housed) can now be kept separate from storage combs (those used solely for honey storage); a mesh of certain size excludes the large queen, preventing her laying eggs in the storage cells, but allows free passage of smaller workers to bring in honey. At the time of honey harvesting all the bees can be excluded from the (usually) upper combs as the wax caps are removed and the honey drained off.

With the mass cultivation of sugarcane, people found another source of sweetness, but honey remains a major industry throughout the world. It also remains an endeavor that crosses cultural and class divides, being practiced by industrial-scale agricultural companies, smallholding farmers, and hobbyists alike.

Richard Jones

Further Reading

Gould, J. L. (1988). *The honey bee.* Houndsmills, UK: Scientific American Library.

Morse, R. A. (1972). *The complete guide to beekeeping.* London: Robert Hale.

von Frisch, K. (1967). *The dance language and orientation of bees.* Cambridge, MA: Belknap Press of Harvard University Press.

Winston, M. L. (1991). *The biology of the honey bee.* Boston: Harvard University Press.

Hornaday, William T.
(1854–1937)

U.S. conservationist

American conservationist and naturalist William Temple Hornaday made important contributions to the development of taxidermy, zoo design, and wildlife preservation. Although sometimes strident in his views, Hornaday played a leading role in fostering concern about and promoting policies to address the decline of North American birds and mammals.

Born in Indiana and raised in Iowa, Hornaday grew up surrounded by a virgin prairie teeming with wildlife. During a visit to one of his Indiana relatives, he discovered a case of mounted birds that captivated his imagination. Left an orphan at age fifteen, Hornaday attended Iowa's Oskaloosa College (a preparatory school) and then spent a year at Iowa State Agricultural College, where he became taxidermist for the school's natural history museum. In 1873 he joined Henry A. Ward's Natural Science Establishment in Rochester, New York, an ideal environment to cultivate his taxidermy skills. He also had the opportunity to develop his field skills during a series of collecting trips that culminated in an expedition to India, Ceylon (Sri Lanka), the Malay Peninsula, and Borneo (1876–1879). After returning to Ward's, he married Josephine Chamberlain of Battle Creek, Michigan, and helped organize the Society of American Taxidermists, a short-lived organization dedicated to improving standards and employment prospects in taxidermy. He and his colleagues received wide acclaim for their experiments mounting animals in habitat groups, a practice that soon became common in museums.

In 1882 Hornaday became chief taxidermist at the U.S. National Museum in Washington, D.C., a part of the Smithsonian Institution. Four years later he led a successful expedition to find specimens of bison for exhibition. Fearful that the bison's days were numbered, he published a pioneering report, *The Extermination of the American Bison* (1889). Partly because of his experience with the bison, he began laying plans for the National Zoological Park in Washington, D.C., which he originally envisioned as a preserve for this and other endangered native species. After serving a year as the initial director, he left in 1890 following disagreements with the secretary of the Smithsonian. For the next six years he sold real estate in Buffalo, New York.

In 1896 a group of wealthy New Yorkers approached Hornaday about directing a new zoo that members were considering. He selected the site in New York City, drew up the plans, oversaw construction, and managed the 261-acre facility, the New York Zoological Park, better known as the Bronx Zoo. Having previously campaigned to reform museum exhibition practices, Hornaday then set out to create a new kind of zoo, one where animals were safely displayed in what appeared to be their natural habitat and where endangered wildlife might be preserved.

During his three decades at the Bronx Zoo, Hornaday immersed himself in conservation work. In 1905 he helped establish the American Bison Society, and two years later he supervised the first efforts to restock bison in western refuges using animals bred and raised in New York. Hornaday also worked to secure passage of the 1902 Alaskan Game Act, the 1911 Bayne Law (which outlawed the sale of native game in New York), the 1912 North Pacific Fur Seal Convention, the 1913 Migratory Bird Act, and other pioneering wildlife initiatives. In 1913 and 1914 he raised $100,000 in private funds to establish the Permanent Wildlife Protection Fund, which became one of his most enduring legacies. Because he rejected compromise and vehemently attacked his enemies, Hornaday often found himself on radical margins of wildlife conservation. Still, through his tireless work on behalf of diminishing species, he accomplished a great deal.

Mark V. Barrow Jr.

Further Reading

Bridges, W. (1974). *A gathering of animals: An unconventional history of the New York Zoological Society.* New York: Harper & Row.

Dolph, J. A. (1975). *Bringing wildlife to the millions: William Temple Hornaday, the early years, 1854–1896. Dissertation Abstracts International, 36,* 09A. (UMI No. AAG7605948).

Henson, P. M. (1997). William Temple Hornaday. In K. B. Sterling, R. P. Harmond, G. A. Cevasco, & L. F. Hammond (Eds.), *Biographical dictionary of American and Canadian naturalists and environmentalists* (pp. 378–381). Westport, CT: Greenwood Press.

Thomas, P. D. (1999). William Temple Hornaday. In J. A. Garraty & M. C. Carnes (Eds.), *American national biography: Vol 11.* (pp. 210–211). New York: Oxford University Press.

Wonders, K. (1993). *Habitat dioramas: Illusions of wilderness in museums of natural history* (Figura Nova Series No. 25). Uppsala, Sweden: Acta Universitatis Upsaliensas.

Horse

The horse is one of the most important animals ever domesticated. Horses belong to the taxonomic order Perissodactyla, animals with an odd number of toes. Perissodactyla contains three families: *Tapiridae* (tapirs), *Rhinocerotidae* (rhinoceroses), and *Equidae* (horses, asses, and zebras).

Evolution

Equidae evolution begins in the Eocene epoch with the appearance of the *Pliolophus* in Eurasia some 50 million years ago. *Pliolophus* was a slightly built, dog-sized mammal with short legs and a curved back. Rather than single, unpadded hooves characteristic of modern equids, *Pliolophus* had four padded toes on its forefeet, three on its hind feet. Its teeth indicate it subsisted by browsing on leafy forest vegetation. *Pliolophus* migrated into North America during the Eocene where its Oligocene descendants evolved larger, more horse-like forms but continued to subsist as generalized browsers.

Equid subsistence changed radically during the Early Miocene. Natural selection on the emerging grasslands of North America produced *Parahippus* with tooth morphology adapted to specialized grazing not browsing. A descendent, *Protohippus*, continued this evolutionary trajectory during the Middle and Late Miocene. Accelerated grassland expansion in North America led to the Late Miocene evolution of *Hipparion*, a tall, long-limbed, three-toed descendant of *Protohippus*. *Hipparion* was the first equid to develop high-crowned, hard, enamel-edged, hyposodont cheek teeth able to efficiently chew hard, silica-rich, abrasive grass fibers. Declining sea level and reemergence of the Bering Straits land bridge permitted *Hipparion*'s spread into the Old World. The three-toed *Hipparion* equid body-plan persisted in the New and the Old Worlds into the Early Pleistocene.

The first true horse, *Pliohippus*, evolved in the Early Pliocene—a small, pony-sized animal. Natural selection on the grasslands lengthened its legs, enlarged the grinding surfaces on its molars, expanded its muzzle to accommodate larger teeth, and reduced the number of its toes to a single functional digit. *Pliohippus* spread from North America to Eurasia until severance of the Bering Straits land bridge during the Pliocene. This severance contributed to the differentiation of Old and New World equine taxa.

Modern Equids

Equus, the genus of modern horses, donkeys, and zebras, evolved from *Pliohippus* in North America during

Beeton's on Cramp in Horses

This is a dangerous complaint in horses unless timely remedies be applied. It comes on very suddenly, and the pain is at times most intense. The general causes of cramp and spasms are drinking profusely of cold water while the horse is heated, exposure to cold, improper food, rank grass, &c. It is hardly possible to mistake the symptoms of it. The horse shows evident marks of uneasiness, shakes, lies down, and rolls about while the fit is on him. He then becomes quiet again; and will perhaps take food. As soon as the complaint is detected, no time should be lost in administering the following anti-spasmodic draught: Mix together 2½ oz. of laudanum, 3 oz. of turpentine, 1 pint of linseed-oil. If the symptoms do not abate shortly, apply hot fomentations to the belly and administer the following laxative ball: 6 drachms of Barbadoes aloes, 1 scruple of croton bean, 1 drachm of calomel. Take the horse off his corn; give him dry bran and cut hay, and keep him warm in a loose box.

Source: *Beeton's All About Everything: Being a Dictionary of Practical Recipes and Every-Day Information.* (1890). London: Ward, Lock And Co., p. 91.

the Late Pliocene. A key evolutionary development in *Equus* is evident in both their fore and hind legs. Whether quadruped or biped, the knee joints of most mammals are structured in such a way that muscular effort must be exerted for them to remain standing. In the absence of such effort, gravity forces the knee joint to flex or collapse. Modern equid legs have "passive stay-apparatus," a complex arrangement of bone, muscle, and ligaments that passively "lock" the knee in extension without calling forth continued high levels

Canadian immigrant Harold Clarke with his eight-horse team in 1920 Saskatchewan. COURTESY OF D. BRUCE DICKSON.

of muscular activity. By enabling them to stand for long periods with reduced muscular activity, this anatomical feature contributes to their energetic efficiency. Skeletal evidence for the passive knee lock is first seen in the hind leg of *Protohippus* around 11 or 12 million years ago. Analogous passive locking mechanisms do not appear in the shoulder region until the evolution of the modern equines between about 3 to 5 million years ago.

Equus dispersed widely over North America during the Pleistocene epoch, reaching South America via the Isthmus of Panama and Eurasia via the Bering Straits. Extinct in New World around 8000 BCE, at the Pleistocene's close, the horse persisted in the Old World where it was eventually domesticated.

Horses Domesticated

The great diversity of mitochondrial DNA in domesticated horses suggests that wild horse domestication was not confined to a restricted geographic area or prehistoric culture. Rather this diversity indicates that wild horses were utilized and domesticated at many different times and places throughout prehistoric Eurasia. One important early center of horse domestication was among peoples of the Tripolye culture who, around 3000 BCE, were located north of the Black Sea on the steppes between Ukraine and Turkestan. They used domesticated horses for milk, meat, and funeral offerings; their use of horses as beasts of burden, draft animals, and mounts came later.

Horses were pulling wheeled carts in Eurasia by 2600 BCE. But evidence that horses were mounted and ridden is not present in the archaeological record until about 2000 BCE (but see Brown and Anthony 1997). Afterwards, "classic" pastoral nomadism—mounted riders driving livestock and moving their belonging on pack animals—emerged in southwestern Eurasia. Efficient use of the horse in hauling demands a special kind of harness. As horses hold their necks erect, they are choked by the oxen's neck yoke. Horse harnesses must fit across the animal's chest. Since their invention sometime before 800 CE in Europe, such harnesses placed formidable traction power at the disposal of humankind and ultimately opened the great grasslands of the world to plow agriculture.

War Horses

Domesticated horses spread rapidly over the Old World and their dispersal profoundly affected patterns of warfare. Mounted warriors strike or flee quickly; mounted bowmen are particularly dangerous opponents. Yet, light cavalry had only limited effectiveness against well-drilled or fortified infantry. Decisive military use of the horse in ancient times came from its traction power. Perfection of two-wheeled, horse-drawn war chariots around 1800 BCE brought radical change to warfare in Eurasia. Mobility, firepower, and battlefield carnage were raised to new levels by teams of galloping horses drawing fast, light, sturdy chariots containing archers and drivers. The peoples best able to use chariot warfare were steppe dwellers, whose way of life assured familiarity with and access to horses. Accordingly, between 1800 and 1500 BCE, waves of barbarians equipped with chariots overran the civilized lands of the southwestern Asia. The effectiveness of cavalry-mounted warriors (as opposed to charioteers) was not much enhanced until the invention of the foot stirrup in China about 500 CE. With this device, cavalrymen could use the shock of their horses' charge to drive their lances against an enemy without themselves being catapulted from the saddle by the force of the blow. Stirrups, arriving in Europe around 700 CE, effected a military revolution. Infantry was eclipsed for five hundred years during the Age of Chivalry and mounted knights dominated Europe's battlefields until the Age of Gunpowder. As its military significance declined, the horse's role in society contracted to symbol of authority, beast of burden, and source of recreation.

D. Bruce Dickson

Further Reading

Agustí, J., & Antón, M. (2002). *Mammoths, sabertooths, and hominids: 65 million years of mammalian evolution in Europe.* New York: Columbia University Press.

Brown, D., & Anthony, D. (1998). Bit wear, horseback riding and the Botai Site in Kazakstan. *Journal of Archaeological Science 25*(4), 331–347.

Evander, R. I. (1989). Phylogeny of the family equidae. In D. R. Prothero & R. M. Schoch (Eds.), *The Evolution of Perissodactyls* (pp. 109–126). New York: Clarendon Press.

Hermanson, J. W., & MacFadden, B. J. (1996). Evolutionary and functional morphology of the knee in fossil and extant horses (Equidae). *Journal of Vertebrate Paleontology 16*(2), 349–357.

Hooker, J. J. (1994). The beginning of the equoid radiation. *Zoological Journal of the Linnean Society 112*(½), 29–63.

Jansen, T., Forster, et al. (2002). Mitochondrial DNA and the origins of the domestic horse. *Proceedings of the National Academy of Sciences 99*(16), 10905–10910.

MacFadden, B. J., & Hubbert, R. C. (1988). Explosive speciation at the base of the adaptive radiation of Miocene grazing horses. *Nature 336*, 466–468.

McNeill, W. H. (1982). *The pursuit of power*. Chicago: University of Chicago Press.

Renfrew C. (1987). *Archaeology and language: The puzzle of Indo-European origins*. New York: Cambridge University Press.

White, L. (1962). *Medieval technology and change*. Oxford, UK: Oxford University Press.

House Sparrow

The house sparrow, or English sparrow *(Passer domesticus)*, like the starling *(Sturnus vulgaris)* and the rock dove *(Columba livia)*, provides an excellent example of a bird that has benefited from the expansion of European civilization during the last centuries. Introduction of the house sparrow around the globe by humans has made it, after the domesticated chicken, possibly the world's most widespread species of bird.

The gregarious house sparrow is a typical representative of the family *Passeridae*: a small, stocky seed eater with a short conical beak and slightly forked tail. It has a body length of 15 centimeters and wingspan of 25 centimeters. The plumage of both sexes is brownish, with a gray crown, chestnut nape, and black bib in the breeding male. The species' song consists of a series of familiar chirping calls. The nesting season varies in length according to climate, but two to three broods are typically raised per year, often in loose breeding colonies. The woven grass nests are usually built within an artificial or natural cavity, but can also be found on open branches.

Native to Eurasia and North Africa, the seed-eating house sparrow formed a special relationship with humans after the advent of agriculture in the Middle East. The house sparrow may originally have been a migratory species, but appears to have evolved the habit of overwintering close to human settlements and relying on grain stores, feedlots, and garbage for foraging. Consequently, the species is encountered over its wide range only in areas inhabited by humans.

During the nineteenth century, settlers of European origin intentionally introduced the house sparrow to North and South America, southern Africa, Australia, and New Zealand. While it was hoped that the species could provide insect pest control, its introduction was also part of the larger attempt to create a familiar landscape for immigrants. A generalist in terms of its diet and an aggressive competitor for nesting sites, the house sparrow was able to expand its range almost everywhere it was introduced. For example, within six decades after its initial introduction to New York in 1851, it had occupied suitable habitats over the entire continental United States and Canada. The exploding sparrow populations became serious pests for grainfields and orchards, created sanitary problems in the cities, and displaced popular native species such as martins and bluebirds. By the beginning of the twentieth century, public opinion had turned against the house sparrow, and measures for its eradication were commonly proposed.

Population numbers of the house sparrow seem to have peaked during the early twentieth century. Before the arrival of the automobile, sparrows thrived in cities, where undigested grains in horse droppings provided an unlimited supply of food. Since the 1960s, populations of the house sparrow have markedly declined over much of its range. Cars have increased the species' mortality in urban settings, while changes in farming practices, such as larger monocrop farms and more efficient livestock feeding practices, have deprived the House Sparrow of much of its former food base. The widespread use of pesticides has also resulted in an absence of insects required by sparrow nestlings.

Mikko Saikku

Further Reading

Barrows, W. B. (1889). *The English sparrow* (Passer domesticus) *in North America, especially in its relations to agriculture* (U.S. Department of Agriculture, Division of Economic Ornithology and Mammalogy, Bulletin No. 1). Washington, DC: Government Printing Office.

Summers-Smith, J. D. (1988). *The sparrows: A study of the genus* Passer. Calton, UK: T. and A. D. Poyser.

Huang River

The Huang (Yellow) River, at 5,400 kilometers in length, is China's second-longest river. It originates in

Qinghai Province and flows northeast and then east across the top of its great bend. At Hekouzhen in Inner Mongolia the river turns south for 800 kilometers before again turning northeast to cross the North China plain and reach the sea at its delta at the Bohai Gulf. The river's drainage area of 745,000 square kilometers ranks it twenty-ninth among the world's rivers, but its discharge of 1,365 cubic meters per second is far less than that of many rivers of comparable drainage area. The Mekong River, for example, has a similar drainage area but more than ten times the flow of the Yellow River.

In spite of its small flow, the Huang River has been infamously difficult to control, repeatedly flooding and changing course throughout history. Two main factors contribute to the river's tendency to flood. The first is a seasonal rainfall pattern that causes extreme and often sudden variations in water levels, particularly in summer and fall.

The second factor is the river's massive silt burden. As the river travels south between Sanxi and Shaanxi Provinces it crosses the highly eroded loess plateau. Loess is a fine-grain, nutrient-rich but easily eroded soil that gives the river its characteristic yellow color. In the rainy season, sudden downpours in the barren erosion gullies of the loess plateau send streams of mud cascading into the river. This results in a silt content that has been measured as high as 37 kilograms of silt per cubic meter of water. When the river leaves the mountains and turns east to cross the relatively flat North China plain, perhaps one-third of this silt settles out, causing the river channel to fill and rise. Eventually the river breaks out of its elevated bed and finds a new, lower course to the sea.

All of China's early dynasties emerged on or near the Huang River, and river control played an important part in imperial politics from earliest times. Emperor Yu, the legendary founder of China's first dynasty, the Hsia (2207–1766 BCE), supposedly established his right to the throne by subduing the Huang River. The Yuan (1279–1368) dynasty marked the beginning of a more active approach to control of the river. The Yuan constructed the Grand Canal to allow the shipment of grain from the Yangtze River valley to the capital at Beijing. Because the canal incorporated part of the Huang River, controlling the river became a central concern of the imperial state. The Ming (1368–1644) and Qing (1644–1911) dynasties created an extensive and growing system of dikes, locks, spillways, and revetments (embankment facings) to keep the river in its bed and the grain flowing north.

By the middle of the nineteenth century, the Huang River control system was one of the largest and most expensive projects of imperial administration, but devastating floods continued to be a problem.

Beginning in the 1950s, the People's Republic of China attempted to use both reforestation of the loess plateau and the construction of dams to reduce silting and regulate the flow of the Huang River. Initial efforts at reforestation failed, and silting behind Huang River dams has severely limited or eliminated their hydroelectric potential. Since the early 1990s soil conservation efforts in the loess plateau have reduced the silt burden carried by the river, but extensive agricultural use of water in the upper reaches has so reduced flow that the downstream bed has gone dry for extended periods. The Huang River valley is also troubled by air pollution, water pollution, and a growing demand for water resources that will only increase as China continues to industrialize.

Randall Dodgen

Further Reading

Dodgen, R. (2001). *Controlling the dragon: Confucian engineers and the Yellow River in late imperial China.* Honolulu: University of Hawaii Press.

Greer, C. (1979). *Water management in the Yellow River basin of China.* Austin: University of Texas Press.

Needham, J., Wang, L., & Gwei-djen, L. (Eds.). (1971). *Science and civilization in China: Vol. 4(3), Civil Engineering and Nautics* (pp. 211–378). Cambridge, UK: Cambridge University Press.

Hudson River

The Hudson River, one of America's richest historical sites, has its source in the Adirondack Mountains in New York State. It flows 507 kilometers from Mount Marcy to the southern tip of Manhattan, where it empties into the Atlantic Ocean. The Hudson River's history in many ways represents America's military, industrial, artistic, and environmental endeavors.

English explorer Henry Hudson "discovered" the Hudson River valley in 1609 while searching for a quick passage to China. He found a beautiful, wooded valley populated by Algonquin Native Americans and wild animals. Dutch colonists later settled the area, which became known as New Amsterdam. The Hudson highlands played an important role during the Revolutionary War when Americans stretched a chain across the river near West Point to prevent British ships from sailing up the Hudson from New York City.

It was not until the early 1800s, the age of the steamboat, that the river gained national economic importance. The Erie Canal, completed in 1825, linked Lake Erie with the Hudson River, the nation's only commercial artery through the Appalachian Mountains. By 1850 more than 150 steamboats carried approximately a million passengers annually along the river.

The Hudson River had more than economic importance. Its forested landscape inspired the nation's first indigenous school of painting, known as the Hudson River School of landscape painting (1825–1870). A group of artists including Thomas Cole, Asher Durand, Albert Bierstadt, and Frederic E. Church painted the river valley's natural grandeur for the world. Contemporaneous writers and poets, including Washington Irving, James Fenimore Cooper, and William Cullen Bryant, also romanticized the landscape.

But the sublime pen and brush barely masked the region's rapid industrialization prior to and after the French and Indian Wars and Revolutionary War. By 1830 most of the river valley had been deforested to supply timber to the local mines, tanning factories, and forges along the river. Troy, Hudson, Cold Spring, and Peekskill became major industrial towns. The mountain valleys above Thomas Cole's studio in Catskill village, for example, supported the largest tannery industry in the country.

Despite this rapid industrialization, health resorts in the Catskills cropped up along the river in the mid–1800s as retreats for urbanites. Hiking, rowing, swimming, and fishing popularized outdoor recreation. Wealthy New York businessmen, including financier J. Pierpont Morgan and railroad baron Edward H. Harriman, built opulent mansions in the hills. By the 1880s railroad lines from New York facilitated access to the Hudson Valley.

Yet, pollution and declining water levels in the Erie Canal and Hudson River generated widespread concern, and the region became the site of one of the nation's first wilderness conservation movements. Adirondack State Park opened in 1891, and Bear Mountain State Park in 1910. The modern era of environmental activism did not start until half a century later, when Consolidated Edison electric company proposed building a giant hydroelectric plant on the river near Cornwall. The federal government decided that protection of natural resources was just as important as economic development, and in 1980 Consolidated Edison designated its purchased land as a park.

Although the Hudson River supports a diversity of wildlife and an estuary in its lower half, pollution still threatens the river's health. But during the past twenty years, local and national legislation has helped to ensure that the Hudson remains a national treasure.

Jessica Teisch

Further Reading

Adams, A. G. (1996). *The Hudson through the years.* New York: Fordham University Press.

Boyle, R. H. (1979). *The Hudson River: A natural and unnatural history.* New York: Norton.

Dunwell, F. F. (1991). *The Hudson River highlands.* New York: Columbia University Press.

Heiman, M. (1989). Production confronts consumption: Landscape perception and social conflict in the Hudson Valley. *Environment and Planning D: Society and Space 7,* 165–173.

O'Brien, R. J. (1981). *American sublime: Landscape and scenery of the lower Hudson Valley.* New York: Columbia University Press.

Van Zandt, R. (1992). *Chronicles of the Hudson: Three centuries of travelers' accounts.* New Brunswick, NJ: Rutgers University Press.

Hudson River School

A group of nineteenth-century realist landscape painters, the Hudson River School was the first coherent school of American art. Their work, which initially focused on panoramic subjects along New York State's Hudson River but eventually depicted subjects as far away as South America and the Arctic, celebrated the wildness and uniqueness of the American landscape. The painters did so through a precise rendering of a location, sketched directly from that spot. Their paintings simultaneously mythologized primitive nature and popularized it.

The roots of the school can be found in European Romanticism and the Romantic writers of the early 1800s. Many of the early Hudson River painters took their cue from the Transcendentalist writings of the day. Thomas Cole (1801–1845), the school's most prominent early member, maintained that if nature were untouched by the hand of people, then people

"A Scene on the Banks of the Hudson" by William Cullen Bryant (1827)

Cool shades and dews are round my way,

And silence of the early day;

Mid the dark rocks that watch his bed,

Glitters the mighty Hudson spread,

Unrippled, save by drops that fall

From shrubs that fringe his mountain wall;

And o'er the clear still water swells

The music of the Sabbath bells.

All, save this little nook of land,

Circled with trees, on which I stand;

All, save that line of hills which lie

Suspended in the mimic sky-

Seems a blue void, above, below,

Through which the white clouds come and go;

And from the green world's farthest steep

I gaze into the airy deep.

Loveliest of lovely things are they,

On earth, that soonest pass away.

The rose that lives its little hour

Is prized beyond the sculptured flower.

Even love, long tried and cherished long,

Becomes more tender and more strong

At thought of that insatiate grave

From which its yearnings cannot save.

River! in this still hour thou hast

Too much of heaven on earth to last;

Nor long may thy still waters lie,

An image of the glorious sky.

Thy fate and mine are not repose,

And ere another evening close,

Thou to thy tides shalt turn again,

And I to seek the crowd of men.

Source: Works by William Cullen Bryant. Retrieved December 30, 2002, from http://www.4literature.net/William_Cullen_Bryant

could become more easily acquainted with the hand of God. In 1825 Cole traveled to the remote Catskill region of the Hudson River valley and made sketches. He painted three astounding landscapes that showed the dense, tangled underbrush, craggy rocks, and broken, twisted trees—the visual embodiments of Transcendentalist ideals. Cole and others also used sky, light, and atmospheric effects to suggest the immanence of God, a technique known as "luminism."

Another early practitioner, Asher B. Durant (1806–1886), pioneered the technique of going outdoors to make oil studies of leaves and bark that gave his paintings a degree of realism not seen before in American art. Cole and Durant also wrote many articles on art and nature urging painters to experience wilderness for themselves and to celebrate America's natural wonders and to foster a sense of nationalism. The two also joined with other artists in 1825 to found the first formal school of painting, the National Academy of Design, to promote an American style of painting "through instruction and exhibition."

The early Hudson River School paintings quickly made the Catskills a popular tourist destination. To find untouched scenery to paint, artists turned first to New York's Adirondack Mountains. Then, in the 1860s and 1870s, the second generation of Hudson River painters, including Albert Bierstadt, Sanford Gifford, Thomas Moran, and Frederick Church, traveled to the Rocky Mountains to find new and larger unseen vistas. The paintings that Moran and Bierstadt produced of Yosemite Valley, Yellowstone, and the Grand Canyon so moved Americans back east that Congress created the world's first national park in 1872 to preserve the Yellowstone area.

The second generation produced its work as America entered the Industrial Revolution. By the time Bierstadt finished *The Last of the Buffalo* in 1889, the art public favored the smaller, more intimate pastoral scenes depicted by the French Barbizon painters. The painting was rejected for a Paris exhibition that year, making *The Last of the Buffalo* ironically one of the last paintings in the Hudson River School style. Although out of favor since, the Hudson River School is remembered for shaping early American nationalism and providing visual support to calls for nature preservation.

James G. Lewis

Further Reading

Asleson, R., & Moore, B. (1985). *Dialogue with nature: Landscape and literature in nineteenth-century America.* Washington, DC: Corcoran Gallery of Art.

Cooper, J. F. (1999). *Knights of the brush: The Hudson River School and the moral landscape.* New York: Hudson Hills Press.

Howat, J. K. (1972). *The Hudson River and its painters.* New York: Viking Press.

Howat, J. K. (Ed.). (1987). *American paradise: The world of the Hudson River School.* New York: Metropolitan Museum of Art.

Lassiter, B. B. (1978). *American wilderness: The Hudson River School of painting.* Garden City, NY: Doubleday.

Powell, E. A. (1990). *Thomas Cole.* New York: H. N. Abrams.

Veith, G. E. (2001). *Painters of faith: The spiritual landscape in nineteenth-century America.* Washington, DC: Regnery Publishing.

Hungary
(2002 est. pop. 10.2 million)

Hungary is located in east-central Europe, sharing borders with Austria, Slovenia, Croatia, Yugoslavia, Ukraine, Romania, and Slovakia. From 1948 until 1989 the Hungarian Communist Party directed production and distribution. In 1989 Hungary went through a major historical restructuring from a state socialist to a market economy. After the political changes of 1989 state-owned companies were sold to private owners. During the five years after the change of systems, unemployment rose to 10 percent. By 2002 unemployment had dropped to 5.8 percent, with higher unemployment in eastern Hungary. Hungary's population has declined over the past fifty years; 17.4 percent live in the capital city of Budapest. Thirty-four percent of the population works in manufacturing of machinery, food, textiles, and other goods. Agriculture and fishing are also important economic sectors.

Magyar, or Hungarian, is the official language. Major ethnic groups are Magyars, accounting for 90 percent of the population, and Roma (Gypsies) with 5 percent. Other ethnicities, such as Croats, Romanians, Slovaks, Germans, and Jews, total 5 percent. Key national symbols include the crown of Saint Stephen and the Chain Bridge spanning the Danube River in Budapest. Hungary's landscape itself is a potent symbol, featured in many poems about the Great Plain and the Danube.

Participation in organized religion dropped after World War II. Over two-thirds of Hungarians are Roman Catholics. The second-largest denomination, Calvinism, accounts for 20 percent of the population. Hungary is also home to smaller congregations of Lutherans, Greek Catholics, Serbian and Romanian Orthodox Christians, and Jews.

Hungary's entire territory falls within the Carpathian Basin. Two major rivers cross Hungary: the Danube and the Tisza. The Great Plain comprises approximately half of Hungary's national territory. Lake Balaton is the largest freshwater lake in central Europe. Hungary has thousands of geothermal sources and caves, including the spectacular caverns at Aggtelek National Park. Important native wildlife populations include the European mayfly (*ephemeroptera galactica*) and the Eurasian otter (*lutra lutra*).

The Hungarian Landscape before World War II

Hungary's landscape and population have changed over time with geopolitical shifts in east-central Europe. Around 896, Magyar tribes swept off the Black Sea steppes into the Carpathian Basin and settled in what is now Hungary. In 1000 King (later Saint) Stephen received a crown from the Vatican and established Hungary as a unified state. By 1301 the Hungarian kingdom included the entire arc of the Carpathians, the Great Plain, and parts of Croatia.

The Ottoman Turks invaded Hungary in 1526, occupying the banks of the Danube as far north as Budapest. Many of the occupied region's inhabitants died or fled during subsequent decades of warfare. When the Hapsburgs defeated the Ottomans in 1686, they resettled the Danube plains with hundreds of thousands of emigrants from northern Hungary, Germany, and Serbia. These settlers drained the Danube wetlands and transformed marshes into agricultural lands.

The reforms and public works projects of Count István Szechényi paved the way for Hungary's industrialization and transformed the Hungarian landscape. In the 1830s Szechényi oversaw the construction of railroads, roads, and bridges. With the assistance of engineer Pál Vásárhelyi, Szechenyi directed large-scale flood-control projects that regulated the flow of the Danube and Tisza Rivers. River regulation led to the intensification of agriculture in Hungary's floodplains. This drive to modernize Hungary culminated in the Hungarian national revolution of 1848–1849. Although the revolution was put down by the Hapsburg army, it led to the 1867 establishment of the Hapsburg's Austro-Hungarian dual monarchy, in which Hungary gained economic resources and control of its domestic affairs.

By the late nineteenth century a few natural historians began to document Hungary's wildlife. Naturalist Ottó Herman published the first scientific guide to Hungarian birds in 1901. Early ornithological societies formed in Austria-Hungary around the same time.

Defeat in World War I shook Austria-Hungary to its foundations. The Treaty of Trianon (1920) established Hungary as an independent nation but ceded 70 percent of Hungary's previous territory to Romania, Croatia, and Czechoslovakia. Hungary lost its forests, mines, and industrial regions. Hungarian leaders directed their energies to recapturing the lost territory. This strategy led the nation into an alliance with Adolph Hitler's Germany in 1940, followed by another military defeat in 1945. In 1947 the Hungarian Communist Party, backed by the Soviet Union, took control of the government and major industries.

Hungarian Environment under State Socialism

From 1947 until the early 1960s Hungarian Communist Party leaders believed that environmental destruction was caused by capitalist industries' exploitation of nature in order to profit in the marketplace. Party officials thought that environmental problems would not occur in socialist countries.

By the early 1960s reformers within the Communist Party recognized the need for environmental regulations. Between 1961 and 1964 the government enacted five major environmental laws regulating forestry, water management, nature conservation, construction projects, and agricultural lands. Although these laws set high standards of environmental quality, they proved difficult to enforce.

The Hungarian government made efforts to protect wildlife and natural habitats. Hungary opened its first national park, Hortobágy, in 1973. In 1979 and 1980 five of Hungary's conservation areas were designated biosphere (the part of the world in which life can exist) reserves by the United Nations Educational, Scientific and Cultural Organization. In 1974 the government permitted the establishment of a major nature conservation organization, the Hungarian Ornithological and Nature Protection Society.

Despite these advances, many Hungarian citizens felt excluded from government decision-making processes on environmental issues. In the early 1980s, when Hungary's government proceeded with a joint project with Czechoslovakia to dam the Danube River between the towns of Gabcikovo and Nagymaros, a small group of Budapest intellectuals formed the Danube Circle. In 1984 the Danube Circle collected signatures on a petition opposing the dam and held the first public debates on the Gabcikovo-Nagymaros dam project. Two of the Danube Circle's founders, János Vargha and Judit Vásárhelyi, were given Sweden's Right Livelihood Award. By the late 1980s the Danube Circle had established a movement that attracted tens of thousands of participants to its protests despite the threat of police violence. In 1989 Hungary's political system changed, and newly elected officials cancelled Hungary's participation in the dam project.

Environmental Issues and Actors after Socialism

After 1989 the movement against the damming of the Danube faded as participants left to join new political parties. Hundreds of environmental organizations formed around the country. By 1997 Hungary had 504 registered environmental organizations. Whereas the Danube movement had been concentrated in Budapest, many new groups were founded in towns in the provinces. New environmental groups worked on diverse issues, including environmental education, waste management, wetlands protection, and public transportation.

The new government revised environmental laws and passed new ones. Harmonizing environmental regulations with those of the European Union has been a major goal because Hungary is projected to enter the European Union in 2004. Important new laws require environmental-impact assessments for potentially harmful projects and hold polluters responsible for environmental cleanup. The national park system also expanded, adding seven parks between 1991 and 2002.

Economic change led to ecological change. As many of the polluting industries from the socialist era closed their doors, air quality improved in many parts of the country. In some cases, however, the shift to a market economy worsened environmental conditions. For instance, growth in personal consumption and wastefully packaged imported goods resulted a glut of consumer packaging waste.

Hungary came into conflict with its neighbors over transboundary environmental issues several times in the 1990s. When the new Hungarian government backed out of the Gabcikovo-Nagymaros dam project in 1990, the Slovak government built a channel and hydroelectric station on the Danube. In late 1993 the Hungarian and Slovak governments brought lawsuits against each other in the European Court; these were not resolved until 1997.

A second transboundary environmental problem developed in early 2000 when a gold-mining operation in Romania spilled cyanide into the Tisza River. As the poisoned water traveled through Hungary, thousands of tons of fish died. The Hungarian government filed suit against the multinational mining corporation operating the mine. Hungarian environmental organizations participated alongside Romanian and Yugoslavian environmentalists in an investigation of the spill, organized by the European Union's Baia Mare Task Force.

During the 1990s Hungary made advances in passing environmental legislation, supporting the growth of citizens' organizations, and improving access to environmental information. At the beginning of the twenty-first century, policymakers must continue working to incorporate public participation and long-term ecological sustainability into Hungary's development strategy.

Krista Harper

See also Danube River

Further Reading

Fitzmaurice, J. (1996). *Damming the Danube: Gabcikovo and post-communist politics in Europe.* Boulder, CO: Westview.

Folch, R. (Ed.). (2000). *Encyclopedia of the biosphere: Vols. 7–8. Humans in the world's ecosystems.* Boston: Gale Group.

Gille, Z. (1997). Two pairs of women's boots for a hectare of land: Nature and the construction of the environmental problem in state socialism. *Capitalism, Nature, Socialism, 8*(4), 1–22.

Harper, K., & Ash, M. (2001). The Tisza chemical spill. In C. Miller (Ed.), *History in dispute: Vol. 7. Water and the environment since 1945: Global perspectives* (pp. 247–255). Columbia, SC: Manly.

Regional Environmental Center. (1997). *NGO directory: A directory of environmental nongovernmental organizations in central and eastern Europe.* Szentendre, Hungary: Regional Environmental Center.

Sugar, P., Hanák, P., & Frank, T. (1990). *A history of Hungary.* Bloomington: Indiana University Press.

Hunting and Fishing

The hunting and fishing practices of recent human cultures are diverse and, where suitable animal resources are available, nearly universal. The amount of animal protein in human diets traditionally varies from 100 percent in high latitudes to as low as 8–30 percent nearer the equator. Virtually every human society displays a strong interest in acquiring meat and bone marrow, owing to the nearly unique nutritional completeness (energy and more than twenty amino acids) that these resources provide. The hunting and collecting of marine shellfish have a long history in human evolution; large game hunting evolved by at least the middle Pleistocene epoch, probably before 500,000 years ago, along with the exploitation of certain small animals.

By roughly 250,000 years ago the products of hunting were deliberately aggregated at some sites and processed and consumed by multiple persons—small social groups for which sharing food may have been an important means for pooling resource risk.

Large Game Hunting

Some prehistoric humans are known to have hunted megafauna (elephants, hippopotamus, and rhinoceros), marsupials, or cetaceans (whales), but in most regions and periods large game hunting has centered on hoofed herbivores (ungulates) of the *bovid* (horned buffalo, bison, wild cattle, and antelopes), *cervid* (deer), and *equid* (horses and asses) families. As predators of ungulates, humans generally are of the "ambush" type, relying to a large extent on stealth and technology. The human hunting niche, with its unusual focus on prime adult animals, became distinct from the niches of other predators of ungulates (i.e., the large cats, wild dogs and wolves, and spotted hyenas) by at least 250,000 years ago. This characteristic of human hunting persists through the historic period and varies surprisingly little with technology.

Small Game Hunting

Small animals were also essential to human diets in lower latitudes from at least 250,000 years ago onward, and probably earlier than this. Small game animals served as supplements to large game resources. The relative emphasis that humans placed on three categories of small animals as defined by predator defense strategies changed dramatically with time: These are slow-moving, easily collected types such as tortoises and marine shellfish; fast-running mammals such as hares and rabbits (lagomorphs); and quick-flying game birds such as partridges and waterfowl. Hunters of the middle Paleolithic (in Eurasia) and middle Stone Age (in Africa) periods seldom took small prey unless they could be collected easily. The upper Paleolithic period was characterized by more even use of high-ranked sluggish, small animals and low-ranked quick-moving types in many regions. This change in subsistence practices, generally known as the "Broad Spectrum Revolution," is taken to indicate a significant expansion in human dietary breadth, beginning around forty thousand to fifty thousand years ago and greatly intensifying by ten thousand years ago. The earliest expansion in human diets took place during a cold climate period, the opposite of what would be expected to result from climate-driven changes in animal community composition and prey availability. The phenomenon was geographically widespread, although perhaps delayed in the continental interiors relative to arid regions. Hares or rabbits, for example, were particularly important by the late upper Paleolithic times in southern and western Europe, Moravia, the central Russian Plain, and Dnestr regions. A surge in lagomorph exploitation took place around the same time in western Asia, but later in north Africa. Environmental change brought about by global warming after 12,500 years ago may have fostered expansions in the availability of lagomorphs in Eurasia, but Mediterranean records indicate that lagomorphs were locally abundant earlier yet largely ignored by humans prior to the upper Paleolithic.

Fishing

Fishing—the capture of free-swimming animals in marine and freshwater habitats—is a more recent development in human adaptations. The first clear evidence of fishing dates from roughly thirty-two thousand to twenty-five thousand years ago, but the rarity and sporadic distribution of evidence indicate only low-level exploitation of fish, such as salmon, during the late upper Paleolithic period in western Europe. Fishing became increasingly important in some upper Paleolithic cultures following the last glacial maximum (when glacial mass and extent were greatest) eighteen thousand to twenty thousand years ago, perhaps first in regions as disparate as the Nile, Jordan, and Danube River valleys. However, it was not until after the Pleistocene-Holocene epoch transition ten thousand years ago that fishing became widespread along coastlines, rivers, lakes, and swamps worldwide with the appearance of Mesolithic cultures (present during a transitional period of the Stone Age between the Paleolithic and the Neolithic periods). Humans' means for capturing fish diversified rapidly, including larger watercraft, nets, and complex lines and weirs (fences or enclosures set in a waterway for taking fish) that facilitated the capture of fish in greater numbers and/or of larger sizes.

Hunting Technology

Most human hunting is tool assisted. Large and small animals pose different capture requirements, and the techniques and equipment for hunting animals have changed greatly over time. Technological evolution has often involved changes from simple to complex designs, with increasing use of spear-throwing boards (atlatls), more elaborate weapon heads, bows and arrows, nets, and unattended and tended traps. These innovations are not linked so much to the emergence of basic abilities to capture animals as they are to humans' attempts to lighten the constraints and energy costs of capture by designing more efficient tools. These changes in human technology are common responses to conditions where access to food is already under strain and the exploitation of alternative resources made necessary by a decline in preferred types of food. The process may have been set in motion as early as eighty thousand to fifty thousand years ago, but it is most apparent after fifty thousand to forty thousand years ago, accelerating noticeably after twenty thousand to eighteen thousand years ago and continuing through the modern era.

Mary C. Stiner

Further Reading

Binford, L. R. (1978). *Nunamiut ethnoarchaeology*. New York. Academic Press.

Bratlund, B. (1996). Hunting strategies in the late glacial of northern Europe: A survey of the faunal evidence. *Journal of World Prehistory, 10*(1), 1–48.

Brooks, S. A., Helgren, C. M., Cramer, J. S., Franklin, A., Hornyak, W., Keating, J. M., Klein, R. G., Rink, W. J., Schwarcz, H., Smith, J. N. L., Stewart, K., Todd, N., Verniers, J., & Yellen, J. E. (1995). Dating and context of three middle Stone Age sites with bone points in the upper Semliki Valley, Zaire. *Science, 268,* 548–553.

Coles, B. (Ed.). (1992). *The wetland revolution in prehistory*. Exeter, UK: Prehistoric Society.

Edinburgh, J. D. (1989). The Mesolithic in Europe. In C. Bonsall (Ed.), *The earliest occupation of Europe* (pp. 103–128). Leiden, Netherlands: University of Leiden Press.

Hayden, B., Chisholm, B., & Schwarcz, H. P. (1987). Fishing and foraging: Marine resources in the upper Paleolithic of France. In O. Soffer (Ed.), *The Pleistocene Old World: Regional perspectives* (pp. 279–291). New York: Plenum.

Jochim, M. A. (1998). *A hunter-gatherer landscape: Southwest Germany in the late Paleolithic and Mesolithic*. New York: Plenum.

Keeley, L. H. (1988). Hunter-gatherer economic complexity and "population pressure." *Journal of Anthropological Archaeology, 7,* 373–411.

Kelly, R. (1995). *The foraging spectrum: Diversity in hunter-gatherer lifeways*. Washington, DC: Smithsonian Institution Press.

Klein, R. G. (1989). *The human career: Human biological and cultural origins*. Chicago: University of Chicago Press.

Kuhn, S. L., & Stiner, M. C. (2001). The antiquity of hunter-gatherers. In C. Panter-Brick, R. H. Layton, & P. A. Rowley-Conwy (Eds.), *Another day, another camp: An interdisciplinary view of hunter-gatherers* (pp. 99–142). Cambridge, UK: Cambridge University Press.

Mellars, P. A. (1985). The ecological basis of social complexity in the upper Paleolithic of southwestern France. In T. D. Price & J. A. Brown (Eds.), *Prehistoric hunter-gatherers: The emergence of cultural complexity* (pp. 271–297). San Diego, CA: Academic Press.

Oswalt, W. H. (1976). *An anthropological analysis of food-getting technology*. New York: John Wiley and Sons.

Stewart, K. M. (1989). *Fishing sites of north and east Africa in the late Pleistocene and Holocene: Environmental change and human adaptation* (B.A.R. International Series No. 521). Oxford, UK: B.A.R.

Stiner, M. C. (1994). *Honor among thieves: A zooarchaeological study of Neanderthal ecology*. Princeton, NJ: Princeton University Press.

Stiner, M. C. (2002). Carnivory, coevolution, and the geographic spread of the genus *Homo*. *Journal of Archaeological Research, 10*(1), 1–63.

Thieme, H. (1997). Lower Palaeolithic hunting spears from Germany. *Nature, 385,* 807–810.

Hunting and Gathering

The history of the hunting and gathering way of life covers 4 million years and begins with the time of emerging humans, covers the millennia when hunter-gatherers constituted 100 percent of the species, and continues through their large-scale disappearance in the face of agricultural life right down to the early contacts with European-style cultures in the seventeenth century and then the beginnings of ethnography (study of human cultures) in the later nineteenth century. In 14,000 BCE everybody was one, and as late as 1500 CE one-third of the Earth's surface was occupied by hunter-gatherers. Groups of hunter-gatherers still exist, although they are affected by the economies of their neighbors. Thus many millennia of their presence are known from excavation and a few centuries from interviews, with the size of the recovery of evidence rather different in each case. In total humans have been hunter-gatherers for over 90 percent of their evolutionary time.

Basic Ideas

The term, often written as *gatherer-hunters* to emphasise a common primacy of reliance on plant material for food, refers to a mode of subsistence that is characterized by the absence of direct human control over the reproduction of exploited species, with the exception of the dog. Such an empirical definition also encompasses the practices of fishing and scavenging. In addition, there is little or no control over aspects of population ecology such as the exploited species' behavior. In essence, therefore, there is no deliberate alteration of the gene pool. However, in the course of utilizing species of living and recently dead organisms, it is possible for hunter-gatherer groups to bring about environmental changes: Sometimes this appears deliberate in its attempt to improve the conditions for resource species, and at other times it may well be an accidental by-product of lifeways, including the nonmaterial aspects of hunter-gatherer cultures.

One outstanding fact is the success of hunter-gatherers in colonizing—over a period from 4 million years ago to 1750 CE—most of the habitats of the planet, with the only exceptions being those permanently covered in ice, such as high mountains, Antarctica and its islands, and the deep oceans far from land. Everywhere else, from the lowland tropical forests to the high Arctic, has housed a population of hunter-gatherers at some stage during the Pleistocene (beginning 1.6 million years ago) or Holocene (beginning ten thousand years ago) epoch. Their range of behaviors and their flexibility were instrumental in this success; yet, a few ecological and social traits seem common to most of their cultures and have relevance for their environmental relationships. Probably the two most significant in terms of environmental interest are low rates of population growth and minor quantities of material possessions. The demographic characteristics of hunter-gatherer populations have either to be inferred from archeological data or reconstructed from periods subsequent to Western contact, and thus there is an someuncertainty. Nevertheless, to say that before the Neolithic (latest period of the Stone Age) period most such populations had annual growth rates of .008 percent, that life expectancy was twenty-four to thirty-seven years, and that recent (i.e., the last 150 years) individual hunter-gatherer populations have been larger than ever before is to summarize their basic demographic history reasonably fairly. The low levels of material possessions clustered around the need for mobility by the human groups, the constant sharing of food and other materials, and a general egalitarianism in which possessions had not of themselves denoted status. Further, their technology was not particularly elaborate (although highly tuned to particular environments), and the lack of a cargo-carrying domesticated animal added to the undesirability of lugging the equivalent of the kitchen sink around the landscape. Also unwanted were too many children who would need to be carried.

Within any set of surroundings, the ecology of food collection is crucial. In the broadest of terms, the degree of dependence upon plant foods declines away from the equator, and there is everywhere a reciprocal relationship between the concentration of food-item calories and the concentration of their source. Thus large fatty animals are usually dispersed and mobile, albeit sometimes with seasonal concentrations, as with salmon and caribou, whereas grass seeds and nuts are abundant and concentrated even if lacking the satisfactions of a belly full of meat. But given the social and ecological adaptability of most groups, a satisfactory diet was often achieved without the sort of back-breaking labor required by subsistence agriculture. The price was, usually, intermittent famines.

Disappearance and Adaptation

All this makes it the more surprising that hunter-gatherers largely disappeared after agriculture was irreversibly established, with survival only in a few areas marginal for agriculture or at least spatially remote from it. Some surviving hunter-gatherers, for instance, were agriculturalists who retreated into forest hunting to escape the Europeans, of which there are examples in Amazonia; in eastern Africa others accepted a degree of contact with colonists so that farming and herding might come and go in their economies in accordance with a variety of climatic, economic, and nonmaterial considerations. Yet, there are still the descendants of ancient hunter-gatherers whose culture is framed by their lineage: The Kalahari San people were nonagricultural from the late Stone Age (8000 years ago) until the late nineteenth century. The perception of hunter-gatherers as being excellently adapted to their environments reflects the notion of them as primitives who were at the mercy of nature, just as in the 1960s they became honorary environmentalists whose ways might be the salvation of the Earth, at least in those places that felt most guilty about the way they had been treated by successor cultures. The notion of adaptation is highly relevant for people moving in a pioneer fashion into post-Pleistocene landscapes or even in the interglacial phases of temperate latitudes. The peripheries of ice sheets are not replete with environmental choices after they are occupied. Similarly, the folk of the northern reaches of North America before European contact either ate animals or they died; there was little cultural choice at that level. Given also the low population densities characteristic of their populations, the relatively simple technologies, and the lack of demand for material possessions, environmental manipulation might well be assumed to be nonexistent. People would gather fruits, seeds, and nuts; they would scavenge on dead meat if they could wrest it from other predators, and they would hunt for a variety of birds, mammals, and reptiles. These latter would have reproductive capacities that would easily fill the gaps left by a human usage that essentially mimicked the natural world: Here was simply a general diversivore, able to eat both plant and animal material, fresh and partially decayed.

Market hunting of waterfowl led to a general decline in America's bird population in the early 1900s. Here a woman displays illegally taken waterfowl in California in the 1930s.
COURTESY U. S. FISH AND WILDLIFE SERVICE.

Impact and Technology, Especially Fire

There are different appraisals of resource bases. The first is that utilized biota (the flora and fauna of a region) are not evenly spread in time and space and that there may be spells when plants or animals are so concentrated that they may be vulnerable to losses that then affect their reproductive rates. Thus if all the pregnant females of a large mammal group cluster in a herd and that group is then run over a cliff, the next generation may be missing in that particular locality. The lowest population density and the simplest technology could bring that about. A stand of wild grasses could be wiped out if the seed heads all ripened simultaneously and were all carefully gathered, an unlikely but not impossible eventuality. But there is another consideration of greater importance in the human-nature relationship from early times onward: the possession and control of fire. The origins of this tool are not firmly known because new evidence constantly accumulates from regions such as Africa, where archeologists are thinner on the ground than the native buffalo, although, according to legend, sometimes equally combative. Fire at the hearth widens the dietary possibilities of hunter-gatherers because it predigests some foods with which the human gut is ill equipped to deal. This is especially true of plants, where cellulose walls are softened by cooking, making chewing and digestion easier. Meat and fish may be culturally more acceptable if cooked, but simply as nutrition, both *tartare* and *sashimi* are as good a source as roast beef or fried cod. More significantly, fire allows the drying and smoking of meat and fish as methods of preservation.

Beyond the circle of the hearth, however, lies the ability to control fire at landscape scale. It seems certain that *Homo sapiens* possessed this skill, but for earlier hominid species the evidence is indirect. However, most archeologists believe that such a proficiency was part of the kit that allowed *Homo erectus* to spread beyond Africa into the rest of the Old World. By the time of modern humans at 150,000–100,000 years ago, the mastery of fire seems undisputed, and life even near Pleistocene ice sheets became possible: *Homo sapiens* could be a fire creature from an ice age, as North American environmental historian Stephen Pyne (2001) graphically puts it.

Once mastered, fire has many uses for hunter-gatherers away from the hearth. Fire can be used to drive animals because most are afraid of it. So predatory species can be scared away from camps and away from fresh carcasses, for instance. All species can be steered into the paths of concealed hunters or driven over cliffs and into cul-de-sacs such as box canyons or crescentic dunes. An advancing fire front also puts up an array of small but edible animals: Locusts and grasshoppers, small mammals, and confused birds may all be added to the menu, as may subterranean lizards and snakes that have been baked. There is then a further stage. The vegetation that springs up afterward, often after the next rainy season or in the spring in a temperate latitude, is usually richer in protein than unburned stands, and so the animals are attracted to the plants and hence concentrated for hunting. Some plants also fruit more heavily after fire, and so direct supplies of, for example, nuts are enhanced: Oak trees were thus managed for acorn yield as far apart as Yosemite, California, and Lerida, Spain. In an overall and longer-term perspective, the way in which repeated fire eliminates intolerant species may often improve sight lines for hunters, especially in woodland and dense savanna. Looked at culturally, a fired landscape is an emblem of human stewardship and hence, very likely, ownership.

Types and Times of Impact

It is essential, therefore, to look closely at the interaction of changes in the natural world with those in human cultures before pronouncing either that hunter-gatherers were inhabitants of a kind of Eden or that they were the precursors of those aspects of today's environmental behavior that are labeled "destructive." The roles of climate and climatic change, for example, cannot be omitted in any discussion of human groups with a preindustrial set of technologies. At the most basic level, there seems to be a human body type that shows the tropical origins of the species (tall and relatively slim) and an adaptation to Arctic conditions seen first in *Homo sapiens neanderthalis*, which was shorter and stockier. The rapid climatic changes of the early Holocene epoch in temperate (extratropical) latitudes led to swift successions of ecosystem type and species composition and thus represented an adaptational challenge: Inhabitants of a tundra-mammoth-migratory reindeer system could find themselves within mere decades in a deciduous (leaf-dropping) woodland-red deer-hazel nut complex with the additional need of a whole new summer wardrobe. Beyond this level of determinism, however, there are instances where climatic change and human action seem difficult to separate. The late Pleistocene-early Holocene period, for example, was often the period when not only did the climate change rapidly but also the first hu-

mans arrived. Many species became extinct, and evidence suggests that humans were largely responsible (the hypothesis of "Pleistocene overkill," in which many species of large mammal died out just after the first colonization by humans) just as there are morsels of evidence and more elaborate models that involve some forms of climatic change. North America and Australia in particular provide stages for the scientists' reenactment of the disappearance of many large mammal herbivore species and genera, together with their dependent carnivores. Although climatic change is likely to have put many species under stress, the coincident arrival of a new carnivore with cooperative capabilities beyond those of the wolf, and with the new tool of controlled fire, seems likely to be significant.

The late Pleistocene-early Holocene uncertainties (pivoting at about ten thousand years ago) about the dominance of either the natural or the cultural provide a transition into the time of more stable ecosystems (never entirely so, of course) that provide a kind of benchmark against which the impact of human communities can be measured up to the disappearance of hunter-gatherers, or at any rate the period of their intensive contact with other economies and cultural types. The main theme of interest here, then, is the hunter, the gatherer, and the fisher as a maker of new genotypes (all or part of the genetic constitution of an individual or group) in the nonhuman biota and as a maker of new ecosystems. In terms of direct breeding only the transformation of some species of wolf into domesticated dogs is recorded, although selective pressures applied to other species must have affected some genetic traits. Research into genetic histories made possible by DNA typing will surely amplify this picture in due course.

Processes of Impact

Thus the focus on hunter-gatherers as makers of landscapes during the Holocene epoch after ten thousand years is on their capacity to alter the ecology of a region in a quasi-permanent fashion. Many examples of this are attested to by the archeological record, by observations from early contacts with literate travelers, and by the oral cultures of the people themselves. A general framework that might encompass the different types of change imposed by human groups might include:

1. Direct changes in animal and plant populations due to hunting or gathering. The effects were variable in time and space but might result in the elimination of a whole species at local, regional, conti-

nental, or even global scales, depending on the abundance and distribution of that species. The use of fire pushed alterations in the direction of permanence as most species reacted differently to repeated burnings: Some were fire tolerant, others largely intolerant.

2. Different technologies might lead to divergent ecologies. In a direct fashion, the adoption of trapping technologies would have a distinct impact on small mammal populations, as distinct from trying to shoot them with arrows or darts. An indirect effect would result from any better technology that allowed greater success in animal hunting that then led to a higher fat intake and thence to lower the age of menarche (the beginning of menstruation) and allow increased rates of population growth.

3. A similar impact type might produce a different ecology if the target populations had different behaviors. If all the pregnant females gather together, and that band is then killed in its entirety for more than a few years in succession, then a decline in its abundance is probable unless there is colonization from adjoining populations. By contrast, if adult males are the target for hunters (killing for status rather than food), then in many mammal species, males on the margins of sexual success may move in and replace those taken out, rather as happens when the school football team goes on tour.

4. There must be space, too, for different cultural attitudes. Clearly, the most important of these is the presence or absence of a "conservationist" approach to animal numbers in which there is a voluntary restriction on off-take (the number of animals killed). (There seems to be no obvious example of plants being viewed in the same way.) Hence, some cultures considered that "resting" an area normally culled for food or furs was important from time to time, whereas others regarded high levels of killing as essential to ensure the perpetuation of the target species: the more deaths, the more animal souls to be reincarnated. The use of fire at landscape scale may have spiritual as well as practical components, as in northern Australia.

5. There are some examples of minimal impacts. In general, wetlands are manipulated less than dry ground, for obvious reasons. But if they dry out seasonally, they can be burned: Early Mesolithic (c. 7000 BCE) people did so to lake-edge reed fringes in northern England, just as Native Americans behaved in prairie Canada within historic times. Yet,

the plants simply regrew on an annual basis. In central Australia channels were dug in swamps to encourage the expansion of eel populations. In Lapland the Saami (who were hunters of reindeer until they took up herding in the nineteenth century) avoided the extensive use of fire lest it consume the precious pine woodlands.

In North America after the Pleistocene epoch, a complex version of these generalities emerged as would be expected in so great a diversity of biomes (major ecological community types). There is not much doubt that many of the cultures were able to exterminate animals on a large scale and that sometimes after contact with external traders they did so, with the classic example being the penetration of the Hudson's Bay Company into what is now Canada. They traded in the valuable beaver pelts and contributed to a condition in which the beaver harvest in North America in the late nineteenth century was only about 10 percent of its level one hundred years earlier because the animal itself had become scarce or locally extinct. Perhaps the most interesting question is the level of the beaver population in, say, 1700 CE, when it was abundant in the interior of the continent but less so in, for example, New England. Was this mostly due to conscious "conservation" of beaver by the inland native people, using a variety of cultural mechanisms such as rotational trapping and moiety totemism (meaning, in this context, a withholding by a sub-group of people), or was it rather a lesser ecological impact from a low population density, an inefficient extraction technology, and the lack of external trade contacts that would have provided a market for pelts? The discussion of these questions is suffused with the language of present-day ecology and politics and so no brief answers are satisfactory; yet, as discussed later, similar questions have implications for today's management policies.

Today's Appraisals of Hunter-Gatherers

The intellectual climate has changed as well in the discussion of the ecological impact of hunter-gatherers in Europe during the millennia of the Holocene epoch before the spread of agricultural practices (the "Neolithic Revolution") from the southeast in about 8000 BCE to the Atlantic fringe in about 4500 BCE. During the 1950s the discussion of the environment of the last preagricultural folk (Mesolithic cultures) was conducted largely in terms of pollen diagrams from peat bogs. The founding document was an account from Denmark by palynologist Johannes Iversen that inferred the importance of *landnam* (land-taking) by means of slash-and-burn agriculture followed by the planting of introduced cereals. Before the Neolithic period, it seemed that there had been no human-induced manipulation of vegetation. This view was the accepted science until the British paleoecologist G. W. Dimbleby published work suggesting the use of fire to alter vegetation communities on the upland areas of northern England, about 300 meters above sea level. He used pollen recovery from podzolic (relating to a group of zonal soils that develops in a moist climate and has an organic mat and a thin organic-mineral layer above a light gray leached layer resting on a dark illuvial horizon enriched with amorphous clay) soils where the stratification is less certain than in bog peats, and so there was a lengthy period of rejection of his ideas. That diminished only when peat sections began to reveal that preagricultural groups were burning in order to encourage grasses and certain kinds of nut- and forage-bearing shrubs and in some places to try to stop the upward progress (under conditions of climatic amelioration) of forests whose resource potential was presumably unfamiliar and less acceptable than that of the open lands that had preceded them. The keeping open of the higher ground had later consequences when the climate shifted to more oceanic conditions. The trees that would have wicked away the precipitation were not present, and so soil waterlogging led to the accumulation of acid peat ("blanket bog") on low but water-shedding slopes, up to depths as great as 6 meters.

It is clear from the study of the history of hunter-gatherers and environments that today's attitudes affect the appraisal of these people and their environmental relations. The recent interest in native populations and indigenous people has enfolded hunter-gatherers as well as preindustrial agriculturalists and has thus become caught up in the preoccupations of the time. Foremost of these has been the revival of the idea of the "noble savage" in which hunter-gatherers are presented as models for a environmental future: people with a strong Earth-bound spirituality who tread lightly on the soil and are thrifty in their use of all types of resources. The ease with which a bogus group (the Tasaday in the Philippines) of "primitive" hunter-gatherers was initially accepted in 1971 is testimony to the desire to exalt such exemplars.

Relevance to Environmental Policies

It is no surprise, then, that the environmental linkages of hunter-gatherers have found their way into management policies. Examples include the omission of Arctic Inupiat people from prohibitions on whaling because the hunting of bowhead whales formed part of their "traditional" culture; the reappraisal of fire management in northern Australia even in monsoon forests; and the rejection of the introduction of many forms of industrial land use that might encroach on hunting and fishing terrains. Some areas in the American West were not ecologically pristine when first traversed by explorers such as Lewis and Clark, but their forests and animal populations had been subject to Native American influences such as fire and the hunting of mammals. Even within regions there seem to be differences in large mammal densities resulting from hunter-gatherer times. Higher population densities seem to have been encountered in "buffer zones" between warring groups, suggesting that human predation was a major factor in game populations in the precolonial era. So if "wilderness" management and restoration ecology generally are desirable in a conservation-oriented, or postproductivist, economy, what is the historical benchmark that should be adopted? Ought managers try to "freeze" a reconstructed landscape ecology at a particular point in time?

The same question is relevant to the moorlands of England and Wales, whose open and treeless aspect had its inception in the Mesolithic times of the mid-Holocene. That state has been maintained ever since by millennia of sheep grazing and fire, together with grouse management for sport since the mid-nineteenth century. The result is a wet desert with low biodiversity (biological diversity as indicated by numbers of species of animals and plants). But it is precisely those areas that have been identified as jewels in the nation's scenic crown and were designated as national parks under a Parliamentary act of 1949. Now that soil erosion, foot and mouth disease (FMD), and overproduction of sheep meat (there is little market for the wool) necessitate a reevaluation of land-use policies, there is a strong rearguard action in favor of the status quo on landscape grounds, that is, the look of the land, not its ecological welfare, is to be preserved.

It is possible to spot the remains of hunter-gatherer environmental linkages outside their remaining identifiable territories. The world's fishing industries have barely embarked on the Neolithic Revolution. They may "voluntarily" restrict their cull, and many examples of herding can be seen, but most often, wild fish are hunted. The lessons of overkill, however, have not noticeably been applied. Slightly less obviously, there is the popularity among human males of killing animals: Fishing and hunting command enormous followings in industrial societies. This seems like a remnant of a time when males proclaimed their desirability as mates by bringing home high-status feast items.

Farewell or Fare Well?

This might lead to the conclusion that although data on hunter-gatherers' environmental bonds are academically desirable, they are not of any practical significance in an electrified world hooked on oil. But maybe all such information is analogous to the protection of biodiversity in the world. These data are like a gene pool and once lost, are gone forever: There is no equivalent of *Jurassic Park*. Even if the knowledge is never of practical value, it enriches current cultures to know of the alternatives that once existed and that were vanishing fast when in 1672 English poet John Dryden formulated a cultural filter for humankind and nature that has resonated ever since. For him the hunter-gatherer was

> . . . as free as nature first made man,
> Ere the base laws of servitude began,
> When wild in woods the noble savage ran.

I. G. Simmons

Further Reading

Alroy, J. (2001). A multispecies overkill simulation of the end-Pleistocene megafaunal mass extinction. *Science, 292*(5523), 1893–1896.

Anderson, A. (1989). Mechanics of overkill in the extinction of New Zealand moas. *Journal of Archaeological Science, 16*(1), 137–151.

Anderson, A. (1989). *Prodigious birds: Moas and moa-hunting in prehistoric New Zealand.* Cambridge, UK: Cambridge University Press.

Anderson, M. K. (1994). Prehistoric anthropogenic wildland burning by hunter-gatherer societies in the temperate regions: A net source, sink, or neutral to the global carbon budget? *Chemosphere, 29*(5), 913–934.

Beck, M. W. (1996). On discerning the cause of late Pleistocene megafaunal extinctions. *Paleobiology, 22*(1), 91–103.

Bettinger, R. L. (1987). Archaeological approaches to hunter-gatherers. *Annual Review of Anthropology, 16,* 121–142.

Cachel, S. (1997). Dietary shifts and the European upper Palaeolithic transition. *Current Anthropology, 38*(4), 579–603.

Choquenot, D., & Bowman, D. M. J. S. (1998). Marsupial megafauna, aborigines and the overkill hypothesis: Application of predator-prey models to the question of Pleistocene extinction in Australia. *Global Ecology and Biogeography, 7*(3), 167–180.

Dryden, J. (1672). *The Conquest of Granada. Part i. Act i. Scene 1.*

Gowdy, J. (Ed.). (1997). *Limited wants, unlimited means.* Covelo, CA: Island Press.

Hicks, S. (1993). Pollen evidence of localized impact on the vegetation of northernmost Finland by hunter-gatherers. *Vegetation History and Archaeobotany, 2*(2), 137–144.

Holdaway, R. N., & Jacomb, C. (2000). Rapid extinction of the moas (Aves: Dinorinthiformes): Model, test and implications. *Science, 287*(5461), 2250–2254.

Jackson, S. T., & Weng, C. Y. (1999). Late Quaternary extinction of a tree species in eastern North America. *Proceedings of the National Academy of Sciences of the USA, 96*(24), 13847–13852.

Kay, C. E. (1994). Aboriginal overkill: The role of Native Americans in structuring western ecosystems. *Human Nature, 5,* 359–398.

Kay, C. E. (1997). Viewpoint: Ungulate herbivory, willows and political ecology in Yellowstone. *Journal of Range Management, 50,* 139–145.

Kay, C. E., Patton, B., et al. (2000). Historical wildlife observations in the Canadian Rockies: Implications for ecological integrity. *Canadian Field Naturalist, 114*(4), 561–583.

Krech, S. (1999). *The ecological Indian: Myth and history.* New York: W. W. Norton.

Lee, R. B., & Daly, R. (Eds.). (1999). *The Cambridge encyclopedia of hunters and gatherers.* Cambridge, UK: Cambridge University Press.

Low, B. S. (1996). Behavioral ecology of conservation in traditional societies. *Human Nature, 7*(4), 353–379.

Lyman, R. L., & Wolverton, S. (2002). The late-Pleistocene-early historic game sink in the northwestern United States. *Conservation Biology, 16*(1), 73–85.

Martin, C. (1978). *Keepers of the game.* Berkeley and Los Angeles: University of California Press.

Martin, P. S., & Klein, R. G. (Eds.). (1984). *Quaternary extinctions: A prehistoric revolution.* Tucson: University of Arizona Press.

Martin, P. S., & Szuter, C. R. (1999). War zones and game sinks in Lewis and Clark's West. *Conservation Biology, 13*(1), 36–45.

Martin, P. S., & Szuter, C. R. (2002). Game parks before and after Lewis and Clark: Reply to Lyman and Wolverton. *Conservation Biology, 16*(2), 244–247.

Meehan, B., & White, N. (Eds.). (1990). *Hunter-gatherer demography: Past and present*. Sydney, Australia: University of Sydney.

Mithen, S., Finlay, N., Carruthers, N., Carter, S., & Ashmore, P.(2001). Plant use in the Mesolithic: Evidence from Staosnaig, Isle of Colonsay, Scotland. *Journal of Archaeological Science*, *28*(2), 223–234.

Moore, P. D. (2002, April 4). Baffled over bison. *Nature*, *416*, 488–489.

Panter-Brick, C., Layton, R. H., & Rowley-Conwy, P. (Eds.). (2001). *Hunter-gatherers: An interdisciplinary perspective*. Cambridge, UK: Cambridge University Press.

Pyalka, J. (2000). Mitigating human effects on European biodiversity through traditional animal husbandry. *Conservation Biology*, *14*(4), 705–712.

Pyne, S. J. (2001). *Fire: A brief history*. Seattle: University of Washington Press.

Shennan, S. (2000). Population, culture history and the dynamics of culture change. *Current Anthropology*, *41*(5), 811–835.

Simmons, I. G. (1996). *The environmental impact of later Mesolithic cultures*. Edinburgh, UK: Edinburgh University Press.

Steadman, D. W., Pregill, G. K., & Burley, D. V. (2002). Rapid prehistoric extinction of iguanas and birds in Polynesia. *Proceedings of the National Academy of Sciences of the USA*, *99*(6), 3673–3677.

Winterhalder, B., & Lu, F. (1997). A forager-resource population ecology model and implications for indigenous conservation. *Biological Conservation*, *11*, 1354–1364.

Ice Ages

Ice ages are epochs of time when massive ice sheets and smaller ice masses called glaciers cover extensive areas of the Earth's surface. During an ice age the planet is cold, dry, and inhospitable. Whereas few forests can be supported, ice-covered areas and deserts are plentiful. Winters are longer and more severe, and ice sheets grow to tremendous sizes, accumulating to thicknesses that measure thousands of feet in depth. These tremendous ice sheets move slowly from higher elevations to lower regions, driven by gravity and their tremendous weight. During that process, they alter river courses, destroy entire regional ecosystems, flatten landscapes, and, along their margins, deposit great piles of glacial debris.

Evidence of Ice Ages

Proof of ice ages—glaciation over continent-sized regions—comes from several sources. There is the widespread deposition of unique sediments of dirt (called "till") found under melting glaciers. These sediments contain a wide variety of rock forms that have been accumulated from disparate areas. In addition, glaciation leaves telltale marks in the form of grooved, striated, polished bedrock pavements, faceted stones in the till, and interspersed layers of gravel containing different rock types. Ice ages also are substantiated by erosional forms believed to have been produced by advancing ice sheets, among them sculptured landscapes, such as glacial uplands or U-shaped valleys.

Such evidence suggests at least five prolonged ice ages: (1) during Precambrian era, 1.7–2.3 billion years ago; (2) during the end of the Proterozoic eon, about 670 million years ago; (3) during the middle of the Paleozoic era, about 420 million years ago; (4) during the Carboniferous period, in the late Paleozoic era, beginning 290 million years ago; and (5) during the Pleistocene epoch of the Quaternary period, beginning 1.7 million years ago. In this most recent era, ice sheets developed in the highlands of North America and Europe and dominated the Northern Hemisphere. Massive ice sheets covered all of present Canada, south of the Great Lakes region, as well as Greenland, Scandinavia, and Russia. Each ice age lasted at least a million years, during which great ice sheets migrated back and forth across a huge paleocontinent (ancient or prehistoric continent). The span of these ice ages totaled 50 to 200 million years, which accounts for only 1 to 4 percent of the Earth's 4.6 billion-year history. Ice ages thus represent unusual, albeit relatively short, episodes in the Earth's climatic record.

Theories about Causes of Ice Ages

Although scientists have extensively studied glaciation, no single theory is widely accepted as explaining the causes of ice ages. However, several theories converge into two categories. First are terrestrial theories. Among these, in 1941 Canadian A. P. Coleman suggested that change in the elevations of continents provided a natural explanation for an ice age. That is, the uplifting of continental blocks creates increases in the height of land areas by mountains rising or sea levels falling, which cooled the land and produced glacial conditions. A second theory is linked to the changing continental positions associated with plate tectonics.

The notion of continental drift, set out by the German geophysicist Alfred Wegener in 1922, proposes that continents sliding around on the globe's surface could be brought into colder climatic conditions, thereby allowing ice sheets to develop, especially because a continent's climate is mainly determined by its latitude and size. A third theory suggests that extensive volcanic activity, which spews out dust and ash into the atmosphere, reflects radiant solar heat back into space, thereby producing cooler temperatures on the Earth's surface. Closely related is the ocean-atmospheric hypothesis. The assumption here is that the only adequate supply of water for massive ice accumulations is the ocean. Because creation of ice sheets on land depends on wind and weather patterns, logic suggests that profound changes between the ocean and the atmosphere could contribute to the onset of ice ages. Another hypothesis was put forward in 1998 by the American climatologist, Maureen Raymo. She proposed the idea that Earth's cooling climate over the last 40 million years was caused by a reduction in atmospheric carbon dioxide due to enhanced chemical weathering in the mountainous regions of the world, particularly the Himalayas, and that the growth of the Himalayas may, in fact, have triggered the start of the ice ages.

The second category of theories to explain ice ages is extraterrestrial. As early as 1875 the Scottish scientist James Croll proposed that astronomical variations in the Earth's orbit around the sun produced conditions for the onset of ice ages. He believed that disturbances by the moon and sun cause periodic shifts in the Earth's orbit, thereby affecting the distribution of solar heat received by the Earth and climatic patterns on the surface. Less heat produces colder climates.

Croll's theory was modified in 1938 by a Yugoslav scientist, Milutin Milankovitch, in what is today the most popularly accepted theory for climate changes during the Pleistocene epoch. Milankovitch believed that the amount of solar radiation is the most important factor in controlling the Earth's climate and in producing ice ages. The amount of radiation varies, he argued, according to three key factors. (1) The Earth doesn't rotate perfectly like a wheel about an axis; it spins like a wobbling top. Every twenty-two thousand years, Milankovitch calculated, there is a slight change in its wobble (called "precession of the equinoxes"). (2) Every 100,000 years there is a change in the Earth's orbit about the sun (which he labeled "eccentricity"). The Earth's almost-circular orbit becomes more elliptical, taking the Earth farther from the sun. (3) Finally, Milankovitch discovered that every forty-one thousand years there is a change in the tilt of the Earth's axis, moving either the Northern or Southern Hemisphere farther from the sun (a process known as "obliquity"). These cycles mean that at certain times less sunshine hits the Earth, so there is less melting of snow and ice. Instead of melting, these cold expanses of frozen water grow. The snow and ice last longer and, over many seasons, begin to accumulate. Snow reflects some sunlight back into space, which also contributes to cooling. Temperatures drop, and glaciers begin to advance. These effects are sufficiently substantial to cause cyclical expansion and contraction of the massive ice sheets. By taking climatic effects and solar insulation of these variations and applying them to computer models of ice sheet behavior, scientists have demonstrated that a correlation exists between these cycles and the cyclic growth and decay of Pleistocene ice sheets over the past 600,000 years. The combination of orbital cycles results in lower summer insulation (exposure to the sun's rays) at fifty-five degrees north latitude. Such cooler summers in high latitudes tend to preserve each winter's snowfall, which over thousands of years leads to snow from successive winters inducing growth in the northern ice sheets, evidentially causing the onset of a new ice age.

A final theory was advanced in 1966 by the American D. W. Patten, who speculated that ice ages may have resulted from "ice dumps" coming from outer space. His theory contends that ice fell directly from space, producing a massive build-up of continental glaciation. That would explain the biblical flood and sudden freezing of wooly mammoths. However, no geological or astronomical evidence has been found to support this theory.

The Earth may be currently in an ice age because within each major glaciation ice caps and mountain glaciers are oscillating between extension and retreat. The last retreat concluded approximately ten thousand years ago and probably represents only an oscillation, not a final ending. The recent trend toward global warming, however, has reduced fears of any imminent return of an ice age.

Christopher C. Joyner

See also Climate; Evolution and Spread of Humans

Further Reading

Andersen, B. G., & Borns, H. W. (1994). *The ice age world.* New York: Scandinavian University Press.

Erickson, J. (1990). *Ice ages: Past and future.* Blue Ridge Summit, PA: TAB Books.

Illinois State Museum, Ice ages. Last updated January 4, 2002: Retrieved January 30, 2003, from http://www.museum.state.il.us/exhibits/ice_ages/

Pielon, E. C. (1991). *The Ice Age*. Chicago: University of Chicago Press.

Ickes, Harold
(1874–1952)
U.S. secretary of the interior

Harold LeClair Ickes served as U.S. secretary of the interior longer than any of his predecessors or successors, from 1933 to 1946. While secretary, he restored public confidence in the scandal-plagued department, enlarged the national park system, increased the power of the Bureau of Reclamation, and revived a moribund conservation program. He simultaneously served as head of the Public Works Administration (PWA) and as oil administrator, positions that allowed him to wield great power during the Great Depression. He succeeded in part because President Franklin Roosevelt and the American public had great confidence in him.

Born in Frankstown Township, Pennsylvania, Ickes graduated from the University of Chicago in 1897, then worked briefly as a journalist before receiving his law degree from the university in 1907. He soon became involved in politics, organizing campaigns for reform-minded candidates in Illinois regardless of party, working for Democratic, Republican, and Progressive Party candidates through the first decade of the twentieth century. He gained a reputation as an embittered crusader while working for several reform causes, including civic betterment, civil rights for blacks, and conservation. His efforts to bring liberal Midwestern Republican voters to the Democratic candidate Roosevelt's side in 1932 won him appointment as secretary of the interior.

Ickes faced a formidable task. The department's reputation had suffered during the Pinchot-Ballinger Affair and the Teapot Dome Scandal of the 1920s; in both cases former secretaries had been accused of misconduct in office. Ickes opposed the department's long-standing position of conservation for the sake of later development and use. Instead, he adopted a concept of wilderness protection and pressed for a comprehensive Wilderness Act, which was not enacted until the 1960s. He expanded the parklands from approximately 3.3 million hectares to over 8 million between 1933 and 1941, and used the Civilian Conservation Corps to make improvements in parks.

As head of the PWA (1933–1939), he used some of its funds to expand the Bureau of Reclamation's dam building, irrigation, and power programs, making the department into the world's largest generator and distributor of hydroelectric power. The PWA also built many public buildings, schools, and hospitals; major highways and tunnels; aircraft carriers and cruisers for the U.S. Navy; and civilian and military installations. He also ended racial segregation in the department and the parks.

Ickes's policies faced their toughest challenge with the coming of World War II. National defense and mobilization for war meant new, intense demands for access to natural resources on public land. With the support of conservationists, Ickes resisted such demands. As petroleum administrator during the war, he coordinated the conservation, acquisition, and allocation of the nation's oil. His only notable failure as secretary came in his attempt to transform the Department of the Interior to the Department of Conservation. He wanted control of all conservation agencies, but failed to get the Forest Service moved, due largely to the efforts of Gifford Pinchot, who had headed the Forest Service from 1898 to 1910.

Roosevelt's death in 1945 left Ickes working for Harry Truman, a man with whom he was never comfortable. A curmudgeon to the end, he protested Truman's nomination of an oil magnate to be undersecretary of the Navy and resigned in 1946. He wrote a syndicated newspaper column for a few years before retiring.

James G. Lewis

Further Reading

Clarke, J. N. (1996). *Roosevelt's warrior: Harold L. Ickes and the New Deal.* Baltimore: Johns Hopkins University Press.

Ickes, H. L. (1935). *Back to work: The story of PWA.* New York: Macmillan Co.

Ickes, H. L. (1940). *Not guilty: An official inquiry into the charges made by Glavis and Pinchot against Richard A. Ballinger, Secretary of the Interior, 1909–1911.* Washington, DC: Government Printing Office.

Ickes, H. L. (1943). *The autobiography of a curmudgeon.* New York: Reynal & Hitchcock.

Ickes, H. L. (1953–54) *The secret diary of Harold L. Ickes* (3 Vols.). New York: Simon and Schuster.

Watkins, T. H. (1990). *Righteous pilgrim: The life and times of Harold L. Ickes, 1874–1952.* New York: Henry Holt & Company.

White, G., & Maze, J. R. (1985). *Harold Ickes of the New Deal: His private life and public career.* Cambridge, MA: Harvard University Press.

Imperialism *See* Colonialism and Imperialism, Ecological Imperialism

India

India is a country whose environment is a study in contrasts. Environmental issues, especially those of forest access, air quality, and the use of water, are keenly contested in a deeply unequal society with a vibrant democracy. Questions of livelihood loom large because more than 33 percent of India's 1 billion people are poor, only 57 percent of adults are literate, and 50 percent of the children are malnourished. Urban middle class groups similar to those in developed countries at times sharply differ with the agendas of empowerment, the livelihood based agendas of the poor. The latter include 6 million coastal fishers, 80 million Scheduled Tribals (indigenous groups who are eligible for positive discrimination under India's Constitution), and others who rely on forest resources. Displacement by development projects is a major public issue.

The legacies of British colonial rule until 1947 and the subsequent model of development are central forces in reshaping the environment. The voter turnout in state and federal elections averages over 60 percent; over 3 million representatives hold office at local, state, and federal levels. But India's people are divided by deep disparities of income, economic opportunity, and privilege. Livelihood in rural settlements, which account for 73 percent of the population, is still heavily reliant on use of land, water, and biomass (the amount of living matter). Conversely, India has been a nuclear-capable country since 1974 and has the third-largest pool of scientific and technical labor power in the world. By 2001 the Indian life span had risen to sixty-four years (from twenty-seven in 1951), but issues of the quality of life and sustainability are more contentious than ever.

Climate and Geography

India has four times the population of the United States on one-third the land area. One-half the land of India is arable (suitable for irrigation). Major regions include the Indo-Gangetic Plain, the Himalaya Mountains, the peninsula, and the Northeast, which borders on Myanmar. The floodplains of the Indus, Ganges, and Brahmaputra Rivers make up one of Asia's largest expanses of lowland river plains. To the north the geologically young Himalayas stretch from west to east. In addition to the sediment that has formed the plains, the Himalayas have other critical consequences. They moderate the cold winds from the Tibetan Plateau; they block the clouds brought in by the southwest monsoon from the Bay of Bengal in the east. The subcontinent is drier to the west, but the pattern does not always hold true. The Western Ghat Mountains, which run parallel to the western coast, form a barrier to the monsoon clouds coming in from the Arabian Sea.

There are significant contrasts between the north and the south. All regions have a well-defined rainy season, the monsoon (from the Arabic *mausam*, meaning "season"). Northern rivers are perennial, fed by the snows of the Himalayas ("the abode of snow"; *him = snow, alaya = home*). Southern rivers, including the Kaveri, Tambrapani, Mahanadi, Godavari, and Krishna, are seasonal, not perennial. The plains and river valleys in the south and peninsula are also less extensive, with no vast expanse that can compare to that of the Indo-Gangetic Plain. The peninsula, lying south of the Vindhya hills, is marked by undulating ground. There are several smaller ranges of mountains and hills—the Ashambu, the Cardamoms, and the Eastern Ghats; much of the peninsula, especially the Deccan Plateau, is composed of older basalt and granite crops.

The Thar Desert lies at the end of the range of the monsoon winds in the Northwest. The Ladahk desert in the Ladakh Plateau has subzero temperatures. Nearly 40 percent of India is semiarid, with fluctuations in rainfall historically being a major factor in determining crop output. In the northeast the hill ranges, by contrast, receive heavy rains, with Cherrapunji recording over 1,000 centimeters a year.

Ecological Diversity

The diversity of terrain and habitats explains why a country of 1 billion people is also one of the world's twelve mega biodiversity (the World Conservation Union designates biological diversity by the numbers of species of animals and plants) regions. India is that rare country where the three great zoogeographic (relating to the geographic distribution of animals) regions—the Ethiopian, the Oriental, and the Alpine—overlap. The Ethiopian is represented by lions in the Gir Forest (their only surviving habitat in Asia) and by gazelle, antelope, and acacia trees. The Oriental is represented by tigers, sloth bears, and a variety of deer species. The Alpine, or Himalayas, are represented by fauna and flora often more typical of Europe: brown bears, a subspecies of the red deer, mountain ungulates, pines, oaks, and rhododendrons. Over forty thousand species of plants and twelve hundred bird species are found, many of them native, especially in the Western Ghat Mountains.

Demographic Expansion and Economic Growth

The increase in the human population and its economy reshaped India's landscape, especially in the twentieth century. India's population density of 300 people per square kilometer masks great variations between regions. The Hindi-speaking states of the North, which cover most of the Ganges River basin or are adjacent to it, make up 45 percent of the population. In the East, Arunachal Pradesh State records densities as low as 13 people per square kilometer.

Much of the population growth is relatively recent. Estimates place India's population in 1596 at 114 million. Even in 1900, India had only 240 million people. The rate of population growth exceeded .5 percent a year only after 1921. In 1951 there were 360 million people, and the population growth rate was more than 2 percent a year until 1981. It has slowed since then, mainly due to better health-care facilities, expansion of women's literacy, better social services, and government-sponsored family planning. The population is now growing at 1.8 percent a year, but large regions, led by Kerala State in southwestern India, record zero population growth.

The transformation of the landscape owes as much to major socioeconomic changes. The advance and retreat of forests due to ax and plow are not new, with the Indus River basin having a first wave of urbanization around 3000 BCE in the Harappan culture. There was a second wave of urban settlement in the Ganges River valley around 600 BCE. Even during the Mughal empire

(1526–1707 CE), Asian elephants were captured in parts of central India where they are now extinct; the greater one-horned rhinoceros was hunted in the Indus River basin. By the late eighteenth century there were already significant and irreversible changes in certain regions. Economic and cultural changes under British rule unleashed new forces of change.

Precolonial Legacies

The advent of British colonialism in the eighteenth and nineteenth centuries marked a major watershed for India. Historians are divided on what colonialism meant and why, and the division arises partly from radically varying views of precolonial society in India. The institution of caste—which entails a division of labor in a sharply unequal system, with closed marriage circles—is central to one view of India's ecological history. Simply put, the division of labor enabled resource sharing at low levels of equilibrium from the eighth century CE until the coming of colonial rule. Colonialism displaced marginal social groups who relied on fodder, game, wood, and other land- and water-based resources. Caste- and kin-based systems underpinned a more ecologically prudent social order.

A contrasting view of India's ecological history shows much more fluidity before the colonial era. Ethnic groups were not fixed in particular sites, and the level of mobility was high because there was more land per laborer. Forests, far from being cut off from wider society, were resources in times of scarcity and a political base for rival claimants for political power. Archival and archeological evidence hardly supports the notion of a long period of stasis, with groups often combining activities, such as hunting, herding, and slash-and-burn cultivation, with settled agriculture. The late nineteenth century was indeed a break but mainly because the British drew a *cordon sanitaire* (security codes) around forests and hills, securing them for timber and for strategic reasons.

Imperial Impact: The Debate

The colonial era marked a break because of the new intensity of resource use and regulation. Although the British first took control of Bengal Province in 1757 and expanded their power steadily, the impact unfolded only over time. Unlike previous Indian regimes, the British had a deep distrust of mobile herders and traders and a strong preference for those who had a fixed home. The British also had a deep prejudice that mobility signified lack of thrift and could damage forests and the land itself.

In one interpretation, strategic and commercial interests shaped British policy. Securing timber for the navy led to forest reservation, the annexation of forest land by the government for teak in Malabar in 1807. Expanding the rail network led to a timber shortage and creation of the Forest Department in 1864. By 1900 one-fifth of British India was administered by foresters who imposed new regulations on customary uses. Commercial interests led to tensions with other rural resource users. The expansion of canal networks proceeded on a parallel course. Although crop yields increased and plowed acreage expanded, salinity, water-logging, and the spread of malaria caused new problems. The building of water-control systems on an unprecedented scale often caused unintended damage in the deltas of peninsular rivers such as the Mahanadi.

In another interpretation, the ideological and scientific currents among British decision makers, rather than British imperial political economy, are emphasized. Colonial regulations aimed to halt the negative impact of denudation on water supplies and agricultural prosperity. The East India Company, which governed India until 1858, had a small but influential cadre of botanists and other scientists. They anticipated many twenty-first-century concerns about species extinction, climate change, and the links between vegetation and water runoff. Policy initiatives were often driven by such concerns. The Indian princes, who ruled over one-third of the land as junior partners of the British, also supported zoology and forestry, often creating the nuclei of modern scientific investigation.

The British had to try and devise methods of irrigation, forestry and game control strategies that suited south Asia's specific ecological and social conditions. But the outcomes and responses were often radically different from what they expected. The canal networks in colonial India were among the world's largest, but often they led to increased water-logging and salinity and contributed to the spread of malaria. In the Himalaya, hill peasants protested levies of forced labor. They also resisted when foresters replaced mixed oak forests with pine monocultures. In central India, there were even sharper tensions, with a tribal uprising in Bastar sparked in part by curbs on shifting cultivation. In central and eastern India, it was not monoculture forestry but denial of access to the forest for wood, hunting, fodder and cultivation that was at issue. In the foothills for the Himalayas shepherds bore the brunt of exclusion.

Independence and Development

After independence in 1947 India drew much from the philosophy of nonviolent resistance developed by nationalist Mohandas Gandhi (1869–1948). India drew less from his critique of development and the ecological insights that led to alternatives. India followed a model of a mixed economy with an emphasis on capital-intensive technology in quest of economic self-reliance. Many middle-class Indians hoped to modernize faster than their former imperial masters had let them.

Environmental concern took a generation to emerge fully, although it had older historical roots. Initially dissent was muted, but since about 1970 the environment as an issue has become central to public debate. Not surprisingly, Gandhi's ideas have often been drawn upon by critics of the dominant model of development. The courts, the media, citizens associations, political parties, and scientists have been prominent in a variety of debates, resulting in a series of reports on the environment by citizens' groups.

Environmental Movements

The fate of the forests has been an issue marked by deep divisions. Two attempts to enact legislation on forests in 1982 and 1994 failed due to protests by tribal and other forest-reliant peoples. Often forests are places of habitation, and many of the protesters were marginal agriculturalists for whom forests were a critical supplementary resource. Underprivileged groups blame industry and urban demand and the commercial orientation of the Forest Department for loss of forest cover. Gender concerns about access and equity have also come into sharp focus. Women have been active in voicing demands for more access to forests and fisheries for sustaining livelihoods. The expansion of cultivated acreage and the growth of human and livestock populations are cited by those who favor stringent measures to protect remaining forest cover, now less than 11 percent of the landscape. Since 1990 many states, especially West Bengal, have attempted more participatory schemes, with resource sharing with villages. These schemes appear to work best in regions with less-polarized land ownership. These schemes, known as Joint Forest Management, will evolve into an alternative or merely complement the dominant model of forestry.

About 5 percent of the Indian landmass is set aside in protected areas, often with intact assemblages of flora and fauna. Many areas are former forest or hunting reserves of the British or of the Indian princes. India, despite its population, has more tigers and Asian elephants than any other Asian country. Here, too, legacies of exclusion clash with the call for more participation by local people. An estimated 3 million people rely on parks and sanctuaries for their livelihood. How increased participation is to be accomplished while retaining biodiversity is still unclear. Alternatives range from microreserves run by communities to resource sharing on the periphery of large parks. Who is to enforce what control regime and how remain contentious issues.

Dams also have been a major issue. After independence they were seen as critical to achieving self-sufficiency in producing food and generating power for industry. The ecological and social costs were to be widely questioned. In 1980 concern about the loss of rain forest stalled construction of a dam in Silent Valley, Kerala. More recently controversy has centered on the displacement of over 100,000 people by large dams on the Narmada River in central India. Most controversial of these is the Sardar Sarovar dam. Whether and under what conditions displacement was justified raise issues of much wider significance. Most of the displaced are from Madhya Pradesh State, whereas many of the benefits of irrigation will flow to the richer state of Gujarat. Many of the displaced are tribal peoples whose social and political assertion is a significant phenomenon of Indian politics. Although the controversial Sardar Sarovar dam is proceeding after a favorable judicial verdict, the wider debate continues.

The Challenge

The central challenge is simple but daunting: to achieve a better standard of living for 1 billion people and to do so in a sustainable manner via a democratic polity. A growing media and a range of citizens' groups are often in conflict with each other in courts and in public spaces. The century ahead will be one of crises but also one of new opportunities.

Mahesh Rangarajan

Further Reading

Agarwal, A., Chopra, R., & Sharma, K. (Eds.). (1982). *The first citizen's report on the environment in India.* New Delhi, India: Centre for Science and Environment.

Agarwal, A., Narain, S., & Sen, S. (Eds.). (1999). *The citizen's fifth report on the environment in India.* New Delhi, India: Centre for Science and Environment.

Agrawal, A., & Sivaramakrishnan, K. (Eds.). (2000). *Agrarian environments: Resources, representations, and rule in India.* Durham, NC: Duke University Press.

Arnold, D., & Guha, R. (1995). *Nature, culture, imperialism: Essays on the environmental history of south Asia.* Delhi, India: Oxford University Press.

Baviskar, A. (1995). *In the belly of the river: Tribal struggles over development in the Narmada Valley.* Delhi, India: Oxford University Press.

Bayly, C. A. (1988). *The new Cambridge history of India: Vol. 2. Indian society and the making of the British Empire, 1780–1870.* Cambridge, UK: Cambridge University Press.

D'Monte, D. (1985). *Temples or tombs? Industry versus environment: Three controversies.* Delhi, India: Centre for Science and Environment.

Dreze, J., Sampson, M., & Singh, S. (1997). *The dam and the nation; displacement and resettlement in the Narmada Valley.* New York: Oxford University Press.

D'Souza, R. (2002). Colonialism, capitalism and nature: Debating the origins of the Mahanadi Delta's hydraulic crisis. *Economic and Political Weekly, 37*(3), 1261–1272.

Gadgil, M., & Guha, R. (1992). *This fissured land, an ecological history of India.* Delhi, India: Oxford University Press.

Gadgil, M., & Guha, R. (1995). *Ecology and equity: The use and abuse of nature in contemporary India.* London: Routledge.

Gilmartin, D. (1996). Scientific empire and imperial science: Colonialism and irrigation technology in the Indus basin. *Journal of Asian Studies, 53*(4), 1127–1154.

Grove, R. H. (1995). *Green imperialism, colonial expansion, tropical island Edens and the origins of environmentalism, 1660–1860.* Delhi, India: Oxford University Press.

Grove, R. H., Damodaran, V., & Sangwan, S. (1998). *Nature and the Orient: Essays on the environmental history of south and southeast Asia.* Delhi, India: Oxford University Press.

Guha, R. (1989). *The unquiet woods, ecological change and peasant resistance in the western Himalaya.* Berkeley and Los Angeles: University of California Press.

Guha, S. (1999). *Environment and ethnicity in India, 1200–1991.* Cambridge, UK: Cambridge University Press.

Guha, S. (2001). *Health and population in south Asia from earliest times to the present.* London: Hurst.

Habib, I. (1982). *An atlas of the Mughal empire.* Cambridge, UK: Cambridge University Press.

Hazarika, S. (1999). *Bhopal: The lessons of a tragedy.* Delhi, India: Penguin.

Jeffery, R., & Sundar, N. (1999). *A new moral economy for India's forests?: Discourses of community and participation.* Thousand Oaks, CA: Sage.

Kothari, A., Anuradha, R. V., Pathak, N., & Taneja, B. (Eds.). (1998). *Communities and conservation in south and central Asia.* New Delhi, India: Sage.

Rangarajan, M. (1996). *Fencing the forest, conservation and ecological change in India's central provinces, 1860–1914.* Oxford, UK: Oxford University Press.

Rangarajan, M. (2001). *India's wildlife history: An introduction.* Delhi, India: Permanent Black.

Rangarajan, M. (2002). Polity, ecology and landscape: New writing on south Asia's past. *Studies in History, 18*(1), 135–147.

Saberwal, V. (1998). *Pastoral politics, shepherds, bureaucrats and conservation in the western Himalaya.* Delhi, India: Oxford University Press.

Saberwal, V., & Rangarajan, M. (Eds.). (2003). *Battles over nature: Science and the politics of conservation.* Delhi, India: Permanent Black.

Seidensticker, J., Christie, S., & Jackson, P. (Eds.). (1999). *Riding the tiger: Tiger conservation in human-dominated landscapes.* Cambridge, UK: Cambridge University Press.

Shiva, V. (1988). *Staying alive: Women, ecology and survival in India.* New Delhi, India: Zed Press.

Singh, S. (1997). *Taming the waters: The political economy of large dams in India.* Delhi, India: Oxford University Press.

Sivaramakrishnan, K. (1999). *Modern forests, state making and environmental change in colonial eastern India.* Stanford, CA: Stanford University Press.

Sundar, N. (1997). *Subalterns and sovereigns: An anthropological history of Bastar, 1854–1996.* Oxford, UK: Oxford University Press.

Sundar, N., Jeffery, N., & Thin, N. (2001). *Branching out: Joint forest management in India.* Oxford, UK: Oxford University Press.

Whitcombe, E. (1995). The environmental costs of irrigation in British India. In D. Arnold & R. Guha (Eds.), *Nature, culture, imperialism: Essays on the environmental history of south Asia* (pp. 237–259). Delhi, India: Oxford University Press.

India, Ancient—Indus Valley

The Indus civilization arose within the greater Indus Valley of Pakistan and northwestern India in the mid-

dle of the third millennium BCE. Its dates have been set using the radiocarbon method and cross ties with Mesopotamia to 2500–1900 BCE. This period saw the emergence of the great Indus cities of Mohenjo Daro, Harappa, Dholavira, Ganweriwala, and Rakhigarhi. The cities, towns and villages of the Indus civilization were inhabited by diverse peoples who lived in a stratified society, engaged in craft and career specialization, and knew the art of writing.

The Extent of the Indus Civilization's Trade Contacts

The Indus peoples had far reaching contacts with Mesopotamia, the Arabian (Persian) Gulf, Afghanistan, Central Asia, and Iran. Much of this interaction was based on the trade of exotic products and raw materials: items made of lapis lazuli, carnelian, copper and bronze, woods, shells, pearls, and the like. In addition to the overland exchanges, we know that the Indus folk were also seafarers. Mesopotamian cuneiform documents of the third millennium speak of maritime contact with Meluhha, reasonably associated with the Indus civilization. There are scores of sites in the Arabian Gulf with Indus pottery and other artifacts, including stamp seals with Indus writing. The remains of maritime fish and shells are represented at Indus civilization sites.

This maritime activity apparently extended to the import of plants to the Indian subcontinent. Millets like sorghum, pearl millet, and finger millet, native to sub-Saharan Africa, were introduced there in the third millennium. Seafaring Harappans who reached the mouth of the Red Sea apparently brought these plants back to the subcontinent.

Geography and Climate

The environment of the greater Indus region is, and was, diverse. Millennia of degradation by man and domesticated animals have brought measurable change. There is no systematic, well-documented environmental reconstruction for the Holocene epoch (the past ten thousand years) in this part of the world. The sense one gets is that tree cover in the region was greater and probably more diversified in prehistoric times. Similarly, the grasslands and savannas were more lush and richer. The river system was considerably different in the third and fourth millennia BCE from the one we see today. In the fourth and third millennia BCE there was a major river flowing out of the Siwalik Hills southwest toward the Indus Valley. This is known as the Sarasvati. A second river, the Drishadvati, joined it near the site of Kalibangan. At that time the Yamuna River was a very small stream. The tectonics of the subcontinent led to changes in the watersheds of these rivers that led to the growth of the Yamuna at the expense of the Sarasvati-Drishadvati system. The Drishdvati dried up in the fourth millennium, its waters going to the Yamuna, which grew in size over this time. The Sarasvati was largely dry by the beginnings of the first millennium BCE.

The precise course of the Indus River during the Indus civilization is not known, but studies of palaeochannels show that it is likely that the channel was to the west of the city of Mohenjo Daro, nearer the foothills of Baluchistan.

The climate of the greater Indus region was entirely stable during the Holocene. There was most likely variation in both the monsoon (June to September) and the winter westerlies that bring rain to the western portions of the Indus civilization. But the evidence for real climatic change (as opposed to variation) is weak. There is insufficient evidence to say that at any point during the Holocene there was enough change in rainfall, for example, to have had a measurable effect on crop yields and the production of grasslands for pasture. (The researchers Singh, Wasson, and Agrawal take a dissenting view in their 1990 article published in *Review of Palaeobotany and Palynology*).

Domestication of Plants and Animals

The key site on the subcontinent for evidence of the early domestication of plants and animals is Mehrgarh, where a settled village community is in evidence in the sixth or seventh millennium BCE. The peoples of Mehrgarh in Period I (7000–5000 BCE) had three forms of domesticated barley and three forms of domesticated wheat, with the barley representing more than 90 percent of the food grains recovered in excavation. The noncereals so far identified for the period include the Indian jujube and dates, represented by stones in Periods I and II. There is also a possibility that cotton was cultivated in the Mehrgarh area at an early date (Period II, 5000–4000 BCE). Cotton fabric was preserved at Mohenjo Daro (2500–1900 BCE).

Humped zebu cattle, a native species, was domesticated at Mehrgarh, native sheep and goats may also have been domesticated. Wild forms of all three of these animals are found in the vicinity of Mehrgarh.

This suite of domesticated animals was of fundamental importance to population growth and diversification in the greater Indus Valley, which eventually led to urbanization and the Indus civilization. Sustained population growth in the greater Indus region cannot be directly observed, but by adding up the size estimates for sites from successive periods in the prehistoric Indus region we get a sense—not very precise, of course, but a rough estimate—of "size." This is not the total "size" since there are many sites yet to be discovered, and some sites have vanished from view, or all together. Moreover, on sites with long-term occupation through many periods, size changes within each period is a critical factor. There are reasons to suggest that these factors apply equally to all sites in each of the archaeological periods that have been defined for the eras prior to the Indus civilization. This being so, one should then look not at the size figures per se, but at the changes between them to see long-term changes in population. (See table 1.)

The Domains of the Indus Civilization

Settlements of the Indus civilization are found over an area of approximately 1 million square kilometers. About 1,060 sites of the Indus civilization are now known to archaeologists. This vast area encompasses considerable cultural and environmental diversity. Based on these factors it has been divided into subregions called domains, which have been developed to facilitate the examination of the cultural diversity of the Indus civilization and to begin to chart out possible internal political units.

TABLE 1.
ESTIMATES OF SETTLED AREA BY STAGE AND PHASE

Period	Total settled area (in hectares)
Indus civilization (2500–1900 BCE)	7940
Early Harappan or Early Indus (3200–2500 BCE)	2113
Sophisticated farmers and herders, the Kechi Beg/Hakra Wares phase (c. 3800–3200 BCE)	1230
Technological innovation, the Togau phase (c. 4300–3800 BCE)	295
First ceramics, the Burj basket-marked phase (c. 5000–4300 BCE)	85
Earliest villages, the Kili Ghul Mohammad phase (c. 7000–5000 BCE)	53

The Kulli and Northwestern domains can be dealt with together, from an environmental point of view. Both are in the mountainous, western edge of Pakistan, along its present borders with Iran and Afghanistan. The area is mountainous with peaks in the 1,800- to 2,7000-meter range and valley floors at 900–1,500 meters. There are many playa lakes in this region that were used for the cultivation of barley and some wheat. Agriculture was dependent on winter rainfall. Orchards and vineyards were also found here. The subsistence regime was dominated by cattle, sheep, and goat pastoralism, with some cultivation. The seasonal migration of men and their animals involved a move from the highlands to the Indus Valley and Punjab in the winter, with a return in the spring.

The Sindhu domain is dominated by the flood plains of the Indus River but extends to Kachchh (Kutch) and the head of the Gulf of Khambhat (Cambay). The Sindhi Harappan peoples practiced a blend of agriculture and cattle pastoralism with considerable subregional diversity. Agriculture predominated in the central parts of the lower Indus Valley. This would have been dependent on the Indus floods. The cultivators in the Sindhu domain do not appear to have had massive, state-controlled irrigation systems. Instead they seem to have relied on the soil and moisture left by the retreating floodwaters. They also used the backwaters, lake margins, and the scars left by river floods for cultivation. Small canals, used to drain land and move water in small amounts relatively short distances were certainly known. Pastoralism predominated in the in the foothills of Baluchistan, the eastern portions of the valley, and in Kachchh. Some documentation for the gathering of wild plants is available at Surkotada in Kachchh, as is evidence for the use of millets, at least one of which is of African origin. There was some hunting in Sind, perhaps more important outside the wetlands of the lower Indus Valley. There is evidence for the extensive use of marine resources, both fish and mollusks, for food and raw materials.

The Sorath domain is roughly the peninsula of Saurashtra in Gujarat, India. It is a land of low hills and low mountains. It would have been a vast savanna grassland in prehistoric times, with forests in the better-watered elevations of the hills, especially in southern Saurashtra. There is a pattern of radial drainage around Saurashtra made up of small seasonal streams, with full flowing water only during and shortly after the monsoon. The subsistence system here appears to have been a complex mix of agriculture and pastoralism, but with cattle predominating as in other do-

mains. There is good evidence for the gathering of wild plants for food and for the hunting of wild ungulates.

The Sorath domain gets essentially no winter rain and is therefore dependent on the southwest monsoon for its moisture. This implies that the winter crops of barley and wheat or both would have been irrigated, either by placing fields inside small riverine entrenchments, or from wells. The Sorath Harappan subsistence regime was based on a wide variety of plants that were hardy and drought resistant.

The Cholistan domain is in the western borderlands of the Thar Desert. The settlements there were apparently occupied during the period in which the Sarasvati River was active. Over 170 settlements of the Indus civilization have been found in the vicinity of Fort Derawar in a former inland delta of the river. The subsistence regime here was a blend of barley and wheat cultivation along with the other domesticates known to the Harappans. Agriculture predominated in the central parts of the domain, with cattle pastoralism in the ascendance to the east and west.

The incorporation of relatively large numbers of sheep and goats into the pastoral economy of this region would have been a feature of the nomads in the more desertlike areas of the Bahawalpur domain, slightly to the north of the Cholistan domain. Seasonal migration into Sind and the greater Punjab by all pastoralists in this region is a likely feature of the ancient adaptive system. Overall the subsistence regime might have been very much like that in Sind, but the density of the sites in Bahawalpur indicate that the Bahawalpur region may well have been something like the Harappan "bread basket."

The Eastern domain, roughly the area of the modern Indian states of Punjab, Haryana and western Uttar Pradesh, seems to have been another area in which there was a blend of agriculture and cattle pastoralism. Wheat, barley, and finger millet are documented and imply double cropping. The following plants were found at Hulas in the Indus civilization levels: wheat, barley, rice, ragi, horse gram, green gram, black gram, and peas.

Like the Harappa domain, the Eastern domain benefited from two seasons of rainfall, both southwest monsoon and winter westerlies. These two independent weather systems are an advantage for peoples here since even if one season of rainfall fails, the other may be plentiful.

The Harappa domain of Pakistani Punjab was composed of two quite different environments: well-watered, entrenched perennial rivers and higher, drier scrub forests between them. The Indus agricultural complex based on wheat and barley was practiced in the riverine environments and cattle pastoralism in the drier areas. The Indus peoples at Harappa also consumed local river fish and imported maritime species.

The Decline of the Indus Valley Cities

The ancient cities of the Indus were no longer functioning urban environments by 1900 BCE. There were successors to these peoples, as documented in the archaeological record, so the Indus civilization did not come to an end so much as it went through a process of transformation. The reason for this transformation is not well understood, but the environmental causes that have been invoked (floods, too much burning of wood for baked brick, climatic change) have all been quite severely and convincingly critiqued. So too has the theory that invading Aryans destroyed the civilization. Archaeologists today are looking for more sociocultural explanations. One position holds that the ideology of these people proved to be impossible to sustain, and that they abandoned it along with their urban ways.

Gregory L. Possehl

Further Reading

Allchin, B., & Allchin, R. (1997). *Origins of a civilization: The prehistory and early archaeology of South Asia.* New Delhi, India: Viking.

Jarrige, C., Jarrige, J.-F., Meadow, R. H., & Quivron, G. (1995). *Mehrgarh: Field reports 1974–1985, from Neolithic times to the Indus civilization.* Karachi, Pakistan: Department of Culture and Tourism of Sind (Pakistan) and Department of Archaeology and Museums, French Ministry of Foreign Affairs.

Kenoyer, J. M. (1998). *Ancient cities of the Indus Valley civilization.* Karachi, Pakistan: Oxford University Press.

Meadow, R. H. (1998). Pre- and proto-historic agricultural and pastoral transformations in northwestern South Asia. *Review of Archaeology 19*(2), 12–21.

Possehl, G. L. (1997). Seafaring merchants of Meluhha. In B. Allchin (Ed.) *South Asian archaeology 1995* (pp. 87–100). Delhi, India: Oxford & IBH Publishing Co.

Possehl, G. L. (2002). *The Indus civilization: A contemporary perspective.* Walnut Creek, CA: Altamira.

Singh, G., Wasson, R. J., & Agrawal, D. P. (1990). Vegetational and seasonal climatic changes since the last full glacial in the Thar Desert, northwestern India. *Review of Palaeobotany and Palynology 64,* 351–358.

Weber, Steven A. (1991). *Plants and Harappan subsistence: An example of stability and change from Rojdi.* Delhi, India: Oxford & IBH Publishing Co. and the American Institute of Indian Studies.

Indigenous Peoples

Indigenous peoples are variously referred to by the terms *populations, ethnic groups, cultural communities, minorities, nationalities, tribals, tribes, little peoples,* and *peasants* in a large body of literature generated by anthropologists, sociologists, psychologists, historians, and other social scientists. These terms have often been used in connection with progressive terminology such as *backward, undeveloped, primitive,* and *uncivilized.* Governments, nongovernmental organizations, educational institutions, business, and organized religion are among those institutions in which these terms have common usage.

As a result of a worldwide social and political movement initiated by indigenous peoples in the 1970s, people have begun to apply new terms that, from the viewpoint of indigenous peoples, more accurately define who and what they are. The word *peoples,* denoting many different peoples, and the word *nation* are the preferred terms of designation, usually modified by the name of the people (i.e., Quechua people, Zulu nation, Ainu people, Sami nation). The terms *indigenous* and *Fourth World* (both of which are widely used) function as terms of art (the meaning of the descriptive word has a political use depending on the context). A growing body of descriptive and theoretical literature generated by indigenous peoples themselves uses the terms *people* and *nation* interchangeably and the terms *indigenous* and *Fourth World* interchangeably. Use of these terms has become more widespread as they have been used in literature and in the formal communications of international bodies such as the United Nations Organization (UNO), International Labour Organization (ILO), European Union (EU), Organization on Security and Cooperation in Europe (OSCE), the Organization for African Unity (OAU), and the Organization of American States (OAS). A "people," according to the Compact Edition of the *Oxford English Dictionary,* is a "body of persons who compose a community, a tribe, a nation." (The Compact Edition of the Oxford English Dictionary, II [1984]: 661) The plural *peoples* is equal to the word *nations.* There-

Selection from the Latest Version of the Draft United Nations Declaration on the Rights of Indigenous Peoples, 1993

ANNEX I

DRAFT DECLARATION AS AGREED UPON BY THE MEMBERS OF THE WORKING GROUP AT ITS ELEVENTH SESSION

AFFIRMING that indigenous peoples are equal in dignity and rights to all other peoples, while recognizing the right of all peoples to be different, to consider themselves different, and to be respected as such,

AFFIRMING ALSO that all peoples contribute to the diversity and richness of civilizations and cultures, which constitute the common heritage of humankind,

AFFIRMING FURTHER that all doctrines, policies and practices based on or advocating superiority of peoples or individuals on the basis of national origin, racial, religious, ethnic or cultural differences are racist, scientifically false, legally invalid, morally condemnable and socially unjust,

REAFFIRMING also that indigenous peoples, in the exercise of their rights, should be free from discrimination of any kind,

CONCERNED that indigenous peoples have been deprived of their human rights and fundamental freedoms, resulting, *inter alia*, in their colonization and dispossession of their lands, territories and resources, thus preventing them from exercising, in particular, their right to development in accordance with their own needs and interests,

RECOGNIZING the urgent need to respect and promote the inherent rights and characteristics of indigenous peoples, especially their rights to their lands, territories and resources, which derive from their political, economic and social structures and from their cultures, spiritual traditions, histories and philosophies,

WELCOMING the fact that indigenous peoples are organizing themselves for political, economic, social and cultural enhancement and in order to bring an end to all forms of discrimination and oppression wherever they occur,

CONVINCED that control by indigenous peoples over developments affecting them and their lands, territories and resources will enable them to maintain and strengthen their institutions, cultures and traditions, and to promote their development in accordance with their aspirations and needs,

RECOGNIZING ALSO that respect for indigenous knowledge, cultures and traditional practices contributes to sustainable and equitable development and proper management of the environment,

EMPHASIZING the need for demilitarization of the lands and territories of indigenous peoples, which will contribute to peace, economic and social progress and development, understanding and friendly relations among nations and peoples of the world,

Continues

Continued

RECOGNIZING in particular the right of indigenous families and communities to retain shared responsibility for the up-bringing, training, education and well-being of their children,

RECOGNIZING ALSO that indigenous peoples have the right freely to determine their relationships with States in a spirit of coexistence, mutual benefit and full respect,

CONSIDERING that treaties, agreements and other arrangements between States and indigenous peoples are properly matters of international concern and responsibility,

ACKNOWLEDGING that the Charter of the United Nations, the International Covenant on Economic, Social and Cultural Rights and the International Covenant on Civil and Political Rights affirm the fundamental importance of the right of self-determination of all peoples, by virtue of which they freely determine their political status and freely pursue their economic, social and cultural development,

BEARING IN MIND that nothing in this Declaration may be used to deny any peoples their right of self-determination,

ENCOURAGING States to comply with and effectively implement all international instruments, in particular those related to human rights, as they apply to indigenous peoples, in consultation and cooperation with the peoples concerned,

EMPHASIZING that the United Nations has an important and continuing role to play in promoting and protecting the rights of indigenous peoples,

BELIEVING that this Declaration is a further important step forward for the recognition, promotion and protection of the rights and freedoms of indigenous peoples and in the development of relevant activities of the United Nations system in this field,

SOLEMNLY PROCLAIMS the following United Nations Declaration on the Rights of Indigenous Peoples:

Source: Commission on Human Rights, Economic and Social Council, United Nations. Retrieved December 26, 2002, from Center for World Indigenous Studies, http://www.cwis.org

---

fore, when people speak of "indigenous peoples," they are speaking of original nations.

More than six thousand Fourth World nations are thought to be distributed throughout the world. Although the total number of such nations is not known, that figure is most often used, based on the number of distinct languages in the world. Of the total number of indigenous nations in the world, 13 percent are in North America; 13 percent, South America; 3 percent, Europe; 26 percent, Africa; 28 percent, Eurasia; and 17 percent, Melanesia and the Pacific region.

Names of Nations

The three most common categories of names for Fourth World nations are geographical (associated with a location or topography), homo exclusive (specifically associated with characteristics of the people), and pejorative. The name used to identify a nation often results from contacts with the outside world. Explorers in the last five hundred years, colonialists, and researchers have all played a direct role in the "naming of nations." When the word *ethnic* is used, one should be suspicious of the source because the word in English has a pejorative meaning (i.e., "heathen" or "pagan"). Also, outsiders contribute to names of nations that have a pejorative meaning, that is, Apache (enemy), Eskimo (flesh eater), Winnebago (people of dirty water). When the name of a specific nation originates with the nation itself, the word used often means simply "people" or "the people." Names of nations such as "Naga," "Yanomamö," "Ainu," "Dogon," "Yup'ik," and "Wanapum" are examples from around the world in which the meaning is "the people" or "people." Variations of this pattern include more descriptive meanings, as in the case of the Oceti Sakowin (known as "Sioux" in the midwestern states of the United States), whose chosen name means "seven council fires."

The diversity of languages reflected in these names illustrates the diversity of nations and, in turn, the diversity of environments in which Fourth World nations reside. Some nations, such as the Inuit, are located around the Earth's North Pole, sometimes called the "circumpolar region." The Inuit live in the Arctic region, as do the Sami in the north of Scandinavia and the Komi, Sakah, and Chuckchee in the Russian Federation. The Sami are reindeer herders who, like many other Arctic peoples, must rely on natural foods and especially foods provided from their herds of reindeer. The Sami frequently have to protect their lands and the lands of the reindeer from development such as road construction and hydroelectric dams. These are the greatest dangers to the health of the Sami people, the wildlife, and the wild plants in their territory, which is made up of the northern parts of Norway, Sweden, Finland, and a little of Russia.

In a scene found in thousands of communities around the world each morning, traders in West Africa bring produce to the local market. COURTESY MARY CORINNE LOWENSTEIN.

The Yanomamö (also known as "Yanomami" and "Yanomam") live deep in the jungles of southern Venezuela and northern Brazil. With an estimated population of 14,500, the Yanomamö are generally understood to be the most successful people in the jungle to achieve a balance between their needs and the needs of the environment in the modern era. Their success for unknown generations is being harshly degraded as a result of gold mining, road building, and logging. Even as diseases such as malaria and the common cold, introduced by miners and other outsiders, ravage the Yanomamö they fight to defend the land and the environment. As Davi Kopenawa Yanomami, a spokesperson for his people, says about the outsiders, "Our work is to protect nature, the wind, the mountains, the forest, the animals, and this is what we want to teach you people. . . . These are the people who want to cut down the forest and sell the wood to Japan and other countries. They are the ones who are interested in minerals to make rings and necklaces. And they are destroying our lands" (Multinational Monitor 1992, 22). Neither the Venezuelan nor the Brazilian government protects the Yanomamö from these corporations, miners, loggers, and road builders, so they have to protect themselves and their lands.

The Jivaro (Ecuador, Colombia), Achen (Sumatra, Indonesia), and Dani (West Papua, Indonesia) also suffer from the same kinds of development threats to their ecosystems in the tropical zones. They, too, receive no protection from the governments and so must defend themselves and their lands on their own.

Fourth World nations range in size from 50 people (the Hoh in the Pacific Northwest of the United States) to 25 million (the Bhil of south-central India). They are as diverse in their economies, social organizations, and political systems, as are the territories they occupy. Some Fourth World nations—such as the Eskudi (commonly called the "Basque" of Spain and France); the Catalans, also of Spain and France; and the Pequot of the United States—are active in the global economy. The environmental challenges to the lands, wildlife, and people in indigenous peoples' territories continue to accelerate as a result of world trade liberalization, which promotes exploitation of more and more of the world's wild regions.

Although the thousands of nations in the world are diverse and different from one another in many ways, they often share political concerns. The two most important political concerns of Fourth World nations are land rights and self-determination. These concerns reflect the growing impact of global economic integration and the increasing development pressures of large metropolitan population concentrations reaching into the remotest regions of the world.

Land, Food, and Self-Determination

The policies of most newly formed states since the early 1960s have been significantly defined by the idea and possibilities of "development." Few of the new states formed in Africa, Melanesia (islands of the southwestern Pacific), Asia, and the Pacific region had the capacity to provide a high standard of living for their citizens. The view that each of the new states required economic, political, and social infrastructure to fully function for the benefit of the newly defined citizens was stimulated by the International Bank for Reconstruction and Development (World Bank) and the United Nations and materialized in the form of loans and development assistance. New forestry, mining, petroleum, fisheries, manufacturing, and service enterprises emerged to exploit the raw materials of new states. In most instances, these enterprises displaced indigenous nations or forced a confrontation between the state government and the affected nations. Rising demands for raw materials created increased pressures on rain forests, jungles, savannas, and prairies where indigenous peoples constituted the primary human residents. While the natural environment was being increasingly exploited for the wealth that would support the state, indigenous peoples who lived in these otherwise-undisturbed regions suddenly found themselves being moved to other lands or living in the midst of a violent conflict with military forces of the state as well as workers whose livelihood would be determined by the success or failure of extracting raw materials.

Confrontations between newly formed states such as Papua New Guinea (1980) and indigenous peoples demonstrated that even when indigenous peoples assumed control over a state apparatus the goals of the state would frequently conflict with the interests of indigenous peoples. For example, the government of Papua New Guinea determined that development of gold deposits through mining in the interior of the country would satisfy the balance-of-payments needs of the state. To develop the gold, however, the indigenous peoples in the interior had to be convinced that such development would benefit them as well. They were not convinced, and the dispute with the government contributed to growing instability that eventually resulted in other indigenous peoples beginning to seek

their independence. The apparently inherent conflict between the aims of the state and the aims of indigenous nations could not be resolved even when all parties to the conflict individually represented indigenous peoples. The conflict ultimately centered on control over land and food by the state or the indigenous nation. Where the state demanded control over the land and food sources the indigenous nation was left to demand its right of self-determination. This is a typical conflict between the interests of a state and the interests of an indigenous nation.

The United Nations Charter (1945) asserts that "a people" has the right to freely determine its social, economic, political, and cultural future without external interference. This right is said to be universal, benefiting all peoples on the planet. Despite the universality of this internationally recognized right, its application to indigenous peoples is tentative and conditional. Before the United Nations Economic and Social Council authorized establishment of the Working Group on the Rights of Indigenous Populations in 1981, there were few internationally recognized guarantees that could be said to apply to indigenous peoples. In the decades after the U.N. Commission on Human Rights study "On the Situation of Indigenous Populations," conducted by José Martinez Cobo between 1973 and 1983, international bodies such as the International Labour Organization, Organization of American States, Organization on Security and Cooperation in Europe, and the United Nations enacted a growing body of declarations and conventions and commissioned conferences and symposia to permanently establish indigenous peoples as a subject of international discourse.

Fourth World Theory

Fourth World geopolitics is the developing field in which students of international relations, environmental policy, developmental studies, and peace studies analyze the relationships between indigenous peoples and between indigenous peoples and other political entities such as states, corporations, and organized religions for their social, economic, political, and cultural impact on human society. From the early 1970s to 2000 a body of literature developed to discuss these relationships from the perspective of indigenous peoples. Fourth World theory has attributes similar to those of environmental theory and feminist theory. The theory has syntax and a vocabulary that fundamentally rearrange the conventional social science analysis used to explain local, regional, and global social, economic, political, and cultural events. Fourth World theory provides analysis in terms of small, local events instead of large, global events. In its acceptance of many chaotic, seemingly unrelated events at the level of Fourth World nations as the focus of change and stability, Fourth World theory introduces a dynamic social, cultural, and political element into the discourse on relations between human beings and the Earth, the role of human beings in the preservation or exploitation of the environment, and the relations between human societies in the arrangement of violent or peaceful relations.

Nations that are incorporated into states without an expression of affirmative consent and that maintain a distinct political identity while remaining internationally unrecognized may be called "indigenous peoples" or "Fourth World nations." The territories of these nations are located inside the claimed boundaries of states—many of which were formed since 1960 as a result of the United Nations adoption of the Declaration on the Granting of Independence to Colonial Countries and Peoples (UN General Assembly Resolution 1514, Session XV). The nations inside these newly formed states—and inside many states formed since the nineteenth century—were not recognized as independent peoples. They soon realized that the distant colonial ruler had been replaced by another ruler not of their choosing inside the newly authorized state. Establishment of new states out of colonies often created boundaries that cut through the historical territories of Fourth World nations. The indigenous peoples now inside new states were obliged to contend with new rulers in pursuit of their own aspirations for self-determination. The new state rulers frequently became more resistant to the desire for self-determination by incorporated nations than had been the distant colonizers who had ruled throughout the nineteenth century. This difference in views has accounted for political and violent disputes between states' governments and indigenous peoples inside most of the 194 modern states for most of the twentieth century and into the twenty-first century.

Rudolph C. Ryser

Further Reading

Battalla, G. B. (1996). *México profundo, reclaiming a civilization* (P. A. Dennis, Trans.). Austin: University of Texas Press.

Bodley, J. H. (1982). *Victims of progress.* Menlo Park, CA: Benjamin/Cummins.

Burenhult, G. (Ed.). (1994). *Landmark series from the American Museum of Natural History: Vol. 5. Traditional peoples today: Continuity and change in the modern world—The illustrated history of humankind.* San Francisco: Harper.

Chagnon, N. A. (1968). *Yanomamö, the fierce people.* New York: Holt, Rinehart and Winston

Ellis, P. B. (1990). *The Celtic empire: The first millennium of Celtic history 1000 BC–51 AD.* London: Guild Publishing.

Haskins, J., & Biondi, J. (1993). *From Afar to Zulu: A dictionary of African cultures.* New York: Walker.

Hyndman, D. (1987). Cystercicosis and Indonesian counter insurgency in a continuing Fourth World war. *Cultural Survival Quarterly, 11,* 8–13.

Yanomami in peril. (1992, September). *Multinational Monitor 13*(9), 22ff. Retrieved January 27, 2003, from http://multinationalmonitor.org/hyper/issues/1992/09/mm0992_12.html

Jones, S. A. (Ed.). (1999). *Simply living: The spirit of the indigenous people.* Novato, CA: New World Library.

Kly, Y. N., & Kly, D. (Eds.). (2001). *In pursuit of the right of self-determination.* Atlanta, GA: Clarity Press.

MacKinnon, C. A. (1989). *Toward a feminist theory of the state.* Cambridge, MA: Harvard University Press.

Moynihan, D. P. (1993). *Pandaemonium: Ethnicity in international politics.* New York: Oxford University Press.

Nietschmann, B. Q. (1994). The Fourth World: Nations versus states. In G. J. Demko & W. B. Wood (Eds.), *Reordering the world* (pp. 225–241). Boulder, CO: Westview Press.

Price, D. H. (1990). *Atlas of world cultures: A geographic guide to ethnographic literature.* Newbury Park, CA: Sage.

Read, J. (1978). *The Catalans.* London: Faber and Faber.

Vick-Westgate, A. (2002). *Nunavik: Inuit-controlled education in Arctic Quebec.* Calgary, Canada: University of Calgary Press.

Wen-chi, K. (1999). *Indigenous peoples and the press: A study of Taiwan.* Taiwan, China: Council of Aboriginal Affairs.

Wouters, H. (1979). *West Asia.* In J. Büttinghausen (Series ed.), *Peoples and customs of the world.* Geneva, Switzerland: Ferni.

Indus River

The Indus River is the principal waterway of Pakistan and one of the geographical focal points of the Indus civilization (2500–1900 BCE), the first period of urbanization on the Indian subcontinent. The ancient name of the river was Sindhu, from which the Pakistani province of Sind takes its name. It is a simple sound shift from Sindu to Indus; from Indus comes the name India.

The Source and Course of the Indus

The source of the Indus River was found by Sven Hedin in 1907 at the sacred spring of Singikabab near Mapam Yumco Lake (Manasarowar Lake) in Tibet. The lake is also the source of the Sutlej River, which joins the Indus after its long course through the Himalayas and Punjab. The Indus initially flows west, then northwest, where it is joined by the Gar Tsangpo, past Skardu and into Gilgit before it makes a great arcing turn to the south, at the same time dropping precipitously out of the confinement of the great mountains. Along this path the river has been fed by many smaller mountain torrents found in this vast watershed. Passing south through the Salt Range it enters the Punjab plains and is joined by the Tochi-Kuram and Zhob-Gomal streams. At this point the modern Indus for the most part flows within a deep entrenchment and is not a widely meandering river.

Below the Salt Range the Indus begins to be navigable, at least by small country craft. Passing the town Dera Ghazi Khan in Punjab, Pakistan, the Indus enters the central region at a point known as the *panjnad*, where the five rivers of the Punjab (Jhelum, Chenab, Ravi, Beas, and Sutlej) join the Indus.

In its lower course in Sind, the Indus flows through, and has filled the geological syncline (trough of stratified rock) formed as the main peninsular landmass of India collided with the rest of Asia. This syncline is the western edge, or scar, resulting from this intercontinental "accident." Its partner is the Ganga Valley, also a deep syncline filled with alluvium on the nose of the intercontinental collision which began in the Mesozoic era (c. 245–66.4 million years ago) and continues unabated today.

Statistical Data

A sampler of statistics gives some impression of the size of the Indus, especially as it compares to other mature rivers. The observations for the Indus have been taken from Pithawala (1959, 74–110):

Total length	2900 kilometers
Length in Sind, Pakistan, with meanders	approximately 1000 kilometers
Discharge, maximum	24,785 cubic meters per second
Discharge, minimum	492 cubic meters per second
Discharge, average maximum	approximately 11,200 cubic meters per second
Maximum highwater at Sukkur, Pakistan	+5.40 meters
Average silt carried	900,000 metric tons per day
Maximum velocity in Sind	3.2 meters/second

In comparison, the Nile, another of the rivers that gave birth to a great civilization of antiquity, has an inundation that is steadier and more deliberate than the Indus. The Nile is measurably smaller, with an average maximum discharge of about 8,400 cubic meters per second. The Indus also carries significantly more silt. The total volume of silt carried by the Indus during the 100 days of inundation has been estimated to be approximately 95 million cubic meters; the same statistic for the Nile would be only 32 million cubic meters.

Flooding

Within the plains of modern Sind, the Indus River is a fully mature stream. It has a reputation as a powerful, violent, unpredictable river. Its floods are mostly dependent on the winter snowfall in the Himalayas, not springtime rain. Flooding during any particular year leads to breaks in the upstream reaches. This diminishes the pressure for breach in the lower reaches of the stream. Floods moving to the east or west of the stream may leave the opposite side of the river wholly or comparatively unaffected, so that in any given year only parts of the valley are likely to be flooded, and some areas go dry for several years in a row. Floods are generally a blessing, and the Indus Valley has been free of famine for as long as we know.

The worst floods are not caused by excessive snowfall and rain but by natural catastrophes in the Himalayan reaches of the river. For example, the flood of 1841 began with the collapse of an ice bridge Shyok tributary, in the Himalayan mountains on the upper course of the Indus in the fall of 1840. This formed a temporary lake 19 kilometers long, 800 meters wide, and 120 meters deep. When the dam was breached, it sent a wall of water down the river. It took two days to reach Campbellpore (Attock) in northern Punjab, where it passed as a wall of thick, muddy water nine meters high. The 1874 flood was not linked to a natural catastrophe, but it washed away eighty towns and villages and a large portion of the city of Jacobabad. The 1942 flood left 400,000 people homeless. The floodwaters spread over 8,000 square kilometers, carrying away everything they encountered before them and destroying roads, bridges, railways, entire villages, farmsteads, and fields.

The Indus and Ancient Civilization

The Indus, its tributaries, and its associated features bring prosperity to the surrounding region. The uncontrolled river inundates vast areas, making agriculture exceptionally productive. The rivers also teem with fish and other useful products. Food production and the Neolithic Revolution in the subcontinent took place in the hills and piedmonts of the western Indus Valley. The productivity of the landscape generally led to the establishment of the Indus civilization, which covered 1 million square kilometers and sent sea traders to Mesopotamia and the mouth of the Red Sea. Mohenjo Daro and Harappa are well known cities of antiquity, but in total more than a thousand Indus sites are known to archaeologists.

Some have also seen the Indus River as the destroyer of the civilization of Mohenjo Daro. There has been a claim that just after 2000 BCE a natural dam formed across the Indus just below Mohenjo Daro, and that this city was engulfed by a mass of mud and water. However, this theory has been discredited since no trace of the dam has been found, and it has become clear that the unconsolidated alluvium of the valley could not withstand the static pressure of the water behind such an obstruction.

The Indus is one of the great rivers of the world. Violent as it may be from time to time, it has been a source of food and inspiration for millennia.

Gregory L. Possehl

Further Reading

Buckley, R. B. (1893). *Irrigation works in India and Egypt*. London: E. & S. N. Spoon.

Burnes, Sir A. (1834). *A voyage on the Indus*. London: John Murray.

Lambrick, H. T. (1964). *Sind: A general introduction*. History of Sind series, vol. 1. Hyderabad, Pakistan: Sindhi Adabi Board.

Meadows, A., & Meadows, P. S. (Eds.). (1999). *The Indus River: Biodiversity, resources, humankind*. Karachi, Pakistan: Oxford University Press.

Pithawala, M. B. (1959). *A physical and economic geography of Sind (the lower Indus Basin)*. Karachi, Pakistan: Sindhi Adabi Board.

Possehl, G. L. (2002). *The Indus civilization: A contemporary perspective*. Walnut Creek, CA: Altamira.

Shroder, J. F. (1993). *Himalaya to the sea: Geology, geomorphology and the Quaternary*. London: Routledge.

Snelgrove, A. K. (1967). *Geohydrology of the Indus River, West Pakistan*. Hyderabad, Pakistan: Sind University Press.

Indus Valley *See* India, Ancient—Indus Valley

Industrial Health and Safety

Industrial health and safety is also described as "occupational health" and "industrial hygiene." The medical treatment of workers and the study of work-related diseases are known as "occupational medicine."

Health and safety concerns of industrial workers are well known in literature. They have also been points of contention for organized labor and important threads within environmental history. In literature, occupational disease has sometimes been portrayed with humor, as in English writer Lewis Carroll's "mad hatter," who was crazy because of mercury poisoning from making hats. A more somber view was taken by English writer Charles Dickens, whose lead factory workers could not get up off the bed, and U.S. writer Upton Sinclair, whose slaughterhouse workers lost fingers and, eventually, their short, brutish lives in *The Jungle*.

The burdens of work-created illness were shouldered entirely by workers and families, rather than industry or taxpayers, until the mid-twentieth century. To this day most workers injured on the job lose most of their income as a result of job injuries. Improving industrial health has long been a primary goal of organized labor.

Historians have noted an overlap between occupational medicine and public health in many instances. For example, deaths of seventeen workers in tetraethyl lead refineries during the period 1924–1925 led to questions about the public health impact of leaded gasoline by scientists who were familiar with occupational impacts of lead poisoning.

The latter part of the twentieth century brought a decrease in the number of worker fatalities and the number of occupational diseases, such as black lung in coal miners and brown lung in textile mill workers. Even so, every day an average of 9,000 U.S. workers have disabling injuries on the job, 16 workers die from an injury, and 137 workers die from work-related diseases, according to the U.S. National Institute for Occupational Safety and Health. The toll comes at a cost of over $100 billion—the equivalent health cost impact of all types of cancer.

Ancient Concerns

Although many of the problems of industrial safety and health have been recognized only during the past 150 years, a duty to protect workers has long been acknowledged. In the Bible, Deuteronomy chapter 22 has the admonition: "When you build a new house, you shall make a parapet for [the] roof, so that you will not bring bloodguilt on your house if anyone falls from it."

A similar social concern existed in ancient Greece. Greek biographer Plutarch (c. 45–125 CE), for example, recommended that only criminal slaves be used in lead and mercury mines. It is not just, he said, to expose noncriminals to the poisons of the mines.

Mercury and lead were well known as poisons, and Greek physicians appreciated their dangers. Greek physician Hippocrates (c. 460–370 BCE) described a severe attack of colic (stomach pain) in lead miners. Around 200 BCE Greek physician Galen observed copper miners and noted dangers. Greek physician Pedanius Dioscorides (c. 40–90 CE) noted in his *Materia Medica* that eating lead would cause colic, paralysis, and delirium.

Romans were also well aware of the dangers of certain occupations. Engineer Marcus Vitruvius Pollio noted in the first century BCE that lead workers had pale gray complexions. "In casting," Vitruvius noted, "the lead receives the current of air, [and] the fumes from it occupy the members of the body, and burning them thereon, rob the limbs of the virtues of the blood" (Hughes 1975, 5). Roman historian and scholar Pliny (23–79 CE) described workers using air bladders as masks to protect themselves from cinnabar (mercury) dust and vapors.

Despite some knowledge of industrial dangers, it was common practice in ancient Rome to sweeten wine and grape pulp with sheets of lead. Most of the problem of lead poisoning in the upper classes could be attributed to this fondness for sweet foods, rather than to lead water pipes, according to modern-day Canadian historian and toxicologist Jerome Nrigau.

Mining Dangers Known in Early Europe

The dangers of mining and smelting metals were well known to workers in the European mining industries that were emerging in the eleventh and twelfth centuries CE. In part, concern about the dangers led to the establishment of the first guilds. One of the first guilds in Europe, for example, was founded among the silver miners of Goslar in the Harz Mountains of Germany in 1188. It was intended to help miners who became ill or to help their families if they died.

Knowledge of the dangers of mining expanded with the publication of *De Re Metallica* by German mineralogist Georgius Bauer, known as "Agricola" (1494–1556). The book concerns techniques of mining and smelting iron, silver, lead, gold, mercury, and other metals. Parts of the book deal with occupational hazards.

Agricola warned that heated rocks give off "fetid vapor" and said miners should not break rocks by fire inside a mine. He noted that mine dust could produce asthma and that if mine dust had "corrosive qualities" it "eats away the lungs and implants consumption" (Agricola 1950, 214). Agricola noted that in some regions—for example, the Carpathian Mountains—women had married as many as seven husbands, all of whom had been lost from premature death in mines.

He recommended that mine shafts be ventilated and that miners wear veils to protect themselves from dust.

Agricola also defended mining in general. "The critics say . . . that mining is a perilous occupation to pursue because the miners are sometimes killed by the pestilential air which they breathe; sometimes their lungs rot away." Agricola discounted these and other concerns. "Things like this rarely happen, and only insofar as workmen are careless," he wrote (Agricola 1950, 6). The idea that workmen are to blame for occupational disease would be repeated into the mid-twentieth century.

Beginnings of Occupational Medicine

German alchemist Paracelsus (1493–1541), also known as "Aureolus Theophrastus Bombastus von Hohenheim," wrote about the diseases of miners in a book published in 1567. Educated as a physician, Paracelsus traveled throughout Europe and settled for a time in Basel, Switzerland, where he lectured on medicine. He was known for attempting to understand disease through direct observation rather than reliance on the theories of ancient physicians, but this approach put him in conflict with the medical authorities of the time.

Italian professor Bernardino Ramazzini (1633–1714) is considered the "father" of occupational medicine. His reputation rests on a book, *De Morbis Artificum Diatriba*, published in 1700, that examines the diseases and problems of fifty-two occupations. As professor of medicine at the university of Modena, Italy, Ramazzini suggested that a doctor should take a medical history by asking the great questions recommended by Hippocrates but to add one more: "What is your occupation?"

"Medicine, like jurisprudence, should make a contribution to the well being of workers and see to it that, so far as possible, they should exercise their callings without harm," Ramazzini said. "So I for my part have done what I could and have not thought it unbecoming to make my way into the lowliest workshops and study the mysteries of the mechanic arts" (Hunter 1976, 34).

In describing occupational disease in the lead mines, Ramazzini noted that the skin of miners "is apt to bear the same color of the metal. . . . Demons and ghosts are often found to disturb the miners. At first tremors appear in the hands, soon they are paralyzed" (Thompson n.d.).

Mercury is the cruelest of poisons, dealing death and destruction to miners, Ramazzini said, noting also that goldsmiths, especially those gilding silver and copper objects through a mercury process, are also susceptible. "Very few of them reach old age, and even when they do not die young their health is so terribly undermined they pray for death," he said (Hunter 1976, 297).

Ramazzini's book reflected an increasing concern for miners in parts of Europe. One of the first programs of occupational medicine for protecting worker health was established in the early eighteenth century in the mercury mines of Idria (Idrija), in what is now Slovenia.

Early Industrial-Era Observations

As new industries and chemicals were introduced, new kinds of problems were observed by physicians and scientists. Benjamin Franklin, for instance, was concerned about lead poisoning in the printing trades and also published a paper on "dry gripes," or stomach cramps, that he found were caused by drinking rum distilled in lead vessels. English doctor Percival Pott (1714–1788) linked a high frequency of nasal and scrotal cancer with the occupation of chimney sweep in 1775 and discovered the first occupational carcinogen. And in 1779 German physician Johann Peter Frank (1745–1821) wrote *A Complete System of Medical Policy* advocating governmental responsibility for clean water, sewage systems, garbage disposal, food inspection, and industrial health under an authoritative "medical police."

A massive social shift from decentralized work in rural settings to centralized workplaces in factory towns took place across Europe in the early nineteenth century with tremendous consequences. Workers who did not move to factory towns found that they had no work, and some took to breaking steam-powered looms in England's Luddite rebellion of 1811–1816. Those who did move to factory towns found no infrastructure for dealing with clean water, sewage, trash, or even personal hygiene. By the 1830s the accumulating damage began to spark investigations and calls for reform.

In 1831 Charles Turner Thackrah (1795–1833), a British physician, published *The Effects of the Principal Arts, Trades and Professions*. Thackrah not only made clinical observations about the incidence of disease in the trades, but also suggested improvements. He wrote that glazers, for example, should avoid dipping their hands into lead glaze mix, or even better, that something only slightly more expensive could be substituted. "Surely humanity forbids that the health of workmen, and that of the poor at large, should be sacrificed to the saving of halfpence in the price of pots," he said. "Evils are suffered to exist even when the means of correction are known and easily applied. Thoughtlessness or apathy is the only obstacle to success" (Hunter 1976, 121).

About the same time during the 1830s, parliamentary commissions began investigating outrageous working conditions common in England. Children were beaten into working sixteen-hour days in textile mills, for example, and were "stunted, diseased, deformed and degraded." The resulting outrage fueled two decades of social and environmental investigations and reform in England and across Europe. The Royal Commission on the Employment of Children in the Mines reported "cruel slaving revolting to humanity" and pushed for passage of the Mines Act of 1842, which prohibited all women and boys under age thirteen from the mines. The Factory and Workshops Acts, passed around this time and amended throughout the nineteenth century, prohibited women from holding dangerous jobs such as lead and brass manufacturing and children under age eleven from grinding metal. Subsequent acts regulated specific occupational diseases, such as the 1875 law preventing child employment of chimney sweeps and the 1883 Prevention of Lead Poisoning Act.

Reformers in the United States were well aware that growing urban populations and a spreading industrial revolution were taking their toll. In 1842 New York City physician John H. Griscom wrote the report entitled "The Sanitary Condition of the Laboring Population of New York City" (Burrows & Wallace 1999, 785). He found that a lack of sanitation, water, and decent housing made it hard for workers and families to keep clean.

U.S. and European Worker Safety Rates

Reform movements in the United States and Europe were spurred by workers, but the U.S. fight between labor and industry was particularly bitter. One impediment to reform was the U.S. myth of a higher standard of living and cleaner factories, which prevailed for many decades into the twentieth century. However, in many industries U.S. workers fared worse than their European counterparts.

"For years we had the comfortable illusion that byssinosis ("brown lung" disease from cotton dust) was not a problem for US workers," a Public Health Service brochure said in 1969 (Rosner & Markowitz 1987, 219). But a survey of 230,000 textile workers had found rates of from 12 to 30 percent in various plants.

U.S. coal miners had an average of 3.4 deaths per 1,000 between 1900 and 1906. This compared with 2.1 in Germany, 1.3 in Britain, 1.0 in Belgium, and .9 in France.

In 1921 the U.S. Public Health Service examined eighteen hundred pottery workers and found a lead poisoning rate of at least 13.5 percent. In comparison, British pottery workers had less than 1 percent. The United States was also slow in legislating technological change for worker protection. White phosphorous matches were well known to produce "phossy jaw," a disfiguring necrotic condition of the face. They were banned in Europe in 1906 but not until 1931 in the United States. Similarly, white lead paint was banned

in Europe in 1922 but not in the United States until much later.

Mine Safety

The fatality rate for coal and hard-rock miners was the worst of all industries. It was 3.4 per 1,000 annually in 1900, dropping by the time of the Coal Mine Health and Safety Act of 1969 to about 1.75 and a late twentieth-century rate of .22 per 1,000.

The worst year on record was 1907, when more than nine hundred coal miners died in seventeen instances, including the worst mine disaster on record, which occurred 6 December 1907, when 362 Fairmont Coal Company workers died in explosions at Monongah No. 6 and No. 8 mines in West Virginia.

Another mining disaster involved over 470 deaths and over 1,500 injuries from silicosis in the period 1931–1933 during construction of the Hawk's Nest hydroelectric tunnel for a Union Carbide power project near Gauley Bridge, West Virginia. Officials on the job were aware that the thick silica dust was killing workers and did nothing. Racism was a factor because most of the dead workers were African American or recent immigrants.

Factory Disasters Spur Legislation

The Triangle Shirtwaist Factory in New York City caught fire 25 March 1911, killing 146 women who were trapped without fire escapes. Public outrage was intense, especially after factory owners were acquitted under New York law. However, the incident led New York State to establish the Factory Investigating Commission, which led to a nationwide era of reform in factory legislation between 1911 and 1914.

Tetra-ethyl lead was a gasoline additive designed by General Motors and Standard Oil to boost engine power. It was dangerous to make, and many workers in one Standard Oil plant near New York went "violently insane" in October 1924. At least seventeen men died from severe lead poisoning in several plants. The incidents drew attention to the larger issue of using a well-known poison in a common article of commerce. Prominent U.S. occupational health advocate Alice Hamilton, like England's Charles Thackrah a century before, insisted that other gasoline additives would have the same anti-knock effect (which increases engine power) without poisoning workers or the public, but a Public Health Service committee was pushed into approving leaded gasoline. Leaded gasoline was banned in 1986, and Hamilton's public health objections and ideas about alternatives were proven to be accurate.

Radium dial painters of New Jersey developed cancer and other problems after working with radioactive watch dial paints that glowed in the dark. At no time during their employment were the painters warned about or protected from the radioactive paint. Their employer, U.S. Radium Corp., tried to forestall lawsuits in the late 1920s with phony medical examinations and inaccurate scientific reports. After a great deal of publicity, in 1928 the painters' lawsuit led to a negotiated court settlement, and their medical bills were covered. Most of the workers died within a few years. Both leaded gasoline and radium dial workplace dangers were diminished after Public Health Service expert conferences identified specific issues.

Major Occupational Diseases

Asbestos was one of the leading causes of occupational death in the twentieth century, with fatality rates still in the range of three thousand per year and continuing to rise as of 2000. Asbestosis and asbestos-related lung cancers were diagnosed as early as 1899 and were considered preventable as early as the 1930s by British occupational health expert Thomas Legge.

Occupational lung cancer is linked to inhaling carcinogens such as asbestos, coal, and petroleum-related compounds in the workplace. In the United States in 1998 about 17,315 lung cancer deaths were attributable to occupational lung cancer, according to the American Lung Association.

Byssinosis (brown lung disease) is a chronic condition severely impairing lung functions. It is caused by dusts from processing hemp, flax, and cotton. Between 1979 and 1996 byssinosis caused only 120 U.S. deaths, but an estimated 35,000 textile workers were disabled.

Black lung disease, or coal workers' pneumoconiosis, is caused by inhaling coal dust. An estimated 4.5 percent of coal miners are affected, according to the American Lung Association. Between 1979 and 1996 in the United States, 14,156 deaths were attributed to black lung disease.

Silicosis results from exposure to silica in mines, foundries, blasting operations, and manufacturing operations involving materials such as stone, clay, and glass. Between 1979 and 1996 in the United States, 2,694 deaths were attributed to silicosis. About 1.6 million workers may have been exposed to silica dust, and almost sixty thousand may suffer from some degree of silicosis, according to the American Lung Association.

Worker's Compensation Laws

Before worker's compensation acts were passed in Europe and various states in the United States, injured workers had to present claims against employers to unsympathetic courts. Usually the claims were denied under common law theories that presumably treated workers and factory owners as equals. A theory of "contributory negligence," developed in the 1830s in England, held it that if an employee's action causes an injury, a factory owner is not responsible. In most cases, even a manager would be considered an employee.

Worker's compensation bills, which guaranteed wages and health benefits to workers who were injured on the job, were passed in Germany in 1884 and Britain in 1897. In the United States, Maryland passed the first state worker's compensation law in 1902. It was declared unconstitutional by a state court.

After the Triangle factory fire, New York State passed a worker's compensation act, but it, too, was struck down by state courts who said that imposing strict liability on a business would deprive it of property without due process.

Taking the workers' side against conservative judges, former President Teddy Roosevelt said these decisions "have been such as almost to bar the path to industrial, economic and social reform. By such decisions they add immensely to the strength of the Socialist Party, they perpetuate misery, they increase unrest and discontent" (Gersuny 1981, 102).

Factory Inspection and Worker Safety

Reforms in Britain during the 1840s led to a series of Factory Acts and amendments designed to end child labor, bring women into safer occupations, and limit workday hours. The 1867 Factories and Workshops Act, for example, excluded boys under age thirteen from the coal mines and glass factories. Women's employment was also curtailed.

Between 1890 and 1920 most states in the United States enacted workplace safety laws, but they were primarily cosmetic and sometimes struck down by reactionary courts. An Illinois law limiting women's employment to eight hours was struck down in 1895 by state courts. When employers did violate weak laws, they were not penalized but were simply asked to stop violating them. In many states, factory inspections were voluntary. Some states enforced tougher laws in response to disasters, such as New York after the Triangle fire, but most did not.

The New Deal of the 1930s brought the National Labor Relations Act (Wagner Act), which guaranteed a right to form unions and bargain collectively, and the 1936 Walsh Healey Act, which set safety and health requirements for government contractors. Safety standards were adopted from panels of government advisors (the American Conference of Governmental Industrial Hygienists [ACGIH]). A 1947 bill guaranteed a right to walk off the job if workers believed it was unsafe, but attempts to pass an act requiring occupational safety and health standards across the board were defeated in the 1950s and 1960s. Organized labor noted that work injury and illness rates increased during this time, with annual fatalities totaling about 14,500.

In 1970 Congress passed the comprehensive Occupational Safety and Health Act (OSHA) with requirements for record keeping, complaint procedures, federal inspections, and regulatory hearings with judicial enforcement. Professional standards for occupational medicine were also included.

Critics say OSHA's impact has been slight enough to be debatable, but some studies suggest that OSHA has managed to limit exposure in newly regulated areas such as asbestos, vinyl chloride, lead, and cotton dust.

In 1977 the Federal Mine Safety and Health Act consolidated all federal mining industry regulations into a single administration, and in 1990 the Mine Safety and Health Administration (MSHA) began programs to help eliminate specific health hazards, such as black lung disease and silicosis.

Government regulation and worker's compensation lawsuits probably decreased the occupational fatality rate from 7.46 to 4.25 per 100,000 workers annually between 1980 and 1995 in the United States, while the 2000 global average is an estimated 14 per 100,000.

According to the International Labor Organization (ILO), 1.2 million men and women worldwide die every year from occupational accidents and work-related diseases. Workers worldwide also suffer 250 million occupational accidents and 160 million occupational diseases each year. These deaths and injuries take a particularly heavy toll in developing countries, the ILO said, where mining, agriculture, logging, and other hazardous industries are concentrated. In addition, only 10 percent or less of the work force in these nations is likely to have any sort of accident or health insurance coverage. Labor organizations and international environmental organizations have made industrial health and safety a twenty-first-century issue for the developing world.

William Kovarik

Further Reading

Agricola, G. (1950). *De re metallica* (H. C. Hoover & L. H. Hoover, Trans.). Mineola, NY: Dover. (Originally published 1556)

Berman, D. M. (1998). *Death on the job: Occupational health and safety struggles in the United States.* New York: Monthly Review Press.

Burrows, E. G., & Wallace, M. *Gotham, a history of New York City to 1898.* Oxford, UK: Oxford University Press.

Corn, J. K. (1992). *Response to occupational health hazards: A historical perspective.* New York: Van Nostrand Reinhold.

Gersuny, C. (1981). *Work hazards and industrial conflict.* Providence, RI: New England Press.

Hughes, J. D. (1975). *Ecology in ancient civilizations.* Albequerque: University of New Mexico Press.

Hunter, D. (1976). *The diseases of the occupations.* London: Hodder and Stoughton.

Ramazzini, B. (1940). *De morbis artificum diatriba* (W. C. Wright, Trans.). Chicago: University of Chicago Press.

Rosner, D., & Markowitz, G. (1987). *Dying for work.* Indianapolis: Indiana University Press.

Somavía, J. (2002, May). Decent work, safe work. *International Labour Organization report.* Retrieved February 24, 2003 from http://www.ilo.org/public/english/protection/safework/decent.htm

Thompson, L. R. (n.d.). Knowledge of industrial hygiene in the early days of history. National Institutes of Health, RG 443 Box 195. Washington, DC: National Archives.

The Industrial Revolution

The Industrial Revolution was the shift from agriculture-based economy and the production of goods in homes to the production of goods in factories and the corresponding growth of population centers and transportation networks for the distribution of those goods. The first Industrial Revolution occurred in eighteenth-century England. Economists generally assign a starting date between 1740 and 1780. Scholars disagree about whether the Industrial Revolution was truly a sudden development or rather the result of changes that had been accumulating for centuries. Similarly, they disagree on the extent to which the Industrial Revolution was a consequence of the development of the steam engine as a source of power. However, from the standpoint of the environment, the significance of the Industrial Revolution was the increased use of fossil energy sources and other natural resources, placing ever-increasing demands on the environment. The increased use of resources resulted not only from the energy needs of manufacturing itself, but also from the higher population densities that industrialized regions could support, as well as the need to transport workers to the workplace and manufactured goods to market.

Preconditions for the Industrial Revolution

The Industrial Revolution could not have occurred until the "agricultural revolution" had gotten underway in England, making it possible to produce increased amounts of food using fewer workers. The agricultural revolution had a number of causes, including the enclosure of grazing lands, the invention of the seed drill and improved plows, and a more productive system of crop rotation. The potato, imported from the Americas, produced a higher yield of food per acre than cereal grains.

Industrialization in its turn had positive effects on agriculture and the economy. Inventions such as the spinning jenny and the cotton gin increased the profit that could be gained by planting cotton. The mechanical reaper increased the speed with which crops could be harvested. The development of machine tools made the manufacture of farm implements easier. Canals and railroads facilitated the transport of food into urban areas and brought manufactured goods to local markets.

Also necessary for industrialization were a stable currency and banking system. Industrial workers needed to be confident that the coins or banknotes with which they would be paid would be generally accepted in exchange for goods and services. Industrialists often needed to borrow the funds to build and equip factories. Banks and other lenders needed to be sure that the currency in which they would be repaid would have the same buying power as at the time it was borrowed.

Also contributing to the Industrial Revolution were the earlier scientific revolution, associated with English physicist and mathematician Sir Isaac Newton, and re-ligious thought of the Protestant Reformation, which established a positive correlation between material prosperity and divine favor.

The Coal Industry and the Steam Engine

A case can be made that the precipitating event of the Industrial Revolution was a change in the ecology of England—the depletion of English forestland resulting from the burning of wood for warmth and cooking and its use in construction and in such activities as glassmaking. Coal, the first fossil fuel to be widely used, was an even more efficient source of heat than was wood, and iron would turn out to be a far more durable building material. But coal and iron had to be mined, and mines tended to fill up with water. A primitive steam engine, known as the "miner's friend," was patented in 1698 by Thomas Savery (1650?–1715), an English engineer from Devonshire, and could be used to remove water from mine shafts. Savery's engine was improved and made much safer by Thomas Newcomen (1663–1729), a Devonshire blacksmith. Newcomen's engine was highly inefficient, however, because much of the energy released by burning coal was wasted reheating the engine's one cylinder, which was cooled as a part of its operating cycle. It remained for the Scottish inventor James Watt (1736–1819) to introduce a second cylinder for condensing the steam, allowing the power-generating cylinder to remain warm. Watt produced a working model by 1775, and Watt's company had installed forty engines in the mines of Cornwall by 1880. Watt continued to improve the steam engine, which found increasing use in factories as well as mines. By 1800 more than five hundred steam engines were in commercial use.

The steam engine represented the first use of heat energy to perform mechanical work. Prior to its invention, the only power sources available to industry were those of human and animal muscle and the energy of flowing water and the wind, the availability of which were somewhat restricted by geography. A steam engine, however, could be installed anywhere water and fuel were available. The steam engine is a good example of the interaction of science and technology during the Industrial Revolution. The earliest versions, those of Savery and Newcomen, were the products of a process of trial and error, with little base in scientific theory. Indeed, a proper scientific theory of heat was not available until the mid-nineteenth century. Watt, although not a university graduate, worked at the Uni-

James Watt—Key Inventor in the Industrial Revolution

Although often credited with the invention of the steam engine, James Watt, the Scottish engineer and inventor born in 1736, actually was responsible for the major improvement in design that made the steam engine less wasteful of fuel energy and therefore cheaper to run. Watt's steam engine was the primary power source for the first stage of the Industrial Revolution, turning England into the first industrialized nation in the modern sense. The impact of Watt's invention on the exploitation of natural resources was immense. Coal had to be mined to supply power to factories and later to run locomotives and steamships. Air pollution became a part of the industrial landscape, and an ever-increasing demand for energy became accepted as an inevitable component of industrialization.

Watt was born in Greenock, Scotland, into a merchant family that had fallen on hard times. Unable to afford a university education, he began an apprenticeship in London to prepare for a career as a mathematical instrument maker. Watt displayed a natural aptitude for machine work but was unwilling to serve the seven-year apprenticeship. He returned to Scotland and was allowed to set up an instrument maker's shop on the grounds of the University of Glasgow. This put him in daily contact with some of the preeminent scientific and engineering minds of his time, notably Joseph Black (1728–1799), whose theory of latent heat would be essential to Watt's invention.

Watt reported that the idea for an improved steam engine occurred to him on Easter Sunday of 1795. He realized at that time that the major flaw of the engine introduced by Thomas Newcomen (1663–1729) was that much of the heat energy contained in the steam was wasted in heating up the its one cylinder during each stroke, only to have the cylinder cooled before the next stroke could begin. By introducing a separate condenser for the steam, Watt allowed the main cylinder to remain hot so that more of the heat energy could be converted to useful mechanical energy. The patent for his invention bore the title "A New Invented Method of Lessening the Consumption of Steam and Fuel in Fire Engines."

To begin the manufacture of steam engines Watt had to overcome a number of obstacles and with limited finances. Watt took on business partners, first Dr. John Roebuck, who went bankrupt within a few years, and then Matthew Boulton, who moved Watt to Birmingham, where the most capable machinists were. Watt produced a working model by 1775, and the company had installed forty engines in Cornwall by 1880.

Watt retired in 1800. He was awarded an honorary doctorate by Glasgow University and elected a member of the Royal Society. In 1814 he became the first engineer to be elected a foreign associate of the French Academy. He declined to be made a baronet, however, and requested a private funeral. He died near Birmingham in 1819 and was memorialized a few years later by a large statue in Westminster Abbey.

Donald R. Franceschetti

Further Reading

Carnegie, A. (1933). *James Watt.* New York: McGraw-Hill.
Crowther, J. G. (1962). *Scientists of the Industrial Revolution.* London: Cresset Press.
Laidler, K. J. (1998). *To light such a candle.* New York: Oxford University Press.

versity of Glasgow and was acquainted with some of the leading scientific minds of his time, in particular Dr. Joseph Black (1728–1799), who introduced the concepts of latent heat and specific heat, which were essential to understanding the operation of the engine. Watt's designs also required that workers be able to produce parts to exacting tolerances, requiring that they master more sophisticated tools and measuring devices.

Building better steam engines would become one of the primary motivations for the development of the science of thermodynamics, which connects heat and mechanical energy. In 1824 the French physicist Sadi Carnot (1796–1832) published "Essay on the Motive Power of Heat," in which he showed that there is a fundamental limit to the efficiency of any heat engine, a limit that is set by the temperature of the environment. Thus any process in which heat is produced for conversion into mechanical energy results in the release of heat to the environment.

The Textile Industry

The climate and terrain of Britain and Scotland were highly suited to sheepherding, and many farm households were involved in the spinning of wool and manufacture of woolen garments. They had also begun the manufacture of cotton cloth. Cotton was available to the English from plantations in the southern United States, the Caribbean, and the Middle East. Whereas the cost of growing a pound of cotton was much less than that of a pound of wool, converting cotton into cloth was a more labor-intensive process. The importation of cotton fabric from India led to interest in the possibility of manufacturing cotton garments in England.

The basic operations in the production of cloth are spinning, in which short fibers are wound into a continuous thread or yarn, and weaving to form cloth. The first major invention in textiles during the Industrial Revolution was that of the flying shuttle loom, patented by the English inventor John Kay (1704–1768) in 1733. The improved loom greatly improved the speed with which thread could be woven into cloth, creating a demand for more production of yarn, a demand met by the spinning jenny, introduced by James Hargreaves (1720–1778) in 1764, making it possible to create multiple strands of yarn at the same time. Hargreaves's spinning jenny produced a relatively weak yarn, however. Sir Richard Arkwright (1732–1792) invented a machine in which, by careful control of tension in the fibers, a much stronger thread was

produced. Both Hargreaves and Arkwright were forced to relocate by their neighbors, who felt that they would be driven out of the market as producers of thread and cloth. By 1778 twenty thousand spinning machines were in operation. Steam engines were installed as "prime movers" in the textile factories, providing mechanical energy to the spinning machines and, later, power looms. In 1793 the American inventor Eli Whitney (1765–1825) began production of the cotton gin, a device that greatly speeded the removal of cotton seeds from cotton fiber, assuring an increased supply of raw cotton, which English textile manufacturers eagerly imported.

The Iron Industry

The extraction of iron from its ores and its use in construction greatly expanded during the Industrial Revolution. Iron production is very costly in terms of energy. Wood does not burn at a high enough temperature to be used directly to heat the ore, so charcoal had been used instead. The copper industry had begun using coke, a purified form of coal, as a more reliable heat source. Abraham Darby (1678?–1717), an English engineer working in that industry, realized that coke could be used effectively in iron extraction as well. In 1708 he opened the Bristol Iron Works Company and within a few years was manufacturing the huge cylinders needed for the Newcomen steam engines being installed in numerous coal mines.

Transportation

The Industrial Revolution was marked by numerous advances in land and water transportation. Canal building by private landowners had been a tradition in England. In 1760, however, Parliament approved using public funds for the construction of the Bridgewater Canal, which was about 16 kilometers long, to carry coal from the coal mines at Worsely to the manufacturing city of Manchester. This reduced the cost of coal to the textile manufacturers by about 50 percent. The success of the Bridgewater Canal was followed by a period of extensive canal building, with nearly fifty additional canals being built by the end of the century and industrialists establishing factories on sites that would reduce their transportation costs.

England also enjoyed a strong navy and a merchant marine fleet. Navigation on the open sea was rendered much safer by John Harrison (1693–1776), a carpenter and clockmaker who invented a chronometer that remained accurate on ship and thus could be used, together with astronomical observations, to determine longitude. Sailing remained dependent on wind, however, and thus somewhat unpredictable until the invention of a practical steamboat by the American inventor Robert Fulton in 1787. By using Watt's steam engine to power a paddlewheel and later a propeller, Fulton made water travel faster and more dependable.

The steam locomotive appeared in 1802 when English inventor and engineer Richard Trevithick (1771–1833) commissioned Darby's Bristol ironworks to produce the first locomotive engine. The railways would become the biggest consumer of industrial iron, required both for the steam-powered trains and the rails they rode on. Although only 320 kilometers of rail were operating in 1820 (all of it in Britain), thousands more would be installed by mid-century.

Social Consequences

The Industrial Revolution occurred in England at roughly the same time as the American and French Revolutions. Although the three revolutions were dissimilar in many regards, they all had the effect of greatly diminishing the power of a landed and hereditary aristocracy: in France by execution, in America by political action, and in England by the accumulation of wealth by a new class of entrepreneur. As a result, social mobility greatly increased, and a new class of technically skilled working men, machinists, draftsmen, and engineers emerged. At the same time the status of unskilled or semiskilled workers diminished. Factory workers were required to report for work seven days a week, ten or more hours a day. Many procedures had to be completed while the machines were still running because it was too costly to interrupt production. Many workers, including many children, were maimed as a result. Eventually child welfare laws and unionization would reduce the human toll of industrialization while more enlightened manufacturers came to appreciate that well-paid and healthy workers would be more productive and ultimately an important part of the market for manufactured goods.

The Developing World

The prosperity of the United States, England, and countries of northern Europe as industrialized nations is widely envied by nations in the so-called Third World, and many poorer nations have set upon an agenda of industrialization. Becoming an industrial power, however, is difficult without a stable currency and government and a literate population. Cultural considerations also come into play; not all cultures

share the European notion of progress. Because industrialization requires energy sources, industrializing nations and the international community must weigh the benefits and risks of the increased use of fossil fuels, if available, against those of nuclear power plants that might be built. There are also limits to the role that governments can play in stimulating industrialization. The leadership of the former Soviet Union was able to industrialize the production of military hardware and farm machinery but had little to offer in the way of consumer goods. Industrialization is making headway in the Pacific Rim as multinational corporations find it easier to manufacture electronic goods in countries with cheaper labor and less stringent environmental laws. How best to facilitate the industrialization process without further deterioration of the global environment remains an issue of international debate.

Donald R. Franceschetti

Further Reading

Crowther, J. G. (1962). *Scientists of the Industrial Revolution.* London: Cresset.

Deane, P. (1965). *The first Industrial Revolution.* New York: Cambridge University Press.

Jacob, M. C. (1988). *The cultural meaning of the scientific revolution.* Philadelphia: Temple University Press.

Schlager, N., & Lauer, J. (2000). *Science and its times: Understanding the social significance of scientific discovery: Vol. 4. 1799–1800.* Detroit, MI: Gale Group.

Sieferle, R. P. (2001). *The subterranean forest: Energy systems and the Industrial Revolution.* Cambridge, UK: White Horse Press.

Thompson, A. (1973). *The dynamics of the Industrial Revolution.* New York: St. Martin's Press.

Toynbee, A. (1923). *Lectures on the Industrial Revolution of the eighteenth century in England.* New York: Longmans, Green, and Co.

Von Tunzelmann, G. N. (1978). *Steam power and British industrialization to 1860.* New York: Oxford University Press.

Insects

Insects (arthropods with three pairs of legs) are small, but they are the most numerous and most diverse creatures on the planet. If an alien intelligence were to land on Earth, charged with surveying its living creatures with limited time and limited resources, it could not do better than study just beetles, dismissing everything else as sampling error.

Despite their small size, insects have had a powerful influence on the world and on humans' relationship with the environment. They have been able to achieve this influence because of their vast numbers, their versatile adaptability, and their mind-numbing diversity.

Insects are thought to have been largely responsible for the explosion of angiosperms (flowering plants) in the Cretaceous period (145–65 million years ago), a basic fact that influences every aspect of the present environment on Earth. These are now the dominant plants on the planet and the most important feature of virtually any landscape in the world. The evolution of flowers has been intricately linked to the evolution of the insects that are attracted to pollinate them. And since that time, too, unimaginable numbers of insect herbivores have mounted a continuous and prolonged attack on plants, bringing to bear a heavy selective load on the evolution of plant defenses, both chemical and physical.

Looking around at the greenness of the world, it is easy to imagine that plants are thriving more or less everywhere and that the nibblings of plant-eating insects have only a minor effect on plant growth. But this belies the fact that these plant-eaters are kept in check by predatory species in an intricate ecological web. The effects of plant-eating insects are best noticed when this web is disrupted. The gypsy moth (Lymantria dispar) is one of many alien species that has been imported into the United States (ironically it was deliberately introduced to test its suitability for silk production). Having left its normal predators and parasites behind in Europe, it has become a serious forestry pest, defoliating vast areas of conifer forest. Likewise, but for the benefit of ecology, the deliberate introduction of the prickly-pear moth (Cactoblastis cactorum) into Australia cleared 24.2 million hectares of the nonnative prickly-pear cactus (Opuntia), which had become an invasive weed squeezing out the native flora.

Plagues and Pests

Insects have most profoundly influenced the environment through their depredations on agricultural crops, forests, domestic food stores, and farmed animals and by their implication in the spread of human and animal disease. (See table 1.)

As soon as early humans changed from being nomadic hunter-gatherers to settled agriculturalists, insects were on hand to take advantage of the ecological niches provided to them. Crop monocultures (forest trees as well as agricultural plants) made it easy for some insects to become major economic, even famine-inducing, pests. Plagues of locusts may have biblical overtones, but they still occur today, and they are still as dramatic and as terrible. Almost all groups of insects have plant-feeding species, and these are considered pests when feeding on cultivated plants. Other well-known agricultural pests include Colorado beetle (Leptinotarsa decemlineata) on potato, vine phylloxera (Viteus vitifoliae) on grapevine, Japanese beetle (Popillia japonica) on horticultural plants, maize weevil (Sitophilus species) on rice and maize, Mediterranean fruit fly (Ceratitis capitata) on soft fruit, cabbage white butterflies (Pieris species) on brassicas (herbs such as cabbage), and bollworms (Diparopsis and Earias species) on cotton. The list is seemingly endless.

Less-obvious but equally devastating attacks come from a wide variety of insects feeding on stored products in silos, warehouses, shops, and homes. Some of the most damaging species are weevils and other beetles that "in nature" eat seeds and nuts, but have adapted to feed on the bountiful surplus of stored grain. Although difficult to measure worldwide, it is estimated that 30–40 percent of all crop produce (currently valued at more than $300 billion) is destroyed by insects, either in the fields or in postharvest storage.

Worse than the damage done to stored products is the damage done to homes constructed of wood. The words termite and woodworm are shot through with the base associations of destruction and worthlessness. The notion that homes, hospitals, universities, libraries, temples, and all the other tokens of a civil society are under gnawing attack from wood-boring insects is a powerful and sobering indictment of what is often viewed as a menacing, malevolent insect nation. Timber continues to evoke feelings of mellow warmth and naturalness as a construction material, but its natural limitations, including its vulnerability to attacks by insects, have led to the use of impervious stone and glass, and later concrete and steel. The imposing strength of important architecture, from cathedrals to castles, was driven by a response to these attacks and the natural decay of wood, thatch, and other previously available materials.

Pesticides and Pollution

The enormous economic impact of insect pests has led to the creation of a massive pesticide industry. And this in turn has enabled the continued development of

TABLE 1.
MAJOR DISEASES SPREAD BY INSECTS

Vector	Disease	Parasite	Transmission	Distribution
Assassin bugs				
Triatoma spp.	Chagas' disease	*Trypanosoma cruzi*	Bite, contamination by feces	S. America
Human lice				
Pediculus humanus	Relapsing fever	*Borrelia recurrentis*	Skin contamination	Europe, Asia, Africa
Tropical rat fleas				
Xenopsylla cheopis	Plague	*Pasturella pestis*	Bite	Pantropical
	Murine typhus	*Rickettsia typhi*	Bite	Pantropical
Mosquitoes				
Anopheles spp.	Malaria	*Plasmodium* spp.	Bite	Pantropical
Aëdes aegypti	Yellow fever	Virus	Bite	Africa, S.
	Dengue	Virus	Bite	America Tropics
Anopheles & Culex spp.	Encephalitis	Viruses	Bite	Africa, America
	Filariasis	*Wuchereria bancrofti*	Africa	Pantropical
Sandflies				
Phlebotomus species	Leishmaniasis	*Leishmania* spp.	Bite, etc.	Africa, Asia, S. America
Tsetse flies				
Glossina spp.	Sleeping sickness	*Trypanosoma* spp.	Bite	Africa
Black flies				
Simulium spp.	River blindness	*Onchocerca volvulus*	Invasion of bite	C. & S. America, Africa
Horse flies				
Chrysops spp.	Loasis	*Loa loa*	Bite	Africa
Chrysops and others	Tularaemia	*Pasturella tularensis*	Bite	Holarctic
Cockroaches				
Blatta etc.	Ameobic dysentery	*Entamoeba histolytica*	Food contamination	Pantropical
Houseflies				
Musca domestica etc.	Bacillary dysentery Conjunctivitis	*Bacillus* spp.	Food contamination	Pantropical
	Typhoid fever	Bacteria		Pantropical
	Cholera	*Salmonella typhi*	Eye visits	Pantropical
	Yaws	*Vibrio cholerare*	Food and water	Pantropical
		Treponema pertenue	Food contamination	Pantropical
			Wound contamination	
	Trachoma	Virus	Contamination	Pantropical
Ticks				
Trombicula spp.	Scrub typhus	*Rickettsia tsutsugamushi*	Bite	S.E. Asia
Ornithodorus spp.	African relapsing fever	*Borrelia* spp.	Bite (or contamination)	Africa
Amblyomma and Dermacentor spp.	Rocky mountain spotted fever	Rickettsia	Bite	United States

Source: D. S. Hill. (1997). *The economic importance of insects.* New York: Chapman & Hall.

an increasingly intensive agriculture. During the twentieth century, in particular after World War II, the industrialization of farming had a major effect on what was previously very much the pastoral ecology of cultivated land, and it changed the visual appearance of the farmed landscape as arable land increased. Modern farming is also driven by mechanization and the availability of chemical fertilizers, but the widespread use of chemical pesticides has played a major role in changing the very look of the land.

Although pesticides have increased yields and improved crop quality to feed a burgeoning population,

Insects that Kill

Though there are no deadly snakes in the country, there are insects that annually cause considerable loss of life. The centipede attains a growth of six or seven inches, and a bite from one of them may prove fatal, if not attended to at once. The Koreans cut up centipedes and make a deadly drink, which they use, as hemlock was used in Greece, for executing criminals. This has now gone out of practice, however, thanks to the enlightening contact with Westerners, who simply choke a man to death with a rope! Among the mountains it is said that a poisonous spider is found; but until this is verified we dare not vouch for it.

Source: Hulbert, Homer B. (1906). *The Passing of Korea*. New York: Doubleday, Page and Co., p. 25.

they have given rise to their own problems—pollution of neighboring ecosystems and poisoning of nontarget organisms, including humans. The best-documented case is the rise in the use of dichlorodiphenyltrichlorethane (DDT) and its subsequent withdrawal because of its toxicity to wild birds, other animals, and humans. New synthetic pesticides continue to be developed, but at the same time many that have been in long use are regularly withdrawn because of new or increasing toxicity fears.

Recent moves away from chemical crop protection by the genetic modification (GM) of plants to induce them to synthesize their own internal insecticides are surrounded by controversy and widespread public skepticism. Fears of the impact of insecticidal GM genes "escaping" into the wider environment are still great, primarily because the possible side-effects are presently unquantifiable.

A smaller number of insect pests attack stock animals, but they can nevertheless wreak major economic havoc. Blood-sucking lice, flies, and fleas spread disease and reduce stock viability. The veterinary pesticide industry is also a major market, and increasing use of chemicals on farm animals and household pets threatens a new ecological side-effect. Systemic pesticides called "ivermectins," injected into the flesh of the animal or given orally against intestinal worms, create what is in effect insecticidal dung. The normal dung-feeding community of beetles and flies that harmlessly recycles this waste material cannot feed, and large quantities of animal excrement build up. Some experts worry that this situation echoes an ecological problem experienced in Australia in the middle of the twentieth century. Native Australian dung beetles, accustomed to feeding in marsupial droppings, were not removing the cow and horse dung that threatened to smother

the fertile meadowland. It was only the deliberate introduction of various African dung beetle species that reversed the build-up of ungulate (mammals with hooves) droppings.

Insects as Disease Vectors

Insects cause vast damage to property and plant and animal foods, but that damage pales beside the sickness and enormous loss of human life caused by insect vectors (transmitters) of disease. At the end of the twentieth century, the World Health Organization (WHO) estimated that malaria, transmitted by mosquito bites, affected 267 million people in 103 countries, killing 1–2 million each year. WHO further estimated that the top five tropical diseases would kill 4 million people a year by 2010. Four of these five diseases—malaria, leishmaniasis, sleeping sickness, and lymphatic filariasis—are spread by insects. (The fifth, schistosomiasis, is carried by freshwater snails.)

Advances in medicine and hygiene have all but eradicated many insect-borne diseases, at least in the West. But historically, and today in some undeveloped countries, there are even bigger killers. Plague, also called the "black death," killed two-thirds of the population as it swept through Europe during the Middle Ages (eleventh to fourteenth centuries). It was transmitted by the tropical rat flea *(Xenopsylla cheopis)* and remains a medical hazard in many tropical regions today.

The humble housefly *(Musca domestica)*, breeding in filth and excrement and then visiting human food in dwelling places, is a prime candidate as the most dangerous animal on the planet. It has been recorded as carrying over one hundred pathogens and transmitting sixty-five of them, including bacteria, helminth

"Killer" Bees

The Africanized honeybee, *Apis mellifera* subspecies *scutellata*, is a superior forager and gives higher yields of honey, but it attacks other bees and occasionally humans or livestock. In the 1950s a few queens were taken to South America for interbreeding and some escaped from domestic captivity. The resulting hybrid race was vigorous and more aggressive, and started to replace the previously docile local honeybees. These so-called killer bees cause alarm because of a few unprovoked attacks on humans, in which people have been stung to death. Deaths from ordinary honeybee stings are well-known, especially as an alarm pheromone (chemical scent) is released with each sting, which labels the "victim" for other bees in the colony to attack. However, the added aggressiveness of the African strain makes it more dangerous. Having started in Brazil, the Africanized bees continue to interbreed and spread and entered the southern United States in the 1990s. However, the race is a warmth-loving one and it is hoped that it will not spread much further north.

Richard Jones

worms, protozoa, and viruses. It is mainly implicated in the spread of diseases such as dysentery, polio, typhoid, cholera, diphtheria, and tuberculosis. Widespread sanitary reform during the nineteenth century and the arrival of the refrigerator in the twentieth revolutionized domestic life in the developed world. They created a modern environment where the housefly is surprisingly scarce in the urban homes where it was once a scourge. However, the housefly and close relatives like the bush fly (*Musca sorbens*) remain major nuisances in Africa, Asia, and Australia.

Beneficial Insects

Not all insects, though, are pests, despite widespread human squeamishness about creepy-crawly "nasties" and the virtually medieval association of "bugs" with dirt and uncleanliness. It has been, after all, more than a century and a quarter since the French scientist Louis Pasteur (1822–1895) disproved the notion of "spontaneous generation" of animalcules from decaying organic matter. Certain insects today are imbued with positive characteristics rather than the usual "yuck" factor. This increasingly positive feeling toward insects as a valuable part of the natural world has great significance for the future of humankind's relationship with the environment.

Honeybees are widely appreciated for their sweet harvest, and bumblebees, even though (contrary to popular opinion) they don't provide honey, are adored for their cuddliness and respected for their earnest hard work. Butterflies are applauded for their bright

natural beauty, and although moths are generally viewed with suspicion for their nocturnal haunts, some of them give us silk, a byword for luxury and wealth. Ladybirds (ladybugs) are the bright subjects of children's rhymes and popular good-luck chants, and fireflies are miraculous glowing wonders of the mysterious natural world. Even some large and rather ominous-looking creatures are revered: dragonflies for their voracious mosquito-hawk prowess and crickets for their shrill but pleasing song.

Today insects are used as biological control agents—parasitoids and predators against crop pests and key herbivores against invasive alien weeds. They are used as indicators of environmental quality, measuring pollution of freshwater and the ecology of ancient forests. The monarch butterfly (*Danaus plexippus*) is an eco-tourist attraction at its mass overwintering sites in Central America. Silk and honey are still major industries. These relatively concrete uses aside, insects are now exerting a more subtle and abstract pressure on human understanding of the environment. They provide a window into the realization that the world is a wondrous and awe-inspiring place.

The Future

Across most of the globe today, humankind's relationship with the environment is a socioeconomic one, based on sovereign ownership of the land, commercial use of the land, and its financial productivity. But re-emerging in the psyche of a relatively educated and wealthy Western population is an awareness of the conflict between unsustainable human activities and the perceived view of wilderness, nature, and life on Earth. The sheer number of insects is bringing an intellectual and moral weight to bear on the wider protection of the environment.

The British scientist J. B. S. Haldane (1892–1964) was reputedly asked by "some solemn ass" what could be inferred of the work of the Creator from a study of the works of creation. "An inordinate fondness for beetles" was his crushing reply.

To some, his reply might at first seem facetious, but such is the magnitude of insect number and insect (especially beetle) variety that scientists are still debating the complex issues. One of these issues—the almost unimaginable diversity of the Earth—is becoming increasingly important in humankind's relationship with the world, particularly in an age of Earth summits and biodiversity initiatives.

At the end of the twentieth century the measure of insect diversity (the number of species in the world) was based on the number of known species housed in the world's museums and on the descriptions of those species that had been published in the scientific literature. By 1980 about 1.2 million animal species were known, 1 million of these being insects. But when entomologists (those who study insects) began to study tropical rain forest trees, this number had to be dramatically increased.

The technique of counting was simple—an insecticide fogging machine, hauled up into the rain forest canopy, knocked down huge numbers of insects (especially beetles) previously unknown to science. Extrapolating the data led to the suggestion that there are perhaps 30 million tropical arthropod species. Other researchers have followed this lead and have reinterpreted the data. But instead of consensus arising, further confusion rules. Current estimates of insect diversity lie somewhere between 3 and 85 million species. Whatever the number, fears are that most of them will become extinct from humanity's unsustainable use of the land before they are ever found or described.

Richard Jones

Further Reading

Arnett, R. H., Jr. (1993). *American insects: A handbook of the insects of America north of Mexico.* Gainesville, FL: Sandhill Crane Press.

Gullan, P. J., & Cranston, P. S. (1994). *The insects: An outline of entomology.* New York: Chapman & Hall.

Hill, D. S. (1997). *The economic importance of insects.* New York: Chapman & Hall.

Naumann, I. D. (Ed.). (1991). *The insects of Australia* (2nd ed.). Melbourne, Australia: Melbourne University Press.

International Law

International environmental law provides the rules and norms that countries must follow when they take actions that affect the human environment. Most of these rules are contained in treaties or other written international agreements that countries have explicitly agreed to. Some of the rules reflect customary international law, which means that they have arisen from a consistent practice among states, which felt obligated to follow that practice. (In international law, the term *state* is used to refer to countries, not subunits—which are often called states—within a country.) Binding international agreements can be referred to as treaties, conventions, international agreements, or sometimes protocols. There are also many other instruments, such as declarations, that countries are not obligated to follow, but often do. These are sometimes referred to as "soft law" or nonbinding legal instruments.

The History of International Environmental Law

International environmental law developed during the twentieth century. Most of it was negotiated after the June 1972 United Nations Stockholm Conference on the Human Environment. In 1972 there were only about three dozen multilateral environmental agreements; in 2002 there were more than 1100 important legal instruments concerned with the environment. There are agreements to control pollution in the oceans, air, and freshwater; to protect regional seas; to conserve biological diversity, wetlands, and world natural and cultural heritage sites; to control international trade in endangered species of fauna and flora, hazardous wastes, and toxic chemicals; and to protect global commons such as the high-level ozone layer, the climate, the high seas, and Antarctica. Many of these are binding agreements, although some are nonbinding legal instruments.

In 1900 international law was based on the principle that countries could exercise almost unfettered national sovereignty over the natural resources within their territory or jurisdiction. International agreements addressed boundary waters, navigation, fishing rights in shared rivers, and the protection of commercially valuable species of birds, fur seals, and other specific species of fauna. The 1909 Boundary Waters Treaty between the United States and the United Kingdom (now Canada) is noteworthy as an early treaty that addressed water pollution. Article 4 of the Treaty provides that water "shall not be polluted on either side to the injury or health or property on the other."

The most famous early adjudication of a pollution problem that crossed national borders is the Trail Smelter Arbitration between Canada and the United States. Settled in the late 1930s, it affirmed Canada's responsibility for the fumes from a copper smelter in British Columbia that harmed crops and acreage in the state of Washington. The arbitral tribunal established for this dispute awarded damages to the United States and set up a regime to monitor the pollution in the future.

During the 1930s and 1940s countries negotiated international agreements that were intended to ensure sustainable harvesting of whales, to protect fisheries, and to conserve other fauna and flora. In the 1950s and 1960s international agreements were concluded that addressed oil pollution of the oceans and liability for nuclear-powered ships.

The surge in bilateral and multilateral environmental agreements came after 1970. In 1972, countries established the United Nations Environment Programme (UNEP), the first international intergovernmental organization dedicated to protecting the environment. It is headquartered in Nairobi, Kenya. Under the UNEP, countries negotiated many regional agreements to protect regional seas, such as the Mediterranean and the Baltic. These were framework agreements that set forth general obligations and usually called for research, monitoring of the conditions of the seas, and exchange of information. The detailed obligations relating to emergencies, land-based sources of marine pollution, or other specific problems were contained in separate agreements (called protocols) attached to the main framework agreement. Countries must join a protocol at the same time that they join the framework agreement for a particular regional sea.

During the 1980s and 1990s countries negotiated international agreements that addressed the problems of high-level ozone layer depletion (by human-made chemicals) and climate change (from human activities); loss of biodiversity; contamination by organic pollutants that persist in the environment, such as dioxin, polychlorinated biphenyls (PCBs), and DDT; and trade in pesticides and in chemicals that have been banned or

severely restricted in the country of production. They concluded regional agreements on air pollution and water quality. In 1982, after almost a decade of negotiations, countries concluded the Law of the Sea Convention, which deals with the multiple uses of the oceans and also sets forth the basic framework for managing marine pollution.

Characteristics of International Environmental Law Since 1990

The international agreements negotiated since 1990 generally contain more detailed obligations than earlier ones (with the notable exception of the Law of the Sea Convention), often recognize the importance of conserving ecosystems in protecting the environment (rather than addressing only the dangers of specific pollutants), frequently assign countries different levels of responsibility based on their level of economic development (as in ozone and climate agreements), and establish a special implementation committee to focus on promoting national implementation and compliance with the obligations in the agreement, or to enforce the obligations if violations occur. Some provide for a special fund to assist developing countries in complying with the agreement or limit trade in designated products with countries that have not joined the agreement, or both.

Most international agreements have secretariats that carry out the administrative work associated with the agreements. The countries party to the agreements usually meet annually or biennially, with special committees meeting more frequently. They often make decisions, issue guidelines, or initiate programs to keep up with changes in the scientific, economic, or political aspects of the environmental problem addressed by the agreement. Sometimes the parties formally amend the agreement (for example, they may add new chemicals to those already covered by an agreement). Each country must consent to the amendment in order to be bound by it. Some of the agreements set up formal procedures for settling disputes, such as by fact-finding, mediation, arbitration, or judicial settlement, although these have been used infrequently.

Nongovernmental organizations (NGOs) have been important in the negotiation and implementation of environmental agreements and in securing compliance with them. Many NGOs are focused on environmental protections; a few represent the interests of indigenous peoples. Other organizations are associated with business, insurance, and other aspects of the private sector.

In 1992, countries met in Rio de Janeiro to celebrate the twentieth anniversary of the 1972 United Nations Stockholm Conference on the Human Environment and to confirm formally the concept of sustainable development. At this Conference, countries adopted the Rio Declaration on Environment and Development, framework agreements on climate and on biodiversity, nonbinding principles on forests, and Agenda 21, a nonbinding document that sets out a comprehensive program of action to promote sustainable development. In September 2002, they met in Johannesburg, South Africa, to review progress since the Rio conference.

International environmental law has become increasingly linked with other areas of international law, particularly human-rights law and trade law. National constitutions in some countries provide for a "right to environment," and some jurists and others have argued that a right to environment also exists in international human-rights law. There is no consensus yet on whether there is a separate right to environment in international law, nor is there consensus on what the right covers. Some argue that the right is included within other human rights.

The World Trade Organization (WTO) has established the Committee on Trade and Environment to look at issues such as whether multilateral environmental agreements that contain provisions limiting trade with countries not party to the agreements are consistent with the provisions of the General Agreement on Tariffs and Trade (GATT, 1994). The committee also examines the extent to which a country's national environmental measures restricting imports or exports are consistent with GATT. Environmental advocates are concerned that panels settling trade disputes may limit measures that countries take pursuant to international environmental agreements or may constrain national initiatives to protect shared environments or resources. The law in this area is evolving.

Principles of International Environmental Law

Unlike in international trade law, in international environmental law, no one document sets forth binding legal principles. The 1972 Stockholm Declaration on the Human Environment and the 1992 Rio Declaration on Environment and Development are the two basic documents that set forth principles of international environmental law, but while some of their provisions represent customary international law and are thus binding, most are not. Neither declaration is an international agreement. The proposed principles include both substantive obligations and procedural ones.

Substantive Obligations

While states have the sovereign right to exploit their own resources pursuant to their own environmental and developmental policies, they also have "the responsibility to ensure that activities within their jurisdiction or control do not cause damage to the environment of other States or of areas beyond the limits of national jurisdiction" (Principle 21 of the 1972 Stockholm Declaration on the Human Environment). This primary obligation has been reiterated in many documents. The International Court of Justice indicated in two decisions in the 1990s that a close variant of the principle now forms part of the corpus of international law relating to the environment and is thus binding. This means, for example, that a country is obligated to prevent pollution from going into a neighboring country if it causes significant damage.

Many jurists argue that states have an obligation to cooperate to protect the health and integrity of Earth's ecosystem. The principle is found in the 1992 Rio Declaration and in many international agreements. The related notion of the common concern of humankind recognizes that the international community has a legitimate interest in issues that affect the community as a whole, such as biological diversity and climate change.

A major environmental problem is the risk of serious future harm from our actions today. There is always scientific uncertainty regarding these dangers. The precautionary principle addresses this. While there are different formulations of the principle, the Rio Declaration's Principle 15 provides an authoritative text: "[w]here there are threats of serious or irreversible damage, lack of full scientific certainty shall not be used as a reason for postponing cost-effective measures to prevent environmental degradation." The principle has been applied to climate change, depletion of the ozone layer, and similar risks.

What we do today affects the well-being of future generations. Some jurists argue that there is a principle of intergenerational equity, which makes it necessary to consider the interests of future generations when we act today. This applies to all areas of environmental activity. Under this principle, future generations are arguably entitled to comparable diversity (options) and comparable quality (on balance) to that which we have in the environment today and to comparable access to environmental benefits and comparable sharing of environmental burdens.

The emerging principle of common but differentiated responsibilities applies among states. Its premise is that while all states must work together to manage certain environmental problems, some states historically have contributed more to the problem and therefore should bear a heavier burden in mitigating it. The principle also covers the different capacities of states to implement their international obligations: Some states may need more time to implement them, their initial obligations may be less, and they may be provided with assistance in implementing them. There is controversy over whether the principle exists or whether it is merely a negotiating tool in concluding certain international agreements, such as those to limit climate change.

Procedural Obligations

If countries engage in activities (such as building power plants or developing mining operations) that could affect neighboring countries adversely, they are obligated to notify those countries before undertaking the activity, to provide relevant information, and to consult with them early on and in good faith. There is disagreement as to whether the country with the project must initiate consultations or only respond to a consultation request by the neighboring country.

Increasingly, there is an obligation for countries to provide an environmental impact assessment for proposed activities that, according to Principle 17 of the Rio Declaration on Environment and Development, "are likely to have a significant adverse impact on the environment and are subject to a decision of a competent national authority." The U.S. National Environmental Policy Act of 1969 (Section 102c) provides for environmental impact statements for "major Federal action significantly affecting the quality of the human environment." The term "federal actions" indicates that the federal government must be involved to some degree, if only by financing or giving approval. The United Nations Economic Commission for Europe has concluded a treaty on Environmental Impact Assessment, which sets forth the obligations in detail, and applies to those countries that have joined the treaty.

For hazardous wastes, chemicals, and pesticides, there are international agreements that require exporting countries or their exporters to obtain the prior informed consent of the importing country before the exporter can send the hazardous goods or wastes into the country.

This general procedural obligation may be evolving into a rule of customary international law, which would then bind all countries.

The Rio Declaration in Principle 10 set forth several other procedural obligations that are phrased as individual rights: the right of each individual to "appropriate access to information concerning the environment" held by public authorities and the "opportunity to participate in decision-making processes." Countries are obligated to make information widely available and to provide effective access to judicial and administrative proceedings. These obligations are sometimes referred to as implementing a "democratic entitlement" of individuals.

Specific International Agreements

Agreements concerned with ozone depletion and climate change illustrate how countries are trying to address global environmental problems.

Ozone Depletion

The 1985 Vienna Convention on the Protection of the Ozone Layer obligates countries to cooperate by monitoring the high-level ozone layer, engaging in scientific research, and exchanging information, and to adopt appropriate legislation or take other measures to control activities that deplete the ozone layer. The 1987 Montreal Protocol to the Convention obligates countries to phase out, or greatly reduce, the consumption and production of chemicals that countries have agreed to list as threats to the ozone layer. Countries that belong to the Protocol are generally prohibited from trading in the listed chemicals with countries that are not party to the Protocol. Developing countries are given ten extra years to comply with the Protocol. A special fund (the Montreal Protocol Fund) is available to assist them with complying.

Climate Change

The 1992 U.N. Framework Convention on Climate Change (UNFCCC) establishes the basic approach for addressing climate change. Among other obligations, all countries must develop and publish "national inventories of anthropogenic emissions by sources and removals by sinks of all greenhouse gases not controlled by the Montreal Protocol" (Article 4 [1] [a]). Forests, for example, serve as sinks for carbon dioxide, a greenhouse gas. Annex I countries—developed countries and those countries in transition to a market economy who have joined the Annex list—agree to adopt national policies and to take measures to limit emissions of greenhouse gases and enhance the sinks for the gases. In different provisions of UNFCCC, the countries recognize that the Convention's objective is to "return by the end of the present decade [1990s] to earlier levels of anthropogenic emissions of carbon dioxide and other greenhouse gases" (Article 4 [2] [a]) and acknowledge as a target the "aim of returning" greenhouse gas emissions to 1990 levels. The 1997 Kyoto Protocol to the UNFCC sets precise targets and timetables for countries listed in Annex 1 to limit their emissions of the six listed greenhouse gases. The Protocol permits Annex 1 countries to engage in joint implementation with other Annex 1 countries, which means that a country can invest in projects in another country that cut emissions and thereby satisfy part of its own obligation to reduce emissions. This provision targets projects between developed countries and countries in transition, such as (at the beginning of the twenty-first century) the Russian Federation. Other provisions permit trading of emissions among Annex 1 countries and establish a Clean Development Mechanism that encourages investment by developed countries in projects to reduce emissions in developing countries. In mid-2002, the Kyoto Protocol was not yet in effect because not enough countries had ratified it.

Edith Brown Weiss

See also Biological Weapons; Global Warming; Greenpeace; International Whaling Commission; Law of the Sea; Nuclear Weapons and Testing

Further Reading

Birnie, P. W., & Boyle, A. E. (1992). International law and the environment. New York: Oxford University Press

Brown Weiss, E. (1988). In fairness to future generations. New York and Tokyo: Transnational Publishers and the United Nations University.

Brown Weiss, E., & Jacobson, H. K. (1998). Engaging countries: Strengthening compliance with international environmental accords. Cambridge, MA and London: MIT Press.

Brown Weiss, E., McCaffrey, S. C., Magraw, D. B., Szasz, P. C., & Lutz, R. E. (1998). International environmental law and policy. New York: Aspen Law & Business.

Kiss, A., & Shelton, D. (2000). International environmental law (2nd ed.). New York: Transnational Publishers.

Morrison, F. L., & Wolfrum, R. (Eds.). (2000). International, regional and national environmental law. The Hague, Netherlands: Kluwer Law International.

United Nations Environment Programme. (1992) Rio declaration on environment and development. Retrieved January 28, 2003, from http://www.unep.org/unep/rio.htm

Sands, P. (1995). Principles of international environmental law: Frameworks, standards and implementation. Manchester, U.K.: Manchester University Press.

United Nations framework convention on climate change (UNFCCC). (1992). Retrieved January 28, 2003, from http://www.sdinfo.gc.ca/docs/en/climate/uncc_p.cfm

U.S. National Environmental Policy Act of 1969. Retrieved January 28, 2003, from http://ceq.eh.doe.gov/nepa/regs/nepa/nepaeqia.htm

International Union for the Conservation of Nature

Founded as the World Conservation Union, the International Union for the Conservation of Nature (IUCN) was created in 1948 as a result of an initiative of the United Nations Educational, Scientific, and Cultural Organization (UNESCO), the Swiss League for Nature Protection, and the French government. Since then it has provided the umbrella for research and conservation work, uniting government agencies, nongovernmental organizations, and individual experts from around the world. Today it employs approximately a thousand people, most of whom are located in its forty-two regional and country offices while a hundred work at its headquarters in Gland, Switzerland.

Awareness of humankind's proclivity to create environmental disasters had grown in the years between World War I and World War II, not least because of the dust bowl disaster on the American plains. Soil erosion was, however, only one symptom of a growing conflict between the planetary ecology and just one of the Earth's myriad species: humankind, whom some people were beginning to see not as Homo sapiens but as Homo "rapiens." These commentators had included writers such as Paul Sears and, after the war, such prescient individuals as Fairfield Osborn and William Vogt. It was their growing concern and that of others that led to the founding of the IUCN.

The IUCN's mission is to influence, encourage, and assist the conservation of the integrity and diversity of nature as well as to encourage a sustainable and equitable use of resources. The protection of forests, wetlands, and coastal areas has been a particular concern. The IUCN gives funds to individual countries to prepare and implement national conservation and biodiversity strategies. It provides guidelines for the establishment of protected areas and publicizes conservation issues. Another major activity is the compilation and publicizing of "red lists" of endangered species. The IUCN also participates actively in the negotiation of international agreements relating to biological diversity and the conservation of resources. Finally, the IUCN is active in the field of environmental education.

In 1980, working with two other conservation bodies, the World Wildlife Fund and the United Nations Environment Programme, the IUCN published *The World Conservation Strategy*, a powerful statement of what needed to be done to reverse the on-going destruction of individual species and ecosystems. This was updated in the 1990s under the title *Caring for the Earth*. In particular, *The World Conservation Strategy* popularized the concept of sustainable development, later taken up by the famous Brundtland Report.

Amongst the IUCN's achievements have been several international conventions concerning the conservation of species. These include the Ramsar Convention on Wetlands (1975) and the Convention on International Trade in Endangered Species of Wild Fauna and Flora, or CITES (1975).

Sandy Irvine

Further Reading

Davoll, J. (1988). Population growth and conservation organisations, with particular Reference to the IUCN. *Population and Environment, 10*(2), 107–114.
IUCN. (1980). *World conservation strategy: Living resource conservation for sustainable development*. Gland, Switzerland: IUCN.
IUCN. (1991). *Caring for the Earth: A strategy for sustainable living*. London: Earthscan.

International Whaling Commission

The International Whaling Commission (IWC), based in Cambridge, England, is an agency made up of member nations that have signed the 1946 International Convention for the Regulation of Whaling. At its founding, the IWC had sixteen members, but over the years, the number of members of the commission has ranged from fourteen to fifty-two; as of 2002, there were forty-eight members. Since 1949, the commission has been holding annual meetings to set regulations for whaling in most of the world's seas, and these meetings have often been the scene of bruising battles among whalers, scientists, and environmentalists. (Each IWC member appoints one commissioner, who is usually a government official and holds voting power, and any number of members to its delegation whose composition typically includes scientists, environmentalists, or whalers.) The whaling commission should be thought of not just as an organization that deals with whaling, but also as one of the first to wrestle with the problems of environmental diplomacy, such as sovereignty issues, scientific uncertainty, and conflicting national interests. However one views the actions of the IWC, its longevity in the face of repeated crises has been remarkable.

The central challenge for the IWC came from the terms of the founding convention, which charged the commission with promoting the orderly development of the whaling industry and the conservation of whales. These two goals have often been in conflict. Through the 1960s, the members of the commission generally split into two groups: scientists who wanted stricter limits on whaling and the whalers who opposed them. As one observer noted, the whaling industry generally had the whip hand in these confrontations. The central point of disagreement was the quota set on Antarctic whaling by the schedule, the part of the 1946 convention that set rules for whaling in the Antarctic seas. The framers of the schedule had established a quota of 16,000 blue whale units for the South Seas, with a unit equaling one blue whale, two fin whales, two and a half humpbacks, or six sei whales. By 1950, the scientists were already leaning toward reducing the quota in the name of conservation, and they succeeded in a small way, but attempts in the late 1950s and early 1960s to make major cuts constantly hit the problem of the objection clause in the schedule. Under this clause, any member could exempt itself from an amendment simply by filing an objection. It thus became impossible to cut the quota without unanimous consent, and the whalers were powerful enough to make sure that the scientists never got their way.

Beginning in the 1970s, the IWC became well known around the world, as the Save the Whales movement blamed it in part for the decimation of the world's whale populations. Driven by their desire to impose a moratorium on commercial whaling, environmentalists slowly gained control of the commission's annual meetings, both by encouraging nonwhaling nations to join and vote against whaling activities and by lobbying the governments of longtime members. Simultaneously, the IWC was becoming a center for extensive research on whales. In a three-cornered debate, the environmentalists prevailed over the scientists and whalers with the 1982 decision to ban all commercial whaling later that decade. Since 1982, debate within the IWC has been focused largely on Japanese efforts to conduct scientific research on minke whales. Most environmentalists see that activity as a screen to cover up commercial whaling, but many scientists see it as a legitimate means of learning about whales.

Kurk Dorsey

Further Reading

Birnie, P. (Ed.). (1985). *International regulation of whaling: From conservation of whaling to conservation of whales and regulation of whale-watching*. Dobbs Ferry, NY: Oceana Press.

Friedheim, R. (Ed.). (2001). *Toward a sustainable whaling regime*. Seattle: University of Washington Press.

Stoett, P. (1997). *The international politics of whaling*. Vancouver, Canada: University of British Columbia Press.

Tønnessen, J. N., & Johnsen A. O. (1982). *The history of modern whaling*. Berkeley & Los Angeles: University of California Press.

Intertropical Convergence Zone

The intertropical convergence zone (ITCZ) is a prominent and important feature of the large-scale wind patterns of the world. The ITCZ is so named because it is the near-equatorial zone where the surface trade winds from each hemisphere flow together. Before reaching the ITCZ, the trade winds blow westward and equatorward across the equatorial flanks of the northern and southern subtropical belts of high surface atmospheric pressure. The trade winds are dominant over all subtropical and tropical oceans and the largest intervening continents (North Africa, southern Asia, and Australia). The ITCZ is part of an ensemble of interrelated surface atmospheric and oceanic features in near-equatorial latitudes that also includes zones where the sea surface temperature is higher, and surface atmospheric pressure is lower than occurs to the north and south. Embedded within these zones is the direction discontinuity (or confluence axis) between the northeast and southeast trade winds that emanate from the northern and southern hemispheres, respectively. All of these features generally are aligned from west to east around the globe. It is important to note that the ITCZ does not necessarily straddle the confluence axis,

nor does the convergence maximum always coincide with that discontinuity.

Because the ITCZ is where the trade winds converge, it is a zone of light and variable surface wind where moisture-laden air often is forced upward to form towering cumulonimbus (i.e., thunderstorm) clouds. This is why the ITCZ appears prominently on imagery of the Earth from satellites—as a near-continuous belt containing thousands of separate cumulonimbus clouds (between which skies are clear) that circles the globe. This west-east-oriented band of broken cloudiness typically has a north-south extent of only 750–1500 kilometers. It is especially well defined and prominent over the oceans, where it contrasts strongly with the relatively cloud-free trade wind regimes immediately to the north and south. The annual latitudinal migration of the ITCZ generally is confined to the low latitudes of the Northern Hemisphere, particularly over the Atlantic and Pacific Oceans. Its southernmost position is reached near the end of northern winter (March), when the ITCZ stalls in the 0°–10° N band around most of the ocean-dominated globe there. The principal exception is across the Indian Ocean, where the ITCZ tends to lie between 0°–10° S. At the other extreme of its annual cycle, the ITCZ reaches farthest north during the core of southern winter (August)—to around 5°–15° N across northern Africa and the Atlantic and Pacific and even more northward above southern Asia (15°–25° N) as part of the summer monsoon system of that subcontinent.

North of the Equator

The ITCZ generally stays north of the equator because air temperatures near the South Pole are much colder than around the North Pole due to the large elevated Antarctic ice surface. This difference makes the southern equator-to-pole temperature gradient considerably stronger than its northern counterpart, which, when coupled with the relative lack of continents in the Southern Hemisphere, causes the midlatitude westerly wind belt to extend farther equatorward in the Southern than in the Northern Hemisphere. The expanded southern westerly winds, in turn, displace the southeast trade winds northward. This is why the southeast trade winds penetrate across the equator at most longitudes in all months, even at the end of northern winter. For the exception of the Indian Ocean noted earlier, a particularly strong northeast trade wind outflow from the cold Asian continent pushes the ITCZ south of the equator in late northern winter. By August the northward cross-equatorial trade wind flow is drawn toward and intensified by the summertime solar heating of northern Africa and southern Asia, which lowers surface atmospheric pressure there. After crossing the equator, and with help from the associated reversal in the Coriolis force wind deflection (from to the left of the motion in the northern hemisphere to the right of the motion in the southern hemisphere) resulting from the Earth's rotation, the southeast trade winds are transformed into southwest monsoons that displace the ITCZ to the extreme northern positions noted earlier.

The importance of the ITCZ was realized as soon as human exploration via the oceans crossed the equator, which occurred when Polynesians began crossing the Pacific more than fifteen hundred years ago and Europeans sailed south through the Atlantic to reach southern Africa, the Indian Ocean and Asia, and South America and the Pacific in the late fifteenth and early sixteenth centuries. Because of the general lack of steady wind, the extensive cloud cover, and regular (but not continuous) occurrence of heavy rainfall accompanied by thunder, lightning, and wind gusts, sailing across the ITCZ was difficult and took many days. This made shipboard life unpleasant and earned the ITCZ the early name of the "doldrums." The carryover of this name into human behavior presumably stems from the relative darkness and lack of progress produced by the cloud cover and absence of wind, respectively. After ships finally left the doldrums/ITCZ, they returned to the domain of the trade winds, where the sky was clear, sunshine prevailed, and the wind was steady and dependable. Sailing was much faster and shipboard life decidedly more pleasant.

Early Scientific Interest

The exploration-based knowledge that the trade winds flow together near the equator to produce the doldrums/ITCZ was incorporated into the earliest scientific ideas concerning the large-scale wind patterns of the world. It was a distinctive feature of schematic models in studies published between the mid-seventeenth and mid- to late nineteenth centuries by several British, German, and American scientists in leading scientific journals. Two informative examples of the titles of those articles are *An historical account of the trade winds and monsoons observable in the seas between and near the tropicks with an attempt to assign the physical cause of said winds*(1686) and *Concerning the cause of the general trade winds* (1735). The names of some of these

scientists have become permanently attached to components of the Earth's atmospheric circulation (e.g., [George] Hadley cell, [William] Ferrel cell). During the twentieth century there was increasing recognition of the pivotal role that the ITCZ plays in the "energy cycle" that sustains all atmospheric motion. Wind is generated by differences in atmospheric heating and resulting temperature. Much latent heat is released to warm the air in the ITCZ when water vapor condenses to form water droplets during the development of the many cumulonimbus clouds there. This latent heat was previously absorbed into the trade winds by their upstream evaporation of water from the subtropical and tropical oceans that, in turn, consumed energy provided by the abundant sunshine permitted by the clear skies there. The convergence of this latent heat in the ITCZ and its subsequent release in towering clouds to warm the air there make important contributions to the equator-to-pole temperature gradients that drive the high-level westerly winds of the subtropics and middle latitudes. Vagaries in those westerly winds, in turn, shape the patterns of daily weather and seasonal climate across the midlatitude continents of both hemispheres that are of great economic importance. During the last twenty-five years, anomalous seasonal locations of the ITCZ have been shown to cause regional rainfall extremes in the tropics. For example, failure of the Atlantic ITCZ to migrate fully to its annual extreme latitudes greatly weakens the rainy seasons in northeastern Brazil (February–April) and the western African Sahel (July–September), causing drought conditions and much-publicized human distress. During Pacific El Niño events, a weakening of the ITCZ over Indonesia-Papua New Guinea suppresses rainfall and induces wildfires there, and an associated southward displacement of the ITCZ across the central Pacific brings copious rainfall to its otherwise dry zone.

Because of the ITCZ's scientific and societal importance, further understanding of it will be sought during the next ten years. An intensive research project is being planned for the Atlantic ITCZ, including its role in the regional climates of bordering continents. This research will attempt to clarify the functioning of the ITCZ from the standpoints of both internal mechanisms (relations between overall ITCZ and its constituent cloud elements) and external linkages (with near-equatorial trade wind strength and direction discontinuity, zone of maximum sea surface temperature, and atmospheric pressure trough). Much remains to be learned about this vital feature of the atmospheric environment.

Peter J. Lamb

Further Reading

Hastenrath, S. (1991). *Climate dynamics of the tropics*. Dordrecht, Netherlands: Kluwer Academic Publishers.

Miller, R. L. (1996). Intertropical convergence. In *Encyclopedia of climate and weather* (Vol. 1, pp. 445–448). New York: Oxford University Press.

Iron

Iron is the earth's second most abundant metal resource, after aluminum. However, extracting iron from its ore requires only a tenth as much energy as does aluminum extraction. Iron's abundance, the relative ease of smelting it, and the varied services it can perform for us make it the most widely used metal. The annual consumption of iron and its alloys in the United States is about 500 kilograms per person. (By comparison, we consume only about 25 kilograms of aluminum). Production of the large amounts of iron used by industrial society places heavy demands on energy and water resources, creates voluminous wastes, and can release undesired effluents. Disposal and recycling end-of-life products containing iron and steel are a significant part of the world's industrial economies today.

The History of Iron Use

People in southwest Asia began smelting iron nearly three thousand years ago. While bronze served as a symbol of wealth and power, iron's abundance and the relatively low cost of smelting it made the peoples' metal. Everyone who wanted iron tools and utensils and knew how to produce them could have them. As more people adopted iron, they initiated an Iron Age, which started around 2000 BCE in the Middle East, 1300 BCE in India, and 800 BCE in China. While the Romans used massive amounts of iron, until about 1000 CE the most sophisticated iron technology flourished in Asia. The Chinese excelled in their use of the blast furnace to make iron to cast into utilitarian, ritual, and decorative objects. Indian artisans specialized in forging iron and making steel (an alloy of iron and carbon), which they exported to the West. This trade relationship was well established by 1000 CE. The African Iron Age, which began around 600 CE, lasted into the early twentieth century. (There is no agreed-upon definition of the end of the Iron Age, but the following factors generally signal the end of what people mean by the Iron Age: (1) a significant increase in the scale of production; (2) adoption of water power for blowing furnaces; (3) adoption of the blast furnace in place of the bloomery forge.) In the New World the peoples of North and South America never used iron before European colonists arrived.

By the sixteenth century Europeans had mastered the techniques for manufacturing the iron and steel they needed to initiate Western industrialization. Subsequent European innovations—the coke-fired blast furnace for smelting iron and the Bessemer and Siemens (open-hearth) techniques for making cheap steel in large quantities—supplied the needs of the rapidly industrializing nations of the Atlantic community. The iron and steel production per unit of gross national product increased around mid-nineteenth century as Western nations put infrastructure in place, and then began to decline in the last quarter of the twentieth century. It remains to be seen if the nations of the developing world can attain Western affluence with a smaller amount of iron per capita.

Uses of Iron and Steel

The widespread use of iron arises not only from its abundance but also from the range of services it can perform. Wrought iron, the earliest form used, is malleable and was traditionally the material smiths forged and welded into complex shapes. Today most products called "wrought iron" are actually made of steel. So-called "mild" steel, which contains up to about 0.5 percent carbon, is made in large quantities and used in buildings, bridges, motor vehicles, and machinery of all kinds. Tool steel contains 0.5 to 1.2 percent carbon and can be hardened by quenching and tempering. Although made in relatively small quantities, it is the essential material used in tools for mining, smelting, and the shaping of metals, stone, and nearly all other materials. Alloy steels develop special properties through additions of relatively scarce metals such as chromium, manganese, molybdenum, or vanadium. Chromium and nickel, for example, give stainless steels their remarkable resistance to corrosion.

Iron alloyed with 1.2 to 4 percent of carbon, known as cast iron, can be easily melted and poured into moulds. From early modern times to very recently it was cast iron that allowed nearly everyone to have pots, pans, and related equipment in their homes. The nineteenth century saw cast iron used to create a distinctive style of architecture for commercial buildings. Because iron foundries find it increasingly difficult to comply with modern air pollution and workplace regulations, relatively few remain active in developed countries. Consequently, many items formerly made of cast iron are now made of steel.

Iron and Steel Production and the Environment

The production and use of iron is relatively benign compared to the deleterious effects on the environment that arise from the use of other metals. Unlike the nonferrous metals, which are extracted from sulfide minerals, iron is made from oxide ores. Therefore, iron mining does not cause problems with acid mine drainage and the release of toxic substances, such as arsenic and sulfur fumes, associated with mining and smelting of metals such as copper, lead, and zinc, which all are extracted from sulfide minerals. Nevertheless, the sheer scale of the iron industry guarantees significant environmental consequences. The exhausted iron mines of northern Minnesota, Michigan, and Wisconsin are now huge holes in the ground. Old mining communities sometimes try to use them as a tourist attraction. Fortunately, slag, the principal solid waste left from ironmaking, can be recycled as aggregate for concrete.

Making large quantities of iron requires large quantities of fuel. Ironmakers' heavy demands on the forest resources of England beginning in Tudor times led them to develop coppicing as a forest management technique. With coppicing, trees are cut down but their stumps are left behind. These then spout many new shoots, which are allowed to grow to a certain size and then harvested. The process can be repeated, assuring a continuous yield of wood. Trees grew to a size suitable for making charcoal in about twenty years. By managing enough acreage of forest so that a twentieth of it was cut each year, an ironmaker secured a continuous fuel supply. Large tracts of woodland held by ironworks in the eastern United States form the nucleus of many of today's state forests.

Beginning in about 1800, substitution of mineral coal for charcoal as the primary fuel for ironmaking initiated the rapid expansion of iron and steel production that we associate with the Western industrial revolution. The sulfur and tar in mineral coal became a source of air and water pollution wherever coke for steelworks was made.

Recycling unwanted iron products is long-established practice, and is the source of nearly half of the steel made in the U.S. today. Mechanized equipment for shredding products such as motor vehicles has increased recycling rates and helped remove junkyards from the landscape. Increased recycling allowed a major restructuring of the steel industry from 1980 onward. New minimills melt scrap steel in electric arc furnaces and roll their recycled steel into the sheets and plates that are the products now most in demand. These mills have freed themselves from the inflexible management practices and restrictive work rules that made the older, established steelworks unprofitable. As a result, many no-longer-useful steelworks are large brownfield sites in urban areas of the industrialized nations.

Robert B. Gordon

Further Reading

Barraclough, K. C. (1984). *Steelmaking before Bessemer: Vol. 1. Blister Steel; Vol. 2. Crucible Steel*. London: The Metals Society.
Barraclough, K. C. (1990). *Steelmaking 1850–1900*. London: Institute of Metals.
Gale, W. K. V. (1967). *The British iron and steel industry: A technical history*. Newton Abbot, UK: David and Charles.
Gordon, R. B. (2001). *American iron, 1607–1900*. Baltimore: Johns Hopkins University Press.
McHugh, J. (1980). *Alexander Holley and the makers of steel*. Baltimore: Johns Hopkins University Press.
Misa, T. (1995). *A nation of steel*. Baltimore: Johns Hopkins University Press.
Tweedale, G. (1995). *Steel city: Entrepreneurship, strategy, and technology in Sheffield, 1743–1993*. Oxford, UK: Oxford University Press.

Irrigation

Irrigation is the artificial application of water to crop and livestock production. Farmers, engineers, and government officials gather water from streams, aquifers, or rainfall and channel it to plants and animals. Irrigation is one of the most important agricultural techniques ever devised. In ancient times it helped generate food surpluses that supported the hallmarks of civilization: social hierarchy, bureaucracy, science and engineering, complex technology, organized religion, powerful militaries, alphabetic writing, cities, and empires.

By the early twenty-first century the Earth's 6 billion inhabitants derived 40 percent of their food from irrigation. However, irrigation also has generated profound environmental transformations and problems. It has made small inland seas and destroyed them, created and eliminated habitats, altered rivers beyond recognition, spread disease, and displaced communities of people.

Ancient Irrigation

Between about 4000 BCE and 1200 CE agricultural societies built irrigation systems in the Middle East, Asia, around the Mediterranean, and in the Americas. The greatest of these early irrigation civilizations used centralized social organization and large-scale technology to divert rivers for crop and livestock production. In the process they created distinctive ecologies that supported a wealth of plants and animals, produced agricultural surpluses, and fed large populations. Some suffered from severe environmental problems.

The German historian and social theorist Karl Wittfogel coined the term *hydraulic civilizations* to describe these distinctive early societies. Wittfogel believed that the diversion of rivers for large-scale irrigated agriculture inevitably required hierarchical, authoritarian government. Only a powerful centralized state could mobilize the resources necessary to build and maintain large dams and canals. Bureaucrats and technical experts designed the hydraulic works, disciplined large numbers of forced laborers, kept records of the operations, repaired and maintained the systems, and collected the taxes necessary to pay for it all. Scholars have attacked Wittfogel's model for being simplistic, static, and deterministic. Among other criticisms, they point out that powerful regimes elsewhere in the world developed without irrigation.

But some scholars concede that Wittfogel's hydraulic civilizations thesis contains a degree of validity. Large-scale irrigation, along with political, economic, and agricultural conditions, probably contributed to the consolidation of governmental authority. Moreover, large-scale irrigation and state power at least evolved together. In Mesopotamia a series of empires built and regulated extensive irrigation systems that tapped the Tigris and Euphrates Rivers for agricultural production, and their kings boasted of their hydraulic achievements. One Babylonian king, Hammurabi, in the period 1792–1750 BCE oversaw the construction of irrigation works and dictated a legal code that in part dealt with irrigation. In Egypt, elites with titles such as "chief of irrigation," "chief of the water office," and "chief of the canal workmen" occupied the top positions in an extensive bureaucracy that guided water from the Nile River through complex irrigation networks. One potentate, the Scorpion King, in about 3100 BCE depicted himself opening an irrigation network. In Peru beginning about 1000 BCE, in Mexico about 320 BCE, and in what is now Arizona in 400 CE, powerful civilizations developed extensive irrigation networks to raise corn and other crops. Irrigation certainly did not evolve into despotism as neatly as Wittfogel suggested, but the control of water and the creation of powerful government certainly influenced one another.

Early irrigation supported an intensification of crop and livestock production. In Mesopotamia irrigators kept sheep, pigs, goats, and cattle; gathered fish from canals; and raised wheat and barley along with flax, dates, apples, plums, grapes, and many other types of fruits and vegetables. Along the Nile in Egypt farmers kept ducks, geese, and asses in addition to other hoofed livestock, which grazed in nearby marshes, swamps, unused lands, and on the stubble of fallow fields. The Egyptians also grew lentils, onions, beans, and cotton along with the more standard staple crops, and they harvested papyrus from wetlands. Chinese farmers, who may have adopted irrigation from Babylon, raised millet and later rice in addition to other types of crops and livestock. Human and animal populations often lived in dense concentrations in the early irrigation civilizations. In about 3000 BCE in Ur, a Sumerian city in Mesopotamia, an estimated ten thousand animals lived in proximity to the settlement's human population of roughly six thousand.

Irrigated fields in the desert in Egypt. In the foreground are the stone ruins of an ancient village, whose inhabitants once farmed the same valley. COURTESY NICOLE LALIBERTE.

Early irrigation on such a vast scale produced enormous quantities of food that supported growing populations, a division of labor, and social stratification. By 3000 BCE Sumeria encompassed eight cities, the most populous of which contained upward of twenty thousand people. Ancient Egyptian irrigated agriculture eventually fed as many as 2.5 million or perhaps even 3 million people. Surpluses allowed some members of society to engage in activities other than agriculture, including writing, record keeping, mathematics, technological innovation (most notably the development of the wheel), craft work, and the priesthood. Social stratification appeared, with administrative, religious, and military officials occupying the highest ranks, and merchants, craftspeople, farmers, and slaves occupying the lower ranks.

Irrigation ecology contributed to the spread of pests and diseases adapted to agriculture and dense settlement. Weeds grew in fields. Rats invaded granaries. Cockroaches, flies, and mice moved in to households. Humans and animals shared parasites and diseases. As early as 1200 BCE Egyptians suffered from schistosomiasis, a debilitating malady caused by bloodworms that pass from mollusks to human hosts through irrigation water. Humans and animals exchanged viruses that evolved into cowpox, smallpox, distemper, rinderpest, measles, and influenza. Viruses were a double-edged sword: Afflicted humans suffered, but eventually their societies developed a degree of immunity that gave them an enormous demographic advantage when they came into contact with virally inexperienced and immunologically defenseless peoples.

Some ancient irrigation civilizations experienced environmental problems that may have weakened them. Although such problems probably occurred in Mesoamerica and along the Indus River, some scholars assert that Mesopotamia best illustrates what can happen when irrigation goes wrong. Several civilizations from about 4000 BCE to about 1200 CE diverted water from the Tigris and Euphrates Rivers into extensive canal networks that ran for miles. Irrigators used the *shaduf*, a simple but efficient device consisting of a lever, a bucket, and a counterweight, to lift water from canals into smaller conduits that ran to the crops. These vibrant civilizations were highly successful, and they established cultural forms, notably alphabetic writing, still practiced by modern people. But erosion, drought, the clogging of canals with silt, and the buildup of poisonous salts in the soil probably contributed to, if not outright caused, their disappearance. Deforestation and overgrazing at the headwaters eroded the soil,

which in combination with drought and reduced river flows caused silt to deposit in the canals. Clearing the canals required intensive labor and resources from societies already under stress from food shortages and other problems. Salt posed an even greater problem. Irrigation water seeped into the ground and dissolved naturally occurring salts. The rising groundwater eventually reached the surface, and as it evaporated it precipitated a toxic white crust harmful to most plants. Laborers scraped away the salt to reach the fresh soil below. Farmers produced more barley, a relatively salt-tolerant grain. But eventually salinization led to land abandonment, a shift in agriculture toward higher ground, usually to the north, and the rise of new civilizations. The process occurred several times: between roughly 2400 and 1700 BCE, in the seventh century CE, and from about 1200 to 1500 CE.

Irrigation was more stable and endured longer in Egypt. For millennia irrigators waited each autumn for the "Night of the Drop," when, in their belief, a celestial tear fell and caused the Nile River to bring forth a flood of nourishing water and silt from the Ethiopian highlands. Although at first the Egyptians relied only on the floodwaters to wet their fields and deposit the fertilizing silt, they eventually built systems of canals, dikes, and basins to capture, move, and impound the flood, helping it to saturate and replenish the soil before they planted. To lift water and increase the area of irrigated land they adopted the *shaduf* around 1500 BCE and the animal-powered waterwheel, the *saqiya*, around 325 BCE. They installed sophisticated measuring devices, *Nilometers*, that recorded the river's level. Some scholars believe that Egypt's many canals and basins were less tied to centralized authority than those in Mesopotamia. Also, Egyptian irrigators never experienced the problems of siltation and salinity that bedeviled their Mesopotamian counterparts. Most important, when the Nile's volume dropped after the annual flood, the water table fell and carried with it most of the harmful salts. Egyptian irrigation works did require much maintenance, especially after floods. Droughts and a weak flood at times meant not enough water, and famines occurred. But through these trials the Egyptian system, attuned to the Nile's annual rise and fall, persisted.

A range of smaller, less-centralized systems existed apart from the great hydraulic civilizations. Some systems involved run-off farming in which irrigators channeled water from slopes or washes and spread it across fields. Nabateans, who inhabited the Negev Desert of what is now Israel from the fourth century

BCE through the first century CE, practiced this technique, as did the Anasazi people who lived in the U.S. Southwest from about 100 CE to 1200 CE, as did the Chagga of Africa's Mount Kilimanjaro, who as early as 1000 CE channeled snowmelt to banana groves. In the Andes in South America and in the Philippines and other Asian regions, farmers created mountainside terraces that collected rainfall for various crops. In China and other parts of Asia, farmers grew rice in *paddies*, using human and animal excrement as fertilizer. Other peoples around the Mediterranean world adopted the ancient Persian practice of excavating a *qanat*, an underground aqueduct that tapped aquifers and carried water to oasis villages. Still other irrigators built stone cisterns and tanks or tapped small springs or rivers and channeled water to their fields. Arab Muslims were instrumental in adopting, synthesizing, improving, and spreading irrigation techniques as far as Spain. The Spanish then transplanted the techniques to the New World, where colonists carried them to the far corners of the empire. By the nineteenth century CE, in what are now New Mexico and Colorado, small communal *acequias* (canals) showed a faint but nonetheless recognizable Arab influence.

Modern Irrigation

Modern irrigation developed in the nineteenth and twentieth centuries when powerful nations, first Britain, then the United States, the Soviet Union, and others, embarked on large-scale dam-building and irrigation projects. The motivation for these ambitious projects included the desire to feed and clothe growing populations, establish colonies, augment national power, and strengthen, with state assistance, capitalist agricultural production. Stunning successes marked these projects, including the damming of major rivers and the vast expansion of the world's irrigated land. But all of the projects contributed to deep environmental problems.

Important developments began in the early 1800s and continued into the early twentieth century. British civil engineers began designing and building canals in India, then under British rule, in 1817. Often these were reconstructions or extensions of conduits dating from the Moghul empire of the sixteenth through the eighteenth centuries CE. The Ganges Canal, completed in 1857, was the largest in the world. The British also focused their attention on diverting water from the Indus River. Between 1870 and 1900 they tripled the area of land irrigated from the Indus and its tributaries. One

of the great British achievements was the development of the barrage dam, a low-level structure with sliding gates that allowed its operators to raise the level of a river to that of the canals. Even during droughts or seasonal low flows, the barrage dam ensured that some water would serve irrigation. The largest such project of its kind, completed in 1932 on the Indus, included sixty-six sliding gates and fed seven canals. By 1940 India encompassed one-quarter of the world's irrigated land.

From the late nineteenth century through the early twentieth century the innovations begun in British India were copied and elaborated upon in Canada, the United States, Mexico, Australia, Africa, and other places. In the United States private irrigation enterprises characterized much development of the nineteenth and early twentieth centuries, but beginning in 1902 the federal government took the lead as the major sponsor of dam construction. By 1935, with completion of Boulder (Hoover) Dam on the Colorado River, the United States became the world leader in the construction of high reinforced concrete dams (150 meters and higher) that stopped floods, generated enormous quantities of hydroelectric power, and stored immense reservoirs for agricultural and urban consumption. The growing power of the U.S. Bureau of Reclamation and its political ties to wealthy agricultural interests and influential members of Congress prompted one U.S. scholar, Donald Worster, to advance the controversial thesis that a hydraulic empire of the sort described by Karl Wittfogel had appeared in the American West. Indeed, Worster suggested that the United States' twentieth-century global reach sprang from its power base in the nation's arid western domains.

Following the American model, nations around the world built enormous concrete dams in ambitious efforts to expand irrigated acreage and increase the food supply for rapidly growing populations. Many scholars highlight Egypt as a case study. Population growth, the prospect of famine, the desire to industrialize, and nationalism encouraged Egyptian leader Gamal Abdel Nasser to build, with assistance from the Soviet Union, Aswan High Dam on the Nile River. Completed in 1970, it superceded an older Aswan dam dating to 1902. The new dam finally brought to an end the practice of flood irrigation that had endured without interruption since the time of the pharaohs. However, the nation's population had outstripped the food supply derived from the old method, and so many people hailed the dam as the key to Egyptian self-sufficiency and independence. Nations in Asia, Africa, and elsewhere attempted to modernize their economies through the construction of similar dams. These developments in dam and irrigation technology increased the total area of the world's irrigated land from 98 million hectares in 1949 to about 240 million hectares in 1984. In combination with the Green Revolution of the 1950s–1970s—the intensive use of hybrid crops and agricultural chemicals—irrigation boosted food production to unprecedented levels.

Despite the vast resources and hopes invested in modern irrigation, and despite its achievements, it resulted in alarming social, environmental, and political problems. Dams inundated large areas and profoundly disrupted human and natural ecologies, submerged sacred sites and cultural relics, destroyed fish runs, spread parasites and other diseases, and displaced entire human communities. Despite the premise that they serve the needs of many people, these structures often concentrated wealth and power in the hands of wealthy farmers and government elites. Where rivers crossed international boundaries, disputes arose over the rights to divert water for irrigation and other kinds of development. Although irrigation created new landscapes and habitats, it also destroyed them. Water pouring from a canal break in 1905 filled up the Salton Sink in southern California, creating the Salton Sea. The new body of water quickly became an important habitat for migrating birds displaced from other habitats by agricultural development. By the late twentieth century the sea had grown so saline and polluted from irrigation effluent that it became uninhabitable to many fish and a serious health hazard to the birds who took refuge there. In the 1950s the Soviet Union tapped rivers that fed the Aral Sea, the world's fourth-largest lake, for the irrigation of cotton. By the 1990s the Aral had shrunk by half, leaving behind extinct fisheries, crop fields poisoned by blowing salt, an altered regional climate, and an ill human population. An irrigation drain on the west side of California's San Joaquin Valley carried toxic concentrations of selenium, a naturally occurring element, along with agricultural chemicals into Kesterson wildlife refuge, where in 1983 it poisoned and deformed thousands of birds. These are but a few of the disasters or impending disasters that modern irrigation has wrought.

At the dawn of the twenty-first century the outlook for irrigation is worrisome, if not grim. Worldwide, soil salinization has diminished the productivity of one in five hectares of irrigated land. Intensive pumping has depleted aquifers. Silt has reduced the storage capacity of reservoirs. Experts fear that the world cannot sustain the production of a sizeable portion of its food supply, an especially serious problem in the face of a growing global population. The hopeful look to simple, small-scale technological innovations that conserve water, maintain the soil, and allow irrigation to continue without heavy infusions of capital, labor, technology, and chemicals. Small, grassroots irrigation systems, some of which have endured for centuries, if not millennia, have become important sources of ideas and inspiration. However, the question of whether large-scale irrigation will endure as in ancient Egypt or collapse as in Mesopotamia remains open.

Mark Fiege

Further Reading

Butzer, K. W. (1976). *Early hydraulic civilization in Egypt: A study in cultural ecology.* Chicago: University of Chicago Press.

Christensen, P. (1993). *The decline of Iranshahr: Irrigation and environments in the history of the Middle East, 500 BC to AD 1500.* Copenhagen, Denmark: Museum Tusculanum Press, University of Copenhagen.

Crosby, A. (1986). *Ecological imperialism: The biological expansion of Europe, 900–1900.* New York: Cambridge University Press.

Doolittle, W. E. (1990). *Canal irrigation in prehistoric Mexico.* Austin: University of Texas Press.

Doolittle, W. E. (2000). *Cultivated landscapes of native North America.* New York: Oxford University Press.

Glick, T. F. (1970). *Irrigation and society in medieval Valencia.* Cambridge, MA: Harvard University Press.

Goldsmith, E., & Hildyard, N. (Eds.). (1984). *The social and environmental effects of large dams.* San Francisco: Sierra Club Books.

Hillel, D. J. (1991). *Out of the earth: Civilization and the life of the soil.* New York: Free Press.

Hundley, N. (1992). *The great thirst: Californians and water, 1790–1990s.* Berkeley and Los Angeles: University of California Press.

Mabry, J. B. (Ed.). (1996). *Canals and communities: Small-scale irrigation systems.* Tucson: University of Arizona Press.

McNeill, J. R. (2000). *Something new under the sun: An environmental history of the twentieth-century world.* New York: Norton.

Postel, S. (1999). *Pillar of sand: Can the irrigation miracle last?* New York: Norton.

Reisner, M. (1986). *Cadillac desert: The American West and its disappearing water.* New York: Viking Penguin.

Stone, I. (1984). *Canal irrigation in British India*. Cambridge, UK: Cambridge University Press.

Wikander, O. (Ed.). (2000). *Handbook of ancient water technology*. Leiden, Netherlands: Brill.

Wittfogel, K. A. (1957). *Oriental despotism: A comparative study of total power*. New Haven, CT: Yale University Press.

Worster, D. (1985). *Rivers of empire: Water, aridity, and the growth of the American West*. New York: Pantheon.

Islam

The importance of Islam as a contemporary world ideology is not yet fully appreciated in the West. Islam is a global faith; the Muslim World spreads from the tropical forests of Indonesia to the semi-arid deserts of Morocco, and from the cool regions of Russia to the Savanna zones of Africa. One person in five in the world today—some 1.2 billion people in more than fifty-five countries—is a Muslim. Accordingly, it is essential to understand the ethics and attitudes of its followers towards their local and global environments. Essentially Islam provides laws and standards regarding use and allocation of natural resources, and has its views concerning ownership, land ethics, pollution, aesthetics, and the role of humankind on earth. Many of these topics have associated with them values that are quite different from Western values, and indeed, very little is known about them in the West.

"Islam" is an Arabic word that means, among other things, surrender, peace, and purity. From a religious perspective, it means submitting to the will of God (Allah in Arabic) and obeying His law. The most fundamental article of the Islamic faith is related to the nature of God as the one, unique, incomparable, merciful deity. He is the sole creator and sustainer of the universe. Muslims also believe in the angels created by God, in the prophets through whom His revelations were brought to humankind, in the Day of Judgment and individuals' accountability for their actions, in God's complete authority over human destiny, and in life after death.

Muslims do not consider their beliefs a new religion, but the same truth that God revealed throughout the history of humankind to every people. Similar to Jews and Christians, Muslims trace their origins to the prophet Abraham and believe that the three prophets of these monotheistic faiths are direct descendants from the patriarch Abraham's sons—Muhammad from the eldest, Ishmael; and Moses and Jesus from Isaac. In addition, they believe that the Holy Qur'an, as it was revealed to the Prophet Muhammad through the Archangel Gabriel, is God's final message to humanity, a reconfirmation of the eternal message and a summing up of all that has gone before.

Development of the Faith

Muhammad was born in Makkah (Mecca) in the year 570 CE. Since his father died before his birth, and his mother shortly afterwards, he was raised by his uncle from the respected tribe of Quraysh. As he grew up, he became known for his truthfulness and trustworthiness.

Muhammad was of a contemplative nature and had long abhorred the moral decay of his society. At the age of forty, while engaged in a meditative retreat, he received his first revelation through the angel Gabriel. This revelation continued for twenty-three years and is known as the Qur'an. When he started to recite and preach what was revealed to him, the people of Makkah resisted and persecuted him and his followers. In 622, he and the Muslim community immigrated to the City of Madinah (Medina), which provided a safe and nurturing haven for them. Gradually, they grew and established the first Islamic state.

Muhammad died at the age of sixty-three. By that time, the greater part of Arabia was Muslim. Less than a hundred years after his death, his followers had advanced from the Arabian Peninsula to create an empire of faith whose global influence was to prevail for a thousand years. The cavalry of Islam conquered the Persian Empire and much of the Byzantine, spreading the faith through north Africa into Spain, and through the Middle East to the Indian subcontinent. From there, devout Muslim merchants later carried the message of Islam to Malaysia, Indonesia, and the Philippines. Other Muslim traders from north Africa introduced the Qur'an to black tribes in east and west Africa.

Similar to other religions, Islam has been diversified over the centuries by theological disagreements among different schools of thought. Today, Islam is divided into two main branches, the Sunni and Shi'te groups. These two major branches resulted from a historical schism over the issue of who should lead the Muslim Ummah (community) following the death of Prophet Muhammad. Mainstream Sunni Islam accounts for nearly 90 percent of all Muslims and is divided into four schools of interpretation. By contrast, the 10 percent of the Shi'te Muslims—located primarily in Iran, Iraq, Yemen, and the Indian subcontinent—are split into various sects and subsects.

Throughout their history, Muslim nations struggled successfully to preserve their lands in the face of foreign invaders including the Mongol armies, European Crusaders, and more recently Western imperialists and Soviet invaders. Today, they are facing different challenges in which their ideological integrity and unique culture are confronting the forces of westernization and globalization.

Muslims Today

Islam is, and has always been, a global religion. Today, the Muslim world encompasses more than fifty-five countries. Recent demographic studies suggest that at the end of the twentieth century, approximately 1.2 billion people from all races, nationalities, and cultures across the globe are Muslims. This makes Islam the second largest religion in the world after Christianity. Having one person in five in the world who adheres to that faith could have a significant impact on the development and management of the world's environment since the shari'a (Islamic jurisprudence) presents specific laws and standards that govern the use and allocation of various resources including land, water, animals, minerals, and plants. Further, Muslims make no artificial division between the secular and the sacred and consider Islam a way of life, not just a religion or a spiritual side of one's life.

The immigration of Muslims to Europe and North America during the twentieth century has marked a new era of relationship between Islam and the West. Today, Islam is becoming the third largest religion in Europe and the United States. In addition, a significant and growing minority of Muslims live in Australia, Latin America, China, India, and Russia.

Islamic Beliefs Regarding the Environment

In addition to its basic and simple doctrine that calls for faith in only one God worthy of worship, Islam repeatedly instructs humans to use their powers of intelligence and observation, to read, and to seek knowledge, and to acquire wisdom from all sources.

As Muslim civilization developed, it absorbed the heritage of ancient nations like Egypt, Persia, and China. Indeed, it was Muslim scholars who first discovered and translated the classical writings of Greece, which were later to spark the European Renaissance.

The synthesis of Eastern and Western ideas, and of new thought with old, brought about advances in arts and sciences, philosophy and theology, literature and poetry, and architecture and landscape design. Many crucial systems were transmitted to medieval Europe from the Muslim schools and universities of Baghdad, Cairo, and Granada. These included algebra, the Arabic numerals, and also the concept of zero in mathematics; water wheels, water clocks, mechanical automate and optics in engineering; magnetic needles, geographic encyclopedias and atlases; astrolabes, observatories, astronomical tables in cosmology; botany encyclopedias; and new crops in horticulture.

The Islamic beliefs toward the environment are gleaned from the Holy Qur'an and the Sunnah (Traditions of Prophet Muhammad), and are usually articulated through the shari'a (Islamic jurisprudence). These environmental beliefs are strengthened by the Muslims' conviction in their divine sources, and as a result, they are considered part of the Islamic faith itself. Five specific concepts are directly related to the Muslims' view of their environment.

First, a Muslim believes that he/she is put on earth for a purpose. Humankind was created to be God's Khalifa (steward or vice-regent) on earth. Accordingly, every believer is expected to contribute to the task of Isti'mar al-ard (the development of the earth). As a Khalifa, a person is expected to interact with nature so as to transform the world from what it is into what it ought to be. Indeed, the Qur'an unfolds clearly the essence and the mission of the human journey in the verse: "Then We appointed you steward in the earth after them, that we might see how you behave" (Qur'an, 10:15).

Second, although Islam encourages people to amass wealth from lawful sources, it applies strict conditions in acquiring and disposing of any wealth. For example, under the shari'a system, God is considered the ultimate owner of the earth and all things on it, and He alone has ordained sustenance for all his creatures. Historically, the delineation of the public and private sectors has been decided by jurists of the Islamic state. They always ruled that indispensable resources, such as pastures, woodlands, wildlife, certain minerals, and especially water, cannot be privately owned in their natural state, nor can they be monopolized. This position is founded on Prophet Muhammad's assertion that all people are partners in pastures, forests, and water, which implies public ownership of certain land, energy, and water resources.

Third, the Prophet's saying, "There shall be no injury, and no inflicting of injury," has been the base of allocating equitable rights of the earth's resources while preserving their carrying capacity. Private property is considered a trust from God and its resources should be managed in accordance with God's purpose. All associated ownership rights may be exercised as long as they don't bring any injury to others or prejudice the long-run interests of the community by depleting and/or polluting natural resources, or diverting their capacities away from fulfillment of primary health, safety, and human welfare needs.

Fourth, Islam urges its followers to strive for *Ietidal* (moderation) in all aspects of their life. The Qur'an stresses this unique character of the Muslim community as being "Ummah Wasata" or a moderate community: "Thus have We made of you a nation justly moderate, that might be witnesses over the nations" (Qur'an, 2:143).

Prophet Muhammad directed his companions against opposing extremes including overextended rituals of worship, celibacy, pessimism, overindulgence, and wasteful extravagance. These directions are stated in many verses of the Qur'an including: "Those who, when they spend, are not extravagant and not mean, but hold a just balance between those extremes" (Qur'an, 2:67).

Another major aspect of the Islamic teachings is related to maintaining the Tawazon (Equilibrium) among all the elements of the environment. The Qur'an refers to this concept in more than nine different places, including: "Verily, all things have We created in proportion and measure" (Qur'an, 54:49). "It is He who created all things, and ordered them in due proportions" (Qur'an, 25:2).

Most significantly, the Qur'an states that humankind is only one community among other equals in the universe, and there is no logical need for humans to conquer others and subdue them arbitrarily. It is, therefore, seen that to violate nature, to destroy its integrity, and to pollute its purity would amount to destroying humanity itself: "There is not an animal (that lives) on the earth, nor being that flies on its wings, but (forms) communities like you. Nothing He omitted from the Book, and they (all) shall be gathered to their Lord in the end" (Qur'an, 6:38).

Islamic Practices Regarding the Environment

Historically, Islam has succeeded in providing a comprehensive set of environmental principles and ethical guidelines. Throughout the centuries, Muslim jurists have developed a series of environmental management injunctions that dealt with different natural resources. These injunctions were always guided by the major objectives of *shari'a* and were systematically added to its evolving body of knowledge. The objectives of *shari'a* include: the universal common goal of all created beings, the wise utilization of the benefit from available natural resources, the elimination of starvation, and the prevention of diseases among humankind and livestock. Implementing the objectives of *shari'a* in the real world was carried out by the Islamic state through establishing a complex system of public institutions. These institutions included, among other things, Hisba (the office of public inspection), Haram (forbidden area), Hema (reserved area), Thya (land reclamation), and Waqf (charitable endowments).

Hisbah (Office of Public Inspection)

The Hisbah is a purely Islamic institution that is directly based on the Qur'anic command of "promotion of good and the prevention of evil." The Qur'an states: "And there may spring from you a nation who invite to goodness, and enjoin right conduct and forbid the reprehensible. Such are they who are successful" (Qur'an, 3:104).

Early in Islam, the Hisbah office was an integral part of the Office of the Qadi (Justice), but when the duties increased and grew in complexity, it was separated. The functions of the office covered both the religious and secular sides of community life including those relating to the rights of God, such as the timing of the five daily prayers and maintaining of mosques; those relating to the rights of people, i.e., ensuring accuracy of weights, enforcing public health standards, inspecting food operations, and regulating the medical professions; and those relating to the rights of other creatures and elements of nature, i.e., preventing any mistreatment of domestic animals, managing wildlife hunting, and protecting nature reserves and water bodies.

Haram (Forbidden Zone)

The primary purpose of declaring any area as a Haram zone is to control its development so that human activities will not damage its unique qualities. Usually, these areas have significant cultural or natural value to the community.

The most inviolate places in Islam are the cities of Makkah (Mecca), Madinah (Medina), and Jerusalem.

The Prophet Muhammad declared the first two as Haram areas. He described their exact boundaries and declared that within their borders no wildlife could be disturbed, no native tree could be uprooted, and no plants could be cut except those used for medicinal purposes.

Hema (Reserve Area)

The institution of Hema can be defined as a set of planning and management standards and guidelines designed to regulate the intensity and the location of different land uses. Historically, five types of Hema existed in Arabia during the early centuries of Islam. They are: (1) Hema for forest trees in which woodcutting is prohibited or limited; (2) Hema in which grazing was prohibited; (3) Hema in which grazing was limited to specific seasons of the year; (4) Hema restricted to certain species and numbers of livestock; and (5) Hema managed for the welfare of needy people who occasionally may suffer from drought or other natural catastrophes.

Waqf (Charitable Endowment)

In Islam, giving charity to the poor or for public welfare is considered one of the highest duties in life. In particular, the Prophet praised the concept of detaining the corpus from a private ownership and granting its income in perpetuity to a noble cause. He said: "Humans' deeds come to an end with their death, and only three things do not discontinue, namely, perpetual charity, useful knowledge, and the prayers of upright offspring."

Ihya (Reclamation)

Ihya translates as "bringing new life" to the land. According to shari'a, four types of land exist: Amer (developed), Mawat (undeveloped), Haram (inviolate), and Hema (protected). The Mawat are those lands that are not settled, cultivated, or zoned, such as Haram or Hema. In shari'a, whoever cultivates a Mawat that does not belong to anyone will acquire the right to possess it if the State approves this agreement.

Human-Environment Relationship

Islam, as a way of life, dominates a person's entire view of the world. A devout Muslim considers Allah to have sovereignty over heaven and earth, power over all creatures, and that He is the direct cause of all things. The creation of this enormous universe indicates numerous signs of God's power and goodness and should spark in every Muslim devotion, praise, and gratitude. These feelings should be demonstrated by treating nature with respect and care.

The Qur'an has numerous verses that deal with nature including various species of animals, plants, and insects, atmospheric phenomena, or geologic features. The Sunnah is also full with implicit and explicit guides to instill a sense of respect for God's creation. In the Hadith (Sayings of the Prophet), four environmental topics are addressed: (1) encouraging Muslims to plant and conserve trees and other kinds of vegetation; (2) instructing Muslims to keep and treat kindly different domesticated animals; (3) requesting Muslims to avoid all kinds of pollution (water, soil, and air), to protect the health of their environment, and to maintain hygienic conditions in terms of food handling and public places; and (4) prohibiting Muslims from deliberate corruption or wasteful action on earth.

Future Challenges

As the Muslim world moves into the twenty-first century, it is becoming more evident that the gap is widening between its people and the Western societies, as well as between the rich and the poor within the Muslim societies themselves. Almost all the Muslim countries are still considered among the developing world economically, physically, environmentally, and socially. Both the colonial era and the last half century of political independence have shown that imported and borrowed development systems have failed in Muslim lands. Unfortunately, leaders of these countries abandoned the shari'a and opted for foreign secular systems of government with laws that may be legally binding but are neither morally obligating nor practically enforceable.

Considering the current suspicion and stereotyping of Islam and everything Islamic, one should expect very little local or international cooperation in reviving the historical Islamic institutions that were proven effective. As a result, Muslim nongovernmental groups and civic societies need to be more involved in political activism in addition to the typical tasks of environmental awareness and natural conservation. Protecting the environment cannot be attained without influencing and convincing both the government and the private sector that Islam is an untapped rich source of environmental ideas and ideals.

Safei-Eldin A. Hamed

Further Reading

Abdel-Ati, H. (1997). *Islam in focus*. Beltsville, MD: Amana Publications.

Ali, A. Y. (Ed.). (1977). *The holy Qur'an: Arabic text, translation and commentary*. Indianapolis, IN: American Trust Publication.

Al-Qaradhawy, Y. (2001). *Ri'ayat Al-Beah Fi shari'at Al-Islam*("Looking after the environment in Islamic jurisprudence.") Cairo, Egypt: Dar Al-Shorouk.

Al-Mawardi, A. (1983). *al-Ahkam as-Sultaniyyah* ("The sultanic rules.") Cairo, Egypt: Dar el-Fikr.

Al Sabbagh, A. L., Al Glenid, M. A., Ba Kader, A., & Ezzidien, M. Y. (1983). *Islamic principles for the conservation of the natural environment*. Gland, Switzerland: International Union for the Conservation of Nature (IUCN).

Dien, M. I. (2000). *The environmental dimensions of Islam*. Cambridge, UK: The Lutterworth Press.

Haleem, H. (Ed.). (1998). *Islam and the West*. London: Ta-Ha Publishers.

Hamed, S. A. Seeing the environment through Islamic eyes: Application of Shariah to natural resources, planning and management. *Journal of Agricultural and Environmental Ethics*, 6(2), 145–164.

Husaini, S. W. (1980). *Islamic environmental systems engineering*. London: Macmillan.

Joma, H. A. (1991). *The Earth as a mosque*. Ph.D. dissertation. Philadelphia: University of Pennsylvania.

Khan, M. M. (1976). *The translation of the meanings of Shaih al Bukhari. Vol. 3*. Chicago: Kazi Publications.

Llewllyn, Othman. (1982). *Desert reclamation and Islamic law*. Jeddah, Saudi Arabia: The Haj Research Centre. (unpublished manuscript)

Nasr, S. H. (1981). *An introduction to Islamic cosmological doctrines*. Albany: State University of New York Press.

Nasr, S. H. (1997). *Man and Nature: The spiritual crisis in modern man*. Chicago: ABC International Group, Inc.

Sardar, Z. (Ed.). (1984). *The touch of Midas: Scientific values and the environment in Islam and the West*. Manchester, UK: Manchester University Press.

Italy
(2000 est. pop. 58 million)

The perception of Italy is squeezed by a double stereotype. Long seen as a land of sun and sea, rich with beauty, mild climates, and tourist attractions, Italy has also been seen—at least until recently—as a pitifully poor country lacking mineral wealth and breeding malaria, with soils eroding and deserts expanding. Each of these stereotypes can be true—and false—depending on one's perspective, interpretation, or political agenda. The nature of Italy cannot be characterized once and for all for everyone. Any single image misses the dynamic evolution of Italy's past environment and of past perceptions of that environment.

While perusing a map of Italy, one can imagine the peninsula without political boundaries or city names in order to recognize the main natural features that have underlain its changing social systems. Its river valleys, mountainsides, and coastlines were already being modified by agricultural societies as early as 5600 BCE. After these scattered societies came the Etruscans, then Greek colonists, Romans, Arabic settlers, city-state residents, and, finally, invading northerners who were, in turn, modified by this country of seas and mountains (the Apennines and the Alps). The Mediterranean Sea rising only a few hundred meters would submerge most of the Val Padana (Po River valley) in the north, leaving a ring of peaks and a chain of ridges extending to the south. All Italian environmental histories follow from these mountains and this sea.

With the Roman Empire crumbling after the fifth century CE, the villages and cities originally built near rivers or harbors began losing inhabitants to the mountainous interior, where people were safe from malaria-infested swamps and coastal invaders. Central Italy's Sanniti and Bruzi people, for example, developed out of these stocks of people, becoming part of a rich mountain heritage that would become fundamental to Italian ways of life. Today the peninsula's rugged spine is still dotted with isolated hamlets and settlements, some abandoned or nearly so, many perched high, protected by rock outcroppings or fortified with castle walls.

But any conclusion about Italians and their mountains is incomplete because there are many kinds of mountains and many ways of living on the mountains. One must distinguish the Alps from the Apennines, for example, while realizing that geology, rainfall, and vegetation vary tremendously across these ranges. Italy's Alps, which cover more area than Switzerland's Alps, have tempered northern winds while helping to keep out Gallic and Teutonic peoples. But this alpine barrier occasionally became quite porous, as when cultural groups pushed by desperation or opportunity migrated through the passes, bringing blond hair to the south and dark hair to the north. The Alps' higher elevations also meant shorter growing and grazing seasons than in the Apennines, along with shorter and steeper transhumance—the seasonal migration of herders and their animals. In late spring, when the Piedmontesi people were pushing livestock vertically, from plain to peak, at the other end of Italy, the Calabresi and Pugliesi were driving their animals horizontally, from south to north along the Apennines spine.

Watersheds

If the peninsula is a series of mountains, then it is also a system of watersheds. Historian Piero Bevilacqua considers Italian hydrographic history to be composed of either rivers or torrents—the former exemplified by the Po River, which drains the southern side of the Alps, the latter exemplified by the smaller water courses that flow down the southernmost Apennines. Large rivers, fed by snowfields from vast collection areas, were more dependable from year to year and from month to month; irrigation cooperatives and farmers organizations were therefore able to flourish in the Po's river plain. Yet, torrents, even if better distributed, were smaller, often drier, and less predictable; these seasonal streams resisted cooperative water management while fostering individual and decentralized approaches to farming. Since at least the Middle Ages, Italy's agricultural modes and productions have reflected the distribution of its rivers or torrents.

All these streams emptied into the sea, reminding one that Italians depended almost as much on the sea as on the land. The "marine republics" of Genoa, Venice, Pisa, and Amalfi were more concerned with what happened in front of the coast than behind it, especially regarding trade. The coasts did not divide human and nonhuman worlds but rather joined peoples and their ways of making a living. Venetian merchants joined Europe to the Levant; Amalfi and Sicilian tuna fishermen joined Tyrrhenian ecosystems to Neapolitan markets.

Italian environmental history can be read as ascension or declension, a story of rising or falling. To a forester, the millennium-long clearing of Apennines forests by wood collectors and charcoal makers—slowed during plagues or accelerated during warfare—meant long-term environmental ruin and human short-sightedness. But to a sheepherder or goatherder, progressive forest clearing meant more pastures and more grass and thus fatter sheep and goats. To a cane gatherer, the draining of the Pontine Marshes near Rome meant destroying productive grounds; to a wheat farmer, these reclamation projects produced arable soils from unhealthy land. The Lombardy region's nineteenth-century economist, Carlo Cattaneo, celebrated the human ability to improve the land, teaching that Italy's most productive lands resulted primarily from cultural rather than natural forces. Yet, his American contemporary, George Perkins Marsh, asserted that Italians had degraded their countryside, pointing to frequent floods issuing from deforested mountainsides. While serving as ambassador to Italy, Marsh elaborated on this declensionist view in *Man and Nature* (1864), a work considered by many to be the fountainhead of the American conservation movement; its translation *l'Uomo e la Natura* (1870) also found a significant reading in Italy. Many Italians agreed with Marsh's message that people need to take better care of natural systems.

Indeed, Italians have a rich tradition of stewarding the natural world. Even though historian Lynn White Jr. suggests that Judeo-Christian doctrines promoted environmental exploitation by instructing the faithful to subdue the Earth and seek dominion over its creatures, Franciscan principles, for example, stress land stewardship and renewal. Indeed, in the thirteenth century St. Francis of Assisi prayed to "Brother Sun and Sister Moon," imploring his listeners to respect all creatures.

Forestry Codes

Along with religious teachings, Italy's early environmental concern was reflected by government policies, particularly those addressing forest and water management. At least by 1600 Venetian officials were placing restrictions on tree cutting in the nearby mountains, citing the forest's ability to stabilize erodible ground and hinder silting of their lagoon. Following the peninsula's political unification (1861–1870), Italy's various forestry codes were unified by the Forest Law of 1877, a measure that was joined in later decades by stronger laws designed to revitalize the forest and guard against flooding watersheds. Administering these laws revealed the difficulty of applying single remedies to enormously varied terrain and regional politics. Members of Parliament, for example, debated whether "mountainland" should be defined by altitude or vegetation and whether low-lying cities or upland communities should bear the responsibility for reforestation. As in the case of forestry, tensions between country and city, or between mountain and lowland, formed the core of many resource disputes.

Italy's first three organizations to systematically advocate resource conservation were the Club Alpino Italiano (founded 1863), a gentlemen's hiking group; the Touring Club Italiano (founded 1894), a bicycle (and later automobile) group; and Pro Montibus (founded 1897), a forest protection group. In 1912 these organizations lobbied for the passage of a law to preserve natural landmarks and historic landscapes. It was perhaps the first Italian law to focus on aesthetic conservation, a law that reflected comparable laws that had been enacted shortly before in France and England. Italy's first national parks, Gran Paradiso and Abruzzo, established in 1922 and 1923 on royal hunting preserves, were aimed at protecting endangered wildlife, especially bear, ibex, and chamois. That these national parks are two of Europe's oldest suggests a special depth to the Italian land ethic.

But in Italian land-use history, neither forest management nor park establishment was as important as *bonifica* (improvement, betterment). *Bonifica* included everything from reclaiming swamps to digging canals, planting forests, and constructing check dams and was financed by cooperatives and governments. Since at least the eighteenth century, Italians refashioned thousands of hectares through *bonifica* projects designed to enhance stability, productivity, or health. The Italian fascist regime's massive Bonifica Integrale program—roughly corresponding to the American New Deal—aimed to improve the rural lifestyle along with the landscape. Dictator Benito Mussolini joined these domestic reclamation projects to imperial land grabs in Africa within a policy that he called "the Battle of Bread," the goal of which was to bring more land into production, helping restore Italy to the status of a great empire reminiscent of ancient Rome. Fascist reclamation projects also continued a long-standing Italian preference to live on the land, not apart from it, to manage the countryside, not degrade it. If Italy can be labeled "the garden of Europe," it is a working garden requiring maintenance, not an edenic garden flourishing without labor.

An Urban Past

The Italian past is also industrial, not just agricultural, also urban, not just rural. Almost every village on the peninsula lies within 100 kilometers of a large city. The Italian urban network is also very hierarchical, with villages orbiting towns and towns orbiting one of a dozen major cities. In almost every town, medieval church planners maintained open space in front of chapels and cathedrals, thereby providing towns with ample room for social gatherings. External threats, share-crop systems, and high land prices also produced compact urban spaces that sharply defined town from country but that also often compromised drinking water with accumulating human or animal wastes. Railroad construction during the nineteenth century reinforced compact urban development when train stations were located at regular intervals near city centers. The Italian sense of place has long been linked to the city: People from, for example, Florence think of themselves as Florentine first, Tuscan second, and Italian third.

By the twentieth century Italy's rural countryside began to depopulate, particularly in mountainous regions lacking good agricultural lands. The Alps lost inhabitants sooner and faster than the Apennines, which lay farther from the attractions of industrializing cities. International out-migration also followed this pattern, first involving northern emigrants and then southern emigrants. Coastal marshlands threatened by malaria initially hindered settlement, but after Mussolini's massive drainage projects, they promoted settlement. With widely fluctuating birthrates and death rates and changing patterns of internal or external migration, Italian demographic history is one of the most complicated of any nation. In 2000 Italy's 57 million inhabitants recorded the world's lowest birthrate.

After thirty years of fascist repression and postwar reconstruction, accumulating threats to human health, natural beauty, and adequate resources accelerated the Italian environmental movement. Across the peninsula, an era of affordable automobiles combined with an expanding economy led to rampant sprawl at the edge of almost every city. The waters, too, were transformed by greater mechanization, higher demands, and industrial pollutants; in both freshwater and saltwater fisheries, removal of big fish led to harvests of small fish, as in Sardinia's sardine catches. With Milan and the surrounding agricultural plains flushing down greater loads of nitrogen, summer algae blooms would soon blight the Adriatic Sea and its beaches. According to many scientists, the Mediterranean is one of the Earth's most polluted seas.

Italy's four principal environmental groups were established between 1955 and 1966: Italia Nostra, Pro Natura, Lega Italiana Protezione Uccelli (LIPU), and WWF (World Wildlife Fund)-Italia. These groups were spurred on by a succession of disasters that was blamed partially or wholly on human negligence: The floods of Polesine (Venice, 1951) and the Arno River

(Tuscany, 1966) were attributed to deforestation; the collapsing dams of Frejus (Provence, France, 1959) and Vaijont (Venice, 1963) were attributed to faulty engineering. The chemical spill at Seveso north of Milan in Lombardy produced an even greater sensation, garnering still more environmentalist support within and beyond Italy: On 10 July 1976, a white cloud of dioxin rose from a chemical plant owned by the multinational company Hoffman-La Roche. Although there were no immediate deaths, hundreds of nearby residents were afflicted, with untold numbers suffering in later years from acute toxicity and possible birth defects. An aftermath of litigation, cover-ups, and ethical dilemmas revealed the ugly side of Italy's postwar industrial miracle. The spill's legacy continues today, as shown by the terminology of a recent European Union law known as the "Seveso Directive" (Directive 96/82/CE), which aims to identify outdated chemical plants in order to prevent environmental accidents of the kind that happened in Italy. In the wake of the Seveso spill and the nuclear accident at Chernobyl (Ukraine, USSR, 1986), Italy's left-leaning environmental groups, such as the Legambiente, which numbered thirty-five thousand members in 1986, gained more support. Leading voices in this new environmental movement included journalist Tina Merlin, biologist Laura Conti, activist Antonio Cederna, and architect Antonio Iannello. Environmental groups orchestrated a successful campaign against nuclear power development and in 1992 also successfully lobbied for the passage of a parks bill (Legge Quadro) that created nine new national parks and consolidated other protected areas. The Italian Green Party gained 3.8 percent of the electoral vote in 1989 before sliding to 2.4 percent in 2000, reflecting a European shift to the right.

Marco Armiero and Marcus Hall

Further Reading

Armiero, M. (1999). *Il territorio come risorsa* [The land as a resource]. Naples, Italy: Liguori.

di Bèrenger, A. (1859–1863). *Studii di archeologia forestale: Dell'Antica storia e giurisprudenza forestale in Italia* [Studies in forest archaeology: Of ancient history and forestry law in Italy]. Venice, Italy: G. Longo.

Bevilacqua, P. (1992). *Storia dell'agricoltura Italiana in et'à contemporanea* [History of Italian agricukture in the modern age]. Bari, Italy: Laterza.

Bevilacqua, P. (1996). *Tra natura e storia. Ambiente, economie, risorse in Italia* [Between nature and history: Environment, economy, and resources in Italy]. Rome: Donzelli.

Bevilacqua, P., & Manlio, R. (1984). *Le bonifiche in Italia dal '700 ad oggi* [Improvement projects in Italy from 1700 to present]. Bari, Italy: Laterza.

Cosgrove, D. (1993). *The Palladian landscape: Geographical change and its cultural representations in sixteenth-century Italy.* Leicester, UK: Leicester University Press.

Fumagalli, V. (1992). *L'uomo e l'ambiente nel Medioevo* [Man and environment in the Middle Ages]. Bari, Italy: Laterza.

Gambi, L. (1972). *I carrateri originale, Storia d'Italia* [The original elements; History of Italy] (Vol. 1). Turin, Italy: Einaudi.

Gaspari, O. (1992). *La montagna alle origini di un problema politico* [Mountains at the source of political problems]. Rome: Ist. Poligrafico e Zecca dello Stato.

Moreno, D. (1990). *Dal documento al terreno: Storia e archeologia dei sistemi agro-silvo-pastorali* [From the document to the land: History and archaeology pf agro-silvo-pastoral systems]. Bologna, Italy: Il Mulino.

Petrarca, Francesco. (1327). *Il Canzoniere* [Petrarch's Sonnets].

Piccioni, L. (1999). *Il volto amato della Patria: Il primo movimento per la conservazione della natura in Italia, 1880–1934* [The country's most-loved aspect: Italy's first nature conservation movement]. Camerino, Italy: Università di Camerino.

Poggio, A. (1996). *Ambientalismo* [Environmentalism]. Milan: Editrice Bibliografica.

Sereni, E. (1961). *Storia del paesaggio agrario Italiano* (History of the Italian agricultural landscape). Princeton, NJ: Princeton University Press.

Sievert, J. (2000). *The origins of nature conservation in Italy.* Frankfurt, Germany: Peter Lang.

Tagliolini, A. (1988). *Storia del giardino Italiano* [History of the Italian garden]. Florence, Italy: La Cas Usher.

Vecchio, B. (1974). *Il bosco e gli scrittori Italiani del Settecento e dell'et'à napoleonica* [The forest and Italian writers from 1700 to the age of Napoleon]. Torino, Italy: Einaudi.

Viazzo, P. P. (1989). *Upland communities: Environment, population and social structure in the Alps since the sixteenth century.* New York: Cambridge University Press.

Ivory-billed Woodpecker

The ivory-billed woodpecker (*Campephilus principalis*) has attained an almost mythical status among Ameri-

717

can ornithologists. The populations of this magnificent bird plummeted by the early twentieth century, and, despite massive searches, no positive sightings of the North American subspecies (*C. p. principalis*) have been documented for years. The Cuban subspecies (*C. p. bairdii*) was rediscovered in 1986 but has since disappeared. Consequently the whole species is today presumed extinct.

At 50 centimeters in length, the ivory-billed woodpecker is one of the world's largest woodpeckers. Its striking plumage is glossy black with white areas along the sides of the head and on the wings, and a prominent red crest in the male. Both sexes have a conspicuous (7-centimeter) creamy-white bill. Unlike other representatives of the genus *Campephilus*, the North American subspecies has been associated with deciduous lowland forests. Its geographical range included the South Atlantic, the Gulf, and the Mississippi Valley states from southeastern North Carolina to eastern Texas and up the Mississippi Valley to southern Illinois.

The populations of the ivory-billed woodpecker began to shrink rapidly during the latter half of the nineteenth century, and by 1880 the bird had disappeared from much of its former range. By the late 1930s, it was known only from a handful of localities in Florida and Louisiana, and from the Santee Swamp of South Carolina. Many of these sites as suitable habitat were destroyed within a few years. Since the mid-twentieth century there have been only unconfirmed reports, and confusion with the relatively common pileated woodpecker (*Dryocopus pileatus*), which is also large (approximately 41 centimeters long), primarily black, and with a red crest, seems evident in most cases.

Compared to the Carolina parakeet (*Conuropsis carolinensis*) and Bachman's warbler (*Vermivora bachmanii*), the two other recently vanished birds of the southern bottomlands (low-lying land along waterways), data on the ecology of the ivory-billed woodpecker is relatively plentiful. This is largely due to the extensive work of late ornithologist James T. Tanner, who studied some of the last known populations of the species. The birds studied by Tanner in the Singer Tract of Madison Parish, Louisiana, showed a high degree of specialization in their foraging habits: Most of their food consisted of larvae of wood-boring insects, found by scaling the bark off dying or recently dead trees. This food requirement postulated a vast territory of old-growth forest for each breeding pair.

The ultimate cause for the disappearance of the ivory-billed woodpecker was the extensive destruction of its habitat by land clearing and logging. The cutting of mature bottomland hardwood forests deprived the species of its main food source. The decreases in the ivory-billed woodpecker's range correlated with the spread of the logging industry, and the populations disappeared after the old-growth timber in the bottomlands had been removed. The decline in area of suitable habitat led to fragmentation of the ivory-billed woodpecker's range, and various causes then exterminated the isolated and sedentary populations. For example, egg and specimen collectors undoubtedly accelerated the decline of the species around the turn of the century. Legislative and other efforts to save the ivory-billed woodpecker, including the 1967 federal listing as endangered, came too late for the recovery of the small and scattered populations.

Mikko Saikku

Further Reading

Collar, N. J., Crosby, M. J., & Stattersfield, A. J. (1994). *Birds to watch 2: The world list of threatened birds.* Cambridge, UK: BirdLife.

Tanner, J. T. (1942). *The ivory-billed woodpecker.* (National Audubon Society Research Rep. No. 1). New York: National Audubon Society.

The Izaak Walton League of America

The Izaak Walton League of America (IWLA) was founded in Chicago in 1922 by a group of fifty-four anglers and hunters. It was named for Izaak Walton, a seventeenth-century British author who wrote *The Compleat Angler* (1653), which praised the pleasures of fishing. During its early years, the League was headed by Will H. Dilg, a public-relations professional who marketed "near beer" for a Chicago brewery during Prohibition. The League soon became the largest U.S. conservation organization, with well over 100,000 members in the late 1920s, when the Audubon Society and the Sierra Club had less than 7,000 members each. The League's rapid growth was based on social demand, Will Dilg's leadership, and the experiences of IWLA founders, many of whom worked in advertising or ran businesses. The League adopted a nested organizational structure, with a national league, state divisions, and local chapters. It was a structure that was successfully adopted by other conservation and environmental organizations later. The League also established a new kind of magazine, *Outdoor America*, to recruit members. Writers such as Zane Gray, James Oliver Curwood, and El Comancho contributed to the magazine, and it also generated income from advertisements targeted to outdoors people. The League's strongest support basis was in the Midwest. Its national influence peaked in the 1920s and the 1930s and started to wane after the Second World War.

The Izaak Walton League promoted the protection of fish, game, wildlife and habitats for recreational and other reasons. It was also concerned with the effects of water pollution on public health, landscape, heritage, and economic development. These broader concerns were partly expressed to justify the interventions required to protect fish life from water pollution. However, they also reflected the breadth of the League's support base, which ranged from middle-class outdoor enthusiasts to prominent professionals, scholars, and politicians. For example, Henry Baldwin Ward, the national president of the IWLA in 1928–30, was a professor of zoology and a pioneer in parasitology at the University of Illinois at Urbana-Champaign. Other scholars, such as William D. Hatfield, future president of the Water Pollution Control Federation, were regular contributors to *Outdoor America*. Politicians such as President Herbert Hoover and conservation leaders such as Aldo Leopold and Jay "Ding" Darling were IWLA supporters or members. IWLA also made explicit efforts to mobilize women and had its first female auxiliary chapter by 1928.

The Izaak Walton League achieved several victories in its early years. After intensive campaigning by the League, in 1924 President Calvin Coolidge established the 140,000-hectare Upper Mississippi River Wild Life and Fish Refuge. In 1927, the League organized a national water quality survey, which found that three-quarters of the nation's waters were polluted. The League raised water pollution to the national political agenda during the 1930s. Its efforts succeeded in directing some of the public funding made available for the alleviation of the effects of the Great Depression to the construction of trunk sewers and sewage treatment plants, as well as to the sealing of old mines. The League's supporters also sponsored a stream of federal water-pollution control bills in Congress. One of these bills passed in Congress in 1939, only to be vetoed by President Roosevelt on the grounds that it was too expensive.

The achievements of IWLA were not limited to the national level. For example, local chapters campaigned successfully in Iowa for the construction of sewage treatment plants on Cedar River in the 1920s. Minnesota Waltonians in turn contributed to the construction of sewage treatment facilities in Minneapolis and St. Paul in the 1930s.

After World War II, the membership of IWLA gradually declined and is presently about fifty thousand members. Nevertheless, it was involved in the successful promotion federal water pollution control program immediately after World War II. Today, the IWLA continues to work for conservation of water, soil, and other natural resources for recreational and other purposes as one of the oldest conservation organizations.

Jouni Paavola

Further Reading

Fox, S. (1981). *John Muir and his legacy: The American conservation movement.* Boston: Little Brown.

Gottlieb, R. (1993), *Forcing the spring: The transformation of the American environmental movement.* Washington, DC: Island Press.

Scarpino, P. V. (1985). *Great River: An environmental history of the upper Mississippi, 1890–1950.* Columbia: University of Missouri Press.

Jainism

Jainism is a south Asian religion that, according to the historical record, began about twenty-five hundred years ago. Since then it has co-existed in India alongside Hinduism and Buddhism and, later, Islam. The word *Jain* comes from the Sanskrit word *jin* or *jina*, which means "to conquer inner enemies such as ego, pride, anger and delusion."

Jainism, as we know it, was founded by Vardhamana (c. 599–527 BCE), later known to Jains as "Mahavir." But according to the oral culture it is believed that there are twenty-four "Great Liberators" in the Jain lineage. Such Great Liberators are called *tirthankaras*. Adinath was the first. Parshwanath was the twenty-third. Mahavir was the twenty-fourth. He revived the Jain religion as it is practiced today. Each of the twenty-four Great Liberators has an associated animal, symbolizing that in Jain teachings the place of animals is central. Love is not love if it does not include love of animals, according to Jain teachings. What kind of compassion is it that reveres human life but ignores the slaughter of animals? This is the challenge of the Jains.

There are about 4 million Jains, most in cities in northwest India. Outside India Jains are found in east Africa, the United Kingdom, and the United States. Almost all of them are of Indian origin. Jains do not convert others to their religion. They believe that there is no one single truth, rather there are many truths. This system of multiple truths is known as *Anekant*, which simply means "no one conclusion, no single reality, no one god." Neither monism nor dualism, but rather pluralism is at the heart of Jain philosophy.

Nonviolence to humans as well as to animals is one of the fundamental contributions of Jainism to world philosophy. Indian nationalist Mohandas Gandhi and French theologian Albert Schweitzer—to name only two—were much influenced by Jain nonviolence, and the origins of vegetarianism are also credited to Jainism.

Humans and Other Species

According to Jain biologists, there are 8.4 million living species on Earth. A list of the species was prepared by Jains over two thousand years ago. The list includes eagles, swans, whales, tigers, elephants, snakes, worms, bacteria, fungi, air, water, fire, rocks, and everything that is natural and alive. Jains are animists—for them everything natural is living, and all life is sacred. Any kind of harm to any form of life is to be avoided or minimized. Of course, the sustenance of one form of life depends upon the death of another, yet the followers of Jainism are required to limit the taking of life even for survival.

Human beings are seen as only one of the 8.4 million species. They have no more rights than any other species. All living beings, human and other than human, have an equal right to life. Not only do humans have no absolute rights—to take, to control, or to subjugate other forms of life—but also they have extra obligations to practice nonviolence and to be humble in the face of the mysterious, glorious, abundant, and extraordinary phenomena of the living world.

Liberation of the Soul

After a long life of meditation and contemplation, Mahavir came to the conclusion that three essential elements bring true liberation of the soul: *ahimsa* (nonviolence), *sanyama* (simplicity), and *tapas* (austerity).

Ahimsa (nonviolence) begins in the mind. Unless the mind is compassionate, nonviolence is not possible. Unless one is at ease in the inner world, one cannot practice nonviolence in the outer world. If the mind is condemning other people, yet the tongue speaks sweet words, then that is not nonviolence. The seeds of nonviolence live within the inner consciousness. Keeping the inner consciousness pure is therefore an essential part of Jain nonviolence. Pure consciousness means consciousness that is uncorrupted by the desire to control others.

Why are people violent? Jains would answer that people are violent because they wish to control others. People who control say, "We own everything here. This world is for our benefit." Those who eat meat say, "Animals and fish are there for our food. Everything is for us, and we are the masters of nature." This is the violence of the mind, which leads to physical violence.

Mahavir saw the world as a sacred place. The birds, the flowers, the butterflies, and the trees are sacred; rivers, soil, and oceans are sacred. Life as a whole is sacred. All of people's interactions with other people and with the natural world must be based on deep reverence for all life.

Nonviolence of the mind should be translated into nonviolence of speech. Harmful, harsh, untrue, unnecessary, and offensive speech is violence. Skillful use of language is a sacred skill. Mahavir insisted that people must understand others fully before they speak. Language can express only partial truth; therefore nonviolence is an essential guide to spoken words. In this context Mahavir put a high value on silence. A Jain monk is called a *muni*, which means "the silent one."

Nonviolence of mind and speech leads to nonviolence of action. Ends cannot justify means. Means must be compatible with ends. Therefore, all human actions must be friendly, compassionate, and unaggressive. Do no harm. Do not compromise. Mahavir's nonviolence is unconditional love to all beings.

Nonviolence is the paramount principle of Jains. All other principles stem from nonviolence. Because all life is sacred, people may not violate or take advantage of those life-forms that may be weaker than people. *Ahimsa* is much more than "Live and let live." It is "Live and love."

The second principle is *sanyama* (simplicity). Being satisfied with less is *sanyama*. The idea that whatever people have, or however much people have, is never enough is the source of anguish. Jains are required to move from "more and more" to "enough!"

For Jains there is nothing lacking in the world. There is the abundance of nature. Only when people want to own, to control, and to possess do people create scarcity. Because people can never possess everything, they always want more. This possessiveness is the source of scarcity. The moment people are satisfied and do not want to control and possess, they have abundance. Paradoxically, this abundance, according to the Jains, is available only to those who can learn to live within the limits of their needs.

The principle of *tapas* (austerity) is one of the most significant contributions of Jain religion. As humans purify their body, they also need to purify their soul. The mind gets polluted by harmful thoughts. The consciousness gets contaminated by ego, greed, pride, anger, and fear. Souls suffer because of desires, attachments, and anguish. So Mahavir devised a way to purify the mind, the soul, and the consciousness, and he called it *tapas*.

Fasting, meditation, restraint, pilgrimage, and service to others fall under the principle of *tapas*. It is a kind of soul exercise to keep the inner world healthy and pure.

Every Jain aspires to four practices to attain inner liberation. The first practice is *satya* (truth), which means understanding and realizing the true nature of existence and the true nature of oneself. It means accepting reality as it is and being truthful to it, seeing things as they are without judging them as good or bad. It means "do not lie" in its deepest sense: Do not have illusions about oneself. Face the truth without fear. Things are as they are. A person of truth goes beyond mental constructs and realizes existence as it is. Living in truth means avoiding manipulating people or nature because there is no single truth that any mind can grasp or tongue can express. Being truthful involves being humble and open to new discoveries and yet accepting that there is no final or ultimate discovery. Truth is what is: People accept what is as it is, speak of it as it is, and live it as it is. Any individual or group claiming to know the whole truth is by definition engaged in falsehood. Ultimately, for Jains, existence is a great mystery.

The second practice is *asteya* (nonstealing), which means refraining from acquiring goods or services beyond one's essential needs. It is difficult to know what the essential needs are, so Jain religion requires that people assess, examine, and question day by day what is need and what is greed. The distinction between

Jain Tale about Humans and Animals

Once Parshwanath, a young prince, arriving as a bridegroom with his marriage entourage to the house of his bride, saw near the house an enclosure of animals, tightly packed, waiting to be slaughtered. Shocked by the cry of the animals, the prince enquired, "Why are those animals being kept in such cruel conditions?" His aides replied, "They are for the feast of the wedding party."

The young prince was overwhelmed with compassion. Arriving at the wedding chamber, he spoke with the father of the princess. "Immediately and unconditionally all those animals enclosed to be slaughtered for the marriage feast must be freed," he said. "Why?" responded the father. "The lives of animals are there for the pleasure of humans. Animals are our slaves and our meat. How can there be any feast without the flesh?!"

Prince Parshwanath was puzzled. He could not believe what he had just heard. He exclaimed, "Animals have souls, they have consciousness, they are our kith and kin, they are our ancestors. They wish to live as much as we do; they have feelings and emotions. They have love and passion; they fear death as much as we do. Their instinct for life is no less than ours. Their right to live is as fundamental as our own. I cannot marry, I cannot love and I cannot enjoy life if animals are enslaved and killed." Without further ado he rejected the plans for his marriage, he discarded the comfortable life of a prince, and he responded to his inner calling to go out and awaken the sleepy masses who had been conditioned to think selfishly and kill animals for their pleasure and comfort.

The animal kingdom welcomes Parshwanath as the prophet of the weak and the wild. They gather around him when he calls for kindness. The birds sit upon the tree nearby; fishes come to the corner of the lake where Parshwanath is seated. Elephants, lions, foxes, rabbits, rats, insects, and ants pay homage to him. One day, finding Parshwanath being soaked by the heavy rain of the monsoon, the king of the cobras stood on his tail and created an umbrella with his huge head.

Thousands upon thousands of people in villages, towns and cities are moved by the teachings of Parshwanath. They renounce meat and take up the work of animal welfare. The princess whom Parshwanath was going to marry was so inspired that she decided to remain unmarried and dedicate herself to the care of animals. Having lost a daughter and would-be son-in-law to the cause of animal compassion, the King himself underwent anguish and yet experienced transformation. He announced that all animals were to be respected in his kingdom, and that there would be no hunting, no shooting, no caging and no pets.

Satish Kumar

---

need and greed can be blurred, and therefore the examination of need should be carried out with honesty. The principle of *asteya* includes "Do not steal." The Jain understanding of this goes further than any legal definition. If people take more from nature than meets their essential need, they are stealing from nature. For example, clearing an entire forest would be seen as a violation of nature's rights and as theft. Similarly, taking from society housing, food, and clothing in excess of one's essential requirements means depriving other people and is therefore theft. If people are using up finite resources at a greater speed than they can be replenished, then they are stealing from future generations.

The Jains would give first and then take. Taking before giving is "stealing."

The third practice is *bramhacarya* (love without lust). This practice has been closely associated with proper sexual conduct. For monks, *bramhacarya* means total abstinence, and for laypeople it means fidelity in marriage. Any thoughts, speech, or acts that demean, debase, or abuse the body are against the practice of *bramhacarya*. The body is the temple of pure being, and therefore no activity that would defile the temple of the body should be undertaken.

The fourth practice is *aparigraha* (nonpossessiveness), which means nonaccumulation of material things. If no one accumulates anything, then no one will be deprived. *Aparigraha* means sharing and living without ostentation. Dress, food, and furnishings should be elegant but simple and minimal. "Simple in means, rich in ends" is a Jain adage. When people spend too much time in the care of possessions there is no time for the care of the soul. *Aparigraha* means not acquiring what is not necessary, recognizing that whatever a person acquires will bind that person tightly. If people free themselves from nonessential acquisitions, then they will be liberated. For Jains it is a moral imperative to live simply so that others may simply live.

Because so much of Jain belief and practice relates to the human-environment interaction, Jainism has been of considerable interest to environmentalists, naturalists, philosophers, and theologians. In India the Jains constitute a wealthy and prosperous urban community. They use their wealth to support causes and institutions whose goals are to relieve human and animal suffering.

Satish Kumar

Further Reading

Bhattacharyya, N. N. (1999). *Jain philosophy: Historical outline*. New Delhi, India: Munshiram Manoharlal Publishing.

Cort, J. E. (Ed.). (1998). *Open boundaries: Jain communities and cultures in Indian history*. Albany: State University of New York Press.

Jaini, Padmanabha (1979). *Jaina path of purification*. Jawahar Nagar, India: Motilal Banarsidas.

Mahaprajna. (2002). *Anekanta: The third eye*. Ladnun, India: Jain Vishva Bhavati.

Pal, Pratapaditya. (1995). *The peaceful liberators: Jain art from India*. New York: Los Angeles County Museum of Art and Thames and Hudson.

Umasvati. (1994). *That which is: Tattvartha sutra* (N. Tatia, Trans.). San Francisco: HarperCollins.

Van Alphen, J. (2000). *Steps to liberation: 2,500 years of Jain art and religion*. Antwerp, Belgium: Etnografisch Museum.

Japan

Sometime around 400 BCE, people in the archipelago that we today call Japan began employing horticultural practices in place of older forager techniques of sustenance. Over the centuries they expanded the acreage under tillage, and their numbers grew, rising from a few hundred thousand to some 7 million by 1200 CE. About then an array of social and agronomic changes began displacing the existing agricultural system with a much more intensive one, and it sustained centuries of accelerated socioeconomic growth, giving Japan a population of some 30 million by 1700. Around then that pulse of rapid growth faded, ushering in a time of demographic stasis and unprecedented environmental stress. But from about 1880 onward, the adoption of industrial techniques based on fossil-fuel use triggered a new pulse of rapid growth that raised the population to more than 125 million by the year 2000. Industrialization established in Japan the full range of environmental issues (including endemic pollution, resource depletion, and loss of biodiversity and natural habitat) that marks industrial society everywhere.

Intensive Agriculture (1200–1880)

Around 1200 CE, the agronomic and social elements of intensified agriculture began falling into place. Most notably, fallowing gave way to fertilizing with ashes, mulch, and manure. Also, regularly irrigated wet rice, which can yield much higher harvests per hectare than do dry grains, came to be planted more widely, with nurturing techniques much improved. And double-cropping, with a summer rice crop followed by a winter dry grain or vegetable crop, spread along Japan's southern littoral and Inland Sea region. These changes required more intensive labor and more communal cooperation in the use of land, labor, and water supplies, which spurred the growth of larger, better-organized villages.

These trends were facilitated by the evolution of smallpox and measles from exogenous, highly fatal, epidemic diseases of adulthood to endemic illnesses of childhood. That change helped stabilize local populations, enabling intensive tillage techniques to become ever more widely practiced despite centuries of violent political turmoil. Towns and trade were growing, which fostered crop specialization and market gardening. In consequence of these developments population kept growing, perhaps reaching some 15 million by 1600.

By then, however, the broader environmental ramifications of growth and turmoil were becoming apparent. Most notably, the expanding village demand for fertilizer, fuel, and fodder had been met by more intensive cutting, raking, and gathering of wood, grass, and leaves from woodland and waste areas, and that activity produced more and more eroded hillsides. In consequence, whereas there earlier had been only desultory government efforts (and those only in the vicinity of Kyoto and Nara) to protect woodland by closing forests and issuing decrees to regulate land use, during the 1500s measures to regulate the exploitation of natural resources—woodland and water supplies in particular—became widespread, pursued most vigorously by villagers and regional barons.

Changes around 1600

The centuries of recurrent warfare ended around 1600 when a powerful dictatorship imposed order on the realm. The synergies associated with this pacification produced a sharp, short-term acceleration in several trends, most notably increases in paddy-field acreage, construction activity, urbanization, mining, and deforestation. The expansion of paddy-field acreage shifted many dry-crop fields into wet-rice production, opened new areas of lowland near major rivers to tillage, gave Japan many new and elaborate irrigation systems, and enabled society to grow rapidly for a few decades.

Meanwhile urban construction work of the late sixteenth and early seventeenth centuries dotted the realm with a vast array of grand wooden monuments—palaces, castles, mansions, temples, and shrines—as well as large cities, lesser towns, and highway stations. This activity was abetted by a boom in gold and silver mining that briefly made Japan the world's greatest bullion producer. By 1630, however, bullion mining was in steep decline as accessible deposits were consumed. By then, too, the construction boom was petering out, in part because much elite demand had been sated, but in part because most of the reasonably accessible high forest from Kyushu (the southernmost of Japan's four main islands) to the northern tip of Honshu (Japan's central island) had been consumed, and the cost of timber provisioning was becoming prohibitive. By 1660, even reconstruction after urban conflagrations was becoming a burden the system could scarcely afford.

The Eighteenth Century: Increasing Environmental Stress

By 1660 the age of land clearance and water works expansion was also passing, because little lowland remained unreclaimed and practically all the controllable water was being used. As decades advanced, the consequences of excessive deforestation and land clearance became more and more evident: soil erosion,

proliferation of bald mountains, flooding, more irregular stream flow, and harvest shortfalls. By the start of the eighteenth century the resulting stresses were starting to work their way through society, spurring remedial measures and adaptations. Deforestation and downstream damage fostered the development of much more elaborate and tightly enforced woodland regulations, the beginnings of plantation forestry, and the emergence of the use of coal. To cope with bullion scarcities, foreign trade was cut back, coinage was debased, and diverse forms of substitution and rationing were developed. To protect its elaborate and costly irrigation systems, society committed itself to a long-term task of continual riparian maintenance: river dredging and dyke, dam, and diversion-ditch construction and repair. To sustain soil fertility despite the scarcity of woodland mulch, farmers utilized more and more nightsoil, industrial waste, and fishmeal, the last of which spurred the expansion of coastal fisheries.

The challenge of surviving on a stressed ecosystem also modified social arrangements in the hinterland in ways that yielded a demographic transformation. Specifically, a large population of struggling agricultural smallholders, tenant farmers, and landless laborers—roughly 75 percent of the archipelago's people—maneuvered to limit family size as a way to sustain their household well-being, and the cumulative effect of their efforts was to replace population growth with stasis. Their maneuvers included delayed and less fecund marriages, outplacement of surplus children, and abortion and infanticide, despite official denunciation. Their efforts were aided by a heightened frequency of famines and epidemics, which decimated the weak.

Villagers acted as they did because their choices were harsh, the harshness evidenced in many ways during the eighteenth and nineteenth centuries. Those ways included increased tenancy and landlessness, as well as greater geographical mobility as more and more people pursued work away from home. There were larger and more frequent peasant rebellions, more forceful armed suppression, increased numbers of urban poor, and larger and more violent urban outbursts. One also sees the blossoming of a hortatory literature that advocated hard work, frugality, and self-discipline along with an intensifying rhetoric of political criticism.

New Pressures and a New Regime in the Late Nineteenth Century

These difficulties notwithstanding, the ruling elite managed to stay in power until the 1860s. But then unprecedented demands from a new quarter—expansionist, early-industrial Europe (and its North American outpost)—presented problems that this elite, as then structured, was utterly unable to handle. During that decade Japan slipped into political turmoil, and elements of the old elite destroyed the existing polity. They replaced it during the 1870s with a more centralized and more powerful regime that started propelling Japan beyond its agricultural order into the age of industrialism, with all its accoutrements of social, cultural, and environmental change.

In sum, then, by the 1880s the lowlands and valley floors of a once thoroughly forested realm had nearly all been opened to tillage, and many of the nearby hillsides were barren or covered with scrub growth. The deeper mountains had surrendered much of their old-growth timber, but most were still verdant, and significant tracts of inaccessible forest—not to mention nearly all of Hokkaido (the northernmost of Japan's four main islands)—remained untouched. Humans and their collaborating species and parasites had displaced earlier occupants from an appreciable part of the realm, mostly lowlands, altering overall biotic composition, and placing some creatures (such as the black bear and the wolf) at risk or near extinction. Having maximized paddy tillage by opening nearly all flood plains to cultivation, the populace found itself locked in an eternal struggle to control river flow. Coastal fisheries were being worked intensively, and the malign effects of mining, notably air and water pollution, were becoming evident as coal and metal mining began expanding from the late eighteenth century onward.

The Rise of Industrialism (1880 to the Present)

Industrial society is as different from agricultural society as the latter is from forager society, being distinguished by two basic environmental changes. One is a shift from material dependence on the society's own terrain to dependence on a global resource base that is made accessible by some mix of politico-military and entrepreneurial means. The other is a radical acceleration in the rate of human-controlled energy cycling, which is made possible by supplementing energy obtained from the living biome (mainly as food, fuel wood, and animal power) with energy obtained from past biomes (mainly as fossil fuel) and other sources (mainly hydroelectric and nuclear).

Japan began the shift to industrialism around 1880 and became a more-or-less "mature" industrial society during the decades after 1960. In its shift to global re-

sources, before 1945 its leaders relied heavily on politico-military means—empire building—to expand their resource base. But after 1950 they favored an entrepreneurial strategy that exchanged finished goods and diverse services for imported raw materials, notably fossil fuel, metals, timber, and foodstuffs. The acceleration in energy cycling was achieved initially by heavy use of domestic coal, supplemented during the second decade of the twentieth century through the 1930s by development of hydropower, after 1960 by a shift to imported fuel oil and coal, and, from the 1970s onward, by the addition of nuclear power.

The shift to a global resource base and new energy sources had a broad range of environmental ramifications. But these—problems associated with urbanization, agricultural practice, mining, fisheries, industrial chemistry, and forest use—are of sorts familiar to all industrial societies and can be noted succinctly.

The explosive growth in Japan's population, roughly a tripling during the century after 1890 or so, was surpassed by the rate of urbanization, so that most Japanese today are city and town dwellers. From the 1880s down to 1950, those cities were breeding grounds for one of the world's worst pandemics of tuberculosis, but with the development of antibiotics that problem was overcome. Today, Japan's cities and towns are some of the safest and healthiest places a human can live, and their residents enjoy, on average, the world's longest lifespans. However, because the rate of material consumption of this urbanized populace is vastly higher than that of their ancestors, these urban sites produce immense quantities of effluent and trash that pollute widely and create chronic problems of waste disposal.

Environmental Consequences of Feeding a Dense Population

To feed this burgeoning population, agricultural leaders spurred domestic food production, achieving major increases in annual output. Since the 1950s, however, the effort has entailed unprecedented reliance on chemical fertilizers and biocides, which have had the usual effect of polluting water and soil, with toxic effluents draining into lakes and coastal waters, in the process injuring diverse organisms. Moreover, surging public consumption has outpaced the increase in output, requiring ever greater food imports: Whereas the people of pre–1860 Japan obtained all their caloric intake from domestic and near-shore production, by the 1990s over half of it came from abroad.

Part of the imported food has been of marine provenance. With motorized vessels, huge nets, and by 1930 cannery ships and catcher boats, Japanese fishermen moved beyond coastal operations into pelagic (open sea) fisheries, in the process making Japan a significant participant in the global marine harvest. Meanwhile, as the twentieth century aged, overfishing and pollution ravaged Japan's coastal and inland fisheries. From the 1980s onward, moreover, the lower-wage pelagic fishing fleets of other countries became able to undersell Japan's own fishermen. These trends led to a gradual decline in the indigenous fishing industry, a decline that continues in the twenty-first century. During the 1990s the level of seafood consumption also began dropping, as global overfishing and marine pollution decimated world supplies and drove up prices.

Industrial Pollution

Much as industrial technology transformed farm and fishery operations, so it changed the mining industry. Metal and coal mining were creating downstream pollution problems by the early nineteenth century, but the rapid expansion of mechanized mining after 1880 led to a countrywide surge in mine output and environmental injury. The most notorious instance involved the Ashio copper mine north of Tokyo during the 1890s, but local, less visible cases of toxic effluent became widespread despite modest legislative attempts to contain pollutants and improve mine safety. By the 1960s, however, with many mines petering out, the government was promoting metal and coal imports, and thereafter the domestic mining industry withered and its environmental impact diminished.

Even as reliance on imports was shifting some of the environmental effects of industrial-age agriculture, fisheries, and mining offshore, the malign impact of other industries continued to grow within Japan. From the early twentieth century onward new types and uses of chemicals produced more and more pollutants that poisoned air, water, and soil, mainly downstream and downwind from factories and smokestacks. During the 1960s a cluster of severe poisoning incidents involving mercury, cadmium, polychlorinated biphenyls (PCBs), petrochemicals, and other industrial products provoked public protests forceful enough to overwhelm industrial and government resistance and win modest remediation and the creation of an environmental regulatory system designed to minimize future problems. More broadly, however, the proliferation of motor vehicles since the 1950s and the use of more and more new chemicals and pharmaceuticals has perpetu-

ated the production of pollutants, many of them unregulated and unmeasured, and their impacts on the biosystem are only gradually becoming apparent.

Japan's Forests in the Industrial Age

Perhaps the most interesting environmental story of industrial-age Japan—interesting because it is the least "normal"—is that of its forests. The modest gains in woodland management and reforestation of the eighteenth and nineteenth centuries were largely undone by the political turmoil of the 1860s and 1870s. From about 1875 onward an explosion in demand for timber to build cities, factories, railroads, and so forth combined with access to new logging technology to produce a surge in timber harvesting that denuded more mountainsides. Together with expanded consumption of mulch and fodder materials, this surge led to escalating erosion, flooding, and downstream devastation. During the early twentieth century remedial measures slowly brought the situation under control as the government employed its powers of regulation, the technology of concrete construction, and a somewhat improved silviculture to manage woodland use, promote reforestation, and control erosion and water flow.

By the late 1930s many areas had been reforested and many waterways effectively controlled. However, the warfare and urban reconstruction of the years 1937 to 1950 consumed most of Japan's timber stands and precipitated a renewed siege of erosion and downstream damage. This situation led during the 1950s and 1960s to a massive nationwide program of reforestation that by 1990 had transformed about 40 percent of the country's woodland into even-aged monoculture conifer stands. By then, however, trends in international trade had made timber imports cheaper than the domestic harvest, and as of this writing Japan has vast acreages of hand-planted conifer stands that are aging poorly, with overcrowded trees growing spindly and becoming subject to windthrow (uprooting and overturning by wind) and snow breakage. But, in a happy trade-off, as the stands disintegrate, the forest floor is exposed to sunlight, varied new growth starts, and a habitat more favorable to birds and other creatures reestablishes itself.

As that last comment suggests, the slow disintegration of hand-planted conifer stands, a trend lamented by professional foresters, constitutes a bright spot—perhaps the only bright spot—in the broader story of biodiversity in industrial Japan. Otherwise the story is the poorly documented one found everywhere of vulnerable species being crippled and consumed by environmental pollution, losing habitat, and being pushed out by exotic competitors. Agricultural and industrial contaminants achieve the first result; diverse forms of urban sprawl accomplish the second; and imports, mainly accidental, introduce the third. As of this writing there seems to be, in Japan as elsewhere, only minimal countermovement to these trends despite the presence of a small but dedicated and sometimes vocal environmentalist movement. So future chapters of the story surely will be instructive.

Conrad Totman

Further Reading

George, T. S. (2001). *Minamata: Pollution and the struggle for democracy in postwar Japan*. Cambridge, MA: Harvard University Asian Center.

Huddle, N., & Reich, M. (1975). *Island of dreams: Environmental crisis in Japan*. Tokyo, Japan: Autumn Press.

Jannetta, A. B. (1987). *Epidemics and mortality in early modern Japan*. Princeton, NJ: Princeton University Press.

Johnston, W. (1995). *The modern epidemic: A history of tuberculosis in Japan*. Cambridge, MA: Harvard University Press.

Kiple, K. F., (Ed.). (1993). *The Cambridge world history of human disease*. Cambridge, UK: Cambridge University Press.

Kurosu, S. (2002). Studies on historical demography and family in early modern Japan. *Early Modern Japan*, *10*(1), 3–21, 66–71.

Morris-Suzuki, T. (1998). Environmental problems and perceptions in early industrial Japan. In M. Elvin & Liu T.-J. (Eds.). *Sediments of time: Environment and society in Chinese history* (pp. 756–780). Cambridge, UK: Cambridge University Press.

Souyri, P. F. (2001). *The world turned upside down: Medieval Japanese society*. New York: Cambridge University Press.

Taeuber, I. (1958). *The population of Japan*. Princeton, NJ: Princeton University Press.

Totman, C. (1993). *Early modern Japan*. Berkeley and Los Angeles: University of California Press.

Totman, C. (2000). *A history of Japan*. Oxford, UK: Blackwell Publishers.

Tsurumi, E. P. (1990). *Factory girls: Women in the thread mills of Meiji Japan*. Princeton, NJ: Princeton University Press.

Walker, B. L. (2001). Commercial growth and environmental change in early modern Japan: Hachinohe's wild boar famine of 1749. *Journal of Asian Studies*, *60*(2), 329–351.

Walker, B. L. (2001). *The conquest of Ainu lands: Ecology and culture in Japanese expansion, 1590–1800*. Berkeley and Los Angeles: University of California Press.

Japan, Ancient

The people of Japan, like people everywhere, have dealt with their environment in three basic ways: as foragers living off the natural yield of their ambient biome, as agriculturalists manipulating that biome to maximize desired yield, or as dwellers in an industrial society, relying heavily on the accumulated energy of past life, mainly as stored in fossil fuels. In Japan the forager system of sustenance lasted for millennia down to about 400 BCE, giving way then to a relatively simple system of agriculture that persisted until around 1200 CE. During the thirteenth century or thereabouts a more intensive agricultural regimen began taking shape, and it lasted into the twentieth century, when it was supplemented and largely supplanted by the arrangements of industrial society.

Forager Society (to 400 BCE)

Archaeologists find appreciable traces of human presence in Japan that date to about 50,000 years ago. Following the final Pleistocene glacial maximum around 18,000 years ago, the small resident population survived global warming, loss of lowland to rising sea level, and the associated disappearance of megafauna. It did so by modifying its hunting, fishing, and trapping devices to capture smaller, fleeter game and inshore seafood. People also developed techniques of maritime travel and, most importantly perhaps, adopted pottery for cooking and storage. The use of pottery made hitherto inedible or perishable foods available for regular consumption, thereby enabling people to diversify their dietary foundation.

During the millennia from around 11,000 to 2,500 BCE, they improved their housing, clothing and foraging techniques. They enlarged and multiplied their settlements, developed local social structures, evinced religious and aesthetic sensibilities in their burial and craft practices, and devised basic trading arrangements that linked coastal and highland populations to mutual advantage. From about 2,500 BCE onward, however, a sustained period of climatic cooling seems to have modified forest composition, reducing the capacity of inland regions to sustain human settlement and causing the overall population to drop, perhaps by half or more, from its earlier peak, estimated at 250,000.

The cooling trend also fostered simple forms of plant nurturing, however, especially along coastal areas where the advance of shorelines created new strips of mixed scrub and grassy growth. This trend then gave way around 400 BCE to the rapid spread of fully developed forms of tillage after their introduction into northwest Kyushu (the southernmost of Japan's four main islands) from the Asian mainland.

Early Agriculture (400 BCE–700 CE)

The fully developed tillage cycle—breaking soil, spreading select seed, nurturing its growth, and harvesting and processing the yield—spread eastward from Kyushu to central Japan by 200 CE or earlier, being disseminated by both immigrants and example. East of the Kinai region (the area around present-day Kyoto and Osaka), however, southwestern Japan's predominantly broadleaf evergreen woodland gave way to cooler deciduous forest that sustained a richer mix of game and edible wild plant matter. Tillage practices, being relatively less advantageous there, were adopted much more slowly and did not spread across the northeast for several more centuries.

Even in western Japan the earlier forager practices persisted for generations, being displaced only gradually as the tasks of agriculture consumed more time; as more and more land was cleared to grow barley, millet, rice, and diverse garden vegetables; and as surviving areas that could yield game and wild edibles diminished. This shift from foraging to horticulture slowly transformed the landscape. Vast sweeps of terrain that had once been nearly uninterrupted woodland became intricately patterned areas of hillside forest intermingled with lowland fields and, here and there, the scattered huts and homesteads of cultivators and their social betters. As centuries passed, more and more of the land was utilized as paddy (irrigated rice) fields, which during the early weeks of cropping would sparkle brightly as sunshine reflected off the water's placid surface.

Land clearance of this magnitude must have changed Japan's biotic composition. Humans, their collaborating flora and fauna—select grains, other domesticated plants, decorative flora, chestnut and mulberry trees, silkworms, horses, oxen, dogs, chickens and so forth—and opportunistic parasites (such as mosquitoes, house mice, and various microbes) clearly expanded their presence. Diverse trees and those understory species that preferred lowland forest canopy clearly lost, being confined to residual sites or less favorable terrain.

On the other hand, because Japan is extremely mountainous, most of the realm remained in high forest, scarcely disturbed by the multiplying humans on the flatlands below. Furthermore, land clearance created uncountable kilometers of forest edge, with its combination of sunlight and nearby shade and shelter, and that change produced a lot of terrain that could support richly diversified and vigorous flora and fauna. Also, as noted above, paddy culture created expanses of relatively warm, shallow water that sustained not only rice plants and mosquitoes but numerous other forms of life, of which frogs may have been the most noisy but stately herons and other water birds are the most well known. In some localities, and especially around urban centers, as we note below, clearance of lowland and adjacent hillside surely reduced species diversity. On balance, however, one suspects (evidence one way or the other being too thin to settle the matter) that as a whole the landscape changes down to 700 CE yielded a net gain in biodiversity and total biomass production, even as they tilted the balance against a number of creatures.

Polity and Ecosystem (700–1200)

The spread of agriculture enabled the realm to support a much larger human population, and as centuries advanced, immigration and domestic fecundity kept the numbers rising, probably to the vicinity of 5 million by 700 CE. As population became more dense, with settlements larger and more numerous, human interaction intensified, manifesting itself in friction, conflict, social stratification, and the emergence of organized groups that engaged in warfare and gradual political consolidation.

By 700 CE these trends had eventuated in the formation of a centralized political order that was headquartered in the Kinai Basin in central Japan and encompassed a realm stretching from the Kanto Plain (the large plain on which present-day Tokyo is located) westward to Kyushu. This polity's highly stratified, hereditary ruling elite managed to retain its position for nearly half a millennium, doing so through an elaborate system of interest-group politics, regulatory oversight, and tribute taking that extracted rice, diverse other products, and corvée labor from the general populace in a regularized manner.

Beginning in the 670s, the regime's hereditary hegemons, known in English as emperors, launched a series of major city-building enterprises, the most famous results being Nara and Kyoto. The cities were intended to give emperors, their hundreds of subordinates, and thousands of service personnel an appropriately expansive and elegant capital. Their existence created in Japan an unusually clear dichotomy between center and hinterland: Power flowed outward from the capital; tribute goods and labor flowed in. And these processes entailed continual movement of people and goods along the highways and waterways of the realm.

Cumulatively this activity served to overload the ecosystem of the Kinai Basin, but it seems to have had little harmful environmental impact more broadly, even though it imposed heavy burdens on the hinterland populace. Thus, in regard to wildlife, the evidence, while very thin, suggests that little changed. Doubtless deforestation of the Kinai region, which accompanied city construction and maintenance, altered its faunal composition. But with most of the realm still forested, and with so much open land consisting of slender strips that ascended forest-girt river valleys, one suspects that few species went extinct or became endangered. The native fauna, which included deer, bear, boar, badgers, wolves, foxes, weasels, rabbits, myriad smaller creatures, and a rich array of birds and marine life, survived into later centuries.

Perhaps the basic reason for this political system's apparently modest environmental impact was that in most respects its creation entailed no noteworthy agronomic or other technological changes that would have increased primary production and, thereby, added to human demand on the ecosystem. In addition, elite pressure was constrained by the difficulty of transport, the limits of government power, and the modest density of population outside the few urban centers.

The Kinai Region: Deforestation and Soil Erosion

On the other hand, two aspects of the system had substantial environmental ramifications. First, the elite's preferred architectural technique made huge new demands on the ecosystem. An older thatch-roof-and-post-hole method of construction that made do with modest quantities of smallish trees and other growth gave way to a monumental style of palace and monastery architecture that required large trees and vast quantities of timber, fuel for tile making, and labor-intensive stone masonry.

Once the great structures had been erected, moreover, they had to be repaired and rebuilt after fire or other calamity. In addition, they housed large, long-lasting concentrations of disproportionately privileged people, who placed heavy, sustained burdens on their surroundings, primarily for foodstuffs, fuel, and textiles. Because of the severe constraints that topography and technological limitations imposed on transport, these burdens were particularly onerous in the Kinai Basin. One by one forests in that region were reduced to fire-prone scrub, and over time areas once celebrated for fine timber became known for their fuel wood. As the eighth century advanced, problems of wildfire, erosion, soil deterioration, stream silting, flooding, and drought became common, prompting government admonitions, decrees, and regulations, and the acquisition of timber from ever farther afield. By the tenth century one sees modifications in construction practice, and a gradual shrinkage in the scale of urban aristocratic splendor.

Disease

The second ecologically significant aspect of the new polity was that the travel associated with it, travel both within Japan and between Japan and the continent, served to disseminate pathogens widely about the realm—smallpox and measles most destructively. Because general immunities within the scattered and periodically exposed populace did not develop until the twelfth century or so, these pathogens precipitated repeated epidemics that decimated the population, stunting its growth and, it appears, causing it to fluctuate in the vicinity of 5 to 6 million for some three centuries after 700 CE.

For a few decades people flocked to Nara, thousands being brought as corvée labor, others coming or staying in hopes of prospering through association with the favored few. By 750, however, disease and hardship were trimming the city populace, and for the next two or three centuries the central and western regions of Japan seem to have experienced net losses. Those were balanced, more or less, by gains in the east.

The Population Shift to the East

Growth in the eastern marches was facilitated by the region's relative backwardness. Much potential arable land was still forested, and the Kanto Plain, Japan's broadest, was blessed with rich volcanic loam that could sustain extensive dry-field cropping—which was taxed little if at all—as well as stretches of paddy fields. In central and western Japan, by contrast, reclamation work entailed more and more the labor-intensive and problem-plagued tasks of terracing hillsides to form small stairlike fields and opening swampland and flood plains where severe downpours could in a few days destroy entire swaths of arable land and irrigation works that had required years to construct. In consequence, a long-term eastward shift in the locus of population and output proceeded, weakening the ruling elite vis-à-vis local leaders and helping usher in the later agricultural age of growth and change.

The general demographic stabilization after 750, together with the lack of substantial change in agronomic technique, severely limited the regime's fiscal foundation, fostering competition for resources within the slowly growing, differentiating elite. Contests for advantage produced a gradual redistribution of power and privilege and, by the tenth century, decay of Kyoto, the capital city whose grandeur had been so central to the whole edifice of hereditary rule.

Insurgencies proliferated; disorder flourished, and by 1200 there had emerged among the favored few a culture of nostalgia for an older, better day, when people understood propriety, beauty prevailed, and life proceeded as it ought to. As this elite was displaced during the twelfth through fourteenth centuries by new claimants to privilege, these latter embraced a more modest aesthetic that placed less demand on the ecosystem, even as cultivators and woodsmen developed more effective ways of exploiting it. Together these developments allowed the rise of Japan's more recent age of social growth and dynamism.

Conrad Totman

Further Reading

Brown, D. M. (Ed.). (1993). *The Cambridge history of Japan: Vol.1. Ancient Japan*. Cambridge, UK: Cambridge University Press.

Farris, W. W. (1985). *Population, disease, and land in early Japan, 645–900*. Cambridge, MA: Harvard University Press.

Imamura, K. (1996). *Prehistoric Japan: New perspectives on insular East Asia*. Honolulu: University of Hawaii Press.

Pearson, R. J. (Ed.). (1986). *Windows on the Japanese past: Studies in archaeology and prehistory*. Ann Arbor: Center for Japanese Studies, University of Michigan.

Piggott, J. R. (1997). *The emergence of Japanese kingship*. Stanford, CA: Stanford University Press.

Shively, D. H., & McCullough, W. H. (Eds.). (1999). *The Cambridge history of Japan: Vol. 2. Heian Japan*. Cambridge, UK: Cambridge University Press.

Totman, C. (1989). *The green archipelago: Forestry in preindustrial Japan*. Berkeley and Los Angeles: University of California Press.

Totman, C. (2000). *A history of Japan*. Oxford, UK: Blackwell Publishers.

Jefferson, Thomas
(1743–1826)
U.S. statesman

Thomas Jefferson championed a scientific view of nature, promoted agrarian stewardship, and intensified western expansion for the early American republic. Jefferson was born in Albemarle County, Virginia, in view of the Blue Ridge Mountains. In 1760 he entered the College of William and Mary and developed an early interest in natural rights philosophy (a branch of philosophy that is based on the notion that nature grants certain political rights to all individuals, which cannot be contradicted by governments) and the natural sciences. Jefferson exemplified this background in natural rights in 1776 with his Declaration of Independence, premising his demands upon "the Laws of Nature and of Nature's God" (Miller 1988, 136).

The Jefferson-influenced 1785 federal Land Ordinance blended his scientific and agrarian ideals. The Land Ordinance asserted that a geometric grid would map the fields, roads, and towns of new American settlements in the West. Jefferson's Land Ordinance designated 160-acre plots specifically for smaller landowners, thus opening the West to more democratic land use among whites. The Land Ordinance translated natural features such as rivers, forests, and mountains into scientifically controlled property.

Jefferson's interest in the natural sciences culminated in his 1787 *Notes on the State of Virginia*. *Notes* offered extensive scientific lists characterizing the flora, fauna, geography, and climate of Virginia. Also in *Notes*, lyrical discussions of navigable rivers and fertile land served as physical evidence for his argument that white, self-sufficient farmers, continually regenerating their freedom through the cultivation of nature, should form the basis of a democratic society.

While serving as president of the United States (1801–1809), Jefferson in 1803 authorized the Louisiana

Purchase, which epitomized his expansive, scientific, and agrarian vision for American western lands. The purchase allowed Jefferson to claim as American space the 1.2 million square kilometers reaching from the Mississippi River to the Rocky Mountains, regardless of numerous Native American claims to the land. In 1804 Jefferson organized the famed Lewis and Clark expedition to the Pacific Ocean. Jefferson requested extensive environmental reporting that would detail the possibility of a "northwest passage," seek the potential existence of unknown animal species, record basic variations of flora and fauna, and report on the river systems of the West—all in hopes of developing markets for the imagined agrarians who would eventually "civilize" Jefferson's West.

After his presidency, Jefferson retired to his family, mansion, and plantation slaves at Monticello, Virginia. Jefferson devoted himself to the business and science of agriculture. He invented an improved plow, experimented with crop rotation and early chemical fertilizers, and continued his close study of climatic and environmental change. He also founded the University of Virginia in 1825 and included natural history, natural philosophy, geography, and botany in the curriculum. Jefferson died on the fourth of July in 1826.

Scholars continue to debate Jefferson's role in environmental history. Some see Jefferson as an early conservationist, citing as evidence his devotion to reducing the intense environmental impacts of tobacco planting and monoculture, his purchase of Virginia's "Natural Bridge" as a public trust, his efforts to popularize nature as a subject of study, and his inquiries into vanishing animal species. Others criticize Jefferson for opening the West to limitless environmental and cultural exploitation, for assuming that nature should be scientifically controlled as a garden, and for theorizing that freedom requires an individualistic system of property.

John Hausdoerffer

Further Reading

Browers, M. L. (1999). Jefferson's land ethic: Environmentalist ideas in Notes on the state of Virginia. Environmental Ethics, 21 (1)43–57.

Engeman, T. S. (Ed.). (2000). Thomas Jefferson and the politics of nature. Notre Dame, IN: University of Notre Dame Press.

Jefferson, T. (1982). Notes on the state of Virginia (William Peden, Ed.). Chapel Hill: University of North Carolina Press.

McEwan, B. (1991). Thomas Jefferson: Farmer. Jefferson, NC: McFarland.

Miller, C. A. (1988). Jefferson and nature: An interpretation. Baltimore: Johns Hopkins University Press.

Johnson, Lyndon

(1908–1973)
U.S. president

Lyndon Baines Johnson was president of the United States between 1963 and 1969, a time when environmentalism emerged as a major social movement in the United States. During his presidency, Johnson signed into law over three hundred pieces of legislation relating to environmental quality. Although this impressive legislative record might suggest that Johnson was an environmental leader, closer examination of the nature of these programs and his views on environmental matters reveals a more complicated picture.

Johnson developed his approach to environmental matters during the Great Depression of the 1930s when he served as head of a federal government youth program in Texas and then as a congressman from that state. He was an avid supporter of President Franklin Delano Roosevelt's New Deal and the president's attempts to alleviate poverty through conservation projects. Like Roosevelt, Johnson believed that the conservation of natural resources and development projects would improve the lives of all Americans.

Johnson brought this belief into the White House when he became president after the assassination of John F. Kennedy in 1963. Johnson proved more successful than Kennedy at passing legislation to protect America's air, water, public lands, and urban environments. During his presidency, he passed the Wilderness Act (1964), Water Quality Act (1965), Endangered Species Act (1966), and Air Quality Act (1967). Many acts passed during these years were later improved and strengthened, but this burst of environmental legislation laid a foundation for the more substantial initiatives approved during the late 1960s and early 1970s.

Johnson often linked environmental concerns to social programs, his primary interest. The Great Society programs that he advocated aimed to improve the welfare of all Americans through initiatives to relieve poverty, promote education, and improve medical care. Environmental protection dovetailed well with these initiatives and was seen as a means to create a more equitable society. Ultimately, the deepening crisis over American military intervention in Vietnam undermined his presidency and prevented him from implementing all social and environmental and social facets of the Great Society.

Although Johnson was not a spokesperson for environmental issues in the manner of Theodore Roosevelt or Franklin Roosevelt, he did have influential supporters for such issues in his administration. Secretary of the Interior Stewart L. Udall (originally appointed by President Kennedy) was well regarded by Johnson and advised him on environmental matters. Johnson appointed his wife, Lady Bird Johnson, to head committees to beautify interstate highways and Washington, DC. Lady Bird's emphasis on aesthetic concerns reflected the greater emphasis that Americans placed on quality of life during the mid-twentieth century.

Given that Johnson was busy directing the Vietnam War and promoting his Great Society programs, it is not surprising that environmental concerns failed to figure highly on his agenda. Yet, because he did not actively oppose many environmental proposals and was an astute politician, Johnson was able to develop a better environmental record than that of most presidents after World War II.

Robert M. Wilson

Further Reading

Dallek, R. (1998). *Flawed giant: Lyndon Johnson and his times, 1961–1973*. New York: Oxford University Press.

Gould, L. L. (1988). *Lady Bird Johnson and the environment*. Lawrence: University Press of Kansas.

Kearns, D. (1976). *Lyndon Johnson and the American dream*. New York: Harper & Row.

Melosi, M. V. (1987). Lyndon Johnson and environmental policy. In R. A. Divine (Ed.), *The Johnson years: Vol. 2. Vietnam, the environment, and science* (pp. 113–149) Lawrence: University Press of Kansas.

Smith, T. S. (1995). John Kennedy, Stewart Udall, and New Frontier conservation. *Pacific Historical Review*, (3), 329–362.

Journalism *See* Media

Judaism

A creation religion like Christianity and Islam, Judaism gives nature a significant role in the relationship be- tween God and humanity. The Jewish calendar and holy days tie Judaism tightly to the cycles of nature. The seven-day week ends in the Sabbath, a day of rest commemorating God's rest after the six days of creation. The Jewish calendar is based both on lunar and solar cycles: The first of each month is the dark of the moon; and the calendar composes a cycle of renewal and regeneration ending with Yom Kippur. Three holy days, Passover, Shavuoth, and Succoth, replay the deliverance from Egypt, with its testing in the desert and promise of a land flowing with milk and honey.

Even so, Judaism emphasizes not nature but the commands of the Torah, the first five books of the Bible. Revealed in the desert amidst numerous miraculous manifestations of God's power in nature, the Torah testifies that nature is not sufficient. Nature tells of God and praises God but cannot guide behavior, conduct, or justice. Indeed rabbis traditionally taught that nature's beauty distracted from study of the Torah. In Judaism, humans are intermediaries between nature and God. Nature is not intermediary between humanity and God. Jews believe themselves to be uniquely responsive to God's commandments and to have a unique role in the future of the earth. The commandments constitute a guide to holiness in everyday life. As a people they must do in thought, word, and deed all the Torah expects. As long as Israel obeys, the land of milk and honey is their heritage, and Earth will be blessed. Disobedience brings natural disaster. Adam's sin resulted in the curse of the Earth. Human violence and corruption produced the Flood. Thus humans link God and creation.

The Torah and its commentaries, the Talmud and Midrash, view nature primarily in terms of its social utility or of human justice. God created humans to take nature and make it useful to mankind (although like tenants or managers, we do not own the earth). Amplified by demands for social justice by Isaiah and the prophets, a significant portion of Jewish commandments constrains individual behavior and action for the common good. Laws with environmental implications include good treatment of animals, sabbatical and Jubilee years of rest for the land, the amount of green space to be kept around settlements, and restrictions on actions that hurt others, such as polluting the air. The two most discussed rules are *za'ar ba'ale hayyim*, cause no unnecessary pain to animals, and *bal tashchit*, do not destroy, derived from Deuteronomy 20:19–20, whose meaning rabbis expanded to forbid the wanton destruction of any socially useful thing. Environmentalist Jews have underlined the environmental implica-

The Sacredness of Trees

Even in times of war, Hebrews received specific prohibitions about how trees could be used, as these passages from the Book of Deuteronomy indicate:

19. When thou shalt besiege a city a long time, in making war against it to take it, thou shalt not destroy the trees thereof by forcing an axe against them: for thou mayest eat of them, and thou shalt not cut them down (for the tree of the field is man's life) to employ them in the siege:

20. Only the trees which thou knowest that they be not trees for meat, thou shalt destroy and cut them down; and thou shalt build bulwarks against the city that maketh war with thee, until it be subdued.

Source: Deuteronomy 20: 19–20 (KJV).

tions of *bal tashchit* and made it a basic principle of Jewish environmental ethics.

Judaic tradition has in general emphasized rationalism and study and shied from mysticism. A major exception is the kabbalah, which like Christian mysticism emphasizes God's immanence in creation, which is a symbol or emanation of God. Kabbalah has had a strong influence mainly on Hasidism. Nevertheless, in contrast to Christians like Schelling, Wordsworth, Emerson, and Muir, to whom the beauty of wild nature led one to the creator spirit, leading Jewish environmental thinkers and leaders rejected mysticism for rationalism. Major American environmental author Paul Ehrlich, of German Jewish descent, in his 1968 bestseller, *The Population Bomb*, advocates government restriction of procreation (restricting the individual for the common good) to prevent disasters overpopulation will cause, and in other books defends the rational, scientific foundations of environmentalism. Jewish environmentalists of Eastern European ancestry tend toward radicalism. Murray Bookchin fiercely resists the mysticism and "biocentrism" of deep ecology and advocates "social ecology," a vision of a world of small, just, democratic, and nonhierarchical communities tied closely to the land. In *The Closing Circle*, the biologist Barry Commoner, a famous antinuclear activist in the 1950s and 1960s, linked social justice and elimination of poverty with socialistic, technocratic solutions to the environmental crisis.

Despite their leadership in social and political reform movements, Jews have not been prominent in nature preservation. Israel is the exception. There a strong feeling of connection with the land, promised by God to Jews in the Bible, created the Society for the Preservation of Nature in Israel in 1953, whose founders included author, photographer, and activist Azaria Alon. Israelis have established parks, in part with the intent to preserve the animals, plants, and landscapes mentioned in the Bible (particularly in the Neot Kedumim preserve). The Israeli organization Israel Union for Environmental Defense helps communities defend endangered ecosystems. In Israel, too, landscape art has flourished (although rare in Jewish art elsewhere), notably in paintings by Reuven Rubin and Anna Ticho. Historically the most successful Jewish back-to-the-land movement is Israel's kibbutz movement. However, in Israel development has always overshadowed environmentalism.

Recently Judaism, especially in the United States, has participated in a greening of religion in general. Several organizations promote an ecologically sensitive Judaism. An early group was Shomrei Adamah ("Guardians of the Earth"), founded in 1990, now mainly a support group for the Teva [Earth] Learning Center in New York City. The most significant group in the United States is the umbrella organization, the Coalition on the Environment and Jewish Life, founded in 1993. Groups such as the Center for Tikkun Olam of New York City have drawn inspiration from *tikkun olam*, a Jewish principle that God created humans to repair the world. In the United Kingdom, the Noah Project, London, promotes environmental awareness in the Jewish community. In Israel, American-born Alon Tal of Arava Institute of Environmental Studies is perhaps the leading environmental activist.

Thus Judaism has produced an environmental theology and ethic that emphasizes rationalism, social utility and justice, and the land of Israel. Inspired by traditional ethics and values, Jews both secular and religious have contributed uniquely to global environmentalism.

Mark Stoll

Further Reading

Bernstein, E. (1998). *Ecology & the Jewish spirit: Where nature and the sacred meet*. Woodstock, VT: Jewish Lights.

Bernstein, E. & Fink, D. (1992). *Let the earth teach you Torah: A guide to teaching Jewish ecological wisdom*. Wyncote, PA: Shomrei Adamah.

Chalier, C. (1989). *L'Alliance avec la nature*. Paris: Les Éditions du Cerf.

Elon, A, Hyman, N. M., & Waskow, A. O. (1999). *Trees, earth, and Torah: A Tu b'Shvat anthology*. Philadelphia: Jewish Publication Society.

Gerstenfeld, M. (1998). *Judaism, environmentalism and the environment: Mapping and analysis*. Jerusalem: Rubin Mass.

Jacob, M. (1999). "Judaism and Ecology Bibliography." Forum on Religion and Ecology Research, Center for the Study of World Religions, Harvard University Website. Retrieved August 22, 2002, from http: //environment.harvard.edu/religion/research/judbiblio.html

Rakover, N. (1993). *Ekhut ha-sevivah: hebetim raFDýyoniyim u-mishpatiyim ba-mekorot a-Yehudiyim*. Jerusalem: Moreshet ha-mishpat be-Yisraýel.

Rose, A. (Ed.). (1992). *Judaism and ecology*. New York: Cassell.

Tal, A. (2002). *Pollution in a promised land: an environmental history of Israel*. Berkeley: University of California Press.

Waskow, A. (Ed.). (2000). *Torah of the earth: Exploring 4,000 years of ecology in Jewish thought*, 2 vols. Woodstock, VT: Jewish Lights.

Keep America Beautiful

Few organizations have had greater impact on mainstream American environmental consciousness during the post-World War II era than has Keep America Beautiful, Inc. (KAB). Since being organized as a nonprofit corporation by an alliance of beverage, cigarette, and container companies in 1953, it has engaged in a variety of efforts aimed at getting individuals to reduce litter and, later, to practice recycling. By the year 2000 KAB had two hundred corporate sponsors and over five hundred community affiliates spreading its influence across the United States. Although acclaimed by some for its success in raising environmental awareness, others have criticized KAB for allegedly distorting environmentalism to serve the interests of its corporate membership.

This paradox is evident in KAB's best-known campaign, which centered around one of the most memorable ads in television history. In the ad, which first aired on Earth Day in 1971, a Native American actor encounters a densely littered landscape. As a narrator's voice-over admonishes, "Some people have a deep abiding respect for the natural beauty that was once this country, and some people don't. People start pollution, people can stop it," the noble Native American turns toward the camera to reveal a large tear running down his cheek.

Although later critics said the "crying Indian" ad perpetuated the "noble savage" stereotype of the ecological Native American, the controversy among environmentalists mostly centered upon the purpose of KAB. To supporters, KAB's ads, combined with its community cleanup drives and educational materials distributed to schools, were important weapons in the fight against litter. To detractors, KAB's slogan, "People start pollution, people can stop it," typified its effort to place the blame for pollution on individuals in order to avert the public's gaze from the more serious problem of industrial pollution produced by KAB's corporate fraternity.

KAB's motives were further questioned when it became a leading opponent of 1970s "bottle bill" legislation to require returnable beverage containers. Although the ten states that enacted bottle bills reported a sharp decline in litter, KAB opposed all state bills and an attempted national bill. Returnable containers cost beverage producers millions of dollars in labor costs, and container manufacturers and solid-waste companies stood to lose a substantial amount of business.

By the late 1970s KAB expanded its antilitter campaign to include recycling. Supporters cheered the movement as a means to reduce the volume of solid waste threatening to overwhelm municipal landfills. Others, however, made a case that KAB's corporations benefited most from community recycling programs. Recycling provided an image makeover for disposable containers, transforming them from waste into productive resources that provided jobs in the recycling industry and raw materials for remanufacturing. In the process, public opposition to disposables diminished. Additionally, community recycling programs meant that cities provided the labor and picked up the tab for sorting and collecting containers, assuring an abundant supply of raw materials at a low cost for bottle and can manufacturers.

Although its efforts appear designed to benefit its corporate membership, KAB, with its well-financed publicity campaigns, has nevertheless planted a seed of environmental awareness in the minds of many Americans who might not have otherwise been reached. It is conceivable that some of those individuals have acted upon that awareness in ways that KAB could not anticipate.

Thomas Jundt

Further Reading

Aleiss, A. (1999). Iron Eyes Cody: Wannabe Indian. *Cineaste, 25* (1), 30–31.

Hays, S. P. (1987). *Beauty, health, and permanence: Environmental politics in the United States, 1955–1985.* Cambridge, UK: Cambridge University Press.

Krech, S., III. (1999). *The ecological Indian: Myth and history.* New York: W. W. Norton.

Paletz, D. L., Pearson, R. E., & Willis, D. L. (1977). *Politics in public service advertising on television.* New York: Praeger.

Weinberg, A. S., Pellow, D. N., & Schnaiberg, A. (2000). *Urban recycling and the search for sustainable community development.* Princeton, NJ: Princeton University Press.

Williams, T. (1990). The metamorphosis of Keep America Beautiful. *Audubon, 92* (2), 124–134.

Kelly, Petra
(1947–1992)
Founder of the West German Green Party

Petra Kelly was a founder of the West German Green Party (*die Grünen*, 1980) and member of the Bundestag (West German parliament) between 1983 and 1990. A charismatic and tireless campaigner for peace, justice, democracy, and environmental protection not only in Germany but also around the world, Petra Kelly became one of the best-known and most influential figures of the twentieth century.

Born Petra Karin Lehmann in Günzburg, Bavaria, on 29 November 1947, she moved to the United States with her mother and stepfather John Kelly in 1959. In 1970 she graduated *cum laude* in international politics from American University in Washington, D.C., then returned to Europe to work in the European Commission in Brussels, Belgium. During the next decade she completed her political apprenticeship, working in the Commission in Brussels and back in Germany, with the political groups that eventually merged to become *die Grünen*. When the first direct elections to the European Parliament took place in 1979, she was elected head of the candidate list for *die Grünen*.

Throughout Europe, but particularly in Germany, the 1979 decision by the North Atlantic Treaty Organization (NATO) to station U.S. "first-strike" nuclear missiles in Europe mobilized a large and vociferous peace movement. Petra Kelly was at the heart of it. She instigated and organized a highly publicized international war crimes tribunal "for the possession of weapons of mass destruction" held symbolically in Nürnberg, West Germany, in February 1983. During this time she met Gert Bastian, a NATO officer who resigned in 1981 over the decision to place the first strike nuclear weapons on German soil, and with whom Petra lived until the time of her death.

In March 1983, Petra Kelly and Gert Bastian were among twenty-seven members of *die Grünen* to be elected to the Bundestag. She was elected one of three speakers of the Green parliamentary group and joined the Bundestag Foreign Relations Committee. Her international work included active support for the emerging dissident movement in East Germany and for the campaign for an independent Tibet. She received several awards, including the Right Livelihood Award (the alternative Nobel Prize) in 1982, and she published a number of books, including *Um Hoffnug kampfen* (Fighting for Hope, 1983) and *The Anguish of Tibet* (1991).

After *die Grünen* lost all its seats in the first post-reunification German election in 1990, Petra Kelly turned her attentions to the Grace Kelly Foundation for the care of children with cancer (her sister Grace died of cancer in 1970). She participated in a wide range of political meetings and conferences, and began to lay plans for a future that included a return to Brussels, possibly as a member of the European Parliament, and a major U.S. television interview series.

When Gert Bastian shot Petra Kelly before turning the gun on himself in October 1992, the news reverberated around the world. It is conjectured that he feared the impending opening of files held by the East German secret police (the Stasi) might reveal contacts the Stasi had with him in the early 1980s. The response to Petra Kelly's death, in Germany and internationally, revealed the extent to which she had inspired others and given practical help to so many during a short but extraordinary life.

Sara Parkin

Further Reading

Kotler, A. (Ed.). (1994). *Thinking green: Essays on environmentalism, feminism and non violence.* Berkeley, CA: Paramax Press.

Beckmann, L., & Kopelew, L. (Eds.). (1993). *Gedenken Heit Erinnern.* Gottingen, Germany: Lamur.

Paige, G., & Guilatt, S. (Eds.). (1992). *Petra Kelly: Non violence speaks to power.* Honolulu, Hawaii: Centre for Global Non Violence.

Parkin, S. (1994). *The life and death of Petra Kelly.* London: Pandora.

Korea

(200 est. pop. 69 million)

Korea, as used to refer to the peninsula, is derived from *Goryeo,* the name of a tenth- to fourteenth-century dynasty. *Daehan Minguk* is the term Koreans use for the Republic of Korea (South Korea), while the Democratic People's Republic of Korea (North Korea) is called *Chosun Minchu-chui Inmin Konghwa-guk.* Korea is remarkably uniform in ethnicity, despite splitting into two countries after World War II. Its historically large population, as in many Asian nations, induced most environmental change with the advent of twentieth-century technology.

The two Koreas comprise a mountainous, peninsular region of 222,073 square kilometers—roughly the size of Great Britain. The Amnok and Tuman Rivers form its northern border with the Chinese province of Manchuria and twenty kilometers of eastern Russia. The Sea of Japan separates Korea from the main Japanese island of Honshu by approximately 200 kilometers, while the East China and Yellow Seas form the south and west boundaries, respectively. Approximately 75 percent of Korea is uninhabitable due to steep topography. The Hangang, which flows through Seoul, is another major river. At 514 kilometers long, it is the largest river in water volume within the Korean peninsula.

The Korean peninsula tilts down from east to west, through a process that began approximately 100 million years ago in the late Mesozoic era. Most of the peninsula has a granite basement overlain with mountains of sandstone and marble. The rugged T'aebaek Sanmaek Mountains drop swiftly to the unbroken shoreline of the east coast, while the west coast is more roll-ing with a highly indented shoreline and strong tidal influence. Volcanic mountains include the highest peaks at the northern and southern ends of the peninsula.

The climate is dominated by late summer monsoons, when half the annual 1,000 millimeters of rain falls, and a dry season from October through March. Precipitation is approximately twice mainland China's and half of Japan's. Temperatures range from subtropical at the southern tip to Siberian at the far north. Vegetation reflects the varied climate, with subtropical vegetation at the southern tip and islands, temperate deciduous forest at low and middle elevations, and coniferous forests at northern latitudes and higher elevations. Forested land comprises 65 percent of the landscape, with almost half of that consisting of coniferous forests. Major tree species include red pine, Korean white pine, larch, and oak.

Common fauna include river deer, fox, and ring-necked pheasant, while black bear, lynx, squirrel, tiger, and weasel are less common. Endangered species include the white-bellied black woodpecker, Japanese crested ibis, white stork, black stork, whooper swan, Manchurian crane, musk deer, and golden eagle. Any remaining tigers are thought to live near Korea's highest elevation of Mount Paekdusan, 2,744 meters above sea level, on the Chinese border.

Early Korea

The first tribal settlers came to Korea approximately 30,000 years ago from central and northern Asia. Both Korean and Siberian creation myths include bears as central figures. Korean folklore dates the birth of the nation at 2333 BCE, associating it with the semi-deity Tan'gun, who was born under a *pakdal* (birch) tree. Since then many altars have been made of birch. His successor, Kija, reportedly planted rows of willows in Pyongyang, the descendants of which still grow there, making it the "willow capital." The Cholmun were hunter-fishers living in coastal zones and rivers from 3000 to 1000 BCE. The Mumun were a Bronze Age people with a more agricultural, sedentary lifestyle that included rice cultivation. Iron Age Koreans assimilated two main Chinese tribes, one agricultural and one nomadic, who arrived in the north from 400 BCE to 100 CE.

Three Kingdoms

Northern tribes united in defense against the Chinese Han dynasty, creating the first Korean kingdom of Go-

A street scene in Seoul, South Korea, showing the contemporary architecture characteristic of the city and a park in the background. COURTESY KAREN CHRISTENSEN.

Chinese Tang dynasty, unified Korea for the first time in the late seventh century, and created a major capital in Gyeongju. From dealing in raw materials only, foreign trade expanded to include manufactured goods.

Goryeo Dynasty

The subsequent Goryeo dynasty (918–1392 CE), contemporary with Mongol dominance in China, called its capital Song-ak (present-day Gaesong, North Korea)—the "pine tree" capital. Pines, with their four points of beauty (color, form, perfume, and resistance to lightning), feature regularly in Korean art. The *pungsu*, or wind and water concept (Chinese *feng shui*), became important toward the end of Silla dominance, influencing the layout of capitals such as Song-ak and the siting of Buddhist temples in scenic mountain locales. The capital of 500,000 was temporarily moved to Ganghwa Island, west of present-day Seoul, to avoid the Mongols.

Yi (Joseon) Dynasty

The Chinese Ming dynasty overthrew the Mongols and the associated Goryeo dynasty in Korea, and the Yi (Joseon) dynasty assumed power in 1392, holding it until 1910. The founding family had the same name as the plum tree, which became the symbol of the kingdom. The Yi dynasty introduced *hanguel* script, simpler than Chinese, which greatly increased literacy. In this period land ownership largely shifted from the monarchy to private ownership by upper-class government officials. Conversion of land to agricultural use increased cropland to three times its Goryeo period extent.

This period brought neo-Confucianism, under which Buddhism was suppressed and never regained its former dominance. Bamboo, featured in Korean art as a symbol of loyalty, commonly grows at Confucian shrines. Korean art also commonly depicted cranes, tigers, and other wildlife. Neo-Confucianism combined Confucius' original ethical ideas with ancestor worship and paternalism. Today it is seen as a conservative ethical system rather than an organized religion, and is a cornerstone of Korean consciousness.

Though repressed during the Yi dynasty, shamanism is another ancient quasi-religion that remains important in Korea. Mostly female *mudang*, or shamans, are intermediaries between the living and spirit worlds. Estimates of the number of South Korean *mudang* as of 2002 range from 40,000 to 100,000.

guryeo in the first century CE. Goguryeo lacked fertile land and so expanded its territory, taking in the more sophisticated Baekje kingdom that occupied fertile ground in southwestern Korea. The less-developed kingdom of Silla (in the southeast) then merged with Goguryeo and Baekje in the fourth century CE. The resulting Three Kingdoms Period saw considerable Chinese influence, and Buddhism became the dominant religion. (Japan felt the influence of Korean Buddhism during this period.) The largest of four Han Chinese commanderies, Nangnang, contained 400,000 Chinese and Koreans. Agricultural implements became mass-produced, new roads were constructed, and cows were brought in for plowing. From being communally owned, land became the property of the monarchy, aristocracy, and Buddhist temples. The Silla kingdom eventually assumed control during the

Japan invaded Korea in 1592, burning palaces and temples and exporting craftspeople and intellectuals. China and the Yi navy eventually expelled the Japanese. Soon afterwards, Manchus overthrew the Ming dynasty in China and also invaded Korea. In reaction, Korea turned inward, becoming known as the "Hermit Kingdom."

Japanese Occupation

Japan defeated China in the Sino-Japanese War of 1894 and Russia in the Russo-Japanese War of 1904 to secure control of Korea. Japan annexed Korea, abolished its monarchy, and ruled the nation harshly from 1910 until 1945. During this period modern technology began severely damaging the environment: road and rail networks were extended in the 1920s, and logging came to affect 72 percent of the forest landscape. Korea's population grew from over 13 million in 1910 to almost 26 million in 1944. Some flora and larger fauna species disappeared, while the populations of others declined. Industrialization and associated pollution was, however, still relatively dispersed and moderate.

Korean War

Post-World War II Korea was to be temporarily divided into Russian (North) and American (South) sectors. The more rural, less wealthy North had long been resentful of the South, but external Cold War factors primarily led to a Russian-supplied invasion in June 1950. In the subsequent war Seoul changed hands four times, much urban and rural landscape was ruined, two million people died, bombing damaged the forest cover, and the partitioning of Korea became permanent. Post-war poverty, exacerbated by an influx of 4.8 million North Korean refugees, led to increased logging to obtain inexpensive fuel. Contemporary photographs reveal denuded hillsides, which frequently suffered erosion and landslides in monsoon rains.

South Korea

South Korean democracy took decades to implement, and former general Park Chung-hee (1917–1979) ruled for eighteen years in the 1960s and 1970s. He oversaw the "economic miracle" whereby South Korea followed a capitalist, industrial path to become an Asian "tiger" and major exporter of cars and electronics. South Korea's labor-intensive industrialization brought rapid urbanization with associated housing and infrastructure problems. The use of industrial coal (*suktan*) caused carbon monoxide and sulfur dioxide pollution, the effects of which were compounded by poor working conditions and the redundant proximity of industrial and residential areas.

An industrial decentralization policy simply relocated pollution, causing problems such as coastal water pollution and acid rain. Farmers increased yields through the green revolution yet suffered from high chemical costs. The environment had become a controversial topic by the late 1970s, but media was controlled and general student protests were violently repressed. Public pressure eventually led to most environmental reforms.

Park Chung-hee oversaw one of the world's most successful reforestation programs. Over 80 percent of Korea's forests had been damaged by the end of the Korean War. In 1961 the Forest Law was enacted, and in 1973 the Forestry Administration embarked on a ten-year National Forest Basic Plan. Since 80 percent of Korea's forests are under 30 years old and are not yet fully productive, Korea produces under 5 percent or its own timber. Korea imports forest products from over twenty countries, including Malaysia, Papua New Guinea, the United States, Chile, and New Zealand.

The late 1980s and 1990s saw continued industrial and economic growth, and sulfur dioxide levels in Seoul, Incheon, and Pusan reached six times permitted levels (0.05 ppm) by 1990. Urban growth in the Seoul region reduced open space and habitats, and construction of deep-water ports reduced the extent of coastal wetlands. Though South Korea is now following the west in building its service sector—which is less polluting—environmental problems persist. Major environmental laws of 1977 were overhauled in the early 1990s to improve pollution control and introduce aggressive recycling incentives.

Kim Dae Jung became the first Korean opposition leader elected to the presidency (1997), and he won the 2000 Nobel Peace Prize for his efforts to repair relations with North Korea.

The two main organized religions in South Korea are Buddhism and Christianity, each followed by approximately 25 percent of the population (estimated at 48.324 million in 2002). Most Buddhist temples are in sites of remote natural beauty, exemplified by Haeinsa in the South and Woljongsa in the Northeast.

North Korea

Post-war North Korea became a closed country ruled by dictator Kim Il Sung (1912–1994) and more recently by his son, Kim Jong Il. Though North Korea occupies 55 percent of the peninsula, its population was estimated at 22.224 million in 2000—less than half of South Korea's. North Korean industry initially grew rapidly, building on a base of pre-existing Japanese infrastructure, but has stagnated under current isolationist, Marxist policy. Industrial pollution, some related to mineral exploitation, has been less severe than in the South, and North Korea has far fewer cars and associated emissions. North Korea, however, has done less reforestation in the post-war period. Recent natural disasters, such as floods, combined with deforestation, erosion, and economic collapse, led to large-scale famine beginning in the 1990s.

Current Environmental Issues

Air and water pollution are major domestic environmental issues in both Koreas. North Korea is especially concerned with inadequate supplies of potable water, water-borne disease, deforestation, and soil erosion. Less modernization in the North means that many important natural sites, including Mount Paekdusan and the Tuman River wetlands, remain relatively unspoiled.

In South Korea, environmental organizations address a full range of issues, including biotechnology, environmental economics, environmental law, genetically modified organisms, industrial ecology, religious (Buddhist and Christian) ecology, sustainable development, urban issues, water, and wetlands. The 40,000-hectare Saemangum wetland reclamation project on the west coast of South Korea is particularly controversial. Green Korea United is a major non-governmental organization with ten chapters and fifteen thousand members. An issue common to both North and South is a proposal, backed by world-renowned biologists, to make the Demilitarized Zone (DMZ) into a nature reserve.

South Korea is party to many international treaties addressing Antarctica, biodiversity, climate change, desertification, endangered species, hazardous wastes, marine dumping, nuclear testing, ozone layer protection, ship pollution, tropical timber, wetlands, and whaling. It has signed but not ratified the Kyoto Protocol regarding climate change. North Korea is party to international treaties addressing Antarctica, biodiversity, climate change, environmental modification, ozone layer protection, and ship pollution. It has signed but not ratified the Antarctic-Environmental Protocol and the Law of the Sea.

Unique international environmental issues that draw attention to Korea include drift-net fishing (South Korea) and nuclear energy and arms (North Korea). Green trade is of particular concern, in view of South Korea's increased ability to import products. Committee discussions within the World Trade Organization and the Association of Southeast Asian Nations (ASEAN) are attempting to curb the detrimental effects of free trade, including the decline of global fisheries and tropical deforestation with its associated loss of biodiversity.

William Forbes

Further Reading

Bae, K. D. (1992). Pleistocene environment and Paleolithic stone industries of the Korean Peninsula. In C. M. Aikens & S. Rhee (Eds.), *Pacific northeast Asia in prehistory: Hunter-fisher-gatherers, farmers, and sociopolitical elites* (pp. 13–21). Pullman: Washington State University Press.

Chung, J. Y., & Kirkby, R. J. R. (2002). *The political economy of development and environment in Korea*. London: Routledge Press.

Edmunds, D., & Wollenberg, E. (2001). Historical perspectives on forest policy change in Asia: An introduction. *Environmental history, 6* (2), 190–212.

Joe, W. J. (1982). *Traditional Korea: A cultural history*. Seoul, South Korea: Chung'ang University Press.

Kim, W. J. (1994). *Natural disaster management in Korea: An analytical study with policy implications*. Seoul, South Korea: Korea Disaster Research and Information Center.

Korea Information Service. (2001). *Koreanet, society and life, environment*. Retrieved February 6, 2003, from http://www.korea.net/directory/List.asp?Category_id=m001

McCune, S. (1956). *Korea's heritage: A regional and social geography*. Tokyo: Charles E. Tuttle Company.

McCune, S. (1980). Geography and natural environment. In H. Kim (Ed.), *Studies on Korea: A scholar's guide*. Honolulu, HI: University of Hawaii Press.

Park, D. W. (1998). The environment of Kyongju. In Korean National Commission for UNESCO (Ed.), *Kyongju: City of millennial history*. Elizabeth, NJ: Hollym International Corporation.

Robinson, K. (2002). *Korean history: A bibliography*. Retrieved February 6, 2003, from http://www.hawaii.edu/korea/bibliography/biblio.htm

Sorensen, C. W. (1988). *Over the mountains are mountains: Korea peasant households and their adaptations to rapid industrialization.* Seattle: University of Washington Press.

Storey, R., & English, A. (2001). *Korea.* Victoria, Australia: Lonely Planet Publications.

Tay, S. S. C., & Esty, D. C. (1996). *Asian dragons and green trade: Environment, economics, and international law.* Singapore: Times Academic Press.

Yang, B. K. (1997). Perceptions of nature in the choson period. *Korea journal 37* (4), 134–155.

Yoo, Y. (1987). *Korea the beautiful: Treasures of the hermit kingdom.* Seoul, South Korea: Samsung Moonhwa Printing Company.

L

Lake Baikal

Lake Baikal is a large lake located in eastern Siberia in the Buriat Autonomous Republic and Irkutsk Oblast (Province) of the Russian Federation. Its name is believed to be derived from the Turkic *bai* (rich) and *kul'* (lake). With its 23,000 cubic kilometers of volume Lake Baikal contains 90 percent of the former USSR's and 20 percent of the world's freshwater. That is as much water as in all of the North American Great Lakes combined. That enormous volume is a consequence of the great depth of the lake; its average depth is 730 meters, with a deepest point of 1,637 meters. The lake's surface lies 455 meters above sea level. Largely oriented north to south with a crescent-shaped length of 636 kilometers and an average width of just 48 kilometers, Baikal has a surface area of a comparatively modest 31,468 square kilometers, but the flush time, the time it takes to replace all the water in a lake or resevoir, for the lake's 23,000 cubic kilometers is four hundred years. After construction of the Bratsk Dam in 1961 on the Angara River, the lake's only outlet, the average level of the lake rose 1 meter, and the lake surface increased by 500 square kilometers. A virtual inland sea, Baikal has 174 capes and 6 major bays or gulfs. Fed by 336 streams, the lake's water is very clear, with visibility up to 40 meters beneath the surface; this is a result of its low mineral content. The lake freezes over from December to May with an ice crust 70–115 centimeters thick, and ice floes may persist into June.

Geological History

Nineteenth-century scientists theorized that Baikal was once a fjord of the Arctic Ocean or even the easternmost part of an ancient Pontic-Sarmatian sea stretching across the West Siberian Plain and Kyrgyz Steppe. Other scientists linked Baikal to the Pacific Ocean or to the Jurassic Sea, which once covered Mongolia. However, geologists and paleontologists rejected the idea of a relict (a relief feature remaining after other features have disappeared) ocean for lack of mineral and fossil evidence.

The most widely accepted theory today is that the lake originated 25 million years ago in a process much like that which created the world's other rift systems. The roots of the lake basin extend to the Earth's upper mantle, about 50 kilometers deep. Below this basin exists an anomalously hot portion of the Earth's core. Light, superheated plasma rose from the core and in places punctured the crust of the Earth, lifting the crust above it to create the mountain ranges that bracket Baikal. At the same time this plasma flowed under the crust to the sides, creating horizontally fissiparous (divisive) forces that widened the rift made by the initial eruption while uncovering previous rifts down to the upper mantle and creating huge new ones and intermontane (between-mountains) abysses. When the crust cooled, the lake basin, with three principal depressions, was formed and filled with both water and sediment. Lake Khubsugul, which is just across the border in Mongolia and is the source of the Selenga River, Baikal's most important tributary, is another rift valley lake.

Native Species

Biologically the lake is rich in native species. Of the 1,550 species of fauna 80 percent are native to the lake.

Crucial to the food chain are the zooplankton (plankton composed of animals), especially the more than 250 species of gammarid amphipods—shrimplike crustaceans. Of these the most important is the epischura, which maintains the purity of the water. Of the lake's 1,085 species of flora, there are 509 species of diatoms (planktonic unicellular or colonial algae) among a large number of algal species. Life, including fishes, exists at all levels of the lake. Because there is no light 1.6 kilometers below the surface, the eyes of bottom-feeding gammarids have atrophied, and they are blind, orienting by antennae. Many of the gammarid and flatworm species are marked by gigantism (abnormal largeness) or nanism (dwarfism), sometimes in the same basin; one flatworm can reach 30 centimeters in length and eats fish. Of the larger fauna, there are fifty-two species of fish, of which twenty-seven are native, including the two species of the transparent, live-bearing genus *Comephoridae (golomianka)*, the Baikal sturgeon, and the *omul (Coregonus autumnalis migratorius Georgy)*. At the apex of the aquatic food chain is the freshwater seal, the *nerpa (Pusa sibirica Gmelin)*, which breeds on the craggy Ushkan'i Islands in the middle of the lake.

The origins of the lake's distinctive biota (flora and fauna) have long intrigued biologists. Vitalii Cheslavovich Dorogostaiskii, the organizer of the Baikal Biological Station, who worked at Baikal during the 1910s and 1920s, developed the theory that most Baikal fauna evolved relatively recently from a small stock of ancestors following an evolutionary bottleneck. In the mid-Tertiary period (25 million years ago) central Siberia was a hilly, even mountainous, area covered with lush subtropical vegetation. At first Baikal was a chain of shallower lakes. With time, major tectonic shifts deepened the rift valley and united the lakes. The climate grew colder, and during the late Tertiary (from about 63 million years ago to about 2.5 million years ago) and Quaternary (from 2.5 million years ago to the present) periods Baikal was covered in ice; shallower lakes froze to the bottom, eliminating existing fauna and flora entirely. The rich subtropical fauna began to disappear, maintaining itself only in the largest lakes such as Baikal. Only cold-hardy fauna survived. Thus the lake maintained itself through the ice ages. With the end of the ice ages and the onset of warming, a rapid speciation (the process of biological species formation) occurred on the basis of those few forms that had survived the climate-driven evolutionary bottleneck. Spurring this adaptive radiation was the host of new habitats that opened up for exploitation. At this time

as well the Angara River provided the opportunity for a small number of Arctic fauna such as the *nerpa* and perhaps *omul* to migrate upstream (from the Arctic Ocean to the lake). Recently humans have influenced the evolution of the lake's fauna with the introduction of three species of fish (Amur catfish, Amur *sazan*—a carplike fish—and perch) and, of course, with the increasingly pervasive effects of economic activity on and around the lake.

History of Human Interaction with the Lake

Although the lake was well known to nomadic Mongol and Turkic peoples (legend has it that Mongol conqueror Genghis Khan was born by the lake), Russian adventurers reached the shores of Baikal and the lake's Olkhon Island only in 1643. One early Russian description of Baikal was that by the exiled archpriest Avvakum, who crossed the lake in July 1662 returning from exile in Dauria (Transbaikalia). With the development of the salt mines at Nerchinsk and Shilka in the nineteenth century, the region around Baikal became a major destination for exiled convicts and political prisoners. These prisoners included Decembrists (people who took part in the failed uprising against Czar Peter I in December 1825), Poles exiled after the revolts of 1830 and 1863, populists, and socialists. One of the best-known Russian songs, "Slavnoe more, sviashchennyi Baikal" (Glorious Sea, Sacred Baikal), commemorates an exile's escape across the lake in the waning days of the czarist empire.

Under Czar Peter I (the Great) the Siberian expedition of Daniil G. Messershmidt, which set out in 1724, produced the first map of the lake. Later exploration was conducted by the Second Northern (Kamchatka) Expedition (1733–1743) and that of Peter Simon Pallas (1768–1774).

In the late nineteenth century scientific stations were established at the lake for the systematic study of its geology and biology. A. V. Voznesenskii, the director of the Irkutsk Geophysical Observatory, organized eleven hydrometeorological (relating to the study of water in the atmosphere) stations at Baikal (1896–1901) at existing lighthouses. Previous measurements of lake levels and temperatures were collected in the period 1868–1872. In 1916 the Academy of Sciences selected a permanent site for its research station at the lake. By the late Soviet period, the following institutes were among those operating at Baikal: the Limnological Institute of the Siberian Branch of the Academy of Sciences of the USSR; Kotinskaia Biological Station of the Institute of Biology of Irkutsk State University; Barguzinskii *zapovednik* (inviolable nature reserve); Baikal'skii *zapovednik;* Baikal National Park; stations of the Siberian Institute for the Study of Earth Magnetism, the Ionosphere, and the Propagation of Radiowaves; Baikal branch of the Institute of Toxicology of the Ministry of the Paper and Pulp Industry; Baikal Institute for Fish Farm Planning of the Ministry of the Fishing Industry; and the Buriat Republic Academy of Sciences.

Soviet scientists first perceived a threat to the lake's integrity in 1957, when they learned of a plan developed by S. Ia. Zhuk's Gidroenergoproekt (Hydropower Construction Agency) to blow up the mouth of the Angara River. The explosion would have lowered the level of Baikal by several meters and would have been 50 percent greater than the atomic explosion at Hiroshima during World War II. The goal of the plan was to allow greater water flow from Baikal to the hydroelectric power stations downstream on the Angara River, where the lake emptied. That same year the Soviet military sought to build two factories on Baikal's southern shore and main tributary, the Selenga River, to make viscose (a solution made by treating cellulose with caustic alkali solution and carbon disulfide) cord for airplane tires using the lake's pure water. The public was not told about the strategic nature of the proposed factories; rather, the factories were depicted as dedicated to producing high-quality paper goods, which, ironically, they eventually did.

The battle against these threats initially was waged on the pages of the pioneering publications *Literaturnaia gazeta, Oktiabr',* and *Komsomol'skaia Pravda.* Prominent scientists and others wrote to the USSR Council of Ministers warning of the devastating consequences of an earthquake at the proposed factories' sites. A collective letter to *Komsomol'skaia Pravda* of 11 May 1966, entitled "Baikal Waits," was signed by some of the most important scientists and writers and described decision makers as having "taken a risk of unheard of scale, turning Lake Baikal into an experimental basin for the trials of a pollution abatement system that has never been tested in actual production conditions and which is not suited to the severe climatic conditions of the Transbaikal region" (Lapin 1987, 80).

In its editorial commentary to the letter, *Komsomol'-skaia Pravda* asked, "Have we really learned nothing from the countless examples when economic bureaucrats in the name of the plan devastated waterways and lakes and poisoned their currents?" (Lapin 1987, 82).

In 1966 the Baikalsk factory started up, and the Selenginsk factory was running by the following year. Hundreds more factories, many of them related to the military and the opening of the Baikal-Amur Mainline Railroad, also began operation in the Baikal basin during the 1970s. Other threats to the lake's natural conditions include the dumping of untreated sewage into the Selenga River and other tributaries, large-scale logging and consequent erosion on the slopes of the mountains surrounding the lake (to keep the pulp and paper factories supplied with raw materials), contamination of regional soils by toxic industrial and radioactive wastes, agricultural waste runoff, and habitat destruction. The protests of scientific and literary public opinion, which continue to the present day, have failed to close the factories or force them to delay production until all pollution-abatement facilities were running. Decades of resolutions and promises of a clean-up by the Soviet and Russian governments have been met with skepticism. The USSR Academy of Sciences had cautioned in 1977 that Baikal was facing irreversible degradation, and although no one knows precisely the tolerances of the lake's life-forms to the growing array of toxic effluents, thermal changes, and changes in dissolved oxygen and other gases, the threats to this natural laboratory of evolution are real.

Evidence indicates that economic activity has already affected the productivity of the lake. The *omul* catch, which reached 9,000 metric tons in 1945, fell to 1,200 metric tons in 1967. A major die-off of *nerpa* seals in 1987 has not yet been explained but is conceivably related to the decline in the *omul.*

Protected Territories

The first protected territory on the lake, the Barguzinskii *zapovednik* (established 1916 with 374,423 hectares), grew out of czarist-era concerns with protecting remaining stocks of sable (*Martes zibellina L.*) and followed the recommendations of the game managers Frants Frantsevich Shillinger and O. V. Markgraf. A new reserve, the Baikal'skii *zapovednik,* was proposed in 1921, but it never functioned. However, a reserve bearing the same name and encompassing 165,724 hectares was established in 1969 on a different part of the lake. The Baikalo-Lenskii *zapovednik* with 659,919 hectares was created in 1986. Additionally, the Pribaikal'skii (418,000 hectares) and Zabaikal'skii (245,000 hectares) National Parks were established in 1986, and there are less-permanent protected areas (*zakazniki*) totaling 86,000 hectares. Finally, a Ramsar satellite observation site occupies 12,000 hectares in the Selenga delta. The entire lake, together with a coastal protection zone of 5.6 million hectares, was declared a World Heritage Site by the United Nations Educational, Scientific and Cultural Organization (UNESCO) in 1996, for a total of 8.8 million hectares.

Douglas R. Weiner

Further Reading

Dorogostaiskaia, E. V. (1994). *Vitalii Cheslavovich Dorogostaiskii (1879–1938)*. St. Petersburg, Russia: Nauka.

Galazii, G. I. (1988). *Baikal v voprosakh i otvetakh* [Baikal of questions and answers]. Moscow: Mysl'.

Galazii, G. I. (1993). *Baikal atlas*. Moscow: Federal'naia sluzhba geodezii i kartografii Rossii.

Josephson, P. R. (1996). *New Atlantis revisited: Akademgorodok, the Siberian city of science*. Princeton, NJ: Princeton University Press.

Pryde, P. R. (1991). *Environmental management in the Soviet Union*. Cambridge, UK: Cambridge University Press.

Weiner, D. R. (1999). *A little corner of freedom: Russian nature protection from Stalin to Gorbachev*. Berkeley and Los Angeles: University of California Press.

Lake Chad

Lake Chad lies in west central Africa, bordering the countries of Nigeria, Cameroon, Chad, and Niger. With a maximum surface area of 2,500 square kilometers—approximately the size of Rhode Island—Lake Chad is the fourth-largest lake on the African continent. Lake Chad is located in a semiarid portion of Africa called the Sahel, known for its bipolar wet and dry seasons. Freshwater supplies from the lake provide sustenance for 8.5 million farmers, fishermen, and cattle herders in the region.

Lake Chad is fed primarily by two rivers originating farther south in the mountainous Central African Republic: the Chari and Logone. The size of the lake varies with the seasons. During the wet season (July–September), Lake Chad receives roughly 38 centimeters of rainfall. The dry season (October–June) is characterized by minimal rainfall and leads to frequent droughts. The northern region of Lake Chad, which straddles an arid climate zone, often receives only half the amount of rainfall as southern Lake Chad. Lake Chad is shallow compared with most African lakes—

only seven meters at its deepest spot—and therefore evaporation during the dry season has a significant impact on lake recession and total surface area.

The severity of recent droughts in the region has contributed to a rapid shrinkage of Lake Chad in the past forty years. Since 1960, Lake Chad has shrunk from 25,000 square kilometers to to its present size, one-tenth the 1960 size. This arises from a combination of factors, including uncharacteristically long dry seasons and the migration of large numbers of people to the area.

In the past, Lake Chad occupied a much larger land area than it does today. Climatologists and hydrologists have divided the climate history of Lake Chad into three eras: Paleo-Chad, Mega-Chad, and present-day Lake Chad. Approximately 55,000 years ago, Paleo-Chad occupied a swath of land with an estimated surface area of 2 million square kilometers. This surface area would comprise the entire northeastern portion of present-day Africa, from Egypt to Nigeria. Between approximately 20,000 BCE and 3000 BCE, the Paleo-Chad Basin underwent multiple periods of aridity and the lake recessed to form Mega-Chad, which was only a quarter the size of Paleo-Chad. Like Paleo-Chad, Mega-Chad faced severe climatic conditions over time and shrank decade by decade. Climatologists believe Mega-Chad shrank significantly as a result of the increasing effects of the harmattan, a seasonal dry wind from the Sahara that has contributed to seasonal droughts in the region. The era of Lake Chad began around 0 CE. In the course of the past two thousand years, Lake Chad has completely dried up on six occasions. In 1908, a severe drought created the Great Barrier, a ridge that has since divided Lake Chad into a northern and southern basin. Up until 1908 the ridge was only visible during the dry season. Two other drought spells from 1973 to 1974 and from 1984 to 1985 forced the lake to recede and caused widespread famine in the region. Since so many people derive their livelihoods from Lake Chad, governments from the bordering African nations have developed large-scale irrigation and water conservation projects, utilizing diminishing water supplies to develop national agricultural schemes and supplying expanding rural populations with adequate water supplies. The rapid shrinkage of Lake Chad has exacerbated problems for small-scale sedentary farmers and pastoralists in the immediate Lake Chad basin region. Large-scale irrigation projects, such as the South Chad Irrigation Project (SCIP), have proceeded (and subsequently failed) regardless of the two shrinkage periods. These projects certainly had political motivations, the primary of which being the perceived need for self-sustainability in terms of food production, relying less on agricultural imports from other West African countries. These import substitution schemes arrived before the export oriented schemes of structural adjustment programs (SAPs) of the World Bank and IMF in the 1980s. Failure of these large-scale irrigation schemes resulted from lack of infrastructure support from the goverment and high failure rates at the community level, where people were used to their own methods of coping with diminishing water resources. Recently, neighboring countries have continued to implement programs for water resource management, but with more grassroots participation in the design process.

Craig Enstad

Further Reading

Gleick, P. H. (2001). *The world's water 2000–2001: The biennial report on freshwater resources*. Washington, DC: Island Press.

Jakel, D. (1984). Rainfall patterns and lake level variations at Lake Chad. In N. A. Morner & W. Karlen (Eds.), *Climate changes on a yearly to millennial basis*. Dordrecht, Holland: D. Reidel Publishing Company.

Sarch, M. T. (2000). Fishing and farming at Lake Chad: Responses to lake-level fluctuations. *The Geographical Journal, 166*(2), 156–172.

Sikes, S. K. (1972). *Lake Chad*. Bristol, UK: Western Printing Services.

Lake Victoria

Located on the border between Uganda, Kenya, and Tanzania, Lake Victoria is the world's second-largest lake. It is both the biggest tropical lake on Earth and Africa's largest freshwater body, with a surface of 69,000 square kilometers. Lake Victoria straddles the equator and forms the source of the Nile, Africa's longest river. The lake probably was formed 400,000 years ago over ancient bedrock in a high, broad depression between East Africa's two great rift valleys. Lake Victoria flowed westward until the Pleistocene epoch (which began 1.6 million years ago), when tectonic uplift turned its flow to the north. The lake level appears to have fluctuated significantly since then, and at the end of the last glaciation, between fifteen thousand and seventeen thousand years ago, the lake may have dried up entirely. This is not surprising because it is shallow, with a maximum depth of 68 meters and a mean depth of only 40 meters. Even during the twentieth century the surface of Lake Victoria has varied by about 2 meters as a result of changes in precipitation and evaporation. The lake receives about 80 percent of its water as a result of rainfall directly onto the surface.

Lake Victoria has also been the site of a spectacular evolutionary event: the adaptive radiation of cichlid fishes from a single common ancestor into three hundred to four hundred species. Cichlids are small, colorful fish frequently bred for aquariums. Mitochondrial DNA evidence indicates that the cichlid species of Lake Victoria are all closely related and that many would even interbreed if they did not segregate themselves by habitat and sexual selection, which is usually based on physical characteristics such as color. Several studies have examined how so many species could have evolved from one progenitor in a single lake. One hypothesis held that populations of cichlids had become isolated in small ponds in the past when the lake level declined, giving them time to diverge from their relatives through genetic drift (random changes in gene frequency, especially in small populations when leading to preservation or extinction of particular genes). Another hypothesis held that the lake had not dried up, that it had been fairly stable over a long period of time, and that cichlids had diversified through sympatric (located in the same area) speciation. Recent evidence indicates that neither hypothesis is correct. It now appears that the cichlids of Lake Victoria radiated into their diverse modern forms only since the lake refilled after the end of the Pleistocene epoch, twelve thousand to fourteen thousand years ago. If correct, this would certainly be a world speed record for vertebrate evolution.

In the twentieth century Lake Victoria and its cichlids have fared poorly. Since the 1920s the formerly clear lake has become increasingly murky and anoxic (oxygen poor) as a result of eutrophication (the process by which a body of water becomes enriched in dissolved nutrients). Eutrophication is caused when nutrients enter an ecosystem and encourage algal blooms, which in turn deprive the water of its dissolved oxygen content. Because sexual selection is largely based on coloration, many cichlid fishes may require clear waters in order to properly identify adequate mates. The water hyacinth, a noxious South American plant, has also colonized Lake Victoria, thriving in nutrient-rich waters and creating dense mats of vegetation that destroy habitat, block sunlight, and render travel impossible. Finally, the enormous and predatory Nile perch was introduced in the 1950s to increase the marketable fishery resources of the lake. The perch's population exploded in the 1980s, and its appetite for cichlids seems insatiable. Over two hundred species of Lake Victoria cichlids have probably become extinct as a result, and many others are considered endangered. In the future scientists, policymakers, and a rapidly growing local population will have to make difficult choices about how best to achieve a healthy and sustainable Lake Victoria.

Peter S. Alagona

Further Reading

Goldschmidt, T., White, F., & Wannick, J. (1993). Cascading effects of the introduced Nile perch on the detritivorous/phytoplanktivorous species in the sublittoral areas of Lake Victoria. *Conservation Biology, 7*(3), 686–700.

Johnson, T. C., Kelts, K., & Odada, E. (2000). The Holocene history of Lake Victoria. *Ambio, 29*(1), 2–11.

Johnson, T. C., Scholtz, C. A., Talbot, M. R., Kelts, K., Rickets, R. D., Ngobi, G., Beuning, K., Ssemmanda, I., & McGill, J. W. (1996). Late Pleistocene desiccation of Lake Victoria and rapid evolution of cichlid fishes. *Science, 273*(5278), 1091–1093.

Seehausen, O., & van Alphen, J. J. M. (1997). Cichlid fish diversity threatened by eutrophication that curbs sexual selection. *Science, 277*(5333), 1808–1812.

Verschuren, D., Johnson, T. C., Kling, H. J., Edgington, D. N., Leavitt, P. R., Brown, E. T., Talbot, M. R., & Hecky, R. E. (2001). History and timing of human impact on Lake Victoria, East Africa. *Proceedings of the Royal Society of London, Series B—Biological Sciences, 269*, 289–294.

Lakes
See Dams, Reservoirs, and Artificial Lakes; Great Lakes and St. Lawrence River; Lake Baikal; Lake Chad; Lake Victoria

Lamprey

The word *lamprey* refers to about twenty-five species of marine and freshwater primitive fish that belong to the class Cephlaspidomorphi, order Cyclostomata, and family Petromyzontidae. Lampreys normally are anadromous fish (migrating into freshwater to spawn), but some populations have become landlocked in freshwater. Most adult lampreys are parasitic, sucking the blood of other fish, attaching to them by horny teeth set in the circular, jawless mouth. The larvae live in muddy river bottoms and eat particles of organic matter.

Some species of lampreys, especially the European river lamprey, are fished during their migration to rivers. For centuries smoked lamprey has been considered a delicacy in some European countries, especially along the Baltic Sea. Today small-scale commercial lamprey fishing has developed in Estonia, Latvia, Russia, France, and Portugal. The Pacific lamprey was important to many of the tribal people of the Pacific coast of North America, who harvested lamprey for food and for ceremonial and medicinal purposes.

However, the benefits derived from lampreys cannot be compared with the harm that lampreys cause to fisheries. Although adult lampreys normally live and feed in the sea, they can completely change their life cycle and invade bodies of freshwater. The best-known example is the invasion of the sea lamprey, *Petromyzon marinus*, from the Atlantic Ocean to the Great Lakes in North America. It appeared in Lake Ontario in the 1830s. Probably the sea lamprey had entered the lake via the Hudson River through the Erie Canal. Later the sea lamprey gained access to Lake Erie via the Welland Canal around Niagara Falls, and from the 1920s to the 1940s it became visible in all the Great Lakes. The lamprey could migrate on boat hulls or on host fish if it could not move freely through the canal. Its introduction was probably aided by the use of larval lampreys as bait by sport fishers.

Invasion of the sea lamprey caused the collapse of commercial fisheries and considerable changes in the whole ecosystem of the Great Lakes. During the 1950s up to 85 percent of large Great Lakes fish, especially lake trout, exhibited lamprey wounds. The alarming decline in the lake trout population was reported, but fishers in the beginning tried to maintain the level of catches, fearing that the sea lamprey would kill all the lake trout anyway. The combined effect of the lamprey invasion and overfishing rapidly caused the collapse of the lake trout population, as well as of white fish and chub populations. The lamprey invasion also was a major factor in the extinction of several species of cisco fish.

To control the sea lamprey, the lampricide 3-trifluoromethyl–4-nitrophenol (TFM) is added to streams in which the lamprey hatch. TFM has reduced the sea lamprey population by 90 percent of its 1961 peak, but control is still necessary. The invasion of sea lamprey shows that introduced species can be detrimental to native species because introduced species have no natural predators or competitors in new habitats. Native species often suffer because they have no experience with exotic species, which rapidly increase and are almost impossible to eliminate once established.

Julia A. Lajus and Dmitry L. Lajus

Further Reading

Ashworth, W. (1987). *The late, Great Lakes: An environmental history*. Detroit, MI: Wayne State University Press.

Fuller, P. L., Nico, L. G., & Williams, J. D. (1999). *Nonindigenous fishes introduced into inland waters of the United States*. Bethesda, MD: American Fisheries Society.

Holchk, J. (Ed.). (1986). The freshwater fishes of Europe (Vol. 1). Wiesbaden, Germany: Aula.

Land Tenure

Land tenure comprises the legal rights and responsibilities defining the use of land and associated natural resources such as forests, minerals, pastureland, and water supplies; the forms of land tenure include communal, tribal, tenancy, private, and state run. These rights derive from the "bundle of rights" concept of property ownership, which delineates rights such as permitting others to use the land or the leasing of its natural resources, and selling or alienating (transferring ownership of) the land. Tenure typically involves land that one uses in return for services or fees rendered to the owners and is therefore subject to control by others. Tenure security has implications for natural resources management, ecological health, and community maintenance.

Land tenure institutions have varied greatly over time, depending on cultural, political, environmental, and geographical conditions. Feudal land tenure in medieval Europe, for instance, evolved to emphasize cultivation of the land through socage tenure, which gave tenants, in some cases, the right to alienate or sell the property. The emergence of market-oriented production and an "enclosure movement" that privatized ownership of common lands disrupted the forest ecosystem, ended community farming efforts, and threw many people into poverty.

Transferred to the New World, European tenure stressing a system of bounded land held in severalty (individual ownership) clashed with indigenous conceptions of communal use, leading first to legal conflicts over property rights and then to violence. In both colonial North and South America, the introduction of domesticated livestock and capitalist-oriented agriculture transformed intercultural social relations and ecological conditions. Latin American land tenure grew to revolve around latifundia (large estates), which steadily replaced indigenous people's communal land practices, such as the Andean kinship-oriented system based on reciprocal labor arrangements (*ayllu*) and the Nahua (Aztec) traditions of *altepetlalli* (the land surrounding an Aztec village and belonging to the community) and *calpollalli* (the land of the community proper). In the United States government policies such as the 1862 Homestead Act promoted settlement of formerly indigenous communal lands through fee simple (absolute) ownership of small family farms. Relegated to reservations, Native Americans adapted to new environmental conditions and land-use patterns while retaining communal tenure until coercive government allotment policies allowing for fee simple ownership resulted in the sale of millions of acres of the tribal estates. Debates on twentieth-century U.S. land tenure have stemmed from conflicts over government control of vast public lands.

The clash between European and communal notions of land tenure continues today in many nations where indigenous people face incursions by ranching syndicates, corporate farmers, and transnational energy corporations. Postcolonial and postcommunist land tenure has suffered from inadequate land registration systems, inefficient land markets, and insensitivity to cultural traditions. The ecological (and cultural) consequences of tenure insecurity are great, especially in regions such as Amazonia and Asia where indigenous groups and their environment face enormous pressure from large state-sponsored development projects. The lack of formal property rights delineated by formal surveys and embedded in land registration systems or statutory procedures inhibits the creation of incentives for private or community investment in soil conservation and other essential land management policies. Without incentives to establish long-term sustainability and productivity measures,

A private home and olive orchard near Sirinca, Turkey in March 2002. COURTESY NICOLE LALIBERTE.

environmental conditions and community well-being will continue to erode.

Paul C. Rosier

Further Reading

Abramson, A., & Theodossopoulos, D. (2000). *Land, law and environment: Mythical land, legal boundaries*. London: Pluto Press.

Alston, L. J., Libecap, G. D., & Mueller, B. (1999). *Titles, conflict, and land use: The development of property rights and land reform on the Brazilian Amazon frontier*. Ann Arbor: University of Michigan Press.

Jacobs, H. M. (Ed.). (1998). *Who owns America: Social conflict over property rights*. Madison: University of Wisconsin Press.

Powelson, J. P. (1988). *The story of land: A world history of land tenure and agrarian reform*. Cambridge, MA: Lincoln Institute of Land Policy.

Spalding, K. (1984). *Huarochiri: An Andean society under Inca and Spanish rule*. Stanford, CA: Stanford University Press.

Sutton, I. (1975). *Indian land tenure: Bibliographical essays and a guide to the literature*. New York: Clearwater Publishing.

Landscape Architecture

Landscape architecture is the study and practice of design in the environment. It is especially focused on the management of land for human use. The most common examples of landscape architecture are found in parks, gardens, and communities. However, landscape architects are involved in almost all aspects of land planning and design. Their work ranges in scale from regional to site specific. For example, landscape architects make recommendations regarding metropolitan growth patterns, advise cities in the planning of new greenway systems, plan for the reuse of former industrial sites, and design neighborhood playgrounds. Landscape architecture is related to but distinct from such professions as architecture, civil engineering, and city planning. Often, on large and complex projects, landscape architects work as part of a team of professionals. For example, they may work with civil engineers to plan and design roadway networks, with planners to guide the expansion of cities and communities, with ecologists to improve damaged habitats, and with horticulturalists to design botanic gardens. Although most landscape architects in the United States work for private companies, many work for governmental parks, planning, transportation, forestry, and conservation departments and nongovernmental organizations.

History of Landscape Architecture

Although the profession of landscape architecture did not organize and take its name until the late 1800s in the United States, and even later in other countries, the history of the ways in which people make changes in the landscape is ancient. For this reason, landscape architectural history includes examinations of early gardens, agricultural practices, settlement patterns, and sacred spaces for burial and ceremony. Like architecture and the fine arts, the landscapes produced by a particular culture reflect its social values, economics, politics, and geography. Teotihuacan, an ancient city in the central valley of Mexico (c. fourth century BCE to eighth century CE), was organized around a complex network of water-delivery systems. The dry garden at Ryoan-ji in Kyoto, Japan (late thirteenth century), made of raked stone, boulders, and moss, was used by Buddhist monks in the religious practice of meditation. Pirro Ligorio designed the elaborate gardens and fountains at the Villa d'Este at Tivoli in Italy (sixteenth century) as a status symbol for its wealthy owner and pleasure grounds for the owner's guests. The English landscape designer Humphrey Repton (1752–1818) designed estates for English gentry, and the before-and-after views in his *Red Books* are some of the best examples of landscape architectural representations. Repton's work was the first to be called "landscape architecture" by Scottish horticultural writer John Claudius Loudon (1783–1843), himself an important designer of estates and parks and a major critic. The French administrator Baron Haussmann cut massive boulevards through the city of Paris as an expression of the power of Napoleon III, and his colleague, J. C. A. Alphand, designed new leisure grounds for the bourgeoisie. The American landscape architect Frederick Law Olmsted (1822–1903) holds an important place in the

history of landscape architecture in America. Olmsted and his partner, the architect Calvert Vaux, planned and built New York City's Central Park (begun in 1853) to be a respite from the noise, pollution, and crowding of the industrial city. Olmsted and Vaux designed parks and park systems for cities including Boston, Chicago, Buffalo, New York, and Montreal, Canada.

The Profession of Landscape Architecture

The first published definition of landscape architecture was by H. W. S. Cleveland (1814–1900) in his book *Landscape Architecture as Applied to the Wants of the West*. Olmsted was the first designer of landscapes to call himself a landscape architect. For this reason he is credited with starting the profession of landscape architecture in North America. Landscape architects like Olmsted and Cleveland played important roles in shaping the United States during the late nineteenth and early twentieth centuries, in particular, in planning and developing public places and communities. In 1899 eleven professionals started an organization called the "American Society of Landscape Architects" (ASLA). The American Society of Landscape Architects is the national professional association representing landscape architects. Today there are more than 13,500 ASLA members, both from the United States and abroad. In 1948 the International Federation of Landscape Architects (IFLA) was founded by national landscape architectural organizations. The constitution of the IFLA expresses the contemporary concerns of landscape architects: human health and welfare and wise use of resources.

Although specific licensure requirements vary from country to country and even state to state, generally to become a landscape architect one must attend an accredited program in landscape architecture, serve an apprenticeship with a licensed landscape architect, and pass an examination. Academic training in landscape architecture includes baccalaureate and master's courses in design, land grading, ecology, construction methods, plant establishment, storm water management, history of landscape architecture, and drawing. The breadth of the training of landscape architects reflects the diverse nature of landscape architectural practice. Reflecting the contemporary concern with promoting ecological practices, many graduate landscape architectural education programs include coursework in wetlands restoration, water resource management, the use of native plant materials, contaminated site remediation, and other sustainable practices. This is not to say that all contemporary landscape architectural methods are ecologically based.

Contemporary practices in landscape architecture reflect and shape cultural values. Landscape architectural practice is tied to legal codes that control natural resources, land use, and housing and political issues such as government spending on transportation planning and the management of national parks. For example, in cities such as Hong Kong and Tokyo, where land resources are scarce and property values are high, designers work to contain sprawl and increase urban densities. In countries that have strict controls on water resources, such as Germany and the Netherlands, landscape architects work with architects to devise systems for collecting and treating gray water on urban sites.

Debates in Landscape Architecture

Because landscape architecture is so tied to culture, politics, and economics, landscape architectural discourse and practice are not without controversies. Some scholars and practitioners argue that the places that receive the most attention in the history of the profession are private spaces designed for only the wealthy. Others argue that although standard texts of landscape architectural history pay close attention to the visual and experiential qualities of particular places, they do not explore the social, ecological, and political impacts of design.

Kristine F. Miller

Further Reading

Cleveland, H. W. S. (1873). *Landscape architecture, as applied to the wants of the West; with an essay on forest planting on the Great Plains.* Chicago: Jansen McClurg.

Cranz, G. (1982). *The politics of park design: A history of urban parks in America.* Cambridge, MA: MIT Press.

Hayden, D. (2002). *Redesigning the American dream: The future of housing, work, and family life* (Rev. ed.). New York: W. W. Norton.

International Federation of Landscape Architects. (2002). *Introduction to the IFLA constitution.* Retrieved October 20, 2002, from http://www.ifla.net/

Jackson, J. B. (1994). *A sense of place, a sense of time.* New Haven, CT: Yale University Press.

Jellicoe, G. A., & Jellicoe, S. (1995). *The landscape of man: Shaping the environment from prehistory to the present day* (3rd ed.). London: Thames & Hudson.

McHarg, I. L., & American Museum of Natural History. (1971). *Design with nature.* Garden City, NY: Natural History Press.

Olmsted, F. L., & Kimball, T. (1922). *Frederick Law Olmsted, landscape architect, 1822–1903.* New York: G. P. Putnam's Sons.

Reps, J. W. (1965). *The making of urban America; A history of city planning in the United States.* Princeton, NJ: Princeton University Press.

Repton, H., Malins, E. G., & Repton, J. A. (1976). *The Red Books of Humphrey Repton.* London: Basilisk Press.

Spirn, A. W. (1984). *The granite garden: Urban nature and human design.* New York: Basic Books.

Tate, A. (2001). *Great city parks.* New York: Spon Press.

Thacker, C. (1979). *The history of gardens.* Berkeley and Los Angeles: University of California Press.

Treib, M. (1993). *Modern landscape architecture: A critical review.* Cambridge, MA: MIT Press.

Landscape Art, American

The paintings of American landscape art may be viewed as historical documents that reveal much about attitudes toward the natural environment. Yet, they should also be viewed as historical actors that have shaped individual and public responses to the land. Since the sixteenth century, with the arrival of European settlers in the Americas, painted landscapes have been powerful agents of cultural change, inspiring economic investment, luring colonists, informing scientists, guiding military ventures, inciting tourism, and encouraging preservation.

The Colonial Era

The idea of "America" began to take shape in the European imagination with the aid of the writings and paintings of adventurers such as John White (fl. 1570s–1593), a participant in the English navigator Sir Walter Raleigh's scheme to found the first British settlement in Virginia. White's paintings, depicting lush forests, peaceful Native American villages, and limpid waters teeming with fish, presented America as a land of abundance, ripe for settlement. All through the colonial era, artists such as the Dutchman Adrian Danckers (fl. 1670s), the London-trained portraitist John Smibert (1688–1751), and the British colonial administrator Thomas Pownall (1722–1805) created images of thriving ports, orderly towns, and scenic wilderness sites such as Niagara Falls, New York. Using the conventions of European landscape art, including framing trees and structured progressions of light and dark, they imposed what was to their audiences a recognizable visual order onto the American land. Although landscape art was still a minor genre in this era, it helped to familiarize both Europeans and Euro-Americans with the appearance and potential of the continent.

After Independence: The National Era (1780–1860)

Landscape painting grew slowly in popularity through the first few decades after the United States declared its independence. With the emergence in the 1820s of the country's first important group of landscape painters—often called the "Hudson River school"—landscape art became a major form of artistic and cultural expression. In the hands of artists such as Thomas Cole (1801–1848), Frederic Church (1826–1900), and Albert Bierstadt (1830–1902), it participated in what was then a central cultural preoccupation: the creation of a distinctive national identity. The artists' expansive, light-suffused wilderness landscapes, painted with careful attention to natural detail, exalted the American land as one of God's most sublime creations, a source of patriotic pride, and the key to national identity.

Although extensive clear-cutting of forests, strip mining, and other industrial and agricultural ventures were then rapidly transforming the face of the American land, the artists of the Hudson River school, and indeed most nineteenth-century American landscape painters, tended to avoid portraying such scenes. They instead favored images that celebrated either the untouched, Edenic character of the American wilderness or, in paintings of settled landscapes, the easy, harmonious relationship between humans and the natural world. Much rarer are artistic expressions of the negative impact that humans could have on the natural environment. These include Sanford Gifford's *Hunter Mountain, Twilight* (1866, Terra Museum of American Art), which depicts sunlight fading over a valley of tree stumps, and Cole's pair of paintings of the landscape near his Catskill, New York, home—*View on the Catskill, Early Autumn* (1837, Metropolitan Museum of Art, New York) and *River in the Catskills* (1843, Museum of Fine Arts, Boston)—painted six years apart to show the depredations wrought by the arrival of the railroad and extensive agriculture.

Late Nineteenth Century–Early Twentieth Century

In the years after the Civil War both nationalist themes and wilderness subject matter faded from American landscape painting as it was transformed by wave after wave of European influences, including the French Barbizon and Impressionist styles. Although some artists continued to seek out rugged natural sites for their subject matter, as did Winslow Homer (1836–1910) in his oils of the wave-pounded margins of the Maine coast, most artists in these years turned to domesticated landscapes. George Inness (1825–1894) and Edward Bannister (1828–1901), for example, both working in a Barbizon-inflected mode, painted rutted roads wending across pastureland and snug farmhouses folded into copses. These paintings, with their gentle colors and soft, misty atmospheric effects, often seem suffused with nostalgia for a vanishing pastoral America.

The more generally upbeat American Impressionists such as Childe Hassam (1859–1935) and William Merritt Chase (1849–1916) embraced warm, blond colors, sparkling light effects, and pleasant, vacation-time subject matter. Their paintings of white sand beaches and clapboarded New England churches offered their viewers a pictorial refuge from the abrasions of modernity. Another group of artists, the New York-based Ashcan school, rejected the pretty canvasses of the American Impressionists as elitist and superficial. These artists, including John Sloan (1871–1951) and George Luks (1867–1933), turned their attention to urban, industrial scenery, painting the grittier aspects of New York life with murky colors and slashing brushwork.

Twentieth and Twenty-First Centuries

Landscape painting never regained in the twentieth century the prestige and prominence it had attained in the nineteenth, yet it continued to be produced in a wide range of subjects and styles. Many artists in the early decades of the century felt the allure of European modernism and sought to apply its lessons in their depictions of the American landscape. Arthur Dove (1880–1946), for example, in his abstract paintings, evoked the sensations and appearances of the natural world through the orchestration of colored forms. Georgia O'Keeffe (1887–1986) created spare images of New Mexico's arid country that convey her spiritual and emotional connection to the land, whereas Stuart Davis (1894–1964) produced raucous, brightly colored, Cubist-inspired evocations of New York City and Rockport, Massachusetts. Other artists chose a more realist mode. The sleek images of the American industrial scene by Charles Sheeler (1883–1965), especially his series of paintings of the Ford automobile factory in River Rouge, Michigan, and the empty streetscapes by Edward Hopper (1882–1967) pose questions about the place of humans in the technologically oriented modern world.

Realist landscape art enjoyed a brief ascendancy during the Great Depression of the 1930s. A number of artists used their landscapes to dramatize the human and environmental traumas of the era. Alexandre Hogue (1898–1994), for example, produced sober images of the abandoned farms, dead livestock, and wind-blown soil of the Dust Bowl. Others, such as Thomas Hart Benton (1889–1975) and Grant Wood (1892–1941), offered soothing and inspiring images of energetic American workers, fertile cropland, and small-town camaraderie.

As abstraction tightened its hold on the American art scene in the years after World War II, landscape almost disappeared from view. Not until the 1970s, with the impetus of the Bicentennial and the environmental movement, did it begin to reemerge. Artists such as Neil Jenney (b. 1945), Alex Katz (b. 1927), Neil Welliver (b. 1929), Jennifer Bartlett (b. 1941), Alexis Rockman (b. 1962), and Jacqueline Bishop (b. 1955) have created extraordinarily varied landscapes, ranging from nonrepresentational to hyperrealistic, from ironic to reverential. Their works offer satiric send-ups of suburbia, metaphorical landscapes of the human psyche, and anxiety-ridden images of a threatened Earth. Running through much of the landscape art of this time is a sense of impending spiritual and environmental crisis.

Rebecca Bedell

See also Hudson River School

Further Reading

Arthur, J. (1999). *Green woods and crystal waters: The American landscape tradition*. Tulsa, OK: Philbrook Museum of Art.

Bedell, R. (2001). *The anatomy of nature: Geology and American landscape painting, 1825–1875*. Princeton, NJ: Princeton University Press.

Corn, W. M. (1972). *The color of mood: American tonalism, 1880–1910*. San Francisco: M. H. De Young Memorial Museum.

Hartigan, L. R. (1985). *Sharing traditions: Five black artists in nineteenth-century America*. Washington, DC: Smithsonian Institution Press.

Howat, J. K., Avery, K. J., Roque, O. R., Burke, D. B., & Voorsanger, C. H. (1987). *American paradise: The world of the Hudson River school*. New York: Metropolitan Museum of Art.

Miller, A. (1993). *The empire of the eye: Landscape representation and American cultural politics, 1825–1875*. Ithaca, NY: Cornell University Press

Novak, B. (1995). *Nature and culture: American landscape and painting, 1825–1875* (Rev. ed.). New York: Oxford University Press.

Nygren, E. J., Robertson, B., Meyers, A. R. W., O'Malley, T., Parry, E. C. III, & Stilgoe, J. R. (1986). *Views and visions: American landscape before 1830*. Washington, DC: Corcoran Gallery of Art.

Weinberg, H. B., Bolger, D., & Curry, D. P. (1994). *American Impressionism and Realism: The painting of modern life, 1885–1915*. New York: Metropolitan Museum of Art.

Wilton, A., & Barringer, T. (2002). *American sublime: Landscape painting in the United States, 1820–1880*. Princeton, NJ: Princeton University Press.

Young, D. (1996). *Destiny manifest: American landscape painting in the nineties*. Gainesville: Harn Museum of Art, University of Florida.

Landscape Art, Chinese

China has long been associated with the production of landscape art, primarily in the form of painting, although apparently an interest in depicting the natural world was somewhat slow to emerge there. Although the archaeological record is incomplete, artifacts from the Neolithic period and early Bronze Age (c. fifth–first millennia BCE) rarely depict nature, and when nature is depicted it generally serves as a backdrop to human activities and not as the focus of the artist's attentions.

The Chinese term that is usually translated as "landscape" in English is made up of the words *shan* and *shui*, literally "mountains" and "rivers" (or "waters"); thus, unlike its English counterpart, *landscape* is a cosmologically (relating to the nature of the universe) loaded term in Chinese, its two elements forming a yin/yang pairing of complementary forces. (Yin is the feminine, passive principle in nature that in Chinese cosmology is exhibited in darkness, cold, or wetness; yang is the masculine, active principle that is exhibited in light, heat, or dryness. When the two principles combine, they produce everything that exists.) In several important early philosophical texts, moreover, water is used as a metaphor for the *dao*, or "way" of nature, whereas mountains (and rocks) are associated with immortality and the primal energy (*qi*) that animates the universe.

Early Representations

In light of these early associations, it is not surprising that the first popular representations of mountains, dating to the Han dynasty (202 BCE–220 CE), are generally found among tomb furnishings, where they frequently appear in the form of incense burners. Made from both clay and bronze and sometimes elaborately inlaid with metals and jewels, such burners usually contained perforations in the mountain-shaped conical lids so that when incense was burning the rising smoke would create the effect of misty peaks.

After the Han dynasty landscape elements begin to appear more frequently, especially in funerary art (such as the scenes depicted on the famous "Nelson sarcophagus"), in religious art (especially in the Buddhist murals at the Dunhuang caves), and in imperially sponsored secular art, such as the Tang dynasty (618–906) blue-and-green landscape tradition associated with the artist Li Zhaodao.

Birth of Monumental Landscape Art

Not until the tenth century, however, after the collapse of the Tang dynasty, did landscape painting finally emerge as an independent genre and the term *shanshui* begin to be used as a separate category in art-historical texts. This new mode of painting is often termed "monumental" both because of the physical size of the works and because of the vast panoramas they typically depict. Although individual and regional styles of landscape painting developed, works in this monumental tradition shared many features in common, such as a preference for the use of ink and wash (rather than the mineral colors generally favored in earlier painting), a clear division and organization of space, the employment of multiple points of view within a single composition, and an emphasis on the use of line as an expressive element.

Traveling amid Mountains and Gorges by the artist Fan Kuan (c. 960–1030), one of the most frequently reproduced examples of early Chinese landscape painting, exemplifies all of these features. A hanging scroll more than 2 meters tall, the work is dominated by a massive granitic mountain in the distance that occupies about two-thirds of the pictorial surface; as the viewer looks more closely, it can be observed that this towering mountain dwarfs a mule team and several figures that occupy the lower-right corner of the foreground, while the outline of a temple roof in the middle distance is silhouetted against a misty gorge just above them. *Traveling* has been praised as a celebration of the raw (if idealized) power of the natural world, and it might be said to demonstrate in a literal sense the proposition that nature is big and humanity is small.

The early masters of monumental landscape art, such as Fan Kuan and his predecessor Li Cheng (c. 919–967), also had in common the fact that they were not associated with the imperial court as artists. That is, they were perceived as amateurs—as scholars who happened also to paint—rather than as professional artists who painted on demand and who were consigned to a much lower social status. The term *literati painting (wenren hua)*, often applied to this tradition (also referred to as "scholar/official's art"), calls attention to the fact that social and intellectual ideals were a large part of its definition. Some modern scholars, in fact, have gone so far as to suggest that literati painting should be understood primarily in terms of shared social class and values and only secondarily in terms of style or shared artistic aims.

The Song Court

If the early landscape masters operated outside of the boundaries of direct court patronage, by the late Northern Song (960–1127) period this kind of painting was also being practiced in imperial settings, where new layers of meaning often accrued. *Early Spring* (dated 1072) by the court artist Guo Xi, for example, stylistically extends the Li Cheng mode; however, in light of the circumstances of its patronage and display, the viewer is clearly encouraged to equate the majestic mountain around which all revolves with the emperor himself.

In the late twelfth and early thirteenth centuries a more intimate mode of landscape developed in the painting academy at the Southern Song (1127–1279) court. Associated primarily with the artists Ma Yuan and Xia Gui, about whom little is known, these paintings tended to employ small formats, such as fans or album leaves, and to focus on scenes that could be taken in at a glance (unlike the complex monumental landscapes that needed to be pored over). The academy also promoted the amalgamation of poetry and painting, and many academy works originally paired a poetic couplet with a painted image (as in Ma Lin's *Reclining Scholar* in the Cleveland Museum of Art).

The Yuan Revolution

The fall of China to the Mongols in 1279 naturally had a major impact on virtually every aspect of Chinese society. Although portions of the country had previously come under foreign control at various points, this marked the first time that all of China was ruled by alien invaders. One effect of this situation was that many scholars (and artists) were reluctant to serve at court for fear of being perceived as collaborators, preferring to withdraw from official life. Many of these retired scholars turned to painting, and especially to landscape painting, as a vehicle for expressing their feelings about the Mongol occupation. For instance, during the Yuan period (1279–1368) Ni Zan (1306–1374) perfected a composition comprising a few trees, some rocks, and an empty hut in the foreground, with a range of mountains in the distance, all executed with a dry and spare technique and with little regard for pictorial illusionism. As one modern scholar writes of his work, "No concessions are made to the viewer; no figures, no boats or clouds enliven the scene, and nothing moves. The silence that pervades the picture is that which falls between friends who understand each other perfectly" (Sullivan 1999, 207).

Although made up of "mountains" and "rivers"—the literal elements of landscape—Ni Zan's paintings were seen by contemporaries (and later viewers) as the outward manifestation of the artist's inner state: the airless, uninhabited, and uninviting world they depict understood as representing the artist's own alienation. Other well-known scholar/artists of the fourteenth century, such as Huang Gongwang, Wu Chen, and Wang Meng, similarly developed individualized landscape styles that they, too, deployed in personally expressive ways. This creation of a mode of landscape painting that emphasized the expression of ideas and personal feelings at the expense of realistic depiction of the external world of nature, a kind of landscape of the self, has often been described as a seminal turning point in the history of Chinese painting that would fundamentally alter the very conception of what a painting can be.

Evolution of Practice and Theory in the Ming Period

After the restoration of Chinese rule in 1368, landscape painting developed along several lines during the Ming period (1368–1644). Professional artists, such as Dai Jin (1388–1452), founder of the so-called Zhe school, revived the earlier court-academy style of the Song period, although on a more monumental scale, whereas scholar/amateur artists, such as Shen Zhou (1427–1509), founder of the Wu school, continued to explore the expressive possibilities first exploited in the Yuan period. In this period, Ming paintings were also increasingly used to mark social occasions—an official's departure to take up a new post or an important anniversary or birthday, for example. At the same time, painting in general became increasingly self-conscious or "art-historical" as artists incorporated deliberate references to earlier styles.

Shen Zhou's famous *Lofty Mt. Lu* exemplifies several of these features and illustrates the way in which Ming artists were able to build multiple layers of meaning into a single work. The painting shows a towering mountain with a rushing waterfall cascading down its face, at the base of which stands the minute figure of a scholar, representing Shen Zhou himself, who gazes up at the peak. On one level, this is a painting about style because Shen Zhou deliberately paints here in the distinctively dense and restless mode associated with the Yuan artist Wang Meng. This is also a painting about "place" in that Mount Lu was a well-known scenic site, famous for the precipitous "flying bridge," which Shen prominently depicts. The artist's inscription reveals that this painting was produced in honor of the birthday of Shen's teacher, thus making this a work with a specific social function as well. Moreover, after one understands the nature of the occasion that sparked the painting, one sees that *Mt. Lu* is also a landscape portrait of the "lofty" teacher and of his former student who still feels dwarfed by his presence.

In the late Ming period the practice of exploring earlier pictorial styles as a goal of painting was codified by the artist and theorist Dong Qichang (1555–1636). Dong divided previous artists into two main camps, primarily in terms of their status as either professionals or scholar/amateurs (the latter of which he considered the orthodox tradition). Presaging twentieth-century modernist views in the West, Dong Qichang asserted that the true subject of painting is painting itself, not the external world. Landscape painting *(shanshui)*, he claimed, ought to be a vehicle for exploring the formal wonders of brush and ink; for those more interested in the natural wonders of actual mountains *(shan)* and rivers *(shui)*, Dong counseled a good hike.

Landscape Art in the Late Imperial and Modern Eras

With the fall of the Ming dynasty and the establishment of the Manchu (Qing) dynasty (1644–1911), China was again placed under foreign domination. As was the case in the Yuan period, many scholars remained loyal to the fallen dynasty, choosing reclusion over participation in official life and using their art as a vehicle to record their feelings and register their dismay. The loyalist painter Hongren (1610–1664), for instance, created spare, empty, nearly lifeless landscapes that immediately evoke the tradition of Ni Zan, whereas the brooding and moody compositions of Gong Xian (1620–1689), with their extreme contrasts of dark and light, suggest an almost apocalyptic vision, "symbolic both of the condition of his native land raped by the Manchus and of his own desperate sense of having, literally, nowhere to turn" (Sullivan 1999, 254).

Many art historians, however, have dismissed the bulk of Qing painting as "stultifying and lifeless imitation" (Fong 1992, 497), although some recent scholarship suggests that such views are beginning to change and that Qing painting is being broadly reappraised. Certainly, with the fall of the Qing dynasty in 1911, painting was revitalized, in part because of the rapid introduction of foreign styles and techniques that accompanied the rush to modernization. One effect of greater exposure to Western art was that painters had to grapple with the question of how "Chinese" their art should be. As a result, a movement known as *"guohua"* (national painting) evolved and stressed the use of traditional Chinese materials and themes, and this term continues to be used today to refer to the works of artists who consider themselves in some sense as heirs to China's classical past.

After the creation of the People's Republic in 1949, many *guohua* painters tried to follow Communist leader Mao Zedong's famous dictum that the past should serve the present and created a hybrid landscape that fused revolutionary values and history with traditional landscape styles. *Sunrise in Yan'an* by Qian Songyan (1899–1985) features a towering pagoda, emblematic of the past, off in the distance, whereas a modern highway bridge with trucks and buses spans the misty gorge at the heart of the composition. "The whole is illuminated by the rosy glow of dawn, or perhaps—to those who wished to read it so—of Communism" (Andrews & Shen 1998, 234).

Landscape art has dominated Chinese painting for most of the past one thousand years, in large measure precisely because it proved to be such an elastic and flexible genre, capable of allowing artists to explore the natural world in a variety of ways while also permitting personal, political, social, historical, and other themes to be included within its domain. Although

landscape painting has been largely relegated to a somewhat peripheral role at present, if history is any guide one might assume that yet another "new" landscape mode will one day occupy center stage again.

Charles Lachman

Further Reading

Andrews, J. F., & Shen, K. (1998). *A century in crisis: Modernity and tradition in the art of twentieth-century China*. New York: Abrams.

Barnhart, R., Xin, Y., Chongzheng, N., Cahill, J., Shaojun, L., & Hung, W. (1997). *Three thousand years of Chinese painting*. New Haven, CT: Yale University Press.

Bush, S. (1971). *The Chinese literati on painting*. Cambridge, MA: Harvard University Press.

Fong, W. C. (1992). *Beyond representation*. New Haven, CT: Yale University Press.

Keswick, M. (1986). *The Chinese garden*. New York: St. Martin's Press.

Munakata, K. (1991). *Sacred mountains in Chinese art*. Champaign: University of Illinois Press.

Sullivan, M. (1999). *The arts of China* (4th ed.). Berkeley and Los Angeles: University of California Press.

Thorp, R., & Vinograd, R. (2001). *Chinese art and culture*. New York: Abrams.

Landscape Art, European

Landscape art is a genre of art in which nature or natural scenery is the primary subject. Landscape art, as expressed through painting, is an articulation of an artist's interpretation of nature. European landscape art developed during the late fifteenth and early sixteenth centuries and occasionally has been influenced by social or intellectual developments as well as by artistic theory.

Origins of Landscape Art

The origins of Western and European landscape art can be found in Hellenistic and Roman art, in surviving examples of landscape murals that adorned the walls of Roman villas. Sometimes painted to look like a view out of a window, these first-century BCE murals depict scenes from the Homeric epic *The Odyssey* or blooming gardens. The presence of landscape art in Roman villas is believed to reflect a celebration of the life in the

Roman countryside that can be found in the poetry and literature of this period.

The Christian art of the Byzantine empire and medieval Europe (c. second century CE to c. fourteenth–fifteenth centuries CE) focused on religious subjects. Nature became the background against which human activity and divine events took place. The shimmering sixth-century CE Byzantine mosaics of churches such as Saint Apollonaire in Classe in Ravenna, Italy, represent an idealized, formal landscape of paradise. In Europe, landscape art could be found in illuminated manuscripts made for nobility and royalty, such as *Les Très Riches Heures du Duc de Berry* (1413–1416), which was a prayer book, or Book of Hours, used for private religious devotions. The French nobleman the Duc de Berry commissioned the Flemish Limbourg brothers to create it for him. A calendar as well as a book of religious devotions, *Les Très Riches Heures* details seasonal human interactions in nature. Palace decorations in southern France and northern Italy also utilized seasonal motifs, usually involving such activities of the nobility as hunting parties. Nature as a background for human activity would continue to be a motif in Renaissance painting.

Italian Landscape Art during and after the Renaissance

Renaissance art is noted for its humanism, a literary and cultural movement that influenced western Europe between the fourteenth and sixteenth centuries. Along with Christian themes, Renaissance art reflected an interest in Classical or mythological subjects. Landscape was utilized extensively in Renaissance art as a backdrop to human activity, often evoking the mood of the painting. In *St. Francis in Ecstasy* (c. 1458), painted by Venetian artist Giovanni Bellini (c. 1431–1516), the landscape is seen in perspective. The clearly drawn rock formations in the foreground almost dwarf St. Francis, and the buildings visible among the hills in the background show carefully depicted topographical details such as trees, fields, and a sunlit sky. Italian artists Leonardo da Vinci (1452–1519) and Titian (c. 1477–1566) also included landscapes as backgrounds in some of their most famous works. Da Vinci created a hazy, dreamlike landscape behind the figure in *Mona Lisa* (1503–1506), and Titian's twilight landscape backdrop to his portrait *Charles V at Mühlberg* (1548) shows King Charles V, mounted on his horse, emerging from a forest.

By the end of the sixteenth century the reintroduction of the pastoral ideal of country life influenced art as well. Italian artists, as well as those from the Netherlands, would, in turn, visit the countryside near Rome and re-create its ruins and its light in paintings depicting landscape far from the classical ruins of Rome.

Northern European Landscape Art

The Italian landscape tradition influenced the artists of northern Europe as well. Some, like Albrecht Dürer (1471–1528) of Germany, made studies of the Italian landscapes, focusing on mountains and atmosphere. Dürer's *Little Pond House* (c. 1497) is a watercolor where landscape and nature alone are the subject of the composition. Dürer began using the term *landscape* in 1520, and his recognition of the ability of a landscape painting to stand on its own as a work of art helped to pave the way for the acceptance of painting nature for its own sake as a form of art.

Flemish painter Pieter Brueghel the Elder (c. 1525–1569), who spent most of his life in Antwerp and Brussels, was one of the first to use landscape as the central focus of a major work. Using the medieval motif of the months of the year, Brueghel's *The Return of the Hunters* (1565) shows a winter village scene where human figures are part of the painting, but they are small against the bare trees, flat snowy plain, distant craggy hills, and gray sky. Prints made from Brueghel's other sketches of the Alps, along with drawings by artists that depicted scenes of forests and of village life, helped to increase the popularity of landscape art by making examples available to the general public.

Seventeenth-Century Italy: Center for Landscape Art

In spite of the fact that landscape art had become a recognized artistic genre by the seventeenth century, it lacked any specific guidelines or theory and remained low on the scale of artistic importance. History painting held the top position in the artistic hierarchy, out of which developed ideal, or classical, landscape painting. Inspired by the beauty of the Roman Campagna, or Roman countryside, artists from France and northern Europe experimented with landscape art, particularly with the effects of light. Many of them, such as French artist Claude Lorrain (1600–1682), sketched from life. French artist Nicolas Poussin (1594–1665) and Lorrain spent significant amounts of time in Italy and used the countryside around Rome as the model for their landscapes. Poussin, who was the first French painter to gain international fame, kept within the classical tradition of painting, using historical or mythological themes. In his *Landscape with the Burial of Phocion* (1648), Poussin details the burial of a Greek hero against a backdrop of a precise and orderly landscape dotted with temple and trees set on gently rolling hills.

Whereas Poussin painted idealized landscapes, Lorrain painted idyllic and pastoral ones. The figures in his landscapes are "meant to intensify the mood of the landscape and bring it into focus for the spectators" (Lucie-Smith 1971, 82). In Lorrain's *A Pastoral Landscape* (c. 1650), the human figures in the foreground are incidental, with the majority of the painting open sky, fields, and trees, lit by either a rising or setting sun.

Golden Age of Dutch Landscape Painting

The seventeenth century was the golden age of Dutch painting, and it was Dutch artists who helped to refine landscape art. Many of the greatest Dutch landscape painters spent many years in Italy, studying the Roman Campagna. Initially, Dutch artists used the unique light of the countryside around Rome when painting their native landscapes. By the mid-seventeenth century, however, Dutch artists recognized the uniqueness of their local landscapes and began to concentrate on capturing a more naturalistic vision of the moist atmosphere and pearly gray skies of northern Europe.

The increasing affluence of the Dutch middle class helped to increase the popularity of landscape art in the region. Middle-class merchants had an appreciation for fine paintings, and although those of the Dutch painter Rembrandt (1606–1669) were out of the reach of many, landscape paintings were not. These paintings' subjects ranged from the familiar, such as Jan van Goyen's *Fort on a River* (1664), which depicted well-known elements of the Dutch countryside, to the more fantastic, such Jacob van Ruisdael's dark and melancholy *The Jewish Cemetery* (1655–1660). Van Ruisdael (c. 1628–1682) is recognized as the greatest Dutch landscape painter, and his more emotional vision of nature would inspire the Romantic landscape painters of the eighteenth and nineteenth centuries. Among its other characteristics, Romanticism focused on human beings' emotional response to nature, which would add further depth to European landscape painting.

Romantic Landscape Art of the Eighteenth Century

In England the tradition of landscape art began with a nostalgic, idealized focus on the English countryside. In eighteenth-century England, "landscape was a cultural and aesthetic object," popular with the English gentry who had the funds to purchase landscape paintings (Bermingham 1986, 9). Thomas Gainsborough (1727–1788), although influenced by Dutch techniques, painted sunlit landscapes (*Robert Andrews and His Wife*, c. 1748–1750) rather than the shimmering gray landscapes of the Netherlands. The landscape paintings of John Constable (1776–1837) were nostalgic recollections of the countryside of his youth. Constable wanted to capture a "pure apprehension of natural effect" and painted numerous outdoor studies with this idea in mind (Janson 1991, 643). Constable was concerned with light, sky, clouds, and atmosphere rather than with the realistic reproduction of the landscape around him.

Eighteenth-century landscape art was influenced not only by Italian and Dutch ideas about light and atmosphere, but also by Romantic aesthetics. British statesman Edmund Burke's 1757 essay "A Philosophical Enquiry into the Origins of Our Ideas of the Sublime and Beautiful" and English writer William Gilpin's 1792 essay "On Picturesque Beauty" gave to Romantic thought three terms through which to explain and examine the observer's relationship to nature. The first was the idea of the *Sublime,* where nature inspired awe, terror, a sense of vastness and of magnificence. The second was the idea of the *Beautiful,* which focused on a characteristic smallness and smoothness of form. The third, the *Picturesque,* suggested ruggedness and rustic landscapes.

Landscape art was meant to convey the internalized, emotional reaction of the artist to nature and to inspire the same in the viewer. The paintings of Joseph Mallord William Turner (1775–1851) reflected his intense interest in the color of light and of inspiring feelings of awe at nature's power and magnificence. This can be seen clearly in *The Slave Ship* (1840). The German painter Caspar David Friedrich (1774–1840) used his paintings to demonstrate that humans are "indissolubly linked to . . . nature" (Stechow 1968, 2). Friedrich's *The Monk by the Sea* (1809) clearly demonstrates the emptiness of the sea and the sky, both of which dwarf the figure of the monk while giving a sense of human beings' powerlessness in nature. Romantic landscape painters were concerned with making nature look "natural" and enhanced that "naturalness" by giving viewers an emotional, subjective experience rather than a rational, objective one.

Nineteenth-Century Landscape Art: Plein Air Painting

Landscape art in nineteenth-century Europe was in many ways defined by developments in France, which affected landscape art not only in Europe but also in the United States. Sketching or drawing nature from life had been an established technique since the late sixteenth and early seventeenth centuries, but it became an important part of an artist's training during the late eighteenth and early nineteenth centuries. The development of paint in a tube, which allowed for easier transportability of an artist's main tool, meant that painting, as well as drawing and sketching, could be done out of doors. Where many artists such as Lorrain had taken their sketches from nature back to the studio and turned them into pastoral visions without a reference to a particular place, the French painter Camille Corot (1796–1875) painted oil paintings of particular views at specific times on the spot. Plein air painting, or painting out of doors, resulted in a more natural vision of nature.

The members of the Barbizon school shared some of Corot's techniques. Between the 1830s and 1870s artists such as the Frenchmen Théodore Rousseau (1812–1867) and François Millet (1814–1875) spent hours contemplating the wooded scenery and rural life of the village of Barbizon, near Paris. Both artists recorded a way of life disappearing before the advancing Industrial Revolution and in turn influenced the next generation of painters, some of whom would paint in a style known as "Impressionism."

Impressionism

Impressionism as an artistic style dates from the 1860s, when artists moved away from more established traditions of painting by focusing on the way light could be represented by bright colors, often through a series of studies at different times of the day. *Impressionism* was a term coined by hostile critics in 1874 in reference to a painting exhibited by the French painter Claude Monet (1840–1926) entitled *Impression: Sunrise*. Impressionists painted "impressions" of the landscape, of the sensations caused by the landscape, rather than the details of the landscape itself. Impressionist painters focused on rural, suburban, and urban landscapes as well as on scenes from modern life. Combined with an unorthodox treatment of colors and shapes, Impressionist landscapes were initially unpopular.

Post-Impressionism

Impressionism, with its emphasis on the personal freedom of the artists, laid the groundwork for modern art. During the late nineteenth century artists who wanted to take Impressionist art beyond what they saw as its limitations have been described as "Post-Impressionists," although there are few similarities between these painters beyond their experiences with Impressionism. During the late nineteenth century the Post-Impressionist French painter Paul Cezanne (1839–1906) influenced the vision of landscape art through his belief that "all forms in nature . . . are based upon the cone, the sphere, and the cylinder" (Langdon 1996, 717), a perception evident in a series of views of Mont Sainte-Victoire painted between 1902 and 1906. The Dutch artist Vincent van Gogh (1853–1890) painted nostalgic agricultural landscapes full of movement, such as the 1889 work *Wheat Field and Cypress Trees*. Paul Gauguin (1848–1903), a follower of Cezanne, turned to rural life as the subject of his landscape paintings, looking for the "hidden world of feeling" lost in modern, industrial society (Janson 1991, 689).

European Landscape Art after Post-Impressionism

Although landscape as a subject for composition remains an important artistic genre, it no longer holds the importance in the first years of the twenty-first century that it held from the sixteenth through the end of the nineteenth centuries. Two world wars, globalization, and the destruction of the natural environment have influenced a reverential view of nature that in many ways recalled the Romantic landscape artists' emotional response to nature. Landscape art in the twenty-first century remains a reflection of human interaction with nature.

Kimberly A. Jarvis

See also Romanticism

Further Reading

Adams, L. S. (1994). *A history of Western art*. New York: Harry N. Abrams.

Andrews, M. (1999). *Landscape and Western art*. New York: Oxford University Press.

Bermingham, A. (1986). *Landscape and ideology: The English rustic tradition 1740–1860*. Berkeley and Los Angeles: University of California Press.

Brown, C. (1996). *Making and meaning: Rubens's landscapes*. London: National Gallery of Art.

Champa, K. S. (1991). *The rise of landscape painting in France: Corot to Monet*. Manchester, NH: Currier Gallery of Art.

Janson, H. W. (1991). *The history of art*. New York: Harry N. Abrams.

Klonk, C. (1996). *Science and the perception of nature: British landscape art in the late nineteenth and early twentieth centuries*. New Haven, CT: Yale University Press.

Langdon, H. (1996). Landscape painting. In J. Turner (Ed.), *The dictionary of art*. London: Macmillan.

Lucie-Smith, E. (1971). *A concise history of French painting*. New York: Praeger Publishing.

Mitchell, W. J. T. (2002). *Landscape and power*. Chicago: University of Chicago Press.

Novak, B. (1995). *Nature and culture: American landscape and painting 1825–1875*. New York: Oxford University Press.

Rosenthal, M. (1982). *British landscape painting*. Ithaca, NY: Cornell University Press.

Rubin, J. H. (1999). *Impressionism*. London: Phaidon Press.

Silver, L. (1993). *Art in history*. Englewood Cliffs, NJ: Prentice Hall.

Stechow, W. (1968). *Dutch landscape painting of the seventeenth century*. London: Phaidon Press.

Turner, A. R. (1966). *The visions of landscape in Renaissance Italy*. Princeton, NJ: Princeton University Press.

Vaugh, W. (1980). *German Romantic painting*. New Haven, CT: Yale University Press.

Wright, C. (1983). *Dutch landscape painting*. Newcastle-upon-Tyne, UK: Tyne and Wear County Council Museums.

Landscape Art, Japanese

Landscape art in Japan was originally developed for garden design. The first recorded residential garden in Japan was the garden of Soga-no-Umako, built in 626 in Nara. This garden had a pond with islands designed not for practical use but for observation. During the Nara period (710–794), because the imperial palace was the center of government in the city, the gardens were designed not only for leisurely observation but also for social events. Today in the ruins of the Heijo Palace, there are traces of a pond with a winding stream, which was once used for poetry parties.

Heian Period

In 794 the capital was moved to Heian (Kyoto), and aristocratic culture flourished during the Heian period (794–1192). Because of its location, the Heian capital had abundant water resources, and many residences of aristocrats had gardens with a pond and a stream. Among the gardens built in Kyoto during the early Heian period, Shinsen-en and Saga-in were famous as large imperial gardens with a beautiful pond. The architecture of gardens was often depicted as being in the Chinese style in scroll paintings during this period. During the late Heian period, the palace style of building *(shinden-zukuri)* became standard for the residences of aristocrats. The interior space of the palace-style building was one room. The southern part of the space was used for ceremony and the northern part for living. The palace style of building had a garden with a pond and stream occupying half of the southern side of its site. Because of the one-room structure, the garden of a palace-style building looked like a picture when it was seen from the inside by opening one of the lifting windows. In order to design the garden of a palace-style building, the first garden-making manual, *Sakutei-ki* (a note of garden making), was written in 1289. No residential gardens built in the Heian period still exist. However, in Kyoto the garden in a Buddhist temple adjoining an aristocratic residence and the garden of a Buddhist monk's residence still remain. The best examples of such gardens are Uji Byodo-in (Kyoto), Enjo-ji (Nara), Joruri-ji (Kyoto), and Hiraizumi Motsu-ji (Iwate). The main characteristics of garden design during this period are elegant layout and functionality. The garden was used for social activities such as aristocratic parties and boating devoted to poem composition and musical performance.

During the Kamakura period (1192–1338), Chinese culture, including Zen Buddhism, was introduced to Japan. Because Zen emphasizes walking meditation as well as sitting meditation, people began to use the garden for strolling as well as for boating. The preference for strolling arose because military society emphasized studying Zen philosophy and literature rather than composing poems and reading aristocratic literature. Thus the garden began to be used for spiritual training as well as leisure. The garden of Saiho Temple (Moss Garden) in Kyoto, designed by Muso Soseki (1275–1351), is one of the best examples that shows the transitional stage between the garden of aristocratic society during the Heian period and the garden of military society during the Muromachi period (1338–1573).

The representative gardens during the Muromachi period are Rokuwan-ji Kinkaku and Jisho-ji Ginkaku (Kyoto). The Muromachi period was a period of civil war. Patrons of gardens had fewer financial resources because of successive conflicts, so gardens were smaller. As a result, the details of each element in the garden, such as the position or orientation of a stone and a tree, became more important. The best examples are stone gardens such as Daisen-in and Ryoan-ji (Kyoto).

The long period of civil war ended with the Azuchi-Momoyama period (1573–1600). As the country became more settled politically and militarily, large castles with sumptuous, large gardens began to be constructed by feudal lords. In the garden of Nijō Castle (Kyoto), for example, many colorful, large, rare stones and rare trees were used to show the power of the lord. Other examples are Daigo-ji Sampo-in (Kyoto) and Onjō-ji Kōjō-in (Shiga). Tea gardens also began to be designed during this period. The tea garden, or *roji*, is not a garden to be observed in its own right, but rather an approach to the teahouse itself. It is a space meant to impart a pure feeling of serenity to guests arriving for the tea ceremony. The tea garden is divided by a small gate into two parts. In the outer garden is a bench where guests await the host's signal that all is ready, a toilet, and stone lanterns to provide light; in the inner garden is a basin for hand washing and mouth rinsing—required etiquette for tea ceremony guests. These features were first elements of the tea garden and gradually became major elements of all Japanese gardens. Unlike the gardens of castles, tea gardens employ simple materials, probably chosen because of the essence of the tea ceremony. Its ideal, coming close to nature, is realized by sheltering oneself in a simple rustic landscape.

Edo Period

During the Edo period (1600–1868), strolling gardens became popular among imperial families and feudal lords. The strolling gardens during this time were gardens with a theme. For example, in Tokyo Koishikawa Kōraku-en of the Mito clan reflects Confucian ideas, and Togoshi Garden of the Hosokawa clan and Toyama Garden of the Owari clan contained versions of the fifty-three scenic points on the Tokaidō Road. The style of the strolling garden reflects all of the styles developed in the previous periods. The garden was designed for leisurely walking with less emphasis on the composition of rocks. During the Edo period, because of advances in printing techniques, many books on garden making were published, and garden making became popular not only among the ruling class but also among the common people.

During the Meiji period (1868–1912), as Western architecture and gardens were introduced to Japan, new designs were sought for gardens. High-ranking bureaucrats and new entrepreneurs created large gardens that showed Western influences. Public parks were planned in cities, and landscape art began to be applied not only to gardens but also to the public spaces. The Taisho period (1912–1926) and Showa period (1926–1989) were the era of small residential gardens. During the Showa period there were two outstanding tendencies in garden design: gardens with abstract design, advocated by garden designer Shigemori Mirei, and gardens with various trees, advocated by garden designer Ogata Kenzo. After World War II, especially during the Heisei period (1989–present), landscape design began to be seen as a way to address environmental and ecological problems.

Seiko Goto

Further Reading

Mori, A. (1964). *Nihon no teien*. Tokyo: Yoshikawa Kobunkan.

Nishizawa, F. (1976). *Teien-ron*. Tokyo: Sagami Shobo.

Shigemori, M. (1971–1974). *Nihon teien-shi taikei*. Tokyo: Shakai Shisosha.

Laozi

(Sixth century BCE)
Chinese philosopher

Laozi was the reputed author of the classic Taoist text known as the *Daode jing* (The Way and Its Power). (Taosim is the indigenous higher religion of China). The name "Laozi" can be translated simply as "Old Master," but the historical identity of this "old master" remains the subject of controversy. The Han dynasty historian Sima Qian (145?–86 BCE) identified Laozi as a southern Chinese archivist known as "Li Er" or "Li Dan." Other early sources, by contrast, identify Laozi as a figure named "Lao Dan," but it is not known

Nature does not hurry, yet everything is accomplished.

—Laozi

whether "Lao" in this case should be understood simply as a surname and "Dan" a forename, or whether in fact "Lao" is an honorific title and the name should be translated as "Old Dan."

According to the *Zhuangzi* (c. 350 BCE; early Taoist wisdom literature), Laozi was the elder contemporary of the Chinese philosopher Confucius (551–479 BCE). British sinologist A. C. Graham (1990) has hypothesized that the lore surrounding the figure of Laozi is in fact a conflation of several personages. It may well be that Lao Dan and Li Er were separate historical figures identified by the later tradition as the "old master."

Historical controversy aside, the figure Laozi has had an important role as a deity in the Taoist religious tradition that may be dated to 142 CE, when Laozi appeared in a revelation to Zhang Daoling, founder of the Way of the Celestial Matters, and established the Way of Orthodox Unity (*Zhengyi dao*), also known as the Way of the Celestial Masters (*Tianshi dao*) or, more pejoratively, as the Five Bushels of Rice sect (*Wudoumi dao*). Taoist priests today trace their lineage back to Zhang Daoling, the first celestial master, and venerate Laozi as one of the chief deities of their pantheon.

The mythology surrounding Laozi underwent further development from the third through the ninth centuries CE, when Taoist traditions expanded and transformed after the dissolution of the original celestial masters community. During this time Buddhism began to be imported into China, and Taoists and Buddhists engaged in debates in order to secure imperial favor. According to an earlier tradition, Laozi had left China on a journey westward and had dictated the *Daode jing* to Yin Xi, the guardian of the Hangu pass separating China from the Western barbarian lands. According to the new version of this story, Laozi had in fact gone to India, where he appeared as the Buddha. Laozi was now to be understood in this new theological interpretation as a cosmic being who manifested throughout the ages and throughout the world in order to bring people into harmony with the Tao, the wellspring of cosmic power for a universe of constant transformation.

Laozi thus became a divine sage associated with political wisdom and harmonious governance. On the basis of his identification as someone named "Li," he was claimed as an ancestor by the Li clan who established the Tang dynasty (618–906 CE). This genealogical act firmly established Laozi and his tradition as key politico-religious icons in imperial Chinese civilization.

James Miller

Further Reading

Ching, J. (1997). *Mysticism and kingship in China*. Cambridge, UK: Cambridge University Press.

Graham, A. C. (1990). The origins of the legend of Lao Tan. In A. C. Graham (Ed.), *Studies in Chinese philosophy and philosophical literature* (pp. 111–124). Albany: State University of New York Press.

Kohn, L. (1999). *God of the Dao: Lord Lao in history and myth*. Ann Arbor: University of Michigan Center for Chinese Studies.

Kohn, L., & LaFargue, M. (Eds.). (1998). *Lao-tzu and the Tao-te-ching*. Albany: State University of New York Press.

Latin America *See* Amazon River; Amazonia, Ancient; Andes; Argentina; Bolivia; Brazil; Cacao; Caribbean; Caribbean Coastlands; Central America; Chile; Columbia; Ecuador; Guano; Manioc; Mendes, Chico; Mexico; Orinoco River; Peru; Peru, Coastal; Rio de la Plata River; Sugar and Sugarcane; Sweet Potato; Venezuela

Law—Biological Conservation

Biological conservation has been a concern of law for as long as there have been scarcity and conflict over biological resources. Well over two thousand years ago the kingdoms of Assyria and Persia established legally protected hunting preserves for the noble classes. Although some sacred areas and moral imperatives to care for nature have religious origins, biological conservation in law grew out of relatively narrow concerns to maintain harvest levels of game and fish. Today the law embraces a far more diverse set of objectives, including preventing extinctions, protecting natural beauty, sustaining ecosystem services, and maintaining biodiversity (the variety and variability of life forms and the ecosystems in which they occur). As regions develop and acquire affluence, biological conservation to maintain economic or subsistence harvest tends to be replaced by recreational, aesthetic, ethical, and long-term ecological concerns. Nonetheless, the more closely economic interests align with legal objectives, the more likely it will be that law operates effectively.

It is important to keep in mind that the law of biological conservation binds only people, not wildlife. To meet the goals of law, the power of the state constrains activities and classes of people. Royal hunting preserves, for instance, are as significant for their maintenance of game as they are for their maintenance of the social order. The aims of law often mix biological goals, such as sustaining deer populations, with social goals, such as limiting the availability of weapons to the ruling class.

This article concentrates on the nondomesticated biological resources—wildlife—of both animals and plants. In contrast to wildlife, domestic cultivars (organisms originating and persisting under cultivation), livestock, and genetically engineered organisms are conserved primarily through traditional property rights. However, as wildlife conservation techniques become more sophisticated, the line between deliberately bred populations and uncontrolled nature blurs somewhat. As people move forward to an era of more active management of species and ecosystems, law will face new challenges in determining what remains wild and what becomes domesticated.

This brief legal survey reviews the three principal mechanisms used to conserve biological resources, in roughly the order in which they emerged in their modern legal guises. Although the article focuses on U.S. law and its English roots, the historical developments find close parallels in other legal systems. The first section discusses restrictions on hunting, trapping, fishing, and other harvest activities. These species-specific restrictions regulate the time, place, and manner in which people can exploit biological resources. The second section describes the approach of protecting particular places that serve as habitat or reserves for biological resources. Public lands, especially parks, have played an especially important role as refuges for wildlife and are increasingly managed actively to enhance ecological attributes. The third section explains how broad-scale regulation, especially of activities on private land, addresses ecological concerns that cross property lines. Limitations on the destruction of wetlands through national regulation in the United States beginning in the 1970s, for instance, have helped sustain a wide range of wildlife, especially migratory birds.

Harvest Activity Restrictions

When threats to sustainable populations of animals and plants come from overexploitation, a simple legal fix is the restriction of harvest. This is sometimes also called a "take limitation." British concern about game populations, as well as social discrimination and a sense of fair play for sport hunting, led to a series of restrictions on hunting in the sixteenth through nineteenth centuries. These restrictions included prohibitions on tracking hare in snow, limitations on which species could be hunted with firearms, "qualification statutes" restricting the kinds of people who could own firearms, and prohibitions on attracting game with lights and sounds. The basic legal elements employed by the British to limit harvest remain the chief elements today. They control who may hunt, when hunting may occur, how hunting may occur, and what may be hunted.

The British restrictions on hunting were not necessary in early colonial America because wildlife was abundant. Beginning on the East Coast, as habitat conversion and harvest took their toll on wildlife, states began to enact laws paralleling the British limitations on take. Hunting permits, closed seasons, bag limits, size limits, reproductive limits, and rules that require hunters to withhold using some forms of harvest technology all emerged in the nineteenth and early twentieth centuries in state hunting and fishing laws. During this time Britain extended these same types of legal restrictions to a wider array of wild animals.

Poor enforcement and spotty coverage of state conservation laws led to dramatic declines of wildlife in mid- to late nineteenth-century America. Sport hunters

Legal Principles for Environmental Protection

Below is the "Summary of Proposed Legal Principles for Environmental Protection and Sustainable Development" adopted by the World Commission on Environment and Development (WCED) Experts Group on Environmental Law.

I. GENERAL PRINCIPLES, RIGHTS, AND RESPONSIBILITIES

Fundamental Human Right

1. All human beings have the fundamental right to an environment adequate for their health and well-being.

Inter-Generational Equity

2. States shall conserve and use the environment and natural resources for the benefit of present and future generations.

Conservation and Sustainable Use

3. States shall maintain ecosystems and environmental processes essential for the functioning of the biosphere, shall preserve biological diversity, and shall observe the principle of optimum sustainable yield in the use of living natural resources and ecosystems.

Environmental Standards and Monitoring

4. States shall establish adequate environmental protection standards and monitor changes in and publish relevant data on environmental quality and resource use.

Prior Environmental Assessments

5. States shall make or require prior environmental assessments of proposed activities which may significantly affect the environment or use of a natural resource.

Prior Notification, Access, and Due Process

6. States shall inform in a timely manner all persons likely to be significantly affected by a planned activity and to grant them equal access and due process in administrative and judicial proceedings.

Sustainable Development and Assistance

7. States shall ensure that conservation is treated as an integral part of the planning and implementation of development activities and provide assistance to other States, especially to developing countries, in support of environmental protection and sustainable development.

General Obligation to Co-operate

8. States shall co-operate in good faith with other States in implementing the preceding rights and obligations.

Source: World Commission on Environment and Development. (1987). *Our Common Future.* Oxford, UK: Oxford University Press, pp. 348–349.

led the effort to tighten restrictions on harvest to protect wildlife. Congress enacted the first federal law restricting take of wildlife in the 1900 Lacey Act. The principal purpose of the Lacey Act was to provide a federal enforcement hook to prosecute interstate commerce involving animals killed in violation of state law.

State conservation concerns were not the only fuel for federal lawmaking. International calls for conservation of transboundary wildlife also spurred legal developments. Beginning with the Convention with Great Britain for the Protection of Migratory Birds in 1916, the United States signed a series of treaties promising protection for animals that cross national borders. Subsequent treaties extended international concern over hunting to fur seals, polar bears, and whales. However, the original Migratory Bird Treaty Act of 1918, providing national authority to meet the obligations of the bird treaties, brought new administrative tools to bear on conservation. In addition to prohibiting certain takes, and even possession, of birds listed under the treaties, it also allowed the federal government to establish harvest restrictions to regulate hunters.

From listed migratory birds in 1918 to listed threatened and endangered species in 1973, federal statutory law traces a steady arc of growth in the range of species (including eagles and marine mammals) protected by take restrictions. The 1973 Endangered Species Act (ESA) broke new ground in two respects. First, it brought new kinds of species under federal harvest restrictions. In addition to the species valuable for sport hunting (such as ducks), commercial exploitation (such as ocean fishes), and national pride (such as bald eagles), the ESA provides protection to any plant or animal on the brink of extinction other than certain insect pests. Such uncharismatic microfauna as the Delhi sands flower-loving fly, the furbish lousewort, and the snail darter received protection under the ESA.

Second, the ESA expanded the traditional scope of take limitations, which formerly covered only direct hunting, collecting, harassing, or pursuing, to include harm. *Harm,* undefined by the act, is a broader term embracing indirect adverse effects to species, such as habitat destruction incidental to otherwise lawful activities (*Babbitt v. Sweet Home Chapter of Communities for a Great Oregon,* 1995). Recent developments in administration of the ESA now employ the harm limitation on habitat modification in a manner that encourages people involved in habitat-disturbing activities to develop conservation and mitigation plans. In this respect, the cutting edge of harvest method restrictions now overlaps the broad-scale regulation of private activities to protect habitat.

Protected Areas

The medieval English "forest jurisdictions" comprised protected areas where ordinary common law did not apply (Lund 1980, 11). Instead, the king's concern for protecting wildlife gave rise to special enforcement officials, special courts, and special rules that afforded rights to animals against harms by people. Plants that were important in providing food and shelter to game animals also received special protection. In many ways, these "forest jurisdictions" are the predecessors of today's protected habitats for conserving biological resources.

The importance of protected areas to conserving biological resources rises as the main threat to species shifts from overexploitation to habitat destruction. This shift occurs as larger-scale agricultural production and industrialization replace subsistence hunting and fishing. The development of protected areas in the United States began first as a response to the Romantic-Transcendentalist and nationalistic conceptions of wilderness value. Popularized by such writers as Henry David Thoreau and John Muir, the Romantic-Transcendentalist philosophy viewed wild nature as a source of sublime inspiration. The United States pioneered many legal innovations in protected area management beginning in the 1870s.

Early protected areas in the United States were public parks declared off limits to certain forms of exploitation, especially homesteading and logging. Among the first were the 1864 federal grant of Yosemite Valley to the state of California for the establishment of a park, the 1872 congressional designation of Yellowstone as a national park, and the 1894 New York State constitutional amendment declaring Adirondack Park to be managed forever wild. These early preserves were selected primarily for their monumental geological attributes and the majesty of their landscapes, not for their habitat value. Nonetheless, an incidental benefit of the parks came to be biological conservation. It was not until the 1934 authorization of Everglades National Park that ecological protection rose to the level of a principal mandate for a national park.

The national forests, established in the wake of widespread timber theft, overcutting, and watershed degradation, were similarly established with purposes other than wildlife protection in mind (other than the floral resources of the forests themselves). Congress first authorized the reservation of federal forests in 1890 and provided a management mandate in 1897. Over time, however, protective overlays, such as the designation of wilderness areas (beginning in 1964), and substantive management criteria, such as the requirement that national forests provide for biological diversity (beginning in 1976), increased the value of national forests for conserving wildlife.

Of all the federal public land designations, it is the National Wildlife Refuge System whose origins most closely align with the purposes of conservation of biological resources. President Theodore Roosevelt, a renowned hunter, designated the first refuge, Florida's Pelican Island, in 1903 to provide habitat for birds. Other early national wildlife refuges were likewise designated to provide habitat for particular animals, such as elk or bison, or relatively narrow categories of animals, such as game or native birds. In the 1970s refuge establishment purposes broadened to include ecological features and plant conservation. Under its 1997 comprehensive statutory mandate, the refuge system now has a mission to "administer a national network of lands and waters for the conservation, management, and where appropriate, restoration of the fish, wildlife, and plant resources and their habitats" (16 U.S.C. § 668dd[a][2]). Substantive statutory management criteria include the maintenance of the "biological integrity, diversity, and environmental health of the System" (16 U.S.C. § 668dd[a][4]). This management mandate is currently the most direct expression of conservation biology goals in U.S. public land law.

During recent decades protected areas of nonpublic land have grown to be significant. The private, nonprofit Nature Conservancy, most notably, manages 5.2 million hectares of land around the world to conserve biological resources. Regional land trusts for biological conservation became widespread in the 1990s.

Broad-Scale Regulation

Protected areas provide habitat but only within designated boundaries. The best habitat is often owned privately, and even large reserves generally cannot provide enough habitat to sustain migratory or large animals. Activities, such as water use, outside of protected area boundaries can thwart conservation goals within the protected area.

The rise of the modern environmental law movement in the late 1960s and early 1970s for the first time brought broad-scale environmental regulation to bear on these problems. This regulation limits activities that adversely affect particular biological resources, wherever they occur. Although harvest method restrictions may be considered a type of broad-scale regulation, what distinguishes the modern developments of the past forty years from traditional take regulation is the focus on activities that incidentally degrade habitat, through pollution or land disturbance.

Early common law cases limiting habitat-degrading pollution focused on the effects on human health or the unreasonable interference with conflicting property rights. Nonetheless, early limitations on the disposal of waste in waterways alleviated some of the worst harms to biological resources. Also, in some settings, fishers and others whose livelihoods directly depended on ecological health were able to recover for harms and strengthen the deterrent for private injury to wildlife.

However, federal statutory innovations have eclipsed common law in the modern era. The two leading examples of broad-scale regulation of private activities in order to conserve biological resources are the 1973 Endangered Species Act (ESA) and the 1972 Clean Water Act (CWA). The ESA regulates private action in two ways. First, it prohibits harm, including forms of significant habitat degradation, without an incidental take permit. In order to get an incidental take permit, a person must prepare a habitat conservation plan that meets a series of requirements, including mitigation. Second, the ESA requires all federally authorized or funded activities, including activities requiring a federal permit, to avoid jeopardizing the continued existence of a species listed as protected under the act. The agency issuing the permit or granting the money must show that the activity will not result in jeopardy to a species through a process of environmental-impact analysis and interagency consultation.

The CWA regulates discharge of pollutants into waters of the United States. Its goals include the restoration and maintenance of the "biological integrity" of waters. Biological criteria help to determine whether any particular discharge will impair water quality standards, established by states but approved by the U.S. Environmental Protection Agency. Permits may be issued for a pollution discharge as long as it will not impair water quality standards.

Another major program of the CWA requires permits to discharge dredge or fill material into waters, including wetlands. Because wetlands are such an important habitat type, this special program is significant for the wide range of wildlife that depends on wetlands or wetlands-spawned species. The CWA dredge or fill permits generally promote locating activities away from wetlands, if possible, and require minimization and mitigation of impacts on wetlands. Because development often requires filling wetlands, this permit program is akin to land use control.

Current Trends

Three trends point toward new developments in the law of biological conservation. First, the emergence of sustainable development in the late 1980s recognized that biological conservation must go hand in hand with poverty alleviation. More affluent groups are more likely to make and abide by laws protecting natural systems. Likewise, ecosystems must remain healthy over the long term in order for societies to prosper over the long term. In addition to shaping international aid decisions, sustainable development also has shaped domestic law decisions, such as the 2000 U.S. Forest Service revisions to its regulations governing planning.

Second, because habitat degradation on privately controlled lands is now the leading threat to biodiversity in the United States, future developments in law will focus on influencing private development. Although people can expect greater regulation through tools similar to the ESA and CWA, financial incentives, such as tax breaks, cost-share programs, and direct subsidies will rise in importance.

Third, global climate change will worsen the weaknesses of isolated protected areas as conservation tools. As habitat zones shift under jurisdictional boundaries, the importance of conservation networks, corridors, and connections among protected areas will become increasingly critical. This trend, along with the other two, suggests that larger-scale, more-comprehensive conservation strategies that incorporate economic and social objectives subject to an ecological bottom line will be needed in future conservation law reform.

Robert L. Fischman

See also Biodiversity; Endangered Species; Endangered Species Act; Zoos

Further Reading

Andrews, R. N. L. (1999). *Managing the environment, managing ourselves: A history of American environmental policy.* New Haven, CT: Yale University Press.

Bean, M. J., & Rowland, M. J. (1997). *The evolution of national wildlife law.* Westport, CT: Praeger.

Davenport, L., & Rao, M. (2002). The history of protection: Paradoxes of the past and challenges for the future. In J. Terborgh, C. Van Schaik, L. Davenport, & M. Rao (Eds.), *Making parks work* (pp. 30–50). Washington, DC: Island Press.

Evans, D. (1992). *A history of nature conservation in Britain.* London: Routledge.

Fischman, R. L. (2002). The National Wildlife Refuge System and the hallmarks of modern organic legislation. *Ecology Law Quarterly, 29*(3), 457.

Hays, S. P. (1959). *Conservation and the gospel of efficiency: The progressive conservation movement, 1890–1920.* Cambridge, MA: Harvard University Press.

Lund, T. A. (1980). *American wildlife law.* Berkeley and Los Angeles: University of California Press.

Musgrave, R. S., & Stein, M. A. (1993). *State wildlife laws handbook.* Rockville, MD: Government Institutes.

Nash, R. (1973). *Wilderness and the American mind* (Rev. ed.). New Haven, CT: Yale University Press.

Nash, R. F. (1989). *The rights of nature: A history of environmental ethics.* Madison: University of Wisconsin Press.

Runte, A. (1987). *National parks: The American experience.* Lincoln: University of Nebraska Press.

Wilcove, D. S. (1999). *The condor's shadow: The loss and recovery of wildlife in America.* New York: W. H. Freeman.

Williams, M. (1989). *Americans and their forests: A historical geography.* Cambridge, UK: Cambridge University Press.

Worster, D. (1994). *Nature's economy: A history of ecological ideas.* Cambridge, UK: Cambridge University Press.

Court Cases

Babbitt v. Sweet Home Chapter of Communities for a Great Oregon, 515 U.S. 687 (1995).

Law—Land Use and Property Rights

Since at least the Dutch scholar Hugo Grotius (1583–1645) and the British philosopher John Locke (1632–1704), political theorists have explored the connections between property rights and government. Explorations of the connections among property rights, land use, and the environment have emerged more recently. Property is popularly taken to denote a thing or the possession of a thing by someone. However, property and property rights are better understood as social relations between people regarding the possession and use of things. That is, property is "a claim to some use or benefit of something" that will "be enforced by society or the state, by custom or convention or law" (MacPherson 1978, 3). Property is generally understood as involving the ability of the property claimant to exclude others from something; however, some argue that property may (or should) river also be an individual right *not* to be excluded by others from the use or benefit of something.

Conceptualizing property as a social relation focuses attention on relations between people and between people and property-related institutions. For example, the ownership, distribution, and use of land in a particular locale may involve relations between land managers and/or relations between land managers and state land-management agencies, banks, private companies, producer cooperatives, and environmental organizations. Recent scholars, drawing on the argument of the economic historian Karl Polanyi (1886–1964) that all economic institutions exist within rather than separate from society, have referred to property as "embedded" in the social, political, economic, and cultural relations between people and institutions. Anthropologist B. J. McCay and sociologist S. Jentoft argue that attention to embeddedness allows for more complex explanations of environmental change/degradation rather than simply "market failure" caused by inadequate property rights. The "misuse and abuse of common resources," they argue, may also result from "community failure" or "situations where resource users find themselves without the social bonds that connect them to each other and to their communities and where responsibilities and tools for resource management are absent" (McCay & Jentoft 1998, 25). The social and institutional dynamics of property, the role of property in society, and the connections between property and environmental change involve several key areas of research.

The Complexity of Property Practice

Because property rights determine, to paraphrase the scholar of law and philosophy Jeremy Waldron, who may be where, when, and doing what, they affect land-use patterns and hence have environmental consequences. To understand the processes that lead to these patterns, it is necessary to move beyond the broad categories of state, private, and common property to more nuanced understandings of the complexity of social relations that constitutes property in practice. The first

complexity is that property is a bundle of rights (e.g., rights to use, sell, lend, give away, lease, destroy, bequeath), which may be held separately by different people at different times. In zoning, for example, the government withholds certain rights from a property owner's bundle of rights. Similarly, different and overlapping kinds of property rights may be asserted against the same physical resource at the same time. This is most easily seen in the case of usufructuary rights, that is, rights restricted to the use of something. Women may have usufructuary rights to the fronds of a palm tree, and, simultaneously, men may have usufructuary rights to the fruit of the same palm tree. The rights to physical attributes (water, trees, minerals, wildlife) of a parcel of land may be held by entirely different people or institutions. A second complexity is that even though legal title may be static, property and tenure relations are dynamic in practice. The form of property under which a physical resource is held may vary seasonally or during ecological stress. For example, private water sources may become common property during drought. A third complexity is that the effects of particular forms of property vary with the social structures in which they are embedded. Thus, for example, although agricultural tenancy is frequently associated with exploitation of the tenant by the landlord, in particular circumstances agriculture tenants have greater control over and benefit from land than do the landlords, sometimes with adverse environmental consequences. For example, when tenants have greater power than landlords, they may refuse to accept clauses in their leases requiring environmentally friendly farming practices. A fourth complexity is that different means of creating the same property rights may have contradictory effects. For example, under some circumstances clearing forest creates rights to the land on which the trees grew, whereas under other circumstances planting trees creates rights to the land on which the trees are planted. In both cases, the rights are rooted in the Lockean notion of labor as the source of property rights, but the environmental consequences are quite different.

Legal Pluralism

Property law is often seen as an instrument for encouraging stewardship or discouraging degradative land-use practices. When such law is being considered, it is worth examining whether state property law is what matters in a particular locality. The field of legal pluralism offers insight in this regard. In contrast to state-centrist approaches, which hold that the state is the sole source of law, legal pluralism recognizes that two or more legal systems (ranging from the customary or traditional law codified and recognized by colonial regimes to religious law to law created and enforced by smaller social groups) may coexist in the same social field. Although the idea of nonstate legal regimes (legal regimes that are not based on legislation or judicial decisions by the state) is generally accepted by most legal scholars, they differ on the boundaries of what counts as "law." An emerging focus on the recognition of more than one kind of law in a group's social practices may resolve this issue. The analytical importance of legal pluralism is clear in the myriad struggles between local people and the state over the use of state-owned forest and parkland. Under national statutory law, national forests and national parks clearly are the property of the state. However, in both industrialized and nonindustrialized nations, local people claim and exercise usufructuary rights based on customary law to collect firewood, cut poles, graze cattle, hunt, gather food and medicines, and farm on national forest and park land. Analysts who wish to understand property in practice, will, in such a situation, direct their attention not just to national statutes but to local customary law as well.

Security of Tenure

It is often taken as given that physical and financial investments in land improvement and/or environmental stewardship depend on secure land tenure (property rights that ensure that the land manager is confident of reaping the returns from investment) under which the land manager is confident of reaping the returns from investment. For some time, enthusiasm for security of land tenure translated into enthusiasm for land registration and privatization. Evidence that such policies did not necessarily have the desired beneficial effects led to a reexamination of what actually constitutes security of tenure and for whom. One approach to security of tenure considers three elements: (1) breadth: the composition of rights (such as the right to sell, the right to use, the right to destroy, and so on), (2) duration: the length of time a right is legally valid, and (3) assurance: the certainty with which a right is held and with which it reflects the predictability and enforcement ability of the tenure-granting regime. Another approach separates the right of ownership from the owner's actual ability to control her or his property. These analytical approaches have

made it clear that private property and security of tenure are not synonymous.

Gendered Property Rights

If security of tenure is important for environmental stewardship, then it is important to know whose tenure is secure and whose is not. When property rights are assumed to be vested in the household rather than in individual members of the household, women's property rights (or the lack of them) are made invisible, often with adverse consequences for women and/or for the environment. On average, women have less land than men and are more likely than men to be landless. Even in households with secure tenure, women's property rights are often insecure. In most of Africa the breadth of women's security of land tenure is narrower than men's because significantly less frequently than men's it includes the ability to rent, give away, lend, lease, sell, or bequeath. In many places women acquire access to land not in their own right but through their fathers, husbands, and brothers. Daughters may have no rights of inheritance from their parents or may be unable to exercise their inheritance rights. The corollary to this principle of access to land is that the fruits of a woman's labor on the land often belong to her husband or his relatives, not to her. Gendered struggles over land rights may also reflect men's desire to control women's labor. The longer a property right is legally valid, the greater the security of duration of tenure. Security of duration of tenure is a matter of particular concern for women living under a gendered property regime in which changes in marital status can be catastrophic for them. It is not uncommon in the case of divorce for property acquired by a woman during marriage to become her husband's property, leaving her destitute. Widows may have limited property rights. They may have no right to inherit their husbands' property, including trees that they themselves have planted and tended. In the face of incursions by younger men, they may not be able to retain control of their property. The environmental effects of gendered property rights have not been widely studied. However, a Zimbabwe study found that in the context of insecure land and tree tenure rights, women, regardless of class, were significantly less likely than men to plant trees on their homestead.

Common Property

The publication of the ecologist Garrett Hardin's "Tragedy of the Commons" in 1968 propelled common property to the foreground of policy, scholarly, and popular debates about land use and the environment. Hardin's famous article concluded, and many policymakers and ordinary people still believe, that common property will inevitably be degraded. This conclusion stemmed from Hardin's confusion of common property resources (in which a set of resource users manages the resource and exclude others) with open access resources (in which no one is excluded, and no one takes responsibility—everyone is a free rider, that is, a user who does not contribute to managing or sustaining the resource). Hardin also separated his imaginary resource users from any social context and hence ruled out any possibility of rules, foresight, monitoring, alternative resource exploitation, or other proactive measures characteristic of actual property institutions. Accordingly, Hardin made it seem as if the only management solutions are either to rationalize individual behavior by privatizing property rights or to protect the property through state intervention. To this day, privatization has persisted as the dominant policy approach, despite many scholars having documented that both private and state managers can degrade resources just as seriously as the public. Moreover, for certain resources "that are sufficiently large as to make it costly (but not impossible) to exclude potential beneficiaries from obtaining benefits from their use" (Ostrom 1990, 30), such as many fisheries, or for unpredictable resources, such as dryland pastures in which the location of rainfall is highly variable, a commons system constitutes the most effective management regime. A large body of research on common property has focused on the conditions under which such efforts succeed and fail, whether due to external factors such as the terms of trade or to internal factors such as class differences within the community. The political scientist Elinor Ostrom's "design principles" (Ostrom 1990, 90–102) regarding the sustainability of common property resources have been particularly influential. These principles consist of (1) clearly defined boundaries for both users and resources, (2) congruence between appropriation and provision rules and local conditions, (3) collective choice arrangements under which most individuals affected by the operational rules can participate in modifying them, (4) monitoring, (5) graduated sanctions, (6) a conflict resolution mechanism that provides rapid access to low-cost local arenas to resolve conflicts among appropriators or between appropriators and officials, (7) at least minimal recognition of appropriators' rights to organize, and (8) nested enterprises (a system in which the commons management

activities are located in multiple organizational layers). In the policy/programmatic realm, community-based natural resource management (CBNRM) has emerged as an alternative to the weaknesses and inflexibility of private and state natural resource management. In contrast to policies of privatization, CBNRM often creates common property out of state property by devolving proprietary rights over specific natural resources to local people. In essence, this approach provides the community with a more central role in the assessment, planning, implementation, monitoring, and enforcement of and benefits from management strategies. Although in the past decade there has been considerable enthusiasm for this approach to natural resource management, the circumstances under which CBNRM does and does not succeed require research.

Louise Fortmann and Dorian Fougères

See also Wise Use Movement

Further Reading

Agarwal, B. (1994). *A field of one's own: Gender and land rights in South Asia.* Cambridge, UK: Cambridge University Press.

Alston, L. J., Libecap, G. D., & Schneider, R. (1996). *The determinants and impact of property rights: Land titles on the Brazilian frontier.* Cambridge, MA: National Bureau of Economic Research.

Berry, S. (1997). Tomatoes, land, and hearsay: Property and history in Asante in the time of structural adjustment. *World Development, 25*(8), 1225–1241.

Bromley, D. (Ed.). (1992). *Making the commons work: Theory, practice, and policy.* San Francisco: ICS Press.

Bruce, J. W., & Fortmann, L. (1988). *Whose trees? Proprietary dimensions of forestry.* Boulder, CO: Westview.

Bruce, J. W., & Migot-Adholla, S. E. (Eds.). (1993) *Searching for land tenure security in Africa.* Dubuque, IA: Kendall/ Hunt Publishing.

Cronon, W. (1983). *Changes in the land: Indians, colonists, and the ecology of New England.* New York: Hill and Wang.

Davison, J. (Ed.). (1988). *Agriculture, women and land: The African experience.* Boulder, CO: Westview Press.

Deere, C. D., & Leon, M. (2001). *Empowering women: Land and property rights in Latin America.* Pittsburgh, PA: University of Pittsburgh Press.

Fortmann, L., Antinori, C., & Nabane, N. (1997). Fruits of their labors: Gender, property rights and tree planting in two Zimbabwe villages. *Rural Sociology, 62*(3), 295–314.

Gordon, H. S. (1954). The economic theory of a common property resource: The fishery. *Journal of Political Economy, 62,* 124–142.

Guyer, J. I., & Peters, P. E. (Eds.). (1987). Conceptualizing the household: Issues of theory and policy in Africa. *Development and Change, 18*(2), 197–328.

Hann, C. M. (Ed.). (1998). *Property relations: Renewing the anthropological tradition.* Cambridge, UK: Cambridge University Press.

Hardin, G. J. (1968). Tragedy of the commons. *Science, 162*(1968), 1243–1248.

Hulme, D., & Murphree, M. (Eds.). (2001). *African wildlife and livelihoods: The promise and performance of community conservation.* Portsmouth, NH: D. Philip and Heinemann.

Hunt, R. C., & Gilman, A. (Eds.). (1998). *Property in economic context.* New York: University Press of America.

MacPherson, C. B. (Ed.). (1978). *Property: Mainstream and critical positions.* Oxford, UK: Basil Blackwell.

McCay, B. J., & Acheson, J. M. (Eds.). (1987). *The question of the commons: The culture and ecology of communal resources.* Tucson: University of Arizona Press.

McCay, B. J., & Jentoft, S. (1998). Market or community failure? Critical perspectives on common property research. *Human Organization, 57*(1), 21–29.

Merry, S. E. (1988). Legal pluralism. *Law & Society Review, 22*(5), 869–896.

Ostrom, E. (1990). *Governing the commons: The evolution of institutions for collective action.* Cambridge, UK: Cambridge University Press.

Ostrom, E., Dietz, T., Dolsak, N., Stern, P. C., Stonich, S., & Weber, E. U. (Eds.). (2002). *The drama of the commons.* Washington, DC: National Academy Press.

Place, F., Roth, M., & Hazell, P. (1994). Land tenure security and agricultural performance in Africa: Overview of research methodology. In J. W. Bruce & S. E. Migot-Adholla (Eds.), *Searching for land tenure security in Africa* (pp. 15–39). Dubuque, IA: Kendall/Hunt Publishing.

Polanyi, K. (1944). *The great transformation.* New York: Farrar & Rinehart.

Schroeder, R. (1999). *Shady practices: Agroforestry and gender politics in the Gambia.* Berkeley & Los Angeles: University of California Press.

Sen, A. (1988). Property and hunger. *Economics and Philosophy, 4,* 57–68.

Suryanata, K. (1994). Fruit trees under contract: Tenure and land use change in upland Java, Indonesia. *World Development, 22*(10), 1567–1578.

Tamanaha, B. Z. (2000). A non-essentialist version of legal pluralism. *Journal of Law and Society, 27*(2), 296–321.

Verdery, K. (1996). *What was socialism, and what comes next?* Princeton, NJ: Princeton University Press.

Waldron, J. (1991). Homelessness and the issue of freedom. *UCLA Law Review, 39*(2), 295–324.

Western, D., Wright, R. M., & Strum, S. C. (Eds.). (1994). *Natural connections: Perspectives in community-based conservation.* Washington, DC: Island Press.

Law—Toxic Waste

National laws and international treaties to control the manufacture, transportation, and disposal of toxic waste emerged primarily in the last quarter of the twentieth century. Also, a few lawsuits involving damages from early varieties of toxic waste were brought. For example, as early as 1831, lawsuits involving disposal of highly toxic waste from coal gas manufacturing plants were successfully brought against gas manufacturers. However, until the late twentieth century, these kinds of actions were sporadic and made little difference in dealing with widespread pollution problems.

National laws and international treaties emerged in part as a response to major environmental disasters involving toxic chemicals, such as the 1984 Union Carbide accident in Bhopal, India, where thousands were killed. Such laws and treaties are also an acknowledgment of a growing problem.

The annual global volume of toxic and hazardous waste was estimated at 400 million metric tons at the beginning of the twenty-first century, as compared to only 4.5 million metric tons fifty years earlier. More than half this volume—over 226 million metric tons—was generated in the United States alone.

Worldwide accumulation of obsolete pesticides—one major category of toxic waste—is over 453,592 metric tons, according to the U.N. Food and Agriculture Organization. Of this amount, perhaps one-quarter is found in African nations.

Dumping industrial waste in developing nations is often seen as unjust and even racist in that developing nations are unprepared to deal with the hazards of the waste, and many people do not understand exactly what they are receiving. Because of this, and because of the damage already being inflicted in some nations, the international trade in toxic waste is high on the list of international environmental priorities.

Efforts to protect public health from toxic wastes have centered around (1) controlling trade of toxic waste from industrial to developing nations through the Basel Convention on the Control of Trans-Boundary Movements of Hazardous Wastes and Their Disposal and (2) controlling generation of toxic wastes at the source through the Stockholm Convention on Persistent Organic Pollutants.

These efforts have been hampered by a lack of funding, by a lack of participation by some important nations (especially the United States), and by discordance with regional trade agreements, such as the North American Free Trade Agreement (NAFTA).

The most acute problems involve existing waste dumps and the growing illegal trade in toxic waste, which was estimated at $1–2 billion in 2002. Laws and treaties against this trade have not been easy to enforce.

The issue is made more complex by the fact that the international community and the United States have taken divergent paths in response to the problem. U.S. legislation includes a variety of laws dealing with toxic waste control and cleanup, and U.S. multilateral agreements such as the North American Free Trade Agreement (NAFTA) promote transboundary movement of some types of toxic waste. Meanwhile, the United States has not ratified the Basel and Stockholm treaties, despite its position as the world's most significant generator of toxic waste.

Although some observers believe that U.S. law is not far removed from international treaty, the divergent paths reflect both conservative U.S. policies about environmental problems and a degree of U.S. isolation from international opinion.

U.S. Law on Toxic Waste

Three major acts administered by the U.S. Environmental Protection Agency control the development and distribution of hazardous and toxic waste.

The first act is the Resource, Conservation and Recovery Act (RCRA) of 1970. This act and its amendments cover solid waste, recycling, and hazardous and toxic waste. Companies handling or shipping hazardous or toxic waste must track its use and disposal. Amendments to the act in 1984 and regulations in 1986 focused on export of toxic wastes. One requirement was that private shipments of waste be formally accepted by host nation governments. However, lax enforcement and loopholes in the definition of "hazardous waste" (some of which encourage recycling) have

led to serious environmental problems in countries receiving U.S. waste. For example, lead is not considered a RCRA waste, but centers in Mexico, Brazil, and Thailand that recycle lead auto batteries from the U.S. have contaminated the groundwater and caused other serious public health hazards. Also, after toxic wastes cross a border, it is difficult for people injured in those countries to bring U.S. lawsuits under RCRA and other laws.

The second act is the Toxic Substances Control Act (TSCA) of 1972, which required that chemicals be tested for health and environmental effects with EPA enforcement through civil proceedings. Critics of the EPA's enforcement point out that of 2,300 new substances reviewed by the EPA between 1972 and 1992, only 13 were withdrawn from the market. Also, with 60,000 existing chemicals in the TSCA inventory, only 4 were fully regulated by the 1990s: dioxin, asbestos, polychlorinated biphenyls (PCBs), and chlorofluorocarbons (CFCs). And of these, only CFCs have been regulated in conjunction with an international treaty (the Montreal Protocol).

The need for a law to specifically deal with toxic waste dumps was apparent by 1980, when studies showed that toxic waste had been found in 24,000 locations. Highly publicized incidents such as those at Love Canal, New York, and Times Beach, Missouri, added momentum to calls for new legislation.

In response, the U.S. Congress passed the third major act—the Comprehensive Environmental Response, Compensation, and Liability Act (CERCLA), as well as the Superfund Authorization and Recovery Act (SARA) of 1980 and 1984. The goal of these acts was to fund the cleanup of abandoned toxic waste sites through a special tax on chemical and petroleum industries. Important cleanup projects would be put on a "Superfund" list, and cleanup would be financed through the special tax.

At the time the tax expired in 1995, the Superfund was contributing about $1.5 billion per year to the cleanup of abandoned dumps. Since then, the number of sites being cleaned up has been reduced, and funding has been depleted. Attempts to pass a Superfund tax reauthorization have not been successful.

North American Free Trade Agreement

The North American Free Trade Agreement is a 1992 treaty between the United States, Canada, and Mexico designed to promote trade in North America. Not only has NAFTA been successful in promoting trade, but also it has tended to promote trade in toxic waste.

Before NAFTA, toxic waste shipments were controlled with bilateral agreements between the United States, Mexico, and Canada. In 1983 the United States and Mexico signed a bilateral agreement on environmental cooperation in La Paz, Mexico. The United States and Canada signed a similar agreement in 1986. At the time, Canada received 85 percent of U.S. hazardous waste exports. In 1988 Mexico banned importation of all hazardous wastes. Exceptions to the Mexican ban include recycling and border area businesses.

When NAFTA was passed in 1992, a major concern was that environment would take a back seat to trade. As a result, the Commission on Environmental Cooperation (CEC) was created to investigate and remedy environmental problems. But the CEC is overwhelmed and underfunded.

NAFTA Cases Show Problems

On the U.S.-Mexico border near Tijuana, a lead smelter operated by Metales y Derivados was abandoned in 1992. Today about 6,000 metric tons of lead slag and other chemicals are poisoning the drinking water of nearby communities. Although the CEC has investigated, nothing has happened to the site. Since 1995 citizens' petitions concerning thirty other sites have been filed with the CEC concerning NAFTA-related complaints. Half have been dismissed, one has had a factual record prepared, and the rest are pending. Environmental advocates have seen these cases as a reflection of the failure to protect the environment under NAFTA.

Another NAFTA case involved a U.S. company, Metalclad, which was in the process of opening a hazardous waste landfill in the Mexican state of San Luis Potosi. In 1996 the governor made the site an ecological preserve, effectively blocking the landfill project. A NAFTA arbitration panel found for the company, and Mexico was compelled to pay Metalclad $16.7 million compensation.

A U.S.-Canadian NAFTA case involved Canada's ban on exports of PCB wastes to the United States. A NAFTA arbitration panel ordered Canada to pay $8.2 million to S. D. Meyers, Inc., which had contracted to treat the wastes. Canada argued that its status as a Basel treaty member posed a direct conflict with NAFTA but still agreed to pay the compensation.

Two other cases show the extent of NAFTA's dominance over environmental law. Methanex Corp. of Vancouver, Canada, sued to recover almost $1 billion in damages because of the state of California's plans to ban the additive MTBE (the gasoline additive methyl tertiary butyl ether, which has had adverse effects on groundwater) from the state's gasoline. That suit was not resolved in early 2003. Finally, the Canadian government had to compensate the Ethyl Corp. after banning a dangerous gasoline additive called "MMT."

All in all, experience with NAFTA shows the difficulty of harmonizing regional free trade agreements with international environmental agreements. In contrast, environmental agreements in Europe have been a springboard for full international environmental treaties, and European Economic Commission (EEC) initiatives cannot be considered separately from U.N.-backed international treaties.

U.N. and EEC Treaties on Toxic Waste

The two major U.N. initiatives concerning toxic waste mentioned earlier have been under development as part of broader initiatives to control environmental pollutants. The Basel Convention on the Control of Trans-Boundary Movements of Hazardous Wastes and Their Disposal aims to control trade of toxic waste from industrial to developing nations, and the Stockholm Convention on Persistent Organic Pollutants aims to restrict and phase out some of the world's most dangerous chemicals—pesticides such as DDT and chlordane, industrial chemicals such as PCBs, and by-product chemicals such as dioxins.

Like many other international agreements, the Basel and Stockholm conventions began as U.N. initiatives and evolved into working conventions. Delegates from U.N. member nations work in conventions that are often named for the cities where they meet, such as Basel, Switzerland, or Stockholm, Sweden. When the delegates recommend treaties and amendments to treaties, their own nations must ratify them. Consequently, the results of some conventions become international treaties rather quickly, whereas others may never attain the full force of international law.

Basel Convention on Waste Trade

Although the original European Economic Commission charter of 1950 did not include environmental regulation, regional agreements about pollution emerged as early as 1963 with the Berne Accord, which was designed to protect the Rhine River from pollution. Treaty members were France, Germany, Luxembourg, the Netherlands, and Switzerland. The accord focused mostly on sewage and industrial waste cleanup.

Additional concern in the area of toxic waste was sparked by a large fire at the Sandoz chemical plant in Basel in 1986. Firefighters using water to combat the fire inadvertently swept thousands of gallons of highly toxic chemicals into the Rhine River, killing millions of fish and making river water temporarily unsafe for drinking.

The origins of the Basel convention treaty are found in a 1982 United Nations Environmental Programme (UNEP) working group to study the hazardous waste trade. By 1987 this led to the Cairo Guidelines, a group of proposals to encourage countries to adopt stronger internal regulations. Building on the Cairo Guidelines, a Rotterdam convention developed an informed consent procedure for trade in hazardous chemicals in 1998.

However, increased trade in toxic wastes led to a need for a legally binding treaty, and in 1989, 116 countries met in Basel to finalize a treaty proposal, which became official in 1992.

The Basel treaty initially limited and (with amendments in 1996) attempted to abolish most kinds of hazardous waste trade between industrial and developing countries. It also put into place a uniform classification system for hazardous wastes and, by 1999, established a system of international liability compensation for damages resulting from hazardous waste transportation. In 2002, 146 nations and the European Union were formally parties to the Basel treaty, although the United States has rejected the treaty, and a complete ban has not been fully ratified.

Despite the progress that the Basel treaty represents, it is severely criticized by some environmental groups and developing nations because it has no "superfund"—that is, it does not finance international protective and remediation efforts, as it was originally meant to do under Article 14 of the convention. Critics also note that the Basel treaty also exempts all waste trade by nonsignatories (such as the United States) and has no international policing mechanism.

Stockholm Convention on Persistent Organic Pollutants

Persistent organic pollutants (POPs) are a class of toxic waste made up of dangerous pesticides such as DDT and other chemicals and process by-products such as PCBs and dioxins. Studies of Arctic ecologies have shown an increasing bioaccumulation of POPs in wild-

life and have raised fears of massive ecological collapse unless control strategies are developed.

In addition, use of banned pesticides in developing nations that export food to industrial nations has been called the "circle of poison" by environmental experts.

The Stockholm Convention on Persistent Organic Pollutants was formally initiated in Sweden in May 2001. Its goal is to ban or restrict POPs, pesticides, and industrial chemicals and avert the development of new dangerous chemicals.

The convention is also proposing a financial mechanism called the "Global Environment Facility" (GEF), through which donor countries can help developing countries clean up waste dumps and shift to safer alternative chemicals.

According to the World Wildlife Fund, POPs pose a particular hazard because of four characteristics: (1) They are toxic, and even small amounts have major impacts on nerve and reproductive systems; (2) they are long-lasting (persistent), and so they resist normal processes that break down contaminants; (3) they build up in the body fat of people and animals and are passed from mother to fetus; and (4) they can travel great distances on wind and water currents.

Moreover, they are not necessary. Chemicals designated as POPs have been replaced in industry and agriculture worldwide but continue to be used simply to give minor economic advantages to some industries. Environmental scientists point out that with an international effort, these major threats to wildlife and people in developing nations could be removed at reasonable costs.

William Kovarik

See also Heavy Metals; Industrial Health and Safety; Toxicity

Further Reading

Boyle, A., & Freestone, D. (Eds.). (2001). *International law and sustainable development: Past achievements and future challenges.* Oxford, UK: Oxford University Press.

Barros, J., & Johnston, D. M. (1974). *The international law of pollution.* New York: Free Press.

Colten, C. E., & Skinner, P. N. (1996). *The road to Love Canal: Managing industrial waste before EPA.* Austin: University of Texas Press.

Schneider, J. (1979). *World public order of the environment: Towards an international ecological law and organization.* Toronto, Canada: University of Toronto Press.

Schreurs, M. A. (1997). *The internationalization of environmental protection.* Cambridge, UK, & New York: Cambridge University Press.

Sellers, C. (1994). Factory as environment: Industrial hygiene, professional collaboration and the modern sciences of pollution. *Environmental History Review, 18*(1), 55–84.

Stone, C. D. (1996). *Should trees have standing?: And other essays on law, morals, and the environment.* Dobbs Ferry, NY: Oceana Publications.

Tolba, M. K. (1998). *Global environmental diplomacy: Negotiating environment agreements for the world.* Cambridge, MA: MIT Press.

Weir, D., & Schapiro, M. (1981). *Circle of poison: Pesticides and people in a hungry world.* Oakland, CA: Food First/Institute for Food & Development Policy.

Weiss, E. B., & Jacobson, H. K. (Eds.). (1998). *Engaging countries: Strengthening compliance with international environmental accords.* Cambridge, MA: MIT Press.

Weiss, E. B. (1992). *Environmental change and international law: New challenges and dimensions.* Tokyo, Japan: United Nations University Press.

Westra, L., & Lawson, B. (Eds.). (2001). *Faces of environmental racism: Confronting issues of global justice.* Lanham, MD: Rowman & Littlefield.

Law—Water and Air Pollution

Environmental problems have plagued human settlements and elicited legal responses since antiquity. For example, in ancient Athens, wastes were supposed to be dumped a mile from the city, and burials were supposed to take place outside the city walls. However, it is better to trace law regarding water and air pollution since the early nineteenth century. Industrialization and urbanization increased pollution problems far beyond their customary levels in the nineteenth century. Increasing production of steel and petrochemicals, the emergence of large-scale textile, pulp and paper, and food industries, and the use of coal-fired steam engines for power also increased pollution problems. Later in the nineteenth century local and state governments began to control water and air pollution.

Water Pollution, Air Pollution, and Common Law

Industrialization and urbanization were the primary reasons for increased water pollution and air pollution in the nineteenth century. Water-powered early industrial establishments such as sawmills and textile mills were located at watercourses, and the easiest way for such establishments to get rid of wastes was to discharge them into water. Other industrial establishments, such as tanneries, were located at watercourses because they needed water for production processes and for the convenience of waste disposal. The smelting of metals and the use of coal for heating and for operating steam engines were the primary sources of air pollution. However, the form of air pollution that most concerned people in the nineteenth century was the odor created by slaughterhouses, rendering plants that recovered fat and other materials from carcasses, and factories that made fertilizers from bones, blood, and other animal tissues.

Early industrial polluters mainly caused property damages. For example, sawmills discharged sawdust and shavings, which could be deposited on downstream riparian (relating to the banks of watercourses) land or clog the waterwheel of a downstream mill. Mines discharged acidic water that spoiled water supplies downstream. Air pollution problems were relatively limited in the early nineteenth century because of the small scale of coal use and the cleanliness of anthracite, the main variety of coal used early on. However, increasing use of bituminous coal and the emergence of new industrial activities increased the damage done by smoke, soot, and dust to neighboring properties. Odors also interfered with the use and enjoyment of properties, but such odors were also understood to indicate health threats in the early nineteenth century.

Urbanization increased the size and density of human populations in cities. This process created problems with the handling and disposal of wastes. In the early nineteenth century human wastes were typically deposited into cesspools or privy vaults from which they seeped into groundwater, polluting the primary water supply of early urban residents. If privy vaults and cesspools were emptied at all, their contents were dumped on vacant lots or into the nearest watercourses. This process polluted surface waters, just as the discharge of human wastes through sewers did later in the century. Pollution of surface waters by human wastes both injured private property and endangered public health.

The urban experience with regard to water and air pollution was broadly similar in Europe and North America. The United Kingdom experienced these urban environmental problems earlier and perhaps more severely than countries such as the United States,

Germany and the Nordic Countries that urbanized and industrialized somewhat later. Many developing countries are still undergoing the processes of urbanization and industrialization and facing their environmental consequences. Legal responses to water and air pollution have varied across legal systems and according to the type and severity of experienced water pollution problems. In what follows, the focus will be on the legal responses to water and air pollution in the United States from the early nineteenth century until the 1970s when the present water and air pollution control policies were established. Exclusive focus on legal responses to water and air pollution in the United States is justified because it helps to discern trends over time. Moreover, the U.S. experience is not qualitatively different from that of other industrialized countries.

In the United States, those people whose private property was injured by water pollution or air pollution could seek damages or an injunction in the courts on the basis of tort (a wrongful act other than a breach of contract for which relief may be obtained) law. If solids such as sawdust or mine tailings physically invaded property, the owner could sue and recover for trespass. Law of private nuisances offered remedies when there was no physical invasion but when the use or enjoyment of property was nevertheless injured by, for example, odors or smoke. Interference with riparians' use of water was actionable under riparian law.

The frequency of litigation against water polluters and air polluters increased steadily during the nineteenth century, but the outcomes of litigation varied because tort law changed several times. In the early nineteenth century the courts protected private property strictly: Even a small interference with another person's property rights was in theory a cause for awarding damages. In contrast, early courts were reluctant to grant injunctions, which required the polluter to stop polluting or to pay a price demanded by the plaintiff for a right to pollute.

In the mid-nineteenth century courts relaxed liability for accidental injuries by adopting the doctrine of negligence: Damages were now due only when the defendant could be shown to have acted negligently. The doctrine of negligence was sometimes used in water pollution and air pollution litigation when the polluters discharged wastes and used fuels intentionally. As a result, their negligence could not be shown, and they were effectively relieved from liability. Injuries that were created by intentional action had traditionally been subject to strict liability. However, strict liability was replaced by the doctrine of reasonable use in *Tyler*

v. Wilkinson (1827), a federal case involving several Massachusetts and Rhode Island textile mills at the falls of the Pawtucket River. Downstream mill owners complained of the injurious diversion of water by upstream mills, arguing that the upstream mills only had a right to residual water not needed by the downstream mills. This doctrine established a common right to a reasonable use of resources such as water and air. It denied the right of other resource users to challenge minor interference with their common rights. A few decades later, the doctrine of reasonable use was transformed into a balancing test in two influential cases. In the Vermont case of *Snow v. Parsons* (1856), a downstream mill owner complained that his waterwheel was clogged by the bark discharged from an upstream tannery. In the New Hampshire case of *Hayes v. Waldron* (1863), a downstream riparian landowner complained that the shavings and sawdust discharged from an upstream sawmill were deposited on his land. The courts of these two cases adopted a balancing test which compared the value of competing uses of environmental resources and endorsed the more valuable one as a right. These changes in tort law favored emerging industry and reflected the priority of industrial development over other concerns. As a result, ordinary property owners could hardly prevail if they complained of industrial pollution.

Industrial development resulted in the emergence of powerful corporations by the end of the nineteenth century. The courts were now more willing to find for those who challenged the actions of industrial polluters because public opinion had turned against big business. The courts also knew by this time that industrial polluters could often abate their discharges at a relatively low cost. Moreover, the courts started to issue injunctions more frequently. For example, in the New York case of *Whalen v. Union Bag and Paper Co.* (1913) the court awarded damages and an injunction to a riparian landowner who had been injured by the discharge of effluents by an upstream paper mill. The riparian landowner refused to bargain with the paper mill, which was either unable or unwilling to abate its discharges and ultimately closed. The granting of injunctions was even more common in litigation over municipal sewage discharges, and comparable cases were litigated over air pollution as well.

However, despite changes in tort law in the late nineteenth-century, it remained a weak tool for controlling air pollution and water pollution. It could be used only for the protection of private property. Moreover, each plaintiff had to weigh the costs of litigation against prospective benefits from damages or an injunction when deciding whether to sue. Also, the award of damages or an injunction did not necessarily translate into improved environmental quality. The primary purpose of common law (the body of law developed in Britain primarily from judicial decisions based on custom and precedent) remedies was to restore the value of injured property rights. They altered the behavior of polluters only if abating discharges or discontinuing the polluting activity was less expensive than compensating the injured parties or buying them off.

In addition to creating disputes over property rights, water pollution and air pollution endangered health and thus provided a cause for public nuisance action. Public nuisance was anything that injured the private property of many people; harmed public rights, such as the right to navigation; or endangered public safety, health, or morals. A public plaintiff, such as the attorney general or an authorized body of the local government, usually initiated a public nuisance suit. However, a suit could also be initiated by individuals who had suffered a special injury, different in kind and not only in degree, from that suffered by the public. Early public nuisance suits were indeed often initiated by private plaintiffs, whereas public plaintiffs were reluctant to do so to abate water pollution or air pollution before the 1860s.

The protection of health by privately initiated public nuisance suits rested on the prevailing understanding of disease. Early nineteenth-century beliefs still associated disease with low morals and God's punishment for sins: Protection of health was a private matter best addressed by prayer and religious devotion. Whereas low morals and sin were thought to predispose one to disease, certain climatic and topographic factors, putrefaction, and odors or miasmas (vaporous exhalations believed to cause disease) indicated an immediate health danger. Epidemiological studies by the British reformer Edwin Chadwick (1800–1890) and the British physician John Snow (1813–1858) and sanitary surveys conducted in Europe and the United States transformed these beliefs in the mid-nineteenth century by establishing the association of disease with environmental degradation and raising health to the public agenda. Still, the exact cause of diseases eluded both medical experts and laypeople until the 1880s, when the bacteriological theory of disease started to gain acceptance.

The early beliefs about the origins of disease had important consequences for legal responses to water

pollution and air pollution. Public nuisance suits were frequently brought against those persons engaged in slaughtering, rendering, and fertilizer production until the last quarter of the nineteenth century. The borderline between air pollution and water pollution was also often thin, if it existed at all. Namely, polluted water was often malodorous and thus considered a health threat. For example, millponds stank because organic wastes carried by water from upstream settled on their bottom and because microbes thrived in their nutrient-rich and shallow waters. Indeed, stinking millponds were the most frequent reason for public nuisance suits such as the New York case of *Mills v. Hall* (1832) and the Massachusetts case of *City of Salem v. Eastern RR Co.* (1868) in the early nineteenth century.

Plaintiffs most often brought public nuisance suits during epidemics. The number of cases and the decisions of those cases litigated in the United States around the 1832 and 1866 cholera epidemics indicate that courts were receptive to the arguments of the plaintiffs during epidemics. Public interventions in water pollution and air pollution became more common after the mid-nineteenth century, when the connection between environmental degradation and disease had been established.

Local and State Responses to Pollution

Public responses to water pollution differed markedly from those to air pollution in the late nineteenth and early twentieth centuries. Local and state governments adopted organizational and institutional responses to water pollution and safeguarded public health by World War I. In contrast, local efforts to control air pollution failed until the 1940s, and the states of the United States became involved only after the federal government forced them to take action.

In the United States, local governments considered water pollution a problem of public health. Their earliest responses included the establishment of local boards of public health and the enactment of public health ordinances. At first local boards of health were temporary divisions of local government or ad hoc civic organizations established to fight an epidemic. However, epidemiological studies and sanitary surveys laid the foundations for sanitary reform in the mid-nineteenth century. Such reform included the establishment of permanent local boards of public health and more elaborate local ordinances. Yet, the enforcement of local ordinances remained sporadic before the late nineteenth century, mainly taking place in response to an epidemic. The courts usually endorsed the local use of police power in these circumstances.

The capability of local boards of public health to control water pollution was, however, limited. The new understanding of the relationship between environmental degradation and disease suggested that the supply of clean water and the construction of sewers for the disposal of human wastes could improve public health. Cities increasingly invested in water supply and sewer networks after the Civil War. Paradoxically, they reproduced the problems that they were supposed to resolve at even grander scale: A community that discharged its wastes into water spoiled the water supply of downstream cities and endangered public health downstream. Local boards of health were powerless when the source of pollution was outside of their jurisdiction.

Local governments first sought to resolve their conflicts over the pollution of water supplies in the courts under common law. However, the courts usually refused to protect water supplies of one city by constraining the sewage disposal of other cities. Instead, the courts directed water companies to use their eminent domain powers to take land and water rights to protect their water supplies. As a result, watershed management became an important tool of water quality management.

Other areas of litigation had a greater impact on water pollution control. Numerous property owners brought private nuisance actions against municipal polluters. The courts did not hesitate to endorse their complaints, creating incentives for the construction of sewage treatment plants. Water companies in turn faced negligence suits because they sometimes delivered contaminated water that caused illness and death. The courts did not require a high standard of care from water companies in the late nineteenth century. In the Wisconsin case of *Green v. Ashland Water Co.* (1898), the court denied compensation because of the contributory negligence of the deceased person Green: He had drunk tap water knowing the prevalence of typhoid in the area. However, when water treatment methods such as filtration and chlorination became available, the courts fostered their adoption by tightening the standard of care they required from water companies.

In the United States, state involvement in water pollution control began when Massachusetts established a state board of public health in 1869. Other states followed in the 1870s, all having a public health organization by World War I. The state boards were almost immediately vested with the task of studying water pollution because it was considered one of the primary threats to public health. The mandates of state boards were gradually expanded to include the review and authorization of plans for waterworks and sewers. The boards also researched the treatment of water and sewage. For example, the Lawrence Experimentation Station of the Massachusetts Board of Public Health developed the first effective methods for water filtration and sewage treatment, which are still used today. The state boards also made recommendations for the improvement of public health such as initiatives for new water pollution legislation. A number of states took up these suggestions at the turn of the twentieth century, when many cities, such as Lowell and Lawrence, Massachusetts; Chicago; Ithaca, New York; Pittsburgh and Scranton, Pennsylvania; and Cleveland, suffered from typhoid epidemics.

The water pollution control statutes of the early twentieth century often prohibited sewage discharges into watercourses that supplied the public. The statutes could also require water companies to submit plans for waterworks for review and approval by the state board. Similar requirements could exist for sewers. The statutes could also require water companies and polluters to report periodically to the state board. However, the statutes often exempted the most polluted industrial rivers, all industrial discharges, or discharges of the industries that were most important for a state's economy. Moreover, the state boards simply did not enforce these statutes vigorously after the typhoid epidemics at the beginning of the twentieth century were overcome.

The state boards of public health could ignore the enforcement of water pollution control statutes in the early twentieth century because they had technological measures for the protection of public health. Slow sand filtration had proven effective in safeguarding water in the end of the nineteenth century, and the effectiveness of chlorine was demonstrated in trials in the first decade of the twentieth century. State boards opted for the filtration and chlorination of drinking water because these measures protected public health at a lower cost than the abatement of sewage discharges. The state boards fostered the adoption of these measures by water companies via their review and approval procedures. Filtration and chlorination of drinking water reduced typhoid mortality and morbidity in many cities to 1 percent of what they had been a few decades before. Indeed, most residents of U.S. cities had safe drinking water by World War I. However, the success extended only this far. Nothing was done to improve water quality of streams, and the success in making drinking water safe for public health had rather negative than positive effect on it.

Local efforts to control air pollution began in the mid-nineteenth century. For example, in 1869 in Pittsburgh the city council prohibited the use of bituminous coal and wood by railroads within the city limits. In the next year the city council prohibited beehive coke ovens, which were used to convert ordinary coal to coke used for the manufacturing of steel. However, as was usual at the time, these ordinances were seldom enforced. Cities could encounter other problems if they did enforce their ordinances. For example, in 1893 the board of aldermen of St. Louis, Missouri, passed an ordinance that declared dense black smoke a public nuisance and created a commission to establish permissible smoke emissions and to test smoke prevention devices. After some initial success, the Missouri Supreme Court declared the city ordinance unconstitutional because the city did not have an authority to determine what constituted a public nuisance. The state legislature used its authority to make such a determination and passed legislation that would have enabled St. Louis to continue its policy, but this did not reinvigorate local activism.

Despite its early difficulties in smoke control, St. Louis ultimately became the first city in the United States to clear its skies. The board of aldermen of St. Louis adopted in 1937 a smoke control ordinance that regulated acceptable smoke and ash emissions as well as the maximum size and quality of coal, mandating use of the Ringelman chart in the measurement of smoke. The Ringelman chart displayed different tones of gray for comparison with the color and density of smoke, providing an important tool for the enforcement of smoke ordinances. The St. Louis ordinance also established a division of smoke regulation with a smoke commissioner and smoke inspectors. Another ordinance passed in the same year established the basis for regulating fuel supplies within the city. After experiencing the worst smoke event in its history in 1939, the city amended and implemented these ordinances under public pressure. The result was a dramatic improvement of air quality within a year.

Pittsburgh adopted the same model for resolving its smoke problem in the 1940s, and other cities followed suit later. The role of local civic organizations such as businessmen's and businesswomen's organizations was central from the mid-nineteenth century until the mid-twentieth century for the establishment and enforcement of local smoke control programs. Cities did not encounter legal obstacles in the enforcement of their smoke ordinances after World War II. For example, the Supreme Court of the United States endorsed the authority of Detroit, Michigan, to enforce its smoke ordinances in *Huron Cement Co. v. Detroit* (1960). However, the success of cities in clearing their skies was largely based on changing technology and fuels. In industry and transport, coal-fired boilers were being replaced by diesel engines and electric motors after World War II. Oil and natural gas in turn became fuels of choice for residential heating, one of the main sources of smoke pollution.

Interstate and Federal Responses to Pollution

Law on water pollution continued to develop differently from law on air pollution during the twentieth century. In the United States, states improved their water pollution control administration and legislation before the mid-twentieth century, and many states also became parties to interstate compacts that managed water quality in interstate waters. Moreover, the federal government increased its role in water pollution control throughout the twentieth century. In contrast, air pollution drew little attention at the state and federal levels before the late 1950s. However, under federal leadership the development of air pollution policy has been faster since the early 1960s than that of water pollution policy.

Water pollution already had interstate effects at the beginning of the twentieth century. For example, New York Bay was badly polluted by oil and industrial effluents in the late nineteenth century, and the Ohio River was polluted by phenols by World War I. States also initiated suits over interstate water pollution in the Supreme Court of the United States. In 1901 the state of Missouri complained about the state of Illinois's endorsement of Chicago's plans to discharge its sewage into the Mississippi River. Chicago pursued the plan to protect water quality in Lake Michigan, its primary water supply. The plan involved the building of a shipping and sanitary canal to divert the Chicago River from Lake Michigan to the Illinois River, which flowed into the Mississippi River. Chicago also diverted water from Lake Michigan to the canal to augment its flow and to flush its sewage down the new route. Chicago was involved in further litigation because its pumping of water lowered the water level in the Great Lakes. The Supreme Court ultimately required Chicago to build a sewage treatment plant—at the time the largest in the world. The states of New

York and New Jersey in turn litigated over New Jersey's plans to construct a trunk sewer to discharge sewage into New York Bay (*New York v. New Jersey,* 1921), as well as over New York's dumping of wastes into the sea off the coast of New Jersey (*New Jersey v. City of New York,* 1931, 1932, 1933).

The U.S. federal government made its first interventions in the issue of water pollution to protect interstate commerce and navigation. Congress enacted the Refuse Act of 1899 to protect navigation from widespread dumping of wastes. The act prohibited the dumping of wastes into navigable waters without a permit issued by the Army Corps of Engineers. In 1924 Congress enacted the Oil Pollution Control Act to clarify the responsibilities for oil spills that occurred in coastal waters. The growth of oil refining and use of petroleum-based products had by this time caused frequent oil spills that threatened navigation, the coastal tourist industry, and recreation. However, these early federal statutes were seldom invoked against polluters. Of more consequence was the establishment of the U.S. Public Health Service in 1912 with an authorization to research water pollution and its effects on public health. This research ultimately established the foundations for understanding the effects of pollution, such as the depletion of oxygen in watercourses. The federal government also funded water pollution control projects, such as the sealing of old mines and the construction of trunk sewers during the Great Depression.

Water pollution rose to the U.S. national political agenda in the 1930s, when the Izaak Walton League and other conservation groups promoted federal legislation and administration as a response to worsening water pollution. A water pollution control bill passed both houses during the 74th Congress in 1935, but proponents of federal water pollution policy ultimately prevented passage of the bill because of its weakness. During the next session of Congress water pollution control bills again passed both houses, only to be vetoed by President Franklin D. Roosevelt, who saw that the bills' grant-in-aid program could not be afforded under the growing threat of war. Instead, the federal government promoted interstate compacts for the management of water quality in interstate waters. A number of interstate compacts were indeed negotiated and established in the 1930s and the 1940s. However, the compacts remained largely ineffective because the interstate commissions did not usually have rulemaking powers and had no or only weak enforcement powers.

Congress established a temporary federal water pollution control program in 1948. The Water Pollution Control Act declared polluting interstate waters so as to endanger public health or welfare in another state to be a public nuisance. The act empowered the U.S. surgeon general to abate such nuisances, but the proscribed enforcement procedures were weak. The act also provided inexpensive federal loans for the planning and construction of municipal sewage treatment plants, but funds were never appropriated for that purpose. The act also authorized the surgeon general to study water pollution problems and their abatement with state authorities.

The Federal Water Pollution Control Act (FWPCA) of 1956 established the permanent federal water pollution control program but declared water pollution control to be a primary responsibility of the states. The act eliminated all references to public nuisance and weakened the already weak federal enforcement powers. On balance, the act transformed the federal loan program into a grant-in-aid program, which promised a maximum of 30 percent or $250,000 of the construction costs of municipal sewage treatment plants. The FWPCA amendments of 1961, 1965, 1966, and 1970 gradually extended the jurisdiction of federal legislation from interstate waters to all navigable waters, simplified and solidified the enforcement provisions, and made important changes to the administration of the program. The amendments also increased federal funding of municipal sewage treatment plants. The FWPCA of 1970 in turn comprehensively revised the Oil Pollution Control Act of 1924.

Despite amendments to the federal water pollution control program, it remained ineffective. Twenty enforcement conferences were held in the early 1960s, but only one resulted in a court proceeding. Even that proceeding, against the city of St. Joseph, Missouri, was settled out of court. Moreover, federal legislation did not respond to the emerging water pollution problems that repeatedly alarmed the public. The linking of Minamata disease (a neurological disorder) to mercury in the 1950s caused alarm when high mercury concentrations proved to be common. The development and increased use of synthetic pesticides and other chemicals caused large-scale fish kills and bird kills that alarmed the public in the 1950s and the 1960s. Nonbiodegradable synthetic detergents produced long-lasting foam that blanketed many watercourses. In 1969 the Cuyahoga River in Cleveland caught fire because of the oil and chemicals discharged into it. The Reserve Mining Company discharged asbestos-containing tailings into Lake Superior, polluting the water supply of several cities with a known carcinogen (*United States v. Reserve Mining Co.*, 1974).

Increased public exposure to and awareness of environmental problems contributed to environmental activism in the 1960s and 1970s. Some activism was channeled into the courts, where citizen groups challenged both polluters and the federal government. For example, environmental activists used the citizen enforcement provisions of the Refuse Act of 1899 to begin court proceedings against industrial water polluters. In part as a response to these pressures, Congress enacted the Clean Water Act of 1972, which established the framework of the contemporary federal water pollution control program.

Air pollution also had interstate effects by the early twentieth century. For example, in 1907 the state of Georgia complained in the Supreme Court of the United States that smelter emissions that originated from the state of Tennessee caused property damage in Georgia (*Georgia v. Tennessee Copper Co.*, 1907). The United States engaged in a dispute with Canada in the 1930s over the sulfur dioxide emissions of a Canadian smelter in Trail, British Columbia, that injured property and other interests in the state of Washington. However, it was the "killer smogs" in Donora, Pennsylvania, in 1948; in London in 1948, 1952, and 1956; and in New York City in 1965 that finally stirred the U.S. federal government to action.

Federal air pollution control legislation saw daylight in 1955. The federal view was still that air pollution is "essentially a local problem" (Davies 1970, 45), and thus the act of 1955 provided funding only for research on air pollution. In 1960 Congress established the Division of Air Pollution to the Public Health Service. In 1963 the federal program was extended to include provisions for abating interstate air pollution and for giving federal grants to state and local air pollution control agencies. However, only one enforcement action—*United States v. Bishop Processing Co.* (1970)—was ever decided in the courts on the basis of these provisions. The federal program developed faster after the mid-1960s. The Clean Air Act amendments of 1965 established federal regulation of new automobile emissions. The New York City killer smog of 1965 expedited reforms included in the Air Quality Act of 1967, such as establishment of air quality criteria for the protection of welfare and public health, ambient air quality standards, air quality control regions, and state air pollution control programs. The Clean Air Act amendments of 1970 then established the framework

of the contemporary federal air pollution control program by increasing federal authority and by moving the administration of the program to the newly established Environmental Protection Agency (EPA).

Historical Lessons

Legal responses to air pollution and water pollution have proceeded in parallel but not at the same pace. Legal responses to water pollution were solidified earlier in part because water pollution was closely associated with public health and because its control was one important reason for the emergence of public health administration. Legal responses to air pollution did not gain similar legitimacy early on. However, more recently the progress in air pollution control has outpaced that in water pollution control. Experience indicates that legal responses have often been made only because of an impending crisis. Often the adopted legal responses have been ignored as soon as the crisis has been resolved by technological or other means. Yet, on another level, the range of interests protected by law has expanded from the interests in the protection of private property to the interests in public health, recreation, and protection of the environment for its own sake.

Jouni Paavola

Further Reading

Anderson, L. (1993). Fire and disease: The development of water supply systems in new England, 1870–1900. In J. A. Tarr & G. Dupuy (Eds.), *Technology and the rise of the networked city in Europe and America* (pp. 137–156). Philadelphia: Temple University Press.

Andrews, R. N. L. (2001). *Managing the environment, managing ourselves: A history of American environmental policy*. New Haven, CT: Yale University Press.

Armstrong, E. L., Robinson, M. C., & Hoy, S. M. (Eds.). (1976). *History of public works in the United States, 1776–1976*. Chicago: American Public Works Association.

Blake, N. (1956). *Water for the cities: A history of urban water supply problem in the United States*. Syracuse: Syracuse University Press.

Bone, R. G. (1986). Normative theory and legal doctrine in American nuisance law, 1850–1920. *Southern California Law Review, 59*, 1101–1226.

Cleary, E. J. (1967). *The ORSANCO story: Water quality management in the Ohio valley under an interstate compact*. Baltimore: Johns Hopkins University Press for the Resources for the Future.

Condran, G. A., Williams, H., & Cheney, R. A. (1984). The decline of mortality in Philadelphia from 1870 to 1930: The role of municipal services. *Pennsylvania Magazine of History and Biography, 108*, 153–177.

Cowdrey, A. E. (1975). Pioneering environmental law: The Army Corps of Engineers and the Refuse Act. *Pacific Historical Review, 44*, 331–349.

Cumbler, J. T. (1995). Whatever happened to industrial waste: Reform, compromise, and science in nineteenth-century southern New England. *Journal of Social History, 29*, 149–171.

Davies, J. C., III. (1970). *The politics of pollution*. New York: Pegasus.

Davis, P. N. (1971). Theories of water pollution litigation. *Wisconsin Law Review*, 738–816.

Duffy, J. (1974). *A history of public health in New York City, 1866–1966*. New York: Russell Sage Foundation.

Flannery, J. J. (1956). *Water pollution control: Development of state and national policy*. Unpublished doctoral dissertation. Madison: University of Wisconsin.

Galishoff, S. (1980). Triumph and failure: The American response to the urban water supply problem, 1860–1923. In M. V. Melosi (Ed.), *Pollution and reform in American cities, 1870–1930* (pp. 35–57). Austin: University of Texas Press.

Galishoff, S. (1988). *Newark: The nation's unhealthiest city, 1832–1895*. New Brunswick, NJ: Rutgers University Press.

Graham, F., Jr. (1966). *Disaster by default: Politics and water pollution*. New York: M. Evans.

Grinder, R. D. (1980). The battle for clean air: The smoke problem in post-Civil War America. In M. V. Melosi (Ed.), *Pollution and reform in American cities, 1870–1930* (pp. 59–82). Austin: University of Texas Press.

Halper, L. A. (1990). Nuisance, courts, and markets in the New York court of appeals, 1850–1915. *Albany Law Review, 54*, 301–357.

Harris, G., & Wilson, S. (1993). Water pollution in the Adirondack Mountains: Scientific research and governmental response, 1890–1930. *Environmental History Review, 17*, 47–71.

Hines, N. W. (1966a). Nor any drop to drink: Public regulation of water quality, part I: State pollution control programs. *Iowa Law Review, 52*, 186–235.

Hines, N. W. (1966b). Nor any drop to drink: Public regulation of water quality, part II: Interstate arrangements for pollution control. *Iowa Law Review, 52*, 432–457.

Hines, N. W. (1967). Nor any drop to drink: Public regulation of water quality, part III: The federal effort. *Iowa Law Review, 52*, 799–861.

Horwitz, M. J. (1977). *The transformation of American law, 1780–1860*. Cambridge, MA: Harvard University Press.

Hughes, J. D. (2001). *An environmental history of the world: Humankind's changing role in the community of life*. London: Routledge.

Hurley, A. (1994). Creating ecological wastelands: Oil pollution in New York City, 1870–1900. *Journal of Urban History, 20*, 340–364.

Judd, R. W. (1990). The coming of the clean water acts in Maine. *Environmental History Review, 14*(3), 51–73.

Kehoe, T. (1997). *Cleaning up the Great Lakes: From cooperation to confrontation*. DeKalb: Northern Illinois University Press.

Melosi, M. V. (Ed.). (1980). *Pollution and reform in American cities, 1870–1930*. Austin: University of Texas Press.

Melosi, M. V. (2001). *Effluent America: Cities, industry, energy and the environment*. Pittsburgh: University of Pittsburgh Press.

Murphy, E. F. (1961). *Water purity: A study in legal control of natural resources*. Madison: University of Wisconsin Press.

Novak, W. J. (1996). *The people's welfare: Law and regulation in nineteenth-century America*. Chapel Hill: University of North Carolina Press.

Paavola, J. (2002). Water quality as property: Industrial water pollution and common law in the nineteenth century United States. *Environment and History, 8*, 295–318.

Reitze, A. W., Jr. (1991). A century of air pollution control law: What's worked; what's failed; what might work. *Environmental Law, 21*, 1549–1646.

Rosen, C. (1993). *A history of public health*. Baltimore: Johns Hopkins University Press.

Rosen, C. M. (1993). Differing perceptions of the value of pollution abatement across time and place: Balancing doctrine in pollution nuisance law, 1840–1906. *Law and History Review, 11*, 303–381.

Rosen, C. M. (1995). Businessmen against pollution in late nineteenth-century Chicago. *Business History Review, 69*, 351–397.

Rosenberg, C. E. (1962). *The cholera years: The United States in 1832, 1849, and 1866*. Chicago: University of Chicago Press.

Rosenkrantz Gutmann, B. (1972). *Public health and the state: Changing views in Massachusetts, 1842–1936*. Cambridge, MA: Harvard University Press.

Scarpino, P. V. (1985). *Great river: An environmental history of the upper Mississippi, 1890–1950*. Columbia: University of Missouri Press.

Scott, A., & Coustalin, G. (1995). The evolution of water rights. *Natural Resources Journal, 35,* 821–979.

Steinberg, T. (1991). *Nature incorporated: Industrialization and the waters of New England.* Cambridge, UK: University of Cambridge Press.

Stradling, D. (1999). *Smokestacks and progressives: Environmentalists, engineers, and air quality in America, 1881–1951.* Baltimore: Johns Hopkins University Press.

Tarr, J. A. (1981). Changing fuel use behavior and energy transitions: The Pittsburgh smoke control movement, 1940–1950: A case study in historical analogy. *Journal of Social History, 14,* 561–588.

Tarr, J. A. (1994). Searching for a sink for an industrial waste: Iron-making fuels and the environment. *Environmental History Review, 18,* 9–34.

Tarr, J. A. (1996). *The search for the ultimate sink: Urban pollution in historical perspective.* Akron, OH: Akron University Press.

Tarr, J. A., McCurley, J., & Yosie, T. F. (1980). The development and impact of urban wastewater technology: Changing concepts of water quality control, 1850–1930. In M. V. Melosi (Ed.), *Pollution and reform in American cities, 1870–1930* (pp. 59–82). Austin: University of Texas Press.

Tarr, J. A., &. Zimring, C. (1997). The struggle for smoke control in St. Louis: Achievement and emulation. In A. Hurley (Ed.), *Common fields: An environmental history of St. Louis* (pp. 199–220). St. Louis: Missouri Historical Society Press.

Whipple, G. C. (1908). *Typhoid fever: Its causation, transmission and prevention.* New York: John Wiley & Sons.

Zwick, D., & Benstock, M. (1971). *Water wasteland.* New York: Grossman.

Court Cases

Beach v. Sterling Iron & Zinc Co., 54 NJ Eq. 65, 33 A. 286 (1895).

Buckingham v. Plymouth Water Co., 142 Pa. 221, 21 A. 824 (1891).

City of Salem v. Eastern RR Co., 98 MA 431 (1868).

Fertilizing Co. v. Hyde Park, 97 U.S. 659 (1878).

Georgia v. Tennessee Copper Co., 206 U.S. 230 (1907).

Green v. Ashland Water Co., 101 Wis. 258, 77 N.W. 722 (1898).

Hayes v. Waldron, 44 N.H. 580, 84 Am. Dec. 105 (1863).

McCarthy v. Natural Carbonic Gas Co., 189 NY 40, 81 N.E. 549 (1907).

Metropolitan Board of Health v. Heister, 37 NY 661 (1868).

Mills v. Hall, 9 Wendell 315 (NY), 24 Am. Dec. 160 (1832, 162).

Missouri v. Illinois, 180 U.S. 208 (1901), 200 U.S. 496 (1906).

Newark Aqueduct Board v. City of Passaic, 45 NJ Eq. 393, 18 A. 106 (1889).

New Jersey v. City of New York, 283 U.S. 473 (1931), 289 U.S. 712 (1932), 290 U.S. 237 (1933).

New York v. New Jersey, 256 U.S. 296 (1921).

Snow v. Parsons, 28 Vt. 459, 67 Am. Dec. 723 (1856).

Tyler v. Wilkinson, 24 F. Cas. 472 (No. 14, 312) (C.C.D.R.I. 1827).

United States v. Bishop Processing Co., 423 F.2d 469 (4th Cir. 1970).

United States v. Reserve Mining Co., 380 F.Supp. 11 (D. Minn. 1974).

Whalen v. Union Bag & Paper Co., 208 NY 1, 101 N.E. 805 (1913).

Wisconsin v. Illinois, 278 U.S. 367 (1928).

Wisconsin v. Illinois, 281 U.S. 179 (1929).

Wisconsin v. Illinois, 289 U.S. 395 (1933).

Law of the Sea

The need for more effective law to govern the world's oceans emerged during the late twentieth century as one of the most urgent environmental issues in international relations. Recognition of the urgency of ocean issues was a reaction to new tensions in international relations concerning claims to ownership and control of ocean space and also to compelling evidence that marine fisheries and other ocean resources were in grave danger from the pressures of human activity.

Massive oil spills at sea from tankers or offshore oil and gas rigs were one source of danger. Unremitting increases in the tonnage of ocean fishing fleets, in the scale and impacts on fish stocks of giant trawlers and factory ships, and in the efficiency of new gear all contributed to a steady increase in the pressures on fish stocks and species. Marine mammals, especially whales, were being decimated with large-scale operations. More generally, the global ocean environment—both in coastal areas and out to sea—was being damaged at an increased level by the rising scale of population growth and the spread of modern industrialization. Marine biodiversity (biological diversity as indicated by numbers of species of animals and plants, and by vitality of habits) was being lost, and scientists and the public by the 1970s were becoming concerned that the damage already done to the marine environment might be irreversible.

Until recent decades, however, little attention was paid to environmental issues that affected the oceans. Effectively addressing these issues was complicated after 1945 by the claims of many nations to the control or even the outright proprietorship of ocean waters beyond their immediate coastal areas. Addressing these issues was complicated also by the various interrelationships of environmental issues, maritime interests in navigation, and military concerns, especially with respect to the transit and operations of submarines during the Cold War.

Historically, from the early eighteenth century until World War II, the question of ownership and control of offshore waters had been a matter of wide consensual agreement in international law. The prevailing doctrine had been set forth, famously, in 1607 by the Dutch jurist Hugo Grotius, who proposed the doctrine of "freedom of the seas," which he declared must prevail in the ocean space that lay outside the control of any nation. The international waters, or "high seas," consisted of all the ocean waters beyond the line that separated the coastal nations' legitimate ocean space from the vast area that must be free to all for fishing, navigation, and all other uses. For over 250 years the world community of nations accepted as rule of law that coastal nations' control should prevail in a "marginal sea," commonly defined as no more than 3 miles (4.8 kilometers) to 12 miles (19.3 kilometers) out from the coastlines. Beyond that, freedom of the seas must govern.

Justifying this open legal order for exploitation of the oceans was the belief, widely held by scientists as well as international lawyers well into the nineteenth century, that ocean fisheries and other marine resources were inexhaustible. Thus the problem of "sustainability" would be taken care of by nature.

Four Departures

Since World War II the history of ocean law has consisted mainly of four vitally important departures from the basic philosophy and specific rules of the Grotian legal order. The first has been a drastic "enclosure movement" by which the coastal nations have extended their jurisdictional claims seaward by expanding the areas of their marginal or "territorial" seas. Beginning immediately after the war, and led by the U.S. government decision in 1945 to claim ownership of the seabed resources (offshore oil) of the entire continental shelf, by the 1970s scores of countries were claiming control of fishing zones or other regulatory powers,

and even outright sovereignty, over more general economic zones out to 321 kilometers (200 miles) offshore.

United Nations conventions on law of the sea in 1958 and the 1960s failed to settle the question of boundaries. The new norm of the 321-kilometer exclusive economic zone (EEZ) finally became codified in international law in 1982, however, with signing of the United Nations Convention on the Law of the Sea (UNCLOS). Even nations that did not ratify UNCLOS, including the United States, accepted the 321-kilometer rule. Hence this marked the formal renunciation of a key element in the Grotian heritage of ocean law. Some 40 percent of ocean space globally thus has come under the control of coastal and island states, and to a large extent foreign operators are excluded for purposes of fishing and many other uses of ocean resources in the EEZs.

Enclosure was driven in part simply by the desire of the coastal states to exclude outsiders and to control more resources. Still, the advocates of enclosure also expressed an environmentalist rationale: If individual states became solely responsible in their EEZs for fisheries and other resources, they contended, it would be likely that sustainable management would prevail, in contrast with what was the practice on the high seas. Unfortunately, EEZ-based controls in fact have not reversed the trend toward depletion of major fisheries.

The second great departure from the long-established doctrine of freedom of the seas consists of a movement since the 1950s toward more effective international law for environmental protection and resource management. To some degree this objective has been pursued through bilateral and multilateral treaties for ocean fisheries management and for regulation of pollution. However, again UNCLOS marked a major change because of its effort at establishing universally accepted new principles of law placing both general and specific obligations on signatory nations for protection of the environment. The obligations specified included a requirement that nations controlling EEZ resources manage them sustainably and share the scientifically established "surplus" with other nations, as well as act cooperatively to advance environmental protection in the high seas.

Formally in force since 1994 and ratified by more than 120 nations, UNCLOS also sought to lay the foundations for controlled exploitation of mineral resources of the seabed beyond national jurisdictions. The original 1982 convention provided for an international agency that would control seabed exploitation as a "common heritage of mankind" and so distribute to all nations in the world community a share of any profits from ocean mining. Subsequently modified, UNCLOS retains elements of cooperation but has veered back toward permitting private companies to take the leading role.

International Institutions

The third major departure in modern ocean law has been an effective reliance upon international institutions for the settlement—through mediation, arbitration, and adjudication—of disputes over ocean uses. The most important forums are the International Court of Justice and a new judicial body established under UNCLOS, the International Tribunal for the Law of the Sea.

Both in UNCLOS and in other new agreements, signatory nations have agreed to broad new principles of law that aim at sustainable use and the protection of marine biodiversity. For example, the "precautionary approach" to uses of marine and coastal environments is articulated in the International Convention on Biological Diversity (signed in 1992), which articulates the obligation to maintain the integrity of ecosystems. Explicit obligations to use the precautionary approach and to protect biodiversity are also incorporated into the important 1995 U.N. Fish Stocks Agreement, which established the legal framework for future "regional" treaties and organizations that, if approved by participating nations, will cooperatively manage fishing in high seas regions formerly outside the reach of any international control. Also under U.N. auspices, numerous "regional seas" agreements already have provided for regulation of polluting activities, coastal habitat protection, and to some degree fisheries management.

Meanwhile, the International Whaling Commission (IWC) since 1986 has adopted a policy of moratorium on whaling activities—one that is continuously challenged, however, by Japan and Norway, among other nations, which conduct what they claim to be "scientific whaling" or which simply ignore the IWC and engage in commercial-scale whale killing.

The fourth major departure in modern ocean law since 1945 is evidenced by new agreements establishing controls over dumping of pollutants, carriage of nuclear materials and other dangerous cargo, ship design, and navigational safety rules. The model approach was provided by the London Dumping Convention of 1973, with later protocols that introduced progressively stronger regulatory requirements. The International Maritime Organization (IMO) further implements antipollution measures through specialized agreements focused on control of specific problems such as oil discharges and transit of nuclear materials.

International law of the sea thus has moved far in a relatively short time from the unregulated order that prevailed until the 1940s. New norms and rules, embodied in the many formal instruments adopted in the last fifty years, give reason for optimism about more effective environmental protection in the oceans. There remain serious difficulties of monitoring and enforcement, however, because of the huge extent of ocean space and because some nations and industries still resist strong international regulations over activities important to them. A more general problem is that only the signatory nations for each of the new agreements, including UNCLOS itself, are obligated to conform. Therein lie the challenges for the future if protection of marine environments and resources is to reach a new level of effectiveness.

Harry N. Scheiber

Further Reading

Attard, D. (1994). *The exclusive economic zone in international law*. Oxford, UK: Clarendon Press.

Burke, W. T. (1994). *The new international law of fisheries*. London: Oxford University Press.

Hey, E. (Ed.). (1999). *Developments in international fisheries law*. The Hague, Netherlands: Kluwer Law International.

Østreng, W., & Vidas, D. (Eds.). (1998). *The order of the oceans at the turn of the century*. The Hague, Netherlands: Kluwer Law International for the Nansen Institute.

Scheiber, H. N. (Ed.). (2000). *The law of the sea: The common heritage and emerging challenges*. The Hague, Netherlands: Kluwer Law International.

League of Conservation Voters

In 1970 Marion Edey, a U.S. congressional staff aide, approached the former Sierra Club director David Brower about creating an organization that could act as the electoral wing of the environmental movement in America. Frustrated by the movement's lack of power in the nation's political sphere, Edey, Brower, and a directorate made up mainly of members of Brower's Friends of the Earth organization organized the League of Conservation Voters (LCV). The LCV was part of the second wave of American environmentalism that arose out of Earth Day 1970 and focused its efforts on influencing politics. Prior to Earth Day 1970, most environmental organizations had been tax-exempt nonprofit organizations forbidden by law from supporting legislation or endorsing a candidate. The LCV took political activism as its mission and focused on influencing Congress to pass environmental protection and resource conservation legislation.

The LCV won its first major victory in the congressional election of 1970, backing Baltimore attorney Paul Sarbanes in the Democratic Party primary against incumbent George Fallon, a Democratic representative who had a record of opposition to mass transit projects as the head of the House Public Works Committee. The LCV used aggressive fund raising and volunteer support to help Sarbanes unseat Fallon, signaling its strength to members of the environmental movement and members of Congress.

A trademark of the LCV became the rating system that the group developed for state and national politicians. The league's National Environmental Scorecard and the environmental grades, begun in 1970, are now well recognized by voters. Between 1972 and 1985 the average grade given was a 33 (or F) to House Republicans and a 60 (or D) to House Democrats. This rating system was partially responsible for giving the two major political parties their environmental (or antienvironmental) identities.

After the administration of President Ronald Reagan, the LCV focused on elections. In 1988 sixty out of seventy-six congressional candidates backed by the LCV won their elections, although the LCV considered the presidential election an embarrassing loss (the LCV gave Michael Dukakis a B and George H. W. Bush a D). In the 1990 election the LCV doubled its spending, but the results gave little support to electoralism as a strategy. Ballot initiatives in California, New York, Oregon, Massachusetts, and Missouri all lost, and only 84 candidates from a slate of 133 LCV candidates won their election. The league had an even worse record in 1992, when only 58 percent of its congressional candidates won election. The LCV and other groups hoping to influence elections began to realize that they could never outspend corporations.

The years spent lobbying for environmental legislation had given the league an institutional presence in Washington by the 1990s, despite the setbacks in individual elections. With the election of Bill Clinton as president and Al Gore, a well-known "green" politician, as vice president, the LCV gained access to the White House. Clinton appointed former LCV president Bruce Babbitt to be secretary of the interior, and a number of lower-ranking positions were also staffed by former LCV directors and officials.

Ryan J. Carey

Further Reading

Gottlieb, R. (1993). *Forcing the spring: The transformation of the American environmental movement*. Washington, DC: Island Press.

Hays, S. P. (1987). *Beauty, health, and permanence: Environmental politics in the U.S., 1955–1985*. New York: Cambridge University Press.

Rothman, H. (1998). *The greening of a nation?: Environmentalism in the United States since 1945*. New York: Harcourt Brace.

Sale, K. (1993). *The Green Revolution: The American environmental movement, 1962–1992*. New York: Hill and Wang.

Scheffer, V. B. (1991). *The shaping of environmentalism in America*. Seattle: University of Washington Press.

Shabecoff, P. (1993). *A fierce green fire: The American environmental movement*. New York: Hill and Wang.

Leopold, Aldo
(1887–1948)
U.S. forester

Aldo Leopold was a U.S. forester and wildlife ecologist best known for his book of nature sketches and philosophical essays, *A Sand County Almanac* (1948), in which he articulated a vision of harmony between people and land and the concept of a land ethic. He is widely considered to be among the most influential environmental writers in twentieth-century United States, as well as the father of the wilderness movement and of the profession of wildlife management in the United States.

Leopold was born in Burlington, Iowa, where he developed his acute powers of observation and love of "things natural, wild, and free" along the bluffs and bottomlands of the Mississippi River. After graduating from Yale University with a master of forestry degree (1909), he joined the U.S. Forest Service, rising to become supervisor of Carson National Forest in New Mexico by age twenty-five and then to assistant district forester in the Southwest (1918–1924). During those years he organized game protective associations in New Mexico and Arizona, laid the groundwork for a new profession of game management modeled on forestry, made important contributions to the ecological understanding of soil erosion, watersheds, and fire, and developed a rationale for the 1924 designation of the Gila Wilderness in New Mexico, the prototype for the national wilderness system given force of law by the Wilderness Act of 1964 and now totaling nearly 40 million hectares.

Leopold left the Southwest to serve as associate director of the Forest Products Laboratory in Madison, Wisconsin (1924–1928), then conducted game surveys of the north-central states, developed the American Game Policy (1930), and wrote his first text, *Game Man-*

"A thing is right when it tends to preserve the integrity, stability, and beauty of the biotic community. It is wrong when it tends otherwise." Aldo Leopold, *A Sand County Almanac*, **1949.** PHOTO COURTESY SUSAN FLADER.

agement (1933), before accepting a chair at the University of Wisconsin (1933–1948), where he trained a generation of leaders in the new profession. He wrote more than five hundred articles, reports, and bulletins addressing conservation issues of the day.

In the final decade of his career he found his voice as an essayist and further developed his conviction of human responsibility for the restoration of land health, expressed most clearly in "The Land Ethic," which is the capstone essay of *Sand County Almanac:* "A thing is right when it tends to preserve the integrity, stability, and beauty of the biotic community. It is wrong when it tends otherwise" (Leopold 1949, 224–225). The book was accepted for publication only days before Aldo Leopold died 21 April 1948 while fighting a grass fire near the farm along the Wisconsin River that he and his family restored to ecological integrity. He left behind his wife, Estella Bergere, and five children—Starker, Luna, Nina (Bradley), Carl, and Estella—all of whom became noted scientists; three won election to the National Academy of Sciences, an unprecedented achievement for siblings.

Leopold's writings won a broad general audience during the ecological awakening of the 1970s, the *Almanac* selling well over 1 million copies. But not until the 1990s was the significance of his ideas of land stewardship, ecological restoration, and ecosystem management acknowledged by the Forest Service and other natural resource agencies and professions among whom he had first articulated them. But even more important is the inspiration that his conviction of individual responsibility as "plain member and citizen" of the land community has provided for conservation efforts on private lands and in local communities.

Susan L. Flader

Further Reading

Flader, S. L. (1994). *Thinking like a mountain: Aldo Leopold and the evolution of an ecological attitude toward deer, wolves, and forests.* Madison: University of Wisconsin Press.

Flader, S. L., & Callicott, J. B. (Eds.). (1991). *The river of the mother of God and other essays by Aldo Leopold.* Madison: University of Wisconsin Press.

Leopold, A. (1949). *A Sand County almanac and sketches here and there.* New York: Oxford University Press.

Meine, C. (1988). *Aldo Leopold: His life and work.* Madison: University of Wisconsin Press.

Meine, C., & Knight, R. L. (Eds.). (1999). *The essential Aldo Leopold: Quotations and commentaries.* Madison: University of Wisconsin Press.

Linnaeus, Carolus
(1707–1788)
Swedish physician and botanist

The Swedish physician and botanist Carl von Linné, usually known by the latinized name Carolus Linnaeus, is generally recognized as the inventor of the system of nomenclature used by biologists to identify plants and animals. The Linnaean system, as it is called, was but one of several proposed during a time when exploration of the non-European world was bringing to light thousands of previously unknown organisms. The Linnaean system defined species and genera more precisely than before, providing the framework within which the theory of evolution would eventually be formulated. Without a taxonomic system like that of Linnaeus, quantitative measures of biodiversity would not be possible.

Linnaeus was born in Rashult, Sweden, the son of a pastor. He developed an early interest in botany and enrolled in 1727 at the University of Lund, boarding at the home of a physician who was himself an amateur naturalist and who granted Linnaeus the use of his immense botanical library. A year later Linnaeus transferred to the University of Uppsala, where he could study medicine and botany. In 1730 he published a short essay supporting the then-new notion that the stamens and pistils of plants have a sexual function. Shortly thereafter Linnaeus was appointed to a temporary post on the medical faculty, a great honor for a young man who still lacked the doctoral degree.

In 1732 Linnaeus participated in a survey of the plants and animals in Lapland. In 1735 he traveled to Harderwijk in the Netherlands, where he passed the necessary examination for his medical degree and submitted a dissertation, defending it a few days later. In the Netherlands, Linnaeus was able to arrange for the publication of his book, *Systema Naturae,* only fifteen pages long, describing a systematic classification scheme, grouping related species into groups called genera, similar genera into orders, orders into classes, and so on. Linnaeus's system included the animal as well as the plant kingdom, grouping humans with other primates and assigning them the scientific name *Homo sapiens.* With a few additions, the scheme remains in use today.

Linnaeus returned to Sweden in 1738 and set up a medical practice in Stockholm. He married the next year. Almost immediately he mounted a campaign to secure a faculty post at Uppsala, where he could devote himself entirely to botany. In 1741 he secured a position as professor. This afforded him the opportunity to supervise the research of advanced students. Nearly 190 students defended dissertations under his guidance. He continued to write extensively and refine his system of classification, publishing the tenth edition of *Systema Naturae,* almost fourteen hundred pages long, in 1758.

Linnaeus was appointed chief royal physician in 1747, knighted in 1758, and raised to the Swedish nobility in 1761. He died of a stroke at Uppsala. A group of English biologists formed a Linnaean society in 1788. He is regarded as a national hero in Sweden, and a crater on the moon is named for him.

Donald R. Franceschetti

Further Reading

Boorstin, D. J. (1983). *The discoverers.* New York: Random House.

Frängsmyr, T. (Ed.). (1983). *Linnaeus: The man and his work.* Berkeley & Los Angeles: University of California Press.

Goerke, H. (1973). *Linnaeus* (D. Lindley, Trans.). New York: Random House.

Literature See Carson, Rachel; Leopold, Aldo; Nature Writing; Thoreau, Henry David

Logging

Early historical evidence of large-scale logging, or timbering, first appears in several early Eastern and Middle-Eastern cultures, including ancient Egypt, Mesopotamia, China, and Greece. The Egyptians, for instance, utilized substantial local timber resources for the building of homes, oar-driven boats, and elaborate tombs in the third millennium BCE. There are accounts of royal family control and overuse of forest resources that document the need to obtain timber from other regions through trade and conquest as local sources became depleted.

Mesopotamian and Middle Eastern cultures also left indications of heavy use of timber during the second millennium BCE for construction of city walls and warships, with statements of great campaigns to distant lands in search of timber resources once local supply dwindled. Likewise, in China early populations removed forests for the development of agriculture, with much of the wood used for domestic fuel. Specialists have reported that the longtime scarcity of fuel wood in densely populated areas of China may have shaped traditional cooking practices. For example, vegetables are often cooked just lightly, and a common cooking pot, the round-bottomed wok, requires less fuel for heating food than do other designs.

Ancient Greek records also indicate a heavy reliance on forests for charcoal as well as for shipbuilding and construction of public and private buildings. In fact, discoveries of skillfully made axes and saws at many ancient Greek settlements, in combination with evidence of large buried construction timbers, support the hypothesis that much of present-day Greece was once heavily forested. The resource was eventually depleted, however, and the scarcity—and consequent value—of wood is poignantly illustrated by descriptions of Greek peasants fleeing from invading Persians in the fourth century BCE, carrying with them the wooden doors of their farmhouses as one of their most valuable possessions.

The Beginnings of European Timber Use

Records of significant timbering exist from early European cultures in present-day Italy, France, Britain, and Germany. In the fifth century CE the Romans are known to have established large areas of European forestlands for harvest, often denying local populations access and requisitioning the resource to reinforce their dwindling supplies near Rome. After the fall of the empire, Christian monastic orders throughout Europe were responsible for the establishment of settlements, the timbering of vast forested areas for wood products, and the clearing of land for agriculture. One estimate holds that during the seventh to fourteenth centuries over half the forestland of France was once owned and timbered by the monastic orders.

As European populations became settled into city-states and kingdoms and timber resources became increasingly scarce, the right to cut a forest was often assigned by chieftains and kings. In Britain and France during the fifteenth and sixteenth centuries CE, these assignments were governed by ordinances protecting the largest and best woodlands, often for the preservation of timber for sailing vessels and warships. Of all industrial requirements for timber cutting, the need to preserve old-growth trees for specific uses influenced

early forest conservation the most. However, the increasing need for timber as a fuel for such activities as the smelting of ore, glassmaking, and cooking ensured the rapid decline of unmanaged forest resources. The degree of forest exploitation varied as leadership and the financial situation of the leader changed. Only the Germanic states were able to maintain adequate long-term forest resources, chiefly due to their lack of a requirement for shipbuilding timber and differing regional forms of government that were more sensitive to local needs as opposed to the more national governance in Britain and France that was slower to adapt and manage resources.

Timber Use in the New World

Evidence of large-scale timbering by North American native cultures is lacking, with most information presenting a picture of land being used mostly for small-scale agriculture and hunting. Undoubtedly native populations used fires to maintain game lands and manage forested areas, but significant logging of the continent was to come later at the hands of European colonists. In fact, less than two hundred years was required to significantly affect the timber resources of the East and Midwest of North America. As the early settlers moved across the continent, they often viewed the lush, dense forests of the new land as an adversary and sought to clear it quickly for safety, agriculture, and travel. In many instances these populations were accompanied by British commercial interests, which exploited what was considered an almost inexhaustible timber resource, harvesting the biggest and best trees for shipbuilding, and shipping much of the resource back to wood-poor Europe. This continued until the American War of Independence in the late 1700s, when the colonies of the Americas began independent harvesting of the forests, just as rapaciously as the Europeans. Indeed, as early as the middle 1800s, common scenes of heavily logged land and fire-scarred earth prompted formal forest conservation efforts.

Modern Timber Management

By the time the United States recognized the need for national timber conservation and institutionalized the effort through federal and state forest reserves in 1891, European endeavors already existed that could serve as a model for frugal timber use and management. As early as 1825, schools of forest science and experimentation had been established in Germany and France to serve

This photo of Oregon shows clear-cutting in which all timber is taken from a specific area.
COURTESY STEVE HILLEBRAND/U. S. FISH AND WILDLIFE SERVICE.

the growing need for scientific management of reduced timber resources. These efforts paved the way for what is now recognized as the modern science of forestry, or the management of forestland for the maximum sustained yield of forest resources and benefits. Today many universities throughout the world provide educational programs in forestry, teaching forest ecology, protection, economics, sustainable harvest techniques, and replenishment. Today much of the public timber resources of Western Europe and North America is scientifically managed, with the goal of a perpetual renewable timber resource for future generations.

Tropical Deforestation

Despite advances in technical, sustainable management of timber resources in the Northern Hemisphere, there is global concern for the equatorial tropical forests of developing nations. Many developing areas of the tropics are currently struggling with familiar historic forest conservation issues, such as overharvesting. At a time when forest cover is increasing in many areas of North America, tropical forests are disappearing at an alarming rate. Although much of Northern Hemisphere forest management can be applied to tropical forests, additional concern is warranted in equatorial areas due to the rapid rate of deforestation and the fragility of the soils.

Tropical forests also contain what many consider a global heritage of species diversity, including many species that have been proven useful for pharmaceuticals and food. Additionally, tropical forests provide an invaluable array of environmental services to larger regions, such as the control of droughts and floods, erosion, and buffering of tropical storm damage. Intact equatorial forests also help reduce global levels of carbon dioxide, a greenhouse gas associated with global warming. With current rates of tropical deforestation many of these benefits are quickly disappearing, and no end to the logging is expected soon. The next phase in the human history of timbering is developing, encouraging our species yet again to adapt and learn.

W. Russ McClain

Further Reading

Clepper, H., & Meyer, A. B. (Eds.). (1960). *American forestry: Six decades of growth.* Washington, DC: Society of American Foresters.

Kricher, J. (1997). *A neotropical companion.* Princeton, NJ: Princeton University Press.

Myers, N. (1992). *The primary source: Tropical forests and our future.* New York: W. W. Norton.

Perlin, J. (1991). *A forest journey: The role of wood in the development of civilization.* Cambridge, MA: Harvard University Press.

Walker, L. C. (1972). *Ecology of our forests.* Cranbury, NJ: A. S. Barnes.

Williams, M. (1992). *Americans and their forests: A historical geography.* Cambridge, UK: Cambridge University Press.

Winters, R. K. (1974). *The forest and man*. New York: Vantage Press.

Lucretius
(c. 99–51 BCE)
Roman philosopher

Titus Lucretius Caro was a Roman philosopher who followed the materialistic views of the ancient Greek philosophers Democritus and Epicurus. Almost nothing is known of his life. His only surviving work is *De Rerum Natura* ("On the Nature of Things"), a philosophical poem in six books. He was a keen observer and perceptive natural historian. Believing that the universe is composed of atoms arranged by chance, he held that change and decay are inevitable—a doctrine perhaps similar to the modern idea of entropy (thermodynamic principle that states that a system moves through time in the direction of randomness, disorder, or chaos). Lucretius subscribed to the antithesis of the idea that history is progress.

Lucretius described ways in which human activities interact with the environment. The arts and sciences, discovered by trial and error, are subject to the same general deterioration as the materials available to them. Agriculture, he maintained, was becoming more difficult because the fertility of the earth was declining. The farmers he knew reported that recent harvests were by no means as good as those in the past. This was not mere rhetoric; Roman agricultural writers also spoke of a decline in productivity resulting either from the senescence (the state of being old) of Mother Earth or from the failure of humanity to care for her.

The search for soil that had not been exploited led people to clear the trees from hillsides, converting woodlands to fields and pastures and killing off the wildlife. Lucretius says that woodcutters made the forests "climb up the mountains" (Humphries 1969, 1370–1378), leaving the foothills to be plowed and planted. Thus, he described the deforestation of Italy that was taking place during the late Roman republic.

Mining, too, was altering the landscape. Lucretius speculated that humans had discovered metals when, after they had set forest fires, they found the ores melting and the molten metals seeping out of cracks in the earth. They experimented and found that they could fashion the metals into tools, weapons, and ornaments. But Lucretius also found that mines and smelters were filled with dangerous forms of pollution that also tainted the air in their neighborhoods. Not only did they smell bad, but also they made the faces of the workers jaundiced and reduced the workers' life expectancy.

Nature, Lucretius believed, is senescent. Humanity's monuments will fall into ruin; no permanent improvement can be expected because history is a process of decline. Nature is guided neither by the gods nor by an Aristotelian purpose. Early humans were stronger and livelier than those of his own time, even if their means of subsistence were more primitive. Humanity did not progress in civilization by following some law of progress, but rather by responding to the trials offered by the circumstances of nature. The best way to cope with such a universe, he concluded, is to seek natural explanations for every phenomenon and to be content with things as they are.

J. Donald Hughes

Further Reading

Asmis, E. (1988). Roman philosophical movements. In M. Grant & R. Kitzinger (Eds.), *Civilization of the ancient Mediterranean* (pp. 1653–1670). New York: Charles Scribner's Sons.

Clay, D. (1983). *Lucretius and Epicurus*. Ithaca, NY: Cornell University Press.

French, R. (1994). *Ancient natural history: Histories of nature*. London: Routledge.

Furley, D. J. (1981). The Greek theory of the infinite universe. *Journal of the History of Ideas, 42*(4), 571–585.

Hughes, J. D. (1994). *Pan's travail: Environmental problems of the ancient Greeks and Romans*. Baltimore: Johns Hopkins University Press.

Humphries, R. (Trans.). (1969). *Lucretius, the way things are: The De Rerum Natura of Titus Lucretius Caro*. Bloomington: Indiana University Press.

Latham, R. E. (Trans.). (1994). *Lucretius, on the nature of the universe*. London: Penguin Books.

Meredith, A. (1986). Later philosophy. In J. Boardman, J. Griffin, & O. Murray (Eds.), *The Oxford illustrated history of the Roman world* (pp. 288–307). Oxford, UK: Oxford University Press.

M

Mackenzie River

The Mackenzie River, known to the aboriginal Dene people as Deh Cho and to the Inuvialuit people as Kookpaic, is North America's second-longest river system, flowing northward 4,266 kilometers from its farthest source, the headwaters of the Finlay River in British Columbia, to the Beaufort Sea. The river basin drains 1.8 million square kilometers, or 22 percent of Canada's landmass. The river below Great Slave Lake is named for Alexander Mackenzie (1763–1820), the fur trader who in 1789 became the first European to descend to the delta.

Much of the Mackenzie system traverses a subarctic region notable for long, cold winters, discontinuous permafrost, and low precipitation falling mainly as snow. As a result, spring breakup of ice and snowmelt flooding are the major hydrological events shaping the river and its immediate surroundings. The basin includes three large lakes (Athabasca, Great Slave, and Great Bear) as well as three major deltas (Peace/Athabasca Rivers, Slave River, and the Mackenzie). A region of overall low biological productivity and species diversity, the lower Mackenzie River valley consists largely of musket with stunted spruce and fir trees, its glacial soils unsuited to agriculture. The huge delta is a maze of alluvial islands, lakes, and back-channels, and the estuary is important beluga whale habitat.

Aboriginal occupancy of the delta began about 2000 BCE, but the original Dorset (archeological designations for the prehistoric cultures occupying the region before 1000 BCE) culture was replaced after 1000 CE by eastward-migrating Thule whaling people, forebears of the contemporary Inuit. The Mackenzie Valley was proba-

bly occupied earlier by northward-migrating paleo-native groups. Precontact Inuit were marine-oriented people adapted to the harsh Arctic environment, whereas Athapaskan (linguistic designation used by anthropologists to refer to a number of northern aboriginal groups, including those of the Mackenzie valley, speaking similar languages) speakers mainly hunted the Mackenzie basin's large terrestrial mammals.

Sustained contact with European culture and economies began with fur trade expansion into the region in the late 1700s. Native peoples trapped muskrat, beaver, and Arctic fox for furs and provisioned forts with "country food" in return for manufactured goods. This trade dominated the region's economy and society until World War II. A rapacious whaling industry arose in the Mackenzie delta in the 1880s, severely disrupting Inuit society and quickly depleting whale stocks.

The Mackenzie region has occupied a contested place in the Canadian environmental imagination, signifying both vast, unspoiled wilderness and a nation-building industrial resource frontier. Industrial development began with an oil discovery at Fort Norman in the 1920s. It intensified during and after World War II, driven both by U.S. security operations across northern Canada and growing markets for minerals and oil.

The resulting social and environmental changes went largely unchallenged until the Mackenzie Valley Pipeline Inquiry in 1975–1976. Public hearings on a plan to pipe Alaskan oil along the valley gave a voice to local critics and stimulated opposition among southern Canadians. Justice Thomas Berger's inquiry report, which recommended the pipeline's delay, was a watershed in Canadian aboriginal and environmental issues. Environmental concerns continue to preoccupy governments and aboriginal and métis (mixed blood) groups as the Mackenzie region faces continued resource development pressure and experiences the effects of pollution and climate change.

Arn Keeling

Further Reading

Berger, T. R. (1988). *Northern frontier, northern homeland: The report of the Mackenzie Valley Pipeline Inquiry* (Rev. ed.). Vancouver, Canada: Douglas and McIntyre.

Bone, R. M. (1992). *The geography of the Canadian North: Issues and challenges*. Toronto, Canada: Oxford University Press.

Coates, K. (1985). *Canada's colonies: A history of the Yukon and Northwest Territories*. Toronto, Canada: James Lorimer.

Cohen, S. J. (Ed.). (1997). *Mackenzie Basin Impact Study (MBIS) final report*. Downsview, Canada: Environment Canada Atmospheric Environment Service.

Hayes, D. (2001). *First crossing: Alexander Mackenzie, his expedition across North America, and the opening of the continent*. Vancouver, Canada: Douglas and McIntyre.

Mackenzie Valley Basin Board. Retrieved January 6, 2003, from http://www.mrbb.ca

Sabin, P. (1995). Voices from the hydrocarbon frontier: Canada's Mackenzie Valley Pipeline Inquiry (1974–1977). *Environmental History Review, 19*(1), 17–48.

Madagascar

(2002 est. pop. 1.5 million)

With a land surface of 587,042 square kilometers, Madagascar is the world's fourth-largest island, approximately the size of Texas. Variations in latitude, altitude, and climate have produced there a number of distinct ecoregions with a high percentage of native species. The island possesses probably the world's greatest concentration of unique flora and fauna: 98 percent of Madagascar's land mammals, 92 percent of its reptiles, 68 percent of its plants, and 41 percent of its indigenous bird species are found nowhere else.

Madagascar's environmental peculiarity stems from its geological origins. Some 150 to 180 million years ago Madagascar split from Africa and settled into its current position in the Indian Ocean, some 400 kilometers from the coast of continental Africa. For millions of years, it has been separated from East Africa by a minimum of 200 kilometers of ocean by the Mozambique Channel notorious for its hazardous winds and currents. Thus many African species, including the elephant, giraffe, lion, and leopard, are unknown in Madagascar. Moreover, its flora and fauna are as much South American as African in origin: Dinosaur remains suggest a land bridge linked Madagascar to South America, probably via Antarctica, until some 65 million years ago.

Arrival and Impact of Man

The natural environment was a stronger force in Madagascar than in most other areas of comparable size as it possessed no human population until the first millennium CE. Even when it began to be settled, its generally mountainous topography (with deserts in the south) ensured scattered and low-density settlement.

Humans have had a major environmental impact over the last 2,000 years. The first settlers introduced new species from Southeast Asia and Africa, some deliberately (such as rice, bananas, dogs, and oxen) and some inadvertently (such as the rat and *plasmodium* protozoa, the infectious agent of malaria). They probably hunted to extinction such species as the pygmy hippopotamus and the world's largest bird species *(Aepyornis maximus)*, among numerous others.

More harmful than hunting has been the burning of forest to create agricultural plots (central and eastern Madagascar) and pasture (in the south and west). Since the 1980s rapid impoverishment and population growth (averaging 3.2 percent per annum from 1990 to 1995) has driven small farmers ever deeper into the forested hills and enfeebled governmental efforts to protect environmentally endangered areas. Forest wood and charcoal still meets 80 percent of domestic fuel needs. Also, economic liberalization has attracted foreign investors eager to exploit Madagascar's valuable mineral and precious-stone reserves, many of which lie within environmentally sensitive areas. Although forest still covers 20.2 percent (12 million hectares) of the island's surface, it is disappearing at an annual rate of 2,000 square kilometers and, except in the northeast, primary forest has been largely replaced by secondary growth.

An estimated 97 percent of the island's dry deciduous western forests have been destroyed by burning and clearing for grazing and agriculture. One-third of

Madagascar's land area is still burned each year to encourage new grass growth for cattle; the practice causes widespread soil erosion. In the central highlands, human activity has reduced Madagascar's sub-humid montane forest to a few fragmented areas where remaining endemic species risk imminent extinction. Moreover, the 14,000 to 17,000 square kilometers of spiny forest in the semidesert of the south, traditionally less threatened than woodlands because of hunting taboos and lower population density, is increasingly threatened by expanding agriculture, timber exploitation, the flower and pet trades, and migration. Also the El Niño Southern Oscillation (ENSO) event, the chief source of global interannual climate variability, occurs every two to ten years, accentuating the south's vulnerability to drought and famine.

Madagascar's marine waters are extensively fished by other national fleets. Its west-coast mangrove forests are threatened by urban development, erosion (due to tree felling in the highlands), rice cultivation, salt production, overfishing, and petroleum and timber exploitation. In addition, global warming has damaged coral reefs that protect mangroves from strong ocean tides.

Endangered Species

Madagascar's primate species, second only to Brazil in variety, are the world's most endangered. The island's endangered plants have considerable potential economic value. Sales of drugs derived from the rosy periwinkle of the south, used to treat childhood leukemia and Hodgkin's disease (remission rates of 99 and 58 percent respectively), have reached about $160 million a year, while the eastern rain forest contains over 50 rare but potentially exploitable species of wild coffee.

Subequatorial East Coast

Warm and wet throughout the year, this ecoregion possesses extensive marshland and on the interior escarpment supported a tropical rain forest. Twenty-two of the forest's twenty-five mammal species are endangered, including such lemurs as the sifaka and the indri; other endangered animal and plant species include the serpent eagle, red owl, and many freshwater fish and orchids.

Central Highlands

At over 1,300 meters altitude, the highlands experience considerably lower temperature and rainfall levels than the east coast. Dominated by mixed savannah and woodland, the highlands possess a number of minor ecoregions. There are fragmented wetlands and semi-humid forests that contain many highly endangered native species, including the Alaotran gentle lemur, several species of shrew, tenrec, and rodent, some twenty-five reptiles, and over twenty amphibians. Of the bird species, the Alaotra little grebe and pochard may already be extinct and several other species are threatened.

The montane zone, comprising ericoid (heathlike) thickets above 1,800 meters on Madagascar's four main massifs, forms another important ecoregion. There, a small number of native mammal, reptile, and amphibian species as well as several native bird species are threatened, mostly by fire used to create cattle pasture.

Western Madagascar

The west supports savannah and woodland, is drier than the center and east, and, as on the plateau, humidity falls progressively as one moves south. Its most vulnerable ecoregion is the coastal mangrove forest, one of the world's ten most endangered forests, only 1.3 percent of which was protected in 2001. There, threatened species include the dugong (an aquatic mammal similar to a sea manatee), turtle species, the Madagascar heron, and other birds.

In the succulent woodlands of the southwest and central regions, hunting threatens the tenrec (a spiny insectivore), fruit bats, and the red-fronted brown lemur. Several endemic bird species are vulnerable, including the Madagascar plover and especially the Madagascar teal, as are the gecko *Paroedura vazimba* and snake *Liophidium chabaudi*. Also threatened are native species of trees, exploited for construction wood.

The few remaining fragmented patches of Madagascar's dry, deciduous forest and associated river systems and wetlands are characterized by very high levels of native plants and animals. Endangered species include four of Madagascar's five native and endangered lemurs and two species of tortoise that are possibly the world's rarest: the ploughshare, or spurred, tortoise and the angonoka tortoise.

The South

Once more humid, southern Madagascar became progressively drier from about 2000 BCE. Much of the interior receives less than 500 millimeters of rainfall, and the southwest coast less than 350 millimeters of rainfall a year. This region is home to the spiny or deciduous thicket, under 3 percent of which is protected. Endangered species include the *Aloe suzannae*, the palm, *Dypsis decaryi*, tiny *Euphorbia* herbs and *Hibiscus* shrubs, Grandidier's mongoose, lemur species, tortoise species, and birds such as the red-shouldered vanga.

Environmental Protection

The government of Madagascar has responded to environmental pressure by designating protected areas (covering over 1 million hectares by 2000) and marine national parks, by trying to develop sustainable levels of forest exploitation and by encouraging alternatives to slash-and-burn agriculture, by teaching about overpopulation and environmental degradation at school, and by trying to control population growth and migration.

However, paralyzed by social and political instability and by financial constraints, the government has relinquished responsibility for protected zones to international agencies, environmental groups, and the private sector. These include the World Wildlife Fund (WWF), the Lemur Conservation Foundation, Primate Conservation Inc., the Madagascar Fauna Group, the Wildlife Trust, Conservation International, the Missouri Botanical Garden, the Wildlife Conservation Society, and the U.S. Peace Corps. In addition, a 1990 World Bank program increased the planting of pine and eucalyptus to satisfy fuel needs. Notable individuals involved in conservation efforts include Henri and Jean de Heaulme, the 1985 Getty Prize Winners for work in preserving Madagascar's wildlife, and Dr. Pat Wright of the State University of New York, whose work in helping to establish the Ranomafana National Park and initiate sustainable agricultural practices among small farmers gained her a MacArthur "genius" grant and a knighthood from the government of Madagascar.

In developing conservation programs, all agencies attempt to involve the local community. Thus in 1990, the World Wildlife Fund brokered a $4.5-million debt-for-nature exchange scheme to help Madagascar's Department of Waters and Forests protect the island's forests, initiate reforestation programs, and train over four hundred local conservation agents. Alongside UNESCO (United Nations Educational, Scientific, and Cultural Organization) and the Kew Botanical Gardens (London), the WWF promotes research into traditional plant remedies and the sustainable harvesting of valuable plants. In addition, it and other conservation organizations help to preserve habitats, establish reserves

of native plants and animals in captivity outside the country, and reintroduce such species to native protected habitats. Both commercial and nonprofit organizations have also initiated ecotourism, designed to compensate for potential revenue lost when commercial exploitation of areas is forbidden and to pay for the required tourist infrastructure and park management.

Poverty and the Environment

Poverty is a major force behind peasant destruction of forest: Madagascar is one of the world's poorest countries, with an annual gross national product (GNP) of $4 billion in 1999 and over 70 percent of its population below the poverty line. Foreign debt (which stood at $3.3 billion in 2001) represented 105 percent of GNP in 1998. The situation has been aggravated by International Monetary Fund and World Bank austerity measures imposed from the mid-1980s and by natural disasters, notably drought and cyclones. For instance, in early 1994 Geralda, the worst cyclone to hit Madagascar since 1927, left 500,000 homeless and severely affected agriculture and infrastructure, especially on the northeast coast, causing an estimated $45 million of damage.

In the early 1980s, the debate over the conflict between human and conservation needs resulted in a recognition that conservation cannot be separated from the human condition. Only timely, well-funded, and competently managed external aid can hope to quickly alleviate poverty and thus remove the major impediment to conserving Madagascar's unique flora and fauna.

Gwyn Campbell

Further Reading

Goodman, S. M., & Patterson, B. D. (Eds.). (1997). *Natural change and human impact in Madagascar*. Washington, DC: Smithsonian Institution Press.

Goodman, S. M., Patterson, B. D., & Sedlock, J. L. (Eds.). (1995). *Environmental change in Madagascar*. Chicago: The Field Museum.

Jenkins, M. D. (Ed.). (1987). *Madagascar: An environmental profile*. Gland, Switzerland: IUCN Conservation Monitoring Centre.

Jolly, A., Oberlé, P., & Albignac, R. (1984). *Key environments: Madagascar*. Oxford, UK: Pergamon Press.

Preston-Mafham, K. (1991). *Madagascar: A natural history*. Cape Town, South Africa: Struik.

Malthus, Thomas
(1766–1834)
British political economist

Thomas Robert Malthus, who provided one of the first warnings of the dangers of overpopulation, put the "dismal" in the "dismal science" of political economy. Malthus's simplistic mathematical models and common-sense observations made his dire predictions about a crowded, starving world a popular fear for generations after his 1798 *An Essay on the Principle of Population.*

Malthus was born of well-to-do English parents. He studied mathematics at Jesus College, Cambridge, taking holy orders, and eventually becoming the first professor of political economy in England at the East India College. In answer to the inevitable question posed to the "father" of population control, he had three children, two of whom survived to adulthood.

Malthus's fame, ironically, arose from his anonymously published *An Essay on the Principle of Population, as It Affects the Future Improvement of Society with Remarks on the Speculations of Mr. Godwin, M. Condorcet, and Other Writers.* Malthus's essay is best understood as a critique of French Enlightenment ideas of progress promulgated by, amongst others, his father, William Godwin, and Condorcet. Where these *philosophes* saw inevitable progress, Malthus saw vice, misery, and starvation. After making some general observations about the fecundity of plants and animals compared to the relative scarcity of the means of subsistence, Malthus went on to offer a mathematical illustration to ground his thoughts on overpopulation. Malthus claimed that whereas population can increase geometrically (e.g., 1, 2, 4, 8, 16 . . .) agriculture is limited to arithmetic increases (e.g., 1, 2, 3, 4, 5 . . .). The result of these differing mathematical limits was that unchecked population would inevitably outrun the food supply. The first edition of *An Essay on the Principle of Population* was indeed a grim document, a stinging tonic to Enlightenment optimism whereby the iron laws of human nature and agricultural productivity trapped humankind in a vicious circle of starvation. By the second edition of his essay in 1803 Malthus offered the meager hope that perhaps humans might shape their destiny through delay of marriage—the only safe (morally and physically) means he could conceive of to prevent conception. Yet overall the Reverend Malthus's population sermon remained the same: Moral restraint was the only possible check to humanity's natural tendency to succumb to animal passion, vice, and despair.

Long a mainstay of economic doctrine, Malthus's influence on the life sciences was, if anything, more pronounced. Both Charles Darwin and Alfred Russel Wallace credited Malthus with providing the mechanism for their near simultaneous co-discovery of evolution by natural selection. Malthus's claims for fecund parents and limited natural resources seemed the ideal engine to drive natural selection. Malthus's links between social class and wanton breeding was also a mainstay of later social Darwinians who shared some of Malthus's prejudices against the lower classes and assistance to the poor.

In the environmental sciences Malthus was no less influential. His population ideas seem directly linked to the later idea of "carrying capacities." In a more popular vein, Malthus provided the intellectual impetus for a Cold War generation of "neo-Malthusians" who once again saw a growing population as the portent of doom. Garrett Hardin was a rigorous hard-hearted cynic in the Malthusian vein whose classic essay "The Tragedy of the Commons" (1968) noted the ecological pitfalls of unchecked population growth, puncturing the optimism of 1960s liberalism as gleefully as Malthus debunked the Enlightenment. Paul Ehrlich's *The Population Bomb* (1968) enjoyed the popular force of Malthus's original essay through its striking mathematical predictions and evocative metaphor of exploding numbers of babies in an increasingly unstable world. In the twenty-first century, there are more than six times as many humans on the planet as the billion souls who so troubled Malthus at his death in 1834, and the debate he began remains contentious. Ironically, for this most influential of population control advocates, his intellectual progeny were numerous.

Mark Madison

Further Reading

Appleman, P. (Ed.). (1976). *An essay on the principle of population: A Norton critical edition.* New York: W.W. Norton.

Ehrlich, P. (1968). *The population bomb.* New York: Ballantine Books.

Hardin, G. (1968). The tragedy of the commons. *Science, 162,* 1243–1248.

Malthus, T. R. (1798). *An essay on the principle of population.* London: J. Johnson.

Vorzimmer, P. (1969). Darwin, Malthus, and the theory of natural selection. *Journal of the History of Ideas, 30,* 527–542.

Mangroves

Mangroves are woody plants that grow between the land and the sea, in the intertidal zone. The plants belong to a number of unrelated families, but have all developed special adaptations to the particular needs of life between the tides. About seventy species of mangrove plants have been recognized. Most are shrubs and trees, but they include ferns and a palm. Many experts list only thirty to forty species as "core" members of the mangrove community, which typically dominate. These include tall red mangroves from the genus *Rizophora* with highly distinctive stilt roots and the black and gray mangroves from the genus *Avicenna*, smaller trees which surround themselves with upward pointing pencil roots and which are capable of surviving in very harsh environments. The Nipa palm, which can only survive in salty waters, is commonly found on the banks of tropical estuaries, and its eaves can reach nine meters in length and are often used to build roofs.

These plants often grow in abundance, forming large forests of mangrove habitat along coastlines and into estuaries in the tropics and near tropics. These areas are variously known as mangrove forests, mangrove swamps, or *mangal*. Numerous other species are found within mangrove forests, including non-mangrove plants, which grow on the leaves and branches of the mangroves (epiphytes), and animals from both land (birds, reptiles, and insects) and sea (fish, mollusks, and crustaceans). These forests are also of considerable importance to people who use them, among other things, for food and timber.

Adaptations

The intertidal zone is a harsh environment, where species have to adapt to regular inundation, interspersed with drying out as the tide rises and falls. The salinity is high, creating significant physiological challenges. In many cases this salinity is also highly variable, ranging from almost fresh to hypersaline. Adaptations that mangroves use include:

Aerial roots. The soils around mangrove roots are usually waterlogged. At high tides waters may rise two meters over the root surface. In order to maintain a supply of oxygen to the roots, many mangrove species have developed specialized aerial roots. These include pneumatophores—upward extensions of roots into the air—which may be long and pointed, such as the pencil roots of *Avicennia*, or the more conical forms of *Sonneratia*. Root-knees are another form of pneumatophore, where more rounded knobs extend up from the soil. Equally characteristic are the prop or stilt roots, typified by *Rhizophora*. Some species also have buttress roots, which may extend into longer sinuous roots known as plank roots. In all cases these aerial elements of the root system provide a critical means of obtaining oxygen and are endowed with large internal spaces for gas storage and a large area of lenticels where gaseous exchange occurs.

Salt exclusion or extrusion. All mangroves have adopted mechanisms to reduce salt uptake. Some may use ultrafiltration at the cellular level to keep salt out from the roots. Others can secrete salt from their leaves using special glands, and salt crystals can often be seen on the leaf surface of species such as *Avicennia*.

Dispersal. Living in the sea it is difficult for small seeds to be dispersed, to find their way into the soil, and to take root. All mangrove seeds or seedlings float, and rely on water to disperse them to new areas. A number of mangrove species have adapted still further and undergo initial development whilst remaining attached to their parent tree. This is known as vivipary, or "live-birth." In species of *Rhizophora* the embryo grows out of the seed coat, and out of the fruit while still attached to the tree. The resulting long propagule is effectively a seedling. It floats upright in the water and is designed to become trapped into the mud on a falling tide.

Associated Species

A broad wealth of species is found living in mangrove communities. These include animals and plants coming from land, sea, and fresh waters. The sheer physical complexity of the mangrove environment, with its tangled roots and with a great network of twisting channels between the trees, makes the mangrove forest an important area for many animal species. These include fish that come in from the open sea to breed, with their young utilizing the shelter and the abundant food as a nursery area. Mudskippers are a familiar resident in mangrove forests from West Africa east to the Pacific

Ocean. These extraordinary fish (a type of goby) are capable of gulping air and spend much of their lives out of water. Many climb onto the base of trees, but they always remain close to water and will race across the water surface if frightened.

Some of the most commonly observed animals in the mangrove forest are crabs. In one Malaysian forest a density of seventy crabs per square meter has been recorded. The larger mangrove crabs take shelter in burrows during periods of low tide. Many are edible and are widely caught. Fiddler crabs are another characteristic group. The males of this group have different sized claws; one highly enlarged claw is used in territorial displays and fighting. Mollusks are also abundant, including mangrove snails, which feed on detritus, but also oysters and mussels, often attached to the mangrove roots, which filter the water for plankton. These are often collected for human consumption.

Microscopic life within mangrove mud is abundant, though poorly known. Many species, including some crabs and mudskippers, feed by filtering through this mud. At the other end of the spectrum, very large animals are rare in the mangrove forest. The estuarine crocodile is a regular inhabitant in mangrove forests of Australia and the islands of Southeast Asia. In the Sundarbans, perhaps the largest continuous mangrove forest in the world, between India and Bangladesh, there are still tigers. And on the island of Borneo the proboscis monkey has a specialized digestive system enabling it to subsist largely on a diet of mangrove leaves.

Importance to People

Although mangroves were mostly probably likely familiar to the ancient civilizations from Egypt to China, the first written record of mangroves were probably those of Nearchus, a commander under Alexander the Great, who undertook a voyage from the Indus River through the Arabian Sea and the Arabian (Persian) Gulf in 325 BCE. Theophrastus, the Greek philosopher and botanist, described mangroves in greater detail, based on observations in both the Arabian Gulf and the Red Sea. It is not so strange that these Europeans should have written down their observations of these trees—for them the concept of a tree growing in the sea was entirely alien.

Mangroves are of considerable importance to people today, most obviously through their role in supporting fisheries and forestry, but also in a less appreciated role as a form of coastal protection.

Fisheries. Crabs, oysters, and shrimps are among the very high value species regularly caught in mangrove forests. In some places farms have been established within the mangrove channels themselves. Even away from the mangrove forests, many fishermen gain considerable benefits, as the fish they catch often use the mangroves as a place to breed. Unfortunately the location of mangrove forests has placed them in direct competition with many entrepreneurs seeking to develop shrimp aquaculture. In many places, but notably across Southeast Asia, mangroves have been cleared to make way for the building of shrimp-ponds. Profits from such ponds are often considerable, but poor design has led to many being abandoned within a few years. The disruption of the ground prevents the return of mangroves to these abandoned farms.

Forestry. Mangrove wood has been used for many years, and is known for its high density and resistance to rotting. Although trees rarely reach very large sizes, smaller trees are used for poles, typically used in the construction industry, while in many areas the wood is also used in the production of charcoal. In a number of places this use of mangrove has been developed as a sustainable industry with regular harvesting on a fifteen- to twenty-year cycle.

Coastal protection. Few people, even amongst those living adjacent to mangroves, are aware of the important role they play in protecting the land from erosion by the sea. Although they are not absolute barriers, mangrove roots bind the sediments and prevent them from being transported by currents and waves. During storms they also reduce the impact of large waves on coastlines.

Despite their importance, it would appear that vast areas of mangroves have been lost. A recent estimate suggested that there are probably 181,000 square kilometers of mangroves in the world, but it seems likely that 100 years ago there may have been double this area. Efforts to protect mangroves remain limited, although there are now over 850 protected areas with mangroves. In some areas mangroves are being actively planted, in recognition of their important commercial value.

Mark D. Spalding

Further Reading

Field, C. D. (1995). *Journey amongst mangroves.* Okinawa, Japan: International Society for Mangrove Ecosystems.

Robertson, A. I., & Alongi, D. M. (Eds.). (1992). *Tropical mangrove ecosystems*. Coastal and estuarine studies, 41. Washington, DC: American Geophysical Union.

Saenger, P., Hegerl, E. J., & Davie, J. D. S. (Eds.). (1983). *Global status of mangrove ecosystems*. IUCN commission on ecology papers, 3. Gland, Switzerland: IUCN (The World Conservation Union).

Spalding, M. D., Blasco, F., & Field, C. D. (Eds.). (1997). *World mangrove atlas*. Okinawa, Japan: International Society for Mangrove Ecosystems.

Tomlinson, P. B. (1986). *The botany of mangroves*. Cambridge, UK: Cambridge University Press.

Manifest Destiny

Manifest destiny is the belief that the territorial expansion of the United States across the North American continent was inevitable and sanctioned by God. The belief was first expressed in 1845; by the end of the nineteenth century a related ideology was utilized to justify the purchase of Alaska, the acquisition of Puerto Rico, and expansion into the Pacific Ocean. Manifest destiny also justified the exploitation of the United States' natural resources, which fueled the growing American industrial and consumer economies.

Manifest Destiny as an American Mission

The mission of the United States as an ideal society began with the arrival of the Puritans during the first decades of the seventeenth century. By the nineteenth century this mission came to be expressed through the concept of manifest destiny. The term first appeared in print in 1845 when John L. O'Sullivan (1813–1895), editor of the *U.S. Magazine & Democratic Review*, declared that it was "[the United States'] manifest destiny to overspread the continent allotted by Providence for the free development of our yearly multiplying millions" (Merk 1995, ix). That the United States had the God-given right to expand as its population and other needs required was a potent idea.

One of the assumptions that underlay the idea of western expansion and manifest destiny was that the land stretching to the Pacific was unoccupied, which was not the case. In addition to the myriad Native American tribes settled on the Great Plains, in the Southwest, and the Northwest, Great Britain, Mexico, and Russia owned a significant amount of territory.

Wars, treaties, or purchase allowed the United States to acquire all of the lands west of the Missouri River by the end of the nineteenth century, led to the displacement of Native American tribes, and allowed for greater exploitation of land and water resources in the region.

Western Expansion in the Nineteenth-Century United States

During the 1820s many Americans took advantage of the Mexican government's offer of land for settlement in the state of Coahuila-Texas. By the mid-1830s, however, Mexico became concerned about the large number of Americans and their slaves in the region. In 1836, after a series of battles, the new Republic of Texas was granted its independence from Mexico and was annexed to the United States in 1845, providing the occasion for O'Sullivan's editorial about the special destiny of the United States. By 1848 the United States had gained territory in Oregon from Great Britain and had acquired the territories of California and New Mexico at the cessation of war with Mexico (1846–1848).

The continued western expansion of the United States between 1840 and 1850 added over 2.8 million square kilometers of territory. During the 1840s promotional literature and the possibility of cheap land assured eager settlers of the boundless opportunities of Oregon and California. Men, and sometimes their families, took to the Overland Trail, at the end of which they found farmland in Oregon and hoped to find gold in California. To encourage settlement and development of western lands, Congress passed the Homestead Act of 1862, which offered almost 32 million hectares of what was essentially free land to settlers willing to farm it for five years. Under the Pacific Railroad Acts of 1862 the U.S. government granted approximately 48 million hectares of land to railroad corporations. This act was meant to encourage the construction of a transcontinental railroad.

Exploitation of Resources

Completed in 1869, the transcontinental railroad, combined with increasing settlement and exploration of the American West, provided access to the vast agricultural, mineral, timber, and water resources of the western United States. The period between 1870 and 1920 included rapid industrial, urban, and population growth in the United States, which necessitated the increasing use of land and raw materials to produce

John L. O'Sullivan on *Manifest Destiny*, 1839

The American people having derived their origin from many other nations, and the Declaration of National Independence being entirely based on the great principle of human equality, these facts demonstrate at once our disconnected position as regards any other nation; that we have, in reality, but little connection with the past history of any of them, and still less with all antiquity, its glories, or its crimes. On the contrary, our national birth was the beginning of a new history, the formation and progress of an untried political system, which separates us from the past and connects us with the future only; and so far as regards the entire development of the natural rights of man, in moral, political, and national life, we may confidently assume that our country is destined to be the great nation of futurity.

It is so destined, because the principle upon which a nation is organized fixes its destiny, and that of equality is perfect, is universal. It presides in all the operations of the physical world, and it is also the conscious law of the soul—the self-evident dictates of morality, which accurately defines the duty of man to man, and consequently man's rights as man. Besides, the truthful annals of any nation furnish abundant evidence, that its happiness, its greatness, its duration, were always proportionate to the democratic equality in its system of government. . . .

What friend of human liberty, civilization, and refinement, can cast his view over the past history of the monarchies and aristocracies of antiquity, and not deplore that they ever existed? What philanthropist can contemplate the oppressions, the cruelties, and injustice inflicted by them on the masses of mankind, and not turn with moral horror from the retrospect?

America is destined for better deeds. It is our unparalleled glory that we have no reminiscences of battle fields, but in defence of humanity, of the oppressed of all nations, of the rights of conscience, the rights of personal enfranchisement. Our annals describe no scenes of horrid carnage, where men were led on by hundreds of thousands to slay one another, dupes and victims to emperors, kings, nobles, demons in the human form called heroes. We have had patriots to defend our homes, our liberties, but no aspirants to crowns or thrones; nor have the American people ever suffered themselves to be led on by wicked ambition to depopulate the land, to spread desolation far and wide, that a human being might be placed on a seat of supremacy.

We have no interest in the scenes of antiquity, only as lessons of avoidance of nearly all their examples. The expansive future is our arena, and for our history. We are entering on its untrodden space, with the truths of God in our minds, beneficent objects in our hearts, and with a clear conscience unsullied by the past. We are the nation of human progress, and who will, what can, set limits to our onward march? Providence is with us, and no earthly power can. We point to the everlasting truth on the first page of our national declaration, and we proclaim to the millions of other lands, that "the gates of hell"—the powers of aristocracy and monarchy—"shall not prevail against it."

The far-reaching, the boundless future will be the era of American greatness. In its magnificent domain of space and time, the nation of many nations is destined to manifest to mankind the excellence of divine principles; to establish on earth the noblest temple ever dedicated to the worship of the Most High—the Sacred and the True. Its floor shall be a hemisphere—its roof the firmament of the star-studded heavens, and its congregation an Union of many Republics, comprising hundreds of happy millions, calling, owning no man master, but governed by God's natural and moral law of equality, the law of brotherhood—of "peace and good will amongst men." . . .

Continues

Continued

Yes, we are the nation of progress, of individual freedom, of universal enfranchisement. Equality of rights is the cynosure of our union of States, the grand exemplar of the correlative equality of individuals; and while truth sheds its effulgence, we cannot retrograde, without dissolving the one and subverting the other. We must onward to the fulfilment of our mission—to the entire development of the principle of our organization—freedom of conscience, freedom of person, freedom of trade and business pursuits, universality of freedom and equality. This is our high destiny, and in nature's eternal, inevitable decree of cause and effect we must accomplish it. All this will be our future history, to establish on earth the moral dignity and salvation of man—the immutable truth and beneficence of God. For this blessed mission to the nations of the world, which are shut out from the life-giving light of truth, has America been chosen; and her high example shall smite unto death the tyranny of kings, hierarchs, and oligarchs, and carry the glad tidings of peace and good will where myriads now endure an existence scarcely more enviable than that of beasts of the field. Who, then, can doubt that our country is destined to be *the great nation* of futurity?

Source: "John L. O'Sullivan on Manifest Destiny, 1839." *Documents Relating to American Foreign Policy, Pre–1898.* Retrieved on February 24, 2003, from http://www.mtholyoke.edu/acad/intrel/osulliva.htm

food and manufactured goods. The threat of the depletion of the natural wealth of the United States, which had seemed inexhaustible, came closer in 1890 when U.S. census data indicated that the American frontier no longer existed. There was also concern that new overseas markets needed to be acquired in order to continue to support the industrial economy of the United States.

American Imperialism

Although the United States bought Alaska from Russia in 1867 and acquired the Midway Islands of the Pacific that same year, it would not be until the 1890s that some of the same ideas that characterized manifest destiny would remerge to support American imperialism. The desire for productive sugar plantations and for a refueling station on the trade route to Asia motivated the United States' annexation of the Hawaiian Islands in 1898.

In that same year the United States acquired Puerto Rico, Guam, and the Philippines and developed a sphere of influence in Cuba, all of which were the result of a favorable treaty that ended the Spanish-American War (1898). The jingoistic (hyperpatriotic) appeal of the Spanish-American War was related not to a desire to expand across the North American continent, but rather to acquire colonial possessions that would allow for expanded trade. The war would also provide the opportunity to bring the American ideal of liberty to

those who needed its civilizing influence. The 1903 acquisition of canal rights on the Isthmus of Panama and the Roosevelt Corollary to the Monroe Doctrine of 1904 served to reinforce a continued interest in Latin and Central American affairs through the expansion of American influence south of the border.

Driven by an increasingly powerful industrial economy, western and overseas expansion of U.S. territory during the nineteenth century resulted in the exploitation of land and resources. Interest in manifest destiny and American imperial ventures faded during the first years of the twentieth century. The jingoistic ideas that informed both nineteenth-century ideologies were influenced by the United States' sense of its divinely inspired destiny to acquire new continental and imperial territories as well as to act as the herald of freedom of justice to the unfortunate peoples of the world.

Kimberly A. Jarvis

Further Reading

Cronin, W. (1991). *Nature's metropolis: Chicago and the great West*. New York: W. W. Norton.
Faragher, J. M. (1979). *Women and men on the Overland Trail*. New Haven, CT: Yale University Press.
Hunt, M. (1987). *Ideology and U.S. foreign policy*. New Haven, CT: Yale University Press.
Kaplan, A., & Pease, D. E. (Eds.). (1993). *Cultures of United States imperialism*. Durham, NC: Duke University Press.

LaFebre, W. (1963). *The new empire: An interpretation of American expansion 1860–1898*. Ithaca, NY: Cornell University Press.

Merk, F. (1995). *Manifest destiny and mission in American history*. Cambridge, MA: Harvard University Press.

Nash, R. F. (1982). *Wilderness and the American mind* (3rd ed.). New Haven, CT: Yale University Press.

Rydell, R. (1984). *All the world's a fair: Visions of imperialism at American international expositions, 1876–1916*. Chicago: University of Chicago Press.

Slotkin, R. (1973). *Regeneration through violence: The mythology of the American frontier 1600–1860*. Middletown, CT: Weslyan University Press.

Trachtenberg, A. (1982). *The incorporation of America: Culture and society in the Gilded Age*. New York: Hill and Wang.

Manioc

The manioc plant (*Manihot esculenta* Crantz subspecies *esculenta*) is also known as "cassava" and "mandioca." Some authorities suggest that there are two separate species: bitter manioc (*M. esculenta*) and sweet manioc (*M. palmata*). This is disputed by the U.N. Food and Agriculture Organization (FAO), which considers that the degree of bitterness, a factor relating to toxicity, varies geographically. Manioc is a member of the spurge family (Euphorbiaceae) and is a perennial shrub whose tuberous roots are valued for its carbohydrate. Manioc is grown in agricultural systems that range from subsistent (providing food/fiber only for the farmer and his/her family) shifting cultivation to permanent cash-cropping in developing countries. It grows well up to elevations of 2,000 meters and tolerates low rainfall and nutrient-poor soils. Prior to consumption, bitter manioc must be boiled and pressed to remove cyanide compounds that are toxic to humans. The tuber is used to make flour, meal, flakes, and tapioca and may be fermented to produce an alcoholic drink. The leaves are consumed as a vegetable and are a good source of vitamins A and B. They are also protein-rich and thus valued where protein sources are limited. Manioc is dried to produce chips, and compressed pellets are used for animal feed. It is utilized as a source of starch in foodstuff, textile, and paper industries to produce glucose, monosodium glutamate, adhesives, plywood, and veneer.

Manioc domestication and the crop's subsequent spread are not well understood. Precisely where and when domestication occurred is unclear, and why it was domesticated is especially enigmatic because of its toxicity. Five species of *M. esculenta* have been identified as the closest wild relatives of domesticated manioc, and *M. esculenta* Crantz subspecies *flabellifolia* (Pohl) and possibly *M. esculenta* Crantz subspecies *peruviana* (Muell. Arg.) Allem are the most likely progenitors. All are natives of Brazil and are present in western Amazonia in forested areas and agricultural lands that have replaced humid forest. This environment could have been a primary locus for manioc domestication. One obstacle to pinpointing the source area, as for other root/tuber crops, is the susceptibility of root/tuber remains to decay, especially under humid tropical conditions. Thus remains are not well preserved in soils, sediments, or archeological contexts. Moreover, manioc may have been selected for purposes other than food; its cyanide content may have become valued as a poison with which to acquire fish, and the residual mash may have been recognized as a source of carbohydrate.

Portuguese invaders in the 1500s recorded that manioc was a staple crop of Brazil's indigenous peoples. From South America it was introduced to the west coast of Africa; it then spread into the humid interior, reaching the Congo River basin by about 1700. By 1800 the crop had spread to East Africa, Madagascar, and then to Asia. Today the significance of manioc is reflected in the following FAO data: In 2000 the area planted was 17×10^6 ha; this produced 177×10^6 tons. The largest producers are Brazil, Nigeria, Democratic Republic of Congo, Indonesia, and Thailand. Manioc cultivation and consumption are likely to increase in the future for commercial and subsistence purposes; the latter will predominate in Africa as populations rise, although increasing use of manioc products in cities will also be important.

A. M. Mannion

Further Reading

Hillocks, R. J., Thresh, J. M., & Bellotti, A. C. (Eds.). (2002). *Cassava: Biology, production and utilization*. Wallingford, UK: CABI.

U.N. Food and Agriculture Organization (FAO). (2002). FAOSTAT. Retrieved July 17, 2002, from http://www.fao.org

Mao Zedong
(1893–1976)
Chinese statesman

Mao Zedong (Mao Tse-tung, Chairman Mao), the dominant force in the People's Republic of China (PRC) from its founding in 1949 until his death, had the greatest negative effect on China's environment—and, because of the severity of the nation's problems and its geographic and demographic size, perhaps the world's environment—of any political leader. Mao presided over a repressive authoritarian system that, under his influence, rejected practices based on science or traditional methods in favor of ideologically driven solutions applied nationwide, regardless of variations in local conditions. Restrictions on discussion and dissent allowed inappropriate policies that often resulted in catastrophe because of the suppression of reports of the consequences.

Mao's authority originated in 1935 with his leadership of the Chinese Communist Party (CCP), which has monopolized political power in mainland China since the CCP's victory in the Chinese civil war (1927–1937, 1945–1949). Victory and the founding of the PRC heralded the end of national humiliation. In Mao's words, China had "stood up" after a century of imperialism and invasion, economic and political instability, and the deaths of tens of millions in rebellions, famines, and war. Mao capitalized on the resultant patriotic fervor to solidify the CCP's hold over the nation and his own hold over the CCP. Mao strengthened support for himself and the CCP through propaganda, repression, utopian promises, improvements in the lives of most Chinese through such measures as female emancipation and the distribution of farmland to the poor, and the maintenance of a siege mentality.

Campaigns mobilizing hundreds of millions of people killed birds to protect grain (leading to crop losses from insect infestations) and supplanted crops with often-unsuitable grains while cultivating hillsides, forests, semiarid grazing areas, and wetlands (resulting in crop failures; deforestation and consequent erosion, siltation, and flooding; desertification; and habitat loss). Campaigns also relocated factories inland and relocated many youths to frontiers (extending ecological damage) and leveled forests, windbreaks, and orchards to fuel crude "backyard" steel furnaces in pursuit of rapid industrialization (the Great Leap Forward, 1958–1961, when inappropriate agricultural practices were intensified). Mao briefly relinquished authority to pragmatists because of famines caused by the Great Leap Forward (20–50 million died). He regained power and returned to ecologically disastrous policies during the Cultural Revolution (1966–1976), having used the army to spearhead a personality cult built around himself to win fanatical support from China's burgeoning youth (Mao had encouraged rapid population growth, silencing demographers who correctly warned of the consequences of overpopulation).

Spurred by Mao, youths led attacks against authorities and institutions of all kinds, heightening environmental damage by disrupting natural resource management. Mao left China with widespread environmental degradation and an immense populace (officially 1.3 billion but perhaps 1.5 billion), most of whom, disillusioned and frightened by decades of government repression and mismanagement, focus their efforts on maximizing their wealth and securing their family's welfare, disregarding the effects of their actions on the environment.

Patrick Caffrey

Further Reading

Edmonds, R. L. (1994). *Patterns of China's lost harmony: A survey of the country's environmental degradation and protection*. New York: Routledge.

Meisner, M. (1999). *Mao's China and after: A history of the People's Republic* (3rd ed.). New York: Free Press.

Ross, L. (1988). *Environmental policy in China*. Bloomington: Indiana University Press.

Shapiro, J. (2001). *Mao's war against nature: Politics and the environment in revolutionary China*. New York: Cambridge University Press.

Short, P. (2000). *Mao: A life*. New York: Henry Holt.

Smil, V. (1993). *China's environmental crisis: An inquiry into the limits of national development*. Armonk, NY: M. E. Sharpe.

Spence, J. D. (1999). *Mao Zedong*. New York: Lipper/Viking.

Mapping and Surveying

Mapping may always have been a human instinct. Originally a mental process, it was associated with spatial awareness for survival—seeking food and shelter and avoiding danger. As these tasks became more complex and as people formed communities, cognitive knowledge may have—instinctively—been externalized as sketch maps in sand or in the dust on a cave floor. Such thinking aids offered a unique form of graphic storage and display and also allowed spatial ideas to be shared, compared, and analyzed. Although this technique of sketching out elements of local environments may have been practiced for forty thousand years or more, the evidence for it is lost. Most early map artifacts (dating from around 2000 BCE) are often pictorial in character, expressing ideas and beliefs, and structured without precise measurement. More specific survey methods were employed by the Egyptians in the Nile River valley around 1400 BCE for property mapping, and the science was advanced at various stages by the Romans, Greeks, and Arabs during the first millennium CE. Not until the eighteenth century did mapmakers begin to develop and apply rigorous scientific survey procedures for military, hydrographic, and national mapping.

Human ancestors must have carefully surveyed their environments visually to expand their spatial knowledge, but surveying has since matured into an established discipline for determining the positions of points (and, by implication, lines and aerial features) at or near the earth's surface, primarily for the production of maps. Maps are now commonplace, but without accurate surveying this situation would not exist. Surveying is employed both on land (topographic) and sea (hydrographic). The principles are the same, but the techniques differ in detail. Although sea navigation charts were among the earliest maps to be used by professionals, this article will concentrate on maps of the land.

Surveying and Reference Systems

Maps are plotted from information surveyed for both control frameworks (an array of points whose positions and elevations have been measured to a high degree of accuracy) at regional and global scales and for the recording of landscape detail. One rule for preserving survey accuracy is to work from the whole (the control) to the part (the detailed mapping). This also reflects the main types of surveying: geodetic, where the earth's curvature is taken into account, and plane, where the reference surface is assumed to be flat and horizontal. To determine location on a plane surface requires only a system of rectangular (x, y) coordinates. The equivalent for the globe is a graticule (grid) of lines, on the earth's reference sphere, of latitude, parallel to the equator, and longitude, at right angles to the equator and passing through the poles.

For the production of small-scale maps the earth can be assumed to be a sphere, although in reality it is flattened at the poles. Acknowledging this, surveyors use a reference ellipsoid (a mathematical shape approximating the true shape of the earth), which approximates reality. However, they also require a separate surface to which ground-surveyed positions in the vertical and horizontal can be referenced. If the earth were of uniform composition and covered with ocean its outer surface would approximately match the ellipsoid. However, the uneven distribution of rock and sea disturbs this simple model and gives, instead, the irregular gravity based surface known as the *geoid*. When map survey measurements are plotted on a flat surface the earth graticule must be transformed to a flat plane. This is done using various forms of map projection. The graticule coordinates of the specific map projection adopted for the country being surveyed can then be converted into the plane coordinate system of that country.

Control Surveys

The holistic approach is provided in geodesy (the study and measurement of the precise shape and size of the earth), and geodetic surveying accounts for Earth curvature in the measurement and computation of the precise locations of widely spaced reference points and the distances between them. Smaller control surveys are also carried out, notably at the national level for mapping programs.

Control is required for both horizontal and vertical measurements. The classic procedure for establishing horizontal control for a large area begins with the determination, using astronomical methods, of the precise latitude and longitude coordinates of two stations defining a baseline that is also measured precisely. A third point is then selected to form a large triangle, and this triangulation is extended to cover the area to be mapped. This primary control can still be identified in some landscapes from the distribution of fixed triangulation pillars (or survey "monuments") that mark out the network.

Although with lower precision, control can also be extended across smaller areas (especially where intervisibility, clear line-of-sight between two points, is poor, such as in forests or urban areas) by creating a traverse of a series of lines through the landscape determined by the direct measurement of distances and angles. The method of trilateration, where triangle side lengths alone are measured, is also possible, but until the introduction of electronic distance measurement (EDM) techniques it was not in extensive use.

Traditionally, vertical control was related to what is called the "mean sea-level datum" for a particular region (the local position of the geoid surface), commonly the average of tidal ranges measured over a nineteen-year period. This is connected using precise leveling techniques to a primary network of local reference points (benchmarks) across the region. In Great Britain, mean sea level was calculated at Newlyn, Cornwall, between 1915 and 1921 as the ordnance datum, with an accessible reference point, the observatory benchmark, established 4.751 meters higher.

Survey Methods for Mapping Detail

By its nature and assumptions, plane surveying has been used mainly for smaller areas, especially for in-filling detailed mapping within a national control framework. It involves the measurement of distances and angles in order to determine the positions and elevations of points.

The two main approaches to such survey measurement are field techniques on the ground and aerial techniques (photogrammetry).

Although other instruments have been employed, the most common instruments for precise ground survey have been steel tape, theodolite, and tilting level. The theodolite is designed to measure horizontal and vertical angles, and the tilting level is designed to determine the differences in elevation between points. Each is mounted on a portable tripod for field use. Methods of locating topographic detail by ground survey have been improved with the development of the "total" station, a theodolite-like instrument consisting of three components—for electronic distance measurement, for electronic angle measurement, and for data processing. It is employed primarily for detailed mapping purposes, either using radiation techniques from one location or tacheometry, where detail is located during a survey traverse. Contour lines can also be located with such equipment.

Photogrammetry is the technique and technology of acquiring measurements from aerial photographs that have been acquired in a special overlapping sequence to permit the accurate determination of relative heights as well as horizontal location. With the development of special cameras and stereoplotting instruments it became so effective for large areas that it was

widely adopted by national governments for their topographical mapping programs. Photogrammetric methods have continued to develop, but the most significant recent change has been to digital (or soft copy) photogrammetry.

Despite the success of photogrammetry, ground survey methods can still be more appropriate for detailed large-scale mapping projects and important for establishing ground control points for photogrammetric mapping.

Effects of Changing Technology

Although the principles behind survey accuracy have been maintained, the instruments and techniques, as indicated, are changing. Today satellite methods (specifically, global positioning systems—GPS) have greatly increased in importance for the rapid and accurate provision of control and even for the detailed revision of topographic maps. For example, the Ordnance Survey of Great Britain has fully adopted GPS for all national coordinate systems, with the old survey monuments now rendered redundant. Although this article has concentrated on metric aspects, other benefits are provided by remote sensing. Aerial photography, developed for intelligence gathering during war, was subsequently employed to improve the mapping and ongoing monitoring of themes such as geology, vegetation, and land use. Infrared photography and side-looking radar have added to the airborne techniques, and, of course, satellite imaging systems such as multispectral scanners, electro-optical, and synthetic aperture radar are also providing a wealth of new spatial data for environmental mapping. Indeed, in some situations and with appropriate spatial rectification (the removal of scale variations and image displacements from aerial photography), the new generation of high-resolution (submeter) scanners, such as on the *Ikonos* and *Quick Bird* satellites, can provide both interpretative and metric data. They can thus provide effective maplike substitutes to support many spatial tasks.

Maps and Spatial Data

Maps are defined as symbolized representations, constructed to reduced scale, of selected features and characteristics, normally of the earth's surface. Unlike photographic or satellite images that record everything that can be detected by a photographic emulsion or scanning sensor, they are always abstractions of reality, designed to improve understanding. Before the arrival of digital computing, topographic maps and plans, plotted directly from field measurements, were the sole sources for all subsequent spatial data and derived maps. Basic scales for the mapping of Great Britain were allocated according to the nature of the landscape and settlement density: 1:1,250 for urban areas, 1:2,500 for agricultural land, and 1:10,000 for the remaining moorland and mountains. Maps at smaller scales (e.g., at 1:50,000) were normally derived from these.

Since the introduction of computing, fundamental changes have taken place. Existing topographic maps are converted into digital form for storage in computer databases rather than on paper, and spatial data captured by ground survey, photogrammetry or remote sensing can also be transferred directly to these databases. Although maps can still be created by accessing these sources, the data are also available for direct use in other spatial tasks. For example, 80 percent of the business turnover at the British Ordnance Survey is for electronic data rather than for the sale of maps. The special value of digital over paper maps is not only an accurate locational record of the features of the physical and cultural landscape (topography), but also the linkage of these to a multitude of other thematic data. Both environmental (e.g., vegetation) and statistical (e.g., population census) data are related to natural or administrative boundaries in the landscape. Databases enriched in this manner offer substantial added value for a range of users through specialized maps or through the data themselves. Geographic Information System software, the established facility for handling such data, is now in use throughout the world. Digital maps can be transmitted electronically, examined on computer screens (desktop or handheld), accessed via the World Wide Web, and need be printed to paper only when required. Not only have these new possibilities increased the potential of maps and spatial data, but also they have released maps from their traditional paper restrictions and rendered them more versatile and accessible to serve a much wider audience and to support many more tasks.

Michael Wood

Further Reading

Campbell, J. B. (2002). *Introduction to remote sensing* (3rd ed.). London: Taylor & Francis.

Dorling, D., & Fairbairn, D. (1997). *Mapping: Ways of representing the world*. Harlow, UK: Addison Wesley Longman.

Harley, J. B., & Woodward, D. (1987). *The history of cartography: Vol. 1. Cartography in prehistoric, ancient, and medieval Europe and the Mediterranean*. Chicago: University of Chicago Press.

Lillesand, T. (1999). *Remote sensing and image interpretation* (4th ed.). New York: John Wiley & Sons.

Longley, P., Goodchild, M. F., Maguire, D. J., & Rhind, D. H. (2001). *Geographic information systems and science*. Chichester, UK: John Wiley & Sons.

Rhind, D. W. (Ed.). (1997). *Framework for the world*. New York: John Wiley & Sons.

Robinson, A. H., Morrison, J. L., Muehrcke, P. C., Kimerling, A. J., & Guptill, S. C. (1995). *Elements of cartography* (6th ed.). New York: John Wiley & Sons.

Wolf, P. R., & Ghilani, C. D. (2002). *Elementary surveying: An introduction to geomantics* (3rd ed.). Upper Saddle River, NJ: Prentice Hall.

Marsh, George Perkins
(1801–1882)
U.S. scholar, statesman, and natural scientist

Born in Woodstock, Vermont, George Perkins Marsh acquired his interest in the environment as a young boy. His childhood home was located at the base of a mountain along the Quechee River. His father pointed out to him how lumbering and sheep grazing caused swift runoff of rainwater from the nearby mountainside. The runoff caused the river to flood in the spring and dry up in the summer. George incorporated such personal observations into his later scientific writings.

Marsh also had interests in European languages and history, became an expert in several languages, and later achieved fame as a linguist. Despite his language aptitude, after graduating from Dartmouth College, he followed his father into law and set up a practice in Burlington, Vermont, in 1825. Never comfortable practicing law, Marsh entered politics. He was elected to the state assembly in 1835 and then to the U.S. Congress in 1843 for two terms. He devoted most of his efforts there to committee work, especially on the Smithsonian Institution, which he helped to found and to shape.

From his reading of history and from personal observation, Marsh formed his ideas on conservation. In September 1847, in a speech on agricultural conditions in New England, Marsh first discussed the human capacity for destruction of the environment. His call for better management of resources and active efforts to restore the land based on European models went unheeded.

In 1849, Marsh was appointed U.S. minister to Turkey. While traveling to Greece, Egypt, and Palestine, he observed the impact of overgrazing and lumbering in the region's arid lands. On a trip to France, he learned about reforestation programs being undertaken. He returned home in 1854 and worked for the state of Vermont. As state fish commissioner, in 1857 he issued a report that linked the decline of Vermont's fisheries to logging, grazing, farming, and industry.

In 1861, Marsh was appointed minister to the new kingdom of Italy. He served until his death in 1882, the longest service of any diplomat before or since. He again had time to research and write. In 1864, Marsh published *Man and Nature; or, Physical Geography as Modified by Human Action*. The first systematic analysis of the impact of human activity on the environment, the book immediately influenced scientific thinking in America and Europe and provided a boost to the conservation movement.

Marsh summarized European and American agricultural practices. He noted how logging, dam construction, and farming damaged the land. Land, subdued and then abandoned, was left impoverished. Nature, he argued, cannot heal itself. But Marsh's faith in science led him to conclude that humans can control the environment for good as well as ill and to argue for conservation strategies. He discussed how Europeans were taking measures to stop or reverse the destruction and could, as France was doing, restore the balance of nature.

Marsh's book not only supplied a spark for the nascent conservation movement in the United States in the twentieth century, but also became the intellectual foundation for the science of ecology.

James G. Lewis

Further Reading

Lowenthal, D. (1958). *George Perkins Marsh: Versatile Vermonter*. New York: Columbia University Press.

Lowenthal, D. (2000). *George Perkins Marsh: Prophet of conservation*. Seattle: University of Washington Press.

Marsh, C. C. (Ed.). (1958). *Life and letters of George Perkins Marsh*. New York: Charles Scribner's Sons.

Marsh, G. P. (1864). *Man and nature; or, Physical geography as modified by human action*. New York: Charles Scribner.

Marsh, G. P., & Trombulak, S. C. (Eds.). (2001). *So great a vision: The conservation writings of George Perkins Marsh*. Hanover, NH: University Press of New England.

Marshall, Robert
(1901–1939)
Cofounder of the Wilderness Society and wilderness activist

Robert Marshall, born in New York City to a wealthy family, developed both his outdoor skills and a love of nature at the family's New York Adirondack Mountains estate. He graduated from the New York State College of Forestry, Syracuse, in 1924 and received a master of forestry degree from Harvard Forest School in 1925. From 1925 to 1928, he worked as a research silviculturalist (forest culture expert) with the U.S. Forest Service in Montana. He received a Ph.D. in plant physiology from Johns Hopkins University in 1930.

Marshall's influential 1930 article, "The Problem of Wilderness," expressed for the first time the idea that wilderness has an aesthetic beauty and that it provides a much-needed place to escape to from the civilized world. He conceded that scientific management on other lands could offset the loss of resources on those preserved lands. To support his agenda, he founded the Wilderness Society in 1935, served on its executive committee and council, and was a major financial supporter.

After school, he traveled to Alaska in 1930 to study tree growth at the Arctic timberline and investigated and mapped the largely unexplored Brooks Range. He received critical praise for *Arctic Village*, his observations on the life of Eskimos and white settlers of Wiseman, Alaska. After returning from Alaska in 1932, he wrote the chapters on forest recreation for the Forest Service's *National Plan for American Forestry*, also known as the Copeland Report. He recommended conducting a survey to determine how much land ought to be set aside for recreation and for what types of recreation.

In his 1933 book, *The People's Forests*, Marshall joined with a handful of other leading foresters in calling for the "social management," or federal and state regulation, of private forests to prevent further forest devastation. Marshall and the others were criticized as socialists, and the government ignored their call. That same year, Marshall became director of the Forestry Division of the Office of Indian Affairs and labored to improve the life of Native Americans. His office encouraged Native Americans to increase their participation in natural resource management on their reservations, including the retention of undeveloped areas.

Based on the Copeland Report, the Forest Service created its wilderness programs in 1937. Marshall agreed to be the chief of its newly formed Division of Recreation and Lands. He urged greater protection for primitive areas in national forests and secured the adoption of regulations for wilderness and wild areas in 1939. He recommended that nearly every large roadless area in a national forest be classified as a primitive area. He also sought to overturn segregated facilities in order to make wilderness accessible to all people.

Although famous for his hiking prowess (he was known for hiking more than 60 kilometers a day), he died of a heart attack in 1939 at age thirty-eight. In just a few short years, Marshall had made recreation an integral part of the Forest Service work and had popularized the cause of wilderness protection. In 1940, the Forest Service reclassified three Montana primitive areas as the Bob Marshall Wilderness Area.

James G. Lewis

Further Reading

Glover, J. M. (1986). *A wilderness original: The life of Bob Marshall*. Seattle: The Mountaineers.

Marshall, G. (1951, Autumn). Bibliography of Robert Marshall, 1901–1938. *Living Wilderness, 16(38)*, 20–23.

Marshall, G. (1951, Autumn). Robert Marshall as a writer. *Living Wilderness, 16(38)*, 14–20.

Marshall, R. (1922). *The high peaks of the Adirondacks*. Albany, NY: Adirondack Mountain Club.

Marshall, R. (1933). *Arctic village*. New York: H. Smith and R. Haas.

Marshall, R. (1933). *The people's forests*. New York: H. Smith and R. Haas.

Marshall, R., & Marshall, G. (Eds.). (1956). *Alaska wilderness: Exploring the central Brooks Range*. Berkeley & Los Angeles: University of California Press.

Nash, Roderick. (1982). *Wilderness and the American mind: The idea of wilderness* (3rd ed.). New Haven, CT: Yale University Press.

Marx, Karl Heinrich
(1818–1883)
German political philosopher

Karl Marx was one of the most influential social and political thinkers of modernity and its most important socialist theorist. Although Marx dealt extensively with environmental issues throughout his writings, until recently his work—alongside that of such social scientists as Emile Durkheim (1858–1917) of France or Max Weber (1864–1920) of Germany—was subject to considerable criticism for allegedly underplaying environmental considerations compared with socioeconomic and political processes. According to critics, his strong confidence in the human capacity for development and material progress would have led Marx to overlook its darker side as manifested in the overexploitation and depletion of natural resources.

Thus critics from a wide range of perspectives, including deep ecology (a radical version of environmentalism promoting a shift from an anthropocentric to a biocentric perspective in environmental values, developed mainly in the United States), sociological theory, and political ecology, have contended that, like most other classical social thinkers, Marx was inescapably trapped in an anthropocentric conception of the natural environment oblivious to ecological concerns. Also, he would have justified the environmental damage done by capitalist industrialization by postulating the primacy of human technological progress over ecological considerations such as the irreversible impact of capitalism's overexploitation of natural resources. Moreover, his allegedly antiecological intellectual legacy would be a crucial factor in explaining the large-scale environmental depletion that took place in communist countries during the twentieth century.

However, scholars now recognize that some of these criticisms have been ill founded, and a more in-depth analysis of Marx's writings has revealed that he made important contributions toward a scientific understanding of environmental questions. He also anticipated some of the key arguments currently associated with the historical sociology of ecological regimes and co-evolutionary theory, whereby human-nature interactions are conceived as interwoven and mutually binding. Thus he analyzed crucial ecological problems of his time, such as the degradation of soil fertility caused by the development of large-scale agriculture, the dangers posed by the increasing use of industrial fertilizers, industrial and urban pollution, and the depletion of forests and mineral reserves. He also put forward what can be considered as precedents of advanced notions of environmental sustainability and intergenerational justice. Most notably, he argued for changes in how the enormous amounts of industrial and urban consumer waste are disposed of and made a strong case for the introduction of recycling practices.

Perhaps Marx's most important contribution in this field has been his concept of socio-ecological metabolism, which he used to describe how the interaction between humans and the natural environment is mediated through the process of labor. This concept reflects a conception of human history in which human interaction with the natural environment is conceived as a mutually binding evolutionary process driven by technological development. He also postulated the notion of intergenerational responsibility that present generations have toward future generations in relation to the preservation of nature and contended that in the more civilized future society that he envisioned, private ownership of natural resources would be superseded by the more advanced social form of common property, by which humans would be caretakers and not owners of nature, and the rights of future generations would be represented.

José Esteban Castro

Further Reading

Foster, J. B. (1999). Marx's theory of metabolic rift: Classical foundations for environmental sociology. *American Journal of Sociology, 105*(2), 366–405.

Grundmann, R. (1991). *Marxism and ecology*. Oxford, UK: Oxford University Press.

Harvey, D. (1996). *Justice, nature, and the geography of difference*. Cambridge, MA: Blackwell.

Parsons, H. (Ed.). (1977). *Marx and Engels on ecology*. Westport, CT: Greenwood.

Redclift, M., & Benton, T. (Eds.). (1994). *Social theory and the global environment*. London: Routledge.

Mayak

Mayak was the first Soviet installation for production of plutonium for atomic bombs. Releases of radioactive waste had substantial health effects on staff, the local population, and the environment in the region. These releases were caused both by technical procedures during the first years of operation and by accidents.

Mayak, which until a few years ago was named Chelyabinsk 65, is located about 80 kilometers to the north of Chelyabinsk, the biggest city in the southern Urals.

Work on the reactor started in September 1946. On 22 June 1948 the reactor's power reached 100 mega-

watts, and in July the reactor started operating according to the production plan.

There are five main reasons for health and contamination problems in the Chelyabinsk region: general working conditions, the dumping of nuclear waste in the Techa River, a storage tank explosion that took place in 1957, the dumping of nuclear waste in Lake Karachay, and storage of nuclear waste in a chain of reservoirs.

Working Conditions

During the first seven years of operation (1949–1956), workers in the reactor, radiochemical plant, and metallurgical plant were subjected to high radiation doses, with direct health effects. Injuries and the ill effects of radiation were detected in 2,089 workers, and more than 6,000 received doses in excess of 1 sievert (the sievert is a unit for measuring doses of radiation [1 sievert = 1,000 millisievrts]), with many receiving more than 200 millisieverts during one year. (In ordinary circumstances, a person would expect to be exposed to about 2–7 millisieverts of natural background radiation.) In more than 2,000 employees an excess of plutonium was detected. A total of 1,596 cases of chronic radiation sickness were diagnosed at the Mayak plants in the period 1949–1989. Of these, 11.5 percent was diagnosed among reactor workers, 73.4 percent among workers in the radiochemical plant, and 15.1 percent among workers in the metallurgical plant.

Dumping of Nuclear Waste in the Techa River

For more than three years starting in 1949, and on a smaller scale for several years after that, nuclear waste was dumped straight into the Techa, a river that flows through densely populated areas. The 124,000 persons living in the river valley were exposed to very high levels of both external and internal radiation; the internal radiation was caused by the consumption of contaminated drinking water as well as contaminated animals and produce from agricultural land. During seven years, from 1949 to 1956, approximately 76 million cubic meters of liquid radioactive waste with a total radioactivity of 2.86 megacuries (the curie is a unit of radioactive discharge; safe levels are measured in the trillionths, or picocuries) were discharged into the river. Over 95 percent of this radioactivity was released between March 1950 and November 1951. The inhabitants living on the shores of the Techa, 28,100 people, received the highest radiation doses: 73 percent received doses up to 200 millisieverts, 12 percent up to 500 millisieverts, and 8 percent up to 1,000 millisieverts. During the first years of the radiochemical plant's operation, the average equivalent effective dose for inhabitants of the Techa River area was 320 millisieverts in the Chelyabinsk region and 70 millisieverts downstream in the Kurgan region. Chronic radiation sickness was diagnosed in 940 persons, mostly residents of villages located in close vicinity to the point of discharge.

The 1957 Storage Tank Explosion

When a storage tank exploded in 1957 it sent more than 20 million curies of radioactive material up in a 1-kilometer plume that then settled over an area of 20,000 square kilometers. Additional, although minor, contamination was caused by a dust storm that in 1967 spread radioactive dust from the shores of Lake Karachay. In the Soviet Union, the number of known accidents caused by chain reaction was thirteen. The total number of fatalities in these accidents is not known and it is not known whether all thirteen caused fatalities. Seven of the accidents took place in Mayak. In these accidents, five persons died, nine suffered from acute radiation sickness, and six received smaller doses.

Dumping of Nuclear Wastes in Lake Karachay

Lake Karachay is a small lake on the Mayak site. Waste was dumped into this lake starting in 1952, when dumping into Techa had to be stopped, not because of public protests, which were not possible in the political system in Chelyabinsk at that time, but because of observed deterioration in the health conditions of the local population. Karachay now contains approximately 120 megacuries of radioactive waste. This is more than twice the total amount released from Chernobyl. Waste solutions from Karachay form a plume of contaminated underground water. Contaminated solutions at first sink vertically down to the nearest aquitard (a layer of clay or silt that does not let water flow through it fast enough to let it be used as a water supply) and only then, at depths of 40–100 meters, form a lateral flow moving to the discharge zones. One of the major problems caused by the waste in Lake Karachay is contamination of groundwater. The velocity of the underground flow between Karachay and a nearby river, the Mishelyak, is 0.39–1.77 meters per day (the average is 0.84 meters per day).

A Cascade of Reservoirs for Storage of Nuclear Waste

Along the Techa, a cascade of reservoirs were constructed between 1950 and 1956 to prevent radionuclides from entering the river. The first reservoirs, constructed above and along the head of the Techa, are Lake Kyzyltash, Lake Tatysh, and Lake Karachay. These lakes were converted into storage dams for liquid nuclear waste in order to avoid releases into the Techa. A cascade of four additional reservoirs was also constructed between 1956 and 1963 to provide storage for additional low-level nuclear waste. On the northern and southern side of the cascade, canals have been constructed to intercept surface runoff and provide a bypass around the cascade. The water from the Mishelyak River, for example, is passed through the canal on the right side. The canal on the left is used as a path for water from Lake Irtyash to Techa below the cascade.

Mayak Today

Manufacturing of plutonium stopped in 1986, and the last operation reactor at Mayak was closed down in 1989. Today, the facility serves mainly as storage and reprocessing facility for spent nuclear fuel. Long-term international health effect studies in the region started in 1993 and are still going on.

Boris Segerstahl

Further Reading

Cochran, T. B., Norris, R. S., & Bukharin, O. A. (1995). *Making the Russian bomb. From Stalin to Yeltsin*. San Francisco: Westview Press.

Egorov, N. N., Novikov, V. M., Parker, F. L., & Popov, V. K. (Eds.). (2000). *The radiation legacy of the Soviet nuclear complex*. London: Earthscan.

Holloway, D. (1994). *Stalin and the bomb: The Soviet Union and atomic energy 1939–1956*. New Haven, CT: Yale University Press.

Kellog, S. L., Kirk, E. J. (Eds.). (1997). *Assessing health and environmental risks for long-term radiation contamination in Chelyabinsk, Russia*. Washington, DC: American Association for the Advancement of Science.

Segerstahl, B., Akleyev, A., & Novikov, V. (1997). The long shadow of Soviet plutonium production. *Environment, 39*(1), 12–20.

Meat Processing

The transformation of livestock into meat by slaughtering has occurred ever since animals were first domesticated (c. 6000 BCE). The meat processing industry originated during the nineteenth century, when industrialization and urbanization increased the demand for meat, which was met by shipping livestock to urban slaughterhouses. This pattern persisted in North America until the last third of the twentieth century, when meat processing companies, in an effort to lower costs, shut down urban plants and opened new facilities close to livestock concentrations.

Historical Background

Slaughtering hogs, cattle, and sheep for meat was confined to farms and urban butchers until the Industrial Revolution, when large slaughterhouses were established. In colonial North America, the Dutch dominated the red-meat trade. Slaughterhouses and cattle pens were major features of the landscape of New Amsterdam (now New York City) in the 1640s, but concerns over odor and effluent from processing led to their relocation outside the settlement and to the public provision of slaughtering facilities. As the population of the island of Manhattan grew, slaughtering moved northward; by the 1830s slaughterhouses and meatpacking plants were banished to north of Forty-Second Street.

Urban residents protested the driving of livestock through crowded streets on their way to slaughter, the dumping of offal, and the stench that accompanied slaughterhouse operations. Local opposition and improvements in water and rail transportation combined to shift the industry westward. By the 1840s, Cincinnati had become the center of the industry. Most of the city's forty plants produced pork and were located adjacent to the Ohio River, which provided an inexpensive means of transporting the finished product and a convenient dump for unused portions of the carcass. This practice ended when packers realized that valuable lard could be obtained from melting down the hog carcass and scraps. By the 1880s the industry's list of by-products included glue, hides, fertilizers, and shaving brushes.

Chicago's rise to prominence at the center of the country's railroad network and the subsequent establishment of the city's Union Stockyards in 1865 resulted in its replacing Cincinnati as the capital of the country's meatpacking industry. Livestock were shipped to the stockyards from surrounding areas, auctioned off, and slaughtered in nearby multistoried multispecies plants. The Midwest dominated the industry after the 1879 introduction of refrigerated rail-

cars, which allowed meat to be shipped throughout the country. Conditions in Chicago's packinghouses were chronicled in Upton Sinclair's *The Jungle* (1906). The public was so appalled by his account that the federal government established a meat inspection program.

Recent Trends in Meat Processing

Urban-based meat processing persisted until the latter half of the twentieth century. In 1961 Iowa Beef Packers (now known as IBP, a division of Tyson Foods) opened a beef slaughter facility in the northwest Iowa town of Denison. The one-story structure incorporated a disassembly line. Because workers were now responsible for only a single task in processing carcasses the company could pay lower wages than its rivals by arguing that the work required less skill than was required in older plants, where workers were expected to perform several tasks. It also enabled the company to raise worker productivity by increasing the line speed. Faster line speeds and thousands of daily repetitive motions led to a rise in worker injuries, and by the 1980s meat processing was the most hazardous industry in the United States. Record fines against the packers for health and safety violations helped reduce the injury rate in the 1990s, as did improved worker training.

In 1967 IBP introduced boxed beef: Instead of shipping carcasses to its customers, IBP "fabricated" them into smaller cuts of meat and vacuum-sealed them. Vacuum packaging appealed to supermarkets since it reduces shrinkage, caused by exposure to air, and adds to the product's shelf life. Supermarkets no longer needed their own butchers, which reduced their labor costs. Demand for boxed beef increased, and IBP responded by constructing several large-capacity slaughter plants close to supplies of grain-fed cattle on the high plains. By utilizing economies of scale, these plants have lower operating costs than smaller plants.

The cost-cutting techniques pioneered by IBP in the beef industry were applied to pork processing in the 1980s and led to competitors closing older urban plants, demanding wage concessions, and constructing large-capacity slaughterhouses close to livestock supplies. More recently, packers have lowered procurement costs by contracting with farmers to supply them with livestock. Under this system, modeled after the poultry industry, processors own the stock and supply it to farmers, who raise it according to the processors' specifications and are paid upon successful completion of the contract.

Meat Processing and the Environment

The westward shift in beef processing reflects a similar shift in cattle feeding. In 1955, Colorado, Nebraska, Kansas, and Texas produced 28 percent of U.S. grain-fed cattle; by 2000 that figure had risen to 76 percent. Large-capacity slaughterhouses require a plentiful supply of livestock. IBP's plant in Finney County, Kansas—the largest in the world—has the capacity to slaughter six thousand cattle a day. To meet this demand and that of other nearby plants, large-scale cattle feeding enterprises (feedlots) have been established. Cattle come to feedlots as yearlings, weighing 240–320 kilograms. At the feedlots they are fed a daily ration of between 9 and 10 kilograms of feed grain, resulting in a daily weight gain of just over a kilogram. Critics charge that diverting grain that might be consumed directly by people to feed cattle in this manner is highly inefficient. In about 120 days, grain-fed cattle reach a slaughter weight of 440–480 kilograms and in the process produce about 1,000 kilograms of manure. Manure is typically stored in piles at feedlots before being spread on fields before planting or after harvest. Stockpiling manure for much of the year creates a major point source of contaminants. Applying too much manure to the soil can cause nutrient imbalances and lead to contamination of surface water and groundwater. Large-scale production of feed grains depends on irrigation, which is depleting the water table.

Today most hogs are raised in barns, spending their lives on slatted concrete floors; their waste falls through slats and is transferred to an outside lagoon. Lagoons are typically emptied once a year by spraying the material on nearby fields. But lagoons leak, threatening groundwater, and occasionally their contents spill and disrupt ecosystems. The health consequences for neighboring residents and workers arising from exposure to gases and odors emanating from these facilities are the subject of ongoing studies.

Michael Broadway

Further Reading

Schlosser, E. (2001). *Fast food nation: The dark side of the all-American meal*. New York: Houghton Mifflin.

Sinclair, U. (1984). *The Jungle*. Cutchogue, NY: Buccaneer Books. (Original work published1906)

Skaggs, J. M. (1986). *Prime cut: Livestock raising and meat-packing in the United States, 1607–1983*. College Station: Texas A & M University Press.

Stull, D. D., & Broadway, M. J. (2003). *Slaughterhouse blues: The meat and poultry industry in North America*. Belmont, CA: Wadsworth.

Stull, D. D., Broadway, M. J., & Griffith, D. (Eds.). (1995). *Any way you cut it: Meat processing and small-town America*. Lawrence: University Press of Kansas.

Media

When the U.S. Department of the Interior Secretary Gayle Norton addressed the national meeting of the Society of Environmental Journalists in October 2001, she could not have expected any easy questions. Norton's department, which oversees the majority of public lands in the United States, had been involved in a number of controversies since George W. Bush had become president the previous January and appointed her to head the Department of the Interior. None of the controversies had been more contentious or had produced more news stories than the Bush administration's plans to allow oil drilling in the Arctic National Wildlife Refuge, a pristine wilderness area whose coastal plain is home to large caribou herds and migratory birds in the summer.

After Norton finished her address, one of the several hundred journalists attending the meeting in Portland, Oregon, asked her about a story in that day's *Washington Post*. The story reported that Norton's staff had switched numbers in a study of caribou calving in the Arctic Refuge, resulting in the false impression that caribou would be less affected by the oil drilling than environmentalists and wildlife biologists contended. "I have to admit we made a mistake," an embarrassed Norton acknowledged.

Secretary Norton did not have to appear in front of this organization. But the very fact that she came to the journalists' meeting—along with Christine Todd Whitman, administrator of the U.S. Environmental Protection Agency—showed that the top federal officials concerned with the nation's environment recognized the influence exercised by journalists who specialize in covering environmental issues. Norton and Whitman had clearly decided that they should make the administration's case to these journalists, who represent newspapers, magazines, television and radio stations, and online publications from around the nation.

Indeed, the parties on all sides of environmental disagreements—from environmental groups to major corporations—try to *use* journalists to convey their messages to the public. Their tactics can include openly disclosing information, developing cordial relations with individual journalists, pursuing public relations campaigns, and seeking to pressure media institutions. Good journalists, on the other hand, try to avoid being used by any special interests and seek to be accurate, fair, and open-minded in their pursuit of information that they will evaluate and ultimately communicate to the public. They share the opinion stated in 1787 by Thomas Jefferson that a well-informed public is "the basis of our government," the basis of democracy (Emery 1962, 167).

The environment—the place in which people live, work, play, and coexist with other species—is, of course, just one of many subjects about which the public needs to be informed. But particularly since the early 1960s, environmental issues have received sustained media attention due in large part to revelations about the way humans are polluting and otherwise harming the environment. Some information about the environment comes from educational or entertainment media such as magazines like *National Geographic* magazine, television programs on the Discovery Channel, and many other print and electronic outlets. But mainstream U.S. news media play the most conspicuous role in informing the public about events and policies affecting the environment, including oil spills and forest fires and efforts to preserve the diversity of species.

Roots of Environmental Journalism

People have a profound desire to know what is happening outside their own lives, and that has come to be known as news. "We need news to live our lives, to protect ourselves, bond with each other, identify friends and enemies," wrote journalists Bill Kovach and Tom Rosenstiel. Broadly defined, then, the environment has been part of the news since humans first developed language by which to communicate with one another about the world around them. With the growth of societies, news affecting public life became more formalized. "Journalism is simply the system societies generate to supply this news" (Kovach and Rosenstiel 2001, 10).

Modern journalism that is focused on environmental issues is rooted in nature writing, investigative reporting, and science journalism, especially that dealing with public health. In nineteenth-century America, writers such as Henry David Thoreau and George Perkins Marsh described the beauty and significance of nature and the need for conservation, while John Muir and others championed the ideals of wilderness in the western United States. Such environmental writing came during a period when scientists began more vigorously studying the relationships between organisms and their environment, a branch of biology termed "ecology" by Ernst Haeckel in 1866 (Worster 1977, 378). By the end of the century, the need to conserve natural resources was deeply engrained in the American public, and national parks had been established around the country.

Public lands and the natural resources they held, such as oil and minerals, also attracted U.S. business executives who had been benefiting handsomely from the Industrial Revolution that began in the nineteenth century. In the early 1900s some of the financiers, who through their monopolistic practices had earned the name "robber barons," set their sights on public land in Alaska, thought to be rich with coal. This caught the attention of investigative journalists who had gained a reputation for exposing corrupt politicians and business executives and who were labeled "muckrakers" by President Theodore Roosevelt in 1906. "A story of robber barons stealing pristine public land with the help of shady government henchmen touched a nerve among conservationists and muckrakers alike," wrote journalism historians Mark Neuzil and William Kovarik, noting that the Alaska land stories raised issues about federal control of public lands that continue to this day (Neuzil and Kovarik 1996, 96, 104).

Muckraking magazines such as *McClure's* published journalists such as Ida Tarbell, whose "History of Standard Oil" series addressed the profitable exploitation of natural resources, and Lincoln Steffens, whose "Shame of the Cities" examined urban environments. Other journalists and writers wrote about the dismal side of workplace environments, as Upton Sinclair did in his famous 1906 novel *The Jungle* about the meatpacking industry in Chicago.

After World War I journalists began writing more about science because the war "showed that science meant power—whether in the killing power of laboratory-developed mustard gas or the transport potential of the monoplane" (Anton and McCourt 1995, 8, 9). In 1921 E. W. Scripps became the first newspaper company to establish a science news service.

Three years later the topics of science and hazardous workplace environments intersected following a report about cancer deaths among young women in a

New Jersey factory who used a radium mixture to paint luminous dials on watches. The women licked their paintbrushes to create fine points for the detailed work. The radium caused cancer. The cases generated considerable publicity, and it turned out that at least nine dial workers at United States Radium Corporation died between 1922 and 1924 and many others contracted cancer (Ackland 2002, 103; Neuzil and Kovarik 1996, 33–52).

Despite the dial workers' story and similar cases, journalists writing about science during the next couple of decades did not spend much time or energy on the potential negative environmental effects from new chemicals and inventions. This was a time of "miracle drugs" like penicillin and chemicals like DDT that promised to wipe out mosquitoes and other pests. Industry's work was praised, not questioned. Journalists did cover events such as the "killer smog" that killed twenty-two people in Donora, Pennsylvania, in 1948, but they often considered such incidents to be isolated aberrations. In most cases, such as the initial controversy over leaded gasoline in the 1920s, journalists failed to examine the scientific issues involved. In the leaded gasoline case, "some papers tended to support industry, whereas liberal papers with a working-class readership extensively quoted public health advocates" (Neuzil and Kovarik 1996, 159).

The fact that the news media would take sides on public issues, including environmental controversies, was not surprising. The U.S. media, with the exception of today's public broadcasting, are private corporations. Although that gives them a valuable independence from the government—impossible in countries where the media are state-controlled—it means that the media owners are part of corporate America. Their goal, like the goal of the businesses that the media write stories about, is to make a profit—and that can get in the way of complete news coverage.

Individual journalists, on the other hand, see themselves as self-appointed, self-anointed public servants. They seek to be accurate, fair, and open-minded in producing stories. At the same time, American journalists generally share their society's ideology. And following World War II, the country's ideological consensus revolved around the titanic Cold War struggle between the United States and Soviet Union, between capitalism and communism. "The world view of the Cold War dominated American thinking about international affairs so totally during those years that it became not merely dangerous, but virtually impossible for most Americans to question or to step outside it," wrote

media scholar Daniel Hallin. "The journalists were no exception" (Hallin 1989, 50). Such ideological blinders caused mainstream journalists to initially miss the biggest environmental story of the twentieth century: the danger of nuclear weapons.

The Environment at Risk

"The Age of Ecology began on the desert outside Alamogordo, New Mexico, on July 16, 1945, with a dazzling fireball of light and a swelling mushroom cloud of radioactive gases," wrote environmental historian Donald Worster in describing the first nuclear bomb test. "For the first time in some two million years of human history, there existed a force capable of destroying the entire fabric of life on the planet" (Worster 1977, 339).

The United States demonstrated the devastating power of nuclear bombs less than a month later, dropping one on Hiroshima, Japan, on 6 August and one on Nagasaki, Japan, on 9 August, killing 210,000 people immediately and poisoning the environment with radioactivity. A year later, Albert Einstein warned, "The unleashed power of the atom has changed everything save our modes of thinking, and thus we drift toward unparalleled catastrophe" (Nathan and Norden 1960, 376).

Instead of people's thinking being changed, Cold War ideology blinded journalists and the public alike about the true nature of nuclear "weapons," devices of mass destruction so powerful and destructive that they weren't really weapons in the traditional sense of the word. After the Soviet Union tested its first nuclear bomb in 1949, the arms race was on. The United States and Soviet Union—soon to be joined by others—tested ever-more-powerful nuclear bombs in the atmosphere. U.S. tests on Pacific islands, and then in Nevada beginning in 1951, stirred concern among scientists and the public, followed by some journalistic coverage.

"The devastation of Bikini atoll, the poisoning of the atmosphere with strontium-90, and the threat of irreversible genetic damage struck the public consciousness with an impact that dust storms and predator deaths could never have had," Worster wrote. "Here was no local problem or easily ignored issue; it was a question of the elemental survival of living things, man included, everywhere in the world" (Worster 1977, 340).

Journalists, particularly in the American West where nuclear tests were occurring and nuclear weapons production was taking place, began asking questions about the consequences of fallout and the risks posed by weapons facilities. But the federal government effectively used the argument of "national security" to conceal the damage that nuclear activities were doing to public health and the environment. And the news media caved in. For example, after a 1957 fire in a plutonium production building at the Rocky Flats nuclear weapons plant just sixteen miles from Denver, journalists did not pursue the report that "spontaneous combustion" had started the fire. The weapons plant provided jobs and hundreds of millions of dollars in contracts for the community, and the media were big boosters of economic development.

On the East Coast, a writer and former U.S. Fish and Wildlife Service scientist named Rachel Carson was worried both about nuclear weapons and about the evidence accumulating in scientific journals about the long-term effects that chemicals such as DDT were having on the environment. "Along with the possibility of the extinction of mankind by nuclear war," Carson noted in her groundbreaking book *Silent Spring*, "the central problem of our age has ... become the contamination of man's total environment with such substances of incredible potential for harm—substances that accumulate in the tissues of plants and animals and even penetrate the germ cells to shatter or alter the very material of heredity upon which the shape of the future depends" (Carson 1962, 8). She brought home the risks by focusing on something everyone could relate to—birds. Robins and other songbirds were dying from pesticides.

Paul Brooks, editor of the company that published *Silent Spring*, wrote that Carson knew she would be "attacked by the chemical industry, not simply because of her opposition to the indiscriminate use of poisons, but—more fundamentally—because she had made clear the basic irresponsibility of an industrialized, technological society toward the natural world." And, Brooks noted, "When the attack did come, it was probably as bitter and unscrupulous as anything of the sort since publication of Charles Darwin's *Origin of the Species* a century before" (Brooks 1987, 15). Carson's research and findings held up.

Carson is widely credited with initiating the modern environmental movement. She also served as an important role model for journalists writing about the environment. Her knowledge of science enabled her to examine scientific journals and translate the obscure language and formulas into words that could be understood by all.

Journalists Grapple with Laws and Science

Silent Spring and the controversies surrounding it stimulated both journalists and policymakers to take a harder look at the contamination of air, land, and water, where pollution was often highly visible. Two *Chicago Tribune* reporters, Casey Bukro and Bill Jones, went to Lake Michigan and saw oily scum on the water. "Jones scooped a handful for a closer look. Black slime and grime coated his flesh," wrote reporter Chris Bowman in describing what led up to the *Tribune*'s 1967 series "Save Our Lakes" (Bowman 1996, 5).

Also in 1967, the nation's most prestigious awards for print journalism—the Pulitzer Prizes—were awarded for the first time for environmental stories. In the Public Service category, the *Milwaukee Journal* won for its articles about water pollution in Wisconsin, and the *Louisville Courier-Journal* won for its "successful campaign to control the Kentucky strip-mining industry, a notable advance in the national effort for the conservation of natural resources" (www.pulitzer.org).

The increased interest by policymakers in environmental issues led Congress to pass the National Environmental Policy Act in 1969. The creation of more environmental groups resulted in the first Earth Day demonstrations in 1970. Congress and the environmental movement were both influenced by journalism coverage and stimulated such coverage. A national consensus had evolved calling for stiffer environmental laws. This resulted in legislation such as the 1973 Endangered Species Act, aimed at preserving both species and the ecosystems they inhabited, and the 1976 Resource Conservation and Recovery Act, intended to discourage companies from producing hazardous wastes and to promote recycling.

The actions in Congress were accompanied by more award-winning journalistic coverage of the environment. In 1978 Gaylord Shaw of the *Los Angeles Times* won a Pulitzer for a series of articles about unsafe dams around the nation, and a year later James Risser of the *Des Moines Register* won for a series about the way farming practices and pesticides were damaging the environment. Extensive news coverage of the toxic Love Canal debacle in New York State pointed out the inadequacy of environmental laws and prompted Congress in 1980 to pass the Comprehensive Environmental Response, Compensation and Liability Act, better known as the Superfund law, requiring the cleanup of hazardous sites.

Environmental journalists increasingly found themselves reporting on issues less visible and more complex than smoke belching from smokestacks or toxic waste pouring from factory pipes. The 1979 accident at the Three Mile Island nuclear power plant in Pennsylvania underlined the need for journalists to understand radiation risks, a need made more dramatic in 1986 when the Chernobyl nuclear plant in the Soviet Union caught fire and air currents transported radioactivity around the world. Scientific reports about the depletion of ozone in the upper atmosphere and controversy over the excessive "global warming" from human emissions of carbon dioxide and other greenhouse gases caused many journalists to admit that they needed to do a better job.

"We often don't do a good job of reporting on the science of complicated issues, and we generally do a lousy job of helping our audience understand uncertainty, which is the central dilemma faced in making environmental policy," journalist Dianne Dumanoski, then of the *Boston Globe*, told her colleagues at a 1993 journalists' conference at Duke University (Lyman 1994, 40).

Environmental Journalism Today

The group to which Dumanoski spoke—the Society of Environmental Journalists—had been formed just three years earlier as a response to the particular demands of environmental reporting, which requires a broad knowledge of science, technology, economics, politics, history, and culture as well as excellent reporting skills. "Through a newsletter, workshops and conferences, the society hopes to train reporters to use the Freedom of Information Act, computer data bases and other investigative tools to probe these kinds of stories," wrote Jim Detjen, then a *Philadelphia Inquirer* environmental reporter and the society's first president (Detjen 1991, 91).

In 1990, when the Society of Environmental Journalists was established, the print media were still producing the largest share of environmental stories, but broadcast media had increased their coverage. "The Cable News Network has given environmental coverage high priority, and National Public Radio regularly provides strong coverage that weaves together the many disparate strands that make environmental reporting so difficult," wrote media scholar Sharon Friedman (Friedman 1991, 17). An increasing number of newspapers had designated environmental "beats," with reporters assigned specifically to cover this subject, and several magazines devoted to environmental coverage were being published.

American journalists in the early 1990s continued to be awarded for extraordinary reporting of environmental issues. In 1990 the *Seattle Times* won a Pulitzer for its coverage of the *Exxon Valdez* oil spill in Alaska, and the *Washington* (N.C.) *Daily News* won for revealing the city's contaminated water supply, "a problem that the local government had neither disclosed nor corrected over a period of eight years" (www.pulitzer. org). A 1992 Pulitzer went to Tom Knudson of the *Sacramento Bee* for his eight-month investigation, using extensive documentation and interviewing, of environmental damage to the Sierra Nevada mountains in California.

It should be noted that Americans are not the only journalists covering environmental issues. By 1993 more than fifty organizations of environmental journalists, both national and regional, existed around the world. Some had been established after the end of the Cold War and the 1991 disintegration of the Soviet Union and its empire, but others had predated those events. Environmental journalists from twenty-six countries met in Dresden, Germany, in 1993 and formed the International Federation of Environmental Journalists, which estimates that between three thousand and five thousand journalists around the world regularly cover environmental issues.

Global environmental issues can, of course, be covered by news media based anywhere. In 1997 the *Times-Picayune* of New Orleans won a Pulitzer for "its comprehensive series analyzing the conditions that threaten the world's supply of fish" (www.pulitzer. org). And in 1999 Richard Read of the *Oregonian* in Portland won a Pulitzer for showing how the Asian economic crisis affected domestic firms by analyzing an Oregon industry that exported frozen french fries. But other global issues get short shrift, for several reasons. By their very nature, the stories are broad and complex. Media companies must spend resources to send reporters abroad. And many stories, for example the pressures of population growth, do not have the kinds of "news hooks" that make headlines or appear on the nightly television news. This problem is not limited to global stories.

"The most valuable environmental coverage is part of a long-haul commitment to journalism that exposes not just one disaster or scandal, but that explains fundamental decisions, large and small, on the way to or from such dramatic occurrences," wrote Melanie Sill, an editor at the *News & Observer* of Raleigh, who shared the 1996 Pulitzer for a series on the environmental and health risks posed by the North Carolina hog industry (Sill 1996, 17–18).

Trying to deal with long-term environmental stories and not just dramatic events is just one of many challenges facing environmental journalists today. They also must contend with credibility issues, deepen their knowledge of environmental science and policy, and confront disturbing changes in the news industry itself.

The credibility question often comes in the form of a debate over whether environmental journalists should be advocates. Advocacy proponents typically argue that "we ought to be advocates for the health and safety of the planet, professionally and personally concerned with global warming, acid rain, destruction of tropical and temperate forests, loss of wilderness and wildlife, toxic wastes, pollution of air and water, and population pressures that degrade the quality of life," as writer and teacher Michael Frome put it (Frome 1998, ix). Journalist Jim Detjen, a Michigan State University professor, countered that "I believe that advocacy journalism, if it means one-sided and unfair reporting, is misguided and in the long run counterproductive" (Detjen 1991, 94). Suffice it to say that someone who disagrees with an environmental story will often try to dismiss it by claiming that the journalist is an "advocate."

The number of American environmental journalists is impossible to measure. Many journalists include environmental issues in their articles even if the articles are placed in a category like business or labor. Many journalists who cover the environment on a regular basis do not like labels or organizations and thus have not joined the Society of Environmental Journalists. But of those who have, according to the society's 2001 survey, out of a total membership of 1,100 people, 651 are full-time journalists, of whom three-fourths are print journalists. The rest are mostly academics or part-time journalists. The society's membership has stayed flat for the past few years, but the reasons for that are unclear. One characteristic of all journalists who produce environmental stories is that they must continually study science and policy if they intend to do good work. That is the main reason why they attend conferences, workshops, and institutes or participate in year-long journalism fellowships offered at universities such as Stanford, Colorado, Harvard, and MIT.

The most serious challenge to American environmental journalism today is presented by the increasing concentration of the news media in fewer and fewer corporate hands. Good, comprehensive coverage of the environment requires journalists to be free to report stories accurately "without fear or favor," as the saying goes. "The notion of a free press is rooted in independence," wrote Bill Kovach and Tom Rosenstiel. "The conglomeration of the news business threatens the survival of the press as an independent institution as journalism becomes a subsidiary inside large corporations more fundamentally grounded in other business purposes" (Kovach 2001, 32).

Len Ackland

See also Earth Day

Further Reading

Ackland, L. (2002). *Making a real killing: Rocky Flats and the nuclear West.* Albuquerque: University of New Mexico Press.

Anton, T., & McCourt, R. (Eds.). (1995). *The new science journalists.* New York: Ballantine Books.

Bowman, C. (1996, winter). Needed: A recommitment. *Nieman Reports, 50*(4), 5–8.

Brooks, P. (1987, January). The courage of Rachel Carson. *Audubon, 89,* 12–15.

Carson, R. (1962). *Silent spring.* Boston: Houghton Mifflin.

Detjen, J. (1991). The traditionalist's tools (and a fistful of new ones). In C. LaMay & E. Dennis (Eds.), *Media and the environment* (pp. 91–101). Washington, DC: Island Press.

Detjen, J. (1996, winter). Overseas activists create own media. *Nieman Reports, 50*(4), 45–48.

Emery, E. (1962). *The press and America: An interpretive history of journalism.* Englewood Cliffs, NJ: Prentice Hall.

Friedman, S. (1991). Two decades of the environmental beat. In C. LaMay & E. Dennis (Eds.), *Media and the environment* (pp. 17–28). Washington, DC: Island Press.

Frome, M. (1998). *Green ink.* Salt Lake City: University of Utah Press.

Hallin, D. (1989). *The uncensored war: The media and Vietnam.* Berkeley & Los Angeles: University of California Press.

Kovach, B., & Rosenstiel, T. (2001). *The elements of journalism: What newspeople should know and the public should expect.* New York: Crown Publishers.

LaMay, C., & Dennis, E. (Eds.). (1991). *Media and the environment.* Washington, DC: Island Press.

Lyman, F. (1994, winter). Mudslinging on the Earth-beat. *Amicus Journal, 15*(4), 39–44.

Nathan, O., & Norden, H. (Eds.). (1960). *Einstein on peace.* New York: Simon & Schuster.

Neuzil, M., & Kovarik, W. (1996). *Mass media & environmental conflict: America's green crusades*. Thousand Oaks, CA: Sage Publications.

Pulitzer Prizes website. Retrieved March 12, 2002, from www.pulitzer.org

Sill, M. (1996, winter). Needed: Long-haul commitment. *Nieman Reports, 50*(4), 17–20.

Worster, D. (1977). *Nature's economy: The roots of ecology*. San Francisco: Sierra Club Books.

Medicinal Plants

Founding myths in all great civilizations mention medicinal plants. One of the Chinese mythical emperors, Shennong (the Divine Husbandman), is presented as the ancestor of Chinese drug lore as well as the ancestor of agriculture. In the *Huainanzi*, a text from the second century BCE, it is said that "he tried all herbs; in one day he found seventy that were toxic." His name was also invoked in the title of the first Chinese drug compendium, composed in the first century CE, the *Shennong bencaojing* (Shennong's Classic of Medical Material).

The close relation between foodstuffs and medicinal plants, on the one hand, and the ambivalence of every drug (with both toxic and beneficial potential effects), on the other hand, is illustrated by these points. The same ambivalence is emphasized by the Greek term *pharmakon* (poison and remedy). However, the presence of medicinal plants in founding myths underlines the importance of the natural products in daily life and in the representations of nature as early as the beginning of human history and probably of human prehistory. Recent researches have even suggested that nonhuman primates acquire the ability to use medicinal plants (zoopharmacognosy). For instance, chimpanzees, when sick, have the habit of chewing the pith of *Vernonia amygdalina* (with antibiotic, antitumor activity) or swallowing the leaves of *Aspilia* species (killing parasitic worms).

The large body of botanical medicine books written in various civilizations since antiquity has shown an important accumulated knowledge of medicinal plants, their gathering, pharmaceutical processing, properties, and medical indications. According to many Mesopotamian clay tablets, diseases were cured, as soon as the first half of the third millennium BCE, with numerous fresh or dried simples (medicinal plants or a vegetable-based drug); more than 850 plant medicines are listed by the ancient Egyptians in the Ebers papyrus (c. 1500 BCE), including such drugs as aloe, castor bean, garlic, and juniper berries. Many centuries later, the great tradition of materia medica treatises was initiated by the Greek physician Dioscorides's *De Materia medica* (first century CE), a precise description of about six hundred plants, with their properties, uses, side effects, and cultivation. It was the major standard reference through the Middle Ages and the Renaissance in Europe. The development, during the Renaissance, of botanical illustrations and the addition of exotic plants to the therapeutic arsenal are also noteworthy.

At the end of the sixteenth century in China the huge *Bencao gangmu* (Classified Medical Material), by Li Shizhen (1518–1593), was printed. Plants form the most important part of the text, with 1,094 out of 1,895 kinds of drugs, the plant kingdom being divided into five sections: herbs (including wormwood, rhubarb, and aconite), grains (hemp, wheat, rice, etc.), vegetables, fruits, and trees. Therapeutic properties have a great diversity, and some plants are regarded as a panacea, often in relation with the Doctrine of Signatures, developed implicitly in China and explicitly in Europe by German alchemist Paracelsus (1493–1551). This is the case with one type of ginseng, the branched roots of which evoke a human body. The Doctrine of Signatures suggests that the medical effects of a plant can be detected by its shape, color, taste, or ecological conditions of growth. For instance, the red color of a leaf is a "sign" of an effect on blood circulation, and the fact that willows (*Salix* sp.) or *Filipendula ulmaria* grow in moist and cool conditions could be interpreted as a "signature" of a possible use for feverish illnesses or rheumatism. The latter example is quite curious because these plants owe their properties to the presence of salicin and other salycilate compounds, the origin of aspirin (acetylsalicylic acid), one of the most-used drugs for pain, fever, and inflammation.

Ethnobotanists (people who study the plant lore of a culture) collect and preserve the knowledge of medicinal plants available in cultures that have no written sources. It is estimated that more than twenty-two thousand plants (often up to 80 percent of the substances used to cure diseases) are used by traditional medicines, and an important part of the world population still entirely depends on these natural drugs as remedies.

Since the nineteenth century Western biomedicine (except homeopathy, which is a system of medicine that treats a disease by the administration of minute doses of a remedy that would in healthy persons produce symptoms similar to those of the disease) has rejected the ancient practices of polypharmacy (prescriptions of many plants together), preferring instead the isolation of active secondary compounds (alkaloids, flavonoids, terpens, etc.) from plants and their industrial production by chemistry. Morphine was isolated from opium in 1805 by Friedrich Serturner, and quinine isolated in 1820 by Pierre Joseph Pelletier and Joseph Bienaimé Caventou from *Cinchona* (any of a genus of South American trees and shrubs whose dried bark was used to treat malaria). Today 40 to 50 percent of all medical prescriptions in Europe and the United States contain at least one plant-derived ingredient, and medicinal plants are of extreme importance as a source of potential medicines. For instance, more than seventy alkaloids have been isolated from a little herb, the Madagascar periwinkle *(Catharanthus roseus)*, and some of them are effective against leukemia and other cancers. The problems of "new" diseases and drug-resistant strains of diseases make essential the research of new drugs from the vegetable kingdom. Traditional knowledge in this way is useful: The leaves of *Artemisia annua*, a wormwood mentioned as a drug for fevers in Chinese texts from the fourth or fifth century CE, are now the source of artemisinin, a compound with major antimalarial activity used as an alternative to chloroquine. A systematic medicinal screening of tropical plants could allow the discovery of new compounds not used in traditional medicines. However, the overexploitation of numerous drugs (*Panax ginseng* or *Eucommia ulmoides*, for instance) may lead to their disappearance. Above all, the dramatic reduction of biodiversity (biological diversity as indicated by numbers of species of animals and plants) around the world is a serious threat to the future research of new drugs: There is a crucial mandate now adopted by many health-related organizations worldwide: "Save the plants that save lives."

Frederic Obringer

Further Reading

Aikman, L. (1977). *Nature's healing arts: From folk medicine to modern drugs*. Washington, DC: National Geographic Society.

Arber, A. (1986), *Herbals: their origin and evolution. A chapter in the history of botany, 1470–1670*. Cambridge, UK: Cambridge University Press.

Aronson, J. K. (1985). *An account of the foxglove and its medical uses*. Oxford, UK: Oxford University Press.

Balick, M. J., Elisabetsky, E., & Laird, S. A. (1995). *Medicinal resources of the tropical forest: Biodiversity and its importance to human health*. New York: Columbia University Press.

Mann, J. (1992). *Murder, magic, and medicine*. Oxford, UK: Oxford University Press.

Obringer, F. (1997). *L'aconit et l'orpiment. Drogues et poisons en Chine ancienne et médiévale* [Aconite and Orpiment. Drugs and poisons in ancient and medieval China]. Paris: Fayard.

Sumner, J. (2000). *The natural history of medicinal plants*. Portland: Timber Press.

World Health Organization (WHO). (1999–). *WHO monographs on selected medicinal plants* (4 vols.). Geneva, Switzerland: WHO.

Mediterranean Basin

The Mediterranean Basin consists of the Mediterranean Sea and the lands that surround it. As the arena within which arose several of the ancient civilizations that influenced the cultures of Europe, North Africa, and the Near East, the basin is of particular importance to the study of environmental history. Historians have remarked that many of the Mediterranean lands, which in early times bore great cities, flourishing farms, and tall forests, later became poor and barren. Scholars have speculated about changes in climate but also about the effects of ancient land practices. Mediterranean societies, like societies everywhere, have always operated within the context of the natural environment, have had various positive and negative effects on it, and have in turn been affected by those effects. Civilizations flourish only as long as the ecosystems they depend on flourish. Among many other examples, cities such as Lepcis Magna, Sabratha, and Thamugadi in North Africa, which were thriving centers in the Roman Empire but later buried by advancing Sahara sands, illustrate this principle.

One of the most damaging effects of human activities in the Mediterranean was deforestation, which occurred to one degree or another in most parts of the basin. The great cedar forests of Lebanon, for example, were cut so intensively during Roman times and earlier that only a few small groves remain. Studies of ancient pollen deposits give evidence of forest removal in many localities around the inland sea. Of course, forests can recover from felling if given the chance, and there is also evidence of regrowth. But all too often, repeated exploitation, fires, the grazing of goats that eat small trees, and the expansion of agriculture meant that forests disappeared over wide expanses of land.

With fewer forests to absorb rainfall and release it in the form of springs, sudden downpours of rain that are common in the Mediterranean Basin swept down the mountainsides, bringing floods and eroding the soil. The resulting effects of erosion, leaving bare rocks and badlands, can be seen in some places such as southern Italy, Spain, and the Levant even today. Certainly it would take centuries to reestablish the same kinds of forest in some of these denuded tracts. Soil from the steeper slopes was deposited by the floods in coastal plains, which became poorly drained, silt-choked marshlands where malarial mosquitoes bred and forced villagers to move to higher elevations where possible. An example is the town of Paestum on the southern Italian coast, which flourished in Greek and Roman times but was uninhabitable by the Middle Ages.

Salinity is a problem wherever irrigation occurs in warm, relatively dry climates. As evaporation takes place in waterlogged fields, salt is concentrated in the soil, making the soil more saline. In some areas this can become so severe that most food crops cannot grow. Salinization has been noted in many places around the Mediterranean, including the Fayum, an Egyptian oasis that is below sea level. This phenomenon is not unrelated to deforestation and erosion because water dissolves more salt from exposed rocks and soil than it does from well-forested, stable slopes.

War and Taxes

Farmers in Mediterranean lands knew remedies for problems such as siltation, salinization, and soil exhaustion through leaching of minerals. But political and military pressures often made the remedies difficult to apply. The tax system made its greatest demands on the agricultural sector of the economy. Farmers were conscripted into armies, making their labor unavailable to care for the land. War ravaged the countryside; farm families were killed, their property requisitioned, and crops, buildings, and terraces destroyed. Antiecological warfare was practiced in order to deny food and other resources to the enemy. These pressures bore more severely on small farmers, who were ruined and became dependents of landlords who,

often having several large estates located in places distant from each other, survived more successfully.

Writers such as the Greek Hesiod and the Roman Virgil described typical Mediterranean farms, and it is evident that they were relatively complex ecosystems. Topography, soil, and exposure mandated that different crops be grown in the locations that most favored them. Portions of the land were left in forest as woodlots, and trees were planted for shelter and other purposes. But the tendency in some periods, especially under Roman rule in Italy and Spain, was to amass land in larger estates under single ownership, where grazing often replaced farming. Single grains such as wheat and barley were planted in extensive fields, a practice called "monoculture." These practices created simplified ecosystems vulnerable to insects and fungi. Because a complex ecosystem is more stable than a simple one—because it has more ways of reasserting its balance if it is subjected to stress—as one species after another is removed, the total complex becomes more susceptible to disaster.

Agriculturalists persecuted predatory animals that sometimes raided their herds and farm animals. The Greek Aristotle and other ancient writers recorded disastrous plagues of rodents. Perhaps they resulted from the fact that wolves, foxes, wildcats, and other predators had been hunted out. Thus by killing off many animals, people were unwittingly undermining their economies. However, these writers did not make the connection between the plagues and the reduced numbers of predators.

These factors affected agricultural productivity in the ancient Mediterranean, where agriculture was the most important sector of the economy. Shortages of food and rising prices were among the debilitating effects. The result of the human failure to support nature was that nature was less able to support humans. During much of antiquity in the Mediterranean, population decline was a continuing problem. Roman emperors tried to counter it by making marriage and childbearing mandatory. A decline in the population would mean fewer workers on farms, so that reductions in population resulted in lower agricultural production, which in turn would fail to feed the population. The Roman emperor Diocletian's Edict on Occupations commanded men to provide sons to fill their positions, and his Edict on Prices set maximum prices for many commodities including food, which is evidence of the economic situation during his reign (the end of the third century CE). Food was scarce, prices were rising, and there was a shortage of labor.

Although sporadic wars and plagues were also to blame, the chronic agricultural decline basically resulted from environmental causes.

The effects of industrial activity were also important in the ancient Mediterranean Basin. Scars left by ancient mines are still visible today. The Greek historian Herodotus remarked that miners on Thasos had turned a whole mountain upside down. The fuel needs of a large smelting operation such as the one that produced silver at Laurium in ancient Greece for Athenian coins or the Roman iron center at Populonium in ancient Italy would each consume annually the growth of wood provided by a forest extending over 404,687 hectares. In addition to these metallurgical factories, the ceramic industry demanded huge amounts of wood and charcoal for fuel.

Pollution

Several ancient writers remarked on pollution produced by industry. The Greek geographer Strabo visited silver-smelting furnaces in Hispania and noted that they needed high chimneys to carry the noxious smoke away because otherwise workers would suffer disability or even death. Lead, the predominant metal in silver ore, was present with other poisonous elements such as arsenic and mercury in industrial procedures, including the processing of other metallic ores, pottery, leather, and textiles, so that workers in these industries were in danger of poisoning. The general population was also exposed to toxic substances. Utensils, dishes, and cooking pots were often made of lead or silver with high lead content. Sweeteners, jam, and fish sauces contained lead compounds, sometimes at high concentrations. Water came through lead pipes, and aqueducts had ceramic channels sealed with lead. Water coming through such conduits could be contaminated by lead if it were acidic, although most water in the Mediterranean Basin contains calcium carbonate and therefore would have been buffered against contamination. Studies of accumulated ice in Greenland have shown that lead in the Earth's atmosphere increased during Roman times. Studies of bones from Roman burials have demonstrated variable, but often high, lead levels. Lead poisoning's effects include interference with reproduction, physical weakness, and dulling of the intellectual faculties, and these are cumulative, slow to develop, and long-lasting. As though that were not enough, mercury was used in gold refining, and arsenic appeared in pigments and medicines. It seems certain that large numbers of people in the Roman Empire suffered from environmental poisoning produced by industrial processes.

Urban dwellers in the ancient Mediterranean Basin found themselves afflicted with problems of pollution. The complaints of poets about conditions in the city of Rome sound remarkably familiar to modern readers. Air pollution from smoke and dust was bad in the larger cities, but noise pollution also generated protests. Indoor charcoal braziers and wood-burning fireplaces were the usual sources of heat in winter and were used for cooking all year. Lamps and torches provided as much smoke as light. Public baths, whose furnaces and hypocausts (ancient Roman central heating systems) were heated with prodigious amounts of fuel, were immensely popular throughout the Roman Empire. Wealthy Romans fled to country villas to escape the polluted atmosphere of Rome. The Roman writer Juvenal catalogued urban nuisances, including traffic, fires, construction projects that destroyed natural beauty, chamber pots emptied into the streets from upper-story windows, and rising crime and vandalism.

Waste disposal caused serious health problems. Many cities had carts to carry the worst of the garbage outside the walls, but in some places dung heaps could be seen and smelled in the midst of town. Even when there was a sewer system, as in Rome, difficulties remained. The *cloaca maxima* (main drain), discharged into the Tiber River, polluting the downstream stretch. Moreover, floods, their frequency increased by the deforestation of the Tiber watershed, backed effluents up the sewers into the city. Sometimes the drain in the floor of the Pantheon temple in Rome spouted like a fountain. Athens channeled sewage out of the city and used it as manure for crops. Materials from latrines were taken to tanneries. Pompeii installed stepping stones so that pedestrians could cross muddy, polluted avenues. The effects of water pollution, vermin, and diseases on the health of urban populations were staggering. The lack of sanitary conditions enabled the spread of the plagues that swept around the Mediterranean Sea in every period of the ancient past.

Questions Remain

Evidence in documents, archeological excavations, and scientific studies indicates that environmental problems were of critical importance in the history of Mediterranean civilizations. These problems may not have been as widespread and rapid as those of more recent centuries, but they were cumulative and mounted to a devastating level by the time of the late Roman Empire. Mediterranean societies could not flourish after their forests had been decimated, their agricultural soil eroded and salinized, their health undermined by the spread of malarial marshes, toxic pollution, and the unsanitary conditions of urban crowding. Of course, these problems were not equally present everywhere throughout Mediterranean history. For some locales and in some periods evidence is available, but for other locales and periods all too little is known. Why did ancient Mediterranean people act in ways that produced erosion, exhaustion of resources, debilitating pollution, the spread of disease, food shortages, and ruinous inflation? There is no simple answer, but several observations can be made.

First, ideas and beliefs affect the way people regard and treat the environment. A prevailing attitude of common people toward the natural environment was worship. Their gods were gods of nature who were believed to protect at least some aspects of nature such as sacred groves and chosen animals. But immediate needs often cause people to circumvent religious prescriptions. The ancients also had a secular practicality, often found in Greek and Latin literature, that weighed the economic value of natural resources and avoided involving the gods in their calculations. A philosopher such as Aristotle could declare that the highest purpose of everything in nature's order is to serve humankind. In late antiquity, Christianity came to dominate the Mediterranean area, and although affirming that the natural world reflects the glory of God, denied that the creation has intrinsic spiritual value, so that it could be used for the benefit of humankind.

Second, in regard to gaining understanding of the environment, many ancient people were interested in learning what makes the world of nature work. Farmers and others did this through experience, through trial and error. Philosophers and scientists developed many ideas that prefigured some principles of the science of ecology. Aristotle himself was important in this way, as was his brilliant student, Theophrastus. But observational and experimental science did not advance far enough to enable a sound theoretical understanding of the web of life. An intuitive grasp of what needs to be done to care for the Earth existed in agriculture and, perhaps to a lesser extent, in pastoralism and forestry. The Greek historian Xenophon expressed it thus: "Earth is a goddess who willingly teaches justice to those who can learn, for the better she is served the more good things she gives in return" (Xenophon 1923,

5.12). But economic, political, and military factors intervened to upset the balance.

Third, in order to maintain ecological balance, a society must have appropriate technology. It might be thought that the ancients did because they lacked many destructive inventions that later appeared. But their technology made major impacts in the long run. Dependence on wood and charcoal as the only major fuels meant a drain on forests. Water and wind power were discovered but not widely used until the Middle Ages.

Fourth, ability to interact creatively with the environment requires effective social organization. This is true because a community's environmental ends may involve sacrifices on the part of its individual members that they would not make without some degree of encouragement or coercion. That the ancients had social control is clear from the works they constructed, including aqueducts, canals, and roads. These works enabled cities to draw resources from distant lands. Technology and social organization can be directed either to conserve or destroy ecosystems. Unfortunately, it often seems that their dominant tendency is toward destruction. The peoples of the ancient Mediterranean Basin set in motion a wearing away of the landscapes where civilization had its birth on three continents. There was deterioration at the same time of both environment and people, and it was caused to a great extent by the actions of the people themselves.

J. Donald Hughes

Further Reading

Aristotle. (1962). *The politics* (T. A. Sinclair, Trans.). Baltimore: Penguin Books.

Aristotle. (1965). *History of animals* (A. L. Peck & D. M. Balme, Trans.). Cambridge, MA: Harvard University Press.

Herodotus. (1954). *The histories* (A. De Selincourt, Trans.). London: Penguin Books.

Hesiod. (1996). *Hesiod's works and days* (D. W. Tandy & W. C. Neale, Trans.). Berkeley and Los Angeles: University of California Press.

Hughes, J. D. (1994). *Pan's travail: Environmental problems of the ancient Greeks and Romans.* Baltimore: Johns Hopkins University Press.

Hughes, J. D. (2001). *An environmental history of the world: Humankind's changing role in the community of life.* London: Routledge.

Juvenal. (1958). *The satires of juvenal* (R. Humphries, Trans.). Bloomington: Indiana University Press.

King, R., Proudfoot, L., & Smith, B. (Eds.). (1997). *The Mediterranean: Environment and society*. London: Arnold.

McNeill, J. R. (1992). The deep history of Mediterranean landscapes. In *The mountains of the Mediterranean world: An environmental history* (pp. 68–103). Cambridge, UK: Cambridge University Press.

Strabo. (1917). *The geography of Strabo* (H. L. Jones, Trans.). Cambridge, MA: Harvard University Press.

Theophrastus. (1916). *Enquiry into plants and minor works on odours and weather signs* (A. Hort, Trans.). Cambridge, MA: Harvard University Press.

Theophrastus. (1990). *De causis plantarum* (B. Einarson & G. K. K. Link, Trans.). Cambridge, MA: Harvard University Press.

Thirgood, J. V. (1981). *Man and the Mediterranean forest: A history of resource depletion*. London: Academic Press.

Virgil. (1956). *Virgil's georgics* (S. P. Bovie, Trans.). Chicago: University of Chicago Press.

Wertime, T. A. (1983). The furnace versus the goat: The pyrotechnologic industries and Mediterranean deforestation in antiquity. *Journal of Field Archaeology, 10*(4), 445–452.

Xenophon. (1923). *Oeconomicus* (O. J. Todd, Trans.). Cambridge, MA: Harvard University Press.

Mediterranean Sea

The Mediterranean is the planet's largest inland sea. It is very salty because evaporation is high and the freshwater influx from rivers is low. At Gibraltar its heavier, salty water flows out to the Atlantic beneath an incoming current of lighter, less-salty ocean water. It takes about eighty years for the Mediterranean's water to flush out fully. In 2000 its catchment (or basin) was home to about 210 million people in eighteen countries. Biologically, the Mediterranean is rich, home to about ten thousand species of animals and plants. But its waters are thin in nutrients, so its total biomass and biological productivity are extremely low. This is why the water is so clear—when it is not polluted.

Marine pollution is not new. The ancient harbors of Ostia (Italy), Piraeus (Greece), and Alexandria (Egypt) were strewn with wastes. Bays, estuaries, and inlets such as Turkey's Golden Horn, the Venetian lagoons, or the Bay of Naples—were unsanitary in early modern times.

Since 1960 the main pollutants in the Mediterranean have been the same as elsewhere around the aquatic world: microbes, synthetic organic compounds such as dichlorodiphenyltrichloroethane (DDT) or polychlorinated biphenyls (PCBs), oil, and excess nutrients. The main sources are the big cities, big rivers, and a few coastal industrial enclaves.

Until 1920 microbial contamination from sewage existed in rough proportion to human population because sewage treatment scarcely existed. By 1990 about 30 percent of the raw sewage splashing into the Mediterranean received treatment, but the total quantity has tripled or quadrupled since 1900. So the risks of gastrointestinal ailments, typhoid, or hepatitis to people eating seafood or bathing have increased significantly. By the late 1980s, when the European Union developed guidelines for microbial contamination, beach closings had become routine from Spain to Greece.

Oil became a major pollutant with the emergence of Arabian oil fields after 1948. Soon about one-quarter of the world's oil shipments crossed the Mediterranean (1970–1990), leaving behind one-sixth of the world's oil pollution. One-third of that oil washed up on the beaches.

Industry did more than oil to sully the Mediterranean. Mediterranean countries accounted for about 5 percent of the world's industrial production in 1929, about 3 percent in 1950, but 14 percent in 1985. For the quarter-century after 1960, industrial production in Mediterranean countries rose by about 6–7 percent annually. This brought greater pollution. Industrial pollution concentrated where industry concentrated: in Italy, France, and Spain. Despite the rapid growth of industry in northern Africa, by 1990 it still accounted for only 9 percent of Mediterranean industry; the several countries ranging from Israel to Croatia accounted for another 10 percent. Italy generated 66 percent of the industrial production of the Mediterranean basin; Spain (mostly Barcelona), 10 percent; France (where little industry is in the Mediterranean catchment), only 5 percent. The greatest pollution problems therefore arose in the northwestern area of the Mediterranean basin, around the mouths of rivers with industrialized basins, such as the Ebro, Rhone, and Po, and around the centers of heavy industry, such as Barcelona, Genoa, and the northern Adriatic coast from Mestre to Trieste.

Eutrophication (the process by which a body of water becomes enriched with nutrients) derives mainly from agricultural runoff and municipal sewage. From time to time algal blooms, also known as eutrophic

An indoor fish market in Barcelona, Spain, displays some fruits of the Mediterranean Sea.
COURTESY SARAH CONRICK.

blooms, occur naturally in the Mediterranean, as else-where in enclosed waters. (Algal blooms occur when excess nutrients allow algae populations to proliferate, sometimes covering the water surface in sheets or "algal mats.") Although algal blooms occurred in the Mediterranean prior to 1950, they happened much more often after 1950 because of urbanization and un-treated sewage and because of the growing use of chemical fertilizers. The most affected areas were France's Gulf of Lions, which suffered its most serious blooms after 1980; the Saronic Gulf around Athens, which experienced its first in 1978; and the northern Adriatic. Between 1872 and 1988, the northern Adriatic recorded fifteen eutrophic blooms. Their frequency in-creased after 1969, which probably reflected greater nutrient loadings but might have reflected warmer water temperatures—perhaps both. Algal blooms played havoc with fish populations, seabed life in gen-eral, and the tourist trade.

As in much of the world, explicit environmental awareness and politics around the Mediterranean date mainly from the 1970s. Most countries by 1975 had tiny bands of ecologically concerned citizens. By 1980 some countries had green parties. Mediterranean countries in 1975 launched the Mediterranean Action Plan (MAP); under the auspices of the U.N. Environment Programme (UNEP), Mediterranean countries agreed to an ongoing process of environmental management for the entire basin. The plan supported scientific re-search and integrated environmental planning. It pro-duced several protocols to limit pollution. Enforce-ment usually left something to be desired: About 2,000 kilometers of coastline were "sacrificed" to develop-ment through lax enforcement or special dispensa-tions. But the plan, together with national regulations and European Union restrictions, helped limit Medi-terranean pollution after 1976. MAP helped in the con-struction of sewage treatment plants for Marseilles, Cairo, Alexandria, and several other cities. Although twenty-five years later the sea was more polluted than when the MAP began, it surely would have been much more so without the MAP.

Any plan involving Greece and Turkey, Syria and Israel, and other pairs of enemies (as of the 1970s) ranks as a high political achievement. In this case some credit goes to scientists who forged something of a pan-Mediterranean community. Scientific wisdom, normally quickly ignored when hard bargaining begins in international environmental politics, carried weight because hundreds of billions of tourist dollars were at stake. In the last quarter of the twentieth century, about one-third of international tourism involved visits to Mediterranean countries, usually to beaches. The quest for tourists, who contributed to pollution, paradoxically helped stabilize—and in some cases improve—the quality of coastal waters of the Mediterranean.

J. R. McNeill

Further Reading

De Walle, F. B., Nikolopulou-Tamvakli, M., & Heinen, W. J. (Eds.). 1993. *Environmental condition of the Mediterranean Sea*. Dordrecht, Netherlands: Kluwer Academic.

Haas, P. (1990). *Saving the Mediterranean: The politics of international environmental cooperation*. New York: Columbia University Press.

Stanners, D., & Bourdeau, P. (1995). *Europe's environment*. Copenhagen, Denmark: European Environment Agency.

Mencius

(c. 371–c. 289 BCE)
Chinese philosopher

Mencius was a follower of the teachings of Confucius and is also regarded as an important Chinese philosopher in his own right. He was born in the same region of China as Confucius (the state of Lu). His original name was Meng Ke, but he is often known in the West by his latinized name, Mencius. There appear to be few details of his youth, but it seems likely that he was well educated and destined to become a teacher. He sought to find a political ruler who would accept and implement his teachings, but had difficulty in achieving this. It does appear that at one stage he was employed as a minister in the state of Qi, but he did not remain in that post for very long. He then continued with his profession of teaching.

The fundamental precept of the teaching of Mencius is that human beings are morally good. They possess an innate virtue, which they should try to develop through self-discipline and through education that values and respects all life. Translating this into the political sphere, Mencius asserted that political rulers who adopted his philosophy would be able to rule not through force, but by the power of their ethical authority. Mencius also extended his view of ethics to the economic sphere, arguing strongly that a sound economic basis was necessary for securing a good quality of life. Mencius himself was born into the upper classes, and yet he appears to have been concerned about those less fortunate than himself. He particularly stressed that rulers should implement policies that assured a reasonable quality of life for ordinary people. In this sense he may be regarded as a social philosopher and an advocate of social reform. Mencius was very much in the tradition of Confucius, in that he respected Chinese traditional teaching and sought to transmit it without a great deal of modification. Part of the Confucian tradition emphasized human beings existing in harmony with their environment; Mencius supported that principle. After his death, the dialogues between Mencius and his students were compiled in the *Mengzi (Mencius)*.

Mencius did not believe in the absolute authority of rulers. He argued that it was the responsibility of rulers to behave justly and to treat all citizens in a fair manner. If the ruler did not behave in an ethical manner, then citizens had the moral right to seek to overthrow the ruler. It is, of course, one thing to advocate the citizens' right to overthrow a ruler as a theoretical position and another to implement it in practical terms. Mencius was in general terms a theoretician rather than a pragmatist when it came to governance.

Perhaps the greatest contribution of Mencius was that he sought to analyze the inherent qualities of human beings, a subject that was given little emphasis by Confucius. In addition, although he sought to transmit traditional Chinese teaching, he succeeded in making that teaching address the social conditions of the time.

Paul Oliver

Further Reading

Fairbank, J. K. (1992) *China: A new history*. Cambridge, MA; Harvard University Press.

Hucker, C. O. (1975) *China's imperial past*. London: Duckworth.

Mencius. (1976) *Mencius* (D. C. Lao, Trans.). New York: Penguin.

Mendes, Chico
(1944–1988)
Brazilian labor leader and environmental activist

Chico Mendes (born Francisco Alves Mendes Filho) became famous in the 1980s for organizing rubber tappers (people who locate and collect rubber sap and process it for sale to the proprietor of the forest from which the rubber was extracted) in the far western Brazilian Amazon River basin to confront cattle ranchers and land speculators who were clear-cutting and burning the rain forest, destroying the livelihood of those who lived there. Together with other rubber tappers, Mendes used nonviolent resistance and capitalized on worldwide concern over the burning of the Amazon rain forest to convince Brazil's government to set aside extractive reserves. In these reserves the forest could not be cut and could be used only in sustainable ways, such as for the extraction of rubber and the harvest of nuts, fruits, and tropical herbs. With the creation of these reserves, Mendes "pulled off one of the most significant feats in the history of grass-roots environmental activism" (Revkin 1990, 4). He became a martyr to that activism in 1988 when he was gunned down by frustrated cattle ranchers.

Born in the Brazilian state of Acre in the Seringal Ecuador, a tropical rain forest containing rubber trees only 6 kilometers from the Bolivian border, Mendes followed in his father's footsteps and became a tapper at the age of nine. As rubber tappers, members of the Mendes family suffered an existence of marginalization, exclusion, and exploitation, as did the majority of inhabitants of the Amazon River basin. Dependent on the sale of rubber and other products extracted from the forest, they lived at the mercy of those who claimed title to the forest and had absolute power over them. During the 1970s the Brazilian military dictatorship sought to develop the Amazon basin and sold huge tracts of the rain forest to powerful national and international investors. In turn, these investors sold the rain forest to cattle ranchers who began to evict the tappers and native communities in order to cut down the forest, burn it, and convert the land to pasture. To protect their homes and livelihoods, the tappers, under the leadership of Wilson Pinheiro, organized the first chapter of the Rural Workers Union in 1975. Greatly influenced by Pinheiro's vision, Mendes became a union leader and helped organize empates (standoffs against the ranchers in which the tappers and their families formed human chains in areas where ranchers attempted to cut the forest). These empates gained the rubber tappers worldwide attention and brought violent reactions from the ranchers and their financial backers. Scores of tappers were killed, among them Pinheiro in 1980. Mendes took his place as head of the Rural Workers Union and, working with Brazilian anthropologists and environmentalists over the next seven years, formed the National Council of Rubber Tappers.

The council's primary purpose was to preserve the rain forest through the creation of extractive reserves. It also established health clinics, schools, and cooperatives. Mauro Leonel, a friend of Mendes, said he "saw Chico often at conferences to decide the fate of the people of the forest. . . . He had a magnetic presence and a real way with words." A "truly selfless man, he respected everybody, whether old or young," said his brother Francisco de Assis (Shoumatoff 1990, 22–23, 29). Mendes won international recognition for his work, and in 1987 the Environmental Defense Fund and the National Wildlife Federation invited him to Washington, D.C., where he persuaded the directors of the Inter-American Development Bank to suspend funding for road-building projects in the Amazon. With this achievement came a violent reaction from ranchers who saw their lands expropriated and set aside as extractive reserves by the Brazilian government. After numerous death threats and attempts on his life, Mendes was shot to death 22 December 1988 as he stepped out the back door of his house in Xapuri. Two years later cattle rancher Darli Alves Da Silva and his son Darci were found guilty of the murder and sentenced to nineteen years in prison. They escaped after serving three years but were captured and returned to prison in 1996.

Many labor leaders were assassinated in Brazil during the last forty years of the twentieth century. Chico Mendes, however, became a symbol for peaceful resistance to social injustice and the destruction of the environment. For his work he received the U.N.'s Global 500 Environmental Prize and the Ted Turner Better World Society Prize. His legacy is in the establishment of extractive reserves in seven Brazilian states totaling more than 8 million acres.

Errol D. Jones

Further Reading

Dwyer, A. (1990). *Into the Amazon: The struggle for the rainforest*. San Francisco: Sierra Club Books.

Hecht, S., & Cockburn, A. (1989). *The fate of the forest: Developers, destroyers, and defenders of the Amazon*. London: Verso.

Mendes, C. (1989). *Fight for the forest: Chico Mendes in his own words*. London: Latin American Bureau.

Revkin, A. (1990). *The burning season*. Boston: Houghton Mifflin.

Shoumatoff, A. (1990). *The world is burning*. Boston: Little, Brown.

Mesopotamia

Mesopotamia is the region in southwestern Asia that stretches between the highlands of Anatolia, Turkey, in the north and the Persian Gulf in the south, the Zagros Mountains in the east, and the Syro-Arabian desert in the west. The word *Mesopotamia* is Greek for "(land) between the rivers"; the region was named for the two great rivers that flow through it, the Euphrates and the Tigris. Northern Mesopotamia—especially the foothills and hilly flanks of the Taurus and Zagros Mountains—has a wetter climate than southern Mesopotamia, allowing for rain farming without artificial irrigation. It is in the eastern part of the "Fertile Crescent" that runs from Palestine through Syria and northern Mesopotamia to southeast Iran. The first farming villages in Mesopotamia emerged in the north around 8000 BCE. In the flat alluvial plain of southern Mesopotamia, agriculture needed artificial irrigation. Settlements began later there than in the north.

Mesopotamian history began with the advent of urbanism in the middle of the fourth millennium BCE and ended in 532 BCE, when Mesopotamia was incorporated into the Persian Empire. During the third millennium BCE, the Sumerian culture in southern Mesopotamia was predominant. Later the power shifted north to Babylonia and Assyria.

Mesopotamia represents one of the most important regions in the early development of culture and technology. There is evidence of the origins of numerous and revolutionary innovations such as agriculture, irrigation, beer brewing, urbanism, writing, codified law, mathematics, astronomy, and metallurgy. These subsequently spread to the Mediterranean coast, Anatolia, and Greece and became the foundations of Western civilization.

Mesopotamian Attitudes toward Nature

The Mesopotamian view of nature was twofold. On the one hand, humans stood within the natural world, not separate from it. People felt a personal connection to nature, and their natural environment was guided by divine powers. On the other hand, the same environment consisted of countless material objects, which were at human disposal and could be manipulated by human actions. Pure spring water, for instance, was used for drinking without any mythological meaning, but it could also be revered as a manifestation of the Sumerian water god Enki. The date palm occurred as a simple tree in the orchards of southern Mesopotamia but also as a disputant in Sumerian philosophical dialogues. Salt was regarded both as a mineral for food preparation and as a personal being addressed in prayers and incantations. All natural phenomena, such as mountains, rivers, winds, or trees, possessed unique powers. They were regarded as manifestations of deities or demons, and explanations for them often took the form of narratives in myths, epics, and incantations. In short, the universal order represented a fragile equilibrium between a multitude of individual powers.

Nature was also seen by the Mesopotamians as a means of staying in contact with the world of the gods. Because any natural phenomenon could be the result of divine action, it was necessary to pay attention to everything that occurred in nature. Eclipses, celestial movements, the shape and behavior of animals, ant tracks on walls—all these could carry a divine message that people had to heed. Religious experts decoded these messages and gave advice regarding actions to be taken, life conduct to be changed, or rituals to be performed.

Agriculture and Irrigation

Mesopotamia was chiefly an agrarian-based society. Barley was the main crop, although other crops were grown as well. They included wheat, sesame as a source of oil, flax for linen, dates, and various vegetables. In much of the country agriculture depended on irrigation. The water levels of the Euphrates and the Tigris fluctuated considerably throughout Mesopotamian history. They rose in the spring due to melting snow from the mountains in the north, causing large areas to be flooded. Such flooding probably gave rise to the idea of a deluge found in several Mesopotamian epics. During summer and autumn, too late for sow-

Symbols from the ancient Sumerian "Farmer's Almanac." The story tells of the arrival of spring (see bird in bottom center) and what is to be done in the summer months.

ing, the water levels sank. This made water management necessary to secure regular harvests and sufficient yields. Dikes protected the fields against spring tides, and a network of large and small canals diverted the water from the great rivers. The water reached the fields by exploitation of its natural flow. Transverse supply furrows brought it to the irrigation furrows running parallel to the seed furrows across the fields. Water sweeps (*shaduf* in Arabic; a contraption with two long poles used to pull water from a lower to a higher level), waterwheels, and wells with pulleys were used to lift water.

In the northern and eastern areas, other methods were in use. In Assyria and Urartu (modern eastern Anatolia) systems of rock-cut canals and aqueducts brought water from distant rivers and areas of rain collection to the major cities. Ancient Iran originated the use of horizontal underground canals (*qanat*) that carried water over long distances from mountainous regions to fields and villages. This system was later adapted in Arabia, Egypt, and northern Africa.

According to a Sumerian school text called the "Farmer's Almanac" from the end of the third millennium BCE, fields were first irrigated during the summer. After that oxen were driven over a field to tread down the weeds. It was then plowed, harrowed, and raked. Sowing was done by means of a seeder plow. This plow created a furrow into which a seed was dropped using a vertical funnel above the plowshare. During the following months the field was irrigated three or four times according to the height of the growing barley. One of the biggest problems for farmers was the heat. Palm trees were often planted to shade the crops and to reduce the heat.

As soon as the barley was fully ripe it had to be harvested. Harvesting teams usually consisted of three men: one to reap the barley, one to bind the sheaves, and one to gather the sheaves into piles. The threshing and winnowing took place on a special threshing floor. The grain was extracted from the ears by use of a threshing sledge that was dragged over and over the sheaves by oxen. The resulting mixture of grain, chaff, and dust was thrown into the air when strong winds were blowing. The chaff and dust were carried away, and the grain fell back to the floor. Outside the crop-growing season, fields were opened for herds of sheep and goats to graze the stubs.

Regular maintenance of the canals was essential to the efficiency of the Mesopotamian irrigation network. This was mainly the task of the state. It required a high level of organization and much labor and expense. Throughout Mesopotamian history kings and governors expressed their concerns about the irrigation systems. Appointed officials had to make sure that canals were kept in good condition, with mud and silt constantly being cleaned out, and the banks kept high enough to keep the high waters away from the fields. According to Mesopotamian law codes, the care of the canals also figured prominently among the legal responsibilities of private landowners.

But irrigation also had its dangers. The irrigation water had a relatively high concentration of salt and minerals, and its evaporation caused heavy salinization, making the soil sterile. On the other hand, the water supplies for irrigation were limited to leach the salts from the fields. In spite of various efforts throughout the third millennium BCE to delay salinization through improved irrigation techniques, the salinity of the soil reached such harmful concentrations that fields became unusable. This loss of agricultural land, combined with a reduced stream flow of the Euphrates and the Tigris, may have contributed to the decline of the Sumerian civilization around 2000 BCE. At the same time, new political centers (Babylon, Ashur, Nineveh) emerged in northern Mesopotamia that were not infected by salinization.

Deforestation and War Damage

From the beginning of ancient Near Eastern civilization, wood was used as household and industrial fuel and as building material. Only in the southern parts of Mesopotamia was it replaced by reed. Many Neolithic sites such as Jericho, Çayönü, and Nevali Çori show evidence of architectural timbers. For the first half of the second millennium BCE, one can estimate the use of over two thousand trees for a 150-room palatial building. The mountains surrounding Mesopotamia, especially the Zagros, Taurus, and Lebanon ranges, provided most of the quality timber. This timber then was floated down the Tigris and the Euphrates to Mesopotamian cities. Assyrian and Babylonian kings regularly used military force to secure their timber supply.

The *Gilgamesh* epic describes the dangerous journey that the hero made to the far-off "Cedar Mountain," the killing of the guardian-demon Huwawa, and the cutting down of cedars for the temple of the god Enlil. Timber also figures prominently among the items listed as war booty or tribute in the Assyrian royal inscriptions. King Shalmaneser III (859–824 BCE) demanded three hundred cedar logs annually from a Syrian ruler, and the Babylonian king Nebuchadrezzar II (605–562 BCE) tells in his Wadi Brisa inscription that he had a special road built from Mount Lebanon to the Euphrates to carry cedar logs—some of them already over four hundred years old when they were cut—for his palace in Babylon. Large-scale shipbuilding carried out by the Phoenicians for Egyptians, Assyrians, or Greeks further exploited the Lebanon forests. The Macedonian general Antigonus Monophthalmos employed eight thousand men and two thousand draft animals for his shipbuilding operation during the siege of Tyre in 315 BCE. In spite of all this deforestation, however, large wooded areas in Syria and Anatolia could still be found in the middle of the first millennium BCE. The current absence of forests in this region is a post-Roman phenomenon.

The cutting down of trees in gardens and orchards was common practice in wartime, as was the total devastation of agricultural land and the destruction of irrigation facilities in defeated territories. Assyrian royal inscriptions regularly mentioned these practices, and the Assyrian palace reliefs provide vivid pictorial evidence. Especially severe was the destruction of orchards that needed years of special care before they could produce sufficient yields, such as the vineyards in the northern highlands or palm groves in the southern plains. During the first millennium BCE, however, there were several cases where these environmental destructions were used as strategic instruments of warfare, with the intention of punishing or creating fear among enemies. In these cases the annihilation of the enemy's habitat was part of the calculated frightfulness of Assyrian kings. Its effectiveness resulted from the widespread belief that disasters—natural or human-made—were divine sanctions for individual or collective sins. The Assyrians incorporated this belief into their political ideology, according to which Assyria was the realm of order that had to expand into the surrounding territories of chaos. Nature became part of this concept. The ecological order within the Assyrian Empire corresponded to the ecological chaos within the enemy countries, and the destruction of the natural environment in enemy territories was the ultimate sign of divine approval for Assyrian supremacy.

The Royal Hunt

Hunting and fishing were practiced in Mesopotamia from earliest times onward. Hunters used a range of devices, such as pits, traps, nets, snares, bows, and spears. Fishing methods included the casting of nets with stone or lead sinkers and the use of line and hook. The *Legend of Adapa*, an epic from the second millennium BCE, describes how Adapa went out fishing in the open sea for the god Enki, how he was drowned by the south wind, and how in his anger he broke the "wing" of the wind.

From the third millennium BCE there is evidence of hunting as a royal sport. Assyrian royal inscriptions mention kings hunting lions, wild bulls, and elephants during their campaigns, and depictions of hunts and accompanying offerings are found on Assyrian palace reliefs. Hunting was not only a source of amusement for Assyrian kings but also a demonstration of their power and physical strength.

During the seventh century BCE Assyrian kings hunted mainly in a specially laid-out game park. The lion-hunt reliefs of King Ashurbanipal (669–627 BCE) in his palace in Nineveh (now in the British Museum in London) have become world famous. They show the king—on foot, on horseback, on his chariot, and on his boat—pursuing and killing hundreds of lions. The whole scene is set within the courtly atmosphere of the residence with the hunting ground fenced off and guarded by soldiers with dogs, while spectators climb a nearby hill. The lions have been brought in wooden cages. Servants are depicted angering the lions until they charge and the king can kill them. At the end Ashurbanipal is seen pouring out libations over the dead lions.

For the Assyrians, lions symbolized kingship, and the killing of lions was restricted to the king himself. But lions also symbolized the threatening forces of chaos surrounding Assyria. By ritually killing the lions the king fulfilled his duty as a guardian of civilization and as a "good shepherd." The close connection between the lion hunt and the Assyrian concept of kingship is illustrated by the fact that the official Assyrian royal seal was decorated with a representation of the king killing a lion with his sword.

Horticulture and Pleasure Gardens

Pleasure gardens in Mesopotamian temples and palaces existed since the third millennium BCE; some of them—for example, in Ashur and Uruk—have been excavated by archaeologists. Certainly these gardens originated from a genuine interest in horticulture and exotica, but from Assyrian times on they also had an ideological function. One of the main duties of Assyrian kings was securing the productivity and prosperity of their country. In this context the palace gardens in the Assyrian residences, which starting from the eleventh century BCE included exotic trees and bushes from all parts of the known world, represented symbolic images of the Assyrian Empire—its expansion, its wealth, and its power.

Texts from the ninth century BCE mention forty-one botanical species growing in the pleasure gardens of the Assyrian capital Calah (modern Nimrud). Among them were cedars, palm trees, fig trees, and frankincense trees. One and a half centuries later King Sennacherib (705–681 BCE) had his palace in Nineveh surrounded by several botanical gardens with exotic trees and by natural parks with swamps where birds and wild boars lived.

These horticultural projects heavily increased the demand for water, and Sennacherib had the water supply system of Nineveh enlarged. By means of aqueducts and rock-cut canals with a total length of over 150 kilometers, water was brought from the mountains in the northeast and from several rivers in the east. It was collected in reservoirs near Nineveh and then distributed among the gardens and the city.

The downfall of the Assyrian Empire was not the end of Mesopotamian royal horticulture. Babylonian kings imported the idea of the designed botanical garden. The famous Hanging Gardens of Babylon became one of the ancient wonders of the world. Unfortunately the German excavators of Babylon were not able to determine their exact location. Under Achaemenidae and Sasanian rule the concept of the royal garden was further developed. The artificial botanical gardens as symbols of an orderly world became a specific element of Persian cultural tradition in the form of the famous rose gardens of Shiraz and Isfahan. The Assyrian game parks developed into walled-in hunting grounds, for example, at Bisutun and Taq-i Bustan, where many types of plants and animals were kept for royal pleasure. Located in the open countryside and surrounded by walls, they became models for Jewish-Christian concepts of paradise. The Old Persian term *pairidaeza* meant an "enclosed preserve." The term became *pardes* in Hebrew and *parádeisos* in Greek, eventually leading to the English word *paradise*.

Implications

Throughout Mesopotamian history close human-environment interactions can be found. These interactions resulted in revolutionary changes in the techniques of agriculture and irrigation but also in environmental damages, such as the salinization of southern Mesopotamia and the dying out of the Syrian elephant. Mesopotamian agricultural experiences and innovations were passed on to the Greeks and the Persians, as was the symbolic use of nature in religious and ideological concepts.

Hannes D. Galter

See also Egypt, Ancient; Irrigation

Further Reading

Anderson, J. K. (1985). *Hunting in the ancient world*. Berkeley and Los Angeles: University of California Press.

Bagg, A. M. (2000). *Assyrische Wasserbauten: Assyrische Wasserbauten im Kernland Assyriens zwischen der 2. Hälfte des 2. und der 1. Hälfte des 1. Jahrtausends v. Chr* [Assyrian waterworks: Assyrian waterworks within the heartland of Assyria between the second half and the first half of the first millennium BCE]. Mainz, Germany: Baghdader Forschungen.

Civil, M. (1994). *The farmer's instructions: A Sumerian agricultural manual*. Barcelona, Spain: Aula Orientalis.

Dalley, S. (1989). *Myths from Mesopotamia*. New York: Oxford University Press.

Fauth, W. (1979). Der königliche Gärtner und Jäger im Paradeisos. Beobachtungen zur Rolle des Herrschers in der vorderasiatischen Hortikultur [The royal gardener and hunter in paradeisos. Observations on the role of the king in ancient near eastern horticulture]. *Persica* [Persia], *8*, 1–53.

Finkel, I. L. (1988). The Hanging Gardens of Babylon. In P. A. Clayton & M. J. Price (Eds.), *The seven wonders of the world* (pp. 38–58). New York: Routledge.

Galter, H. D. (1999). Enkis Haus und Sanheribs Garten. Aspekte mesopotamischer Natursicht [Enki's house and Sennacherib's garden. Aspects of Mesopotamian attitudes toward nature]. In R. P. Sieferle & H. Breuninger (Eds.), *Natur-Bilder. Wahrnehmungen von Natur und Umwelt in der Geschichte* [Views on nature: Concepts of nature and environment in history] (pp. 43–72). New York: Campus.

Jacobsen, T. (1982). *Salinity and irrigation: Agriculture in antiquity*. Malibu, CA: Bibliotheca Mesopotamica.

Klengel, H., & Renger, J. (Eds.). (1999). *Landwirtschaft im Alten Orient* [Agriculture in the ancient Near East].

Berlin, Germany: Berliner Beiträge zum Vorderen Orient.

Meiggs, R. (1982). *Trees and timber in the ancient Mediterranean world*. Oxford, UK: Claredon Press.

Oded, B. (1997). Cutting down orchards in Assyrian royal inscriptions—the historiographic aspect. *Journal of Ancient Civilizations, 12*, 93–98.

Oppenheim, A. L. (1978). Man and nature in Mesopotamian civilization. *Dictionary of scientific biography, 15* (Suppl. 1), 634–662.

Potts, D. T. (1997). *Mesopotamian civilization: The material foundations*. London: Athlone Press.

Scholz, B. (Ed.). (1989). *Der Orientalische Mensch und seine Beziehungen zur Umwelt* [Oriental man and his relation to his environment]. Graz, Austria: Grazer Morgenländische Studien.

Wiseman, D. J. (1983). Mesopotamian gardens. *Anatolian studies, 33*, 137–144.

Wiseman, D. J. (1984). Palace and temple gardens in the ancient Near East. In T. Mikasa (Ed.), *Monarchies and socio-religious traditions in the ancient Near East* (pp. 37–43). Wiesbaden, Germany: Harrassowitz.

Metals *See* Heavy Metals, Silver, Iron, Gold

Mexico
(2000 est. pop. 100 million)

The environmental history of Mexico shows how humans and nature have interacted over time to forge what is today a vibrant and diverse country. However, Mexico has severe environmental dilemmas. Its history helps explain the roots of those dilemmas and why they are so difficult to solve.

Mexico is the second-largest country in Latin America (after Brazil). Its 1.9 million square kilometers cover the area between the United States on the north, Guatemala and Belize on the south, the Gulf of Mexico on the east, and the Pacific Ocean on the west. The Sierra Madre mountains dominate Mexico's physical landscape; the Sierra Madre Oriental mountains run north to south on Mexico's eastern side, and the Sierra Madre Occidental mountains form a spine from north to south on the western side. Between the ranges are plateaus, deserts, and valleys with dry, harsh climates—meaning that only 10 percent of the country is arable (good for agriculture), and much of that requires intense irrigation. In Mexico's southern region are more mountains, some of which are active volcanoes, and dense tropical forests. Like appendages sticking out from both ends, Mexico's two peninsulas have unique characteristics. The Yucatan in the Southeast is flat and dominated by low scrub forest, and Baja California in the Northwest is characterized by the Sonoran Desert. The deserts, mountains, tropical forests, and lack of any major, navigable rivers have all created geographic barriers to transportation, communication, and development over time. However, with such a diversity of regions, climates, and ecosystems the country is often considered to be "many Mexicos."

The population is equally diverse. Mexico is a federal republic with thirty-one states, the larger ones located in the less-populated North. Mexico City, the nation's capital, is in the Distrito Federal and is now the largest city in the world with over 21 million people. Other large urban areas include Guadalajara, Monterrey, and the border cities of Ciudad Juarez and Tijuana. That Mexico shares a 3,218-kilometer-long border with the United States means that there has been a great deal of migration to the Borderlands from within the country. The growth has been so swift that social services have not been able to keep pace with it.

Indigenous Mexico

How Mexico's pre-Columbian indigenous population survived in such diverse environmental conditions merits attention. In the northern deserts some groups, such as the Chichamecs, were nomadic—they moved around for optimum hunting and gathering. Others, such as the Yaquis, practiced floodgate irrigation by diverting river water for their crops. In southern Mexico great cities flourished in the Mayan and Aztec Empires—cities that required considerable quantities of food. To meet those demands for food, the natives created an intercropping system: They planted corn (maize) in rows, nitrogen-fixing beans beside the corn to restore nutrients to the soil, and a variety of squashes between the rows. The squash leaves provided cover for the beans and acted as a natural pest control.

In the Valley of Mexico, where the invading Aztecs established the great city of Tenochtitlán (where Mexico City is today), the local natives had developed a unique form of agriculture called *chinampas*. This highly productive farming method used beds of mud and decayed plant material in the region's lake shal-

lows for the planting of an array of grains and vegetables. The natives could get several harvests a year from the *chinampas* that supported Tenochtitlan—a city of an estimated 235,000 people by the mid-fifteenth century. Further, as one historian notes, "the *chinampas* aided soil and forest conservation by reducing pressures to burn steep wooded hillsides for farming" (Simonian 1995, 25). This efficient farming practice continues today near Xochimilco, but much of the *chinampas* land has been destroyed by urban sprawl.

Farther south, the Mayans of Yucatan and Chiapas (the state bordering Guatemala) used *milpa* (corn plot) farming—fields that were cleared and burned from the tropical forests. With efficient intercropping they, too, were able to sustain large populations until the tenth century CE, when their advanced civilization collapsed. Some scholars argue that the Maya had exceeded the carrying capacity (the population that an area will support without deterioration) of the land as their population grew, but others suggest that a cataclysmic event hastened their collapse. Despite these environmental impacts, the Maya, like all indigenous societies, maintained a spiritual relationship with nature. For them the ceiba tree was sacred—it held up the four corners of the world; also, the souls of their dead went under

Homero and Betty Aridjis, Mexican environmental writers and activists, cofounders of El Grupo de los Cien Mexico City, Mexico, in Reno, Nevada, February 1988. COURTESY SCOTT SLOVIC.

it, and therefore it was not to be felled. Their respect and fear of the forest helped to protect it.

Colonial Era

Spanish explorer Hernán Cortés and his crew entered Mexico in 1519. They came with riches and domination in mind and set out immediately to conquer Mexico for Spain. With the help of indigenous groups who had suffered under Aztec control, firearms, horses, and the Aztec belief that Cortés was perhaps a returning deity, by 1521 Cortés was triumphant. The Spanish monarchs then established "New Spain" in Mexico and sent other conquistadors, explorers, and priests to secure the colony. This was facilitated by diseases that the Europeans brought with them against which the natives had no immunities. Epidemics of influenza, measles, typhus, and especially smallpox caused such high mortality that by the mid-seventeenth century the indigenous population of the region was between 5 and 10 percent of what it had been in 1500. Thus in great part the conquest was a biological one.

Other environmental changes occurred when the colonizers introduced crops and livestock that produced food that they were used to from Europe. Wheat, malt barley, and wine grapes became new staple crops. Mediterranean fruits and olives replaced some local produce. A variety of weeds competed with, and often overtook, native plant habitats. Cattle and sheep, however, caused the greatest transformations. What has been called "ungulate irruptions" (Melville 1994, 6) occurred when livestock exceeded the carrying capacity and caused plant communities to crash until a plant-animal accommodation plateau was reached. This was especially noted with sheep in the Mezquital Valley northeast of Mexico City by the late 1500s when intensive grazing caused severe erosion and deterioration of the environment.

The Spaniards also introduced plantation agriculture in areas that were conducive to growing sugarcane and, with even greater environmental implications, began large-scale mining ventures. Gold and silver were in high demand in Europe, and Mexico's vast underground reserves were soon found and exploited. The colonial labor system for these enterprises was based on the *encomienda*—a grant of native labor to colonizers for use in developing the region. Similar to slavery, the process exploited indigenous people and helped transform landscapes. Mining, with its demand for timber to support shafts and food to feed miners, was especially damaging. Finally, exporting sugar, minerals, and other raw materials during the colonial era set Mexico on a dependency pathway that continued after independence.

Independence and the Nineteenth Century

When Mexicans won their independence in 1810 their national map did not look as it does today. It included all of New Spain—from Guatemala to the California-Oregon border. Granted, there were few Spanish settlements in the vast area that is now the U.S. Southwest, only settlements along the California coast and in northern New Mexico. However, Mexico lost that land, nearly half its territory, in the Mexican-American War by 1848—just before gold was discovered in California. The lost resources and land became a boon for an expanding United States.

During the formative years of its new nationhood, Mexico was ruled by General Antonio López de Santa Anna (1833–1855), under whose command the country lost so much land and suffered from stagnant economic growth. A revolt against his dictatorship brought Benito Juárez to power in 1858; he believed in liberal economic policy. Liberalism in those years implied modernization, material progress, and development of natural resources. Thus Mexico began to disburse funds for railroads, mines, and other national projects, which often were at the expense of indigenous communities and altered the natural environment. Forests were cleared, mountainsides were often overgrazed and were studded with mining operations and tailings piles, and vast open areas were converted to intensive agriculture.

This pattern accelerated during the dictatorship of Porfirio Díaz (1876–1911, a period known as the *porfiriato*), whose advisors were schooled in European positivism—a belief that economic development follows private property, modernized agriculture, expanded transportation, and communication and an educational system bent on science and engineering. Thus Díaz's policies converted much native land to plantation agriculture to sell cotton, sugar, henequen (a fiber crop grown in Yucatan and used to make twine and rope), and later vegetables on the international market. He emphasized mining, especially that of copper, which was in high demand due to a growing world market for electrical conduit. He also expanded Mexico's railway system, nearly quadrupling its number of miles, to transport the agricultural and mineral commodities to ports.

Despite the social and ecological changes (e.g., eroded hillsides, clear-cut forests, polluted streams and rivers from mining operations, and dammed valleys) that these developments caused, the expected economic benefits never materialized. The projects were dependent on foreign investment, 80 percent from the United States, meaning that profits went to large land and business owners. By 1910 half of Mexico's land was controlled by three hundred families (20 percent of the country was owned by seventeen people). Likewise, the railroads made it easier for people to relocate, as observed by the thousands of landless peasants who traveled to the cities to seek work. The newcomers, often having to live in slums on the outskirts of cities, helped Mexico City become a metropolis. Thus a radically changing urban environment, and all its resource pressures, were outcomes of the *porfiriato*.

Twentieth Century

The tyranny and economic malaise of the Díaz years prompted Mexico's revolution and civil war (1910–1920). Along with political reforms, limiting presidents to one six-year term, central to the revolution was agrarian reform to return lands that had been taken from *campesinos* (rural peasants) and natives. As a result, Article 27 of the Constitution of 1917 made foreign ownership of land and subsurface resources illegal. It restored much of the land to *ejidos*—communal lands cooperatively operated by *campesino* or Indian groups.

President Lázaro Cárdenas (1934–1940) accelerated this process by enacting 66 percent of all the agrarian reforms between the revolution and 1940. The largest *ejido* established, 3.2 million hectares, was in the Laguna cotton-growing district of the northern state of Coahuila. Cárdenas further encouraged these communal ventures by creating *ejido* credit banks (for loans to purchase seeds and farming equipment) and by supporting large irrigation projects. By the 1950s and 1960s dams and hydroelectric projects sprouted up all over Mexico, forever changing rivers, valleys, and the lives of people who were displaced by the dams' reservoirs. Finally, in 1938 the Cárdenas government nationalized oil reserves to form Petróleos Mexicanos (PEMEX), a move that infuriated U.S. oil companies and that hastened Mexico to become a petroleum-exploring, -consuming, and -exporting country, with all the ecological changes that those activities bring.

Cárdenas was also the first Mexican president to take an active interest in conservation by pushing for the country's first forest reserves and national parks.

To assist him in this, he selected Miguel Angel de Quevedo to head the new Department of Forestry, Fish, and Game. De Quevedo, who founded the Mexican Forestry Society in 1922, was an expert on hydrology and watershed management and believed strongly in protecting forests. He advocated sustainable logging, and he worked to establish forty national parks.

Mexico continued to modernize its agriculture and to industrialize in the 1940s and 1950s. The country was the first site of the "Green Revolution"—a program developed in the United States to increase crop yields by exporting chemical fertilizers, pesticides, and herbicides to less-developed nations. However, most of the program was directed to monocrops for export, and it started Mexico on the road to dependency on synthetic, often foreign-made, chemicals that have caused many health problems and deaths of agricultural workers over the years. As the country further developed its manufacturing industries, millions of citizens flocked to the cities for factory jobs. As Mexico City grew at alarming rates (from an area of 116 square kilometers in 1940 to 1,250 square kilometers by 1990, and then growing at an estimated one thousand persons a day), pollution became a severe environmental and health problem. Smog, an especially visible representation of the problem, accounts for why 80 percent of all days in the Distrito Federal have unacceptable ozone levels, with an estimated 3.9 million metric tons of pollutants emitted into the air every year. Likewise, 40 percent of the city is without an adequate sewage system. The crisis did spawn the development of an environmental movement in Mexico, however. One of the most active groups is the Grupo de Cien (Group of One Hundred), which lobbies for environmental policies.

Outlook for the Twenty-First Century

Urban, agricultural, and conservation problems will continue to plague Mexico in the twenty-first century. Some scholars cite Mexico's involvement in the North American Free Trade Association (NAFTA) as a way to improve the nation's economy, but others argue that increased trade means more chemical-dependent export agriculture, ecologically unsound mining and logging, and an increase in the *maquiladora* (foreign-owned assembly plants where workers are paid far less than in the United States) in Mexico's border cities. The *maquiladoras* operate with fewer and less-enforced environmental regulations than U.S. factories. In 1994 NAFTA also prompted an uprising by the Zapatista

Army for National Liberation in Chiapas that continues off and on into the twenty-first century. The Zapatistas claim that neoliberal economic policies like NAFTA eat away at their natural resources without benefiting the residents of Chiapas. They demand more local control and want to protect the tropical environment of their state. At issue in Mexico also is a concern with genetically modified corn from multinational agrobusinesses that can pollute the gene pool of native varieties. Finally, tourism now is the country's top earner of foreign currency and is at the root of many environmental problems along Mexico's coasts. Environmentalists there worry about its continued effects.

Sterling Evans

Further Reading

Aboites Aguilar, L. (1998). *El agua de la nación: Una historia política de México (1888–1946)* (The nation's water: A political history of Mexico ([1888–1946])). Mexico City: CIESAS.

Collier, G. A. (1998). *Basta!: Land and the Zapatista uprising.* Oakland, CA: Food First Books.

Crosby, A. W. (1972). *The Columbian exchange: Biological and cultural consequences of 1492.* Westport, CT: Greenwood Press.

Humphrey, R. R. (1987). *90 years and 535 miles: Vegetation changes along the Mexican border.* Albuquerque: University of New Mexico Press.

Joseph, G. M. (1988). *Revolution from without: Yucatan, Mexico, and the United States, 1880–1924.* Durham, NC: Duke University Press.

Katzenberger, E. (Ed.). (1995). *First world, ha ha ha: The Zapatista challenge.* San Francisco: City Lights Books.

León-Portilla, M. (1990). *The broken spears: The Aztec account of the conquest of Mexico.* Boston: Beacon Press.

Lorey, D. E. (1999). *The U.S.-Mexican border in the twentieth century.* Wilmington, DE: SR Books.

MacLachlan, C. M., & Beezley, W. H. (1999). *El gran pueblo: A history of greater Mexico.* Upper Saddle River, NJ: Prentice Hall.

Mader, R. (1998). *Mexico: Adventures in nature.* Santa Fe, NM: John Muir Publications.

Melville, E. G. K. (1994). *A plague of sheep: Environmental consequences of the conquest of Mexico.* Cambridge, UK: Cambridge University Press.

Meyer, M. C., & Beezley, W. H. (Eds.). (2000). *The Oxford history of Mexico.* New York: Oxford University Press.

Meyer, M. C., Sherman, W. L., & Deeds, S. M. (2002). *The course of Mexican history.* New York: Oxford University Press.

Radding, C. (1997). *Wandering peoples: Colonialism, ethnic spaces, and ecological frontiers in northwestern Mexico, 1700–1850.* Durham, NC: Duke University Press.

Richmond, D. W. (2002). *The Mexican nation: Historical continuity and modern change.* Upper Saddle River, NJ: Prentice Hall.

Ross, J. (1995). *Rebellion from the roots: Indian uprising in Chiapas.* Monroe, ME: Common Courage Press.

Ross, J. (1998). *The annexation of Mexico: From the Aztecs to the I.M.F.* Monroe, ME: Common Courage Press.

Ross, J. (2000). *The war against oblivion: The Zapatista chronicles.* Monroe, ME: Common Courage Press.

Ruiz, R. E. (1992). *Triumphs and tragedy: A history of the Mexican people.* New York: W. W. Norton.

Simon, J. (1997). *Endangered Mexico: An environment on the edge.* San Francisco: Sierra Club Books.

Simonian, L. (1995). *Defending the land of the jaguar: A history of conservation in Mexico.* Austin: University of Texas Press.

Sklair, L. (1993). *Assembling for development: The maquila industry in Mexico and the United States.* San Diego, CA: Center for U.S.-Mexican Studies, UCSD.

Wright, A. (1992). *The death of Ramón González: The modern agricultural dilemma.* Austin: University of Texas Press.

Microorganisms

Microorganisms (or microbes) are microscopic organisms. Bioscientists use the term *microorganisms* for lifeforms in diverse biological phyla (major divisions of the animal kingdom). Basically there are "lower" microorganisms, such as viruses, bacteria, and cyanobacteria (blue-green algae), and "higher" microorganisms, such as algae, fungi, and protozoa. Microorganisms are systematized basically by cell wall structures, cell nucleus structures (if any), and their cell organelles (specialized cellular parts that are analogous to organs). Microorganisms are observed, analyzed, and classified by microbiologists, although applied sciences such as medicine add substantially to knowledge about them.

Microorganisms live in all media on Earth, mainly soil, freshwater, and saltwater, but specialized forms are adapted to live under extreme pH, extreme temperatures, and high pressures, such as volcanic environments, polar ice zones, and the deep sea. Some microorganisms, such as viruses, chlamydiae (intracellular bacteria), and mycoplasmas (nonmotile microorganisms without cell walls), can survive only in other microbes or even in higher organisms. The spores of microorganisms, which are durable instars (forms existing between molts) produced to allow microorganisms to survive suboptimal living conditions, are dispersed by air and can be carried to the highest mountains and other remote places and even across continents. Of course, microorganisms are also spread by animals, air raiding seeds (such as in dandelions), and human activities, such as migration and trade.

The first microorganisms, procaryotes, developed probably 3.5 billion years ago. They lived on organic compounds and were anaerobic (living without oxygen) because the atmosphere contained methane instead of oxygen. The first microorganisms to produce oxygen were cyanobacteria (about 3.4–2.5 billion years ago). The oxygen was slowly enriched by cyanobacteria activities in the oceans and afterward in the air. This development must have led to the extermination of most anaerobic life-forms, causing the first environmental disaster on Earth by biological processes. Anaerobic microorganisms still exist and are considered to be the oldest life-forms on Earth.

Most microorganisms today depend on the degradation of organic material. However, a few are autotrophic—they can turn sunlight energy and carbon dioxide into complex, energy-rich organic compounds and oxygen, contributing to the basis of the global food web and benefiting oxygen-based life-forms.

All life-forms, especially the higher ones, depend on the influence of microorganisms. Also, the spread of plants, animals, and humans is limited, between other determinants, by the microbial burden in given areas. Microorganisms acquired early in phylogeny (the evolutionary history of an organism) of higher cells became cell organelles, which are included in all cells of higher life-forms. Two of these organelles are mitochondria, which provide energy within higher cells, and chloroplasts, which produce carbohydrates and oxygen by using carbon dioxide and sunlight energy in green plants. Microorganisms help to digest nutrition in the intestines of higher animals, some of which, for example cattle, live off of microorganisms in their digestive tracts rather than from their actual nutrient uptake. The fodder that the cattle eat serves the microorganisms and allows them to propagate at sufficient rates for the cattle to consume them and subsist on the nutrients they provide.

Higher Plants

Higher plants depend on microorganisms that live around and even inside their roots. Such microorganisms provide salts of minerals, sulfur, iron, and nitrogen, which are essential to plants.

Microorganisms are concentrated in topsoils. Estimates of numbers of microorganisms (per gram) in A_1–horizon soil (nutrient-rich topsoil found from the surface to approximately 10 centimeters of depth) are: aerobic bacteria, 7.8 million; anaerobic bacteria, 1.9 million; actinomycetes, 2.1 million; fungi, 119,000; and algae, 25,000. Numbers decrease with depth, reducing microorganisms to almost none in the B_2–horizon (approximately 30 to 60 centimeters from the surface). However, the amount of microorganisms in the upper soil strata makes topsoils the medium on Earth with the highest biomass (the amount of living matter). Microorganisms help break up the lithosphere (the outer part of the Earth composed of rock) and decompose organic matter, turning it into inorganic compounds and thus recycling biomolecules to the inorganic sphere.

Life-forms can be endangered by microorganisms because many of them are parasites, both on other microorganisms and on higher life-forms. Pathogenic (disease-causing) microorganisms produce toxins harmful to host organisms or affect the genetic material of host organisms. Microorganisms reach their hosts by uptake (with nutrition), by microbial burden (concentration of microbes) of the surrounding medium (via air or water), by aerosols, or by contact between infected and noninfected organisms.

Plants and animals have innate capabilities (immune system) to cope with pathogens. The acquisition of an immune system is a result of a co-evolution process between microorganisms and hosts. As humans began to domesticate animals, which brought both into closer contact, opportunistic pathogens from animals were acquired by humans and became human pathogens, causing specific diseases (for example, tuberculosis). The absence of specific pathogens in the environment of indigenous populations meant an absence of specific genetic-based immune responses, allowing epidemics after contact with organisms from other biomes (major ecological community types), such as continents. An example is the decimation of Native Americans by disease after European contact; similarly, Europeans contracted syphilis as a venereal disease new to them, as well as the bubonic plague and influenza.

The spread of pathogens depends on the density of host organisms, some of which can persist only in large populations with close individual contact (e.g., groups of wild animals and plant communities dominated by few species), in densely populated areas such as towns, in domesticated herds of animals, and in plants under cultivation (monocultures).

However, contact between continents leads to new anthropogenic licenses (ecological niches made by humans), allowing pathogens to affect human interests, as in the case of the mosquito-transmitted West Nile virus, which entered the United States from the Old World recently. Environmentally important are recent attempts to incorporate immunity-providing DNA sequences into organisms that have lost immunity during their domestication. Other attempts use genetic engineering of microbe-transmitting vermin (e.g., mosquitoes) to reduce disease risks.

Control of Pathogens

Human culture depends in many ways on the control of pathogens. Control strategies are developed in epidemiology and follow basic principles of hygiene, including clean drinking water, clean food, proper sewage and refuse disposal, inoculation, and separation (quarantine) or extermination of diseased individuals. Minimal differences in hygiene standards must have been decisive for political and economic success in history. For example, many wars were more influenced by the health of the soldiers than by war technology.

The exploitation of microorganisms has influenced human history profoundly. Storage of food is possible only if microbial deterioration of staples can be avoided. All storage techniques are based on two processes. The first is to dehydrate the stored food because microorganisms depend on water. Dehydration is accomplished by drying (including freeze drying around the frost border in the Andes Mountains) or by adding salt or sugar (honey). The second is to introduce antimicrobial substances by smoking (e.g., meat) or using chemicals. Both processes must have been used early in human history. After the development of durable containers people could control microorganisms for food production, refinement, and conservation. Another important development was the controlled treatment of raw milk with microorganisms (fermentation), thus introducing cow-, sheep-, and goat-based cultures even in those human populations that are genetically not able to digest raw milk. The discovery of fermentation of alcohol also was important because beer and wine consumption was probably less dangerous than uptake of drinking water, at least in dryer areas of the world, for thousands of years because of the antimicrobial nature of alcoholic solutions. Storage of vegetables

became possible by using lactic acid fermentation, as, for example, is used to pickle cabbage, which became the nutritional foundation of early European ship travel because it prevented scurvy. Lactic acid fermentation is also used in preparing sausages.

A recent breakthrough in molecular biology uses an enzyme extracted from thermophile (growing at high temperatures) microorganisms to amplify DNA in vitro (outside the living body). The invention of the so-called polymerase chain reaction (PCR) allows molecular scientists to specify the genetic code of any organism, which is the prerequisite for altering organisms genetically.

Bernd Herrmann

Further Reading

Alexander, M. (1961). *Introduction to soil microbiology*. New York: John Wiley.

Campbell, N. A., & Campbell, B. (2001.) *Biology*. San Francisco: Benjamin Cummings.

Herrmann, B., & Hummel, S. (Eds.). (1994). *Ancient DNA: Recovery and analysis of genetic material from paleontological, archaeological, museum, medical, and forensic specimens*. New York: Springer.

Schlegel, H. G. (1993). *General microbiology*. Cambridge, UK: Cambridge University Press.

The Middle East

The geography of the Middle East, comprising western and southwestern Asia as well as North Africa, is variously delimited. In this article, the Middle East is defined as Algeria, Egypt, Libya, Morocco, and Tunisia in North Africa, and the countries of the Levant and the Arabian Peninsula, including Bahrain, Iran, Iraq, Israel, Jordan, Lebanon, Oman, Qatar, Saudi Arabia, Syria, the West Bank and Gaza, the United Arab Emirates (UAE), and Yemen. It does not include Turkey.

This complex region has one of the longest known histories of human occupation and is considered one of the birthplaces of human societies. Consequently, the Middle East also has a long history of human use of the environment, including many important events such as the domestication of wheat, barley, sheep, and goats. It is not surprising, then, that many scholars have claimed that the environment of the Middle East has long been abused by humans and their herds of animals. Recent research has shown, however, that the vegetation in this region is well adapted to many human uses (and to grazing) and it is actually quite a resilient and dynamic environment. Although in the past the environmental issues believed to be most important for the Middle East have included deforestation, overgrazing, and desertification, this article suggests that in actuality the most pressing environmental problems at the beginning of the twenty-first century are those of degradation of available water resources, pollution, and other effects of unbridled and unregulated attempts at economic development in a rapidly urbanizing region.

Overview of the Middle East

Despite the fact that the Middle East is often conceived as a single region, it is actually a highly diverse and differentiated conglomeration of nations, peoples, languages, and physical environments. Out of a total population of approximately 295 million people, the majority speaks Arabic and approximately 90 percent are Muslim. Many people, however, speak other languages, including Persian, Berber, Hebrew, Kurdish, Azeri, and so forth. In addition to Islam, other religions in the region include Judaism, Christianity, and Zoroastrianism. The fact that many different ethnicities also exist in the Middle East and that local people may identify themselves by many different combinations of these languages, religions, and ethnicities further complicates the region.

The physical environment is equally complex. More than 80 percent of the Middle East is classified as desert or semidesert. Although aridity and infrequent rainfall are the norm in the region as a whole, some places, such as the mountains in Yemen, receive plentiful rainfall, while some parts of the Sahara desert in Algeria receive practically no rainfall at all for years at a time. As a result, the vegetation in the Middle East can differ greatly from one place to another, largely depending on rainfall. For the region as a whole, only approximately 7 percent of the land is capable of growing crops. The majority of the local plants and animals in the Middle East are well adapted to arid environments and species diversity is high in several Middle Eastern countries, including Morocco and Lebanon.

Although some oil-producing countries, such as Saudi Arabia, are very wealthy, 33 percent of the population of the Middle East lives below the poverty line. Poverty levels are rising, real wages are declining, and unemployment is at an average of 15 percent and ris-

ing. Literacy rates in the Middle East are below the average of the underdeveloped countries, and 40 percent of the population lacks access to sanitation services. The majority of the population, approximately 60 percent, lives in Middle Eastern cities, which are concentrated along coastlines, rivers, and other sources of water. The Middle East has one of the highest rates of urbanization in the underdeveloped world, second only to Latin America. Most of these countries have authoritarian governments, are highly indebted to organizations such as the World Bank and other lending organizations, and import large amounts of food. In summary, everyday living conditions for the majority of Middle Eastern peoples are difficult and have worsened during the last fifteen to twenty years. These political and economic realities have a direct bearing on the state of the environment in most Middle Eastern countries today.

Land Degradation

Deforestation and overgrazing have long been blamed for land degradation in the Middle East. New research, however, has demonstrated that these two forces have not had a significant impact on most Middle Eastern environments now or in the past. Rather, the vegetation in the Middle East is highly resilient and is well adapted to drought and grazing. Approximately 5 percent of the Middle East's rural population (about 6 million people) are estimated to be nomadic pastoralists. Deforestation in the region over the last decade has been only 0.1 percent (approximately 16,800 hectares) on average, and in some places, such as Algeria, the forested area has actually increased. In Algeria the increase is more than a million hectares; in Morocco it is 1.5 million hectares, and in Syria forests have increased by 82,000 hectares during the last 40 years, according to the United Nations Food and Agriculture Organization (FAO). Hard data demonstrating desertification are very rare. It is important to understand the environments of the Middle East, for the most part, not as deforested, overgrazed, and desertified, but rather as naturally arid lands that are being used by humans and their livestock in a largely sustainable manner.

One recent cause of land degradation of growing concern across the Middle East is the expansion of dryland cereal cultivation into marginal areas where average rainfall is too low to support reliable cereal harvests. The process of plowing these dry lands desiccates the soil, and most fields are soon abandoned, leaving the local vegetation severely degraded.

Much of the Middle East is desert. This scene is the Valley of the Kings in Luxor, Egypt.
COURTESY NICOLE LALIBERTE.

In North Africa, for example, cereal cultivation has increased dramatically in the last twenty years, nearly doubling in area in both Morocco and Algeria. In the other Middle Eastern countries, the area under cereal cultivation has also expanded but only by approximately 50 percent. Most of the increases in Morocco, Algeria, and Syria have been in marginal areas that were previously grazing lands. Experts are concerned that this may produce long-term land degradation in large areas of the Middle East. Despite these problems, most Middle Eastern governments feel they have no choice but to continue to expand dryland cereal cultivation to provide basic foods to their population as their economies are squeezed by structural adjustment policies (SAPs). SAPs are policies enforced by the IMF, which include cutting subsidies on basic foods, privatizing business and industry (job losses), cutting of social services such as health care and education, etc. They nearly universally make the poor poorer, increase the number of people going hungry, and they have a negative impact on the environment.

Irrigated agriculture has nearly doubled in some areas in the Middle East during the last forty years. Much of this expansion has been made possible by the building of large dams on major rivers as well as by the increased pumping of groundwater resources. With this increase in irrigation, often year-round, has come a host of problems. One of the most important is that of salinization of agricultural soils. Due to a variety of factors, salts commonly build up in perennially irrigated soils, and this is harmful to plant growth. The growing problem of salinization from irrigation is directly related to a multitude of water resource problems throughout the Middle East.

Water Resources

Although the Middle East is home to approximately 5 percent of the world's people, it contains only about 1 percent of the world's fresh water supplies. Fresh water supply per person in the Middle East is only 14 percent of the global average (1,145 cubic meters per person per year, as opposed to a global average of 8,240 cubic meters). Many countries in the Middle East have far less water than this. For example, Jordan, one of the poorest countries, has one of the lowest per capita water supplies, less than 250 cubic meters per person per year. Although several other countries have lower per capita water supplies, they are primarily the wealthy Persian Gulf oil countries, such as Saudi Arabia, the UAE, and Kuwait, which have desalination plants that can supply the needed fresh water. Eighty percent or more of the Middle East's water is used in agriculture. Approximately half the countries in the Middle East use their renewable water supplies at or above the rate of natural recharge today. Given recent data, which shows overall downward trends in average annual rainfall amounts in the Middle East, water shortages will most likely worsen in the future.

Because major rivers are rare in the Middle East, a substantial amount of water is taken from underground water sources (aquifers). In areas such as the Arabian peninsula, aquifers provide most of the water for domestic use, industry, and agriculture. Countries in this region currently use the water from these aquifers faster than the aquifers are being recharged, thus exceeding the renewable supply of water. Overuse has lowered the water table in many areas, causing natural springs to dry up and necessitating deeper wells. This overwithdrawal (mining) of aquifers is not confined to the Arabian peninsula, however. Other countries that mine their aquifers in an unsustainable manner include Bahrain, Kuwait, Oman, Qatar, Saudi Arabia, the UAE, Yemen, Israel, the West Bank and Gaza, Jordan, Syria, Morocco, and Tunisia.

As a result of this overuse, the intrusion of salty water from the sea into many coastal aquifers has made them unusable for drinking and often for irrigation. Aquifers throughout the Middle East are also degraded and polluted by heavy metals such as mercury, by pesticides and fertilizers, and by raw human sewage (which carries disease-causing microbes), which seep down into these aquifers from the surface. The resulting pollution is a serious threat to public health. Aquifers are very difficult to clean of these pollutants, since the rate of recharge is slow and they are largely confined underground bodies of water. Due to overuse, pollution, and short supply, several Persian Gulf countries, including Saudi Arabia and the UAE, rely on desalinization plants to produce water. This is expensive, and the plants create air pollution as well as water pollution from the rejected brine and heat accumulation.

On many major rivers in the Middle East such as the Nile, the Euphrates, and several rivers in Morocco, large dams have been built to try to store water and to generate electricity. These large dams have caused a host of problems, including increases in waterborne diseases such as schistosomiasis, salinization in areas of perennial irrigation, deterioration of downstream water quality, lowering of the water tables downstream, siltation of the dam reservoir, adverse effects on deltas and wetlands, coastal erosion, decline in river fish population, river channel degradation, and loss of arable land downstream due to decreased sediment load in rivers. The Aswan High Dam in Egypt has caused a number of serious problems of this nature, including the salinization of at least 50 percent of all arable land in Egypt, significant erosion of the delta area, and an increase in schistosomiasis. A complication of schistosomiasis treatment in Egypt over the past 30 years has been a dramatic increase in hepatitis C, spread when contaminated syringes were used to give anti-schistomosiasis drugs. The environmental impact of this dam has been especially wide-ranging.

Pollution

Surface waters such as rivers, reservoirs, and lakes are also suffering from pollution. Four lakes in northern Egypt known as the Four Sisters are very polluted with a variety of industrial toxins, agricultural runoff, and sewage. High percentages of the fish caught in these lakes register alarming levels of contaminants such as DDT, polychlorinated biphenyls (PCBs), heavy metals, and pesticides. In many other Middle Eastern countries water pollution is also a serious problem. Sources for 60–70 percent of drinking water in Lebanon are contaminated with fecal bacteria. Significant water pollution is reported in nearly every Middle Eastern country from these sources and from petroleum products. As rivers discharge into seas and oceans, significant pollution of the Mediterranean, the Red Sea, the Atlantic coastal waters of Morocco, and the Persian Gulf has also occurred.

Air pollution is a large and growing problem across the Middle East. The main sources of air pollution are industry and automobiles. Leaded automobile fuel is widely used and produces airborne lead that settles out onto soil and water, polluting them too. The problem of lead contamination from automobiles and industries is so grave in Cairo and other parts of the Middle East that playground dust has been found to contain lead levels that exceed those for hazardous waste sites in the United States. Cairo also has some of the worst air pollution in the world. The level of particulate matter in Cairo's air is five to ten times higher than health standards and was higher than the level in any other large city in the world in the mid-1990s. Large cities throughout the Middle East such as Casablanca, Beirut, Amman, Tunis, Tehran, and Jidda have similar air pollution problems. Unregulated dumping of solid waste and industrial toxins has contaminated water and soil in many areas of the Middle East. Contaminated soil and water can contaminate local food with dangerous levels of bacteria, pesticides, and other toxins.

Present State of Affairs and Prognosis

In response to the Middle East's growing environmental problems, many countries have created new branches of government for the protection of the environment, especially during the 1990s. This has resulted in new environmental legislation, as well as ratification of international treaties such as those emerging from the 1992 Rio Earth Summit, in several countries, including Morocco, Egypt, Iran, Jordan, Lebanon, Oman, the UAE, and Tunisia. The results of the new environmental legislation have been minimal. Due to high poverty levels and high rates of indebtedness across the Middle East, governments have chosen to put their meager financial resources toward economic development rather than toward regulation and enforcement of environmental policies. As a result, new environmental protection laws are not enforced, and basic regulations on industrial air and wastewater emissions are still nonexistent. Outside of a few major cities, organized solid waste collection and disposal do not exist. Across the Middle East, it is estimated that only 35 to 40 percent of wastewater is treated; the remainder is dumped. The lack of basic infrastructure and lack of regulation of industry are directly linked to the countries' political and economic problems. Without addressing those basic underlying factors, it is unlikely that the environmental problems confronting the Middle East will improve.

Diana K. Davis

Further Reading

Blumler, M. A. (1998). Biogeography of land-use impacts in the Near East. In K. Zimmerer and K. Young (Eds.), *Nature's economy: New lessons for conservation in developing countries*. Madison: University of Wisconsin Press.

Bush, R., & Sabri, A. (Fall 2000). Mining for fish: Privatization of the "commons" along Egypt's northern coastline. *Middle East Report, 30*(216), 20–23, 45.

Hopkins, N., & Mehanna, S. (Winter 1997). Pollution, popular perceptions and grassroots environmental activism. *Middle East Report, 27*(213), 21–25.

Jabbra J., & Jabbra, N. (Eds.). (1997). Challenging environmental issues: Middle Eastern perspectives. [Special issue]. *Journal of Developing Societies, 13*(1), 18–134, 150–168.

Nicholson, S. E. (1994). Recent rainfall fluctuations in Africa and their relationship to conditions over the continent. *The Holocene, 4* (2), 121–131.

Perevolotsky, A., & Seligman, N. (1998). Role of grazing in Mediterranean rangeland ecosystems. *BioScience, 48*(12), 1007–1017.

Swearingen, W., & Bencherifa, A. (1996). *The North African environment at risk*. Boulder, CO: Westview Press.

Thomas, D. S. G., & Middleton, N. (1994). *Desertification: Exploding the myth*. West Sussex, UK: John Wiley & Sons Ltd.

Watkins, E. (1995). *The Middle Eastern environment*. Cambridge, UK: St. Malo Press.

White, G. F. (1988). The environmental effects of the High Dam at Aswan. *Environment, 30*(7), 4–11, 34–40.

Midgley, Thomas
(1889–1944)
American chemist

Thomas Midgley was a brilliant industrial chemist and had more impact on the atmosphere than any other single organism in the history of life on Earth.

Midgley was born 18 May 1889 in Beaver Falls, Pennsylvania. He studied engineering at Cornell University and learned chemistry on his own. In 1916 he joined the laboratory of Charles Kettering in Dayton, Ohio, sponsored by the General Motors Research Corporation, where he sought additives for gasoline that would reduce 'knocking' and thereby allow higher-compression engines. In late 1921 he found that lead did the job admirably. Soon tetraethyl lead became a standard gasoline additive, first in the United States and eventually around the world. A public health controversy arose in 1924, and lead gasoline was briefly withdrawn from the U.S. market. But by 1926 authorities found the risk acceptable. Thereafter, millions of tons of lead entered the atmosphere with vehicle exhausts, some of which found its way into plant and animal tissues, and into human bodies, where, in sufficient doses, it caused disorders in nervous systems and brains, especially those of children. Ambient lead derived from several sources, but mainly from vehicle exhausts. Most countries phased out leaded gasoline gradually in the late twentieth century, and ambient lead concentrations dropped dramatically, as did the lead levels in human bloodstreams.

In the late 1920s Midgley took up research on refrigerants. At that time, chemical refrigeration involved dangerous gases, such as ammonia. Midgley in 1930–1931 developed the first of the chlorofluorocarbons, Freon (dichlorofluoromethane), an inert gas that made safe refrigeration feasible and air-conditioning practical. Chlorofluorcarbons (CFCs) also proved useful in solvents, spray propellants, and insulation. CFC production remained small until after World War II, but by 1970 some 750,000 tons of CFCs entered the atmosphere annually. They drifted up to the stratosphere intact (because as inert gases they react with very few chemicals), where ultraviolet radiation broke up CFC molecules, releasing agents that in turn ruptured ozone molecules. Stratospheric ozone has for roughly a billion years formed a shield that minimizes the amount of ultraviolet-B radiation reaching the earth's surface, making life as it has evolved possible. Enhanced UV-B radiation endangered phytoplankton (the basis of the oceans' food web), human immune systems, and raised skin cancer rates. By the year 2000, perhaps two million excess cases of skin cancers were attributable to the thinning of the ozone shield.

In the 1970s scientists suggested that CFCs might erode the ozone layer, and in the 1980s careful measurements showed this had indeed happened. International agreements followed quickly, limiting further CFC production. But, as inert gases, CFCs linger in the atmosphere for about a century, so that some of those released in the twentieth century will still be rupturing ozone molecules late in the twenty-first century.

Midgley won most of the prizes an industrial chemist can win in the U.S. and became president of the American Chemical Society. He died in 1944, strangled by the ropes of a rope-and-pulley system he had invented to help him in and out of bed after he contracted polio.

J. R. McNeill

Further Reading

Kauffman, G. B. (1989). Midgley: Saint or serpent? *Chemtech*, Dec., pp. 717–725.

Loeb, A. (1995). Birth of the Kettering doctrine: Fordism, Sloanism, and the discovery of tetraethyl lead. *Business and Economic History, 24*, 72–87.

McNeill, J. R. (2000). *Something new under the sun: An environmental history of the 20th-century world*. New York: W. W. Norton.

Rosner, D. & Markowitz, G. (1985). A 'gift of God'?: The public health controversy over leaded gasoline during the 1920s. *American Journal of Public Health, 75*, 344–352.

Migration

Human beings did not begin as a global species. We began as an extremely small population (perhaps no more than a few thousand) living in East Africa, and we had to grow in number and migrate in order to cover the planet as we do today. This expansion was perhaps inevitable given the nature of our species and our place in the biosphere. Nevertheless, our journey was not fast, easy, or cheap. To travel from East Africa to the southernmost limits of South America (the last place on Earth that humans populated) required a journey of more than one hundred millennia. It is a journey that has not been without consequences, both for our own species and others, and for the environment at large.

Human Migration in Historical Perspective

As one of the world's most mobile species, *Homo sapiens* have exploited their mobility in two ways. First, we have moved ourselves, and second, we have acquired the ability to move objects, including other organisms, along with us. From the very beginning of our odyssey some 100 to 150 millennia ago, we had the ability to do both these things over long distances provided our numbers were small and time was not a factor. As time passed and we added bulk flow technologies and social organization to our cultural repertoire, we were able to move ourselves and our companion organisms not only long distances but in large numbers and at increasing speeds. As our speed and volume have increased exponentially in the last 500 years or so, so has our impact.

The long-distance movement of humans across Earth's surface has been, and will always be, heavily conditioned by the availability and distribution of en-

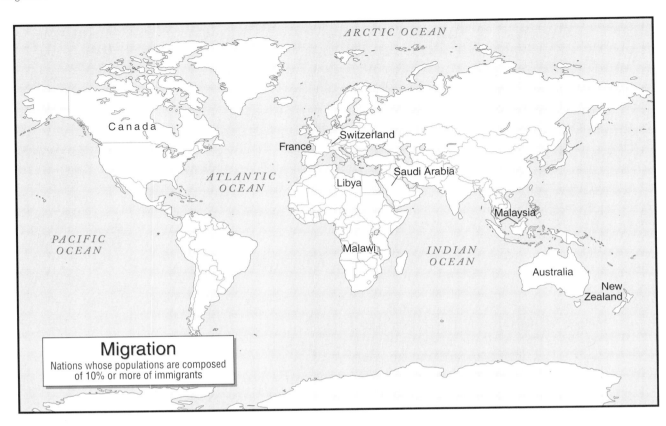

Migration
Nations whose populations are composed
of 10% or more of immigrants

ergy. Earth is a closed system for virtually all resources except energy. Nearly all the energy on which we depend comes to us as solar radiation in enormous and continuous quantities, reaching us through a food web or chain that includes photosynthesizing plants, herbivores, carnivores, and, at the end of the chain, humans.

Some of the earth's energy—what is called real-time energy—is used fairly soon after it arrives on Earth; that is, within days, months, or perhaps years at the most. This energy is available from four sources: wind, moving water, animal muscle, and human muscle. Stored energy, in contrast, arrived on Earth perhaps 200 to 300 million years ago, and was stored in plant and animal tissue that was later fossilized under layers of sediment and rock. This energy is available today as fossil fuels: coal, petroleum, and natural gas.

Self-Powered Migration

Changes in the form, volume, and accessibility of energy over the past 150 millennia are reflected in changes in human migration volumes and patterns. From the beginning of our time on Earth, perhaps 150 millennia ago, human migration was fueled by real-

time energy channeled through human muscle power. That is, we moved then as we still move today, by walking, running, swimming, or climbing. From our origins in East Africa, small populations of no more than 50 individuals migrated gradually at the rate of perhaps a kilometer a year. Some members of our ancestral population migrated south, to the southernmost tip of Africa, while others walked north toward the place where Africa joins Eurasia. From here, groups moved in several different directions. Some walked north and then turned west into Europe; some turned north and east across South or Central Asia; while others (much later) acquired the ability to use the waters of the Arabian Ocean and the Indian Ocean to migrate along the South Asian coastline. There were ancestral human populations in Europe perhaps 35,000 to 40,000 years ago, in East Asia by about 60,000 years ago, and in Australia perhaps as long ago as 40,000 to 60,000 years. From East Asia, human beings crossed the Bering Straits between 15,000 and 35,000 years ago, and then turned south to populate the Americas, reaching the southernmost point in Chile by about 12,000 years ago.

Wind- and Water-Powered Migration

About ten thousand years ago, in a transformation known as the Neolithic Revolution, human beings began to domesticate a select number of other species (both plant and animal). At that point, we began to acquire the ability to tap the energy stored in animal muscle as well as human. The domestication of the horse about 4000 BCE in what is today Ukraine was a breakthrough in the growth of human mobility. Moreover, our ability to fabricate technologies such as sleds, canoes, and (later) sail-driven vessels enabled us to exploit the transport capabilities of wind and moving water.

As a consequence of these technologies, human migration experienced significant increases in all dimensions: speed, volume, and distances covered. Trade and war stimulated the first large-scale movement of populations, principally across the vast interior expanses of Eurasia and by sea across the Indian Ocean. By the early fifteenth century CE, civilizations on either end of Eurasia—China, and the mercantile states of Europe (Venice, Genoa)—had acquired the technologies required to move populations in the range of a few hundred to several thousand. With the arrival of Europeans in the Western Hemisphere in 1492, the stage was set for the first long-distance migration of large masses of people: the transatlantic slave trade of the sixteenth to eighteenth centuries. Between 1531, when this trade was begun by Portuguese traders, to the close of slave trafficking in the 1870s, more than 10 million human beings were transported in captivity from their homes in West Africa to the Western Hemisphere. Perhaps as many as 10 million more perished in the journey. The second wave of migration was that of the Irish, about a million of whom were forced from their homeland in the mid-1840s by the repeated failure of the potato crop.

Migration Powered by Fossil Fuels

The third stage in human migration began during the first quarter of the nineteenth century when humans acquired the ability to connect a source of stored energy—specifically, the coal-fired steam engine—with a transport device. In 1803, Robert Fulton demonstrated the first successful steamboat on France's Seine River; and a year later, Richard Trevithick installed a steam engine on a rolling platform to move heavy loads around an iron works in South Wales, in Britain. By 1869, there was a steam railroad line from one coast of North America to the other, and in 1890 the steam-ship *Lucania* was crossing the Atlantic Ocean in about 125 hours.

For the first time, people had access to mobility that transcended that provided by the forces of nature. The availability of the steamship and the railroad, coupled with a massive population increase in Europe, stimulated an unprecedented migration of Europeans abroad, to the United States and Canada, to Argentina and Brazil, and to Australia and New Zealand. In all, some 50 million Europeans left their homelands between the 1840s and World War I, and another 50 million or so Asians emigrated after 1880 in search of a better life in the Americas. These two population movements changed forever the population distribution patterns of the Earth.

In the twentieth century, the global movement of people has continued to grow, sparked this time by the use of the internal combustion engine to power transport technologies: automobiles and airplanes. Tourists, business travelers, refugees, and immigrants are on the move in numbers and at speeds that are unprecedented. Each day, about two million people cross an international border. Each year, international tourist arrivals equal about 10 percent of the world's total population. Global international refugees fleeing from war, environmental crises, or economic collapse are at an all-time high of nearly 50 million. The United States alone receives nearly one million new immigrants each year (not counting those who arrive without documentation), and the flow shows little sign of abating (although there was some temporary decline in the months following the terrorist attacks of 11 September 2001).

The Environmental Consequences of Human Migration

All animals have the potential for migration; indeed, migration as a means of adaptation to changes in environmental conditions is a fundamental property of all forms of life. One of the first responses of any organism to stress in its environment is to seek to move away to find more a congenial setting in which to live. As the biologist Niles Eldredge puts it,

> By far the most common response of species to environmental change is that they move. . . . In the face of environmental change, organisms within each and every species seek familiar living conditions. . . . This is "habitat tracking," the constant search for suitable habitat going on continuously, generation after gen-

847

eration, within every species on the face of the earth. (Eldredge 1995, 94–95)

Whatever else one might think of our species, we cannot deny our extraordinary biological achievements. In the last ten thousand years, we have increased our numbers from about six million to more than six billion, and our density from about 0.04 persons per square kilometer to more than 40, in both instances an increase of three orders of magnitude. We have experienced a threefold increase in life expectancy, from 25 years to 75. And we have expanded our range from a small corner of East Africa to live virtually every place on Earth where people can live.

Biological Packages and Loss of Biodiversity

We could never have accomplished these things alone; we had to have help from our companion organisms, which joined with us to provide us with food, transport, assistance in the hunt, and even simple companionship. Some scientists refer to these interconnected species as "packages" or "suites" of organisms. Together they confront the challenges of all organisms: the acquisition and processing of energy, defense against attackers, and reproduction. Fortunately, the biosphere is structured so as to provide a basis for these unions of humans, plants, and animals. The fundamental principle at work here is *coevolution*, a term that means the process by which two or more species evolve together, for mutual benefit.

Over the course of the last ten millennia, many such packages of species have come into being, each living more or less in balance within its own geographic range. In the Old World, for example, the Mediterranean system included humans, wheat, grapes, olives, sheep, cattle, and smallpox; while the Chinese system comprised humans, rice, horses, swine, and bubonic plague. In the New World, the Powhatan system included humans, maize, squash, and hunted animals such as deer, while the Incan system contained humans, tubers (especially potatoes), and the llama.

For many centuries, these biological packages remained self-contained and relatively isolated. Although there was contact between them, it was sporadic and took place over long spans of time, which allowed for gradual adaptation by all parties concerned. As long-distance migration accelerated and began to involve mass populations (two thousand years ago in the Old World, five hundred years ago globally), these sets of species began to intrude on one another with increasing speed, scope, and violence.

The ultimate consequence of ten millennia of migration, contact, competition, and adaptation has been the emergence of a system of people, food, and diseases that has become nearly global in scope.

Large-scale human migration has affected the biosphere in many ways. For example, as populations grew and cities became the preferred habitat for greater and greater percentages of the total, humans had to open new lands for food, dwelling space, and other resources. As the biologist Paul Ehrlich asserts, "the primary cause of the decay of organic diversity is not direct human exploitation or malevolence, but the habitat destruction that inevitably results from the expansion of human populations and human activities" (Ehrlich 1988, 21). As Europeans, Africans, and their plant and animal companions (including microbes) spread out from the Old World to occupy an increasing proportion of the earth's surface, their packages of organisms have driven out those they did not incorporate.

Humans now appropriate for their use each year an estimated 40 percent of the earth's production of energy via photosynthesis (that is, the annual production of biomass). Those parts of the biosphere that we do not need, we push aside or destroy. The process affects both flora and fauna. Five millennia ago, for example, forests covered an estimated 50 percent of the earth's land surface; by 1978, that figure had dropped to 20 percent. In *The Covenant of the Wild: Why Animals Chose Domestication* (1992), Stephen Budiansky estimates that in 1860 humans and their domesticated animals accounted for 5 percent of the total weight of all animal life on earth. By 1990, that figure had reached 20 percent; and if our population doubles again to reach 12 billion, it will be 60 percent.

The biological invasion by Europeans of eastern North America between 1600 and 1800 occasioned the near-total destruction of such indigenous species as the beaver and the wolf, and replaced them with cattle, pigs, and sheep. Wheat, oats, and barley were planted in European-style fields, replacing the native crops of beans, squash, and maize. In the nineteenth century, the industrial cities of Europe and North America fed themselves by drawing on the temperate-zone grasslands of the entire planet. The wheat of Kansas and Nebraska fed Chicago and New York in a system that was merely continental, but when the grasslands of Australia and Argentina were transformed to supply British cities with meat and wheat, the system had become truly global. In the process, indigenous systems (including native peoples) were swept aside, replaced by species more familiar to Europeans, including wheat, cattle, sheep, and pigs.

Disease

Moreover, as human beings invade ecosystems, we come face to face with new diseases. The spread of the bubonic plague through Asia and Europe in the fourteenth century resulted from the invasion of what is today Myanmar (formerly, Burma) by Mongol troops. They spread the disease back to China, from where it was carried through Central Asia to the Mediterranean by traders and soldiers. From there it went on to Europe, where it killed as much as one-fifth of the population. The modern equivalent is the AIDS pandemic, first observed in the human population in 1981 and still spreading through Africa and Asia at an increasing rate. There is still some controversy about the origin of AIDS and how it got into human populations. But the scientific consensus today seems to be that the disease was spread from some nonhuman primate species (perhaps gorillas) in West or Central Africa as human populations invaded these regions in search of food, living space, and hardwood forests from which to harvest timber for export.

Interplanetary Human Migration

What comes next; where do we go from here? The final chapter in human migration may well see the transport of small but self-sustaining populations to live on other planets, beginning perhaps with Mars in the next century or two. Although astronomers have located more than two dozen planets outside our own star system, we know of no other with a biosphere capable of supporting our life and the life of the species we will take with us. We will need to transform the environment of our next habitat in a process known as terraforming. This will take to a new level the actions of human populations in changing our environment so that we can live there. Unless our descendants learn from their ancestors' mistakes, such terraforming may occasion yet another round of environmental damage as well, this time on a distant world.

Robert P. Clark

Further Reading

Cavalli-Sforza, L. L., & Cavalli-Sforza, F. (1995). *The great human disaporas: The history of diversity and evolution*. Reading, MA: Addison Wesley.

Clark, R. (2001). *Global life systems: Population, food, and disease in the process of globalization*. Boulder, CO: Rowman & Littlefield.

Crosby, A. (1993). *The Columbian exchange: Biological and cultural consequences of 1492*. Westport, CT: Greenwood Press.

Ehrlich, P. (1988). The loss of diversity: Causes and consequences. In E. O. Wilson (Ed.), *BioDiversity* (pp. 21–27). Washington, DC: National Academy Press.

Eldredge, N. (1995). *Reinventing Darwin: The great debate at the high table of evolutionary theory*. New York: Wiley.

Gungwu, W. (Ed.). (1997). *Global history and migrations*. Boulder, CO: Westview Press.

Mascie-Taylor, C. G. N., & Lasker, G. W. (Eds.). (1988). *Biological aspects of human migration* Cambridge, UK: Cambridge University Press.

Millennialism

The word *millennialism* (or *millenarianism*) follows from the word *millennium*, with Latin roots, meaning "one thousand years." As a religious term, *millennialism* refers to the belief, expressed in the Book of Revelation, that Christ will establish a one-thousand-year reign of the saints on Earth before the Last Judgment. *Chiliasm* is a word with Greek origins with the same meaning. Belief in an ultimate divine justice has provided meaning for life in countless generations over a wide spectrum of religious persuasions in every age, bolstering both conservative ideologies and revolutionary activism. Millennialists envision a time of supernatural peace and abundance on Earth at the end of time. In various guises millennialism is found everywhere and provides insight into the historical relationship between human society and the natural environment.

Secular Significance

The British sociologist Stephen Cotgrove's book *Catastrophe or Cornucopia* (1982) distinguished the new wave of environmentalism of the 1960s and 1970s from the earlier nature conservation movements that began in the 1890s in the anglophone (English-speaking) West. The message of the new wave was that industrial development and population growth could not continue without irrevocably damaging natural life-support systems. The new wave advocated a radical cure: the total overhaul of materialist values and social institutions through personal redemption and political activism. Utopian thought about alternatives enjoyed a renaissance. This shift in worldview was so profound that Cotgrove suggests that organizations such as Friends of the Earth resemble sects. He notes that such worldviews led to a swift reaction, such as the book *The Doomsday Syndrome* (1972) by the former editor of *Nature*. Significantly, *Nature* provided a platform for the environmental historian Richard Grove's case that environmental concern arising from British expansion had much deeper antecedents than U.S. literature and historiography (writing about history) acknowledged. Conservationism initially found expression in studies of island ecology during the 1600s, and the Cape in South Africa was an important site for such advocacy from 1811 onward. The Reverend John Croumbie Brown (1808–1894) was employed by the Cape Colony government from 1862 to 1866 to advise on the biological aspects of colonial settlement. His words, writes Grove, "thundered from a Cape Town pulpit with all the energy of Scottish ecological redemption" (1997, 151). However, such imperatives fell on deaf ears and did not correspond with policy or significant currents of social change. Another scholar who picked out Scottish ideas of nature in imperial history is John Mackenzie. He traced a global strand of apocalyptic thought that fueled popular green histories such as that of C. Ponting, which painted "a strikingly doom-laden picture. . . . This dramatic counter-progressivism views world history as one long free fall, with imperialism as its global accelerator. The entire past is coloured with fear of the future" (Mackenzie 1997b, 220).

Apocalypticism

Millennialism is closely related to apocalypticism—the belief in an impending transformation of epic proportion, about which a select few have forewarning so they can make appropriate preparations. The word *apocalypse* comes from a Greek root word suggesting the unearthing of hidden information about unfolding human events. Although burdensome and dangerous, such information offers immediate rewards; converts see themselves center stage in the ultimate universal drama with their every act carrying cosmic significance. Passionate apocalypticism in second temple Judaism (586 BCE–210 CE) dealt not only with fear, but also with ethics—the responsibility of humanity's relationship with God and fellow humans. Feminine spirituality also found room to bloom in this period. Apocalyptic readings of environmental history have

comparable concerns with ethical behavior toward the earth. Ideological and scholarly developments such as deep ecology, the Gaia hypothesis, and ecofeminism evoke passion with spiritual echoes into such a past.

Cornucopian Postmillennialism

Not all millennial thought is apocalyptic. The majority of people leading industrial society are confidently cornucopian (that is, they have faith in a robust natural bounty). The outcome of the World Summit on Sustainable Development (Johannesburg, South Africa, 2002) shows adherence to this pursuit of everlasting economic growth, despite dissenting voices pointing out its ecological fallaciousness. This adherence is scarcely surprising because it is, as the French historian of development Gilbert Rist has shown, the global faith (1997). People live under a secular regime that contemporary Christian theologians call "postmillennialism": The savior comes after the church and saints have built a kingdom toward which believers can and should work. Postmillennialism is often associated with optimistic views of human progress and the United States in the nineteenth century, when optimism in the Industrial Revolution and the Gospel had not been dampened by world wars. Whether capitalist or communist, industrial ideologies share faith in progress and infinite natural resources to exploit.

2000's Cusp

Global millennial anxiety was at its height at the end of the twentieth century with the perceived, if unfounded, crisis of the millennium computer bug Y2K. Specters of terrorist attacks have become vividly real in the United States since 11 September 2001. This single-day carnage provided fundamentalist religious groups with potent recruitment material. Another apocalyptic response is the global insurance industry's resolution of the twenty-first century: a refusal to cover nuclear incidents, terrorism, and computer breakdown. The depth of modern society's dependence on science and technology brings a correspondent fear of failure. Notions of the end of time, and thus of history, have great appeal. They are found under vastly varying contexts and in books that become best-sellers.

Back to the Sacred

As the scholar Donna Haraway puts it, "the line between a secular crisis and a sacred apocalypse is a very thin one in U.S. American discourse, where millennial matters are written into the fabric of the national imagination from the first Puritan City on a Hill to Star Trek and its sequelae" (Haraway 2003). Global environmentalist ideas can seamlessly blur into millennialist science fiction, particularly in the more mystical shades of green on the New Age fringes.

Millennialism is a pervasive worldview that is likely to continue to win converts by providing explanations about the human predicament. Millennialism is clearly evident in issues of nature and perceptions of environmental crisis, even if there is much divergence in content. Ancient doctrines about the supernatural provide a durable structure to modern people's view of the natural world. Environmental history and millennial studies have much to learn from one another.

Malcolm Draper

See also Ecology, Deep; Ecofeminism; Gaia Theory

Further Reading

Callenbach, E. (1975). *Ecotopia*. New York: Bantam.

Cotgrove, S. (1982). *Catastrophe or cornucopia: The environment, politics and the future*. New York: John Wiley.

Grove, R. (1990, May 3). The origins of environmentalism. *Nature, 345,* 11–14.

Grove, R. (1994). *Green imperialism*. Cambridge, UK: Cambridge University Press.

Grove, R. (1997). Scotland in South Africa: John Croumbie Brown and the roots of settler environmentalism. In T. Griffiths & L. Robin (Eds.), *Ecology and empire: Environmental history of settler societies* (pp. 139–153). Pietermaritzburg, South Africa: University of Natal Press.

Haraway, D. (2003). Cyborgs to companion species: Reconfiguring kinship in technoscience. In D. Ihde & E. Selinger (Eds.), *Chasing technoscience: Matrix of materiality*. Bloomington: Indiana University Press.

Mackenzie, J. (1997a). *Empires of nature and the nature of empires: Imperialism, Scotland and the environment*. East Lothian, UK: Tuckwell Press.

Mackenzie, J. (1997b). Empire and the ecological apocalypse: The historiography of the imperial environment. In T. Griffiths & L. Robin (Eds.), *Ecology and empire: Environmental history of settler societies* (pp. 215–228). Pietermaritzburg, South Africa: University of Natal Press.

Maddox, J. (1972). *The Doomsday syndrome*. London: Macmillan.

Moos, R., & Brownstein, R. (1977). *Environment and utopia*. New York: Plenum Press.

Ponting, C. (1991). *A green history of the world*. Harmondsworth, UK: Penguin.

Rist, G. (1997). *The history of development: From Western origins to global faith*. New York: Zed Books.

Mining

Mining is the extraction of useful materials from surface or underground operations. However, mining can also encompass downstream processing to recover and refine the valuable fraction contained in the extracted material. Mining is distinct from other industries because the raw materials that are extracted—such as sand, gravel, stone and rock, coal, or metal-bearing ores—cannot in general be worked indefinitely because deposits are finite.

In the past the availability of rich geological resources in tandem with market conditions largely outside the control of metal-producing enterprises resulted in an industry characterized by a low level of technological innovation. Corporate strategies traditionally focused on the discovery and acquisition of high-grade and easily accessible mineral deposits and on increased scale of production to offset declining ore grades. In the past, health and safety regulation was a major driver behind technological innovation alongside the need to improve process energy efficiency. However, the focus has now altered: After a period of limited technological innovation a spur to technology development in mining has been applied by public concern over environmental damage and the design of environmental regulation that obliges firms to mitigate or prevent such damage.

Metals and other mineral resources are rarely found in a sufficiently pure state to be sold in an "as-mined" form. Metals are often found in chemical combination with oxygen (as oxides), sulfur (as sulfides), or other elements (e.g., chlorides, carbonates, arsenates, phosphates, etc.) and physically mixed with less valuable or valueless minerals (e.g., silicates). Nonmetal mineral resources (e.g., coal, industrial minerals) also normally contain impurities in their undisturbed state. Valueless or low-value minerals associated with valuable minerals are generally known as "gangue." Inputs from mining (extraction) to mineral processing/extractive metallurgy contain gangue that exits the process in a number of forms (e.g., as contaminants in the primary product, as separate salable by-products, solid wastes, gases, fumes, and suspended particulates). During the extraction and processing of ore, mass is conserved. However, the physical and chemical characteristics of inputs may be modified by interactions with process chemicals and/or the process itself. For example, depending on the point at which it is rejected from the process, gangue may be disposed of in an as-mined state (e.g., waste rock), as tailings (residues) (e.g., mineral processing), as glass-like slags (e.g., after smelting), or as other waste products (e.g., dusts, sludges from water treatment, spent ore from leaching, etc.). These wastes may also contain significant quantities of the target mineral or metal due to inefficient processing, technological limitations, or mineralogical factors. Therefore, the disposal of solid and liquid wastes in the mining industry is a major issue. Chemicals are also widely used in the process of moving from as-mined material to the finished salable product, and these chemicals may also give rise to environmental and social issues and impacts.

Extraction is the first operation in the commercial exploitation of a mineral resource. Extraction is the act of removing one or more components of the target material. There are three types of extraction: surface, underground, and in-situ (solution mining). The latter is somewhat limited in its application, although it is sometimes used to exploit residual mineralization as grades drop at surface or underground mines. Surface extraction is dominated by open-pit (e.g., base and precious metal ore) or open-cast (e.g., coal) operations. Surface and underground extraction usually occur independently of one another, although open-pit extraction does occasionally occur in areas already partly worked by underground methods. Similarly, underground methods are sometimes used to extract ore from beneath or in the vicinity of pits where further extension of the pit itself is not economically or technically feasible.

Underground Extraction

Underground extraction methods are usually employed to exploit richer, deeper, and smaller ore bodies where open-pit methods would be impractical. Underground extraction operations are a complex combination of tunnels, rock support, ventilation, electrical systems, water control, and hoists for the transportation of people, ore, and materials. Consequently, underground extraction is less flexible than surface extraction, and deviations in the production rate are more difficult to accommodate. Because extraction may proceed in several underground locations to ensure an appropriate level of production, planning and control of mine development are important.

Compared to underground extraction methods, surface extraction methods allow a higher degree of worker safety, greater flexibility in extraction (the capacity to practice selective mining and grade control), and lower development and maintenance costs (due to the requirement for fewer specialized systems). However, the major benefit lies in economy of scale because large-capacity earth-moving equipment can be used to generate high productivity.

The decline in ore grades over the last ten years has also increased competitive pressures in the mining industry. It has forced many companies to reassess corporate strategy, prompting the adoption of more sophisticated technologies and increased mine sizes. Indeed, the major thrust of innovation in extraction aspects of mining has been the development of open-pit techniques and exploitation of the economies of scale created by developing larger mining equipment and larger-scale extraction techniques. For example, major developments have included improved ventilation equipment and improved visibility; larger and more efficient hoisting machinery, compressors, pumps, and so forth; improved mine development equipment and procedures for mechanized shaft sinking, shaft freezing, raising, and drifting; larger and heavier equipment with better drill-bit and blasthole-drilling techniques; trackless mining equipment, initially to mechanize ore loading and transport; improved blasting agents and techniques for greater efficiency and safety; and electric mining shovels and draglines with significantly greater bucket capacities. Other developments have been 181-metric-ton diesel-electric haul trucks and front-loading equipment; portable and mobile in-pit ore-crushing and overland conveyor systems, allowing more continuous mining operations and the elimination of truck haulage where hauls are long and adverse; self-propelled scalpers and scrapers to integrate extraction and transport operations; online/automated production monitoring and control to optimize extraction and truck and shovel capacity utilization through scheduling/dispatching and route selection; and computerized and remote control systems for underground train haulage and mine pumps.

Some of these developments, of course, also apply to underground mining. In underground mining, advances have also been made in the use of "right-in-space" mining methods, which seek to ensure that drill holes, stopes (steplike excavations for the removal of ore), and other underground workings are placed more accurately in relation to the ore body during both development and production. These methods allow high ore recovery and reduce dilution by unwanted gangue, reducing waste that requires disposal and management.

Regardless of the method employed, mining is always accompanied by processing. For relatively pure materials processing may be limited to crushing and sizing (e.g., quarried rock) or washing (e.g., some coal operations). Such simple processing is possible only when the target mineral forms the majority of the material mined. In such cases the main environmental impacts are associated with the mining itself rather than with subsequent processing.

Although any mining operation has the potential to produce environmental impacts, typically the potential arises from discharges of solid, liquid, and gaseous waste products. The characteristics of the discharges, the nature of the receiving environment, and the distance over which the discharges are transported are major factors in determining the magnitude of the impacts. Societal values and preferences also play a significant role in determining how certain discharges are viewed by various stakeholders (those affected by the actions of another). This more subjective aspect of the discharges and receiving environment characteristics therefore determines, in part, the site-specific environmental footprint of an operation.

Ore Extraction

Ore extraction and processing are the sources of major environmental impacts by releasing solid, liquid, and gaseous wastes into soil, air, and water. With the possible exception of water contamination, arguably the most significant impact arises from the disposal of solid wastes, particularly in relation to soil and water pollution. In mining, as in most industries, less than 100 percent of the raw material is the target product. Average figures (based on a survey of Canadian metal mines) indicate that 42 percent of the total mined material is rejected as waste rock, 52 percent is rejected from the mill as tailings, 4 percent is rejected from the smelter as slag, leaving as a valuable component only 2 percent of the originally mined tonnage. At many gold operations, the concentration of valuable material is so low that effectively all of the mined ore is disposed of as waste. In effect, such operations are as much about waste disposal as they are about resource extraction.

The significance of this dual extraction/disposal role in mining of base and precious metals is seen in global estimates of the annual generation of solid and gaseous wastes from copper and lead production, with the amounts being dominated by solid waste. Although waste disposal directly sterilizes a significant land area, it is the presence of potentially harmful elements, minerals, and other contaminants in the solid (and liquid) wastes generated during mining, mineral processing, and other downstream processes (e.g., waste rock, tailings, slags, smelter flue dusts, and precipitates from the chemical treatment of metal-contaminated liquid effluents) that determines the wider environmental impact. The contaminants may be organic (e.g., flotation reagents [substances used because of their chemical or biological activity]) or inorganic (e.g., metals). Their original source may be the ore body itself or chemicals applied during extraction and processing of the ore. The contaminants may cause a number of related environmental impacts, including contamination of ground and surface waters and soil resources, sustained ecosystem degradation, and atmospheric suspension of respirable (breathable) dusts. These impacts can combine to extend the spatial and temporal footprint of a mine site, an example being the long-term generation of acid rock drainage (ARD) from surface wastes and from underground and open-pit workings. ARD is one of the most intractable problems in the mining of nonferrous metals and coal, a fact reflected by the increasing volume of research published in conference proceedings, journals, and books. ARD is both the most serious environmental impact caused by mining and the industry's greatest environmentally related technical challenge.

At a site-specific level, the extent of the environmental impacts of mining and mineral processing depends on a number of variables, including size of the site, method of ore extraction, ore mineralogy, processing and treatment routes, process efficiency, volume and nature of wastes, hydrology (the properties, distribution, and circulation of water), hydrogeology, local environmental conditions, nature of the regulatory framework, and the timing of any remediation.

Acid Rock Drainage

ARD includes drainage of water originating in underground mines and runoff from open-pit workings, waste rock dumps, mill tailings, and ore stockpiles, sometimes in flows measured in millions of gallons per day. Although normally mines extracting coal or nonferrous metals suffer the greatest problems, similar problems may arise during construction or other engineering activity on certain rock types. ARD results from the exposure of pyrite (FeS_2), marcasite (FeS_2), and pyrrhotite (FeS_{1-x}) to oxygen and water, resulting in the formation of sulfuric acid, ferrous iron (Fe^{2+}), and ferric iron (Fe^{3+}). Ferric iron is a powerful oxidizing agent and oxidizes insoluble metal sulfides to water-soluble sulfates. These may then be dissolved and transported in the acid medium. The rate of ferric iron and acid generation is increased dramatically by the presence of certain bacteria (e.g., *Thiobacillus ferrooxidans, Thiobacillus thiooxidans*). Metals commonly found in ARD include copper, zinc, nickel, cadmium, arsenic, aluminum, and manganese, although the concentrations are largely dependent on the mineralogy of the ore body, the surrounding host rock, and attenuation reactions. The nature of ARD originating from waste products is also influenced by process efficiency and economics because these in turn partially determine the concentration and type of residual metal contaminants (present as sulfides or other species) in waste rock and tailings and in the unexploited host rock.

The dominance of waste management today is perhaps a reflection of the prevailing attitude toward closure, namely that a civil engineering-style remedial approach is sufficient to properly decommission a site *and* avoid possible liability in the future. Although this approach may have been valid twenty years ago, technology, legislation, and the expectations of stakeholders have moved on. If there is a generic "thread" that ties current waste management approaches it is the

possibility of future litigation and liability associated with what might be considered short-term (but relatively cheap) solutions to long-term environmental problems. The threat of incurring financial penalties in the future has helped to catalyze the industry into exploring alternatives to current practices, to establish "best practice" standards, and to move toward preventive action, particularly within the mineral processing arena. This is not to say that waste management has no role in optimizing future environmental protection. However, in a legislative framework increasingly leaning toward preventive rather than remedial measures, any environmental benefits of remedial approaches relative to alternative approaches need to be quantified rather than relying on empirical and historical precedent.

At local and regional levels stakeholder groups may balance the environmental and social impacts with the socioeconomic benefits that often accrue (at these levels and at the national level) from mining, for example: (1) contribution to local economies. Mining may form a vital part of rural economies in particular. (2) Contributions to the macroeconomy: Mining forms a vital part of the gross domestic product (GDP) of some countries. (3) Provision of consumer products: Many products that are not directly associated with mining but that are essential to a modern lifestyle depend on tin products (e.g., food containers).

Consequently, social and environmental impacts may be mitigated by a willingness to accept a certain degree of environmental impact in return for other benefits. Therefore, a social-impact analysis may be required at the site level to fully understand an operation's contribution to social effects and the level of significance that stakeholders attach to them.

The legacy of mining that took place before environmental and social issues were considered is a universal problem that the mining industry faces, and the industry is often criticized in terms of today's regulation for practices that were legal at the time. Dealing with this legacy is problematic—companies are loath to address the legacy for fear of being seen to admit or accept liability and responsibility. Some experts suggest that the mining industry should explore regulatory, voluntary, and fiscal approaches to the gradual reclamation of abandoned operations that are likely to impact its ability to operate in the future. This approach has been examined in the United States to assess the potential to rework abandoned sites, with the liability for environmental impacts remaining with the state or federal government, removing the liability risk as a major obstacle to restoration through reworking (this approach applies to sites where the reworking is undertaken by a company other than that originally responsible for the environmental impact).

The remediation of existing mine sites represents a significant opportunity to develop innovative technologies for reprocessing mine wastes and to develop policy and technical procedures to promote the utilization of secondary wastes rather than primary resources where possible. Increased constraints relating to the exploitation of primary resources have elevated wastes into potential resources themselves. Regulatory standards and quality standards may impede the use of innovative technologies, and there may also be technical barriers to the reprocessing of certain complex waste materials. Innovative technologies may also have cost and performance drawbacks that in turn generate a lack of incentive to invest in such technologies.

Alyson Warhurst and Paul Mitchell

Further Reading

Hester, R., & Harrison, R. (1994). *Mining and its environmental impact.* Cambridge, UK: Royal Society of Chemistry

Institute of Mining and Metallurgy. (1992). *Minerals, metals and the environment.* London: Elsevier Science.

Ripley, E. A., Redmann, R. E., & Crowder, A. A. (1996). *Environmental effects of mining.* Delray Beach, FL: St. Lucie Press.

Sengupta, M. (1992). *Environmental impacts of mining: Monitoring, restoration and control.* Boca Raton, FL: Lewis Publishers.

United Nations, United Nations Department for Development Support and Management Services & United Nations Environment Programme. (1994). *Environmental management of mine sites, technical report No. 30.* Paris: author

United Nations Environment Programme, Industry and Environment Programme Activity Centre. (1991). *Environmental aspects of selected non-ferrous metal ore mining: A technical guide.* Paris: author.

United Nations Environment Programme & Comisión Chilena del Cobre. (2001). *Abandoned mines: Problems, issues and policy challenges for decision makers.* Paris: author.

United Nations Environment Programme, World Bank, & the Mining, Minerals and Sustainable Development (MMSD) Project. (2002). *Financing, mining and sustainability.* Paris: author.

Warhurst, A., & Noronha, L. (Eds). (1999). *Environmental policy in mining: Corporate strategy and planning for closure.* Boca Raton, FL: Lewis Publishers.

Mississippi and Missouri Rivers

Draining two-thirds of the continental United States, the system of the Mississippi (3,782 kilometers) and Missouri Rivers (3,967 kilometers) is the longest waterway in the world. It is also among the most transfigured by human engineering.

Centuries before the arrival of European settlers, these rivers formed the basis of a vast trade network that supported some of the most technologically advanced civilizations in North America. French colonists exploited and modified this network in organizing an extensive trade in fur during the eighteenth century. Following the transfer of political authority to the United States in 1803, the Lewis and Clark expedition the next year, and the advent of steam power in the 1810s, river traffic increased considerably. The Missouri became the great highway to the West, charting a path of European settlement and Native American subjugation. A flourishing trade in lead, flour, and lumber spurred the growth of towns up and down the Mississippi, most of which were located on high bluffs that offered protection from rising waters. Colorfully portrayed by writers such as Mark Twain and artists such as Karl Bodmer, these rivers became central to the popular imagery and mythology of the nineteenth-century West.

The environmental impact of steamboat traffic, the expansion of commercial agriculture, and urbanization presented western settlers with a host of new problems. The felling of forests to fire steamboat boilers destabilized riverbanks and contributed to unpredictable channel migration. Runoff from plowed fields added considerably to the sediment load in the rivers and facilitated the formation of dangerous sandbars. Floods became more menacing, as well as towns spread onto low-lying land. Meanwhile, direct discharges of industrial and domestic waste damaged the health of downstream users.

It was not until the twentieth century that these problems were attacked systematically. Floods on the Mississippi in 1927 and the Missouri in the 1940s provided the political impetus for federal involvement in

Indian-European Trade on the Missouri

In the 1700's when the trade and travel records were written, the Missouri River was a main artery of European-Indian trade. Commercial companies centered in St. Louis maintained regular contact with trade centers up the river, and in the 1800's steamboats plied their way upstream with goods and guns to exchange for furs. Trade centers for exchange were an ancient tradition of American Indian life, and now they eagerly made their way to the trade centers of the European where new goods and materials could be gotten. But the price was dear. For besides the new goods, there came new and fatal diseases—measles, smallpox, cholera, and a variety of fevers—wiping out hundreds and even thousands of people at one blow. Whole tribes that had lived in the region for hundreds of years were wiped out or left in such a fragmentary condition that they joined with other tribes and lost the knowledge of their past identity.

The Pawnees who lived outside the mainstream of commercial traffic were less affected than the others by this holocaust. They lived along the outlying tributaries of the Missouri—the Loup, the Platte, and the Republican—that flow eastward across the present State of Nebraska and join the Missouri at their eastern ends.

Source: Weltfish, Gene. *The Lost Universe; With a Closing Chapter on "The Universe Regained."* New York and London: Basic Books, 1965, p. 3.

river management. Under the principles of multiple-use planning that had been established during the Progressive Era, river channels were straightened and deepened, levees were raised, and water was impounded in reservoirs for irrigation and the generation of electricity. These large-scale modifications brought economic benefits but imposed heavy environmental and social costs. Fish, wildlife, and human habitats were destroyed; Native American tribes along the Missouri River lost thousands of acres of land to dam and reservoir construction. Embankments and walls squeezed higher volumes of water through narrower channels and increased the risk of inundation for downstream communities that were unable to procure federal flood protection funds.

In the wake of the post–World War II environmental movement, there have been attempts to restore the rivers to their natural condition, including several wetland preservation projects and a plan to reintroduce seasonal fluctuations in flow to the Missouri River. Stricter pollution regulations have resulted in cleaner effluents from industries and cities, although pesticide and herbicide runoff from farms continues to raise health concerns.

Andrew Hurley

Further Reading

Colten, C. (Ed.). (2000). *Transforming New Orleans and its environs*. Pittsburgh, PA: University of Pittsburgh Press.

Colten, C. (2002). Reintroducing nature to the city: Wetlands in New Orleans. *Environmental History, 7*(2), 226–246.

Kelman, A. (2003). *A river and its city: An environmental history of New Orleans*. Berkeley & Los Angeles: University of California Press.

Scarpino, P. V. (1985). *Great river: An environmental history of the upper Mississippi River, 1890–1950*. Columbia: University of Missouri Press.

Thorson, J. E. (1994). *River of promise, river of peril: The politics of managing the Missouri River*. Lawrence: University Press of Kansas.

Moa

Moa is a word used by the Maori (Polynesian inhabitants of New Zealand) for a unique group of birds native to the main islands of New Zealand in the southwestern Pacific Ocean. Moa are classified with the ostrich (Africa and formerly Europe-Asia), rhea (South America), cassowary and emu (Australia), and kiwi (New Zealand) as ratites, so named for the flat, raftlike breastbone. However, characters as diverse as the structure of their chromosomes, eye and egg-white proteins, and nuclear and mitochondrial DNA show that these birds, with the tinamous of South America, form a distinct group often referred to as Paleognaths—the most primitive of recent birds.

Moa were large, flightless birds ranging from 15 to 20 kilograms in weight and about 0.5 meter in height at their back for the smallest species to perhaps 160 to 200 kilograms and nearly 2 meters at their back for the largest of the biggest species. They therefore include some of the largest birds to have ever lived, matched in weight by only the dromornithids (mirihung birds) of Australia and aepyornithids (elephant birds) of Madagascar. It is now generally accepted that moa and their relatives had a common ancestor on the supercontinent of Gondwana and that as that landmass split apart, birds marooned on each segment evolved to become the modern forms. The ancestors of moa were marooned on New Zealand 82 million years ago.

Eleven species of moa are recognized in six genera. (See table 1.) They differed markedly in size, relative stoutness, and especially in the shapes of their bills. The latter reveal specializations in feeding. All moa were vegetarians; some are known by gizzard contents

to have browsed on coarse leafy and twiggy material (*Dinornis*), whereas others preferred soft leaves and fruit (*Euryapteryx*). Different species lived in different areas, so that normally only three or four species coexisted, with feeding niches separated by body size and bill shape. On South Island of New Zealand there was segregation by altitude, with specialists for both the lowlands and uplands. Most species lived in forest or shrubland, as during the Holocene epoch (the last ten thousand years) the small area of grassland was confined to the dry rainshadow zones (sides of the mountains that face the direction of prevailing water-laden winds that drop rain on the opposite, upwind side) and to the subalpine areas.

The moa fossil record extends only about 2.5 million years, so most of their evolution within New Zealand is unknown. All known species survived until humans colonized New Zealand about seven hundred to eight hundred years ago. Within 250 years all moa were extinct, and Europeans, who arrived beginning in 1769, never saw any. Moa extinction was caused primarily by hunting—their remains are known from hundreds of middens (rubbish dumps at old campsites and villages) throughout the country—but habitat loss through burning of vegetation contributed to their rapid decline.

Moa bones first came to the attention of European naturalists in 1839 and excited their curiosity in that golden age of natural history discovery. When the next consignment of bones arrived in England, the scientists were flabbergasted. How could such large birds with apparently so many forms have lived on a tiny island in the middle of a vast ocean? Moa became symbolic of island novelty in the new evolutionary understanding of life. And moa have taken center stage in the studies of New Zealand prehistory ever since.

Trevor H. Worthy

TABLE 1.
SPECIES OF MOA, THEIR HIGHER CLASSIFICATION, AND THEIR DISTRIBUTION ON NORTH ISLAND (NI) OR SOUTH ISLAND (SI) OF NEW ZEALAND ORDER STRUTHIONI FORMES (RATITE BIRDS)

Suborder Dinornithii (Moas)
Emeidae
  Anomalopteryginae

Anomalopteryx didiformis	Little bush moa	NI, SI
Megalapteryx didinus	Upland moa	SI
Pachyornis elephantopus	Heavy-footed moa	SI
P. australis	Crested moa	SI
P. mappini	Mappin's moa	NI
Emeinae		
Emeus crassus	Eastern moa	SI
Euryapteryx geranoides	Stout-legged moa	NI, SI
E. curtus	Coastal moa	NI
Dinornithidae		
Dinornis struthoides	Slender moa	NI, SI
D. novaezealandiae	Large bush moa	NI, SI
D. giganteus	Giant moa	NI, SI

Source: Worthy & Holdaway (2002).

Further Reading

Anderson, A. J. (1989). *Prodigious birds: Moas and moa-hunting in prehistoric New Zealand*. Cambridge, UK: Cambridge University Press.

Archey, G. (1941). The moa: A study of the Dinornithiformes. *Bulletin of the Auckland Institute and Museum,1*, 145.

Cooper, A., Lalueza-Fox, C., Anderson, S., Rambaut, A., Austin, J., & Ward, R. (2001). Complete mitochondrial genome sequences of two extinct moas clarify ratite evolution. *Nature, 409*, 704–707.

Cracraft, J. (1976). The species of moas (Aves: Dinornithidae). *Smithsonian Contributions to Paleobiology 27*, 189–205.

Worthy, T. H. (1990). An analysis of the distribution and relative abundance of moa species (Aves; Dinornithiformes). *New Zealand Journal of Zoology 17*, 213–241.

Worthy, T. H., & Holdaway, R. N.(2002). *The lost world of the moa: Prehistoric life of New Zealand*. Bloomington & Indianapolis: Indiana University Press.

The Montreal Protocol

The Montreal Protocol (MP) is the foremost example of successful international environmental policy making. Signed in 1987, it started regulating ozone-depleting substances (ODS) such as chlorofluorocarbons (CFCs) globally, with the goal of eventually phasing them out. CFCs had been invented in 1928 and became very popular after World War II when their production and consumption rose steadily.

In 1974, Mario Molina and F. Sherwood Rowland, two scientists from the University of California at Irvine, advanced the hypothesis that CFCs could damage the ozone layer. Their hypothesis called for a revision of the long-held belief in the harmlessness of CFCs, which were considered a wonder chemical for numerous domestic and industrial appliances (as propellants in spray cans, as coolants and insulation in refrigeration, as cleaning agents in electronics manufacturing) since they seemed to be chemically inert, nontoxic and noncorrosive. According to the Molina-Rowland hypothesis, CFCs could deplete stratospheric ozone and hence lead to an increase in ultraviolet-B (UV-B) radiation, which in turn would have severe effects on biological systems (causing skin cancer in humans, crop damage, and algae diminution) and on global climate.

International Negotiations

In the United States, this hypothesis was taken seriously early on. As a consequence, the Clean Air Act of 1977 introduced a ban on CFCs in spray cans. Several other countries followed, but not the other large producers of CFCs, such as the Soviet Union, Japan, or the nations of the European Community (EC). They pointed to the unknowns of the causal relationships. International negotiations started in 1977 on the initiative of the United States. At an international conference organized by United Nations Environmental Programme (UNEP), the World Plan of Action for the protection of the ozone layer was adopted.

In the early 1980s, the problem of the ozone layer seemed to have gone away. Computer models predicted only small long-term reductions of ozone, and observations of ozone concentrations showed no significant trend. Also, the CFC consumption in the United States had dropped, and therefore global emissions were seen as declining. Negotiations for an international convention on the ozone layer, started by UNEP in 1981, made little progress. While the United States favored forbidding the use of CFCs in some applications (for example, as propellants in spray cans), Europe argued for a cap on production capacity only. The differences could not be bridged. Eventually, a nonbinding treaty, the Vienna Convention for the Protection of the Ozone Layer, was signed in March 1985. It contained only pledges to cooperate in research and monitoring, to exchange information on CFC production, and to agree to binding control measures only if and when justified.

The Road to Montreal

Throughout the process, political controversy merged with scientific controversy. The question was how to act under uncertainty. The United States and few other countries pushed for significant international controls while others rejected cuts from current production levels. After a protracted negotiation period, a compromise was reached in September 1987. It envisaged a 50 percent cut of ozone-depleting substances by the year 1999 for developed countries. In the years that followed, those goals were made more ambitious, resulting in a complete phase-out of these substances in the industrialized countries by 1996. Developing countries were granted a ten-year grace period in order to meet their basic domestic needs. They are now scheduled to phase out most ozone-depleting substances by 2010. By May 2000, a total of 176 countries had ratified the 1985 Vienna Convention and 175 the 1987 Montreal Protocol.

In 1985–1986 the ozone hole—abnormally low ozone concentrations that were completely unexpected—was discovered over Antarctica. This introduced an element of drama into the ongoing international negotiations and changed the perception of the problem completely. As Professor Rowland told the *New York Times*, "The big loss of ozone over Antarctica has changed this from being a computer hypothesis plausible for the future to a current reality and cause for concern" (7 December 1986). Whether this discovery influenced the international negotiations in Montreal is contentious. The architects of the protocol portray the discovery as precautionary in character, while others argue that the ozone hole did in fact have an influence on the negotiations.

The Amendments

Apart from reduction targets, the Montreal Protocol institutionalized a formal structure with the annual conference of the parties as its highest decision-making body, and several other bodies, including the Multilateral Fund, the UNEP secretariat, technical, scientific and socioeconomic working groups, and the implementation committee also part of the structure. As implementation of the Montreal Protocol is the responsibility of national governments, the task of the implementation committee is mainly to monitor noncompliance on the part of member countries. While it is accepted that some countries may not be able to meet their reduction targets, they are expected to be frank in their reporting and also to refrain from exporting any of their ongoing production.

In June 1990, during the second conference of the parties in London, delegates agreed to phase out CFCs by the end of the century, and to include a series of other ozone-depleting substances in the list of controlled substances. They also agreed to establish a multilateral fund to help developing countries to comply with the MP. In 1992, the parties met in Copenhagen and agreed to advance the phase-out date for the five substances already controlled by the Montreal Protocol. For the first time, HCFCs (hydrochloroflourocarbons; a replacement chemical with a smaller ozone depletion potential) were included on the list of regulated substances. In Vienna 1995, the phase-out date for HCFCs was brought forward to 2020, and methyl bromide was set to be phased out by 2010. In Beijing in December 1999, $150 million was approved to fund the shutting down of CFC production in China by 2010. Likewise, $82 million was earmarked to phase out of CFC production in India. (India and China had become the world's largest producers of CFCs.) Overall the Montreal Protocol has brought about a dramatic reduction of CFCs, while at the same time HCFC production has increased.

Lessons

Global environmental issues cannot be solved unilaterally. However, damage to a common pool resource (like the atmosphere) can be done unilaterally. Therefore, control measures have to be binding on all main parties to an international treaty. International regulations for the protection of the ozone layer seem to be quite successful. Mostafa Tolba, one of the architects of the Montreal Protocol and former UNEP executive director, has gone so far as to say that the Montreal Protocol may be a blueprint for regulations dealing with other global environmental problems, such as climate change.

Reiner Grundmann

Further Reading

Benedick, R. E. (1991). *Ozone diplomacy: New directions in safeguarding the planet*. Cambridge, MA: Harvard University Press.

Brack, D. (1996). *International trade and the Montreal Protocol*. London: Royal Institute of International Affairs.

Grundmann, R. (2001). *Transnational environmental policy: Reconstructing ozone*. London: Routledge.

Harremoës, P., et al. (2002). The precautionary principle in the 20th century. Late lessons from early warnings. London: Earthscan.

Molina, M. J., & Rowland, F. S. (1974). Stratospheric sink for chlorofluormethanes: Chlorine-atom catalysed destruction of ozone. *Nature, 249* (28 June), 810–812.

Tolba, M. K., with Rummel-Bulska, I. (1998). *Global environmental diplomacy*. Cambridge, MA: MIT Press.

United Nations Environmental Programme. (2000) *Action on ozone*. Retrieved June 19, 2002, from http://www.unep.org/ozone/pdf/ozone-action-en.pdf

Mountaineering

Mountaineering is the sport of climbing mountains. It began in Europe during the eighteenth century. Although people climbed mountains before the eighteenth century, they climbed for spiritual or utilitarian purposes, not for sport. Two dates are usually cited for the birth of mountaineering. The first is 1741, when a group of Englishmen made a special trip to climb peaks near Montanvers, France. The second—and more commonly referenced—is 1786, when Frenchmen Jacques Balmat and Michel-Gabriel Paccard made the first successful ascent of Mont Blanc (4,807 meters) on the border of France, Italy, and Switzerland, the highest peak in the European Alps. The word *mountaineer*, from the words *montagnier* and *montainier* in Old French, dates to the seventeenth century, when it referred to a mountain dweller. By the 1870s, after recreational mountain climbing had become popular in Europe, English speakers commonly used *mountaineers* to refer to climbers and *mountaineering* to refer to the sport.

Origins

Mountaineering developed due to changing perspectives about nature in general and mountains in particular. Prior to the 1700s Europeans generally feared mountains, believing that the Alps were home to witches, dragons, and demons. However, European thought shifted during the eighteenth century as a result of the Enlightenment (a period during the 1700s when people in Europe and the United States embraced rationality, science, and respect for humanity more systematically and profoundly than previously) and Romanticism (a literary, artistic, and philosophical movement originating in the eighteenth century that celebrated nature and the human senses). Enlightened thinkers sought to classify the natural world, understand it through mathematics and science, and, essentially, control nature through rational thinking. Romanticism, a reaction against the Enlightenment, focused on emotions, imagination, and human freedom, which, for many, could be attained in mountains. Both Romanticism and the Enlightenment influenced early mountaineers, who wanted to conquer and measure mountains while basking in their glorious, sublime beauty.

Mountaineering Phases

Mountaineering evolved through distinct phases. During its first phase, from the late 1700s to the mid-1800s, mountaineering was primarily a European phenomenon. Europeans' ultimate goal was the Matterhorn (4,478 meters), the most famous and feared peak in the Alps. The English climber Edward Whymper made the first successful ascent in 1856, although the death of four climbers during the descent (one of the most famous mountaineering accidents in history) tarnished Whymper's accomplishment. Many mountaineers be-

fore the 1850s combined climbing with scientific study; they conducted meteorological experiments and analyzed geological formations on their climbs.

An imperialist phase of mountaineering occurred during the late nineteenth and early twentieth centuries, when European mountaineers began climbing outside Europe. British mountaineers in the 1850s, for example, explored the Himalayas to both climb and survey their empire's colonial lands in India. In 1911 Yale University professor Hiram Bingham planted two flags on the summit of Mount Coropuna (6,613 meters) in Peru: The Yale University flag represented the triumph of Western, rational education over both nature and Peruvian "backward" and "superstitious" beliefs about mountains; the U.S. flag metaphorically exerted the U.S. claim over South American lands.

Women mountaineers, who have been recognized in the sport ever since Marie Paradis, of Chamonix, France, ascended Mont Blanc in 1808, also climbed for equal rights and suffrage, especially during the early 1900s. The U.S. climber Annie Smith Peck, a prominent advocate, furthered her cause when she reached the summit of Peru's Huascarán Norte (6,768 meters) in 1908, going higher in the Andes than any male mountaineers had. In the early 1900s, the U.S. women's rights activist Fanny Bullock Workman had herself photographed on a Himalayan mountain while carrying a banner reading "Votes for Women." Not until the 1970s, however, did sexism wane sufficiently so that men regularly accepted women on expeditions.

By the 1920s another phase of mountaineering began: massive army-style (and army-sized) "assaults," as they were called, on high-altitude mountains in the Himalayas, Andes, and elsewhere. The goal: climb the world's highest peaks, especially the highest of them all, Mount Everest (8,850 meters) in Nepal. The first ascent of Mount Everest by Nepalese sherpa Tenzing Norgay and New Zealander Sir Edmund Hillary in 1953 invigorated mountaineering worldwide.

Throughout the 1960s and 1970s winter mountain sports, including mountaineering, grew in popularity among middle-class people worldwide. During the 1990s adventure travel and ecotourism gave mountaineering another boost. Although changes have occurred, mountaineering still embodies ideals from the Enlightenment and Romanticism: In their quest to escape modern society, climbers rely on rational thinking, they conquer peaks, and they feel the spiritual magnificence of mountains.

Nonmountaineering Mountain Climbing

Not all mountain climbing is mountaineering. Before the sport was born, the Italian poet Petrarch made his famous ascent of Mount Ventoux (1,909 meters) in France "to see the view" in 1336. After the Spanish conquistador Hernando Cortés invaded Mexico in the 1520s, he ordered climbers to the summit of Popocaté-petl volcano (5,452 meters) to find sulfur, which Cortés used in making gunpowder for his cannons. Sacred peaks have also attracted people to their summits. Incas prayed for rain atop many Andean peaks in the 1400s and 1500s. Native Americans in North America also made spiritual journeys to mountain summits. In Japan groups called "Fuji-ko" were making annual sacred ascents of Mount Fuji (3,776 meters) by the 1800s. In Peru religious pilgrims still climb Mount Ausangate (6,384 meters) annually.

Local Mountain People and Environments

For local mountain people and environments, mountaineering has had both positive and negative impacts. On the positive side, mountaineering has infused local economies with jobs, infrastructure, and financial investment. Mountain climbing has also offered new recreation possibilities. For example, Mexicans in the 1920s—after witnessing thirty years of foreign climbing on Mexican volcanoes—established their own climbing clubs. Mountaineering has also inspired people to protect sensitive alpine environments in national parks, such as Sagarmatha in Nepal, Huascarán in Peru, Kilimanjaro in Tanzania, Rainier and Denali in the United States, and Fuji-Hakone-Izu in Japan.

On the negative side, local guides and porters risk their lives but earn little or no recognition. The influx of revenue, although helpful to many, has often disrupted social norms. Local residents sometimes blame mountaineers for triggering catastrophes by committing spiritual transgressions against mountain deities. Additionally, mountaineering has environmental impacts. These include use of natural resources, trampling of fragile mountain ecosystems, an increase in litter and pollution, and the buildup of human waste at high altitudes, such as at climbing camps on Mount Rainier, where 7.2 metric tons of human waste are generated annually and removed by helicopter. Although conservation measures can help protect local ecosystems, national parks often restrict local access to traditional lands and resources. These issues have some-times fed local resentment of foreign mountaineers and heightened tensions within local societies.

Mark Carey

Further Reading

Ardito, S. (1997). *Mont Blanc: Discovery and conquest of the giant of the Alps.* Seattle, WA: Mountaineers.

Bernbaum, E. (1990). *Sacred mountains of the world.* San Francisco: Sierra Club Books.

Fleming, F. (2000). *Killing dragons: The conquest of the Alps.* London: Granta Books.

Jenkins, M. (2000). *The white death: Tragedy and heroism in an avalanche zone.* New York: Random House.

Mazel, D. (Ed.). (1994). *Mountaineering women: Stories by early climbers.* College Station: Texas A&M University Press.

Ortner, S. (1999). *Life and death on Mt. Everest: Sherpas and Himalayan mountaineering.* Princeton, NJ: Princeton University Press.

Poole, D. (1998). Landscape and the imperial subject: U.S. images of the Andes, 1859–1930. In G. M. Joseph, C. C. LeGrande, & R. D. Salvatore (Eds.), *Close encounters of empire: Writing the cultural history of U.S.-Latin American relations* (pp. 107–138). Durham, NC: Duke University Press.

Potterfield, P. (1996). *In the zone: Epic survival stories from the mountaineering world.* Seattle, WA: Mountaineers.

Stevens, S. (Ed.). (1997). *Conservation through cultural survival: Indigenous peoples and protected areas.* Washington, DC: Island Press.

Unsworth, W. (1981). *Everest: A mountaineering history.* Boston: Houghton Mifflin.

Mountains

The word *mountains* may conjure up an image of gigantic rock precipices, sharp peaks, glaciers and snow, and a team of grim-faced mountaineers, roped together, risking avalanches, rockfalls, and blizzards in their arduous upward progress—the sort of scene one might see in the upper sections of the Alps or the Himalayas, or in the many other dramatic high landscapes of the planet. However, that scene represents only a small fraction of our mountain environment. While there has been much debate among academics over how to define mountain, no simple statement has evolved. The

Selection from Lord Byron's "Alpine Scenery"

Above me are the Alps—most glorious Alps—

The palaces of Nature, whose vast walls

Have pinnacled in clouds their snowy scalps,

And throned Eternity in icy halls

Of cold Sublimity, where forms and falls

The avalanche—the thunderbolt of snow!

All that expands the spirit, yet appalls,

Gather around these summits, as to show

How Earth may pierce to Heaven, yet leave vain man below.

[. . .]

Clear, placid Leman! thy contrasted lake

With the wide world I've dwelt in is a thing

Which warns me, with its stillness, to forsake

Earth's troubled waters for a purer spring.

This quiet sail is as a noiseless wing

To waft me from distraction; once I loved

Torn ocean's roar; but thy soft murmuring

Sounds sweet as if a sister's voice reproved,

That I with stern delights should e'er have been so moved.

It is the hush of night; and all between

Thy margin and the mountains, dusk, yet clear,

Mellowed and mingling, yet distinctly seen,

Save darkened Jura, whose capped heights appears

Precipitously steep; and drawing near,

There breathes a living fragrance from the shore,

Of flowers yet fresh with childhood; on the ear

Drops the light drip of the suspended oar,

Or chirps the grasshopper one good-night carol more.

Source: Parker, Richard Greene, & Watson, J. Madison. (1866). "Alpine Scenery." In *National Fifth Reader: Containing A Complete and Practical Treatise on Elocution; Select and Classified Exercises in Reading and Declamation; With Biographical Sketches, and Copious Notes: Adapted to the Use of Students in Literature.* New York, Chicago, and New Orleans: A. S. Barnes & Company, p. 467.

people of Wales and northwestern England would insist that they live among mountains, yet their highest summits barely exceed 1,000 meters above sea level. Nomads of Tibet or agricultural peasants of southern Peru who live above 4,000 meters above sea level would be classified as mountain folk, yet their local landscapes may be as flat as the North American prairies.

Nevertheless, a varying combination of high altitude and steepness of slope make for short growing seasons and slow soil formation processes. The variation in mean annual temperature with altitude and latitude has combined to give the Lofoten Islands of North Norway, close to sea level and 70 degrees north, and the upper reaches of the Swiss Alps, above 2,000 meters and in latitude 46 degrees north, similar landscapes, referred to as "alpine." Both are above the limits of tree growth (timberline) and have been molded by glaciers. In contrast, locations at high altitude (above 3,500–4,000 meters) close to the equator, such as in

Ethiopia, Kenya, or Ecuador, rather rounded landforms may support flourishing agriculture. Carl Troll (1900–1975), the famous German mountain geographer of the twentieth century, made the remark that above 3,000 meters in Indonesia, for instance, there are high mountains without a high mountain (alpine) landscape.

In its efforts to ensure a critical assessment of the importance of mountains to sustainable human progress, the United Nations adopted a pragmatic approach in its declaration of 2002 as the "International Year of Mountains" (IYM). Thus it is claimed that mountains occupy about 20 percent of the world's terrestrial surface and provide the direct life-support base for about 10 percent of humankind. Indirectly, in terms of their resources, such as provision of more than half of all fresh water, forest products, minerals, grazing lands, and hydropower, mountains are vital to survival of over 50 percent of the total population. Furthermore, mountains have provided the spiritual essence of all major and many minor religions. Second only to coastal areas, they are the major focus of tourism, the largest and most rapidly expanding industry in the world. Mountains shelter some of the world's most important centers of biodiversity and a large share of its cultural diversity. Finally, climate change, especially the currently anticipated global warming, would have some of its earliest and most noticeable effects in mountain regions. It follows that mountains are becoming a serious object of concern.

Geographical Distribution of Mountains

Mountains are found on every continent, from the equator to the poles as far as land exists. Taken together as a single great landscape category or ecosystem, they encompass the most extensive array known of landforms, climates, and flora and fauna, as well as human cultural diversity. From a geological and tectonic point of view they comprise the most complex of the earth's underlying structures.

Mountains and uplands incorporate the inhuman and extremely cold and sterile high ice carapaces of Antarctica and Greenland as well as the high, dry, hypoxic, and almost uninhabitable ranges of Central Asia and the south central Andes. They also include richly varied and even luxuriant ridge and valley systems of the humid tropics and subtropics, such as the eastern Himalayas, the Hengduan Mountains (Yunnan, China), Mount Cameroon, sections of the northern Andes, and parts of New Guinea. In East Africa and

Ethiopia, the flanks and valleys of the high mountains have long been the preferred human habitat compared with the arid lowlands that surround them. An enormous array of other mountains must be included— for instance, the high volcanoes of the Caribbean and Central America, Indonesia, Japan, and Hawaii, where humans have long benefited from access to rich soils regardless of exposure to extreme fiery hazards. There are also what are usually called "middle mountains" (German: *Mittelgebirge*), ranging from Tasmania to South Africa and from central and northern Europe to the Urals and Siberia. While these latter contrast with the Alps (the epitome of "high mountains," German: *Hochgebirge*) because of their more subdued relief, their other mountain attributes warrant special policies to ensure sustainable resource use and preservation of their traditional landscapes.

The high mountains of the world are associated with the most recent, or Tertiary to present, geological period of mountain building resulting from movement of Earth's tectonic plates. This has established two great systems of mountain ranges: the circum-Pacific and the transverse Atlas-Pyrenees-Alps-Caucasus-Hindu Kush-Himalaya-Indonesian arc. Collectively they form the loci of most of the world's active volca-

Some 60 inches of rain in three days caused thousands of landsides in Darjeeling, West Bengal, India in 1968. Here, local people are employed by the Indian military to clear landsides and reopen roads. COURTESY JACK D. IVES.

noes and the majority of seismic epicenters (earth-quakes). Mountains are dangerous places to live, given the combination of gravity, steep slopes, often very high levels of precipitation, tectonic disturbance, and volcanic activity. Many mountain regions are also dangerous because of the actions of people.

Changing Attitudes Toward Mountains

Let us try to picture the classical image of a mountainous landscape. The physical characteristics, together with relative inaccessibility and remoteness from the mainstreams of world society, provide images of indestructibility, ruggedness, and hostility to most human endeavor. Yet these same characteristics over a long time scale have led to unparalleled biodiversity and cultural diversity. Mountain communities evolved in semi-isolation, developing and preserving local languages, costumes, customs, and intricately adapted farming and grazing practices. They frequently retained high levels of independence. The independence of mountain communities, however, was bought at a price: hard physical labor for survival, the risk of natural hazards, and periodic forced out-migration as population growth depleted local resources.

Many mountain communities became famous as providers of fiercely effective mercenaries for the national armies of lowland powers. For example, the Swiss mountain contingents contributed to many premodern European armies, a surviving remnant being the Vatican's Swiss Guard. More recently, during two world wars and the Falkland Islands campaign, the Gurkhas of Nepal won international fame. They continue to supply contingents to the Indian and British armies.

Prior to the early twentieth century, remoteness, lack of "modern" communication links, and low population densities led to mountain regions being established as buffer zones with only roughly surveyed frontiers between powerful lowland-based empires. Those imperial conflicts and compromises left many present-day states with irrational frontiers, such as that possessed by Afghanistan—a nineteenth-century product of the rivalry between the British Empire and imperial Russia. As far as the affluent West was concerned, until the last decades of the twentieth century, mountains were virtually the preserve of mountaineers and tourists, especially winter sports enthusiasts and warmer-season trekkers, and a relatively small number of scientists. The people who

lived and made their livelihood in the mountains were largely ignored.

In Europe, as nations industrialized and modernized during the nineteenth century, roads and railways were built, and the first waves of affluent tourists and mountaineers began to penetrate the Alps, bringing with them money. Today we think of Switzerland and Austria as regions of great wealth, but even now, national government policy recognizes that mountain agriculture, essential to the conservation of the beauty that makes the mountains a tourist attraction, depends upon heavy subsidy. In this sense a broad division can be made between the development of mountain regions in the industrialized countries and those of the developing world. The difference being that industrialized countries have money to help preserve the scenic nature of the mountains whereas developing countries focus on exploitation. A further subdivision must be made between mountain regions of the Old World (Europe) and those of the New World (the North American West, New Zealand, and Australia). In contrast to the European Alps, for example, that have a very long history (pre-Roman) of settlement and environmental adaptation, mountain regions of the New World have experienced colonization and development only very recently (little more than 150 years ago).

Globalization has spread mass tourism from industrial countries into selected areas of the mountain regions of developing countries. Where tourism, especially mountaineering and trekking, has selectively penetrated parts of the developing world's mountain regions, it has brought about significant change. Tourism does bring increased wealth, but very selectively, and most of the commercial profits go back to the industrialized countries investment profits. Tourism can and has caused serious disruption to local cultures. (The outstanding example is the Mount Everest region of Nepal, whose inhabitants, the Sherpas, have become relatively affluent.) By the 1970s and 1980s there was a growth in awareness of the need to preserve the Alps and to avert a perceived imminent environmental catastrophe in the Himalayas. In the Alps, uncontrolled growth of two-season tourism threatened the traditional mountain landscape. In the Himalayas, it was assumed that massive deforestation was being caused by "ignorant" mountain subsistence farmers. Their rapid population growth (Nepal, for instance, at 2.7 percent per year) and their dependency on the forests for construction materials, firewood, and fodder, led to the assumption that the perceived impending environmental collapse was due entirely to imprudent indigenous land use on the mountain slopes. Furthermore, increased numbers of landslides and acceleration of soil erosion, influenced by gravity and torrential monsoon downpours, was widely believed to cause downstream siltation and an increase in severe flooding in Gangetic India and in Bangladesh. Thus the potential for international dispute was added to the threat of environmental disaster. Regardless, prior to 1992 concern remained limited.

Why, as recently as the 1970s or even the 1980s, were mountains not afforded a more prominent place on the world's political agenda, when environmental movements had been in full swing for some time? A partial answer is that mountains had not yet attracted an effective constituency. During the 1972 U.N. Stockholm Conference on the Environment, great strides were made in recognizing the growing gap between the have and have-not regions of the world and by the establishment of ministries of the environment in numerous member countries. Yet mountains did not even merit a footnote. It was not until the 1992 United Nations Conference on Environment and Development (UNCED; the Rio de Janeiro Earth Summit) that a real breakthrough appeared possible with the inclusion of a special chapter for mountains in Agenda 21. Chapter 13 (which deals with managing fragile ecosystems and sustainable mountain development) of Agenda 21 led ten years later to designation by the U.N. General Assembly of 2002 as the "International Year of Mountains."

Problems Facing the World's Mountains

Undoubtedly, mountains are threatened by general overuse of natural resources—water, forests, grasslands, and minerals—that can lead to soil erosion, water and air pollution, and downstream damage. This is particularly severe on steep slopes (as compared with regions of gentle relief). Indiscriminate road construction on unstable slopes and erection of high dams, usually for the sole benefit of downslope communities, are aggravating factors. Unregulated mass tourism can also lead to environmental degradation, loss of biodiversity, disruption of mountain cultures, and an augmented sense of deprivation as well as actual deprivation on the part of many poor mountain people. These are the topics that hit the news headlines. But they are frequently overdramatized. Too often the causes, as outlined in the case of the Himalayas, are misunderstood, oversimplified,

or even falsified for political advantage. Regardless, mountain communities, whether in the Alps or in the Himalayas, are in economically marginal positions compared with their lowland counterparts. A large proportion of the world's poverty, especially in Asia and South America, is located in mountain regions. It is difficult to make a precise statement because demographic and related data are usually aggregated so that specific information is unobtainable.

The entire complex of mountain problems has been further exacerbated by an apparent unwillingness, until very recently (principally after the terrorist attacks of 11 September 2001), to publicize the single most devastating process that is occurring within mountains: warfare in all its forms. This includes conventional armed conflict, guerrilla insurgencies, drug wars, and terrorism. Moreover, mistreatment of mountain peoples has caused a great increase in the number of internal and international refugees. The U.N. Food and Agriculture Organization (FAO) claimed during the launch of the IYM on 11 December 2001 that of the 27 wars affecting the world, 23 were located in mountain regions. This disproportionate burden that the mountains and their people carry signals real disaster—human, economic, environmental, political—on an unprecedented scale.

In terms of overall conflict, mountain peoples, often ethnic minorities, are frequently victimized by the central governments. In northern Thailand, western China, and the Himalayan countries, they are unfairly and wrongly blamed for catastrophic environmental degradation. The real culprits are frequently large commercial interests intent on resource exploitation and central governments seeking access to resources at the expense of the local people who are often marginalized minorities with little political clout. Nevertheless, poverty often leaves the local mountain people with little alternative but to over-exploit their own environment. Regulations, such as logging bans, are imposed by the bureaucracies in the lowlands. This cannot lead to satisfactory solutions and may further exacerbate mountain poverty, thus generating further unrest.

Future Directions

The vast extent of the world's mountainous territory, together with its extreme complexity, both in terms of the inherent natural phenomena and the innumerable ways in which human communities have adapted to them, are a challenge indeed to sustainable development. Mountains as a whole are among the least known and least understood areas of the world. It was hoped that the International Year of Mountains would provide an unprecedented opportunity for expanding research and for rapid growth in communication. The first task, however, is to reduce the burden of conflict and, related to this, to facilitate involvement of mountain people in management of their local resources and in development of relations with society at large.

Jack D. Ives

Further Reading

Bowman, W. D., & Seastedt, T. R. (Eds.). (2001). *Structure and function of an Alpine ecosystem*. Oxford & New York: Oxford University Press.

Funnell, D., & Parish, R. (2001). *Mountain environments and communities*. London & New York: Routledge.

Gerrard, A. J. (1990). *Mountain environments*. Cambridge, MA & London: MIT Press.

Ives, J. D., & Messerli, B. (1989). *The Himalayan dilemma: Reconciling development and conservation*. London & New York: Routledge and United Nations University Press.

Messerli, B., & Ives, J. D. (Eds.). (1997). *Mountains of the world: A global priority*. London & New York: Parthenon.

Muir, John
(1838–1914)
U.S. naturalist

John Muir was born in Dunbar, Scotland, and moved to frontier Wisconsin with his family at the age of eleven. His father, Daniel Muir, was a fervent Christian whose preaching and Bible study left little time for farming, which fell to his children. Daniel Muir also forbade his children frivolous pastimes and books. A talented inventor, John Muir hand-built many instruments, including a thermometer, clocks, and an "early-rising" bed that tumbled its occupant to the floor. In 1860 Muir exhibited his inventions at the state fair and gained entry into the University of Wisconsin, whose faculty introduced him to botany, geology, journal writing (which Muir mined for publication throughout his life), as well as Unitarian Christianity and Transcendentalism. A faculty wife, Jeanne Carr, became a longtime friend and mentor. A new world opened to him.

In 1864, Muir traveled and botanized in Canada. He returned to the United States and in 1866 became a factory manager in Indianapolis. An industrial accident caused temporary blindness, sending Muir into deep depression and soul-searching. He resolved to spend his life not in dark factories among the inventions of man, but in nature amidst the ongoing creation of God. During a walk to the Gulf of Mexico he contemplated nature's relationship with humanity, concluding that nature was not made for man but had value in itself. He continued on to California and lived much of the next decade in the Sierras, studying their flora and geology. He published scientific articles establishing the glacial origins of Yosemite Valley and found a wide audience for his writings about his adventures and the value of wild things. In 1879 he married, and in the next decade ran a fruit farm, raised two daughters, and wrote nothing.

Muir began writing again to advocate a national park to protect the damaged, exploited Yosemite area, leading to creation of Yosemite National Park in 1890, the nation's second national park after Yellowstone; he would be largely responsible for the establishment of four other national parks. Later, he camped with President Theodore Roosevelt and guided President William Howard Taft in Yosemite. To defend the park against special interests, Muir founded the Sierra Club in 1892. Books like *Our National Parks* (1901) promoted a transcendentalist idea of national parks as places of wild and inspirational beauty. A battle to build a reservoir in Hetch Hetchy, a beautiful but little-known valley in Yosemite Park, marred Muir's last years. Bitter debate ended in 1913 when Congress approved it. Muir died a year later. He left a legacy of love of wilderness, inspirational writings, and a national park system. Earth Day occurs on his birthday, 22 April. For many environmentalists and nature lovers, John Muir is the American patron saint of wilderness.

Mark Stoll

Further Reading

Cohen, M. (1984). *The pathless way: John Muir and the American wilderness*. Madison: University of Wisconsin Press.

Selections from John Muir's *My First Summer in the Sierra* (1869)

June 18

Another inspiring morning, nothing better in any world can be conceived. No description of Heaven that I have ever heard or read of seems half so fine. At noon the clouds occupied about .05 of the sky, white filmy touches drawn delicately on the azure.

The high ridges and hilltops beyond the woolly locusts are now gay with monardella, clarkia, coreopsis, and tall tufted grasses, some of them tall enough to wave like pines. The lupines, of which there are many ill-defined species, are now mostly out of flower, and many of the compositæ are beginning to fade, their radiant corollas vanishing in fluffy pappus like stars in mist.

We had another visitor from Brown's Flat to-day, an old Indian woman with a basket on her back. Like our first caller from the village, she got fairly into camp and was standing in plain view when discovered. How long she had been quietly looking on, I cannot say. Even the dogs failed to notice her stealthy approach. She was on her way, I suppose, to some wild garden, probably for lupine and starchy saxifrage leaves and rootstocks. Her dress was calico rags, far from clean. In every way she seemed sadly unlike Nature's neat well-dressed animals, though living like them on the bounty of the wilderness. Strange that mankind alone is dirty. Had she been clad in fur, or cloth woven of grass or shreddy bark, like the juniper and libocedrus mats, rightful part of the wilderness; like a good wolf at least, or bear. But from no point of view that I have found are such debased fellow beings a whit more natural than the glaring tailored tourists we saw that frightened the birds and squirrels.

July 5

The clouds of noon on the high Sierra seem yet more marvelously, indescribably beautiful from day to day as one becomes more wakeful to see them. The smoke of the gunpowder burned yesterday on the lowlands, and the eloquence of the orators has probably settled or been blown away by this time. Here every day is a holiday, a jubilee ever sounding with serene enthusiasm, without wear or waste or cloying weariness. Everything rejoicing. Not a single cell or crystal unvisited or forgotten.

September 7

About sundown saw a flock of dun grayish sparrows going to roost in crevices of a crag above the big snow-field. Charming little mountaineers! Found a species of sedge in flower within eight or ten feet of a snow-bank. Judging by the looks of the ground, it can hardly have been out in the sunshine much longer than a week, and it is likely to be buried again in fresh snow in a month or so, thus making a winter about ten months long, while spring, summer, and autumn are crowded and hurried into two months. How delightful it is to be alone here! How wild everything is,—wild as the sky and as pure! Never shall I forget this big, divine day,—the Cathedral and its thousands of cassiope bells, and the landscapes around them, and this camp

Source: Muir, John. (1911). *My First Summer in the Sierra.* Boston and New York: Houghton Mifflin, pp. 77–79; 100–101; 338.

Muir, J. (1901). *Our national parks.* Boston: Houghton Mifflin.

Muir, J. (1911). *My first summer in the Sierra.* Boston: Houghton Mifflin.

Wolfe, L. M. (1945). *Son of the wilderness: The life of John Muir.* New York: A. A. Knopf.

Murray River

The Murray River is Australia's second-longest river (2,530 kilometers). Together with the Darling (2,740 kilometers) and Murrumbidgee (1,690 kilometers) Rivers, the Murray comprises the Murray-Darling Basin. The

Murray-Darling Basin covers 1,061,469 square kilometers, equivalent to 14 percent of Australia's total area. The basin extends over the states of New South Wales, Victoria, Queensland, South Australia, and the Australian Capital Territory. The basin accounts for over 40 percent of Australia's gross value of agricultural production. Approximately 70 percent of all water used for agriculture in Australia is used by irrigation in the basin.

The Murray River is of immense cultural, economic, and environmental significance. Gravesites at Roonka and Big Bend demonstrate that aboriginal communities lived there continuously for at least thirty-five thousand years. The river was discovered by explorers Hamilton Hume and William Hovell in 1824. Originally named the Hume River, in 1830 Captain Charles Sturt renamed it the Murray after Sir George Murray, British secretary of state for the colonies. The publication in London in 1833 of Sturt's account of his river explorations indirectly led to the establishment of the colony of South Australia.

In 1852 the first paddle-steamer boat from South Australia, traveling up the Murray from Goolwa, a port town at the mouth of the Murray, reached Echuca in Victoria. Such was the economic importance of the Murray that in 1863 a conference was held between New South Wales, Victoria, and South Australia regarding improving the navigability of the river. Despite further meetings and the development of irrigation schemes from the 1880s on, it was not until the severe drought of 1895–1902 and the creation of the Commonwealth of Australia in 1901 that the colonies/states were able to reach limited consensus on river regulation.

The River Murray Waters Agreement, providing for the construction of water storage, weirs, and locks and agreed shares of water usage, was signed in 1915 by the governments of Australia, New South Wales, Victoria, and South Australia. In 1917 the River Murray Commission was established to implement the agreement. The powers of the commission were primarily concerned with water quantity. However, by the late 1960s its powers spread to quality issues as a result of increased water salinity.

Amendments were made to the agreement in 1982 and 1984 to take account of environmental issues. However, these amendments were unsatisfactory as resource management problems, including salinity and species and wetland loss, continued to worsen. As a result, new institutional arrangements were agreed to by the Commonwealth and the three states in 1987, and in 1992 the Murray-Darling Basin Agreement replaced the previous River Murray Waters Agreement. Queensland becoming a signatory in 1996.

The agreement provides for the establishment of a commission, a ministerial council, and a community advisory committee to coordinate the equitable, efficient, and sustainable use of the water, land, and other environmental resources of the Murray-Darling Basin. According to the commission, the public-private initiative is the largest integrated catchment (drainage basin) management program in the world. But despite the initiative, the Murray's environmental problems continue to worsen as water usage outstrips availability, and, as during the drought year of 1982, it seems likely that in the future the Murray will fail to reach the sea.

C. Michael Hall

Further Reading

Eastburn, D. (1990). *The River Murray history at a glance*. Canberra, Australia: Murray-Darling Basin Commission.

Murray-Darling Basin Commission. Retrieved October 25, 2002, from http://www.mdbc.gov.au/

Powell, J. M. (1993). *The emergence of bioregionalism in the Murray-Darling Basin*. Canberra, Australia: Murray-Darling Basin Commission.

Senate Standing Committee on Science and the Environment. (1979). *Continuing scrutiny of pollution: The River Murray* (Parliamentary Paper No. 117/79). Canberra, Australia: Government Printer.

Sinclair, P. (2001). *The Murray: A river and its people*. Carlton, Australia: Melbourne University Press.

N

Narmada Dam Project

The Narmada dam project is an ambitious river valley irrigation and hydroelectric project under construction on the Narmada River in western India. The Narmada, considered by many to be one of India's holiest rivers, is India's fifth longest river and most important west-flowing river. Ninety percent of the river and its drainage area is in the state of Madhya Pradesh, and the rest is in Maharashtra and Gujarat. The river begins in central India in the Maikala ranges in Madhya Pradesh before flowing 1,312 kilometers to drain into the Arabian Sea near Bharuch, Gujarat. Along the way, the river passes through vast fertile plains and hilly tracts that have sustained many groups for centuries.

Plans to dam the Narmada go back to the late nineteenth century, but several controversies and interstate conflicts prevented the project from being realized. Several commissions, including the Khosla Committee of 1965 and the Narmada Waters Dispute Tribunal of 1967, were appointed to resolve questions concerning the height of the dam, the extent of submergence, and the sharing of costs and benefits among the riparian states. Finally, in the 1980s the Narmada Valley Development Plan was formulated. It includes 2 megadams, the Narmada Sagar Project (NSP) and the Sardar Sarovar Project (SSP), 30 large dams, 135 medium dams, and over 3,000 small reservoirs and dams. All these projects, if realized, will most certainly transform the river and its surrounding areas.

The SSP, one of the world's most controversial dams, is under construction in Gujarat. According to project plans, it will generate 1,450 megawatts of power, irrigate 1.8 million hectares of land, and pro-
vide drinking water to 40 million people. Critics maintain that the benefits are exaggerated and that the dam will submerge 37,000 hectares of forest and prime agricultural land as well as harm the homes, lands, and livelihoods of 1 million people. At least 250,000 people will be directly affected and lose their homes due to submergence. The rest will be indirectly affected by canal construction and downstream impacts of the dam.

The World Bank withdrew its funding from the project in 1993 due to national and international criticism. Crucial also was the report of the first World Bank–appointed independent review team. The team, led by the late Bradford Morse, former head of the United Nations Development Programme, concluded that the project was badly flawed on both social and environmental grounds and advised the bank to withdraw its funding. The Indian Supreme Court also passed a stay order on the dam's construction for six years. In 2000 a controversial Supreme Court judgment allowed the dam's construction to go ahead. In late 2002 thousands of farmers in Madhya Pradesh faced the threat of submergence of their homes and lands without receiving adequate compensation in land.

In recent years attention has also focused on the Maheshwar dam in Madhya Pradesh, one of the thirty large dams on the Narmada and India's first privately financed hydroelectric project. If the dam is built, about forty thousand farmers, fisherfolk, and sand quarry workers would lose their homes, lands, or livelihoods. Many people affected by the project have questioned the financial viability of a privately financed hydroelectric plant and the ability of implementing agencies to fulfill the land for land compensation measures. Protests and financial problems encountered by the private company, S Kumars, have led to time and cost overruns, and at the time of writing, the dam's construction had stopped.

The Narmada River valley is known as a site of resistance because of the protest activities of the Narmada Bachao Andolan (Save the Narmada Movement), a coalition of project-affected people, urban activists, and supporters. This coalition has attracted significant international attention and media interest. Since the late 1980s its members have faced arrests and beatings, staged hunger strikes, and even refused to vacate the submerging zone, facing the rising waters created by the dams because they believe the dams are an infringement of their rights and livelihoods. In contrast, some civil society members, academics, and government officials believe that the project is the solution to Gujarat's water problems and Madhya Pradesh's power shortages. Thus the controversies surrounding the Narmada dam project raise issues concerning the financial, environmental, and social viability of large dams. Within India, the controversies have sparked debates concerning "development" models entailing high social costs that, may outweigh the predicted benefits, which are widely contested and may disproportionately benefit more elite groups. At the global level, the antidam movement (along with the World Bank and the International Conservation Union) played a key role in the formation of the World Commission on Dams. In 2000 this commission presented a framework for options assessment and decision-making processes in energy services and water resources development.

Lyla Mehta

Further Reading

Bissell, R., Singh, S., & Warth, H. (2000). *Maheshwar hydroelectric project: Resettlement and rehabilitation.* Report prepared for the German Ministry of Economic Cooperation and Development.

Dreze, J., Meera, S., & Satyajit, S. (Eds.). (1997). *The dam and the nation: Displacement and resettlement in the Narmada Valley.* Delhi, India: Oxford University Press.

Fischer, W. (Ed.). (1995). *Towards sustainable development: Struggling over India's Narmada River.* Armonk, NY: M. E. Sharpe.

Friends of the River Narmada. (2003). Retrieved March 3, 2003, from http://www.narmada.org

Mehta, L. (2001, December). The manufacture of popular perceptions of scarcity in Gujarat, India: Dams and water-related narratives in Gujarat, India. *World Development*, 29(12), 2025–2041.

Morse, B., Berger, T., Gamble, D., Brody, H., & Sarovar, S. (1992). *Report of the independent team.* Ottawa, Canada: Resource Futures International.

World Commission on Dams. (2000). *Dams and development: A new framework for decision-making.* London: Earthscan.

National Park Service

The National Park Service manages the 367 national parks, monuments, and historic sites in the United States. Congress established the National Park Service in 1916 as a bureau within the Department of the Interior. The park service took shape under Stephen T. Mather, its first director, and Horace M. Albright, who was Mather's assistant and then the second director. The two defined the philosophy and authority structure that characterized the service into the twenty-first century. That philosophy is best expressed by one of the service's first publications, *National Parks Portfolio*, written by Robert Sterling Yard and published in 1917. Yard described Yellowstone National Park in Wyoming, Montana, and Idaho as having "great hotels and . . . two hundred miles of excellent roads." Yard said of Yellowstone that it is "the fitting playground and pleasure resort of a great people; it is also the ideal summer school of nature study" (Yard 1917, 3–21).

The mission of the service has been the education and recreation of the public, with an institutional emphasis on natural resource management, landscape architecture, and engineering (for roads and campgrounds). The service has sought to create gentle and majestic settings for the enjoyment of tourists.

The service expanded along with the national park system. During the Great Depression of the 1930s the service absorbed a number of monuments and historic sites that had remained outside of the system. Parks added during the New Deal included Kings Canyon in California, Olympic in Washington, and Everglades in Florida. During World War II the service fought developers to uphold the sovereignty of the parks. One developer sought rights to harvest sitka spruce within Olympic National Park by claiming that the wood was of aeronautical grade and thus necessary for winning the war.

The number of annual visitors to the service's parks steadily increased through the 1940s. In 1954, 47.8 million visitors entered the parks—more than double the number in 1941—in part because a new interstate highway system and the proliferation of automobiles made it easier for urban and suburban residents to visit. Needing more services, employees, and roads to accommodate vacationers, the service proposed Mission 66—a program of facilities construction and promotion intended to bring the parks into the automotive era.

But more than tourist access concerned the service in the 1960s. A report, "Wildlife Management in the National Parks," issued by a committee headed by Starker Leopold of the University of California in 1963, questioned the service's policy toward animal habitat. The committee recognized the parks as dynamic ecosystems yet recommended that habitat be maintained "as nearly as possible, in the condition that prevailed when the area was first visited by the white man" (Runte 1979, 198–199, 205). The debate over fire ecology is an example of how the service struggled to function within that contradiction. A series of articles published in the 1960s warned that massive forest debris, accumulated over a half-century of official fire suppression, would fuel fires so large that they engulf the crown or canopies of forest trees, as opposed to fires that remain on the forest floor that never destroy large trees. The giant sequoia groves in California were particularly threatened. The trees required small fires, which did no damage, every so often in order to reproduce, but great fires would consume them. Responding in 1967 to this new research, the service proclaimed that fire resulting from natural causes would be tolerated as part of wilderness environments.

The new ecological perspective was tested in the summer of 1988 when fire burned thousands of acres in Yellowstone National Park. Seven years later, in March of 1995, the service took the lead in returning gray wolves to Yellowstone, nearly a century after their eradication under a policy of predator control. In between these two events came the "Vail Agenda," a self-critical report published in 1991 that redirected the park service toward ecological management. The greatest challenge of the service in the coming years will be to accommodate 300 million annual visitors and their automobiles. The service is searching for ways to virtually eliminate automobiles from Yosemite (California) and the Grand Canyon (Arizona) without compromising the easy access and comfortable accommodations that the public has come to expect of the national parks.

Steven Stoll

Further Reading

Albright, H. M. (1985). *The birth of the National Park Service: The founding years, 1913–33.* Salt Lake City, UT: How Brothers.

Runte, A. (1979). *National parks: The American experience.* Lincoln: University of Nebraska Press.

Sellers, R. W. (1997). *Preserving nature in the national parks.* New Haven, CT: Yale University Press.

Yard, R. S. (1917). *National parks portfolio.* Washington, DC: U.S. Department of the Interior.

National Wildlife Federation

The National Wildlife Federation (NWF) was founded in 1935 by Jay Darling, a former member of the Izaak Walton League conservation group. The NWF began as a conservative hunting- and recreation-based organization. Although Darling hoped to unite hunting interests and wildlife management in a single organization, the NWF immediately experienced controversy between sportsmen and the more strident advocates of wildlife protection. The NWF sided with sportsmen, even limiting the voting rights of "individuals and nonhunter groups" within the organization (Gottlieb 1993, 157). Initially tied to corporations in the sportsman industry such as DuPont, Hercules Powder Company, and Remington Arms Company, the NWF has retained a corporate atmosphere throughout its existence. By the 1970s it had become one of the largest and most highly professionalized environmental organizations in the country.

More focused on service than on activism, the NWF was a latecomer to many of the environmental issues of the 1960s. The NWF was initially opposed to the Wilderness Act of 1964 because it did not protect the rights of hunters in designated wilderness areas. Only after the NWF's second executive director, Ernest Swift, convinced the Wilderness Society president Howard Zahniser to guarantee hunting rights in protected areas did the NWF agree to support the act. The controversy over Grand Canyon dams such as those in Echo Park, Utah, and Glen Canyon, Arizona, was even more indicative of the federation's conservatism. The Arizona and Utah state chapters of the NWF initially supported the U.S. Bureau of Reclamation's plans in the Colorado River watershed, arguing that the reservoirs created by the dams would provide additional opportunities for sportsmen. The issue, seen differently from local and national perspectives, threatened to split the NWF. Only after a bitter debate at the NWF's national meeting did the organization officially oppose Colorado River dams.

In the 1960s the NWF maintained its corporate ties under the leadership of its executive director Thomas Kimball. The organization favored working within the political and corporate channels of power instead of taking adversarial stands. Although Kimball wanted to broaden the scope of the NWF, he still described the majority of environmentalists as "extremists and kooks" (Gottlieb 1993, 158). As a result, the NWF maintained its ties to industry and began to cultivate new connections with the energy industry as well as policymakers in Washington.

In the 1980s the NWF took this position one step further. Accepting overtures from President Ronald Reagan's administration (which had been heavily criticized by environmental groups), the NWF maintained a direct link with the White House. Yet, the newest NWF director, Jay Hair, represented a break from what he considered the NWF's "good-old-boy hunting club approach" (Gottlieb 1993, 158). Hair criticized the administration and was one of many who called for the resignation of Reagan's secretary of the interior, James Watt. Hair tried to forge a moderate position by establishing the Corporate Conservation Council, an institutional bridge between environmentalists and industry, made up of NWF executives and representatives from the oil and chemical industries.

The NWF's embrace of corporate and Washington-based power demonstrates the split between grassroots environmental activism and the highly professionalized environmental organizations. The NWF represents an older conservationist impulse in the environmental movement, criticized not only for its six-figure CEO salaries, but also for its narrow focus on wilderness at the expense of social justice concerns such as environmental racism and the link between environmental degradation and poverty.

Ryan J. Carey

Further Reading

Allen, T. B. (1987). *Guardian of the wild: The story of the National Wildlife Federation*. Bloomington: Indiana University Press.

Gottlieb, R. (1993). *Forcing the spring: The transformation of the American environmental movement*. Washington, DC: Island Press.

Hays, S. P. (1987). *Beauty, health, and permanence: Environmental politics in the U.S., 1955–1985*. New York: Cambridge University Press.

Scheffer, V. B. (1991). *The shaping of environmentalism in America*. Seattle: University of Washington Press.

Shabecoff, P. (1993). *A fierce green fire: The American environmental movement*. New York: Hill and Wang.

Natural Gas

This fossil fuel now supplies about a quarter of the world's primary energy, the category that includes all fossil and biomass fuels as well as hydro, nuclear, solar, and geothermal electricity. Its importance will rise in the future because of its abundance and relatively clean combustion.

Much like crude oil, natural gas was known for millennia from "burning pillars" encountered by travellers in the Middle East. The only instance of the fuel's use in antiquity was the remarkable practice of burning it in order to evaporate brines in China's landlocked Sichuan province. This usage dates to at least the beginning of the Han dynasty (200 BCE) and it was made possible by the Chinese invention of percussion drilling, whereby heavy iron bits attached to long bamboo cables from bamboo derricks were raised rhythmically by men jumping on a lever. Boreholes were only 10–30 meters deep during the Han dynasty, but they reached 150 meters by the tenth century, and culminated in the one-kilometer-deep Xinhai well completed in 1835. Natural gas was distributed by bamboo pipelines, and the evaporation of brines took place in huge cast iron pans. Some of the piped gas was also used for lighting and cooking.

Rising Importance of Natural Gas

For decades after the beginning of modern oil production most of the natural gas that is commonly associated with crude oil deposits was flared (burned) on site because without compressors and steel pipes it could not be moved over longer distances. Only the availability of large-diameter pipelines and turbine-driven compressors, and the growing demand for clean household and industrial fuel and for convenient petrochemical feedstocks, led to increased natural gas extraction. The United States pioneered the shift before World War II but the dense North American network of natural gas pipelines was built only after 1945 as new gas resources were tapped in states ranging from Pennsylvania to Wyoming and from Alaska to the Gulf of Mexico.

Beginning in the early nineteenth century many European countries produced relatively large volumes of town gas by gasification of coal whereby the fuel, heated to high temperatures in the absence of air, releases a mixture of hydrogen, carbon monoxide, methane and ethylene. A virtually continent-wide shift toward natural gas (mostly just methane) began only during the 1960s. The greatest milestones in this European transition were the discovery (in 1959) and the development of the giant Dutch gas field in Groningen, deliveries of Russian gas from giant fields in western Siberia (which began in 1978 via the world's longest gas pipeline), emergence of the North Sea as a major natural gas province, and the completion of the first gas pipeline connecting Africa and Italy (Transmed from Algeria via Tunisia to Sicily in 1975). Exploitation of huge Siberian and Central Asian fields also boosted Russia's domestic natural gas consumption. The rising demand for energy in the Middle East led to greatly reduced flaring of the gas in the region, and to its use in water desalination, chemical syntheses, and steelmaking.

As a result, the share of natural gas in the world's total primary energy supply rose from about 10 percent in 1950 to 25 percent by the year 2000 when more than 2.3 trillion cubic meters were extracted. U.S. and Russian shares of this total were, respectively, 25 percent and 53 percent and even Japan, where all natural gas is imported in expensive liquefied form from Brunei and from the Middle East, got nearly 15 percent of its primary energy from this fuel. The two main reasons that explain this growing worldwide importance of natural gas are the relative abundance of the fuel and its clean combustion. The world's known reserves of conventional natural gas (the fuel that escaped from its parental rocks and accumulated in nonpermeable reservoirs, either associated with oil or alone) nearly tripled between 1975 and 2000, and in spite of the doubled extraction since 1970 the global reserve/production ratio is now above sixty years, compared to just over forty years in the early 1970s. Principal concentrations of gas reserves are in Russia (about one-third of the total), Iran (about 15 percent), Qatar (over 7 percent), and Saudi Arabia and United Arab Emirates (4 percent each).

The best available global assessment puts the world's known reserves of natural gas at nearly 150

Natural gas and water conduit covers in a Boston sidewalk, 1993. COURTESY CATHLEEN FRACASSE.

trillion cubic meters in the year 2000 but the most likely total of recoverable resources is nearly three times as large and in addition there are enormous deposits of nonconventional natural gas. This category includes methane in coalbeds, and much larger deposits in tight reservoirs, high-pressure aquifers, and in methane hydrates. Global resources of geopressured gas were estimated to be about 110 times the current proven reserves of the fuel, and methane hydrates (CH_4 trapped inside rigid lattice cages formed by frozen water molecules) in all coastal U.S. waters may contain as much as 1,000 times the volume of the U.S. conventional gas reserves. Eventual recovery of even a tiny share of these deposits would multiply the global gas supply.

Environmental Advantages

No fossil fuel is more environmentally friendly than natural gas, which is extracted either as a virtually pure methane (CH_4), or as a mixture of methane, ethane, and propane with the merest trace of sulfur (mostly as H_2S) that can be easily removed before the fuel is put into pipelines. Low energy density of the fuel—typically around 34 megajoules per cubic meter compared to 34 gigajoules per cubic meter for oil, or a thousandfold difference—obviously limits its use as a transportation fuel, but its stationary combustion produces no sulfur gases, and it proceeds with higher efficiency (up to 97 percent in the best gas furnaces) and emits less CO_2 per unit of energy than is the case with any other fuel. Typical carbon emission ratios per gigajoule are about 25 kilograms for bituminous coal, 19 kilograms for refined fuels, and less than 14 kilograms for natural gas. At the same time, methane is itself a greenhouse gas. Though the losses from pipelines should not exceed more than 1–2 percent of the carried gas, pipelines in the former USSR leak 6–9 percent of total extraction.

Low air pollution emissions are the main reason why natural gas is increasingly preferred not only for household and industrial uses but also for electricity generation using stationary gas turbines. Combined-cycle plants that use waste heat to produce more electricity, and whose overall conversion efficiency is well above 50 percent, will be increasingly common as will be the use of natural gas to generate electricity indirectly via fuel cells. This conversion should also eventually make the gas an important automotive fuel. Modular phosphoric acid fuel cells are already used for small-scale electricity generation and in experimental vehicles. Another option is to use methane to produce methanol (CH_3OH), a liquid at ambient temperature that can be stored and handled much like gasoline but is much less flammable. Finally, methane is also the most important feedstock, as well as energy source, for the synthesis of ammonia from its elements as well as for the production of many plastics.

Vaclav Smil

See also Fertilizers; Haber, Fritz

Further Reading

British Petroleum. (2002). *BP statistical review of world energy*. Retrieved August 20, 2001, from http://www.bp.com/worldenergy

Energy Information Administration. (2001). *U.S. natural gas markets: Recent trends and prospects for the future*. Retrieved December 18, 2002, from http://tonto.eia.doe.gov/FTPROOT/service/oiaf0102.pdf

Kleinberg, R. L., & Brewer, P. G. (2001). Probing gas hydrate deposits. *American Scientist*, 89, 244–251.

Laherrère, J. H. (2000). *Global natural gas perspectives*. Retrieved December 18, 2002, from http://www.hubbertpeak.com/laherrere/ngperspective/

Lowrie, A., & Max, M. D. (1999). The extraordinary promise and challenge of gas hydrates. *World Oil*, 220(9), 49–55.

Odell, P. R. (1999). *Fossil fuel resources in the 21st century*. London: Financial Times Energy.

Rogner, H-H. (2000). Energy resources. In J. Goldemberg (Ed.), *World energy assessment* (pp. 135–171). New York: United Nations Development Programme.

Smil, V. (1994). *Energy in world history*. Boulder, CO: Westview.

Smil, V. (2003). *Energy at the crossroads*. Cambridge, MA: The MIT Press.

Vogel, H. U. (1993). The great well of China. *Scientific American*, 268(6), 116–121.

Natural Resources Defense Council

The Natural Resources Defense Council (NRDC) was founded in 1970 by a group of activist lawyers from Yale Law School's class of 1969 and a handful of Republican attorneys from the Wall Street law firm of Simpson, Thatcher, and Bartlett. Both groups began discussions with the Ford Foundation about the possibility of inaugurating, in the words of one of the Yale graduates, "an NAACP Legal defense fund for the environment" (Shabecoff 1993, 117). The Ford Foundation agreed to fund the venture, provided that the two groups worked together. Part of a shift toward professionalization in the environmental movement, the NRDC, according to environmental historian Robert Gottlieb, created a niche within the movement as the organization "most identified with the technical expertise needed to draft legislation, issue reports, and use litigation as a tool in the policy process" (Gottlieb 1993, 143).

The NRDC's original agenda was eclectic, according to one of its founders, John Adams, formerly with the U.S. District Attorney's office in New York. Yet, the NRDC's creation coincided with the congressional debates on sweeping environmental legislation, and its focus quickly coalesced around those debates. The NRDC immediately became part of a larger coalition that lobbied for the passage of the Clean Water Act and became integral in implementation of the Clean Air Act. The NRDC provided technical assistance in these efforts and employed a large number of scientists in addition to the lawyers already on staff. For example, through the work of Richard Ayres, the group's expert on air pollution, the NRDC filed thirty-five of the first forty Clean Air Act–related lawsuits.

The professionalization of the environmental movement, represented by organizations such as the NRDC, also signaled a shift from traditional issues of conservation toward a vision of the environment that encompassed more than just so-called wilderness spaces. Gus Speth, one of the founders from Yale, wrote that "unregulated discharge pipes, fish kills, urban air pollution, all kinds of industrial pollution—those were the issues that originally turned my head" (Shabecoff 1993, 117). The NRDC increasingly became known for its advocacy for the urban environment, an advocacy that positioned it well for the debates over environmental racism that would occur in the early 1990s.

The NRDC became one of the leaders in the fight over environmental problems associated with industrialization. Its criticism centered squarely on corporations. In 1987 the NRDC successfully prosecuted a suit against Bethlehem Steel using the Clean Water Act. The federal government forced the steel giant to pay out over $1.5 million in penalties for water pollution—including $200,000 to the Trust for Public Lands, $100,000 to the National Fish and Wildlife Federation, and $50,000 to Save Our Streams. Monetary penalties at the corporate level, however, were often passed on to the workers, and the success of the NRDC has helped reinforce a growing separation between laborers and environmentalists.

Since its founding, the NRDC has become one of the largest and most powerful environmental organizations in America. Part of the "Group of Ten" (ten influential environmental advocacy groups that have worked together since the early 1970s), the NRDC currently boasts over 500,000 members and a budget in excess of $40 million.

Ryan J. Carey

Further Reading

Gottlieb, R. (1993). *Forcing the spring: The transformation of the American environmental movement.* Washington, DC: Island Press.

Hays, S. P. (1987). *Beauty, health, and permanence: Environmental politics in the U.S., 1955–1985.* New York: Cambridge University Press.

Rothman, H. K. (1998). *The greening of a nation?: Environmentalism in the United States since 1945.* Fort Worth, TX: Harcourt Brace College Publishers.

Scheffer, V. B. (1991). *The shaping of environmentalism in America.* Seattle: University of Washington Press.

Shabecoff, P. (1993). *A fierce green fire: The American environmental movement.* New York: Hill and Wang.

Nature

Aldo Leopold (1887–1948), the U.S. environmentalist, wildlife manager, and nature writer, acquired in 1935 an abandoned farm on the banks of the Wisconsin River. In *Sand County Almanac* he tells the story of a spring flood that marooned his land. Along with a lovely description of the enthusiastic responses of geese and carp to high water, he recounts his own human attraction to the flood: "The spring flood brings us more than high adventure; it brings likewise an unpredictable miscellany of floatable objects pilfered from upriver farms. An old board stranded on our meadow has, to us, twice the value of the same piece new from the lumberyard." For carp and geese, the flood opens a "new and watery world." Likewise, the flood expands Leopold's understanding of the place in which he lives: "Our lumber pile, recruited entirely from the river, is . . . an anthology of human strivings in upriver farms and forests. The autobiography of an old board is a kind of literature not yet taught on campuses, but any riverbank farm is a library where he who hammers or saws may read at will. Come high water, there is always an accession of new books" (Leopold 1949, 24–25).

Leopold's essay relies on a vernacular understanding of nature as what people experience outside themselves—seasonal rotation, physical terrain, the sensory world of rushing water, wild bird calls, flashing fish, and an attendant element of unpredictability, surprise, and mystery. Humans are embedded in this natural world—Leopold finds himself filled with "inner glee" that the flood strands him on the farm, providing the opportunity to share in the enthusiasm of geese and carp for the moment (Leopold 1949, 25). But people are also set apart from that nonhuman world by their striving—their efforts to control and remake nature. And people are removed by another kind of striving— the urge to understand nature and themselves that

Untitled Poem on Nature by Emily Dickinson (c. 1863)

"Nature" is what we see—

The Hill—the Afternoon—

Squirrel—Eclipse—the Bumble bee—

Nay—Nature is Heaven—

Nature is what we hear—

The Bobolink—the Sea—

Thunder—the Cricket—

Nay—Nature is Harmony—

Nature is what we know—

Yet have no art to say—

So impotent Our Wisdom is

To her Simplicity.

Source: *The Complete Poems of Emily Dickinson*. Retrieved March 10, 2003, from http://www.incipitario.com/incipitdidz.html

yields books, libraries, and universities such as the one where Leopold taught wildlife management.

"Nature" enjoys a history of more than two thousand years in Western thought. In twentieth-century scholarship it is common to use such long history to call attention to the necessary ambiguities, paradoxes, and dangers of the word. Until the rise of environmental history in the last half of the twentieth century, most examinations of the concept of nature by historians focused on its place in the history of ideas—in religious cosmologies, creation stories, as a benchmark in periodizing human history. Thus R. G. Collingwood's *The Idea of Nature* embeds nature within the history of scientific discovery, asserting "that no one can answer the question what nature is unless he knows what history is" (Collingwood 1945, 177).

Although the emphasis on "nature" as an abstract concept like "truth" or "virtue" is useful to environmental history, the field also takes a more materialist approach. One of the most influential American environmental historians, Donald Worster, in *The Wealth of Nature*, suggests that the eighteenth-century English tradition of natural history—in which "antiquities and natural curiosities lay jumbled together in the same country cupboard" (Worster 1993, 31)—was lost in the late nineteenth and twentieth centuries with increasing fragmentation of specialized knowledge. History moved to archival research in urban institutions, and science took over consideration of the nonhuman world: "There is little history in the study of nature, and there is little nature in the study of history" (Worster 1993, 30). Aldo Leopold's confidence in the fundamental reality of the world out there and his sense that the entangled history of humans and the rest of the natural world is best understood by "reading" the sandbar-abraded pieces of barn that periodically wash up in his meadow lyrically call attention to environmental history's interest in nature conceived as itself contingent in time and space and as a material force in human history.

The Birth of Nature

All human societies rely on the nonhuman world of sun and ocean and weather and plants (nutritious and weedy) and insects (beneficial and harmful) for their sustenance, and all human cultures have vibrant creation stories offering categorizing systems for, and ethical concepts about, their place and role in the biophysical environment. But it has been Western culture that regards the complex multitude of universal laws, physical matter, and blooming, buzzing life and attempts to express it as a singular entity—nature. Scholars of the history of conceptions of nature most often point to China, Japan, and other Asian cultures to make the contrast clear. Ole Bruun and Arne Kalland's essay collection, *Asian Perceptions of Nature*, finds that none of these cultures has a singular term encapsulating all of

Poets, Philosophers, and Others on Nature

One touch of nature makes the whole world kin. (William Shakespeare)

If you violate [Nature's] laws you are your own prosecuting attorney, judge, jury, and hangman. (Luther Burbank)

The universe is not required to be in perfect harmony with human ambition. (Carl Sagan)

God never made his work for man to mend. (John Dryden)

Nature always strikes back. It takes all the running we can do to remain in the same place. (Rene Dubos)

The world is mud-luscious and puddle-wonderful. (e.e. cummings)

Nature, to be commanded, must be obeyed. (Francis Bacon)

If one way be better than another, that you may be sure is Nature's way. (Aristotle)

Look deep into nature, and then you will understand everything better. (Albert Einstein)

Let us permit nature to have her way. She understands her business better than we do. (Michel de Montaigne)

It appears to be a law that you cannot have a deep sympathy with both man and nature. (Henry David Thoreau)

I love to think of nature as an unlimited broadcasting station, through which God speaks to us every hour, if we will only tune in. (George Washington Carver)

Humankind has not woven the web of life. We are but one thread within it. Whatever we do to the web, we do to ourselves. All things are bound together. All things connect. (Chief Seattle)

When one tugs at a single thing in nature, he finds it attached to the rest of the world. (John Muir)

The poetry of the earth is never dead. (John Keats)

There is a pleasure in the pathless woods,
There is a rapture on the lonely shore,
There is society, where none intrudes,
By the deep sea, and music in its roar:
I love not man the less, but Nature more.
(Lord Byron)

Any man that walks the mead
In bud, or blade, or bloom, may find
A meaning suited to his mind.
(Alfred Tennyson)

Adopt the pace of nature: her secret is patience. (Ralph Waldo Emerson) nature. For example, when Klas Sandell asked Sri Lankan villagers if they had one word "which means things such as forests, wild animals, trees, birds, grass and flowers," responses varied, including "thick jungle," "all sentient beings," and "sanctuary" (Bruun & Kalland 1995, 153). And Kalland and S. N. Eisenstadt add that among the Japanese, "reality is structured in shifting contexts and even in discrete ontological entities, as opposed to the absolutist Western approach" (Bruun & Kalland 1995, 11).

The literature on the etymology (history of a linguistic form) of nature, so ancient and so central to Western thought, is enormous and complicated. Arthur O. Lovejoy's classic study of nature in Greek and Roman history, *A Documentary History of Primitivism*, outlines the birth of the idea. *Natura* meant "genesis, birth, origin." The Greek poet Homer (c. 700 BCE), rendering a physical description of an herb, provides as well its character, its "nature." To the Greek dramatist Aeschylus (524–456 BCE), nature referred to visible characteristics that are assumed to be innate. The contrast between reality (nature) and appearance occurred as well, as with the pre-Socratic philosophers' distinction between the appearance of a couch and its true nature—the wood from which it is constructed. During this period nature also came to mean the cosmic system as a whole and the laws of that system.

With philosophers like the Greek Euripides (480–406 BCE), nature takes on moral purpose, gaining a sacred quality. Clarence Glacken's *Traces on the Rhodian Shore* offers the most comprehensive review of the force of the design argument in the history of nature from its emergence as early as the Greek historian Herodotus (484–425 BCE) through the seventeenth century CE. Teleological (relating to design or purpose) conceptions of the "purposefulness in the creation—that it was the result of intelligent, planned, and well-thought-out acts of a creator," including a strong sense of the fitness of nature to human needs, have been key in Western constructions of nature (Glacken 1967, 39). English writer C. S. Lewis's *Studies in Words* neatly sums the result: "A comparatively small number of speculative Greeks invented *Nature*—Nature with a capital," which required "taking all things they knew or believed in—gods, men, animals, plants, minerals, what you will—and impounding them under a single name; in fact, of regarding Everything as a thing, turning this amorphous and heterogeneous collection into an object or pseudo-object" (Lewis 1967, 35, 37).

From its earliest inception, then, "nature" referred to the whole material world and to intrinsic form and elemental creative forces. Raymond Williams's *Keywords* provides a concise history of changes in usage in English from the thirteenth to eighteenth centuries. Williams famously states: "Nature is perhaps the most complex word in the language" (Williams 1976, 184). Complexity arises from an enfolding of one meaning within another. *Nature* as "the essential quality or character *of* something" took on the additional sense of "inherent force" in the fourteenth century, and by the seventeenth century, *nature* as material world shared significant overlap with intrinsic form and creative force. Thus *nature*, which refers to a "multiplicity of things and creatures, may carry an assumption of something common to all of them" (Williams 1976, 185).

Nature is subject to abstraction and personification. The ancient Greek philosophers, articulating a stance common in paganism worldwide, believed the natural world to be alive, an all-encompassing animal with both soul and mind, binding plants and animals (including humans) in physical, intellectual, and psychic kinship. Plato's (428/7–348/7 BCE) *Timaeus* conceived of the soul as female. Lovejoy suggests that the Roman orator Cicero (106–43 BCE) carried the concept of nature as goddess from the Greeks into the eighteenth century, whereas Carolyn Merchant, in *The Death of Nature*, follows the tradition from the Neoplatonism of Roman philosopher Plotinus (204–270 CE) to twelfth-century Christianity, which placed a female nature "as more powerful than humans, but . . . subordinate to God" (Merchant 1980, 10). Nature personified as female contains much ambiguity—seen as a practical expression of the divine order, as chaotic and destructive, as innocent and tainted. Although C. S. Lewis argued that this specific personification of nature as mother has been "the hardest to kill" (Lewis 1967, 42), many environmental historians identify the seventeenth and eighteenth centuries as the point during which nature was, momentarily at least, most rigidly confined and its long history of vitalism reduced.

Nature in Modern Times

Carolyn Merchant locates "the death of nature" in the rise of mechanical philosophy associated with Rene Descartes (1597–1650) in France and Francis Bacon (1561–1626) in England. Critical of organic worldviews in which the world is personified as a forceful, living body, these scientists viewed nature as inert, passive matter acted upon by physical laws set in motion by a clockmaker deity. One result of the Scientific Revolution was the transformation of female nature "from an active teacher and parent . . . [to] a mindless, submissive body"—submissive first to God and through God to humankind (Merchant 1980, 190). Raymond Williams sees the goddess replaced by a constitutional lawyer whose role was not "an inherent and shaping force" but rather "an accumulation and classification of cases" (Williams 1976, 187).

Strongly influenced by the explanatory power of physics and mathematics, natural history continued to search for stable order in the exponentially increasing numbers of plants and animals resulting from the voyages of discovery from the fifteenth to the nineteenth century. The Swedish botanist, Linnaeus (1707–1778), developed the first universally accepted system for organizing the profusion of living nature into an arrangement apparently revelatory of God's design. Continuing a tradition strong among the Greeks, however, Linnaeus viewed change in nature as fundamentally cyclical, always returning to the same start point.

Mechanical philosophy located nature in mathematically based laws played out in the physical world, in which "the earth [can] be understood through a series of deductions from abstract premises" with little consideration for final causes and less interest in the plenitude of life (Glacken 1967, 406). Although Linnaeus participated in the urge to render a nature ordered by abstract laws, he also inspired the rise of natural history by giving naturalists tools for organizing their botanical discoveries. Obsession with documenting and organizing the plenitude of life derives as well from a group of writers, many influenced by Linnaeus, who return to classical ideas of organic nature, argue for final causes and design in nature, and seek them in observations of the sensory world. The leading natural theologian, Englishman John Ray (1627–1705), in his influential *The Wisdom of God in the Works of Creation* (1691), emphasized the interrelatedness of plants, animals, and habitats as evidence of a wise creator. Later naturalists continued to probe the intricacies of relationships in nature even as they moved away from the argument from design.

Throughout the sixteenth to eighteenth centuries, one of the most persistent characteristics of nature was the law of subordination. Arthur O. Lovejoy's *The Great Chain of Being* outlines the belief that the deity had appointed each species a fixed place in an eternal chain of being from the lowliest worm through humans to God. The task of natural history was to fit new discoveries into the related links on the chain. Donald Worster, in *Nature's Economy*, traces as well the history of nature as at once a sacred and an economic system from the Greek word for *house (oikos)* through its amplification to refer to household management, the political "oeconomy" of human societies, and nature's economy. Thus Linnaeus, in his influential essay, "The Oeconomy of Nature" (1749), described nature as the "earth household" in which God was the "Supreme Economist" who rationally ordered the cosmos and "the housekeeper who kept it functioning productively" (Worster 1985, 37).

By the beginning of the nineteenth century two scientists—the German geographer, Alexander von Humboldt (1769–1859) and the English geologist, Charles Lyell (1797–1875)—initiated a discovery process that would sweep away the singular chain and the stable taxonomy (scientific classification) as well as lead to questions about the central role of a designing deity. In their footsteps came the naturalist who discovered a fundamental key to understanding the history of nature. Benefiting from Humboldt's discoveries of geographical diversity and mutual dependency in plant groupings and from Lyell's understanding of the age of the earth's crust and its history of sometimes-violent change, the English naturalist Charles Darwin (1809–1882) went on a voyage to the New World, arriving in 1835 at the Galapagos Islands, an isolated archipelago off the coast of Ecuador. The creatures he saw there, so like and yet so different from South American species, ultimately led him to theorize that chance migration, isolation, and fit with a specific environment lead to evolution of new species.

An Essay on the Principle of Population by the English economist Thomas Malthus (1766–1834) provided Darwin the mechanism for evolution—the elimination of the weak and survival of the most fit, which Darwin called "natural selection." When Darwin finally published *On the Origin of Species* in 1859, the static, objectified view of material life of the mechanical philosophers, as well as the eternally fixed singular chain of being of the natural theologians, was challenged by a world that Darwin described as "an entangled bank, clothed with many plants of many kinds, with birds singing on the bushes, with various insects flitting about, and with worms crawling through the damp earth." The result was nature that, although partaking of universal, unchanging physical laws, also had a distinctive history: "whilst this planet has gone cycling on according to the fixed law of gravity, from so simple a beginning endless forms most beautiful and most wonderful have been, and are being, evolved" (Darwin 1964, 489–490).

Nature in the Age of Ecology

In gaining history, nature regained some of the vitality lost under the reign of mechanical philosophy. In *Problems in Materialism and Culture*, Raymond Williams argues that the late nineteenth-century personification of nature replaced the constitutional lawyer with Darwin's "selective breeder" (Williams 1980, 73). Others have located more complicated vitalism in post-Darwinian nature. Donald Worster emphasizes the shift in the late nineteenth and early twentieth centuries to an imperfect nature—communities of competing lives contingent along axes of space and time. Darwin took the Linnaean conception of a stable chain of being and put it in motion through competition and coadaptation. Paul Sears situates Darwin's centrality to ecology in his observation that "environment had from the beginning built itself into the very form and organization of all forms of life" (Sears 1950, 56). The German comparative anatomist and zoologist, Ernst Haeckel (1834–1919), is generally credited with coining the term *oecologie* (by 1893, *ecology*) in 1866. Worster agrees with Sears that Haeckel grounded the web of life in Darwin's theory that the economy of nature is governed by relationships deriving from the struggle for existence.

The lack of a designer did not imply that there is no order in nature conceived as ecological. During the early twentieth century plant geographers and botanists in Europe and the United States gradually discovered in plant communities an active, changeful nature defined by the 1930s most forcefully in the work of the U.S. botanist Frederic Clements (1874–1945). Nature, he argued, is dynamic, but change occurs in patterns of "successional development" over time. Innovation through competition is progressive in the sense that a specific habitat "begins with a primitive, inherently unbalanced plant assemblage and ends with a complex formation in relatively permanent equilibrium with the surrounding conditions" (Worster 1985, 210). This most stable moment in plant history Clements termed a "climax" and a "complex organism." By the end of the 1930s Clements, in collaboration with the U.S. animal ecologist Victor Shelford, had arrived at a vision of living nature as a "biotic community" (Worster 1985, 214).

Both the earlier natural history and ecology understated the roles of inorganic forces in the creation and maintenance of life. Under the ecosystem concept developed by the British botanist Arthur George Tansley (1871–1955) in 1935, mechanical philosophy returned through twentieth-century thermodynamic physics as a powerful approach to constraining nature. Uniting living and nonliving aspects of the world under the processes of energy flow emphasized nature's processes as historical while repudiating the organic community posited in Clements's version of nature. Nature as ecosystem is as linear as nature as climax community, but time's arrow moves in the direction of entropy (gradual decline into disorder) rather than progress. As Donald Worster describes it, "the ecosystem of the earth, considered from the perspective of energetics, is a way-station on a river of no return. Energy flows through it and disappears eventually into the vast sea of space; there is no way to get back upstream" (Worster 1985, 303). Both Clements and Tansley, however, assume a predictable trajectory in natural history.

By the end of the twentieth century historical nature had acquired chaos, chance, randomness. Daniel Botkin's *Discordant Harmonies* posits an organic nature, a "living system, global in scale, produced and in some ways controlled by life" (Botkin 1990, 189), which may be modeled through computer programs, uniting Clements and Tansley, but with a critical twist. Nature's history is essentially ambiguous, variable, and complex; time's arrow is not singular but is rather a sheaf whose arcs and marks are defined by probability. Nature abstracted is essentially ambiguous, variable, and complex; time's arrow is not singular but is rather a sheaf whose arcs and marks are defined by probability, "always in flux, changing over many scales of time and space, changing with individual births and deaths, local disruptions and recoveries, larger scale responses to climate from one glacial age to another" (Botkin 1990, 62). Nature in the twenty-first century has a radically contingent history and one that proves particularly troublesome in light of the role of nature in human history.

Humans and Nature

Exploring the other side of the equation—how to place nature in history—requires finally considering the place of humans in nature. Clarence Glacken's *Traces on the Rhodian Shore* fulsomely covers the preindustrial history of humans and nature. Glacken posits that, throughout time, the West has regarded the natural world with several questions in mind, all of which arise from the sense that the earth is an inherently habitable place for humankind. Is this Earth apparently so fitting an environment for organic life, "a purposely made creation"? What is the influence of the earth's climates, physical terrain, and continental configuration, that is, the environment in which life is embedded, on individual health and morality and on the shape of human culture? Lastly, and coming increasingly into play from the eighteenth century to the present, in what manner have humans through their artifice acted as "geographic agents" changing nature "from its hypothetical pristine condition" (Glacken 1967, vii)?

As is apparent from the preceding discussion, much of the attempt to describe the history of nature has centered on the first issue—on teleological aspects of nature. Although the idea of nature as a product of design arose independently of the concept of environmental influence (which Glacken credits to early medical theory), each reinforced the other. Organic life (including humans and their societies) was seen as adapting to "purposefully created harmonious conditions" (Glacken 1967, vii). And human artifice, distinct from "first" nature and exemplifying the human place in the chain of being just below the creator, constituted a "second" nature cultivating and adding improvements to the design. From the Greeks until the eighteenth century, Western conceptions of nature in human history portrayed it as the world out there to which humans adapted—but part of that adaptive move was to order nature. Human creations of second nature, through hunting and domesticating animals, cultivating crops, and digging canals, settled unknown, wild lands, but, until the seventeenth and eighteenth centuries, such activity assumed an inviolate stability in first nature.

During the modern era, as nature itself began to develop a contingent history, humans began to recognize their role as agents of geographic change. Emerging during the Renaissance out of a growing self-consciousness about the power of human control over nature and pushed by the belief that such power marks humans off from the rest of nature, human history became a narrative about harnessing the elements (through arts such as alchemy) and transforming the landscape (for economic and aesthetic purposes). Just as the Age of Exploration contributed to an emerging sense of nature's history, it also offered comparative evidence of the interactions between natural history and human history. In addition to new plants and animals, the discovery and exploration of the New World offered an aspect of nature seemingly untouched by human artifice. Glacken explains that, by the eighteenth century, the French naturalist George Louis Leclerc, Comte de Buffon (1707–1788) relied on the contrasts between Europe and the Americas to construct his history of the earth as ultimately "seconded" by the history of human strivings. For Buffon, who had little appreciation for the wild, uninhabited places on Earth, second nature was at once an improvement of first nature and a sign of improvement in human civilization.

Although anthropologists, such as the American Shepard Krech in *The Ecological Indian* have explored the extent to which native peoples' artifice had seconded nature in the Americas by the time of European arrivals, in contrast with the more visibly modified landscapes of eighteenth-century Europe, America was, indeed, an exemplar of first nature. European immigrants to America took pride in Western domination. William Cronon in *Changes in the Land* and Carolyn Merchant in *Ecological Revolutions* probe the extent to which most immigrants set out to fully second nature with many of the same techniques and ideologies prevalent in Europe. But other immigrants (also in consort with European counterparts) were less celebratory of human power over this seemingly more pristine nature. The forces driving skepticism about the Western urge to powerfully transform first nature into second nature were many. Most environmental historians isolate several historical shifts that began in the eighteenth century but came to fruition in the nineteenth.

Agents of Change

The import of modern humans as agents of geographic change was more visible in the New World. Early commentators like the Swedish botanist Peter Kalm (1716–1779), the U.S. botanist John Bartram (1699–1777), and the U.S. horticulturist John Lorain (1753–1823) noted that settlers were replacing old environments with new and raised questions about the impact on first nature and whether second nature improved the prospects for human habitation. Industrialization in Britain and the United States accelerated the transformations of nature, sharpened the distinctions between city, country, and wild places, and radically dislocated increasing populations from labor on the land to work inside factories.

The most influential critique of such attempts to second nature came from Romanticism, a transcontinental philosophy that granted privilege to first nature as an organic force in human history. Where Buffon argued that Earth history is improved and furthered by the shift from first to second nature, the American Romantic transcendentalist and nature writer, Henry David Thoreau (1817–1862), countered that Earth has its own history, which humans destroy in the act of seconding nature. In a journal entry considering the effects of settlement around Concord, Massachusetts, Thoreau poses "primitive" or first nature as a "poem" he is privileged to read only to discover "that my ancestors have torn out many of the first leaves and grandest passages, and mutilated it in many places. I should not like to think that some demigod had come before me and picked out some of the best of the stars. I wish to know an entire heaven and an entire earth. All the great trees and beasts, fishes and fowl are gone. The streams are . . . shrunk" (Thoreau 1906, 220–221). For the Romantics, humans who embedded themselves in first nature—returning at least to the countryside and at best to more untrammeled spaces—countered what they viewed as the growing dominance of mechanical philosophy and its attendant materialism and repression of the innate spirit in all life.

One of the other key figures in the effort to place nature in history was a contemporary of Thoreau—the U.S. scholar George Perkins Marsh (1801–1882). Marsh's *Man and Nature: or, Physical Geography as Modified by Human Action* (1864) has been widely credited by environmental historians as the first comprehensive analysis of the detrimental effects of human modifications on the natural environment. Comparing soil erosion and forest destruction in his native Vermont with degraded environments in the Mediterranean basin and histories of land and resource use in Europe and Asia, Marsh concludes "man [sic] is everywhere a disturbing agent. Wherever he plants his foot, the harmonies of nature are turned to discord" (Marsh 1965, 36). Based on his analysis of the history of humans as agents of ecological change, Marsh called on his contemporaries for caution in seconding nature, always with an eye to what must be learned from the priorities of first nature. In this he considered both the history of nature and nature in history.

But Marsh's image of humans as disturbers of a pristine nature raises one of the most controversial meanings of nature for contemporary environmental history. Marsh and Thoreau, in keeping with many Americans of the nineteenth and twentieth centuries, make sharp contrasts between a world of nature out there and humans. The question of the human place in nature has been ambiguously answered for the past two thousand years. One of the dangerous ambiguities about nature is that it may at once contain and exclude humans. Nineteenth-century critics of industrialism often argued, as Marsh and Thoreau do, that the artifices of humans had shifted from improvement to de-

struction and were not seconding but rather disturbing nature's history. Humans and their arts then become unnatural, alien to nature. Similarly, in the early twentieth century two of the key figures in the age of ecology, Clements and Tansley, radically disagreed on the role of humans in nature, with Tansley arguing that ecologically sound "anthropogenic" (human-caused) climaxes could be created by human artifice, and Clements making a sharp distinction between the disturbance brought by the plow and presettlement prairie biota (the flora and fauna of a region).

Thoreau, Marsh, and Clements shared Aldo Leopold's sense that the twentieth century would require an ecology-based "land ethic" that "changes the role of *Homo sapiens* from conqueror of the land-community to plain member and citizen of it. It implies respect for his fellow-members, and also respect for the community as such" (Leopold 1949, 204). These are the values Leopold more lyrically expresses in the preceding passage about sharing his flooded fields with geese and carp. And they are the values that led him and likeminded people into the twenty-first century to advocate preserving remnants of the wild, in large part because such places seemed to offer different trajectories for both historical nature and nature in history.

This controversy over the role of nature in human history continues into the early twenty-first century. Most fundamental is the question of whether one may speak of a nature existing free from human modification. Raymond Williams asserts that "we have mixed our labor with the earth, our forces with its forces too deeply to be able to draw back or separate either out" (Williams 1980, 83). Drawing on Williams, William Cronon suggests that the "trouble with wilderness" is its erasure of the history of human striving from natural history (Cronon 1995, 69), and Richard White poses nature in contemporary times as an "organic machine"—a symbiotic meld of human artifice and natural processes (White 1995, ix). But for Williams the second nature that people have now created is materialist, socially repressive, and polluted—toxic for humans and the rest of the organic world. J. R. McNeill's *Something New under the Sun* reinforces the troubling reciprocity between recent understanding of the history of nature as not only changeful but also unpredictable and the disruptive forces of human history. McNeill argues that during the twentieth century humans took a planet whose future was inherently uncertain and made change even more volatile, primarily through economic and technological imperatives, creating a "total system of global society and environment . . . more uncertain, more chaotic than ever" (McNeill 2000, 359). The most pressing global issue for the twenty-first century is the environmental future.

Such troublesome nature and controversial human history were hardly on Aldo Leopold's mind that day in the early twentieth century when a welcome flood washed up evidence of human striving into his fields along with carp and geese. He did, however, pose an enduring challenge to people to educate themselves in the material worlds of first and second nature. The future will be forged in synergy between the history of nature and nature in history.

Vera Norwood

See also Conservation

Further Reading

Botkin, D. (1990). *Discordant harmonies: A new ecology for the twenty-first century.* New York: Oxford University Press.

Bruun, O., & Kalland, A. (Eds.). (1995). *Asian perceptions of nature: A critical approach.* Surrey, UK: Curzon Press.

Collingwood, R. G. (1945). *The idea of nature.* London: Oxford University Press.

Cronon, W. (1983). *Changes in the land: Indians, colonists and the ecology of New England.* New York: Hill and Wang.

Cronon, W. (Ed.). (1995). *Uncommon ground: Rethinking the human place in nature.* New York: W. W. Norton.

Darwin, C. (1964). *On the origin of species.* Cambridge, MA: Harvard University Press. (Original work published 1859)

Eisenstadt, S. M. (1995). The Japanese attitude to nature: A framework of basic ontological conceptions. In O. Bruun & A. Kalland (Eds.), *Asian perceptions of nature: A critical approach* (pp. 189–214). Surrey, UK: Curzon Press.

Evernden, N. (1992). *The social creation of nature.* Baltimore: Johns Hopkins University Press.

Flader, S. (1974). *Thinking like a mountain: Aldo Leopold and the evolution of an ecological attitude toward deer, wolves, and forests.* Madison: University of Wisconsin Press.

Glacken, C. J. (1967). *Traces on the Rhodian shore: Nature and culture in Western thought from ancient times to the end of the eighteenth century.* Berkeley & Los Angeles: University of California Press.

Krech, S. (1999). *The ecological Indian: Myth and history.* New York: W. W. Norton.

Leopold, A. (1949). *A Sand County almanac and sketches here and there.* London: Oxford University Press.

Lewis, C. S. (1967). *Studies in words.* Cambridge, UK: Cambridge University Press.

Lovejoy, A. O. (1936). *The great chain of being: A study of the history of an idea.* Cambridge, MA: Harvard University Press.

Lovejoy, A. O., Chinard, G., Boas, G., & Crane, R. S. (1935). *A documentary history of primitivism and related ideas.* Baltimore: Johns Hopkins University Press.

Malthus, T. (1890). *An essay on the principle of population.* London: Ward. (Original work published 1798)

Marsh, G. P. (1965). *Man and nature.* Cambridge, MA: Harvard University Press. (Original work published 1864)

McNeill, J. R. (2000). *Something new under the sun: An environmental history of the twentieth century world.* New York: W. W. Norton.

Merchant, C. (1980). *The death of nature: Women, ecology and the Scientific Revolution.* San Francisco: Harper & Row.

Merchant (1989). *Ecological revolutions: Nature, gender, and science in New England.* San Francisco: Harper & Row.

Plato. (1952). *Timaeus, Critias, Cleitophon, Menexenus: Epistles.* Cambridge, MA: Harvard University Press.

Ray, J. (1759). *The wisdom of God manifested in the works of creation.* London: John Rivington, John Ward, Joseph Richardson. (Original work published 1691)

Sandell, K. (1995). Nature as the virgin forest: Farmers' perspectives on nature and sustainability in low-resource agriculture in the dry zone of Sri Lanka. In O. Bruun & A. Kalland (Eds.), *Asian perceptions of nature: A critical approach* (pp. 148–173). Surrey, UK: Curzon Press.

Sears, P. (1950). *Charles Darwin: The naturalist as a cultural force.* New York: Scribner's.

Soule, M., & Lease, G. (Eds.). (1995). *Reinventing nature? Responses to post-modern deconstruction.* Washington, DC: Island Press.

Thoreau, H. D. (1906). *The writings of Henry David Thoreau: Journal VIII.* Boston: Houghton Mifflin.

White, R. (1995). *The organic machine: The remaking of the Columbia River.* New York: Hill & Wang.

Williams, R. (1976). *Keywords: A vocabulary of culture and society.* London: Fontana/Croom Helm.

Williams, R. (1980). *Problems in materialism and culture.* London: Verso.

Worster, D. (1985). *Nature's economy: A history of ecological ideas.* Cambridge, UK: Cambridge University Press.

Worster, D. (1993). *The wealth of nature: Environmental history and the ecological imagination.* London: Oxford University Press.

The Nature Conservancy

The Nature Conservancy (TNC), founded in 1950, is an international, nonprofit organization that works to protect important habitats for plants and animals. The Nature Conservancy's mission is to preserve biological diversity by saving lands and waters that are integral to the life of native species. The Conservancy was founded by a group of scientists who wanted to form an organization that would take constructive action on conservation-related issues. The group has helped protect over 12 million acres in the United States and Canada, as well as 80 million acres in Latin America, the Caribbean, Asia, and the Pacific. The preserved land includes forests, marshes, prairies, deserts, mountains, and islands. The Nature Conservancy owns and manages more than 1,500 nature sanctuaries in the United States.

The Nature Conservancy is concerned about species of flora and fauna threatened by the loss of their native habitat. In 1974, the Conservancy began establishing a nationwide system of State Natural Heritage Programs. These systematic ecological inventories use an integrated network of computer, map, and manual files to identify and prioritize species and natural communities that are endangered. The resulting data guides development decisions, resource use, and other conservation initiatives. The Heritage Programs, now in all fifty states, help establish priorities for protection. The Conservancy scientists advise state and town governments as well as developers about the presence of rare species on their land.

Virtually all of the Nature Conservancy's financial support comes from private, tax-deductible contributions. Corporate contributions, foundation grants, and membership dues also fund the organization. The Conservancy acquires land by gift or purchase. Private landowners or corporations sometimes donate critical land to TNC, and the group raises money to purchase other natural areas. The Conservancy often arranges bargain sales, land exchanges, joint ownership, and other creative real estate transactions with landowners who cannot afford to donate their property but want to see it protected. When the price of a land acquisition is prohibitive, TNC seeks conservation easements, management leases, or voluntary landowner agreements to ensure the protection of a natural area. A unique characteristic of the Conservancy is that it is capable of rapidly leveraging large amounts of money to purchase tracts of valuable land. When an area faces an imminent threat, TNC uses a revolving, internal loan fund to buy the land immediately, then repays the loan once permanent funding has been secured.

The Nature Conservancy is responsible for the long-term stewardship costs of land it acquires. Volunteer local land stewards assist Conservancy staff and consultants in maintaining TNC preserves. The Conservancy attempts to protect the preserves' natural features while allowing opportunities for human visitors to enjoy the sanctuaries with minimal impact. Most preserves are open for educational uses and recreation, such as hiking, nature study, birdwatching, and photography. Conservancy naturalists offer field trips to some preserves; however, the protected land tends not to have amenities as state parks do and is not capable of supporting large numbers of visitors.

The Nature Conservancy differs from other private conservation organizations in that it avoids political action, rarely becoming involved in public policy issues. The group does offer expertise and assistance on legislative matters that affect threatened species and lands. However, opponents criticize TNC for its refusal to engage in environmental activism and its eagerness to compromise with industry.

The Nature Conservancy tends to encounter public opposition in situations where residents make their living from the land, such as through logging or other natural resource extraction. In these cases, TNC works with a variety of groups—including schools, land trusts, government agencies, and businesses—in an attempt to achieve mutually beneficial conservation goals.

The Nature Conservancy has one million members worldwide. There is an open membership policy and an elected Board of Governors. The organization has over 2,000 employees with backgrounds in various fields including ecology, biology, forestry, real estate, business, and law. Its international headquarters are in metropolitan Washington, D.C. The Nature Conservancy is the umbrella organization for individual state Nature Conservancies. Professionally staffed offices are located in all fifty states.

Robin O'Sullivan

Further Reading

The Freshwater Initiative. Retrieved October 4, 2002, from http://www.freshwaters.org/tnc.html

Grove, N. (1992). *Preserving Eden: The Nature Conservancy.* New York: Harry N. Abrams.

Halperin, E., & Williams, L. A. (1993). The cycle of cost-effectiveness: The Nature Conservancy. In G. L.

Schmaedick (Ed.), *Cost-effectiveness in the nonprofit sector* (pp. 79–92). Westport, CT: Quorum Books.

Hill, R. A. (1989). *Maine forever: A guide to Nature Conservancy Preserves in Maine*. Topsham, ME: The Nature Conservancy.

Nature Photography

Nature photography is photography that takes nature as its subject and represents nature for its own sake. The "nature" in nature photography can range widely—from mountains, grasslands, seas, and plants to animals such as birds, fish, and insects. Nature photographs usually do not include human beings or objects made by humans, but the subjects chosen are often influenced by social, cultural, or historic events.

Origins of Nature Photography

The origins of photography can be traced back to China during the fifth century BCE. Although the modern photographic process was developed in the nineteenth century, a type of camera had been in use prior to that time. The camera obscura is a darkened room or tent into which the image of an object—a scenic view, the sky, a building—can be projected using reflected light, a pinhole, or a lens. Although there is no permanent reproduction, the image can be projected onto a wall opposite the pinhole or lens. Scientists and artists used the camera obscura in their work.

Modern photography dates from 1827, when Joseph Nicéphore Niépce (1765–1833) of France exposed a chemically treated plate to light through a camera obscura, and an image was created on the plate. By 1839 Louis Jacques Mandé Daguerre (1789–1851) of France had built upon Niépce's process to produce a much clearer image in a shorter time. Perhaps most important for the increasing popularity of photography was the paper negative, invented by William Henry Fox Talbot (1800–1877) of England. The paper negative allowed photographs to be reproduced without limit. Talbot's 1844 book *The Pencil of Nature* also helped add to the increasing popularity of photography because it included text as well as photographs of everything from Parisian boulevards to haystacks near Talbot's home in England.

Photography and Art

Photography was believed to be a more scientific and objective interpretation of both the natural and human-made environment and photographs "an exacting and unsentimental view of the landscape" (Davenport 1991, 60). Photography and art, although the former responds to a moment in time and the latter to a lengthier process of the artist's interpretation, influenced each other from the beginning. Some artists would use photographs as a basis for a painting, similar to the way a sketch would be used, and photographers often took pictures of the same views that attracted landscape painters. Nineteenth-century landscape photography was an aesthetic that eventually gained the same acceptance as landscape painting.

Uses of Nature Photography

Commercial photography developed quickly and produced views of locales throughout the world. Roger Fenton (1819–1868) of England, known for his photographs of the Crimean War, also photographed the Welsh landscape, and other photographers concentrated on the Alps or the Himalayas. Stereograph views of Egypt, the Holy Land, and Niagara Falls in the United States for the first time gave audiences a sense of the wonders of the world. Although photography was viewed at first as an objective interpretation of the natural environment, limitations in the technical aspects of photography necessitated the "doctoring" of some photographs, such as combining one photograph of the sky with another of the landscape.

Nature Photography and the American West

The spectacular scenery of the American West became known through the efforts of both commercial and documentary photographers. As members of the U.S. Geological Survey teams who explored the American West beginning in the 1860s, photographers produced work that had cultural as well as political and economic implications. Lacking the centuries-old history and architecture of Europe, some nineteenth-century Americans saw their country's history in its natural exceptionalism evident in western landscapes.

Three of the best-known early American landscape photographers were Carleton Eugene Watkins (1829–1916), Timothy O'Sullivan (1840–1882), and William Henry Jackson (1843–1942). Watkins took some of the earliest photographs of the Yosemite Valley in California, working at one point with the California State Geological Survey (1866). His 1861 photographs were hailed as magnificent and won awards at the Centennial Exposition in Philadelphia in 1876. O'Sullivan joined the U.S. Geographic Survey team who went to document the land along the fortieth parallel and photographed Panama and then the American Southwest. Jackson, who was a trained artist, did some of his best work in Yellowstone during the late 1860s and 1870s, and his photographs of the region captured the region's unique geological and thermodynamic features. These photographs were as dramatic as the paintings of the American West executed by artists such as Albert Bierstadt (1830–1902).

Twentieth-Century Nature Photography

The publication of Englishman Peter Henry Emerson's *Naturalistic Photography* (1886) changed the perception of nature photographers from that of mere recorders of the landscape to that of artists who should study nature in order to achieve the best results from their work. Emerson himself followed the techniques of English landscape artists when composing his landscape photographs. By the 1930s some American nature photographers began to focus on a precise and objective photographic representation of nature. Among these photographers was Ansel Adams (1902–1984). Adams's photographs of the American West and Southwest have remained some of the dominant images of the region and have been exhibited in galleries and used by the Sierra Club in support of its conservation measures.

Adams was concerned that the critical acclaim and popular appeal of his photographs had resulted in an increase in tourism to some of the locations of his photographs. Nature photography—whether it be wildlife, underwater, plant, or landscape photography by professionals or amateurs—has, in recent years, been a cause for concern among wilderness protection organizations throughout the world. Increasing numbers of visitors have caused some damage to ecologically fragile regions. Nature photography in the twenty-first century remains popular for some of the same reasons it was popular in the nineteenth century, including the desire to see exotic locales and flora and fauna as well as a desire for an objective representation of nature.

The increasing number of new glossy coffee table books, calendars, and magazines filled with high quality photographic reproductions of landscapes and wildlife are indicative of the growing popularity of nature photography. Similarly, this interest has led to the production of nature films and documentaries as well as television series. Nature photography workshops and guided excursions have encouraged novice and experienced photographers alike to learn new photographic techniques. Organizations such as the Sierra Club and the Nature Conservancy have utilized this popular interest to encourage greater awareness of the dangers posed to nature by modern society. Nature photography has become a popular hobby as well as a serious art form that offers the opportunity to gain greater appreciation for the beauty and complexity of nature.

Kimberly A. Jarvis

Further Reading

Andrews, M. (1999). *Landscape and western art*. New York: Oxford University Press.

Davenport, A. (1991). *The history of photography: An overview*. Albuquerque: University of New Mexico Press.

Dawson, R., et al. (1992). *Ansel Adams: New light: Essays on his legacy and legend*. San Francisco: Friends of Photography.

Hales, P. B. (1988). *William Henry Jackson and the transformation of the American landscape*. Philadelphia: Temple University Press.

Janson, H. W. (1991). *The history of art*. New York: Harry N. Abrams.

Jeffrey, I. (1981). *Photography: A concise history*. New York: Oxford University Press.

McDarrah, G. S., McDarrah, F. W., & McDarrah, T. S. (1999). *The photography encyclopedia*. New York: Schirmer Books.

Mitchell, W. J. T. (2002). *Landscape and power*. Chicago: University of Chicago Press.

Neaf, W. (1975). *Era of exploration: The rise of landscape photography in the American West 1860–1885*. New York: Buffalo Free Arts Academy, Albright Knox Art Gallery, and the Metropolitan Museum of Art.

Novak, B. (1995). *Nature and culture: American landscape and painting 1825–1875*. New York: Oxford University Press.

Nature Writing

During the past half-century, and particularly from the late 1960s to the present, the genre of literary expression known as "nature writing," sometimes described more broadly as "environmental literature," has become one of the most vigorous and significant branches of world literature—this is particularly true in the United States and in other English-speaking cultures such as the United Kingdom, Canada, and Australia. But throughout the world significant writers are concerned with the workings of the physical and biotic world ("nature"), with the degradation of the planet through human actions, and with a broader assortment of interactions between the "human and more-than-human worlds," as philosopher and essayist David Abram puts it (Abram 1996, 7). Virtually every culture on Earth, it seems, has traditions of thinking about the relationship between human culture and nonhuman phenomena, but these traditions have not always been expressed in ways accessible to scholars and others trained in Western (European) styles of expression and analysis and have thus sometimes been overlooked or disregarded.

A Brief History of the Genre

The term *nature writing* itself began to be used in the United States during the first decade of the twentieth century, according to scholar Don Scheese, who claims that the term was coined by the journalist Dallas Lore Sharp to describe the work of natural history writers such as John Burroughs and Ernest Thompson Seton. Robert Finch and John Elder, editors of *The Norton Book of Nature Writing*, likewise emphasize the roots of contemporary nature writing in the British and American traditions of nonfiction (essays) concerned with scientific and philosophical aspects of how nature functions—the anatomy and behavior of animals, the locations and growing habits of plants, the geological processes that formed canyons and mountains. The major scholarly organization for research on nature writing and related topics is the Association for the Study of Literature and Environment (ASLE); ASLE was founded in 1992 in Reno, Nevada. In one of the keynote presentations at ASLE's first conference in 1995, the literary scholar John Elder defined *nature writing* as "a form of the personal, reflective essay grounded in attentiveness to the natural world and an appreciation of science but also open to the spiritual meaning and intrinsic value of nature" (Armbruster & Wallace 2001, 2). Independent branches of ASLE, devoted to the study of environmental literature in cultures outside of North America, exist in Japan, the United Kingdom, South Korea, and Australia.

The 1990 first edition of the Norton anthology begins with the writings of eighteenth-century British "parson naturalist" Gilbert White, who spent much of his time walking the grounds of his rural home in the village of Selborne, observing snakes and birds and plants and then writing about them in letters to a friend. *The Natural History and Antiquities of Selborne* (1789) has been identified as one of the original examples of "nature writing" in the English language. In North America, many scholars have tended to point to Henry David Thoreau's *Walden* (1854) or to his personal journal (maintained from 1837 to 1861 and first published in its entirety in 1906) as pivotal to the American approach to thinking about the workings of nature and the relationship between the human mind and the larger universe. In his 1989 book, *Nature Writing and America: Essays upon a Cultural Type*, critic Peter Fritzell defined nature writing as a combination of Aristotelian natural history writing and Augustinian spiritual autobiography, tracing the genre's contemporary combina-

The environmental writer Terry Tempest Williams in Castle Valley, Utah, in November 1995. COURTESY HIROFUMI OHUE AND SCOTT SLOVIC.

tion of empirical (scientific) observation, first-person stories, and philosophical and spiritual meditation back to ancient Greece and Rome. In the late 1960s and early 1970s American writers such as Wallace Stegner, Edward Abbey, Wendell Berry, and Annie Dillard, building on the mid-century works of the U.S. forester Aldo Leopold and the U.S. anthropologist Loren Eiseley, began to develop a distinctive mode of American nature writing attuned to the social, political, and environmental situation in the United States. The Australian scholar Peter Hay, in his book *Main Currents in Western Environmental Thought*, argues that "poets, novelists, and essayists have long made the idiosyncratic especialness of place a prominent literary theme, but the elevation of place to 'genre' status is predominantly the achievement of a robust North American tradition of nature writing" (Hay 2002, 153). For Hay and other international scholars and authors, the tendency to think freshly and provocatively about specific places in the world is the major contribution of recent American nature writing; this notion has been articulated forcefully in Barry Lopez's essay "A Literature of Place" (1997).

From "Nature Writing" to "Environmental Literature"

Although Gilbert White and Henry David Thoreau continue to be regarded as major figures in English-language traditions of writing about nature, there are strong inclinations today to decentralize these two authors and their writings, to argue that significant writing about humans and nature began well before White and Thoreau, and to maintain, further, that by emphasizing the genre of so-called nonfiction (essays, journals, letters, treatises), there has been a tendency to marginalize people (including entire ethnic, national, and socioeconomic groups) who have communicated their observations and visions through other media, ranging from written poetry and fiction to oral narratives and song and dramatic presentations. Patrick D. Murphy, in his 2000 book, *Farther Afield in the Study of Nature-Oriented Literature*, provides a forceful argument for expanding the notion of what nature writing is and its potential to guide contemporary culture; he tries to push readers to move beyond the natural history musings and observations of John Burroughs's nineteenth-century *Birch Browsings* by offering environmental readings of the poetry of contemporary Mexican-American writer Pat Mora and the experimental, journalism-fiction narratives of Japan's Mi-

chiko Ishimure. In another recent study, *American Indian Literature, Environmental Justice, and Ecocriticism* (2001), Joni Adamson argues that authors such as Leslie Marmon Silko and Simon J. Ortiz have deeply explored environmental justice issues through their novels and short stories. By "environmental justice," she means the impact of particular government policies and laws and mainstream economic trends upon poor and disenfranchised communities, such as those who dwell on Native American reservations. It would be difficult to find much nonfiction nature writing that addresses the specific impacts, for instance, of uranium mining in southern Utah and northern New Mexico upon local, rural communities. However, Silko's 1977 novel, *Ceremony*, evokes the wrenching psychological implications of such mining in that part of the world. Daniel G. Payne examines the political implications of nature writing in his 1996 book, *Voices in the Wilderness: American Nature Writing and Environmental Politics*.

For scholars and teachers, the term *nature writing* has come to mean literary nonfiction that offers scientific scrutiny of the world (as in the older tradition literary of natural history), explores the private experience of the individual human observer of the world, or reflects upon the political and philosophical implications of the relationships among human beings and between humans and the larger planet. Nonfiction nature writing continues in the early twenty-first century to be a particularly vibrant mode of literary expression in the books and magazine publications of the South African Breyten Breytenbach, the Australian William Lines, the Mexican Homero Aridjis, the American Terry Tempest Williams, the Taiwanese Liao Hong-Ji, and dozens of other essayists. However, it is increasingly popular for people who once focused exclusively on nonfiction to spend their time now reading and studying works that fall into the broader category of "environmental literature"—this term encompasses nonfiction nature writing, eco-fiction, nature poetry, eco-drama, and various modes of oral storytelling and rhetorical exhortation.

It is important to realize that environmental literature is not the same as what some might call "environmental*ist* literature." Environmental literature is seldom simply propaganda on behalf of conservation causes—it is different from the "literature" (pamphlets, newsletters, requests for financial support or political action) that might be prepared and distributed by environmental organizations. Environmental literature, although it frequently expresses a particular political orientation and a concern for social reform in pursuit of environmental protection, also tends to be exploratory, questioning, and celebratory—in other words, it is much more than simple argumentation against typical environmental ills, such as destruction of wildlife habitat, pollution, urban sprawl, and excessive extraction of natural resources. In 2001, when Karla Armbruster and Kathleen Wallace published the scholarly collection *Beyond Nature Writing: Expanding the Boundaries of Ecocriticism*, the contributors to their book offered studies of a broad range of authors, literary forms, and other media, including the poetry of Geoffrey Chaucer, John Milton, Robert Frost, and Michael Harper; the fiction of Samuel Johnson, Harriet Beecher Stowe, Thomas Hardy, Mary Wilkins Freeman, Franz Kafka, Virginia Woolf, Nadine Gordimer, Russell Hoban, Ursula K. Le Guin, and Toni Morrison; and various examples of popular film and twentieth-century drama. Another recent scholarly anthology, Steven Rosendale's *The Greening of Literary Scholarship: Literature, Theory, and the Environment* (2002), offers studies by more than a dozen scholars of a similar assortment of writers and genres. For a quick glimpse of many examples of environmental literature (mostly American and mostly from the twentieth century), it is possible to check such anthologies as *Literature and the Environment: A Reader on Nature and Culture* and *Literature and Nature: Four Centuries of Nature Writing*, both of which contain poetry and fiction as well as nonfiction. One of the major collections of nonfiction nature writing is Thomas J. Lyon's *This Incomperable Lande: A Book of American Nature Writing*. Likewise, for examples of the latest research on environmental literature, one could consult the journal *ISLE: Interdisciplinary Studies in Literature and Environment*. The best contemporary environmental writing appears routinely in *Orion* magazine.

The Purpose of Environmental Literature

Although explorations of human attitudes toward, and experiences of, the natural world appear in the various subcategories of environmental literature discussed earlier (such as poetry and fiction), it remains true that nonfiction nature writing emerged in the late twentieth century as a leading strand of environmental expression, prompting anthologist and nature writer John A. Murray to suggest in the introduction to "Nature-Writing Symposium" in the autumn 1992 issue of the Hawaiian journal *Manoa*, "Since the first Earth Day on April 22, 1970, a once obscure prose genre—nature writing—has steadily grown in stature and popularity,

attracting more and more of the best writers and larger and larger portions of the reading public until, in 1992, it is arguably the major genre in American literature" (73). So what are the basic aims of this genre, and who are some of its main exemplars?

On the one hand are nature writers who explore fundamental epistemological questions, trying to understand how the human mind comes to know the world and the place of human experience within the world. Annie Dillard, author of one of the classic works of modern American nature writing, the Pulitzer-Prize–winning book *Pilgrim at Tinker Creek* (1974), exemplifies this exploratory, epistemological mode of writing; as she explains in the introduction to a book called *Living by Fiction* (1982), "The mind fits the world and shapes it as a river fits and shapes its own banks" (Dillard 1982, 15). Dillard's many books, including *Teaching a Stone to Talk* (1982) and *An American Childhood* (1987), investigate the delightful and startling ways in which the individual human mind encounters the outside world. On the other hand are nature writers for whom the ultimate purpose of writing about nature is to subtly, slowly, indirectly change how humans perceive their own species and the planet, aiming to bring human civilization eventually into a more sustainable relationship with the nonhuman world. Former poet laureate of the United States Robert Haas argued in 1996 that it makes sense for the United States to be both a major environmental culprit and a leader in producing fine environmental literature: "All of the processes of industrial society that are destroying the natural world are accelerating. The World Bank this morning issued a report on the state of the environment—they talked about automobiles in developing cities. Where there's now acid rain, in the future there will be acid rainstorms. We simply can't have it. America has, to a large extent, exported that technology. It's also the case that because of our national heritage we're exporting a literature of thinking about it" (Crystal 1996). A third prominent form of contemporary nature writing—exemplified by the work of Edward O. Wilson, John Hay, Ann Zwinger, Robert Michael Pyle, and Chet Raymo in the United States—is literary natural history, science writing laced with personal, spiritual, political, or philosophical meditations.

Why would writers want to do this sort of work when there are so many other exciting and urgent "human topics" to address? Many of the prominent American nature writers have responded directly to this question by writing book-length essays on how and why they work in this field for the *Credo Series*, published by Milkweed Editions. As of 2002 Rick Bass, Pattiann Rogers, William Kittredge, Scott Russell Sanders, Ann Zwinger, Robert Michael Pyle, Alison Hawthorne Deming, John Nichols, John Elder, John Daniel, and Gary Paul Nabhan had contributed to this series by expressing their personal "credos" on the subject of environmental writing and sometimes, more specifically, nonfiction nature writing. Other prominent nature writers, such as Wendell Berry, Joseph Bruchac, David James Duncan, Linda Hogan, Barry Lopez, Bill McKibben, Peter Matthiessen, Richard K. Nelson, Mary Oliver, Pattiann Rogers, Gary Snyder, and Rebecca Solnit, assert their personal visions of the world and their work routinely in their essays, novels, short stories, and poems. Scott Russell Sanders stated his own position on this literary work—a position that would be shared by many of the writers mentioned earlier—quite poignantly in an earlier essay called "Speaking a Word for Nature." He wrote:

> However accurately it reflects the surface of our times, [literature] that never looks beyond the human realm is profoundly false, and therefore pathological. No matter how urban our experience, no matter how oblivious we may be toward nature, we are nonetheless animals, two-legged sacks of meat and blood and bone dependent on the whole living planet for our survival. Our outbreathings still flow through the pores of trees, our food still grows in dirt, our bodies decay. Of course, we all nod our heads in agreement. The gospel of ecology has become an *intellectual* commonplace. But it is not yet an *emotional* one. For most of us, most of the time, nature appears framed in a window or a video screen or inside the borders of a photograph. We do not feel the organic web passing through our guts, as it truly does. While our theories of nature have become wiser, our experience of nature has become shallower. . . . Thus, any writer who sees the world in ecological perspective faces a hard problem: how, despite the perfection of our technological boxes, to make us feel the ache and tug of that organic web passing through us, how to situate the lives of characters—and therefore of readers—in nature. (Sanders 1987, 226)

In other words, Sanders writes to help his readers feel and appreciate their own naturalness, their involvement with the physical world, the more-than-human world. Humans are animals—nothing more or less. And yet humans strive increasingly to suspend themselves above nature, to enclose themselves within human-constructed spaces and technologies, to estab-

lish abstract, virtual relationships with other humans, other species, and even with the natural resources that people rely upon for their daily existence. Fewer and fewer people in industrialized nations such as the United Kingdom, Germany, Italy, Australia, Japan, Taiwan, and, of course, the United States actually know where their food, fuel, and building products (wood, steel, glass, and so forth) come from. The subtext of contemporary writing about the natural world, sometimes explicit but often simply implicit, is that people's personal lives may be enriched by revivifying a sensory awareness of what it means to be alive in a world that is not merely a human creation. At the same time, the subtext continues, quietly or vociferously, to suggest that the future of society—indeed, of the human species—is contingent on learning (or relearning) how to rein in many of the excesses of modern human society in order to establish a more balanced and sustainable relationship with the planet.

Scott Slovic

See also Carson, Rachel; Leopold, Aldo; Thoreau, Henry David

Further Reading

Abram, D. (1996). *The spell of the sensuous: Perception and language in a more-than-human world*. New York: Pantheon.

Adamson, J. (2001). *American Indian literature, environmental justice, and ecocriticism*. Tucson: University of Arizona Press.

Anderson, L., Slovic, S., & O'Grady, J. P. (Eds.). (1999). *Literature and the environment: A reader on nature and culture*. New York: Addison Wesley Longman.

Armbruster, K., & Wallace, K. R. (Eds.). (2001). *Beyond nature writing: Expanding the boundaries of ecocriticism*. Charlottesville: University of Virginia Press.

Crystal, L. M. (Executive Producer). (1996, April 22). *Jim Lehrer news hour* [Television broadcast]. Washington, DC: MacNeil/Lehrer Productions.

Dillard, A. (1974). *Pilgrim at Tinker Creek*. New York: Harper & Row.

Dillard, A. (1982). *Living by fiction*. New York: Harper & Row.

Dillard, A. (1982). *Teaching a stone to talk*. New York: Harper & Row.

Dillard, A. (1987). *An American childhood*. New York: Harper & Row.

Elder, J. (1996). Introduction. *American nature writers*. New York: Scribner's.

Elder, J., & Wong, H. D. (1994). *Family of Earth and sky: Indigenous tales of nature from around the world*. Boston: Beacon Press.

Finch, R., & Elder, J. (Eds.). (1990). *The Norton book of nature writing*. New York: W. W. Norton.

Fritzell, P. A. (1989). *Nature writing and America: Essays upon a cultural type*. Ames: Iowa State University Press.

Hay, P. (2002). *Main currents in Western environmental thought*. Sydney, Australia: University of New South Wales Press.

Keegan, B., & McKusick, J. C. (Eds.). (2001). *Literature and nature: Four centuries of nature writing*. Upper Saddle River, NJ: Prentice Hall.

Lopez, B. (1997, Summer). A literature of place. *Portland: The University of Portland Magazine, 16*(2), 22–25.

Lyon, T. J. (Ed.). (1989). *This incomperable lande: A book of American nature writing*. Boston: Houghton Mifflin.

Mabey, R. (1995). *The Oxford book of nature writing*. New York: Oxford University Press.

Murphy, P. D. (Ed.). (1998). *Literature of nature: An international sourcebook*. Chicago: Fitzroy Dearborn.

Murphy, P. D. (2000). *Farther afield in the study of nature-oriented literature*. Charlottesville: University of Virginia Press.

Murray, J. A. (1992). The rise of nature writing: America's next great genre? *Manoa, 4*(2), 73–96.

Payne, D. G. (1996). *Voices in the wilderness: American nature writing and environmental politics*. Hanover, NH: University Press of New England.

Rosendale, S. (Ed.). (2002). *The greening of literary scholarship: Literature, theory, and the environment*. Iowa City: University of Iowa Press.

Sanders, S. R. (1987). Speaking a word for nature. In *Secrets of the universe* (pp. 205–227). Boston: Beacon Press.

Scheese, D. (1996). *Nature writing: The pastoral impulse in America*. New York: Twayne.

Slovic, S. (1996). Politics and epistemology in American nature writing: Embedded rhetoric and discrete rhetoric. In C. G. Herndl & S. C. Brown (Eds.), *Green culture: Environmental rhetoric in American culture* (pp. 82–110). Madison: University of Wisconsin Press.

Slovic, S. (1999, March). Giving expression to nature: Voices of environmental literature. *Environment, 41*(2), 6–11, 25–32.

Thoreau, H. D. (1906). *The journal of Henry D. Thoreau* (B. Torrey & F. H. Allen, Eds.). Boston: Houghton Mifflin.

Thoreau, H. D. (1971). *Walden*. Princeton, NJ: Princeton University Press. (Original work published 1854)

Torrance, R. M. (1998). *Encompassing nature: A sourcebook*. Washington, DC: Counterpoint Press.

Netherlands

(2000 est. pop. 15.6 million)

The Netherlands has a special position on the globe, and that position has influenced the Dutch environment and environmental history. The country is located at the mouth of several rivers (Rhine, Meuse, Scheldt, IJssel), which makes part of the country a delta. This location at the mouth of rivers means that the country has to deal with much more waste than it produces itself. It receives also the waste, mostly chemical, that is dumped into these rivers in other countries.

A great part of the country lies below sea level, which has caused great problems in getting rid of superfluous water. The general impression is that the Netherlands has had to deal with only the dangers from the sea. However, besides the sea there is the water within: superfluous rain water, seepage water. For many centuries the Dutch have been controlling these waters just to keep their land habitable.

A great part of the country is rather flat, which means that there are no fast-running waters and that people have had to cope with stagnant waters. This fact had important consequences for the sanitation of the country. Discharging waste in water didn't mean that one had done away with the problem; at best one had merely put it on a neighbor's doorstep.

Because a great part of the country lies near the sea, most of the time a fresh wind blows. For this reason the Netherlands has less air pollution than several other countries. Its flatness is an advantage because the wind is not hindered by mountains. But because of specific wind directions in the eastern and southern parts of the country, people suffered from air that was polluted elsewhere.

The Netherlands has a rich variety of types of soil. A great deal of the western part of the country (the provinces of North and South Holland) is a mixture of clay and bog peat, whereas the province of Sealand consists mainly of marine clay. However, some parts of these provinces are sandy; there is a difference between old and new marine clay; and there are mixtures of sand and clay. The eastern part of the country is built up from sand, bog peat, and peat moor, and brook dales have a mixture of clay, sand, and peat. Most of the great peat bogs have been cut off. In the West this process started during the Middle Ages and in the East, after the sixteenth century. In some regions the former peat bogs were converted to arable (suitable for cultivation) land and in other regions, to pastures. (Today the Netherlands tries to regain some of the peat by transforming agricultural land.) This variety had consequences for agricultural use, especially when people didn't dispose of artificial fertilizers. As a matter of fact, the quest for manure was a theme during at least four centuries before 1900. By and by an elaborate system for gathering waste (manure) and distributing it to various agricultural regions was developed.

Belated Industrialization

Compared to other western European countries the Netherlands began the Industrial Revolution rather late—in the second half of the nineteenth century. However, this belated industrialization did not mean that the Dutch took advantage of the lessons of the past from other countries—the same problems (e.g., overcrowding of cities and polluted air and water) occurred in the Netherlands.

The Netherlands did not exist as a unified nation before 1789. Before that date the country north of the rivers Meuse and Rhine was split into seven provinces, each with a great measure of autonomy. Within each province the towns were the real centers of legislation; or, in some of the eastern provinces with only a few towns, there were other legislative bodies. Environmental measures had a local or regional impact but had some general characteristics. One of these characteristics was the habit of getting rid of waste at the expense of neighbors, for example, by discharging wastewater in a way that wouldn't harm local citizens but might harm other locales. This practice was continued into the twentieth century.

The fact that the Netherlands has been densely populated for centuries has had consequences: Many large industrial, agricultural, and building projects could not be undertaken in a vacuum. Through the ages this problem has become worse, especially since 1900. The construction of roads and railroads was increasingly accompanied by protests. For example, during the nineteenth century an environmental objection was raised against one of the first railroads—between the Hague and Rotterdam. Conflicts also occurred between several governing boards, for example, between water authorities and communities over draining the effluent of the latter into the waters of the first or between one municipality and another over dumping of refuse.

The Netherlands consumed much more than its basic agriculture and natural resources could provide. Beginning in the Middle Ages the Dutch had to import wheat, furs, wood, and other commodities. The Dutch used a great part of the world for their needs: cereals from the Baltic, furs from Russia and other parts of Europe, wood from Norway, Germany, and eastern Europe, wine from France and southern Europe, metals from Sweden and Germany, and so on. A system that has become common worldwide in the twentieth century was already customary for the Dutch nearly seven hundred years ago. This system had serious ecological consequences, for example, during the seventeenth and eighteenth centuries Germany clear-cut forests to accommodate trade of the so-called *Holländerstämme* (tree trunks destined for the Netherlands).

Dutch Environmental History

During the Middle Ages the Dutch in the western part of the country drained the peat bogs in a way that had a lasting effect not only on the landscape, but also on the water level. The works of the early Dutch had effects that have continued into modern times. Compacting of soils started in the eleventh century and is still of current interest to the present inhabitants. The landscape also was changed by the digging of peat. In the regions where peat was found, it was cut below the groundwater level. As a result large lakes developed, in some cases causing serious problems for people living on the surrounding lands. A lasting effect was caused by the *darinkdelven*, an activity that was practiced especially in the southwestern coastal part of the country whereby saliferous (containing salt) soil or peat was dug to extract salt. However, sometimes too much was dug, allowing the sea to enter. In fact, the coastline of the provinces of Sealand and North Brabant would look different now if the inhabitants of those provinces during the Middle Ages would have been more prudent in their salt production.

Another problem during the Middle Ages was environmental pollution, mainly in the cities. Many *keurboeken* (local laws) were passed against water pollution caused by industries such as tanneries, breweries, and textiles. Individuals also were regulated, for example, concerning the disposal of solid and fluid waste. Livestock kept in cities also created problems. For instance, pigs were used to clean up debris in the mostly unpaved streets, but they left behind their feces. The waste of fish and vegetable markets were another problem. Authorities did their best to control these problems but generally with little result.

With time these problems increased. Especially during the seventeenth and eighteenth centuries many new industries arose, mainly in Holland (the western part of the country). Many of these industries (vinegar factories, sugar refineries, gin distilleries, cement factories) caused serious environmental problems. Especially in Amsterdam, the country's most important trade and industrial center, water pollution and stench became serious problems. The city board tried to handle these problems with town planning whereby tanneries and dying industries were placed in special quarters of the city. Other municipalities tried to do likewise.

Several places in the countryside suffered from pollution. The growing of hemp in the provinces of Utrecht and Holland and flax in the Southwest, mainly for the shipbuilding industry, had serious environmental consequences. During processing, both crops have to be soaked in water for several weeks. This soaking caused a heavy stench. Later hemp and flax were grown in the northern part of the country with comparable consequences.

Population Growth

The prosperity of these times attracted many people to Holland, and the fast-growing population was difficult to accommodate in a hygienic way. In several towns a kind of waste-removal system developed to clean up at least the worst filth. Rich people escaped the towns, preferably in summer, when odors were worst. They had country seats where they could breathe fresh air and where pleasure gardens rendered life agreeable. Of course, these amenities of country life were reserved for a happy few.

During the second half of the eighteenth century people developed an interest in fighting air pollution—which was, in fact, fighting stench. Research was done into the kinds of trees and shrubs that would absorb bad air and into the way towns should be planned to stimulate the movement of air or to prevent air from becoming stagnant.

The growing concern for public health during that age led to a greater awareness of the sanitary conditions of communities. A striking example is the *Rapporten . . . betrekkelijk de aanstelling eener Commissie van Geneeskundig Toevoorzicht, te Amsterdam* (Reports . . . Concerning the Appointment of a Committee of Health in Amsterdam), published in 1798. The *Reports* contained many cases of polluted and unhygienic places and circumstances in Amsterdam. The height of the

houses, the broadness of the streets, the form and size of trees, and the walls surrounding the city affected the quality of the air. The health conditions were worsened by how people dealt with their environment and by the way of sanitation. Amsterdam was full of cess pits, which polluted the soil and the air. People polluted canals by throwing waste into them, refuse disposal was badly organized, and many injurious factories were located within the city walls. The dredging of canals caused an enormous stench and was generally done insufficiently. Residents were forced to throw their waste into the canals because there was no system for gathering refuse. The city itself had been reluctant to enforce rules for many decades.

The situation underwent little change during the first half of the nineteenth century. During the occupation of the country by the French (1795–1813) several attempts were made to enforce hygiene laws, but after the French departed old circumstances returned. During the years 1816–1820 a medical topography (overview of hygienic and sanitary circumstances) of Amsterdam was published, and in 1827 a treatise by physician J. G. Mulder on the water and air of Amsterdam was published. The medical topography shows that most of the problems mentioned in the *Reports* of 1798 still existed. Although the collecting of waste was better organized now, rubbish dumps were located within the built-up area. These dumps were looked upon as manure reservoirs and not as a hygienic provision, and thus when manure prices were low, the heaps were not removed, notwithstanding the hygienic risks such as dust or vermin.

Upon his arrival as a physician in Amsterdam, Mulder was struck by the bad smell of the canals. In his research into its causes he enumerated the waste matter in the water: Human excrement; voidance of distilleries, vinegar factories, and sugar refineries; dirt from the streets; refuse of vegetables and fish; household refuse; ashes; and garbage from stables and butcheries contributed to putrefaction. He concluded that the main reason for the canal water pollution was stagnation, and he suggested some ways to stimulate the flow of the water.

Water pollution was in part responsible for pollution of the air, but also responsible was the presence of so many people in a small area. According to Mulder, each adult consumed 850 liters of oxygen a day. In Amsterdam this led to a consumption of 170,000 cubic meters a day. This oxygen was replaced by carbon dioxide, which had a noxious effect on drinking water. To supplement the oxygen supply

Mulder suggested the planting of trees. Factories, not only by the vapors and smoke they belched, but also by their oxygen-consuming fires, were another cause of deterioration of air quality. Mulder had far-reaching ideas concerning the establishment of factories: They should prove that they were not injurious to health before they could receive permission to operate.

During the second half of the nineteenth century a general discussion of health and environment evolved. The bad state of public health and the protests of physicians persuaded the government to pass sanitary laws in 1865. For some decades there was a strong hygiene movement, and many abuses were denounced. However, the movement met with little success, and in 1897 a state committee to investigate the pollution of public waters was established. Its report, published in 1901, was alarming: Water pollution was ubiquitous in the Netherlands. Although people were now convinced of the gravity of the situation, in the end nothing was done. There were too many diverging interests and too many administrative competences involved. For example, the committee proposed a law against water pollution. However, not until 1970 was such a law passed.

During the first half of the twentieth century the situation was not better. Water pollution decreased only during times of economic depression, when factories slowed or closed and as a consequence released less effluent. The situation grew worse after World War II. The country faced strong industrialization, especially in the chemical sector. With little or no regulation of the pollution of air, soil, or water, factories had rather free play. After some decades and many protests on all levels of society, especially since the mid-1960s, laws were enacted to handle these problems. Since the 1980s the legislative power of the Dutch government has been diminished, and rules are issued more and more by European authorities in Brussels.

Henk van Zon

Further Reading

Ali Cohen, L. (1872). *Handboek der openbare gezondheidsregeling en der geneeskundige politie, met het oog op de behoeften en de wetgeving van Nederland (Handbook of public hygiene in medical policy, with respect to the needs and the legislation of the Netherlands)*. Groningen, Netherlands: Wolters.

Barneveld, W. van, & Muller, J. F. (1785). *Antwoord op de vraag . . . wat heeft men te denken aangaande het planten van boomen, binnen en rondom de steden? Is dit voordeelig of nadeelig voor de gezondheid der menschen? Wordt de lugt door derzelver uitwaseming gezuiverd, of besmet? En welke soort boomen is meest, of minst voordeelig of nadeelig? (An answer to the question . . . how we should think about the planting of trees, within and around towns? Will this be advantageous or harmful to the health of the people? Will the air be purified or polluted by the exhalations of trees? And what kind of trees are the most, or the least advantageous, or harmful?)*. Utrecht, Netherlands: De Waal.

Dekker, C. (1996). De moernering op de Zeeuwse eilanden (The extraction of salt in the islands of Sealand). *Tijdschrift voor Waterstaatsgeschiedenis, 5*, 60–66.

Geuns, M. van (1801). *De staatkundige handhaving van der ingezeetenen gezondheid en leven, aangepreezen, en in eenige proeven voorgedragen (The maintanance of health and life of the inhabitants recommended, and presented in some essays)*. Amsterdam: Allart.

Hofstee, E. W. (1981). *Korte demografische geschiedenis van Nederland van 1800 tot heden (Short demographical history of the Netherlands from 1800 to the present)*. Haarlem, Netherlands: Fibula-van Dishoeck.

Houwaart, E. S. (1991). *De hygiënisten: artsen, staat & volksgezondheid in Nederland, 1840–1890 (The hygienists: physicians, state and public health in the Netherlands, 1840–1890)*. Groningen, Netherlands: Historische Uitgeverij.

Keuning, H. J. (1979). *Kaleidoscoop der Nederlandse landschappen: de regionale verscheidenheid van Nederland in historisch-geografisch perspectief (Kaleidoscope of the Dutch landscapes: The regional differentiation of the Netherlands in historical-geographical perspective)*. The Hague: Nijhoff.

Lambert, A. M. (1985). *The making of the Dutch landscape: An historical geography of the Netherlands*. London: Academic Press.

Leenders, K.A.H.W. (1989). *Verdwenen venen: Een onderzoek naar de ligging en exploitatie van thans verdwenen venen in het gebied tussen Antwerpen, Turnhout, Geertruidenberg en Willemstad (1250–1750) (Disappeared peat-moors: An investigation into the situation and exploitation of nowadays disappeared peat-moors in the region between Antwerp, Turnhout, Geertruidenberg and Willemstad (1250–1750)*. Brussels/Wageningen, Belgium: Gemeentekrediet van België/Pudoc

Leenders, K.A.H.W. (1999). Ecologische aspecten van de middeleeuwse zoutwinning in de Delta (Ecological aspects of the extraction of salt in the Delta [of Sealand]). *Jaarboek voor Ecologische Geschiedenis*, 43–60.

Mulder, G. J. (1827). *Verhandeling over de wateren en lucht der stad Amsterdam en aangrenzende deelen van ons vader-*

land (*Treatise concerning the waters and the air of the city of Amsterdam and adjacent parts of our country*). Amsterdam: Sulpke.

Zanden, J. L. van, & Verstegen, S. W. (1993). *Groene geschiedenis van Nederland* (Green history of the Netherlands). Utrecht, Netherlands: Spectrum.

Zon, H. van (1986). *Een zeer onfrisse geschiedenis: Studies over niet-industriële verontreiniging in Nederland, 1850– 1920* (A very dirty affair: Studies in non-industrial pollution in The Netherlands, 1850–1920). The Hague: Ministry of Housing, Planning and Environmental Conservation.

New Zealand

(2002 est. pop. 4 million)

New Zealand holds a special place in environmental history for at least two reasons. First it is a fragment of the ancient super-continent of Gondwana, cast adrift before the advent of mammals. The Australian ecologist Tim Flannery refers to it as "a completely different experiment in evolution to the rest of the world," showing how things might have looked had the birds been left "to inherit the globe." The birds inhabited a landscape of extremes, one that is geologically vigorous and mountainous from its location astride two great tectonic plates, but also having extensive wetlands, coastlines, and offshore islands. It was 80 percent clothed in forest, ranging from the subtropical to subalpine, at the time of first human contact. Such recent contact—within the last thousand years—is the second reason for the distinctiveness of its environmental history, as successive waves of human immigrants have moved into this unusual biotic setting and produced dramatic impacts.

So dramatic, in fact, that the geographer Kenneth Cumberland alleged in 1941 that the landscape transformation from forest to grassland farm had occurred in little over a century in New Zealand, compared to 400 years in North America and two millennia in Europe. Cumberland published his essay 101 years after the signing of the Treaty of Waitangi between representatives of the British Crown and tribal leaders of the Maori, New Zealand's indigenous people. The essay was, therefore, largely a celebration of European settler environmental "progress," although Cumberland was by no means unaware of its costs, publishing

only three years later the first comprehensive assessment of the extent of soil erosion on deforested lands. However he did perhaps underestimate the extent of the pre-European landscape impacts of the Maori, whose forest burn-offs and hunting activities led to the extinction of over thirty species of native birds, including those of the famous flightless moa, larger than a modern ostrich.

Nonetheless the intensity of environmental impacts has been greater since European arrival. Europeans first sighted the "large land, uplifted high" in 1642, and Captain James Cook began the process of acclimatization of northern hemisphere flora and fauna on his first visit in 1769. The incorporation of New Zealand into an international division of labor as Britain's southern farm after the 1850s initiated the development of today's tidy geometries of farming and exotic forestry. Its native forests have been reduced to a coverage of less than a quarter of the land area, and 85 percent of the wetlands have been drained (compared to less than half in the United States). Just over half of New Zealand is covered in grass, most of it imported pastures from Britain, compared to a global average of 37 percent. Much of the remainder, mountains and some native forests, is held in the national conservation estate, the designation reflecting its negligible value for productive purposes.

A relatively small population, that is, less than 1 million before 1910 and having passed 4 million in 2002, carried out this extraordinary transformation, much of it caught on canvas and camera and written about at length in a readily accessible archive. Little wonder that this transformation has attracted the gaze of overseas scholars since at least the 1940s. The Canadian geographer Andrew Clark spent a wartime sabbatical researching the acclimatization of exotic species in the South Island, subsequently publishing *The Invasion of New Zealand by People, Plants and Animals* (1949). This theme was elaborated by Alfred W. Crosby, who used New Zealand as a prominent case study in his volume *Ecological Imperialism* (1986). Other American environmental historians, such as Stephen Pyne, John McNeill, and Thomas Dunlap have worked on, or in, the country. Recently, William Cronon has republished Herbert Guthrie-Smith's *Tutira*, attributing to this volume his own early interest in the field.

Guthrie-Smith's book, first published in 1921, is the story of the ecological impact of his own land reclamation activities on his run, or large sheep farm, in Hawke's Bay, in the east of the North Island. It is widely quoted as an example of the realization of the unintended consequences of European impacts in settler lands, with loss of habitat leading to the decline of native bird populations, and land disturbance hastening the spread of exotic weeds as well as erosion (Wynn 1997). In recent years New Zealand geographers, ecologists, and historians have written thematic environmental histories. Archeologists and anthropologists have contributed to lively discussions on pre-European Polynesian impacts.

The *New Zealand Historical Atlas* (McKinnon 1997), drawing on these disciplines, took the understanding of environmental change to a new level. It uses dramatic representations of Maori construction and use of territory, alongside archeologists' maps of the traces of such activity in the landscape. Thereafter, it portrays the dispossession of Maori from their lands by Pakeha (European) methods of colonization, illustrates the progressive outcomes of this colonization, and maps some of the environmental hazards that ensued. This project was one of the prompts for an interdisciplinary exploration of the main themes of New Zealand's environmental history, in the form of a book of essays organized chronologically and thematically (Pawson & Brooking 2002). It, along with the *Atlas*, are the most comprehensive single coverage treatments available. Some of their main findings are summarized in the remainder of this entry.

Maori Impacts

Recent scholarship confirms that the Maori impacted the environment in more substantive ways than is often realized, particularly given the tendency today to romanticize the relationship between indigenous peoples and environments. Migrants began arriving from the Polynesian islands in the Pacific from about 800 years ago, according to the evidence of the latest dating techniques, although there has been much debate over the exact timing. They found the new land lacking in familiar staples, and too cold for many of their tropical crops. Consequently, like new colonists everywhere, they used the richest, most accessible resources with pitiless energetic efficiency. Widespread vertebrate extinctions and deforestation occurred until environmental learning brought about adaptive change, at different rates in different parts of New Zealand. In the interests of long-term survival, Maori family (*hapu*) and tribal (*iwi*) units adopted rules of guardianship (*kaitiakitanga*) within well defined, but frequently disputed territories.

European Colonization

Such disputes intensified once regular European incursions began in the 1790s, after the British annexation of New South Wales. Maori were keen traders, and competition for tradable commodities, such as flax, sold in exchange for muskets and agricultural goods, destabilized social organization and its territoriality. At the same time, European diseases began to wreak a terrible toll, as Crosby's *Ecological Imperialism* makes clear. The stories of the impacts of European colonization depend on who is telling them, Maori or Pakeha, and whose perspectives amongst Maori or Pakeha are given voice. This has been the case ever since the signing of the Treaty of Waitangi, which was written in both Maori and several English language versions. To Maori it guaranteed *rangatiratanga*, or chieftainship, over lands they wished to keep; to Europeans it was the instrument of British sovereignty and the imposition of individual rights to land held under title from the Crown (Kawharu 1989).

European appropriation of New Zealand's resources was focused at first on coastal regions, with Auckland in the north being a major center of trading. Land settlement, initially usually organized by British-based colonizing companies, proceeded most rapidly in the South Island, from the late 1840s, because of the extensive areas of less rugged, less forested land, and the small Maori populations. In the North Island, competition for and between Maori owners and Pakeha led to war, in the 1840s and subsequently in the 1860s, before the Crown imposed widespread confiscations. As Maori lands shrank in extent, so too, depleted by disease and disease-induced infertility, did Maori population. It reached its nadir in the 1890s, the very decade in which Pakeha acquisitions of tribal lands reached their peak (Brooking 1996). At this point even sympathetic Europeans felt that Maori demise was inevitable, just as it was thought—in keeping with prevalent Darwinian thinking—that the native flora and fauna was retreating before the onslaught of inherently superior northern hemisphere species.

This onslaught was, however, the product of an energetic colonizing process, backed by the hand of law that mandated commodification of land and facilitated exploitation of resources. Individual colonists experimented widely in determining what would and would not grow where, but much was also carried out with little knowledge of the particularities of specific places. Settlers fired South Island high country tussock lands indiscriminately to provide sheep pasture, leading to pest invasions and the collapse of stocking capacity as early as the 1870s. Huge areas of swampland in both islands, powerhouses of indigenous ecologies and rich reservoirs of food for Maori, were demonized as "waste" and converted into what Geoff Park (1995) calls "imperial landscapes," in which the "linear logic" of modernity met and seemed to beat "the chaos of nature." Settlers cut over and burnt off much of the North Island's bush, as Europeans termed its seemingly impenetrable forest, between the 1860s and 1900.

Conservation

Concern quickly developed over the destruction of resources. The New Zealand Forests Act of 1874, informed by George Perkins Marsh's book *Man and Nature* (1864), has been labeled one of the earliest conservation measures in the British Empire (Wynn 1979). Although ineffectual, it attempted to regulate timber use and stave off a "timber famine" in a country dependent on wood for all sorts of purposes. One of the insights of current research is that this was not an isolated initiative: By the 1890s, urban-based conservation bodies succeeded in establishing island bird sanctuaries and scenic reserves. Extensive areas of alpine lands were protected in national parks by the 1920s; the first such park, Tongariro in the volcanic center of the North Island, has its roots in the 1880s. Mountains became an important symbolic resource, featuring prominently on the first national issue of pictorial postage stamps in 1898. Motives and meanings were often mixed however. Such moves reflected pride in "possession" of spectacular scenery and its value for tourism, as often as any interest in conserving scenery or habitat.

Twentieth Century

Environmental transformation intensified in the twentieth century. A "grasslands revolution" underpinned massive expansion of stock numbers from 1920. Superphosphate (made by mixing sulphuric acid with concentrated bird droppings from the Pacific Island of Nauru) revived soil fertility that flagged after the initial clearance of bush. Delivery of fertilizer by airplanes after 1949 underwrote soaring sheep numbers, which peaked at 70 million in 1980. Prosperity encouraged a belief in the capacity of applied science to solve all problems cheaply and expeditiously, which the growing incidence of environmental hazards, such as soil erosion, did little to dent. In part this blind faith was reinforced by the ongoing investment of the state in programs of "wise use" of resources. These set out in particular to manage soil and water issues, alongside reforestation using fast growing Californian *pinus radiata* (Roche 1994, 1990). At the same time, urban areas, in which a majority of people have lived since 1911, have had to be insulated by an increasingly elaborate infrastructure of flood and earthquake proofing, to protect investment in and the amenity values of what has long been a predominantly suburban nation (Pawson 2000).

Contemporary

Contemporary New Zealand environmental histories focus on three main themes. The first is the extent to which processes of colonization and modernization persist as the driving dynamics of agriculture and forestry. Diversification of land use is now widespread, given the long-term decline in terms of trade for basic commodities such as wool and sheep meat, and the need to find a wider range of markets for a broader range of products. Often this leads to intensification: for instance the conversion of land for dairying, with its concomitant demands for irrigation water and intensified production of solid wastes and gaseous emissions.

The second theme concerns the continued prominence of conservation initiatives. In the last twenty years, the national conservation estate has considerably expanded, to include large areas of native forests, although the success of urban-based environmentalist campaigning to this end has been facilitated by the loss of commercial value in these forests as more readily worked plantations come on stream. The estate is of inestimable value for branding the country as "clean and green" in promotion of the tourist industry, now the largest single source of foreign exchange earnings. At the same time, New Zealand has been a leader in the adoption of sustainability, in the form of the Resource Management Act of 1991, although whether this has fundamentally shifted the bias of law from exploitation is subject to much debate.

Thirdly, Maori resource claims, arising from perceived breaches of the Treaty of Waitangi, have become numerous. The body charged with examining such claims, the Waitangi Tribunal, has commissioned extensive research into each case it has heard over the last twenty years. Its reports are a record of the ways in which *iwi* and *hapu*, growing in size and confidence, have maintained ties to territory, even where land has long since been lost and landscapes remade (Kawharu 1989). These reports, largely available on-line, are testimony to the many voices and multiple perspectives that construct environmental histories, and place a radically different perspective on standard accounts of environmental transformation. In turn there is a parallel realization that Pakeha relations to land in postcolonial New Zealand are more layered than usually represented (Dominy 2001).

Tom Brooking and Eric Pawson

Further Reading

Brooking, T. (1996). *Lands for the people? The Highland clearances and the colonisation of New Zealand. A biography of John McKenzie.* Dunedin, New Zealand: Otago University Press.

Cumberland, K. B. (1941). A century's change: Natural to cultural vegetation in New Zealand. *Geographical Review, 31*(4), 529–554.

Dominy, M. (2001). *Calling the station home: Place and identity in New Zealand's high country.* Lanham, MD: Rowman & Littlefield.

Kawharu, I. H. (Ed.). (1989). *Waitangi: Maori and Pakeha perspectives of the Treaty of Waitangi.* Auckland, New Zealand: Oxford University Press.

McKinnon, M. (Ed.). (1997). *The New Zealand historical atlas.* Auckland, New Zealand: David Bateman.

Park, G. (1995). *Nga Uru Ora the groves of life: Ecology and history in a New Zealand landscape.* Wellington, New Zealand: Victoria University Press.

Pawson, E. (2000). Confronting nature. In J. Cookson & G. Dunstall. (Eds.). *Southern Capital: Christchurch. Towards a city biography* (pp. 60–84). Christchurch, New Zealand: Canterbury University Press.

Pawson, E., & Brooking, T. (Eds.). (2002). *Environmental histories of New Zealand.* Melbourne, Australia: Oxford University Press.

Roche, M. (1990). *History of forestry.* Wellington, New Zealand: New Zealand Forestry Corporation in association with GP Books.

Roche, M. (1994). *Land and water: Water and soil conservation and central government in New Zealand, 1941–1988.* Wellington, New Zealand: Department of Internal Affairs.

Wynn, G. (1979). Pioneers, politicians and the conservation of forests in early New Zealand. *Journal of Historical Geography, 5*(2), 171–188.

Wynn, G. (1997). Remapping Tutira: Contours in the environmental history of New Zealand. *Journal of Historical Geography, 23*(4), 418–446.

Niger Delta

The Niger is Africa's third largest river, 4,167 kilometers long. The delta into which the Niger drains before it enters the Atlantic Ocean in a complex of streams is a huge floodplain in southeastern Nigeria. The Nile delta is a vast sedimentary basin constructed over time through successive thick layers of sediments dating back 40–50 million years to the Eocene epoch. Its immense coastal plain covers almost 70,000 square kilometers.

The Niger delta has been defined for a variety of political, ecological, and geological purposes, but the conventional geographical perimeter extends from the Benin River in the west to the Imo River in the east and from the southernmost tip at Palm Point near Akassa to Aboh in the north, where the Niger River bifurcates into its two main tributaries. This area represents roughly 25,900 square kilometers, about 2.8 percent of Nigeria's land area. It is a classic arcuate (bow-shaped) delta, typically below the 15-meter contour across its entire extent.

The Niger delta has four major ecological zones: coastal sand barrier islands, mainly along the coastline; western African lowland equatorial monsoon, marked mainly by vast stretches of floodplain and riverine swamp; western African freshwater alluvial equatorial monsoon, a levee forest area; and western African brackish-water alluvial equatorial monsoon, dominated by mangroves and an area of transition between mangroves and freshwater alluvial equatorial monsoon. Nigeria's mangroves are the largest in Africa, and over half of them are in the Niger delta.

The Resource Wealth of the Niger Delta

The delta is endowed with very substantial hydrocarbon deposits. Crude-oil production from the delta runs at almost 2 million barrels per day; this accounts for roughly 90 percent of Nigerian export revenues. Nigeria is the largest producer of petroleum in Africa, is among the world's top ten oil producers, and is a member of the Organization of Petroleum Exporting Countries (OPEC). The major drainage systems of the delta consist of seven discrete river systems that lie squarely in the wet equatorial climatic belt. Cloud cover is high, relative humidity is always above 80 percent, and rain falls year round with the exception of a short dry spell in January and February. Soils are hydromorphic (poor in oxygen due to their development in a wet environment) and poorly drained. There are few remaining areas of pristine vegetation, and the contemporary biogeography is largely composed of a mosaic of arable farmlands (planted in cassava, maize, and yams), tree crops (oil palm, rubber, cocoa, plantain), and patches of natural vegetation. The remaining natural vegetation includes lowland rain forest, freshwater swamps, tidal mangroves, salt marsh and tidal mudflats, and coastal forest on the barrier sand ridges.

The Effect of Dams

The construction of dams on the Niger, beginning with Kainji Dam in central Nigeria in 1968, triggered a process that began to alter the Niger delta's hitherto-dynamic and self-regulating ecosystem. Prior to Kainji and several other dams in its wake, there was a fine balance between the constant flooding, erosion, and sediment deposition. Upstream dams led to the loss of 70 percent of sediment transport from the Niger and its tributaries. Sediment deposits are rising again, however, due mainly to the accumulation of silt in the dams, which has led to the decrease in the capacity of the reservoirs to obstruct river flow.

The Human Geography of the Niger Delta

It is difficult to estimate the current population, but since the 1960s population has been growing at about 2.7 percent per annum, and the combined population of the states of Delta, Rivers, and Bayelsa (all of which form the administrative heart of the Niger delta) is in excess of 7 million. The settlement pattern is largely nucleated and rural, with villages typically occupying isolated dry sites within the deltaic swamps. Cities such as Warri and Port Harcourt are found inland where better drainage exists, located at the heads of navigable estuaries. Yenagoa, the capital of the recently founded Bayelsa State, has emerged as a boomtown of several hundred thousands seemingly overnight. Farming systems are predominantly peasant, characterized by small land parcels, short-fallow systems of cultivation (i.e., keeping the land unplanted for one to two years) and diversified forms of rural livelihood, including hunting and fishing.

The delta is a region of enormous ethnic and linguistic complexity. While there are five major linguistic categories (Ijoid, Yoruboid, Edoid, Igboid, and Delta Cross), each embraces a profusion of ethnolinguistic communities (in excess of one hundred across the greater delta). The history of the delta is reflected in this linguistic and cultural complexity; precolonial

trade across the region was linked to a social division of labor rooted in occupation and microecology. Early European explorers commented on the transdeltaic trade networks, but those patterns were radically compromised by the Portuguese in the fifteenth century, and subsequently by French, Dutch, and British slavers. The rise of so-called legitimate trade in rubber and cocoa, which developed under British auspices after Britain abolished slavery in its colonies in 1833, helped create the Oil Rivers Protectorate in which commercial life thrived. One adverse effect of the establishment of the Nigerian colony and the imposition of indirect rule, however, was the marginalization of the multiethnic communities of the delta. Indeed, in the transition to independence in the 1950s, the so-called ethnic minorities voiced their concerns to the departing British that they were largely peripheral in a Nigerian federation dominated by three ethnic majorities (the Hausa, the Yoruba, and the Ibo).

The Political Economy of the Oil Industry

Oil production and related infrastructure development have severely disrupted the natural equilibrium of the Niger delta ecosystem since 1958, when Royal Dutch/Shell opened its first oil field in the area. Several Western multinational oil companies operate in the Niger delta, the most prominent of which are Shell, Chevron-Texaco, Mobil, Elf, and Agip. The oil exploration and production of these companies are almost entirely onshore. This means that the bulk of their operations—oil fields, production stations, and several thousand kilometers of pipelines—takes place in the same ecosystem inhabited by the various local communities, including the flora and fauna.

The consequences of this coexistence have been devastating to the delta's ecology. The highest gas flaring rates in the world, massive contamination of deltaic waterways, and more than 4,640 oil spills between 1976 and 1996 (totaling 3 million barrels). The ecological crisis in the delta is coupled with a deepening political-economic crisis. The oil producing states in Nigeria—all in the Niger delta—generate 90 percent of Nigeria's oil revenues (the remainder comes from ocean drilling), yet they receive only 19 percent of the statutory revenues that the Federal government derives from petroleum sales. Local people complain that they suffer from air pollution resulting from the oil industry's emissions of poisonous gases. Incessant oil spills from old and damaged pipelines also endanger plant life, animals, and humans. Agricultural land and fish-bearing rivers and creeks are also contaminated, leading to significant decrease in yields. International and local environmental groups charge that the oil companies do not conduct adequate environmental-impact studies before operations commence to determine what potential harmful effects such activities are likely to have on the area and how to avoid or minimize them. They also accuse the companies of committing widespread human rights abuses and collaborating with the Nigerian government to suppress legitimate protest and to subvert the quest of local people and their leaders for a new political arrangement in the country, which would give them a fair portion of the revenue from the oil taken from their land.

Not surprisingly, by the 1970s and 1980s, a number of ethnic communities had begun to mobilize against the so-called slick alliance of oil companies and the Nigerian military. A foundational role was played by Ken Saro-Wiwa and the Ogoni people, a small ethnic group of 400,000, who established a political wing (Movement for the Survival of the Ogoni People, or MOSOP) to challenge Shell—one of the transnational companies with a large stake in Nigerian oil—for environmental compensation and the Nigerian state for direct control of their oil. Saro-Wiwa and the MOSOP leadership were hanged by the Nigerian military in 1995, an action that drew the attention of the international community to the growing environmental and social crisis in the area.

Since that time the Niger delta has become a zone of conflict and heightened struggles as more minorities (among them, the Adoni, the Itsekiri, and the Ijaw) organize. Indeed, the central political issue in Nigeria currently is resource control, which refers directly to the question of who controls the oil resources and how ethnic minorities in the delta will determine their futures in a reformed federation.

Prospects

The Niger delta is one of the most complex and fragile ecosystems in the world. It is also a source of vast wealth. These two characteristics have come into open conflict as increasingly enfranchised and militant oil-producing ethnic minorities are confronting the state and the oil companies in order to rehabilitate their environment and to regulate their resource base. At the same time this political mobilization around oil and the environment has generated powerful forms of ethnic identification and conflict that threaten to convert the delta into an unstable and volatile zone. The future of the environment of the Niger delta unfortunately rests in part on the enormous strategic significance and the vast wealth generated by a single commodity that happens to be the fuel of the modern world economic system—hydrocarbon capitalism.

Ike Okonta and Michael Watts

Further Reading

Ashton-Jones, N., & Arnot, S. (1998). *The human ecosystems of the Niger delta*. Benin City, Nigeria: Environmental Rights Action.

Niger Delta Environmental Survey. (1999). *Niger Delta Environmental Survey*. Lagos, Nigeria: author.

Okonta, I., & Douglas, O. (2001). *Where vultures feast*. New York: Sierra Club Books.

Rowell, A. (1996). *Green backlash: Global subversion of the environment movement*. London: Routledge.

Saro-Wiwa, K. (1995). *A month and a day*. London: Penguin Books.

Watts, M. (1997). Black gold, white heat. In S. Pile & M. Keith (Eds.), *Geographies of resistance*. London: Routledge.

Nile Perch

The Nile perch (*lates niloticus*), more commonly known as *mbuta* or *capitaine*, is one of the most important food fish in Africa. It can be found in Lake Chad and in the Congo, Niger, and Nile river systems as far south as Lake Victoria. The Nile perch, a fierce predator of other fish, is one of the largest freshwater fish in the world, with record catches of more than 120 kilograms. A historically important food fish throughout Western and Central African lakes and rivers, controversy surrounds the Nile perch's introduction into Lake Victoria.

Around 1960, local Ugandan fishers or fisheries officials made a clandestine transfer of a small founder population of perch from Lakes Albert and Turkana to Lakes Victoria, Kyoga, and Nabugabo. This introduction caused dramatic transformations in Lake Victoria's ecosystems and fishery economies. Feeding on numerous indigenous species, the Nile perch expanded rapidly in Lake Victoria in the 1980s. Its population increased from less than 5 percent of the estimated total catch combination of the lake's fishery in 1980 to above 80 percent annually from 1985 to the present. Scientists blame the extinction, through both predation and competition, of two hundred to three hundred species of small local fish known as haplochromine on this massive proliferation of Nile perch. The decreased number of algae-eating fish in the lake has caused algae blooms, increased detritus, loss of oxygen in deeper waters, and a subsequent decrease in biomass at lower levels of the lake. While the 1980s witnessed a boom in Nile perch population and average size, in the 1990s average size declined from over 24 kilograms to under 6 kilograms.

The exploding new fishery generated local economic opportunities for some, but also led to a shift to a capital-intensive commercial fishery and to overfishing. In the 1980s the fisher population around Lake Victoria doubled to over thirty thousand as the developing regional and export market in fish attracted immigrants and small-scale investors. Fishers target Nile perch primarily with gill nets, but also with some seine nets and longlines. (Gill nets are hung vertically in the water; they have openings that allow fish to swim partway, but not completely, through the net. Their construction is such that the fish cannot escape by swimming backward. Seine nets are also hung vertically, with sinkers on the bottom and floats on the top; fish are trapped when the ends of the net are pulled together. Longlines are fishing lines with baited hooks hanging off them down their length, which can be several kilometers.) In Lake Victoria, the size and deeper-water location of Nile perch resulted in local investments in larger gill nets and outboard motors.

Beginning in the 1990s, the Nile perch fishery was driven by exports of filets to Israel and Europe. Commercial fleets out of Kisumu (Kenya), Mwanza (Tanzania), and Entebbe (Uganda), fish beyond the range of local outboard fishers. Currently, a dozen factories each in Kisumu, Mwanza, and along the Ugandan coast process the yearly catch of 360,000 to 45,000 metric tons of fish to frozen and fresh filets that are sent by refrigerator truck to the East African coast or to airports for export. The plants also sun dry swim bladders for export to Asia. Industrial Nile perch processing on the shores of Lake Victoria is a new unregulated source of pollutants in the lake.

Perhaps up to three quarters of a million people around Lake Victoria now depend on Nile perch fishing and processing for their livelihoods. A new urban processing economy has emerged, dominated by women who purchase bare fish frames from the processing plants, fry them, and sell them locally. However, for the most part the Nile perch and the commer-

cial export of perch filets have disrupted local fishing economies. The perch have devastated other species. Beyond the processing plants, demand and prices for Nile perch are low. The size and oil content of the fish necessitate that local processors dry the fish over wood-burning fires, but high local fuel costs make this process prohibitively expensive for most people.

Regional and national development boards in Africa promote the Nile perch as a valuable export commodity that attracts foreign capital investment. In contrast, many scientists, local people, and conservation groups argue that the tragedy of local-species extinctions, the drastic changes in the lake itself, and the sudden boom and then rapid decline of the Nile perch fishery due to overfishing and to the population cycle of this exotic predator have created a massive environmental crisis for Lake Victoria and an economic crisis for local people.

Kirk Arden Hoppe

Further Reading
Pitcher, T. J., & Hart, P. B. (Eds.). (1995). *The impact of species changes in African lakes*. London: Chapman and Hall.
Reynolds, J. E., Greboval, D., & Mannini, P. (1992). *Thirty years on: Observations on the development of the Nile Perch fishery in Lake Victoria*. Rome: UNDP/FAO Regional Project for Inland Fisheries Planning.

Nile Valley (Aswan Dam)

The Nile River is one of the natural and romantic wonders of the world and the world's longest river, flowing 6,800 kilometers over 35 degrees of latitude. The Nile stops at the Sadd al-Aali, the High Dam at Aswan, the southern frontier of Egypt. Behind the dam lies the world's largest reservoir, Lakes Nasser and Nubia. Downstream from the dam, the Nile flows as a canal through Egypt to the Mediterranean.

In September 1952, Colonel Gamal Abdel Nasser and his Revolutionary Command Council decided to build a great dam at Aswan to be a monument to their revolution and to provide a constant supply of water for the future security of Egyptians. Engineering and environmental studies were followed by complicated political negotiations with the Sudan about the division of the water. These negotiations were successfully concluded on 8 November 1959 by the Nile Waters Agreement, which made possible the beginning of construction. When the United States and Britain withdrew their offer to finance the dam in July 1956, the Russians agreed to do so in October 1958. On 9 January 1960 President Nasser detonated 9 metric tons of dynamite to demolish 18,100 metric tons of granite on the east bank of the Nile to begin construction of the High Dam.

The technical and engineering obstacles in building the world's largest dam were formidable. The flow of the Nile was predictable but difficult to control even for the Russian engineers with experience on powerful rivers in the Soviet Union. Millions of cubic meters of rock and sand had to be excavated, requiring the organization of Egyptian laborers unfamiliar with the Russians, who were working in an unfamiliar cultural and desert environment. Egyptian contractors took over the construction and recruited over thirty thousand Egyptians to complete the High Dam in September 1970. President Anwar Sadat and President Nikolai Podgorny of Russia inaugurated the dam in January 1971. The dam provided water security for Egypt but at a great environmental cost.

Archeological Impact

After the decision to build the dam had been made, the United Nations Educational, Scientific, and Cultural Organization (UNESCO) launched a massive international campaign in 1955 to preserve the ancient temples, tombs, fortresses, and ruins of Nubian history that would be flooded by the great reservoir (482 kilometers long, 12.8 kilometers wide, and 6,600 square kilometers in area) behind the High Dam. Archeologists and experts in restoration from twenty-three countries directed by an international committee of experts under the aegis of the Nubian Salvage Scheme rescued from oblivion an array of monuments at a cost of $87 million. Some temples, churches, and forts were moved to higher ground. Others were donated to foreign museums in gratitude for their cooperation in the project. The most dramatic rescue was that of the great temple of King Ramses II at Abu Simbel, which was cut into sections and carefully reconstructed above the reservoir, financed by donations of $19 million from many nations.

Social Impact

The rescue of the monuments received international acclaim, but few people were concerned about the fifty thousand Nubians who were forced by the rising waters of the reservoir to leave their historic lands on the banks of the Nile. Their discontent was violent and suppressed by the Sudanese army. They were forcibly relocated to the Sudanese town of Khashm al-Qirbah on the Atbara River, where they became rivals for the land with the traditional herdsmen of the Butana Plain, creating hostility between the immigrants and the owners of the land. The water to irrigate their land comes from the Khashm al-Qirbah Dam, whose capacity has been drastically reduced by the heavy sedimentation from Ethiopia that has severely aggravated the incompatible demands between the pastoral Shukriyya of Sudan and the Nubian cultivators.

Environmental Impact

The environmental impact of the dam had long been studied but not fully realized until the dam's completion. The Nile carries 90 million metric tons of Ethiopian soil annually, depending on the volume of the Nile flood. Upon reaching the quiet waters of the reservoir the heavy silt is deposited at the head of Lake Nubia, the finer grains being deposited throughout the 482 kilometers of Lake Nasser. Between 1978 and 1990 the Nile deposited a billion and a half cubic meters of soil into the first 160 kilometers of the reservoir. This enormous quantity of soil creates what hydrologists call "dead storage." As the reservoir inexorably fills with Ethiopian soil, the "live storage" of water steadily diminishes, giving the High Dam an estimated life of from four hundred to five hundred years.

Moreover, the reservoir is located in one of the most arid deserts in the world where evaporation consumes over 10 billion cubic meters of Nile water, or 12 percent of the total Nile flow, an enormous loss for Egyptians, who are always short of water. The water that remains in Lake Nasser becomes semistagnant and cannot sustain large numbers of fish and plankton, which require oxygen from free-flowing waters for survival. The vast reservoir has become a major obstacle to the fierce sandstorms that blow out of the Western Egyptian Desert. No longer able to pass over a free-flowing river, tons of sand accumulate in big dunes on the bank of the reservoir to add to the dead storage at its bottom. Below the reservoir in the Nubian sandstone south of Aswan is a network of fault lines that has been disturbed by the great weight of water over it. On 14 November 1981 an earthquake measuring 5.3 on the Richter scale occurred, and many locations recorded lesser earthquakes.

Economic Impact

When the nutrient-rich soils from Ethiopia could no longer pass through the dam to nourish their fields, Egyptians had to resort to expensive chemical fertilizers. Only sluggish water was running in northern Egypt to sweep away municipal, industrial, and agricultural waste. Salinity in the delta was increased by the intrusion of brackish water no longer flushed out to the Mediterranean by natural drainage, diminishing productivity in the delta. Also, the absence of sediment has allowed the sea to intrude upon the coast, which has receded. Furthermore, without the annual addition of nutrients, the once profitable sardine industry of Egypt has become extinct. The Egyptian brick industry, which produced a billion bricks a year from Ethiopian sediment, now must buy at premium prices thousands of tons of precious Egyptian agricultural land.

Environmentally and hydrologically the Aswan Dam of the Nile River valley may be the wrong dam in the wrong place, but it has sustained the people of Egypt during the decade of drought in the 1980s, protected them from the enormous floods of the 1990s, and created the illusion that Egypt is free from the danger of being a hostage to upstream riparians from whose countries the Nile flows downstream to the High Dam at Aswan and Egypt.

Robert Collins

Further Reading

Abate, Z. (1994). *Water resources development in Ethiopia: An evaluation of present experience and future planning concepts: A management method for analysing a key resource in a nation's development.* Reading, UK: Ithaca Press.

Cheesman, R. E. (1968). *Lake Tana and the Blue Nile: An Abyssinian quest.* London: Macmillan. (Original work published 1936)

Collins, R. O. (1990). *The waters of the Nile: Hydropolitics and the Jonglei Canal, 1900–1988.* Oxford, UK: Oxford University Press.

Collins, R. O. (1991). *The waters of the Nile: An annotated bibliography.* London: Hans Zell.

Collins, R. O. (2002). *The Nile.* New Haven, CT: Yale University Press.

Erlich, H., & Gershoni, I. (Eds.). (2000). *The Nile: Histories, culture, myths.* Boulder, CO: Lynne Rienner.

Howell, P., & Allan, J. A. (Eds.). (1994). *The Nile: Sharing a scarce resource.* Cambridge, UK: Cambridge University Press.

Howell, P., Lock, P. & Cobb, S. (Eds.). (1988). *The Jonglei Canal: Impact and opportunity.* Cambridge, UK: Cambridge University Press.

Hurst, H. E. (1951). *The Nile: A general account of the river and the utilization of its waters.* London: Constable.

Little, T. (1965). *High Dam at Aswan: the subjugation of the Nile.* New York: John Day.

Said, R. (1993). *The river Nile: Geology, hydrology, and utilization.* Oxford, UK: Pergamon Press.

Sutcliffe, J. V., & Parks, Y. P. (1999). *The hydrology of the Nile.* Wallingford, UK: International Association of Hydrological Sciences.

Tevdt, T. (2002). *The river Nile and its economic, political, social, and cultural role: An annotated bibliography.* Bergen, Norway: Centre for Development Studies.

Waterbury, J. (1979). *Hydropolitics of the Nile Valley.* Syracuse, NY: Syracuse University Press.

Nixon, Richard
(1913–1994)
U.S. president

Richard Milhous Nixon was the thirty-seventh president of the United States. His nearly two terms in office (1969–1974) included the passage of significant environmental legislation, including the Clean Air Act (1970), creation of the Environmental Protection Agency (1970), the Endangered Species Act (1973), and the bill authorizing construction of the Alaskan oil pipeline (1973).

The publication of Rachel Carson's *Silent Spring* in 1962 caused debate over the effects of pesticides on public health, which gave rise to a variety of environmental issues during the 1960s, including concerns over pollution. By the last years of the 1960s, a variety of new environmental groups began to lobby for federal legislation on environmental issues.

Richard Nixon had not supported conservation issues prior to his first term as president. His presidential platform in 1968 focused much more on the war in Vietnam. By the time of his inauguration in January 1969, however, Nixon had read reports that recommended better environmental management. With strong Democratic support behind them, Nixon signed into law the Endangered Species Act of 1969 and the National Environmental Policy Act (NEPA). The NEPA required that an environmental-impact statement be completed for any major federal project.

In his 1970 State of the Union address Nixon spent a considerable amount of time discussing the state of the environment, including environmental issues such as pollution, while at the same time presenting himself as "a champion of efficiency and technological improvement [who was] making peace with nature" (Gottlieb 1993, 109). Recognizing the dangers of air pollution, Nixon supported the Clean Air Act of 1970, which strengthened the Clean Air Act of 1967. In 1970 Nixon also supported and saw created the National Oceanic and Atmospheric Administration (NOAA) and the Environmental Protection Agency (EPA). NOAA's mission was to deal with issues of ocean and marine policy and that of the EPA was to establish and enforce better air and water quality and to deal with solid and toxic waste.

Although Nixon proposed and supported important environmental legislation during 1970, he failed to support the first Earth Day, a popular expression of environmental issues. Perhaps seeing the event's connection to the radical antiwar movement, Nixon lost the opportunity to show that he understood the popular roots of environmental activism. The environmental legislation passed in 1972 and 1973, the Water Pollution Control Act and the Endangered Species Act, did not have Nixon's support due to his concerns over the Watergate scandal and excessive appropriations for both bills. The energy crisis of 1973 promoted the passage of the bill approving the construction of the Alaskan pipeline.

The environmental legislation passed during Nixon's tenure was significant for its efforts to deal with air and water pollution and for its introduction of federal agencies to institute and regulate federal policy.

Kimberly A. Jarvis

Further Reading

Carson, R. (1962). *Silent spring.* Boston: Houghton Mifflin.

Flippen, J. B. (2000). *Nixon and the environment.* Albuquerque: University of New Mexico Press.

Gottlieb, R. (1993). *Forcing the spring: The transformation of the American environmental movement.* Washington, DC: Island Press.

Hays, S. (1987). *Beauty, health, and permanence: Environmental politics in the United States, 1955–1985.* Cambridge, UK: Cambridge University Press.

Hays, S. (2000). *A history of environmental politics since 1945.* Pittsburgh, PA: University of Pittsburgh Press.

Nongovernmental Organizations

Modern governments play a significant role in many areas of society. In west European countries such as the United Kingdom, France, and Germany, this role has included extensive activity in fields such as education, welfare, economic development, and, increasingly, environmental protection. Government intervention and provision of services such as health care have been less marked in North America, but governments there still affect many aspects of the ordinary citizen's life.

However, there is another tradition in which volunteers form an organization to work for a cause. At times they organize because they feel that governments are not doing enough to relieve a problem. At other times they organize because they feel that governments are actually part of the problem. In both cases, the organizations usually try to maintain their independence.

Unlike commercial organizations, these volunteer organizations are nonprofit. They dedicate themselves to what are felt to be intrinsically good causes, such as human rights, animal welfare, conservation, and peace. An early expression of this new social force was the movement against slave trade in the nineteenth century. Other early organizations campaigned closer to home on issues such as poverty and child welfare. Such organizations sometimes constituted themselves on a more formal basis and hired full-time workers to expand the organizations' work. One of the first international examples was the Red Cross, which formed to attend to the suffering of wounded soldiers, regardless of their nationality.

Citizens Organizations

These nonprofit voluntary organizations work outside of government and in recent years have become known as "nongovernmental organizations" (NGOs). They are also called "citizens organizations" and "pressure groups." Some commentators even go so far as to talk of "new social movements" or even a "global civil society" composed of such organizations, in contrast to the world of national governments, traditional political parties, and business corporations.

NGOs might be distinguished from what have been called "quasi-autonomous nongovernmental organizations" (QUANGOs). QUANGOS are set up and financed by governments but, in theory at least, with a degree of autonomy from direct political interference. Another distinction might be made between organizations that campaign and those that provide a service, although a number of organizations, especially in the field of social welfare, do both.

Today's NGOs address a far wider range of issues than do traditional charitable bodies. The United Nations estimates that twenty-five thousand NGOs act at the international level (with twenty-five hundred NGOs having formal consultative status with the U.N.), but many more NGOs focus on the local level.

Diversity of NGOs

NGOs range from loose networks, sometimes just "clearinghouses" to facilitate communication between activists, to organizations with branches and full-time workers in many parts of the world. Some NGOs devote their efforts to raising awareness about certain issues, whereas others engage in practical work. Some are prepared to engage in militant confrontations, whereas others concentrate on in-depth research that will demonstrate the inescapable need for reform. There are campaign groups that "name and shame" those who threaten public well-being, such as companies causing pollution. Then there are NGOs that provide legal expertise and other resources to help individuals and communities to defend themselves. Most NGOs are not seeking power but rather are trying to pressure politicians and business leaders to change their policies.

Some NGOs are well known. Amnesty International, for example, campaigns on behalf of political prisoners, and Oxfam works to reduce hunger and poverty. Friends of the Earth and Greenpeace are leading environmental NGOs with branches in many countries. Many NGOs are conspicuous at fringe meetings outside the official conference halls at events such as the United Nations Earth Summit (Rio de Janeiro, Brazil, 1992). The Fourth World Conference on Women in Beijing, China, in September 1995 attracted thirty-five thousand NGO representatives.

The growth of such organizations was most rapid in the 1990s. This growth reflected a widespread perception that global economic change (globalization) was creating new social, economic, and environmental problems while intensifying old ones. This new economic order was felt by some to be taking power away from citizens. Powerful transnational business corporations were particularly seen as both the cause and the beneficiaries of such change, whereas the losers were local communities and local environments. Furthermore, conventional political parties were increas-

ingly regarded as either accomplices of these business interests or simply impotent in the face of the challenge. Such concerns led an increasing number of citizens to look for other avenues to bring about changes.

Many NGOs exist to oppose particular organizations and policies. For example, various groups campaign against the World Bank and measures such as the North American Free Trade Agreement. Certain technologies, such as nuclear power, have also led to the formation of NGOs to oppose their development.

NGOs tend to be nonaligned in terms of political affiliations. Their reason for existence usually is a cause, perhaps a single issue (e.g., genetic engineering) or a related family of issues (e.g., women's rights). Labor or trade unions might be defined as NGOs, but they tend to focus first and foremost on the wages and conditions of their own members, whereas NGOs tend to work on behalf of exploited and oppressed groups or on behalf of society as a whole.

Valid Role?

However, some NGOs have been attacked for acting selfishly, for engaging in what in Britain is called "NIMBYISM" (from the acronym *NIMBY*, standing for "not in my backyard"). An example would be a group opposing a road project simply because it will have bad effects on the group members' property. That said, it seems only fair to note that most NGOs are composed of individuals working on projects from which they will receive few, if any, direct personal benefits.

Some NGOs are now big organizations. Amnesty International, for example, is said to have over 1 million members with local groups in over ninety countries. Its London headquarters has a staff of over three hundred. Some critics allege that there is the danger of NGOs becoming bureaucratized, more concerned about their own existence than the causes they should be promoting. However, it could be argued that such organizations have to develop their expertise and administrative systems if they are to be effective.

A deeper criticism is that NGOs are not accountable. Politicians have to submit themselves to the judgment of the electorate when elections come around. To that extent, they are answerable for their actions. By comparison, NGOs never have to face that test, even if they claim to be speaking on behalf of the public or at least significant sections of it. Some business leaders refer to NGOs as "no good organizations." In their eyes and perhaps those of government leaders, NGOs irresponsibly stir up trouble but offer no practical alternatives.

However, it should also be noted that there is much evidence that ordinary members of the public place greater trust in NGOs than in politicians. Furthermore, there are few proven cases of corruption and other malpractice among NGOs, despite the large sums of money that pass through the hands of the bigger organizations. They also face the accountability test in that, if they were failing to do their job, members would resign, and public donations would dry up.

Some NGOs have been criticized for being too soft in their criticism of, for example, business corporations or senior decision makers in government. Certainly some of the more traditional environmental protection and animal welfare groups try to work closely with private companies and government departments. Their strategy is usually defended on the grounds that there is more to be gained by opening channels of communications and creating a dialogue than by engaging in militant confrontation.

A more complex issue is the source of funding. Some multinational businesses such as oil and chemical firms regularly donate money to social and environmental projects, for example. The question of whether NGOs should seek funding from such sources is perhaps one that will never be fully resolved. It might be argued that such funding compromises the recipients, but the reply might be made that, in the real world, some concessions are unavoidable.

There is one other area of contention. Some NGOs undertake practical work either in addition to or instead of campaigning. Critics might say that these NGOs are conducting activities that really ought to be delivered by full-time and properly funded public services. Yet, there is the counterargument that governments cannot—and should not try to—substitute for voluntary work undertaken by citizens willing to become socially involved. Furthermore, it could be said that many problems are too urgent to wait for government action.

Although they have few formal powers, NGOs have achieved much and have an impressive record. In recent years they have successfully fought for new environmental and weapons agreements. For example, measures to protect the ozone layer (the 1987 Montreal Protocol) and reduce the use of land mines owed much to work by NGOs. Similarly they have helped to win greater rights for women and groups such as tribal peoples. Awareness of the burden of debt on poorer countries owes a great deal to the work of the Jubilee

2000 Campaign. Perhaps the assessment by Kofi Annan, United Nations secretary-general, that NGOs are "the conscience of humanity," sums up their role in the modern world.

Sandy Irvine

Further Reading

Bennett, J. (1995). *Meeting needs: NGO co-ordination in practice.* London: Earthscan.

Cohen, R., & Raij, M. S. (Eds.). (2000). *Global social movements.* London: Athlone Press.

Edwards, M., & Gaventa, J. (Eds.). (2001). *Global citizen action.* London: Earthscan.

Ekins, P., & von Uexkull, J. (1992). *Grassroots movements for global change.* New York: Routledge.

Florine, A. M. (Ed.). (2000). *Third force: The rise of transnational civil society.* Washington, DC: Carnegie Foundation.

Hancock, G. (1989). *The lords of poverty.* New York: Atlantic Monthly Press.

Lischutze, R. D., & Mayers, J. (1996). *Global civil society and global governance: The politics of nature from place to planet.* Albany: State University of New York Press.

Stokke, O. S., & Thommeson, O. B. (Eds.). (2001). *Yearbook of international cooperation on environment and development.* London: Earthscan.

Trzyna, T., & Didion, J. (Eds.). (2001). *World directory of environmental organisations.* London: Earthscan.

North America—California
(2000 est. pop. 34 million)

California has changed dramatically over the past fifteen thousand years. Some of the changes, such as climatic warming and glacial retreat at the end of the Ice Age, were entirely natural. Others were caused by human activity, for example, the devastation wrought the Gold Rush. Often the environment was affected by a combination of natural and cultural forces. The mass extinction of animal species soon after 12,000 BCE is a case in point. The end result of these changes over time is modern California, a place far different than the primeval land found by the Indians who first settled here.

Environmental Overview

California lies on the Pacific coast of North America between 32 and 42 degrees north latitude. The state is

And how should a beautiful, ignorant stream of water know it heads for an early release—out across the desert, running toward the Gulf, below sea level, to murmur its lullaby, and see the Imperial Valley rise out of burning sand with cotton blossoms, wheat, watermelons, roses, how should it know?

—Carl Sandburg, *Good Morning America*, 1928

1,351 kilometers long (north to south), but its shoreline totals more than 2,400 kilometers. Its width varies from 257 to 405 kilometers (west to east), respectively at the latitudes of Sacramento and Point Concepcion. Covering 409,741 square kilometers (41 million hectares), California is third in area among the 50 states. Its population and economy, however, rank first.

The Golden State is a land of great environmental diversity; indeed, its varied regions are aptly called "the Californias." The state encompasses all or parts of eleven natural provinces, each distinctive in terms of geologic origin, landforms, climate, soils, vegetation and wildlife. Typical features are parallel mountains and valleys aligned north to south, among them the Central Valley, Coast Ranges, and Sierra Nevada. The maverick Transverse Ranges, however, trend west to east from the northern Channel Islands to the western edge of the Mojave Desert. Relief within California is extreme. The highest and lowest points in the contiguous 48 states—Mt. Whitney (4,418 meters above sea level) in the Sierra Nevada, and Badwater (85 meters below sea level) in Death Valley—are only 128 kilometers apart.

In far northwestern California granitic and metamorphic rocks form the rugged Klamath Mountains whose slopes rise to 2,400 meters. Rainfall there can exceed 250 centimeters per year, the heaviest in the state. To the east, volcanic peaks of the Cascade Range are dominated by Mt. Shasta (4,316 meters) and Mt. Lassen (3,187 meters). Both the Cascade and the Klamath uplands are densely forested. East of the Cascade Range, lava beds and shallow lakes at elevations above 1,200 meters typify the Modoc Plateau. Along the eastern edge of the state, on the arid leeward side of the Cascades and Sierra Nevada, are the faulted ranges and valleys of the western Great Basin, part of a vast desert province that sweeps from California across Nevada and well into Oregon and Utah.

South of the Cascades and west of the Great Basin a huge mass of granitic rock (640 by 110 kilometers) has been uplifted to become the Sierra Nevada, California's loftiest range. Nearly 500 peaks along the crest are more than 3,000 meters high. Nestled between the Sierra and the Coast Ranges is the Central Valley (640 by 80 kilometers), drained from the north by the Sacramento River and from the south by the San Joaquin River. With its long growing season, deep soils and ample water, the Valley is America's premier agricultural region. Between the Valley and the Pacific shore are the Coast Ranges, a geologically complex series of old mountains rising to 2,100 meters. The North Coast Ranges meet their South Coast kin at San Francisco Bay, the state's largest estuary, through which the combined waters of the interior rivers flow to the sea.

South of the Coast Ranges, Central Valley, and Sierra Nevada, the Transverse Ranges divide central from southern California. Deep, faulted sediments there contain abundant petroleum. Los Angeles sprawls over hills and valleys in the southwestern part of this province. Down the coast in the San Diego vicinity are the Peninsular Ranges, so named because they continue into Mexico as the backbone of the Baja California peninsula. These mountains were formed when granitic magma was intruded into older metamorphic rocks. Farther inland on both sides of the international border, the Colorado Desert (including the Imperial Valley and Salton Sea) occupies a trough between forks of the San Andreas Fault. Finally, the Mojave Desert covers a large area east of the Transverse Ranges and Colorado Desert and south of the Sierra Nevada and Great Basin. The Mojave province consists of isolated mountain ranges and expanses of low and high desert pocked by the dry beds of ancient lakes.

Natural Environmental Changes

Nature is constantly busy reshaping California. The earth moves along countless faults; mountains erode, even as they push upward; and volcanoes erupt, spewing ash and rock. Climates fluctuate, bringing now ample moisture and then prolonged drought. Glaciers

Runaway population growth in the twentieth century brought urban sprawl and freeways to Los Angeles leading to habitat loss, air pollution, water shortages, and other environmental problems. COURTESY MICHAEL J. MORATTO.

wax and wane, sculpt and polish; streams flood, carve valleys, and deposit sediments; coastal features emerge or disappear as sea levels fall or rise; and lakes fill, only to evaporate in arid times. As well, vegetation adjusts to shifting climate and available moisture. These are some of the ways by which California's land and life-forms have come to be. Because change is perpetual, and has been for millennia, no single time period can represent California's primal landscape.

Prior to 11,600 BCE, California was gripped by ice age climates of the Pleistocene epoch. On the coast, waves pounded beaches as far as 35 kilometers west of the present shoreline, a result of water trapped in continental ice sheets and lower sea levels worldwide. Glaciers were entrenched in the high Sierra, on Cascade peaks, and in the Klamath Mountains. Heavy precipitation, cool temperatures, and minimal evaporation kept life zones (areas characterized by specific plants and animals) at low elevations and created lakes in the deserts and Central Valley. Pine forests stood in the hill country where oaks now grow, and the Mojave Desert was a region of deep lakes and fertile marshes surrounded by cold steppes and woodlands. Roaming the land were bison, musk oxen, camels, horses, giant sloths, mastodons, and mammoths along with such predators as the dire wolf, saber-toothed cat, lion, cheetah, and short-faced bear. Collectively these ancient beasts are the Rancholabrean fauna, named after the Rancho la Brea tar pits and fossil beds in Los Angeles.

By 9000 BCE the Pleistocene epoch was ending. As ice fields melted and sea levels rose, California's shoreline crept inexorably landward. Warm temperatures and declining precipitation led to retreat of glaciers in the mountains, shrinking of lakes in the lowlands, and the upward march of biotic (relating to flora and fauna) communities. Most Rancholabrean species had vanished by this time due to hunting pressure and habitat loss driven by climatic warming. The modern fauna—

deer, elk, pronghorn, coyote, and grizzly and black bear—promptly filled open niches in the mosaic of emerging habitats.

Warm temperatures prevailed during the early Holocene (postglacial) epoch. By 6000 BCE the sea had risen enough to enter the Golden Gate and begin filling San Francisco Bay. Other estuaries up and down the coast similarly began to form when marine waters invaded the lower reaches of streams. While the sea advanced, lakes retreated. Sustained high temperatures caused lakes and marshes to evaporate, leaving behind only playas and wave-cut terraces to mark their beds and high stands. Alpine glaciers continued to wane, and life zones migrated northward and to higher altitudes. As xerophytes (plants adapted to live with very little water) colonized the arid lowlands of southern California, the Mojave and Colorado provinces became true deserts.

Between 6000 and 2500 BCE drought and high temperatures prevailed in California, and surface water was often scarce. Vegetation series moved yet farther north and upslope, while tree lines and lower forest borders reached their highest elevations. At this time of ecologic stress the carrying capacity (the population that an area will support without deterioration) of many habitats declined, particularly in areas away from the coast. Sea levels continued to rise, pushing the shoreline ever upward and filling estuaries. By about 2500 BCE San Francisco Bay had nearly achieved its maximum extent of 1,800 square kilometers. As bay waters rose, the velocity and sediment-load capacity of the lower Sacramento and San Joaquin Rivers fell, resulting in widespread deposition of sediment and creation of the delta with its labyrinth of sloughs and marshes.

Beyond these changes the stupendous eruption of Mt. Mazama (now Crater Lake, in southern Oregon) in 4890 BCE blanketed the northern half of California with volcanic ash. Volcanoes in California also were active during the Holocene epoch, for example, the eruptions of Mono Craters (6010 BCE, 1950 BCE, 80 CE, 760 CE), Inyo Craters (1250 CE) and Mt. Lassen (1914–1917 CE). The effects of the California eruptions were local and not of the magnitude represented by the Mazama event.

Between 2500 BCE and 1850 CE the overall climatic trend in California was toward cool and moist conditions. This trend was punctuated twice, first by the Medieval Warm Interval (900–1350 CE) and then by the unusually wet regime of the Little Ice Age (1350–1850 CE). The former witnessed two episodes of severe drought (912–1112 CE and 1210–1350 CE) separated by ninety-eight years of relatively moist climate. The extreme aridity tested the drought tolerance of plants and animals, and reduced species diversity and density in ecosystems. Before and after the warm interval, however, the character and distribution of vegetation resembled those of the later historic period.

Effects of Native American Activities

People have lived in California for at least 135 centuries and over time have adapted to every part of the state, from the north coast forests to the southern deserts. When resources were optimal, the human population reached 300,000 to 450,000; in hard times the numbers were smaller. By 1500 CE native Californians were among the most advanced hunter-gatherers on Earth. Although subsistence modes varied geographically and seasonally, native peoples typically gathered a wide range of fruits, seeds and nuts (especially acorns), greens, roots, and bulbs. They hunted or trapped diverse mammals, took waterfowl, collected shellfish, and engaged in both freshwater and marine fishing. Only in parts of southern California, and only in late prehistoric times (after 1000 CE), was agriculture practiced to a limited extent.

These activities, along with the use of building materials, firewood, and tool stone, generally had little impact on the environment; but there are three notable exceptions. The first is the demise of Rancholabrean species at the end of the Ice Age. These animals died out not only because habitats were disrupted by climatic shifts but also because of intense hunting. The second exception is that as human settlements grew, the abundance and size of local prey animals often declined. This in turn led to exploitative pressure on other resources. And third, by using "proto-agricultural" methods, native peoples managed fire frequency and intensity, plant succession, and species composition. Thus, for millennia California was as much a cultural landscape as a "wilderness" untouched by humans.

Except for the mass extinction, long-term effects of native land use were relatively slight. Given their modest numbers (equal to about 1 percent of California's population today) and simple technology, the native Californians did not impact the environment very much. Moreover, their relationship with nature was viewed as sacred: All life was spiritual, and people were obliged to use resources only when needed and then respectfully, sparingly and in such a way as to ensure future supplies. Sustainability as a focal concept was thus imbued with religious conviction. Flowing from this ethic were many subtle practices, notably burning to control brush, create browse for game, and maintain meadows; sowing seeds; tending plots to increase yields of food and fiber; using game efficiently, wasting nothing; and abiding by fishing seasons to foster an equitable and lasting reliance on salmon. In sum, California's bounty was nurtured rather than depleted by the natives. Their ways of life might have persisted indefinitely, albeit with cycles of growth and recession, had they not been disturbed by outsiders.

Spanish and Mexican Period

Even before 1769, when Spanish settlement began, waves of infectious diseases had swept through California, devastating native societies. This had the effect of releasing harvest pressure on fish and game animals, allowing their numbers to rebound; but it also curtailed traditional land management. Between 1769 and 1822, the Spanish in California established twenty missions, four presidos (military forts), several pueblos (towns), and connecting roads—all to bolster the northern frontier of New Spain. The goals were to "civilize" the natives, convert them to Catholicism, and forge a society loyal to the Crown as a bulwark against the threat of foreign occupation.

In realizing these goals, the Spanish changed the landscape in many ways. With draft animals, plows, steel tools, and native labor they tilled the earth and planted crops. They dammed streams to supply water for domestic needs and irrigation. Their sheep, cattle, horses and swine variously overgrazed range land, caused soil erosion, devoured the mast (nuts accumulated beneath trees) of oak groves, and consumed young trees. The livestock also spread exotic diseases and competed with wild animals for forage. Moreover, the Spanish brought to California, either intentionally or otherwise, numerous alien plants. Some, for example, olive and citrus trees, maize and onions, were contained in orchards, plowed fields, and gardens. Others, including storksbill (*Erodium botrys*) and the notorious wild oats (*Avena barbata* and *A. fatua*), quickly spread and overwhelmed native bunch grasses. The most devastating environmental impact of Spanish tenure, however, was the removal of native people from their traditional land stewardship roles. Altogether, more than 70,000 native Californians were forced to abandon

homelands that they and their forebears had tended for centuries.

Spanish land-use tactics were continued and expanded by Mexicans after 1822. When the last mission was founded at Sonoma in 1823, California belonged to Mexico. The missions were agricultural centers, known for their fruitful orchards and yields of barley, wheat, and corn and for their abundant livestock. In the 1820s herds of five thousand to ten thousand cattle and even larger flocks of sheep grazed at a number of the missions. These burgeoning herds only added to the impacts mentioned above. Although the missions were secularized between 1834 and 1836, their lands continued to be used for farming and ranching by the new owners.

Mexican land grants strongly influenced the environmental history of California. Between 1824 and 1846, approximately 813 land claims were filed. A few parcels were in the Central Valley, but most were in western California between San Diego and Sonoma County. An immediate effect was the geographic spread of ranching well beyond the reach of former settlements. The size of the land grants is remarkable: many were of 8,100 to 22,300 hectares, and a few were much larger: Simi (45,733 hectares); the former Mission San Fernando (47,290 hectares); and Santa Margarita y las Flores (54,001 hectares). These grants were the foundation of the great ranchos with their cattle herds as large as fifty thousand head. During the annual *matanzas* (slaughters) when cattle were killed for their tallow and hides, thousands of carcasses littered the countryside. With access to such a prodigious supply of meat, and with the removal of human competitors (that is, native people) from the ecosystem, grizzly bear populations surged during the rancho era. Even though *Californios* (the Spanish colonists of California and their descendants) often killed bears outright or captured them to fight with bulls, the number of grizzlies remained exceptionally high in the vicinity of ranchos until the early 1850s.

The Gold Rush

Mexican rule ended in 1846–1848 with the Bear Flag Revolt and U.S. conquest. The non-native people in California then numbered about eight thousand. In January 1848 gold was discovered on the American River east of Sacramento. The ensuing Gold Rush caused more environmental damage than did any event in the previous ten thousand years. Six thousand men swarmed to the diggings in 1848; in the next year eighty-nine thousand more arrived from all over the world; and by 1850 the number of gold seekers had surpassed 150,000. Cities sprang up almost overnight. San Francisco exploded from two thousand residents in early 1849 to thirty thousand in 1850. Sacramento and Stockton kept the pace. The urbanization of California had begun. In the first dozen years of the gold frenzy California's non-native population skyrocketed to 380,000—forty-eight times the previous number!

In every gully and canyon of the Sierra mining districts, from the Feather River down to Mariposa Creek, men worked feverishly to overturn the landscape. At first pay dirt was shoveled into pans or other devices operated by individual miners. Then, as the digging gained momentum, streams were diverted, flumes and ditches built, and the potential of water pressure realized. Using large canvas hoses and iron nozzles, miners after 1853 "hydraulicked" stream banks and entire hillsides with powerful jets of water to extract gold from sediments. (A single twenty-centimeter nozzle could discharge 5,240 cubic meters of water per hour at a velocity of forty-five meters per second!) Soon river dredging, quartz (hard rock) mines, and ore mills were operating. Gold seekers obliterated streamside habitats, clear-cut woodlands, polluted streams, and despoiled hundreds of miles of spawning beds. They destroyed salmon runs in the Sierra foothills, and washed several billion tons of sediment into the delta and San Francisco Bay. Not until 1884 did the Court issue a "perpetual injunction" against hydraulic mining. Beyond such monumental direct impacts, the Gold Rush set into motion the forces of resource extraction and rapid population growth that have dogged California ever since.

Late Nineteenth Century

The pace of environmental change after the Gold Rush has only accelerated. Native people were driven from their lands and confined to reservations throughout the state. Starting in the 1860s, the Central Pacific, Southern Pacific, and other railroads quickly built hundreds of miles of track in California for which they received U.S. land grants totaling 4.6 million hectares—more than 20 percent of the public domain in the state. Much of this land was then sold to settlers who cleared natural vegetation and planted crops in soils never before plowed. Farming, together with the demand for wood to fuel steamboats, took its toll. Riparian (relating to watercourses) woodlands once covered more than 364,000 hectares in the Central Valley;

today less than 12,000 hectares remain. In a positive vein, late in the nineteenth century the federal government established in California a system of forest reserves and three national parks: Yosemite, Sequoia, and Kings Canyon. By 1900, the state's population had climbed to 1.6 million, setting the stage for unprecedented growth and change in the twentieth century.

Early Twentieth Century

In the name of progress, monumental efforts were made to tame wild California and to harness its resources. Market hunters nearly obliterated many fish and game species. By 1915, only about thirty sea otters remained of an earlier population estimated at upward of twenty thousand animals. Tule elk, pronghorn, mountain sheep, and the California condor vanished regionally, while the wolf and California grizzly bear was pursued to extinction. Most of the old-growth redwoods in the Coast Ranges were logged off, as were huge tracts of virgin pine and fir forest in the Sierra and Cascades. Thousands of miles of paved roads shaped the automotive landscape and contributed to the sprawl of Los Angeles and other cities. Incredibly rich ecosystems in the San Joaquin Valley were sacrificed when Tulare and Buena Vista lakes were drained to make way for agriculture. After an unsuccessful fight led by naturalist John Muir, in 1923 the spectacular Hetch Hetchy Valley in Yosemite National Park was dammed to quench the thirst of San Francisco. Huge dams were built on the Sacramento, San Joaquin, and Colorado Rivers to generate hydropower and provide water to the state's rapidly growing cities and farms; again, unique ecosystems were lost in the bargain. This momentum reached a peak in California's expansion during World War II. Farms, mines, aircraft factories, shipyards, port facilities, military bases and cities all experienced phenomenal growth between 1941 and 1945. The direct environmental costs of this growth are measured in terms of habitat loss, watershed damage, pollution, destruction of wetlands and attrition of native species, not to mention the burden of 1.9 million new California residents. By 1950 the state's population had surpassed 10 million and amid signs of growing environmental strain.

Late Twentieth Century

During the last five decades, as the population surged to over 34 million, California's environmental problems mounted. Urban sprawl, abetted by an expanding network of freeways and airports, consumed millions of hectares of wild lands and led to severe air pollution. Laws, such as the National Environmental Policy Act (1969) and the California Environmental Quality Act (1970), were passed to address a wide range of issues in the context of planning. Although these laws have reduced the environmental impacts of individual projects, the totality of landscape modification has been staggering. Looming water shortages "justified" creating new dams on myriad rivers and building the California Aqueduct to move water from north to south. Family farms gave way to large-scale agribusiness evinced by land leveling, stream channeling, and irrigation along with heavy reliance on fertilizers, pesticides, and herbicides. Cattle ranching similarly evolved from dispersed grazing to centralized feedlot operations. Consequently, farming in the late twentieth century became a significant source of soil and water pollution. Timber harvests often proceeded at unsustainable rates, and poor fire-management strategies led to conflagration of forests. Throughout the state, ecosystems were collapsing.

California's landscape today is far different than the one seen by the Spanish 230 years ago. As Michael G. Barbour sums it up,

> Desert scrub is degraded by overgrazing, purposely set fires, ORVs [off-road vehicles], and changed by invasive forbs, grasses, and shrubs. Montane forests have abnormally flammable dense understories because of fire supression and resultant overstories that are weakened by drought and atmospheric pollutants. Square miles of chaparral have been converted to grassland of homesites, coastal scrub to annual grassland and suburbs, and perennial grasslands to weedy annual pastures or farmland. Only 5–25% of our old-growth forests remain (depending on the forest type), less than a fragmented 10% of coastal wetlands and a meager 2% of interior wetlands are still with us. . . . About one-fourth of our native plant species and one-fourth of our plant communities are threatened with extinction. . . . One-seventh of our flora is non-native and—in such cases as grassland—the non-natives constitute >90% of the cover and biomass. (Barbour 1996, 5)

Today California is beset by environmental challenges. High on the list are supplying enough water to meet the needs of cities, agriculture, fish, and wildlife; ensuring air and water quality; limiting urban sprawl and habitat loss; proper disposal of solid waste; sound forest management; and preserving native biodiversity in the path of land development and alien species invasion. These problems are being faced systematically, with varying degrees of commitment, by agencies and decision makers. Also critically important, however, are curbing the human population explosion, habitat restoration, and planning to cope with severe drought—three challenges that so far have not evoked the level of political concern merited by their implications for California's future.

Michael J. Moratto

Further Reading

Bakker, E. S. (1984). *An island called California: An ecological introduction to its natural communities* (2nd ed.). Berkeley & Los Angeles: University of California Press.

Barbour, M. G. (1996). California landscapes before the invaders. California Exotic Pest Council, *1996 Symposium Proceedings*. Davis, CA: Department of Environmental Horticulture, University of California.

Barbour, M., Pavlik, B., Drysdale, F., & Lindstrom, S. (1993). *California's changing landscapes: Diversity and conservation of California vegetation.* Sacramento, CA: California Native Plant Society.

Bean, L. J., & Blackburn, T. C. (1976). *Native Californians: A theoretical retrospective.* Ramona, CA: Ballena Press.

BioSystems Analysis, Inc. (1994). *Life on the edge: A guide to California's endangered natural resources. Wildlife.* Santa Cruz, CA: BioSystems Books in collaboration with Heyday Books.

Blackburn, T. C., & Anderson, K. (Eds.). (1993). *Before the wilderness: Environmental management by native Californians.* Menlo Park, CA: Ballena Press.

Duane, T. P. (1999). *Shaping the Sierra: Nature, culture, and conflict in the changing West.* Berkeley & Los Angeles: University of California Press.

Evarts, J., & Popper, M. (Eds.). (2001). *Coast redwood: A natural and cultural history.* Los Olivos, CA: Cachuma Press.

Fradkin, P. L. (1995). *The seven states of California: A natural and human history.* Berkeley & Los Angeles: University of California Press.

Gutierrez, R. A., & Orsi, R. J. (1998). *Contested Eden: California before the Gold Rush.* Berkeley & Los Angeles: University of California Press in association with the California Historical Society.

Heizer, R. F., & Elsasser, A. B. (1980). *The natural world of the California Indians.* Berkeley & Los Angeles: University of California Press.

Holliday, J. S. (1999). *Rush for riches: Gold fever and the making of California.* Berkeley & Los Angeles: University of California Press.

Merchant, C. (Ed.). (1998). *Green versus gold: Sources in California's environmental history*. Washington, DC: Island Press.

Paddison, J. (Ed.). (1999). *A world transformed: Firsthand accounts of California before the Gold Rush*. Berkeley, CA: Heyday Books.

Peters, G. L., Lantis, D. W., Steiner, R., & Karinen, A. E. (1999). *California* (3rd ed.). Dubuque, IA: Kendall/Hunt.

Preston, W. L. (1981). *Vanishing landscapes: Land and life in the Tulare Lake basin*. Berkeley & Los Angeles: University of California Press.

Rawls, J. J., & Bean, W. (2003). *California: An interpretive history* (8th ed.). Boston: McGraw-Hill.

Sawyer, J. O., & Keeler-Wolf, T. (1995). *A manual of California vegetation*. Sacramento, CA: California Native Plant Society.

SNEP Science Team and Special Consultants. (1996). *Status of the Sierra Nevada: Sierra Nevada ecosystem project, final report to Congress*. Davis, CA: Wildland Resources Center.

North America—East

Physical, biological, and cultural environments of eastern North America have been profoundly shaped by global climatic oscillations during the most recent series of ice ages of the Quaternary period. The Quaternary period of geologic history extends over the past 2 million years and consists of the Pleistocene epoch (2 million to 11,500 years ago) and the Holocene epoch (11,500 years ago to the present). During the Quaternary period, continental ice sheets have waxed and waned over about twenty glacial-interglacial cycles, each cycle 100,000 years in duration. The most recent ice age, or Wisconsinan continental glaciation, reached its maximum about twenty-one thousand years ago (19,000 BCE) and was followed by climate warming that resulted in the retreat of continental glaciers in both North America and Europe. Humans entered the North American continent near the end of the Pleistocene epoch.

Environments

During the Wisconsinan continental glaciation's maximum, the Laurentide continental ice sheet extended southward in eastern North America to the present-day confluence of the Ohio and Mississippi Rivers. South of the ice sheet, climates were cold enough to support growth of evergreen boreal (cold-requiring) forests of spruce and jack pine across extensive portions of the continental interior. Warmth-requiring vegetation, including forests composed of deciduous trees, was confined to latitudes south of about 34°N, along the Gulf Coastal Plain and peninsular Florida. Mammal communities were unlike those of today, with northern and southern species intermingled across middle latitudes. This rich and diverse fauna of the Pleistocene ice ages included numerous species of now-extinct megafauna (those with adult body weight greater than 45 kilograms), such as giant beaver, ground sloth, saber-toothed tiger, short-faced bear, mammoth, and mastodon.

Cultures

Archeological evidence to determine when the first Paleo-Indians (early American hunting people of Asian origin living during the late Pleistocene) immigrated is sparse, but current evidence indicates that initial immigration could have begun before fifteen thousand years ago (13,000 BCE). Earliest sites in Pennsylvania, Virginia, South Carolina, and Florida contain human artifacts that have proved difficult to date accurately. Initial colonists were failed migrations of limited populations who were unable to persist and flourish and hence left only a sparse archeological record.

Culture-Environment Interactions

The locations of ice sheet margins and shorelines of freshwater lakes flanking glaciers, river courses fed by summer meltwater from glacial ice, and wide continental shelves exposed by lowered sea levels (as water was stored in great ice sheets) would have influenced the routes by which Paleo-Indians first entered the continent and later spread southward throughout the Americas. Initial entry may have been on foot via the Bering land bridge connecting Siberia with North America. Alternatively, Paleo-Indians may have explored the coastline of the eastern Pacific Ocean, island-hopping via skin boats. Some of the earliest substantiated human artifacts, including both triangular and lance-shaped projectile points, are found in the southeastern United States. It has been suggested that in addition to Asia, Europe was a possible source of human immigrants who may have crossed the North Atlantic Ocean along the pack-ice margin that linked Portugal with the Carolinas.

A Traveler's Impression of the Flora of Eastern North America in the Eighteenth Century

I went to-day accompanied by Mr. *Jacob Benston*, a member of the *Swedish* consistory, and the sculptor *Gustavus Hesselius*, to see the town and the fields which lay before it. (The former is brother of the rev. Messrs. *Andrew* and *Samuel Hesselius*, both ministers at *Christiana* in *New Sweden*, and of the late Dr. *John Hesseliu* in the provinces of *Nerik* and *Wermeland*). My new friend had followed his brother *Andrew* in 1711 to this country, and had since lived in it. I found that I was now come into a new world. Whenever I looked to the ground, I every where found such plants as I had never seen before. When I saw a tree, I was forced to stop, and ask those who accompanied me, how it was called. The first plant which struck my eye was an *Andropogon*, or a kind of grass, and grass is a part of Botany I always delighted in. I was seized with terror at the thought of ranging so many new and unknown parts of natural history. At first I only considered the plants, without venturing on a more accurate examination.

Source: Kalm, Peter. (1972). *Travels into North America*. Barre, MA: Imprint Society, p. 24.

Middle Paleo-Indian Times

By middle Paleo-Indian times circa 11,500 BCE, climate and vegetation of eastern North America were undergoing rapid changes. A warmer and more highly seasonal climate resulted in changes in distributions of species. Biotic (flora and fauna) communities were pulled apart as some species became extinct, and others emigrated from full-glacial refuges to take their place. Thus destabilization of environments was followed by disassembly, then reorganization of the biota as boreal conifer forest moved north into Canada and temperate deciduous forest spread over much of eastern North America.

Cultures

Beginning about 13,500 years ago (11,500 BCE), distinctive fluted projectile points are found abundantly throughout eastern North America. Named for the archeological site of Clovis, New Mexico, where they were first discovered, these Clovis points were specialized bifaced fluted points used as tips of spears to hunt large mammal prey. Clovis technology was widespread during the middle Paleo-Indian cultural period, a time interval when mobile bands of hunter-gatherers ranged widely. Clovis peoples were particularly concentrated along major river systems such as the Mississippi, Ohio, Cumberland, and Tennessee, a region rich in game, plant foods, and other resources such as chert (a rock resembling flint), which was used to make high-quality fluted points.

Culture-Environment Interactions

Along with climate warming and possibly the introduction of diseases, Clovis hunters may have been partly responsible for extinction of many species of megafauna at the end of the Pleistocene. These Paleo-Indians were keystone predators who may have aided in the destabilization of already environmentally stressed populations of large carnivores and herbivores.

Late Paleo-Indian Times

During late Paleo-Indian times, from about 12,900 to 11,500 years ago (10,900 to 9,500 BCE), the transition from Pleistocene glacial-age climates to Holocene interglacial-age climates resulted in the stabilization of the biota in middle latitudes of eastern North America. Deciduous forest containing oak, hickory, and hornbeam became widespread from the Appalachian Mountains to the Ozark plateaus. Prairie expanded throughout the Great Plains.

Cultures

During late Paleo-Indian times a number of subregional cultural traditions began to develop. As human populations increased, bands of hunter-gatherers became less mobile. The Paleo-Indian tool kit became more diverse, including fluted, basally thinned, serrated, and notched projectile points used in hunting small game such as white-tailed deer and birds. These Paleo-Indians are known regionally in the southeastern United States as the Dalton people. Their tools also included the true adze, a cutting tool used in the construction of dugout canoes. Dalton-age sites include camps in rock shelters, base settlements along rivers, and cemeteries. Dalton people were organized into bands of some twenty-five individuals bound together through intermarriage.

Culture-Environment Interactions

Dalton people exploited small game, fowl, and fish along local watersheds and used plant resources for making canoes. Their impact upon their environment were probably localized because their small populations consisted of bands who were widely dispersed along relatively long reaches of stream valleys.

Archaic Cultural Period (11,500 to 3,200 Years Ago)

By Archaic times, which directly followed the Paleo-Indian Cultural Period, the eastern deciduous forest had emerged as a major vegetation type with a rich and diverse flora of woody trees and shrubs and non-woody herbs. The Archaic period extended through the time of midinterglacial, warm climatic conditions, which were relatively droughty in the Midwest and relatively wet in the Southeast. With melting of much of the continental ice sheets, sea level rose to its modern level, flooding the mouths of major rivers in estuaries, which became productive wetlands for shellfish. Shellfish also became abundant along upper reaches and shoals of streams in the interior highlands.

Cultures

Distinctive tools of early Archaic times include a series of side-notched, corner-notched, and basally-stemmed projectile points. Archaic people gradually abandoned previous tool kits, which had included carefully made stone tools used for scraping, cutting, and piercing hides, and began to use tools that could be made quickly from locally available raw materials. Bands of people became more localized within watersheds, and people began to rely more on foraging as the climate warmed and a variety of wild plant food sources became abundant. Walnuts, hickory nuts, and acorns were gathered and eaten, along with a variety of native herbaceous plants with starchy and oily seeds.

During middle Archaic times a number of cultural changes occurred. The atlatl (spear-throwing device) was used to hunt small game. Grooved stone axes were used to fell trees. Cooking was done in earth ovens. During this time, shell and earthen mounds were constructed, indicating an increase in complexity of local cultures as well as an increase in resources such as shellfish available in river shoals and coastal estuarine marshes. During this time of variable climate, with frequent droughts that made the harvest size of wild edibles unpredictable, people cooperated in mound-building and increased their exchange networks for trade goods.

During the late Archaic cultural period archeological sites included spatially bounded sites such as Poverty Point, Louisiana, which occupied 150 hectares with a large, central earthen mound surrounded by six concentric earthen ridges—evidence of tribal organization. Deep midden (refuse heap) deposits indicate that late Archaic people lived in permanent houses within stable villages that were occupied at least seasonally. Fiber-tempered pottery and stone bowls came into use. Such villages were locations for horticulture, growing squash and other cultigens (cultivated organisms for which a wild ancestor is unknown) that were originally native to riparian (along water courses) environments. These edible native plants are known as the "Eastern Agricultural Complex" and included sunflower, marsh elder, goosefoot, maygrass, knotweed, and little barley. The size of marsh elder seeds preserved in hearth sites increased through the late Archaic cultural period, and the seed coats of goosefoot thinned over time, indicating human selection for edible seeds. The late Archaic cultural period was thus a time of true plant domestication and horticulture.

Culture-Environment Interactions

Early Archaic hunter-gatherers practiced a logistically organized foraging strategy. They established semipermanent base camps but also conducted forays over a distance of several kilometers in search of prey or nut resources. Archeologists have suggested that Archaic peoples may have tended groves of especially productive nut trees and that they may have been responsible for advancing the ranges of trees by planting acorns, walnuts, or hickory nuts beyond their previous native ranges.

By late Archaic times Native Americans began to have an ecological impact on native riparian plant species. Villages were sites of increasing human disturbance as people created openings in the canopies of floodplain forests and trampled along pathways. These open-ground locations became the sites for establishment of weedy floodplain herbs that were harvested for their edible seeds as well as for their fiber, which was used as thread to make twined fabrics. Human-environment interactions on this local scale thus began to influence the structure and composition of floodplain vegetation.

Woodland Cultural Period

During the Woodland cultural period (thirty-two hundred to one thousand years ago) modern patterns of climate and vegetation were established as conditions became more equable and droughts less frequent. Southern pine, bald cypress, and tupelo gum trees expanded northward, and deciduous forest expanded westward at the expense of prairie, which had reached its maximum extent during the warm but dry middle Holocene (Archaic) interval. In the Great Lakes region, wetlands expanded in response to cooler temperatures and increased lake effect precipitation.

Cultures

During Woodland times people developed a new cooking style that included use of food bowls and cooking jars used directly over the fire hearth, in addition to continued use of earth ovens. By the middle Woodland period, in the midwestern United States a Hopewell culture emerged, expanding outward from its geographic base of the Hopewell Mound Group in Ohio. It was based upon construction of mound and earthwork complexes and the use of exotic ceremonial artifacts. During the late Woodland period nucleated villages developed to accommodate growing human populations.

Culture-Environment Interactions

With the transition from late Archaic to Woodland times, landscapes were progressively impacted by human activities. Native Americans used stone tools such as ground-stone celts (tools shaped like a chisel or ax head) and adzes along with fire to clear patches of forests both along stream corridors and adjacent to rock shelters. These patches of cleared land were used for garden plots in which crops of native plant species were grown. Throughout the Woodland period, humans impacted both local vegetation and broader landscapes. Their impact stretched from river bottoms to ridge tops in the southern Appalachian Mountains, where fire-tolerant forests of oak, chestnut, and pine expanded in response to human-caused burning of upper hill slopes.

Mississippian Cultural Period

The Mississippian cultural period (one thousand to five hundred years ago) developed during a time of climatic instability and variation in the flow of major river systems such as the Mississippi and its tributaries. After about six hundred years ago (1400 CE), colder and more variable climate conditions of the "Little Ice Age" decreased the length of the growing season throughout much of eastern North America and made growing conditions increasingly unfavorable for maize agriculture.

Cultures

The transition from the Woodland to the Mississippian cultural period was marked by the wide adoption of the bow and arrow (which made both hunting and fighting more efficient), introduction of maize (from Mexico) as an agricultural crop new to eastern North America, and construction of major civic-ceremonial centers with temple and mortuary mounds arranged around plazas. These cultural developments characterized the emergence of chiefdoms, which were large political organizations that were particularly well developed in the central and lower Mississippi River valley. Woodworking tools became increasingly sophisticated, indicating increased skill in using forest resources. Mississippian villages were dispersed across floodplain environments to take advantage of tillable soil and supplemental food reserves in nearby lakes and swamps. The diet included not only maize but also white-tailed deer, waterfowl, and fish. Strong, light jars were made of shell-tempered pottery fashioned from backswamp clay. Salt was processed from aquatic plants and traded widely.

By late Mississippian cultural times, across much of southeastern North America simple chiefdoms directed by local councils developed into more complex chiefdoms with paramount chiefs. Log stockades with bastions protected Mississippian villages during increasingly frequent times of warfare. Carbon-isotope analysis of human bone from Mississippian burials in the Mississippi River valley indicates that people grew increasingly dependent on maize in their diet. A socially stratified culture is evidenced by increased use of exotic artifacts such as ornamental shell gorgets (neck ornaments), large chert maces, and ceremonial spears, documented from Mississippian sites in Oklahoma, Alabama, and Georgia. Near the end of the Mississippian cultural period, large fortified towns grew in nucleated concentrations of populations in response to increasing competition among powerful chiefdoms. Many of the largest chiefdoms, including the prehistoric city of Cahokia, situated today within East St. Louis, and American Bottom of southern Illinois, were abandoned just prior to contact with Spanish explorers in 1540 CE. Remaining populations were vulnerable to diseases introduced by Europeans.

Culture-Environment Interactions

Construction of log palisades (defensive fences) increased the impact of Native Americans upon forests that were already being fragmented through slash-and-burn (felling and burning trees to clear land) agriculture. Overexploitation of resources and growing dependence on nutritionally deficient maize in the diet, combined with increasing climatic variability and destabilization of river systems, led to crop failures, warfare, and collapse of major Mississippian chiefdoms.

Since their initial immigration to North America during the late Pleistocene epoch, Native Americans had many kinds of interactions with their environment. Paleo-Indians were keystone predators who contributed to the extinction of large Pleistocene mammals. In late Paleo-Indian times, people adapted to climate change by adopting a diverse hunting-gathering lifeway. By Archaic times, in addition to small game, fish, and shellfish, hunter-gatherers ate acorns, hickory nuts, and walnuts along with starchy and oily seeds of native herbs. The social organization of Archaic people in villages along streams resulted in local disturbance of floodplains, where the first domestication of native food plants took place. By Woodland and Mississippian times, Native American societies were organized into complex villages and chiefdoms that utilized increasing areas of landscape. With development of maize agriculture, overexploitation of forest and soil resources resulted in broad landscape degradation, one of many factors that led to eventual collapse of the Mississippian culture.

Paul A. Delcourt and Hazel R. Delcourt

Further Reading

Anderson, B. G., & Borns, H. W., Jr. (1997). *The Ice Age World*. Oslo, Norway: Scandinavian University Press.

Anderson, D. G. (2001). Climate and culture change in prehistoric and early historic eastern North America. (2001). *Archaeology of Eastern North America, 29*, 143–186.

Anderson, D. G., & Sassaman, K. E. (1996). Modeling Paleoindian and early Archaic settlement in the South-

east: A historical perspective. In D. G. Anderson & K. E. Sassaman (Eds.), *The Paleoindian and early Archaic Southeast* (pp. 16–28). Tuscaloosa: University of Alabama Press.

Chapman, J. (1994). *Tellico archaeology: 12,000 years of Native American history* (Rev. ed.). Knoxville: University of Tennessee Press.

Delcourt, H. R. (2002). *Forests in peril: Tracking deciduous trees from Ice-Age refuges into the greenhouse world*. Granville, OH: McDonald & Woodward.

Delcourt, H. R., & Delcourt, P. A. (1991). *Quaternary ecology: A paleoecological perspective*. New York: Chapman and Hall.

Delcourt, H. R., & Delcourt, P. A. (2000). Eastern deciduous forests. In M. G. Barbour & D. W. Billings (Eds.), *North American terrestrial vegetation* (2nd ed.) (pp. 357–395). Cambridge, UK: Cambridge University Press.

Delcourt, P. A., & Delcourt, H. R. (1987). *Long-term forest dynamics of eastern North America, ecological studies 63*. New York: Springer-Verlag.

Delcourt, P. A., Delcourt, H. R., Morse, D. F., & Morse, P. A. (1993). History, evolution, and organization of vegetation and human culture. In W. H. Martin, S. G. Boyce, & A. C. Echternacht (Eds.), *Biodiversity of the southeastern United States* (Vol. 1) (pp. 47–79). New York: John Wiley & Sons.

Dixon, E. J. (1999). *Bones, boats, & bison: Archeology and the first colonization of western North America*. Albuquerque: University of New Mexico Press.

Hudson, C. (1997). *Knights of Spain, warriors of the sun: Hernando de Soto and the South's ancient chiefdoms*. Athens: University of Georgia Press.

Martin, P. S. (1984). Prehistoric overkill: The global model. In P. S. Martin & R. G. Klein (Eds.), *Quaternary extinctions: A prehistoric revolution* (pp. 354–403). Tucson: University of Arizona Press.

Milner, G. R. (1998). *The Cahokia chiefdom: The archaeology of a Mississippian society*. Washington, DC: Smithsonian Institution Press.

Minnis, P. E., & Elisens, W. J. (Eds.). (2000). *Biodiversity and native America*. Norman: University of Oklahoma Press.

Morse, D. F., & Morse, P. A. (1983). *Archaeology of the central Mississippi Valley*. New York: Academic Press.

Pielou, E. C. (1991). *After the Ice Age: The return of life to glaciated North America*. Chicago: University of Chicago Press.

Redman, C. L. (1999). *Human impact on ancient environments*. Tucson: University of Arizona Press.

Smith, B. D. (1992). *Rivers of change: Essays on early agriculture in eastern North America*. Washington, DC: Smithsonian Institution Press.

North America—Great Basin and Columbia Plateau

The Great Basin and Columbia Plateau are adjoining major physiographic and environmental regions in western North America, together comprising over 675,000 square kilometers in area. The plateau is bounded on the west by the Cascade Mountains, on the east by the northern Rockies, and on the north by the Oakanogan Highlands. The two regions merge in the High Lava Plains of south-central Oregon. The Great Basin is bounded on the west by the Sierra Nevada and on the east by the Wasatch Mountains and Colorado Plateau. On the south the Great Basin merges into the Sonoran Desert section of the Basin and Range Physiographic Province, which extends southward into Arizona and northern Mexico.

The Great Basin and the Columbia Plateau were first occupied by ancestral American Indian hunter-gatherer populations about twelve thousand years ago. Populations adapted to local resources, principally fishing along the Columbia River system and local lake and valley-upland environments in the Great Basin. As climates and environments fluctuated at the end of the Pleistocene Ice Age (ten to nine thousand years ago) and during the Later Holocene (from nine thousand years ago to the present), so, too, did local cultural and economic adaptations. These populations remained hunter-gatherers until the advent of white explorers and settlers after 1800 CE. Both regions were settled by white populations after 1840, and economies of mining, cattle and sheep ranching, and farming were developed differentially according to subregional environmental conditions and distributions of natural resources.

The Great Basin Region

The Great Basin is part of the Basin and Range Physiographic Province of North America. It was recognized in the 1840s as having no rivers draining to the sea, hence the term *Great Basin*. The are of internal drainage, covering about 47,000 square kilometers, is actually composed of over 150 individual basins, usually called *valleys*, separated by some 160 north-south–trending mountain ranges. Mountain ranges and associated valleys vary from 50 to over 350 kilometers in length.

The region generally slopes downward in elevation from north to south. Mountain peaks range from 1,500 to over 4,340 meters in elevation. Elevations of valley floors range from 1,840 to 1,100 meters in the north and from 800 to minus 85 meters on the floor of Death Valley in the south. There are two major biogeographic (of or relating to the geographical distribution of animals and plants) subregions: the High Desert, north of 36°30' N latitude, with valley floors between 1,840 and 1,100 meters, and the Low Desert to the south, with valley floors 800 meters and below in elevation. Each subregion has a characteristic biome (major ecological community type) within which temperature- and moisture-sensitive ecological zones of plant and animal communities occur in vertical succession from valley floors to mountain tops. For example, in the High Desert subregion, major zones would include (1) sagebrush (*Artemisia spp.*) and grasses, (2) pinyon pine-juniper, (3) conifers, such as ponderosa pine, and (4) alpine. The overall floristic makeup of each biome and its constituent communities varies in species composition from north to south.

During the Pleistocene epoch, many valleys were filled by pluvial (characterized by abundant rain) lakes, some of great size. Lake Bonneville at its largest extent covered 50,000 square kilometers and had a maximum depth of 330 meters. Its major remnant is the shallow, highly saline Great Salt Lake, covering approximately 4,550 square kilometers with a mean depth of 9 to 11 meters. The Great Salt Lake Desert, 10,400 square kilometers, including the Bonneville Salt Flats, is a portion of the Lake Bonneville playa. Lake Lahonton at its maximum covered about 22,000 square kilometers with a maximum depth of about 270 meters; its major remnants are Pyramid and Walker Lakes. In addition to Bonneville and Lahonton, there were over one hundred other smaller pluvial lakes in the various valley/basins. Presently, some forty pluvial lake remnants have semipermanent water; surface areas vary yearly according to local precipitation regimes. On the east side of the basin, the Bear and Weber Rivers and the Utah Lake/Jordan River system drain the west flanks of the Wasatch Mountains and empty into the Great Salt Lake. On the west side of the basin, the Truckee River originates in the Sierra Nevada at Lake Tahoe (which has an area of 1,300 square kilometers and a maximum depth of 500 meters) and discharges into Pyramid Lake; the Walker and Carson Rivers originate in the Sierras and drain to Walker Lake and the Carson Sink, respectively. The Humboldt River, about 480 kilometers in length, originates in mountain ranges in northeastern Nevada and empties into the Humboldt Sink in western Nevada.

Population

The total population of the hydrographic Great Basin (based on 2000 U.S. Census) is approximately 4.1 million. Over 3.6 million live in six U.S. Census metropolitan statistical areas (MSAs) with population densities ranging from 16 to 250 persons per square kilometer. The rural populations, about 470,000 people, range in density from 0.7 to 6.0 persons per square kilometer. Many areas of eastern Oregon, central Nevada, and western Utah have densities of less than 1 person per 75 square kilometers.

Economy

Historically, the Great Basin economy was based on cattle and sheep ranching, irrigation agriculture where possible, and mining, especially gold, silver, copper, iron, and rare earths. Since the 1930s the Nevada economy has also included tourism and gaming. Irrigation agriculture along the western slopes of the Wasatch Mountains in Utah was established by the early Mormon settlers in the 1850s and 1860s, and such agriculture continues. Beginning in early World War II the region as a whole became a major location for federal military and energy installations. Since the 1970s warehousing of consumer goods, high-technology manufacturing, and computer software production have centered in the MSAs in Nevada and Utah. The Oregon section of the Great Basin is very sparsely settled and is characterized by a pattern of widely dispersed cattle ranches.

The Columbia Plateau

The Columbia Plateau, covering about 210,000 to 235,000 square kilometers (boundary definitions vary), consists primarily of lava (mainly basalt) deposits ranging up to 3,050 meters thick in places and in geological age from Middle Tertiary to Early Quaternary times. The plateau is divided into four subregions: the Columbia Basin, Blue-Ochoco Mountains, High Lava Plains, and the Snake River Plain. The Columbia Basin, ranging from 100 to 600 meters in elevation, is mantled by loess (loamy deposits). In the central part of the basin, the surface loess and underlying deposits of lava were extensively and repeatedly eroded by melt waters from glacial Lake Missoula during the Pleistocene epoch into coulees, or vertical-walled canyons, ranging up to 150 meters deep, called channeled scablands.

The plateau is drained by the Columbia River and its tributaries, most notably the Snake River. The Columbia River originates in the Rocky Mountains of Canada and flows generally south across the Columbia Basin in a loop called the Big Bend before cutting through the Cascade Mountains and draining into the Pacific Ocean. The Snake River, over 1,670 kilometers long and draining 282,000 square kilometers, originates in western Wyoming and extreme southeastern Idaho and flows in a long arc across the Snake River Plain before turning north through the 200-kilometer-long Hell's Canyon gorge. Over 65 kilometers of the gorge is more than 1.6 kilometers deep, the deepest point being 2.5 kilometers.

The Columbia River system is controlled by twenty major dams and over four hundred smaller ones, providing hydroelectric power, flood control, and recreation and irrigation water for major agricultural projects in the Columbia Basin and parts of the Snake River Plain. Canal locks along the Columbia and Snake Rivers allow barge traffic as far as Lewiston, Idaho, 470 kilometers inland. The dams and locks effectively block the annual salmon runs up the rivers. Historically, up to 16 million salmon swam yearly to the headwaters of the river system to spawn; less than 2 percent of that number now make it. Irrigation, erosion, pollution, and population growth have caused the Columbia River to be named one of the nation's most imperiled rivers by the Environmental Protection Agency.

Population

The total population (based on 2000 U.S. Census) of the Columbia Plateau is approximately 2 million. Over 1.3 million live in five MSAs with population densities ranging from 130 to 660 persons per square kilometer. The rural population, about 700,000 people, ranges in density from 0.6 to 12.5 persons per square kilometer. Some areas of east-central Oregon have densities of less than 1 person per 75 square kilometers.

Economy

The Washington State section of the Columbia Plateau has extensive irrigated agricultural production, principally wheat, soybeans, hops, apples, and potatoes. The Oregon section is focused on cattle ranching, with lumber production in the Blue-Ochoco Mountains. The Snake River Plain has extensive irrigated agricultural production, particularly potatoes and cereal grains. There is a wide range of manufacturing in both the Columbia Basin and Snake River Plain subareas. Federal military and energy installation payrolls provide major sources of income in the region.

The basin and plateau regions share major environmental pollution problems created by nuclear waste. Hanford Engineer Works (now Hanford National Laboratory) was established on 202,000 hectares of land at Richland, Washington, in 1943 to produce materials for atomic weapons. The National Reactor Testing Station (now the Idaho National Engineering and Environmental Laboratory) was created in 1949 on 230,000 hectares west of Idaho Falls. Both facilities have severe and potentially disastrous pollution problems from underground and other storage of radioactive waste, heavy metals, organic chemicals, and nitrates. Cleanup and monitoring activities are projected to last forty years (from 2002) at the Idaho facility and indefinitely at Hanford.

An Army Air Corps facility was created in 1940 on 1,300,000 hectares in southern Nevada. In 1950, 175,000 hectares of the facility became the Nevada Atomic Test Site; the remainder, on three sides of the test site, became the Nellis Air Force Bombing Range. Between 1951 and 1962, ninety-nine above-ground nuclear tests were detonated on the test site, with major negative effects on human health and the environment. From 1962 through 1992 more than eight hundred underground tests were conducted, leaving the surface of the site pockmarked with major and minor subsidence craters, resembling a lunar landscape. The Yucca Mountain Nuclear Waste Facility in the southwestern corner of the test site will store millions of kilograms of high-level nuclear waste for ten thousand years, according to the federal government. The Nellis range is littered with the remains of millions of kilograms of exploded munitions; an estimated 320,000 kilograms of unexploded munitions are dropped each year. The Fallon Naval Air Station ranges in central Nevada, totaling over 97,500 hectares in size, receive over 30 million kilograms of exploded and unexploded munitions per year. The Herlong Army Depot northwest of Reno, Nevada, is a major source of downwind air pollution through the disposal of hundreds of thousands of kilograms of out-of-date munitions by surface burning each year. Vast areas of the Tooele Ordinance Depot and adjacent Dugway Proving Grounds in western Utah are seriously polluted by conventional and chemical warfare munitions and attempts to dispose of them.

Some of the largest surface and open-pit gold and copper mines in North America are located in the Great Basin. Great Basin open-pit mines require removal of billions of kilograms of material to extract minerals in minute quantities. For example, the Round Mountain Mine in central Nevada, the largest open-pit mine in North America, recovers on the average 0.5 grams of gold per 907 kilograms of matrix (the natural material in which something is embedded) and overburden (overlying material). In the year 2000 the mine produced 19.9 million grams of gold extracted from over 18 billion kilograms of matrix and overburden. Gold processing, especially in Nevada, has resulted in serious environmental and groundwater pollution from cyanide, chlorides, and mercury used in various ore-processing technologies at several major mines across the region.

Both the plateau and the basin have been seriously affected since the 1950s by invasive exotic plant species that move rapidly into areas burned by range fires or impacted by overgrazing by cattle, sheep, and wild horses. These plants, together with development of suburbs in MSAs, mining, off-road vehicles, and other human-caused disturbances, have seriously harmed desert biomes. The draining of Owens Lake in Owens Valley by the Los Angeles Aqueduct after 1913 created the largest dust pollution area in North America from the now-dry lakebed. All the major MSAs in the Great Basin suffer periodically from moderate to severe air pollution problems.

Don D. Fowler

Further Reading

Baker, V. R. (1981). *Catastrophic flooding: The origin of the channeled scabland.* New York: Academic Press.

Cronquist, A., Holmgren, A. H., Holmgren, N. H., & Reveal, J. A. (1972–1977). *Intermountain flora: Vascular plants of the intermountain West, U.S.A.* (Vols. 1–6). New York: New York Botanical Garden.

d'Azevedo, W. L. (Ed.). (1986). *Handbook of North American Indians: Vol. 11. Great Basin.* Washington, DC: Smithsonian Institution Press.

Dietrich, W. (1995). *Northwest Passage: The great Columbia River.* New York: Simon & Schuster.

Fiege, M. (1999). *Irrigated Eden: The making of an agricultural landscape in the American West.* Seattle: University of Washington Press.

Fiero, B. (1986). *Geology of the Great Basin.* Reno: University of Nevada Press.

Fowler, D. D., & Koch, D. (1982). The Great Basin. In G. L. Bender (Ed.), *Reference handbook on the deserts of North America* (pp. 7–66). Westport, CT: Greenwood Press.

Grayson, D. K. (1993). *The desert's past: A natural prehistory of the Great Basin.* Washington, DC: Smithsonian Institution Press.

Hitchcock, C. L., Cronquist, A., Ownbey, M., & Thompson, J. W. (1955–1969). *Vascular plants of the Pacific Northwest.* Seattle: University of Washington Press.

Hunt, C. B. (1967). *Physiography of the United States.* San Francisco: W. H. Freeman.

Kimberling, A. J., & Jackson, P. L. (Eds.). (1985). *Atlas of the Pacific Northwest* (7th ed.). Corvallis: Oregon State University Press.

Trimble, S. (1989). *The sagebrush ocean: A natural history of the Great Basin.* Reno: University of Nevada Press.

Walker, D. E., Jr. (Ed.). (1998). In *Handbook of North American Indians:* Vol. 12. *Plateau.* Washington, DC: Smithsonian Institution Press.

North America—Northwest Coast

Extending from northern California northward to southern Alaska and pinned between the Pacific Ocean on the west and the Cascade Mountains and northern coast ranges on the east, the Northwest Coast of North America presents one of the most rugged and densely vegetated temperate coastal environments in the world. Home to indigenous communities for at least ten thousand years, the region came into the orbit of European and U.S. commercial and imperial development only after the late eighteenth century. Since then development in the region has focused on extraction of rich natural resources in the form of forests and fisheries. The resulting history includes a series of environmental crises due to depletion of those resources and a boom-and-bust economic cycle. Since World War II population in the region has shifted from struggling rural areas to a relatively small number of prosperous urban centers such as Portland, Oregon; Seattle, Washington; Vancouver, British Columbia; and Anchorage, Alaska. Throughout the region's changing history of development, the presence of the Pacific Ocean and its influence on climate, transportation, and the economy remain the central factors in defining this region and its land-use patterns.

Natural History

The Northwest Coast began to emerge from under the Cordilleran ice sheet—the last of the Ice Age glaciers of the region—seventeen thousand years ago. The topographical impact of those glaciers is one of the most visible characteristics of the region, especially north of 48° N latitude. They left deep valleys extending from the various mountain ranges toward the coast and wide troughs between the mountains. The Puget Sound basin in Washington State was at the southern foot of the last continental ice sheet between the Cascade and Olympic Mountains. By ten thousand years ago ocean water returned to fill the resulting trenches to depths of 283 meters. Waters are even deeper in the Strait of Georgia, which separates the mountains of Vancouver Island from the Coast Range in southern British Columbia. An extensive series of fjords extends ocean water far into the interior of British Columbia.

The mountainous regions are a product of a complex combination of geologic forces. As part of the Pacific Rim "ring of fire," the region has a long history of volcanic eruptions and earthquakes as the Pacific tectonic plate slides under the North American plate. The Cascade Mountains reflect the legacy of ancient volcanoes in the southern portion of the range in northern California and Oregon but shift to a steeper, granitic composition from central Washington State northward to the range's terminus in southern British Columbia. Volcanic Mount Rainier in Washington State is the high point of the Cascades at 4,393 meters. The coast ranges of British Columbia and southeast Alaska are the legacy of a combination of uplift and the addition of various geologic formations shoved into North America through the force of continental drift. Whereas the Cascades and the northern coast ranges define the eastern boundary of the Northwest Coast, other significant mountain ranges stand closer to the Pacific Ocean on British Columbia's Vancouver Island, the Olympic Peninsula in Washington, and the coast of Oregon.

The most distinct climatic feature of the Northwest Coast is its abundant rainfall. Weather patterns come from off the North Pacific laden with moisture. The mountain ranges force the air mass upward in elevation, causing it to cool, which precipitates the moisture into rain and snow. Mount Baker, in the northern Washington Cascades, received 28.96 meters of snowfall from July 1998 to June 1999, the most ever recorded for a single year anywhere. The region also has the highest average annual snowfall on Earth. The abundant snowfalls provide for consistent water supplies and river flows throughout the year and feed the extensive system of glaciers that remains in higher elevations throughout the region. In the northern stretches of the coast, these glaciers reach sea level.

The Tlingit Salmon Ceremony

The plentiful salmon were a primary food resource for the Tlingit and other native peoples of the Northwest Coast. To ensure a good harvest, salmon fishing was accompanied by considerable religious ritual, as described below.

. . . Salmon, the all important foodstuff, lived in a house under the sea in a far place. There they existed in human form and lived a way-of-life akin to that enjoyed by the Tlingit. At the proper time these spirit-people turned themselves into salmon and traveled across the ocean to the rivers and streams of the Tlingit territory. If the bones of the salmon were returned to the water, just as the carcasses of the many salmon who could not be caught by the Tlingit returned to the sea, then these spirit people would once again sacrifice themselves for the benefit of the Tlingit. Careless treatment of salmon bones was a sure way of irritating salmon spirits and would cause them to sacrifice themselves elsewhere.

The First Salmon Ceremony lead by a "Salmon Chief" did not reach the elaborate ritual proportions in this area that it did among the central and southern tribes of the Northwest Coast. The first salmon caught was greeted by the Tlingit as if it were a visiting "chief." Formal speeches were given and it was prepared and cooked in a prescribed manner. Salmon were particularly concerned with how their carcasses were handled. Again this was an outgrowth of the belief that the salmon species were people who assumed an animal body and sacrificed themselves for the benefit of the Tlingit. To not treat the salmon as honored guests was an insult that the salmon people would not soon forget, and, if they failed to return to the Tlingit territories, could lead to starvation in a society so highly dependent upon this food resource.

Source: Rathburn, Robert R. (1976). *Processes of Russian-Tlingit Acculturation in Southeastern Alaska.* Ann Arbor, Michigan, University Microfilms: pp. 36–37.

For most of the region precipitation falls as rain, mainly during winter. Rain is heaviest in the inland valleys near the coast, where clouds funnel inland before rising and releasing their moisture. Henderson Lake, on Vancouver Island, records the highest average annual rainfall in North America, 650.24 centimeters, higher than that found in any other temperate region. Most all of this abundant precipitation arrives during winter, from November to May, and summers are relatively dry. This pattern is quite different from that in the interior of North America, where rain falls most during the growing season. Agricultural settlers in the moist climate of western Oregon in the mid-1800s found that their desire to grow corn struggled in the face of the dry summers. Much of the forest vegetation of the region is determined not so much by a plant's ability to take advantage of the heavy rainfalls as by its ability to withstand summer droughts. Such is the case with the Douglas fir, the dominant tree of much of the region's forests.

Most of the human occupation of the region has been in the low-elevation forested region due to the consistent presence of the western hemlock in undisturbed, old growth forests in the region. Dominant trees in this zone also include western red cedar, sitka spruce, and Douglas fir, which can grow to a height of 100 meters. The skylines of today's cities, naturalists note, are often lower than the tops of the forests that the urban development replaced. In the northern sections of this region in southeast Alaska, sitka spruce and yellow cedar become increasingly prevalent, whereas the Siskiyou region of southern Oregon contains a unique mix of conifer and broadleaf trees.

Two factors make the forests in the western hemlock zone of the Northwest Coast unique among the temperate forests of the earth. First, the dominance of coniferous evergreen trees over hardwood deciduous trees is the reverse of most forests in other temperate regions. Only on rocky slopes or sites of frequent disturbance will forests of the western hemlock zone consist mainly of deciduous big-leaf maple, vine maple, sitka alder, or red alder. Second, the size and life span of the dominant coniferous trees surpass those found in any other forest community in the world. The mild

Cape Meares National Wildlife Refuge is located on the northern Oregon coast, and encompasses one of the few old growth coastal forests in Oregon. COURTESY ROY W. LOWE, U.S. FISH AND WILDLIFE SERVICE.

winters provide an advantage to evergreens, which continue to grow year around, and the deciduous trees struggle through the dry summers. Undergrowth in these climates is an extremely dense combination of huckleberry, ferns, devil's club, salmonberry, and a variety of other woody shrubs. Measured in terms of biomass (the amount of living matter), these are among the most productive ecosystems on Earth, one hectare producing up to 30 metric tons of plant material per year.

Although prevalent, fire—ignited by both human and nonhuman sources—has been less influential in the Northwest Coast than in most of North America. Historical patterns of fire in the lowland coastal forests typically establish a cycle of intense, stand-replacing conflagrations that repeats on average every 230 years. Most indigenous communities did not use fire on a large scale to clear land because it was not a controllable or beneficial tool in such conditions. They did use fire selectively, however, to maintain meadows for root and berry production. Important exceptions stand out in Oregon's Willamette Valley and the prairies of the southern Puget Sound region, where local villages used fire broadly on an annual basis to clear underbrush and to promote the growth of camas (plants of the lily family) and other food sources.

The mountains create a complex mix of vegetation zones with changes in elevation; climate changes occur more rapidly ascending into the interior mountain ranges than traveling northward along the coast, where climate changes occur gradually. Higher elevations have more Pacific silver fir, Alaska yellow cedar, mountain hemlock, and subalpine fir. Forests are less dense at these higher elevations, often existing in scattered clusters separated by open meadows. Heavy snows, shorter growing seasons, and more frequent fire regimes help to shape these montane (relating to the zone of moist, cool upland slopes below the timberline dominated by coniferous trees) environments.

Indigenous Land Use

Indigenous communities of the Northwest Coast used resources in all these vegetation zones. Although a diversity of land- and resource-use patterns exists, anthropologists identify the Northwest Coast as a single cultural region. Most of the precontact (before the arrival of Europeans) communities practiced little or no horticulture. They were mostly hunting and gathering societies, but fishing remained the major food resource for all indigenous groups of the region. Indigenous peoples (commonly referred to as First Nations in Canada and Native Americans in the United States) harvested all five species of anadromous (ascending rivers to breed) salmon on the Northwest Coast using hooks and nets on the open waters and various forms of weirs, traps, nets, and harpoons along the rivers.

Between 8000 BCE and 6000 BCE coastal tribes became more sedentary and more reliant on specific resources. One result is that regional boundaries of resource use between tribes became more distinct and strongly defended. Communities claimed and defended their privileged use of salmon fishing sites and shellfish beds. Coastal communities of Nootka and Makah tribes (both members of the Nuu-chah-nulth nation) hunted whales from large canoes off the coast of Vancouver Island and the Olympic Peninsula. Inland tribes such as the Upper Skagit, Sauk, and Skykomish in the Washington Cascades hunted elk, bear, and mountain goat to supplement their fishing of salmon and to trade with coastal tribes.

Native Americans throughout the region made extensive use of plant materials for clothing and shelter needs. They cut massive cedar trees to serve a variety of needs. Villages established permanent winter settlements of cedar longhouses. Cedar logs were carved into canoes of a variety of shapes, depending on their uses. Coastal peoples, such as the Haida on the Queen Charlotte Islands, carved large, elaborate ocean-going canoes for hunting and warfare. Upland communities used a smaller, shovel-nosed canoe to ply the mountain rivers as far as they were navigable. They all wove cedar bark into baskets, clothing, and summer shelter. People used fire focused at the base of a tree to help in felling the cedar and in logs to help carve out canoes, although they rarely used fire as a more extensive land-management tool.

Due to the abundance of resources and improving ability of First Nations and Native American people to exploit diverse elements of their resource base, a population boom occurred in the region between 5000 BCE and 4000 BCE. The Northwest Coast developed into the most crowded region of North America at the time of European arrival. By 1774, when Spanish ships under the command of Juan Perez made contact with villages on Vancouver Island and the Queen Charlotte Islands, as many as 183,000 people lived in the region. It was one of the most densely populated nonagricultural societies in world history.

Coastal culture also developed strongly hierarchical societies, ruled by an elite whose members maintained their power through hereditary lineage and distribution of material wealth. These societies stand out among early Americans for their material culture, particularly their elaborate artwork. Wood carvings, from ceremonial masks to totem poles, demonstrate the intricate skill levels of native craftsmen and played a role in maintaining social status. All communities along the coast north of the Columbia River practiced the potlatch ceremony, by which influential families enhanced their position with the ritual distribution of material wealth. Slavery was widely practiced, and ownership of slaves was an important display of wealth and social power.

European Exploration and Contact

The earliest documented contact on the Northwest Coast between European explorers and Native American villages came in 1741 with the second North Pacific voyage of Vitus Bering, the Danish captain of a Russian expedition. Although Bering died on one of the islands along the northern coast, his crew returned with charts of the coastline of southeast Alaska and several hundred sea otter pelts. Spanish ships arrived in 1774 and 1775 to assert their claim to the region and also traded with coastal villages. In 1778 the British explorer James Cook's last voyage of exploration stopped in Nootka Sound on Vancouver Island, where he traded with the local Nuu-chah-nulth village for sea otter pelts. Although he, too, did not survive to return home, having been killed in the Sandwich (Hawaiian) Islands by natives, his crew sold the otter pelts for a high profit in the Portuguese territory of Macao in Asia. News spread to other European and U.S. sailors, instigating the first major resource boom on the Northwest Coast. These international traders valued sea otter pelts as "soft gold," and the earliest significant understanding of the Northwest Coast among Europeans was of a region rich in lucrative natural resources. This would be a hard label to shake and one that more than any other influenced the region's future.

From 1778 into the early nineteenth century, the sea otter trade dominated European–Native American relations on the Northwest Coast, and native hunters and traders played a central role in trade and the eventual demise of the otter population. Native Americans traveled through the coastal kelp beds hunting sea otter. The economic exchange brought increased material wealth to the coastal tribes as they used their role as suppliers of pelts to demand increasingly high prices from the European and U.S. traders, who competed against one another for access to the pelts.

By 1820 the sea otter along the coast was nearly extinct, its population having dropped from 500,000 to less than 2,000 in the entire North Pacific. Destruction of the sea otter led to devastation of the kelp beds along the coast and the diverse ecosystem that thrived in their shelter. Sea otters were the main predator of sea urchins, which fed on kelp and algae along the ocean floor. The sea urchin population exploded, thus replacing the productive kelp beds with "urchin barrens." In 1968 the provincial government of British Columbia began a project to reintroduce sea otter from Amchitka Island in the Aleutian Islands to the northwest coast of Vancouver Island. The otter thrived among the abundance of urchins, and kelp bed ecosystems quickly returned. The otter population has since spread along the west coast of Vancouver Island as far south as the Olympic Peninsula of Washington.

The sea otter trade brought material benefits to coastal tribes, but European ships also brought with them waves of infectious diseases that decimated the densely populated coast. Because of the relatively recent arrival of Europeans to the Northwest Coast compared to other regions of the Western Hemisphere and the frequent contacts by fur traders, the impact of epidemics is well documented. From an estimated population of over 180,000 in 1774, the indigenous population of the region dropped to less than 40,000 within one hundred years. Smallpox and malaria were the biggest killers, and epidemics recurred about once every generation. Smallpox first hit the coast from Oregon to southeast Alaska in the 1770s. Explanations of how it arrived and from whom, including theories that some epidemics arrived overland from the Great Plains, remain under debate. By 1830 malaria arrived in the lower Columbia River region as a land-based trade in beaver pelts developed there, killing 88 percent of native inhabitants within a decade. These epidemics cleared the way for American settlement of the Oregon country and were the most powerful force in shifting the population from Native American to Anglo-American by the time of the founding of Oregon Territory in 1848.

As the sea otter disappeared, economic development of the region's resources shifted to trade in beaver pelts, particularly in the lower Columbia River region. The American-based Pacific Fur Company founded Fort Astoria in 1811 at the mouth of the river. British traders of the Northwest Company bought out Astoria, and it eventually moved upriver to Fort Vancouver, near present-day Portland, Oregon, in 1824 as the seat of the Hudson's Bay Company's Columbia District.

Hunting of beaver had more impact in the inland regions of the Northwest, but many of the furs were transported to international markets via the Columbia River. In 1845 the Hudson's Bay Company decided to move its regional headquarters to Victoria on Vancouver Island, thus shifting British presence and the social and environmental impacts of the fur trade farther north, into the Fraser River country.

As the fur trade declined in the 1840s, the Hudson's Bay Company began to develop additional commercial ventures in the region. It promoted agricultural settlement at its Puget Sound Agricultural Company and at farms around Victoria. These two sites joined the Willamette Valley in Oregon as the first major pockets of agriculture on the Northwest Coast in the 1840s. Farmers transformed the botanical life of their surroundings by introducing crops such as wheat, hops, and fruit orchards as well as nonnative flowers. The Hudson's Bay Company developed commercial ventures in coal mining on Vancouver Island near Fort Rupert in 1849 and Nanaimo in 1852. The company also built lumber mills at Fort Vancouver in 1827 and at Victoria in 1848. It also began to export barrels of salted salmon. These changes represented the diversification of the company and were the first commercial efforts to exploit the mineral, timber, and fish resources of the region.

Timber Industry

Timber became the dominant coastal industry beginning in the 1850s, and no industry so strongly shaped the regions identity. By 1851 five water-powered mills operated along the Willamette River in Oregon City. Entrepreneurs from California and Maine established mills in bays along Puget Sound beginning in 1853, when Andrew Jackson Pope and F. C. Talbot funded construction of a steam-powered sawmill at Port Gamble. They came to cut timber to sell to markets in San Francisco. Mills also opened in the 1850s in Coos Bay, Oregon, and Gray's Harbor, Washington. The ocean-going lumber trade grew through the remainder of the nineteenth century and served markets around the Pacific Rim. The impact of logging remained focused on sites along the coastlines and rivers and in the proximity of settlements. This early commercial logging affected the environment of only a tiny fraction of the region.

The industrialization of the logging industry at the turn of the century vastly increased its environmental and social effects. The arrival of the transcontinental railroad was the galvanizing moment in the industrial transformation of the region. Direct railroad connections with eastern North America reached Portland, Oregon, in 1883; Tacoma, Washington, in 1887; Vancouver, British Columbia, in 1887; Seattle, Washington, in 1893; and Prince Rupert, British Columbia, in 1914. These connections opened the natural resources of the region to the demands of growing markets throughout North America. These connections also attracted vast sums of capital investments to the timber industry. In 1900 the Minnesota lumber baron Frederick Weyerhaeuser bought 364,218 hectares of land in western Washington from the Northern Pacific Railroad on his way to creating the largest private timber holdings in the United States. Weyerhaeuser's example, the reduced shipping rates on railroads after 1900, and government policies to attract outside capital spurred additional investments to land and technology. In British Columbia, where public ownership of natural resources was maintained under the Crown lands, the province by 1911 had leased timber rights on 4.4 million hectares of public land, mostly to large U.S.-based corporations. Small-gauge logging railroads allowed access to timber away from the shorelines and river banks and helped to boost the volume of wood brought out of the forests. Steam technology, replacing animal and water power, also improved the output of both logging and milling operations. It also vastly increased the frequency of fires in these forests.

Improved technology and heated competition in the timber industry led to the rapid deforestation of the most productive lower-elevation forests in the central and southern portions of the Northwest Coast by the 1930s. Concerns over the environmental impact of commercial forestry led conservationists in the United States to push for government retention of much of the upland forests as forest reserves beginning in 1891. These reserves in 1905 became part of the national forest system, which was to be managed under scientific principles of modern forestry. British Columbia sought to establish professional management and regulations over timber harvests on its Crown lands with the Forest Act of 1912.

Permanent public ownership of timber lands did not solve the problems of overcutting and depletion of the region's native forests and timber supply. By World War II the timber industry in Oregon, Washington, and Alaska began to harvest more timber from public national forest lands than from its own private holdings because the industry had depleted most of the private forests by 1940. Cutting accelerated rapidly on these public lands and continued through the 1980s until a diminishing supply of large trees and lawsuits by environmentalists decreased the sale of old-growth timber from public lands in the Northwest.

Increased logging after World War II spawned a concern for conservation that grew within the region to become an influential environmental movement. From organized efforts to preserve wilderness by local Sierra Club chapters in Oregon and Washington in the 1950s to the founding of Greenpeace in Vancouver in 1970 (to oppose nuclear testing in the Pacific), the regional environmental movement challenged the image of the Northwest Coast as a land of inexhaustible natural resources. The remaining old-growth forests symbolized for a new generation the last stand in a fight against corporate power and environmental destruction. In Oregon, Washington, and northern California this political battle over logging on public lands focused on protection of the northern spotted owl, an old growth-dependent raptor, which was listed as a threatened species in 1990. Clayoquot Sound came to symbolize the same fight in British Columbia in 1993 when the provincial government granted Canadian timber giant MacMillan-Bloedel permission to clear-cut up to 70 percent of the 350,000 hectares of forest there. More than eight hundred protesters were arrested that summer in Clayoquot Sound in demonstrations that brought international attention to the remaining forests of the coast.

Fishing Industry

The fishing industry of the Northwest Coast has followed many of the patterns of growth and decline of the timber industry, but these two resource industries have come into conflict with each other in recent years as logging in the interior degrades spawning habitat for a decreasing supply of salmon.

From the barrels of salted salmon shipped out by the Hudson's Bay Company, the fishing industry turned to canning operations, beginning on the lower Columbia River in 1866. By 1883 more than fifty canneries operated in the lower Columbia River system, and many more operated in the Puget Sound area. The industry expanded to the lower Fraser River by 1870 and farther north to the Skeena River delta by 1877. Native American and Chinese immigrants provided the labor for many of the canneries, but beginning in 1903 mechanization began to reduce the need for labor.

Like the timber industry, the salmon canning industry suffered from cutthroat competition and unsustainable harvests. High profits by the original operators created a series of new canneries, leading to periods of overproduction for the industry. Fishing operations often laid nets across the mouths of rivers to harvest all the fish swimming upstream, allowing few to spawn. Fish wheels on the Columbia River scooped salmon directly out of the river to canneries. State conservation measures as early as 1877 in Washington reflected growing concerns for the survival of salmon stocks, but the measures were not fully enforced.

The salmon population in the region declined steeply during the twentieth century. Improved technology in harvesting, including open ocean trawlers in the North Pacific, took their toll, along with hydroelectric projects in the interior, which cut off much of the salmon spawning habitat. The heavily dammed Columbia River system was once the most productive salmon river in the world, but that distinction went to the undammed Fraser River after dams took their toll on the Columbia's fish runs beginning in the 1930s. In the 1990s salmon stocks on the Fraser began to decline as well. As salmon numbers declined, tensions arose between interest groups involved in the industry. Many of the strongest tensions have arisen between U.S. and Canadian fishers. Canadian fishers claim that foreign vessels in the Gulf of Alaska intercept much of the salmon returning to British Columbia streams. Spawning habitat for salmon remains far more healthy and productive in British Columbia than it does in the United States. A 1937 treaty between the United States and Canada failed to resolve these tensions. In response to both lingering cross-border resentments and diminishing supplies of salmon, the two nations agreed to the Pacific Salmon Treaty in 1985, which sought to promote conservation and well as production. Implementation of the treaty continues to be a difficult process as all sides compete for a valuable and limited resource. Disagreements also arose in both countries over the rights of Native American and First Nations fishers to harvest salmon and other fish species. Canadian and U.S. regulatory agencies have restricted or occasionally eliminated fishing seasons to promote conservation. The Canadian government has employed a program to buy out some of the salmon fishing fleet as a way to reduce pressure on the salmon runs. As native stocks decline, hatcheries have failed to fully replicate the genetic strengths of native fish. Aquaculture systems along the British Columbia coast raise Atlantic salmon in pens for sale, but escaped schools of these nonnative fish raise grave fears of an additional threat to native fisheries. Both timber and

fishing are heavily consolidated fractions of their once-dominant roles in the region's economy. High technology, aerospace, and tourism have all far surpassed resource extraction industries in regional economic importance.

The Northwest Coast of North America continues to take its identity from the lush resources of the region, but for the sake of biodiversity and recreation, the local public increasingly favors preservation rather than extraction of those resources. Efforts at conservation and preservation grew correspondingly with the increasing impact of resource extraction. An increasing demand for recreational opportunities arose from the growing urban populations of the region beginning in the late nineteenth century. National parks were created at Crater Lake in Oregon in 1897 and Mount Rainier in Washington in 1899. Most of these preserved areas represented high elevation regions, where valuable economic resources were less abundant; their existence usually did not challenge the dominance of natural resource industries such as timber harvesting. Washington's Olympic National Park, established in 1947, did raise strong opposition from the regional timber industry, because it contained valuable temperate rain forests within its protective borders. As the industry moved into higher elevations in search of further supplies of raw materials, conflicts with recreational and preservation interests increased after World War II. In Oregon and Washington states, this conflict corresponded with a dramatic rise in logging on public forest lands from the 1940s to the 1980s. A regional wilderness preservation movement arose beginning in the 1950s as a way to protect some old growth forests of the Northwest Coast from industrial logging. In British Columbia, these debates centered on the forests of the coastal islands, such as the Queen Charlotte Islands in the 1970s, and they often were led by First Nations groups. Other environmental concerns focused on limiting the damage of dams on river systems throughout the region. Salmon and forests, the two dominant symbols of the Northwest Coast, have both been a source of tremendous wealth for resource industries and a rallying cry for environmental protection.

The result of these movements has been to heighten awareness and appreciation in the region of natural resources and biodiversity. They have also protected significant portions of the landscape. Roughly 9 percent of the state of Washington is protected as wilderness under United States law, as of 2003, and the provincial government of British Columbia set a goal in

1992 to preserve 12 percent of the province under the Protected Areas Strategy.

Although the region is often celebrated for its scenery and wild landscapes, enormous environmental challenges continue to face the Northwest Coast. Continued logging and mining, dwindling salmon runs, and urban sprawl make this a battleground for high profile environmental debates well into the future.

Kevin R. Marsh

Further Reading

Barman, J. (1996). *The West beyond the West: A history of British Columbia* (Rev. ed.). Toronto, Canada: University of Toronto Press.

Boyd, R. (1999). *The coming of the spirit of pestilence: Introduced infectious diseases and population decline among the Northwest Coast Indians, 1774–1874.* Seattle: University of Washington Press.

Cannings, R., & Cannings, S. (1996). *British Columbia: A natural history.* Vancouver, Canada: Greystone Books.

Goble, D. D., & Hirt, P. W. (Eds.). (1999). *Northwest lands, Northwest peoples: Readings in environmental history.* Seattle: University of Washington Press.

Rajala, R. A. (1998). *Clearcutting the Pacific rain forest: Production, science, and regulation.* Vancouver, Canada: UBC Press.

Robbins, W. G. (1997). The great raincoast: The legacy of European settlement. In P. K. Schumaker, B. von Hagen, & E. C. Wolf (Eds.), *The rainforests of home: Profile of a North American bioregion* 9 (pp. 313–28). Washington, DC: Island Press.

Sturtevant, W. C. (Ed.). (1990). *Handbook of North American Indians:* Vol. 7. *Northwest Coast.* Washington, DC: Smithsonian Institution.

North America—Plains

The Great Plains is a vast, relatively flat, nearly featureless grassland that occupies the midcontinent of North America. It stretches from Texas into Canada and from the edge of the Rocky Mountains east to approximately the ninety-eighth meridian. It is a landscape that receives just enough precipitation to qualify as semiarid, at least at present. During the eleven thousand years that humans have been on this landscape, however, the environment has changed radically—from a well-watered, lush grassland spotted with tens of thousands of freshwater lakes to a parched and dusty, drought-stricken moonscape. Before embarking on a discussion of past conditions, a brief review of the present climate and ecology will highlight the challenges faced by past and present peoples in the sometimes-harsh and often-unpredictable environment of the Great Plains.

Present Environment

The high mountain ranges of western North America, especially the Rocky Mountains, profoundly influence the climate on the Great Plains. For by the time the dominant westerly air masses from the Pacific Coast reach the Great Plains, much of the moisture originally contained is lost, having fallen as rain or snow on the windward slopes of the mountains. As a result of being in the "rain shadow" of the Rocky Mountains, annual precipitation on the Great Plains is low overall but increases from west (less than 40 centimeters a year) to east (about 71 centimeters a year). These are averages, but few years on the Great Plains are average. Instead, annual precipitation is often well above or well below the average, and drought is a regular occurrence. Most precipitation falls during the summer in late afternoon thunderstorms fed by moisture-laden air coming up from the Gulf of Mexico. Winters are usually dry; snowfall is rare and mostly confined to the northern Great Plains.

The climate is warm, too, with the average annual temperature increasing from north (just over 4° C) to south (over 15° C). Because the region is in the interior of North America and relatively high above sea level (ranging from 610 meters to over 1,500 meters), it has a continental climate that cycles daily, seasonally, and annually between hot and cold extremes. Summers—especially on the southern Great Plains—are marked by long, hot sunny days and cool nights; winters are marked by weeks or months of dry, cold weather (bone-chilling cold on the northern Great Plains). Throughout the year, there is abundant sunshine, low humidity, and strong and persistent winds that over the millennia have eroded and sculpted the landscape.

Because precipitation is low and evaporation is high, surface water is limited. Few rivers cross the Great Plains, and few lakes dot its surface. The western portion of the Great Plains, known as the High Plains, represents the largest, most intact and least altered portion of the Plains as originally deposited during the late Miocene period (around 5 to 6 million years ago). It is topographically higher and flatter than the remainder of the Great Plains to the east, and is underlain by a vast (350,000 square kilometers) aquifer—the Ogallala aquifer—which at one time held a volume of freshwater about equal to that of Lake Huron, the second largest of the Great Lakes. Water flows from the aquifer to the surface, emerging in springs, lakes, and rivers. The Ogallala aquifer filled slowly over a long time, and because it is fed primarily by precipitation seeping into the ground, water levels in it rise and fall in response to periods of greater or lesser rainfall.

The Great Plains is covered in grassland: short-grass steppe on the drier, High Plains and mixed-grass and tall-grass prairie in the increasingly better-watered central and eastern Great Plains. Trees are generally rare on this landscape and mostly grow in river valleys and other low spots on the landscape where more water is available.

This landscape has relatively few species of animals compared to, for example, a tropical rain forest. However, the species that occur there are sometimes found in enormous numbers. Before the encroachment of humans, the Great Plains supported herds of bison (American buffalo) that numbered in the tens of millions, perhaps as many as 50 million pronghorn antelope, and perhaps several billion prairie dogs. There were also untold numbers of jackrabbits, smaller mammals, birds, amphibians, reptiles, and insects. These animals had developed sometimes-elaborate adaptations to cope with scarce water and recurrent drought and the challenges of living in a harsh and treeless environment in which animals cannot readily hide or find refuge from the weather or predators.

The modern climate and environment of the Great Plains developed in just the last few thousand years, but even during that time have varied considerably. And before the onset of modern conditions, the climate and environment were even more distinct.

Ice Age Great Plains

The Pleistocene epoch (Ice Age) was marked by the advance of massive continental ice sheets, which buried the northern Great Plains and strongly influenced the climate and environment of the unglaciated Great Plains farther south. Overall, global air temperatures were cooler, but the annual swings in temperature were probably not as pronounced then as now. The severe winters that the Great Plains currently experiences are a consequence of frigid Arctic air that sweeps down into the United States. In full glacial times, that frigid air was trapped in the Arctic behind glaciers looming 3–4 kilometers high. As a result, Pleistocene climates were more equable than today, with cooler summers and warmer winters.

The Great Plains was also wetter then: During glacial times the jet stream was shifted south and brought moist air into the Great Plains, producing more cloud cover, lower evaporation, and higher precipitation—perhaps twice as much as at present. That increase in precipitation helped fill tens of thousands of freshwater lakes on the Great Plains and saturated the sand and gravel of the Ogallala aquifer.

Roaming that grassy, well-watered landscape were dozens of now-extinct large mammals—or megafauna—including camels, horses, mammoths, large-headed llama, antelope, an ancestral species of bison, and their formidable predators, including the giant short-faced bear. Humans, too, occupied this landscape and even occasionally hunted mammoth at sites such as Clovis, New Mexico, and Colby, Wyoming, which are radiocarbon dated to between 11,500 and 10,900 years ago. However, these humans were not specialized mammoth hunters because their diets also included a variety of other, smaller animals, including Pleistocene and turtles.

Although humans have been blamed for hunting the megafauna to extinction, there is no archeological evidence to support that accusation. There is, however, ample evidence of dramatic climatic change at the end of the Pleistocene epoch, which assuredly had a significant impact on these animals. The Great Plains climate became warmer and drier, less equable, and more continental; in turn, the vegetation changed as cool-loving plants gave way to more warm-adapted plants. Perhaps one of the most significant changes was a sharp increase in warm-season grasses (which grow in the summer when temperatures are highest) at the expense of cool-season grasses (which complete most of their growth in the fall, winter, and spring). The dominant warm-season grasses on the Great Plains produce strong antiherbivory toxins (their defense against grazers), which probably made them unpalatable to most of the large animals except one. Bison, it turns out, thrive on warm-season grasses, one of which is the aptly named buffalo grass.

With the extinction of the megafauna at the end of the Ice Age (about 10,600 years ago), bison populations multiplied—after all, they were now the only grazers on the Great Plains. As bison numbers increased, human groups increasingly came to rely on these animals as the basis of their diet. At the site of Folsom, New Mexico, 10,500 years ago hunters killed approximately thirty-two bison. Just a thousand years later, at sites such as Jones-Miller and Olsen-Chubbuck (both on the plains of eastern Colorado), several hundred bison were slaughtered at one time, the kill providing sustenance and raw material for clothing and tools enough for dozens (if not scores) of people.

The Great Plains during the Altithermal

But good bison-hunting times would not last. Beginning around seventy-five hundred years ago and intensifying over the next millennium, a drought—known as the Altithermal—laid waste to the Great Plains. The Altithermal was probably a summer drought, if only because most Great Plains precipitation (at least at present) falls during the summer. Unlike any historically known drought, however, the Altithermal lasted two thousand years. During that time, freshwater virtually disappeared from the Great Plains surface, save for a few deep lakes and the few rivers that originated in the snowfields of the Rocky Mountains. Otherwise, groundwater-fed seeps and springs declined and disappeared as water levels in the Ogallala aquifer fell. Vegetation changed; as drought-tolerant forms expanded, and those requiring more water withered and died, parts of the landscape must have been laid bare. The reduction in available moisture and surface cover allowed the ever-present winds to scour exposed surfaces and pile up the eroded sediment to form dune fields and sand sheets that marched across the Great Plains landscape. To be sure, there was variation in the severity of the Altithermal's effects, with conditions worsening in the more southerly warmer and drier portions of the High Plains.

These drought conditions had a profound impact on animals. During the Altithermal, many species declined in number or shifted their range in response to changes in vegetation; species that required more water were replaced by ones that could survive on less. Bison, which need large amounts of both forage and water, declined in number, and their populations were under such environmental stress that they underwent rapid reduction in body size and evolutionary change. The bison that emerged after the Altithermal was a different species than the one that had entered the drought (*Bison antiquus* became the modern *Bison bison*).

Human hunters who relied on bison naturally had to alter their lifeways as well. This they did in different ways, depending on the local severity of drought. On the southern Great Plains, at sites such as Mustang Springs, Texas, people had to dig wells to reach water

tables that had fallen at least 3 meters since the onset of the Altithermal. For food they continued to take bison when the animals were spotted, but with fewer bison available, people expanded their diet to include smaller animals and drought-resistant plants (such as cacti but also mesquite, sunflower, and other seed-bearing plants). Altithermal-age sites on the central and northern Great Plains also show an increase in the number of foods in the diet, but in more northerly areas bison populations did not decline so drastically and continued as a mainstay of the human diet.

Although there is evidence that humans occupied the Great Plains throughout the Altithermal, their numbers, too, may have declined because researchers have found far fewer archeological sites from this time period than from earlier or later periods. Of course, this was also a period of severe erosion, so the scarcity of Altithermal sites may simply reflect poorer conditions for preservation. Even so, there is reason to suspect that the most drought-stricken parts of the Great Plains (notably the central and southern regions) were probably abandoned for periods of time: A scarcity of surface water is also a potentially dangerous situation for people, who must drink often to maintain hydration. Travel across waterless landscapes could have been risky, particularly when temperatures rose and the water available for transport decreased.

Historic and Modern Great Plains

Around five thousand years ago the Altithermal drought finally broke, and the climate and environment of the Great Plains improved—although there was never a return to the well-watered conditions of the late Pleistocene epoch. Indeed, during the last five thousand years the Great Plains climate has undergone cycles of drought, and during that time bison and other animal populations have ebbed and flowed with the changes in vegetation and available water. None of these droughts has been as severe as the Altithermal—although many of them have been more severe than the historic droughts of the twentieth century, such as the Dust Bowl of the 1930s. Among the harshest droughts were those of the thirteenth century and one that lasted through much of the last half of the sixteenth century.

Native Americans—descendants of the people who had weathered the Altithermal—weathered these later droughts as well by shifting their subsistence practices to cope with changing availability of food and water. Their diets were broad based: Bison, always a preferred resource, continued to be hunted when available, but by then many Great Plains people also hunted small game and gathered a wide variety of plants; some even farmed small plots of corn—a domesticated crop originally from Mexico introduced onto the Great Plains less than a thousand years ago. When conditions were suitable, corn was farmed in the low-lying valleys of the Great Plains, where it could take advantage of rainfall runoff and greater soil moisture. During dry periods, people shifted their reliance back to more drought-tolerant foods.

Euro-Americans began moving onto the Great Plains in the early 1800s. Yet, the first of these people viewed this as dry, barren land to be crossed, not settled. Their agricultural practices were geared toward the wetter eastern United States, and the Great Plains was still home to Native Americans, who resisted Euro-American incursion onto their lands.

By the late nineteenth century, however, following several decades of often-intense conflict between the U.S. Army and Native American tribes, many of the Great Plains peoples were decimated (disease took its toll as well) and shifted onto reservation lands. Bison, too, having survived ten thousand years of hunting by people, were at the same time pushed to the brink of extinction by Euro-Americans and virtually cleared from the landscape. In their wake, tens of thousands of farmers streamed onto the Great Plains, lured by the promise of free and easily plowed fields (no trees or rocks to clear!) and buoyed by the assurance that "the rain follows the plow." The latter claim was a bit of climatic quackery, based on the dubious notion that plowing would release soil moisture, which would then return to the fields as rain.

Demand for Wheat

A few brief droughts at century's end burst that bubble, but those who managed to hang on were richly rewarded at the beginning of the twentieth century, when World War I closed Russian ports and stopped the flow of Russian wheat onto the world market. That created a huge global demand that more than doubled the price of wheat, and farmers on the Great Plains raced to plow and plant wheat. Much of the land that was plowed was virgin grassland—and too much of it was easily eroded land, better suited to pasture, not cropland. However, those were unusually wet years on the Great Plains, and farmers enjoyed bumper crops and financial gain, which they in turn used as down payments for more farm equipment and land.

Of course, after World War I ended, Russian wheat once more moved to market, and with that increase in supply wheat prices plummeted. On the Great Plains, farmers responded by plowing and planting even more, expanding their production to help pay for land and equipment they had purchased to keep pace with wartime demand. But then drought began in the early 1930s. Crops shriveled, pastures were scorched, and the topsoil of the Great Plains—once held tightly in place by thick roots of native grasses—began to blow away. There were hundreds of dust storms—"black blizzards." One, on 10 May 1934, began on the Great Plains and moved east, dropping tons of sediment in Chicago, blocking out the sun in New York City, and raining dust on ships in the Atlantic Ocean hundreds of miles off the coast. The Dust Bowl of the 1930s, worsened by the Great Depression, wrought deep social change and economic ruin on the Great Plains as farmers fled to greener fields elsewhere.

Unable to depend on water from the sky, Great Plains farmers—especially those on the High Plains—began to look underground at the vast Ogallala aquifer. Windmills had long been used to bring that water to the surface, but these could not bring up water fast enough to irrigate a large farm field. Farmers needed a more efficient means of tapping the Ogallala. That means came in the decade after World War II with the invention of stronger pumps, the widespread availability of inexpensive engines, and especially the newly invented center-pivot irrigation system. All of which could pump water out of the aquifer at the rate of 3,800 liters a minute and distribute it over a circular area of 64 hectares (or more) of cropland daily.

Irrigation and Its Effects

Irrigation was first used as an emergency response to drought, but it quickly became an essential tool. Many farmers, weary of waiting for fickle rains, came to depend on Ogallala water. Irrigation pivots sprang up throughout the High Plains, and farmers began irrigating year around. In the latter half of the twentieth century, as many as 5,000 new irrigation wells were being drilled a year; by century's end, nearly 5.7 million hectares were being irrigated by almost 200,000 wells. The green circles visible as one flies over the Plains are from center pivot irrigation systems and have become, perhaps more than anything else, the symbol of the Plains (it is not the buffalo anymore).

Thanks to widespread irrigation the Great Plains produced during the last half-century bumper harvests that filled great grain elevators and helped feed the world. This was accomplished, however, at considerable cost, not least of which was a precipitous and perhaps irreversible decline in the Ogallala aquifer. Water levels in the aquifer, always slow to rise, began to fall with the advent of irrigation, the natural rate of recharge unable to keep pace with the heavy demands of irrigation. Like a bank account from which money is withdrawn faster than deposits are made; pumping is now removing water from the aquifer at rates that are twelve to forty times higher than local rates of recharge—particularly on the southern High Plains, where precipitation and aquifer recharge rates are especially low. At some point in the future—how near or far depends on how we use the resource and the vagaries of climate—the underground water in this area will run out. In 1970, it was estimated that farmers would have irrigation water for another 300 years; some estimates after 2000 suggest there may be only thirty years of irrigating left (at least on the southern High Plains).

There are other costs as well. Irrigation systems are expensive to install and maintain, and to compensate for their investment, farmers often keep their cropland in use almost continuously, plant high-value but thirsty plants (like corn and alfalfa), and invest heavily in fertilizer, herbicides, and pesticides, the runoff from which became a significant source of groundwater pollution. Although most of the water drawn from the Ogallala is used for irrigation, there are other demands on this source. Cattle and hogs are nowadays largely raised in giant feed lots and high-density hog farms, and fattened on a high-tech diet of feed. Roughly 600 gallons of water goes into the production of a single head of beef, and large cattle feedlots that process upwards of a million animals a year annually consume upwards of hundreds of millions of gallons of water. Coupling all this with water used in oil drilling (on the southern High Plains) and in electrical power generating plants (where Ogallala water is turned to steam in coal- and gas-fired plants), the result is heavy demand for groundwater as well as substantial chemical runoffs that further exacerbates pollution of the aquifer.

Recognizing their impact on the quantity and quality of groundwater, some farmers and ranchers have over the last couple of decades adopted new techniques to stretch the irrigation water supply, and/or shift to dryland production. In terms of the former, less thirsty crops are being planted, and there are also efforts to develop more efficient irrigation technologies

(to reduce the loss of water to evaporation and time its use to critical stages of plant growth), more tightly monitor and enhance soil moisture, and more effectively recover water runoff. In addition, the federal government through its Conservation Reserve Program is actively encouraging (through financial incentives) the retirement of land unsuitable for cultivation to return it to natural grassland and pasture. Even though this is a nationwide program, nearly half of the funds for this $1.35 billion program are spent in just the states of the Great Plains.

Although important measures, these are being done against the backdrop of an already diminished groundwater supply and an unreliable and unforgiving climate in which the only certainty is that the rains will one day cease. As has so often happened before, the Great Plains will be visited by drought. No one knows how long and how severe the next drought will be—especially given the possible compounding effects of global warming.

Prehistoric foragers responded to drought by expanding and shifting their subsistence practices, by selectively abandoning hard-hit areas, and by tapping groundwater sources, which, relative to the foragers' technology, were essentially limitless. Today and into the future, with the considerably greater populations living on the Great Plains, the amount of land and economic investment in irrigation agriculture, and the significantly lowered water levels in the Ogallala aquifer, it is doubtful we will enjoy such a full range of options.

David J. Meltzer

Further Reading

Borchert, J. R. (1950). The climate of the central North American grasslands. *Annals of the Association of American Geographers*, 40(1), 1–39.

Holliday, V. T. (2000). Folsom drought and episodic drying on the southern High Plains from 10,900–10,200 14C yr B.P. *Quaternary Research*, 53(1), 1–12.

Meltzer, D. J. (1999). Human responses to middle Holocene (Altithermal) climates on the North American Great Plains. *Quaternary Research*, 52(3), 404–416.

Opie, J. (2000). *Ogallala: Water for a dry land* (2nd ed.). Lincoln: University of Nebraska Press.

Woodhouse, C. A., & Overpeck, J. (1998). 2000 years of drought variability in the central United States. *Bulletin of the American Meteorological Society*, 79(12), 2693–2714.

Worster, D. (1979). *Dust Bowl: The southern Plains in the 1930s*. Oxford, UK: Oxford University Press.

North America—Southwest

The ancient Southwest of North America provides an excellent arena for studying human adaptations to an arid, desert environment from the arrival of the first humans around 10,000 BCE until the arrival of colonial Spaniards in 1540 CE.

The North American Southwest encompasses the U.S. states of Arizona, New Mexico, and southern Colorado and Utah and the Mexican states of northern Chihuahua and Sonora. The Southwest may be divided into three major physiographic subareas—the southern Basin and Range, the Montane Transition Zone, and the Colorado Plateau. During the ancient period this area encompassed at least thirty Native American ethnic groups, five major archeological areas, and at least twenty-five major biotic (relating to the flora and fauna of a region) provinces that varied from low-altitude subtropical deserts to montane (relating to the biogeographic zone of moist, cool upland slopes below the timberline dominated by large coniferous trees) tundras.

Paleo-Indian Period (10,000–8,500 BCE)

Human occupation of the Southwest began roughly twelve thousand years ago. Nonarcheological bone beds and archeological sites have produced the remains of extinct Pleistocene epoch (beginning 1.6 million years ago) fauna, such as bison, camels, dire wolves, four-pronged antelope, horses, mammoths, and tapirs. Studies of bone beds (naturally occurring layers of bone in geological deposits), pollen samples, and packrat middens (refuse dumps) indicate that the Southwest was generally moister and cooler than it is today. Grasslands were more extensive, and the lower limits of major biotic provinces, such as pinyon-juniper-oak woodlands and montane conifer forests, extended to lower elevations than they presently do.

The earliest human occupants of the New World are collectively referred to as "Paleo-Indians." Their chipped-stone tools, knives, and spear points have been found throughout the Southwest as well as in the rest of North America and parts of Central and South America. In the Southwestern archeological sites of the Paleo-Indian period (10,000–8500 BCE) are typically concentrations of chipped-stone tools that include spear or dart points, knives, bifacial (having opposite sides or faces worked on to form an edge for cutting) tools, and the debris from their manufacture. These artifact scatters have in some cases been found with the bones of extinct mammoth or bison, as at the Sulphur Springs localities in Whitewater Draw and at the Lehner Ranch localities, both in southeastern Arizona.

In general, scholars agree that Southwestern Paleo-Indians were hunter-gatherers who made their living hunting wild game and gathering wild plant foods. Scholars disagree about the relative dietary importance of large game animals as opposed to smaller animals and plants. The consistent association of distinctively shaped spear points with the bones of extinct mammoth and bison has led some to speculate that Paleo-Indians were specialists at hunting big game. In the face of Pleistocene and early Holocene (the current geologic epoch) environmental changes, however, Paleo-Indians probably had to remain flexible in their use of large and small game and the seeds of wild plants.

Archaic Period (8500–1700 BCE)

After the Pleistocene epoch, the North American Southwest featured generally increasing temperatures and varying amounts of summer moisture for a period of sixty-eight hundred years. The discharge rates of streams initially increased, as did the surface areas of lakes. Grasslands spread, and warmer temperatures forced the spread of conifer woodlands and forests to higher elevations. The Pleistocene fauna so prominently and exotically featured at many Paleo-Indian sites became extinct, either as a result of human hunting, climatic changes, or both. Within a thousand years effective moisture, watershed discharge rates, and lake surface areas began to decrease, and average temperatures increased, reaching record highs during the Altithermal (high heat) period around 6000 BCE. Water was a limiting resource, and people tended to settle or establish base camps near the most reliable sources of water—typically along watercourses and lake margins. Archeologists suspect that many archeological sites were lost in episodes of down-cutting and erosion that occurred during the middle and late parts of the Archaic period (8500–1700 BCE), at the end of the Altithermal period. Few intact open-air archeological sites have been discovered that date to the late Archaic period. Substantial archeological deposits tend to be limited to cave sites. Noncave sites are mostly limited to chipped-stone scatters that lack subsurface features.

It is difficult to assess how prehistoric groups responded to the temperature fluctuations, increasing aridity, successional migrations of biotic provinces, and the extinction of major terrestrial mammals. In part the difficulty lies in not having a clear model of Paleo-Indian resource use. The difficulty is worsened by the lack of Archaic period sites. Archeologists are, however, generally impressed by the rapid increase in the number of types (used for different purposes) of ground-stone tools and their increased proportional frequency in archeological assemblages. These tools are often referred to as "manos" (hand-held milling stones) and "metates" (larger, anvil-like grinding surfaces), although they bear little resemblance to the manos and metates of more recent prehistoric and Spanish colonial times. The earliest manos are small and round, rarely greater than 10 centimeters in diameter, and were used in basin-shaped metates. Most archeologists agree that their primary purpose was to grind seeds, although nonfood items such as pigments made from crushed ore may also have been prepared in them.

Given the expansion of milling stones in the tool assemblages, archeologists tend to infer that dependence on wild plant foods increased, although hunting large mammals such as antelope, bighorn sheep, bear, deer, and elk remained a vital source of nutrition. Nets and baskets made from dry caves in the Southwest and to the north in the Great Basin of Nevada and Utah suggest that Archaic period foragers made increasing use of birds such as ducks and geese.

Early Agricultural Period (1700 BCE–150 CE)

Sometime in the mid-second millennium BCE, maize (*Zea mays*) or corn, which had been developed in central Mexico by 4000 BCE, made its way northward into the southern Basin and Range. The best-documented archeological sites with maize in the North American Southwest—the Clearwater, Las Capas, and Los Pozos sites—occur along the Santa Cruz River in Tucson, Arizona. In these sites maize cob fragments have been found in large quantities in large, underground storage pits and in features in pithouses (houses with floor surfaces below ground level). The occupants of Las Capas used canals—the oldest known canals in the New World—to irrigate their crops. Grinding tools include larger basin metates and circular or oval-shaped manos. Chipped-stone tools include spear or dart points, arrow points, and general purpose bifacial tools. Clay figurine fragments with braided hair, processed pigment "cakes" made of crushed ore, Pacific Coast shell jewelry, polished cruciforms (objects shaped like a cross), and spherical basalt balls of varying sizes point to a rich, if poorly understood, social, ceremonial, and economic life.

The particular combination of irrigation agriculture and the oldest detectable remains of houses in the Southwest has led many scholars to conclude that Early Agricultural period (1700 BCE–150 CE) subsistence was a sedentary (people lived in one place for the entire year, usually for several years) and agriculturally focused (depending primarily on crops augmented by hunting) economic system. This conclusion, however, presents several major problems. Early southwestern maize does not resemble modern corn with respect to productivity or yield. Early Agricultural period maize cobs were tiny. For comparison, imagine a new piece of blackboard chalk. The chalk is substantially larger than most of the maize cobs grown at this time. Because the early maize was a small-cobbed, low-yield variety, people used a wide range of harvested wild plants and large, upland mammals. Some of these plants were not available in the immediate vicinity of the sites in which they were found. To obtain these wild resources, people had to leave their villages for substantial intervals, perhaps months at a time, each year.

Independent evidence of high mobility among Early Agricultural period forager-farmers may be found in human skeletons. Comparative metric (measurement) studies of human leg bones from Early Agricultural period sites and modern hunter-gatherers and farmers show that Early Agricultural period forager-farmers spent as much time traveling as most hunter-gatherers and substantially more time traveling than sedentary farmers.

The environmental circumstances in which the introduction of agriculture occurred may have been exceptionally favorable. The occupation of the Tucson Basin sites occurred during a period of alluvial floodplain stabilization and increased rainfall, and the Santa Cruz River (which has the least-steep gradient of any local drainage around Tucson) provided a discontinuous series of ideal locations for irrigation agriculture. These ideal farming conditions were interrupted at least twice by episodes of arroyo (a watercourse in an arid region) formation followed by massive flooding, but on the whole the Santa Cruz River in the Tucson Basin remained a highly productive farming locale.

Although maize cultivation in the Southwest was first practiced near Tucson, it quickly spread to other areas. On the Colorado Plateau irrigation canals with maize pollen and charcoal dating to the first millennium BCE have been found near the modern town of Zuni Pueblo, New Mexico. In the Montane Transition Zone, maize cob fragments have been found west of Silver City and in the San Agustin Plains of New Mexico. The rapid spread of maize into the southern Basin and Range, the Colorado Plateau, and the Montane Transition Zone shows that early agriculture was suitable for widely differing microenvironments. Agriculture was attractive enough that people rapidly incorporated maize farming into their range of options for obtaining food.

Agricultural Intensification and Sedentism (150–1338 CE)

Archeologists have noted increasing evidence for substantial dependence on agriculture throughout the first millennium CE in the southern Basin and Range, Montane Transition Zone, and Colorado Plateau. Evidence includes higher frequencies of cultigens (organisms of a variety or species for which a wild ancestor is unknown) such as maize, beans, gourds, squash, cotton, and agave.

Studies of plant remains are particularly crucial because of three important trends. First, throughout the first millennium CE, there is evidence for biological changes in maize, probably caused by selective breeding, that produced new varieties with much greater yields (weight of grain per unit of farmed land). Second, the number of varieties of maize, beans, and squash increased. This expansion in the range of available cultigens is consistent with increasing specialization in the production of crops and with efforts to tailor cultivars (organisms originating and persisting under cultivation) that were better adapted to highly localized environmental circumstances in different parts of the Southwest. Third, most of the wild plants that were consumed during the Early Agricultural and Archaic periods are observed much less frequently after 150 CE. By 550 CE some plant taxa (names applied to a group in a system of classification) disappeared completely from the suite of plants that was routinely used. The shortage of formerly common wild plants in archeological sites suggests that wild plants became much less important as staple foods. Instead, when they were

used they may have been important as "famine foods" or backup resources that were used only when crops failed to meet basic needs.

The period 150–1338 CE included the rise of the major archeological culture areas of the Southwest—the Anasazi, Hohokam, and Mogollon. Large villages with hundreds of occupants, intensive agriculture, widespread trade or exchange networks, and complicated social systems flourished. In the Colorado Plateau the first pueblos sprang up, were occupied, and abandoned, and the baseline belief systems of the modern Native American puebloan peoples were established. In the southern Basin and Range the Hohokam culture flourished, culminating in societies with complex irrigation-management hierarchies and establishing the baseline belief systems of the O'odham and related peoples of southern Arizona and northern Mexico.

Throughout this period the timing and availability of water set limits to human settlement. One consistent problem for prehistoric southwesterners was the relatively unpredictable nature of rainfall. Throughout the Southwest the timing and distribution of precipitation were affected by long-period and short-period environmental fluctuations, El Niño (an irregularly occurring flow of unusually warm surface water along the western coast of South America) and La Niña (the cold counterpart of El Niño, causing abnormally cooler sea surface temperatures in the tropical Pacific) events, and insolation (exposure to the sun's rays). The result was that farmers at any given southwestern village knew that rain would probably fall somewhere nearby in any given year, even if rain did not fall directly on their own fields, but they could not count on sufficient local water to produce a good harvest. For those who lived along watercourses, all water eventually had to flow along the drainages that fed their fields, so the problem of unpredictable precipitation was greatly alleviated by the use of stream-fed irrigation canals. However, those for whom irrigation was not possible and for whom rainfall farming was the only option had to establish broad social networks and trading partnerships with people in other villages. Allison Rautmann's research in the Colorado Plateau shows that reciprocal social relationships existed between some villages that experienced complementary rainfall patterns and were reasonably close to one another.

The agricultural way of life in the Southwest harmed the environment in several locations. Studies of the wood charcoal from cooking hearths and studies of riverine silt and sand deposits show that farmers of the Mimbres Valley, New Mexico (1000–1150 CE), exhausted supplies of riparian (relating to the banks of watercourses) plants, possibly causing erosion. In other areas archeologists have documented the depletion of local wood supplies and soil nutrient depletion caused by persistent farming.

Late Adaptations and Chaotic Circumstances (1339–1438 CE)

In 1339 CE the climate throughout the Southwest changed in ways that probably escaped the collective memories of generations handed down through oral tradition. Researchers at the University of Arizona Laboratory of Tree Ring Research have established that spatial patterns in annual precipitation broke down catastrophically from 1339 to 1438. This interval of southwestern prehistory featured unprecedented shifts in the geographic centers of population, both on local and greater scales. The ensuing migrations, wars, and social reorganizations are too complicated to enumerate in detail. It must suffice to note that social ties broke down, and some areas within the Southwest that had been continuously occupied for a millennium were abandoned. In the southern Basin and Range there was a population shift into southern Arizona and northern Sonora, with abandonment of the Phoenix Basin. Populations in the Montane Transition Zone decreased as people immigrated to other areas. Colorado Plateau populations shifted eastward, concentrating in three groups centered on the Hopi mesas in northeastern Arizona, the ancestral villages of the Zuni in west-central New Mexico, and Rio Grande pueblos in New Mexico.

Throughout this period of environmental unpredictability and frequent migrations, agriculture remained the primary means of obtaining food. In the fifteenth century migrating Athabaskan peoples arrived from the Northern Plains states, filtered into the Southwest, and concentrated in the Montane Transition Zone. Although the Navajo and Apache peoples acquired agriculture from their pueblo-dwelling neighbors, they made a greater effort at hunting and gathering. Their relationship with established southwestern peoples is perhaps too simply described as "raiding and trading," but in the absence of a detailed exploration of the nature of Athabaskan-Puebloan interaction, that characterization will suffice.

After the arrival of the Navajo and Apache, scarcely a century passed until colonizing Spaniards arrived on the scene in 1540 to fundamentally, radically, and permanently change social, economic, and subsistence relationships throughout the Southwest through the introduction of cattle, horses, sheep, and Iberian (the peninsula on which Spain is located) crops such as wheat.

Michael W. Diehl

Further Reading

Brown, D. E. (Ed.). (1994). *Biotic communities: Southwestern United States and northwestern Mexico*. Salt Lake City: University of Utah Press.

Cordell, L. S. (1997). *Archaeology of the Southwest*. New York: Academic Press.

Dean, J. S. (1996). Demography: Environment and subsistence stress. In J. A. Tainter & B. B. Tainter (Eds.), *Evolving complexity and environmental risk in the prehistoric Southwest* (pp. 173–188). Reading, MA: Santa Fe Institute Studies in the Sciences of Complexity, Addison-Wesley Publishing.

Diehl, M. W., & Waters, J. A. (forthcoming). Aspects of optimization and risk during the early agricultural period in southeastern Arizona. In D. Kennett & B. Winterhalder (Eds.), *Foraging theory and the transition to agriculture*. Washington, DC: Smithsonian Institution Press.

Mabry, J. B. (Ed.). (1998). *Paleoindian and Archaic sites in Arizona*. Tucson, AZ: Center for Desert Archaeology.

Minnis, P. E. (1991). Famine foods of the North American desert borderlands in historical perspective. *Journal of Ethnobiology, 11*, 231–257.

Rautmann, A. E. (1996). Risk, reciprocity, and the operation of social networks. In J. A. Tainter & B. B. Tainter (Eds.), *Evolving complexity and environmental risk in the prehistoric Southwest* (pp. 197–222). Reading, MA: Santa Fe Institute Studies in the Sciences of Complexity, Addison-Wesley Publishing.

Northern Spotted Owl

The northern spotted owl (*Strix occidentalis caurina*), a subspecies of the spotted owl (*Strix occidentalis*), is one of the world's most controversial birds and the center of heated disputes among logging companies, government agencies, and land managers. It closely resembles another North American owl, the barred owl (*Strix varia*), with brown plumage, dark eyes, and a barking call. However, the entire underparts of the northern spotted owl are barred (rather than just the breast), and its call more typically consists of only four to five notes ("Whooo . . . are you, you-all?") rather than the distinctive nine-note call of the barred owl. The northern spotted owl also differs strongly in its habitat preference, distribution, and rarity.

The northern spotted owl primarily inhabits large tracts of old-growth conifer forest (at least one hundred years old) from southwestern British Columbia, Canada, through the mountains of Washington, Oregon, and California in the United States. These undisturbed old-growth conifers, including Douglas fir (Pseudotsuga menziesii) and redwoods (Sequoia sempervirens), provide the required high nest sites (average of 27.3 meters), preferred foods of northern flying squirrels (Glaucomys sabrinus) and wood rats (Neotoma sp.), and elevated roosting sites needed for survival. Additionally, the minimum required area for each breeding pair has been estimated to range between 400 and 1,000 hectares, depending upon the amount of old-growth forest present.

This same old-growth forest has historically been of value to the timber industry in the Pacific Northwest as well, such that many local economies have been built around the resource. So valuable is this resource that by the early 1970s logging companies had reduced the old-growth forest in the region by 85 to 90 percent. Today less than 10 percent of the original old-growth forest remains. Concern for the owl arose from this crossroads of resource depletion and reduction of critical habitat. Unfortunately, the result of this concern was primarily contentious protests and lawsuits (most heated in the 1980s), many of them between environmental groups and loggers whose livelihood was being threatened.

The U.S. Fish and Wildlife Service officially recognized the concern for the northern spotted owl in 1990 when it placed the owl on the federal threatened species list, thereby affording it protection under U.S. federal law (it is listed as endangered in southwestern Canada). Currently a multiagency U.S. management team is evaluating the owl's habitat availability via Earth-imaging satellites and ground surveys, which should soon provide a model of the well-being of the owl over more than 10 million hectares of the Pacific Northwest. Proponents hope that this information, together with appropriate considerations of the local timber economy, will ultimately provide for the protection of the habitat necessary for the owl's survival.

However, despite the best attempts to protect the northern spotted owl, the plan may be partially foiled before completion. The barred owl, the close relative of the spotted owl, has in recent years taken advantage of the changes in habitat and invaded the Pacific Northwest. The barred owl is more aggressive than the northern spotted owl, better able to adapt to changing forests, and occasionally will interbreed with the northern spotted owl. The long-term effects of this mixing will likely remain unclear for many decades, further confusing an already contentious debate over the future of the species.

W. Russ McClain

Further Reading

Dietrich, W. (1992). The final forest. New York: Simon & Schuster.

Johnsgard, P. A. (1988). North American owls. Washington, DC: Smithsonian Institution Press.

Sibley, D. A. (2001). The Sibley guide to bird life and behavior. New York: Chanticleer Press.

Terres, J. K. (1991). The Audubon Society encyclopedia of North American birds. Avenel, NJ: Random House.

Weier, J. (1999). Spotting the spotted owl. Retrieved February 25, 2003, from http://earthobservatory.nasa.gov/cgi-bin/texis/webinator/printa ll?/Study/SpottedOwls

Yaffe, S. L. (1994). The wisdom of the spotted owl: Policy lessons for a new century. Washington, DC: Island Press.

Nuclear Power

When the first nuclear weapons exploded over Japan in 1945, observers all over the world knew that human life had changed in an instant. In the years since, nuclear technology has struggled to define itself as a public good when the public seemed more inclined to view it as an evil. Its proponents argue that electricity made from nuclear reactors has the capability to power the world more cleanly than any other resource can. Opponents are less sure. As the debate rages, nuclear power has become an increasingly important part of world energy.

Beginning as a Bomb

By the late 1930s World War II threatened the globe. Leaders of every nation searched for any edge that would defeat the enemy forces. Scientists in the United States and Germany experimented with nuclear reactions. In Germany leaders felt that such a technology might be a decisive force in the war effort. In reaction, U.S. scientists enlisted the U.S. physicist Albert Einstein to write a letter about their research to President Franklin D. Roosevelt. In his letter Einstein stressed the technology's potential—particularly if it were developed by the enemy. In October 1939 Roosevelt authorized government funding for atomic research.

Eventually science and the military would be linked in a way never before seen. However, first scientists needed to demonstrate the viability of an atomic reaction. Of course, today the concept of force generated by separating atomic particles is fairly well known; however, in 1940 such a concept smacked of science fiction. In 1940 the U.S. physicists Enrico Fermi and Leo Szilard received a government contract to construct a reactor at Columbia University. Other reactor experiments took place in a laboratory under the west stands of Stagg Field at the University of Chicago. In December 1942 Fermi achieved what the scientists considered the first self-sustained nuclear reaction. It was time to take the reaction out of doors, and this process would greatly increase the scope and scale of the experiment.

Under the leadership of General Leslie Groves in February 1943, the U.S. military acquired 202,343 hectares of land near Hanford, Washington. This land was one of three primary locations of Project Trinity, which was assigned portions of the duty to produce useful atomic technology. The coordinated activity of these three locations under the auspices of the U.S. military became a pathbreaking illustration of the planning and strategy that would define many modern corporations. Hanford used water power to separate plutonium and produce the grade necessary for weapons use. Oak Ridge in Tennessee coordinated the production of uranium. These production facilities then fueled the heart of the undertaking, contained in Los Alamos, New Mexico, under the direction of the U.S. physicist J. Robert Oppenheimer.

Oppenheimer supervised the team of nuclear theoreticians who would devise the formulas using atomic reactions within a weapon. Scientists from a variety of fields were involved in this complex theoretical mission. After theories were in place and materials delivered, the project became one of assembling and testing the technology in the form of a bomb. All of this needed to take place on the vast Los Alamos compound under complete secrecy. However, the urgency of war con-

vinced many people that this well-orchestrated, corporate-like enterprise was the best way to save thousands of U.S. lives.

By 1944 World War II had wrought a terrible destruction on the world. The European theater of war would soon close with Germany's surrender. Although Germany's pursuit of atomic weapons technology had fueled the efforts of U.S. scientists, German surrender did not end the U.S. atomic project. The Pacific theater of war remained active, and Japan did not accept offers to surrender. Project Trinity moved forward, using the Japanese cities Hiroshima and Nagasaki as the test laboratories of initial atomic bomb explosions. The U.S. bomber *Enola Gay* released a uranium bomb on Hiroshima on August 6, and the U.S. bomber *Bock's Car* released a plutonium bomb on Nagasaki on August 9. Death tolls vary between 150,000 and 300,000, and most were Japanese civilians. The atomic age, and life with the bomb, had begun.

Atomic Futures

Experiments and tests with nuclear and hydrogen bombs continued for nearly twenty years after World War II. Many of the scientists who worked on the original experiments, however, hoped that the technology could have nonmilitary applications. Oppenheimer eventually felt that the public had changed its attitude toward scientific exploration because of the bomb. "We have made a thing," he said in a 1946 speech, "a most terrible weapon, that has altered abruptly and profoundly the nature of the world . . . a thing that by all the standards of the world we grew up in is an evil thing."

Many of the scientists involved believed that atomic technology required controls unlike those of any previous innovation. Shortly after the bombings a movement began to establish a global board of scientists who would administer the technology with no political affiliation. However, wresting control of this new tool for global influence from the U.S. military proved impossible. The U.S. Atomic Energy Commission (AEC), formed in 1946, placed the U.S. military and governmental authority in control of the weapons technology and other uses to which it might be put. With the "nuclear trump card," the United States catapulted to the top of global leadership.

In the 1950s scientists turned their attention to applying nuclear reaction to peaceful purposes, notably power generation. The reaction is a fairly simple process. Similar to power generators fueled by fossil fuel, nuclear plants use the heat of thermal energy to turn turbines that generate electricity. The thermal energy comes from nuclear fission, which is made when a neutron emitted by a uranium nucleus strikes another uranium nucleus, which emits more neutrons and heat as it breaks apart. If the new neutrons strike other nuclei, chain reactions take place. These chain reactions are the source of nuclear energy, which then heats water to power the turbines.

Soon the AEC seized this sensibility and began plans for "domesticating the atom." It was quite a leap, though, to make the U.S. public comfortable with the most destructive technology ever known. The AEC and other organizations sponsored a barrage of popular articles concerning a future in which roads were created through the use of atomic bombs and radiation was employed to cure cancer.

In the media the atomic future included images of atomic-powered agriculture and automobiles. There were optimistic projections of vast amounts of energy being harnessed, without relying on limited natural resources like coal or oil. For many Americans this new technology meant control of everyday life. For the administration of President Dwight Eisenhower the technology meant expansion of U.S. economic and commercial capabilities.

As the Cold War took shape around nuclear weapons, the Eisenhower administration looked for ways to define a domestic role for nuclear power even as Soviet missiles threatened each American. Project Plowshares grew out of the administration's effort to turn the destructive weapon into a domestic power producer. The list of possible applications was awesome: laser-cut highways passing through mountains; nuclear-powered greenhouses built by federal funds in the Midwest to enhance crop production; and irradiated soils to simplify weed and pest management. Although domestic power production, with massive federal subsidies, would be the long-term product of government effort, the atom could never fully escape its military capabilities. This was most clear when nuclear power plants experienced accidents.

Accidents Fuel Public Doubt

A number of nuclear power plant accidents occurred before the late 1970s, but they went largely unnoticed by the U.S. public. Nuclear power became increasingly popular, even though critics continued to argue issues of safety. In 1979 the United States experienced its first nuclear accident in a residential area outside of Harris-

burg, Pennsylvania. The accident at Three Mile Island (TMI) nuclear power plant entirely altered the landscape of American power generation. Although involving only a relatively minor release of radioactive gas, this accident demonstrated the public's lack of knowledge. Panic ripped through the state, and Harrisburg was partially evacuated.

Of course, the international community took notice of the TMI accident; however, it clearly did not present a grave threat to the world. The world's other superpower had even greater difficulty with its atomic industry, which was plagued by accidents throughout this era. None, however, compared to the Chernobyl meltdown that occurred in Ukraine in 1986. During a test the fuel elements ruptured and resulted in an explosive force of steam that lifted off the cover plate of the reactor, releasing fission products into the atmosphere. A second explosion released burning fuel from the core and created a massive explosion that burned for nine days. It is estimated that the accident released thirty to forty times the radioactivity of the atomic bombs dropped on Hiroshima and Nagasaki. Hundreds of people died in the months after the accident, and hundreds of thousands of Ukrainians and Russians had to abandon entire cities.

The implications of nuclear weapons and nuclear power had already been of great interest to environmental organizations before Chernobyl. After Chernobyl international environmental organizations such as Greenpeace dubbed nuclear power a transborder environmental disaster waiting to happen. Interestingly, even within the environmental movement, nuclear power maintained significant support due to its cleanness. Whereas almost every other method for producing large amounts of electricity creates smoke or other pollution, nuclear power creates only water vapor. Yet, at least in the public's mind, there remained the possibility of atomic explosions.

Growth in the International Market

Although accidents decreased the U.S. domestic interest in nuclear power generation, the international community refused to be so quick to judge the technology. Since the early 1990s nuclear power has become one of the fastest-growing sources of electricity in the world. Today 16 percent of the world's energy derives from nuclear power.

Although only eight nations possess nuclear weapons capability, thirty-one nations have 440 commercial nuclear power reactors. As many as forty more reactors are scheduled to be built over the next few years. Nations that depend on nuclear power for at least one-quarter of their electricity include Belgium, Bulgaria, Hungary, Japan, Lithuania, Slovakia, South Korea, Sweden, Switzerland, Slovenia, and Ukraine.

Currently fewer nuclear power plants are being built than were built during the 1970s and 1980s. However, the newer plants are much more efficient and capable of producing significantly more power. Additionally, nuclear power is being used for needs other than public electricity. In addition to commercial nuclear power plants, there are more than 280 research reactors operating in fifty-six countries, with more under construction. These reactors have many uses, including research and training and the production of medical and industrial isotopes. Reactors are also used for marine propulsion, particularly in submarines. Over 150 ships of many varieties, including submarines, are propelled by more than two hundred nuclear reactors.

Regardless of the use to which it is put, nuclear energy continues to be plagued by its most nagging side effect: Even if the reactor works perfectly for its service lifetime, the nuclear process generates dangerous waste. In fact, reactor wastes from spent fuel rods are believed to remain toxic for fifty thousand years. At present each nuclear nation makes its own arrangements for the waste. U.S. nuclear utilities now store radioactive waste at more than seventy locations while they await the fate of the effort to construct and open a nuclear waste repository inside Nevada's Yucca Mountain.

Internationally, the situation is not much clearer. Opponents in Germany have obstructed nuclear waste convoys, and shipments of plutonium-bearing waste to Japan for reprocessing are often placed under dispute. Some observers have voiced concern that less-developed nations will offer themselves as waste dumps for the more-developed nations. The income from such an arrangement may be too much to turn down for many nations.

In the energy industry many observers continue to believe that nuclear power remains the best hope to power the future. The issues of safety and waste removal need to be dealt with. However, in nations with scarce supplies of energy resources, nuclear power—even with its related concerns—remains the most affordable alternative.

Brian Black

Further Reading

Boyer, P. (1994). *By the bomb's early light*. Chapel Hill: University of North Carolina Press.

Brennan, T. J., Palmer, K. L., Kopp, R. J., Krupnick, A. J., Stagliano, V., & Burtraw, D. (1996). *A shock to the system—restructuring America's electricity industry*. Washington, DC: Resources for the Future.

Brower, M. (1992). *Cool energy: Renewable solutions to environmental problems* (Rev. ed.). Cambridge, MA: MIT Press.

Cantelon, P., & Williams, R. C. (1982). *Crisis contained: Department of Energy at Three Mile Island*. Carbondale: Southern Illinois University Press.

Darst, R. G. (2001). *Smokestack diplomacy: Cooperation and conflict in East-West environmental politics*. Cambridge, MA: MIT Press.

Erikson, K. (1994). *A new species of trouble—the human experience of modern disasters*. New York: W. W. Norton.

Garwin, R. L., & Charpak, G. (2001). *Megawatts and megatons: A turning point in the nuclear age*. New York: Knopf.

Hampton, W. (2001). *Meltdown: A race against nuclear disaster at Three Mile Island: A reporter's story*. Cambridge, MA: Candlewick Press.

Hughes, T. P. (1983). *Networks of power: Electrification in Western society, 1880–1930*. Baltimore: Johns Hopkins University Press.

Hughes, T. P. (1989). *American genesis*. New York: Penguin Books.

Josephson, P. R. (2000). *Red atom: Russia's nuclear power program from Stalin to today*. New York: W. H. Freeman.

May, E. R. (1993). *American Cold War strategy*. Boston: Bedford Books.

May, E. T. (1988). *Homeward bound*. New York: Basic Books.

McNeill, J. R. (2000). *Something new under the sun: An environmental history of the twentieth-century world*. New York: W. W. Norton.

Melosi, M. V. (1985). *Coping with abundance: Energy and environment in industrial America*. New York: Alfred A. Knopf.

Moorhouse, J. C. (Ed.). (1986). *Electric power: Deregulation and the public interest*. San Francisco: Pacific Research Institute for Public Policy.

Nye, D. E. (1990). *Electrifying America: Social meanings of a new technology*. Cambridge, MA: MIT Press.

Poole, R. W., Jr. (Ed.). (1985). *Unnatural monopolies: The case for deregulating public utilities*. Lexington, MA: Lexington Books.

Smil, V. (1988). *Energy in China's modernization: Advances and limitations*. Armonk, NY: M. E. Sharpe.

Smil, V. (1994). *Energy in world history*. Boulder, CO: West-view Press.

Weiner, D. R. (1988). *Models of nature: Ecology, conservation, and cultural revolution in Soviet Russia*. Bloomington: Indiana University Press.

Nuclear Weapons and Testing

The development of nuclear fission had a significant impact on global geopolitics and environmental consciousness in the post-1945 period. With international tensions focused on the manufacture and deployment of nuclear weapons, the atomic bomb provided a technological framework for Cold War hostilities. During the 1950s radioactive fallout from nuclear tests dispersed throughout the biosphere (the part of the world in which life can exist), revealing for the first time the fragility of the planet to human interference. For U.S. ecologists such as Rachel Carson and Barry Commoner, the destructive power of the atomic bomb provided a symbol of human arrogance toward nature, an example of technology run amok. Invisible, human-made, and highly toxic, with the ability to affect organic matter on a molecular level, radioactive fallout—like pesticides—embodied a modern environmental threat to the Earth.

"Brighter than a Thousand Suns"

Under the auspices of the Manhattan Engineer District—a covert U.S. government undertaking—an international cadre of scientists detonated the world's first nuclear weapon at a remote location near Alamogordo, New Mexico, on 16 July 1945. Directed by the acclaimed U.S. physicist J. Robert Oppenheimer and overseen by U.S. General Leslie R. Groves, the Manhattan Project met its founding mission: to deliver an operational nuclear device before Nazi Germany could attain nuclear capability. Groves oversaw the creation of a vast military-industrial complex, including the secret cities of Los Alamos, New Mexico; Oak Ridge, Tennessee; and Hanford, Washington. Delayed by an unforeseen thunderstorm, the Trinity test began at 5:29:45 A.M. On observing the gigantic mushroom cloud of ra-

dioactive vapor drifting upward into the sky, Oppenheimer quoted the Hindu sacred text, *Bhagavad-Gita*: "I am become death, the shatterer of worlds." He also described the light of the blast as "brighter than a thousand suns." The invention of the atomic bomb was commonly equated with the attainment of a new level of mastery over nature.

On 6 August 1945, a U.S. Army Air Corps B-29 bomber dropped the second nuclear bomb, nicknamed "Little Boy," on the Japanese city of Hiroshima in an attempt to swiftly bring about the end of World War II. On 9 August 1945, a similar bomb, nicknamed "Fat Man," exploded over Nagasaki. Japan surrendered five days later. By the end of 1946, 140,000 had died as a result of the bombing of Hiroshima, with 70,000 deaths in Nagasaki. Both cities suffered extensive damage from the initial blast wave and from subsequent fires.

Atomic Testing in the 1950s

Large-scale nuclear testing in the 1950s reflected Cold War rivalries. Only gradually came recognition of the environmental and humanitarian implications of such testing. The Soviet Union successfully detonated its first nuclear device at the Semipalatinsk test site in Kazakhstan on 29 August 1949. Semipalatinsk served, as did Novaya Zemlya in the Arctic Ocean, as a center for Soviet testing, with 456 and 130 detonations at these two sites (of a total of 715 tests). Environmental concerns remained of secondary importance to concerns of national defense. Military observers rarely used respirators. Soldiers searched highly radioactive debris for dosimeters and mementos. Residents of towns closest to the proving grounds received scant warnings of impending danger. In an attempt to catch up with developments in the United States, the Russian Ministry of Atomic Energy (Minatom) accelerated its testing program. The Soviets detonated their largest nuclear device—a 50-megaton bomb—over Novaya Zemlya on 30 October 1961.

In the United States the Atomic Energy Commission (AEC) acquired the Nevada Proving Ground for testing purposes in 1951. Originally a 906-square-kilometer stretch of desert, the proving ground (from 1955 onward known as the "Nevada Test Site" [NTS]) encompassed 3,500 square kilometers by 1967, making it larger than the state of Rhode Island. Conceptions of the arid American West as an open, remote wasteland

The Horror of Nuclear War

Women are sleeping out in Whitehall: "Why don't you go home?" We are homeless.

Our homes have been shattered

by cruise missiles, by Tornados, by B52s. "Why don't you go get a job?'

These palaces in Whitehall

have usurped our lives.

Women are sleeping in Bagdad;

they slept out in Tieneman Sq.

In Sofia, in Bucharest, even in Moscow's Red Sq.;

they are presently sleeping out

before the parliament buildings in Vilniers

because our homes, our common hme,

our cities, our civilization

has disintegrated.

So we must sleep and dream

in the woods & in the streets;

look past the lamplight & the stars

and here, in the open, lay hand on hand,

stone on stone, brick on brick,

to build the new palaces

of our new home.

Source: "Elizabeth." (1991, Spring). "The Peace Picket in Whitehall." *Greenham Common Newsletter*, p. 19.

suited nuclear testing purposes. On 27 January 1951, the AEC commenced its first series of atmospheric nuclear tests at the NTS. From October 1951, troops engaged in combat maneuvers following nuclear detonations, taking sorties close to ground zero. Scientists conducted experiments to measure the impact of blasts on military equipment and penned pigs in the path of shock waves to assess radiation burns. The destruction of "doomtowns"—makeshift houses occupied by mannequins—gave some indication of the danger posed by nuclear war to communities. The ability of nuclear weapons to fundamentally transform landscapes also led to experiments into their peaceful application. Project Plowshare posited the idea of using nuclear explosives to irrigate deserts, forge harbors, and even carve a new Panama Canal. In 1962 a 104-kiloton device created a crater 97 meters deep and 400 meters in diameter at the NTS. However, Project Plowshare met with criticism for its insensitivity to issues of environmental contamination and was abandoned.

The AEC also used the western Pacific Ocean for testing in the late 1940s and early 1950s. In March 1954 a hydrogen bomb code-named "Bravo" was detonated at Bikini Atoll. Resulting radioactive debris blew onto the Marshall Islands, causing nausea, burns, and hair loss among residents. The crew members of a Japanese trawler, the *Lucky Dragon*, who were searching for fish in the region, also suffered radiation sickness. Fish stocks taken to Japan were found to be radioactive.

As radioactive rain fell over New York State and scientists discovered traces of the carcinogen strontium 90 in milk, concern grew over the environmental risks of testing. In 1958 the U.S. ecologist Barry Commoner helped form the St. Louis Committee for Nuclear Information with the hope of alerting the public to the dangers of radioactive contamination. Americans gradually became more familiar with the concept of nuclear fallout thanks to the efforts of concerned scientists and education programs. In schools, the affable Bert the Turtle instructed children to "duck and cover" in case

Operation Upshot/Knothole testing included this firing of HARRY, a 32 kiloton weapons-related device, from a tower on 19 May 1953 at the Nevada Test Site. COURTESY U.S. DEPARTMENT OF ENERGY.

The Nuclear Threat and Environmental Doomsday

The threat posed by atomic energy helped crystallize environmental consciousness in the 1960s by demonstrating the delicate ecological connections binding the earth. The invisible and all-encompassing nature of radioactive fallout revealed the planet as an organism incredibly vulnerable to human activity and one in need of protection. In her seminal work, *Silent Spring* (1962), Rachel Carson drew on the analogy of a town hit by nuclear fallout to expose the dangers of widespread pesticide use, and Paul Ehrlich's *The Population Bomb* (1969) drew on the imagery of the atomic bomb to suggest ecological collapse from overpopulation. Scientific findings in the 1970s—such as those contained in the National Academy of Sciences report "On the Worldwide Effects of Multiple Nuclear Weapon Detonations" (1975)—suggested that nuclear weapons pose a threat not only to human life and civilization, but also to the long-term integrity of the global ecosystem. Experts in Europe and North America argued that a conflict involving repeated use of nuclear warheads would disperse radioactive isotopes throughout the atmosphere and lead to the partial destruction of the ozone layer.

With radioactivity threatening to bring an environmental doomsday, citizens began to explore social justice concerns. Plagued by cancers and genetic defects, families affected by the atomic tests of the 1950s (most often military veterans and local communities) demanded compensation from national authorities for their treatment as atomic guinea pigs. Meanwhile, a growing cadre of environmental activists protested the placement of nuclear waste on Native American lands, citing environmental racism. From uranium mining to weapons testing, the nuclear fuel cycle became increasingly criticized for its ecological costs. In 1971 direct action campaigners staged a protest off the Aleutian island of Amchitka, at once canceling the scheduled U.S. nuclear test and ushering in the birth of the Greenpeace environmental movement.

Nuclear Winter, Freeze, and the Second Cold War

During the late 1970s and early 1980s nuclear tensions heightened, and huge increases occurred in defense spending on atomic weaponry. The "second cold war" was characterized by U.S. President Ronald Reagan's hard-line stance toward communism, the Soviet inva-

of nuclear attack. Deteriorating U.S.-Soviet relations raised the specter of nuclear war and spurred a boom in sales of fallout bunkers. Meanwhile, popular B-movies such as *Them!* framed the nuclear threat in terms of mutation and unnaturalness, predicting that radiation would spawn a phantasmagoria of monsters.

Despite the *Lucky Dragon* incident, the Pacific remained a center for experimentation for the world's nuclear powers. Britain conducted tests off the coast of Australia and at Christmas Island between 1952 and 1958. France relocated its nuclear program to Polynesia after an Algerian test spread fallout across the Iberian Peninsula in 1960. The proliferation of tests, coupled with rising concern over environmental effects, led to the signing of the Partial (Limited) Nuclear Test Ban Treaty by representatives of the United States, the Soviet Union, and Britain in Moscow on 5 August 1963. The treaty prohibited nuclear tests in water, the atmosphere, and in outer space due to the danger of radioactive fallout moving beyond sovereign boundaries. Nations responded by moving tests underground.

sion of Afghanistan, the failure of detente, and the advent of new nuclear technology, namely SS20 and Cruise missiles, the B-1 bomber, and the neutron bomb.

The growing likelihood of war spurred protests in Europe and the United States against nuclear armaments. In the United Kingdom, 141 local councils created nuclear free zones that banned the manufacture, use, or deployment of atomic weapons within their confines. In August 1981 a group of women established a peace camp outside Greenham Common Air Force Base in Berkshire to oppose the installation of Cruise missiles. The Campaign for Nuclear Disarmament (CND) experienced a rapid rise in membership (reaching ninety thousand by 1984). In the United States citizen protest galvanized around the idea of the nuclear weapons freeze, a project sponsored by groups including the Committee for a Sane Nuclear Policy (SANE), Friends of the Earth, and American Baptist churches. A 12 June 1982 rally organized by Mobilization for Survival in New York City attracted 1 million people.

Books and movies depicting nuclear holocaust heightened public fears. Edward Thompson's *Protest and Survive* (1980) booklet criticized civil defense initiatives in Britain, and in the U.S., Jonathan Schell's *The Fate of the Earth* (1982) and Helen Caldicott's *Nuclear Madness: What You Can Do!* (1980) highlighted nuclear war as a paramount ecological concern. Movies such as *The Day After* (1983) and *Threads* (1984) detailed communities struggling with the onset of nuclear war and its aftermath of social decay and environmental contamination. The scientific community also explored postnuclear scenarios. Working with information gleaned from the *Mariner 9* mission to Mars (1971) as well as the eruption of Mount St. Helens volcano (1980), scientists developed the idea of nuclear winter. Envisaging a 5–15° C drop in temperature and an 80 percent reduction in solar energy for several months after an atomic war (a product of the huge quantities of dust sucked up into the atmosphere), scientists postulated the possible extinction of life on Earth. According to the "TTAPS Report" (named after the initials of its authors, beginning with scientist Richard Turco and ending with astronomer Carl Sagan), nuclear winter could be triggered by a 100-megaton exchange (1 percent of the global nuclear stockpile at that time). In October 1983 thirty-one citizen groups, including the Sierra Club, sponsored a conference in Washington, D.C., entitled "The World after Nuclear War" hosted by Paul Ehrlich and Carl Sagan.

End of the Cold War, Nuclear Proliferation, and Rogue States

The reforms inaugurated by Soviet premier Mikhail Gorbachev and the subsequent ending of the Cold War in the late 1980s dramatically reduced nuclear tensions between East and West. The superpowers agreed to notable advances in arms limitation. The Intermediate Range Nuclear Forces (INF) treaty (1987) banned all intermediate ballistic and cruise missiles, and the Strategic Arms Reduction Treaty (START I, 1991) limited each side's strategic nuclear weapons. In the 1990s negotiations resumed toward a comprehensive test ban treaty, a process backed by the United Nations General Assembly in December 1993. Although progress stalled—notably because of French testing in the South Pacific (1995), a move widely condemned by environmental groups—the original five nuclear powers (United States, Russia, France, Britain, and China) signed the Comprehensive Test Ban Treaty on 24 September 1996.

Dealing with the environmental consequences of nuclear technology remained a significant issue at the beginning of the twenty-first century. Accidents at nuclear installations such as Windscale, Britain (1957), Three Mile Island, Pennsylvania (1979), and Chernobyl, Ukraine (1986), attested to the risks associated with developing peaceful nuclear energy. Weapons testing and decommissioning engendered similar risks. In May 2002 the Russian premier Vladimir Putin and the U.S. President George W. Bush agreed to reduce numbers of operationally deployed weapons to between 1,700 and 2,200 by 2012. At the peak of the Cold War, the U.S. arsenal contained more than thirty thousand warheads, and the Soviet Union had forty-five thousand. These vast stockpiles of nuclear materials required careful monitoring and safe disposal. In the former Soviet Union, more than seventy ill-maintained nuclear submarines lay rusting off the Kola Peninsula awaiting decommissioning. The sinking of the *Kursk* nuclear submarine in the Barents Sea in August 2000—killing 118 crew members and threatening to contaminate local marine ecology with plutonium—was seen as symptomatic of the long-term dangers posed by Russia's ailing nuclear fleet.

Nuclear proliferation became a major concern to the international community. India exploded a 2–5-kiloton device, code-named "Smiling Buddha," at Pokharan Test Site in the Rajasthan Desert on 18 May 1974. In May 1998 another three tests were undertaken, corresponding with detonation of the first atomic devices by neighbor and adversary Pakistan. Strategic analysts emphasized the danger of theft or sale of nuclear materials from the former Soviet Union to "rogue states," while U.N. inspectors continued to demand access to military facilities in North Korea and Iraq to determine their nuclear capabilities. In response to the threat posed by terrorism, in 2002 the Bush administration made clear its desire to modernize and update the U.S. nuclear arsenal to cope with new, mobile targets.

Interpreting the Nuclear Age

Since 1953 members of the public have visited the Trinity test site, the original ground zero in New Mexico, for glimpses of Armageddon in the twisted structures and desert craters of the region. Hiroshima Peace Park has similarly provided somber reflection on the social and ecological costs of atomic weaponry. The nuclear age brought unrivaled environmental risks. At the same time, secret nuclear installations of the Cold War became de facto wildlife sanctuaries, with restrictions on public access and vast areas of untamed land providing protection for rare species of flora and fauna. On 8 June 2000, President Bill Clinton created Hanford Reach Historical and Ecological National Monument in Washington State, preserving a rare shrub-steppe ecosystem on the site of the former nuclear facility. That coyotes and bald eagles have been seen wandering test ranges testifies to the complexity of the nuclear age and its environmental legacy.

John Wills

Further Reading

Ball, H. (1986). *Justice downwind: America's atomic testing program in the 1950s*. New York: Oxford University Press.

Boyer, P. (1985). *By the bomb's early light: American thought and culture at the dawn of the atomic age*. Chapel Hill: University of North Carolina Press.

Caldicott, H. (1980). *Nuclear madness: What you can do!* New York: Bantam.

Delgado, J. (1999). *Ghost fleet: The sunken ships of Bikini Atoll*. Honolulu: University of Hawaii Press.

Divine, R. A. (1978). *Blowing on the wind: The nuclear test ban debate, 1954–1960*. New York: Oxford University Press.

Ehrlich, P., Sagan, C., Kennedy, D., & Roberts, W. O. (1984). *The cold and the dark: The world after nuclear war*. New York: W. W. Norton.

Feshbach, M., & Friendly, A., Jr. (1992). *Ecocide in the USSR: Health and nature under siege*. London: Aurum Press.

Fradkin, P. L. (1989). *Fallout*. Tucson: University of Arizona Press.

Gallagher, C. (1993). *American ground zero: The secret nuclear war*. Cambridge, MA: MIT Press.

Hevly, B., & Findlay, J. M. (Eds.). (1998). *The atomic West*. Seattle: University of Washington Press.

Kuletz, V. (1998). *The tainted desert: Environmental ruin in the American West*. New York: Routledge.

Rhodes, R. (1995). *The making of the atomic bomb*. New York: Touchstone Books.

Schell, J. (1982). *The fate of the earth*. New York: Alfred A. Knopf.

Solnit, R. (1994). *Savage dreams: A journey into the landscape wars of the American West*. New York: Random House.

Titus, A. C. (1986). *Bombs in the backyard: Atomic testing and American politics*. Reno: University of Nevada Press.

Veldman, M. (1994). *Fantasy, the bomb and the greening of Britain: Romantic protest, 1945–80*. Cambridge, UK: Cambridge University Press.

Weart, S. (1988). *Nuclear fear: A history of images*. Cambridge, MA: Harvard University Press.

Nutrition and Diet

Human beings require forty to fifty nutrients to survive and are remarkably omnivorous in design and capable of occupying—and obtaining necessary nutrients from—a wide range of ecological niches. Human design, however, begins with a series of largely irreversible limitations related to primate ancestry in rain forest environments. Having evolved in an environment with abundant vitamin C, humans are incapable of synthesizing their own. Because human ancestors evolved in an environment rich in steady sources of water, humans are severely limited in their ability to imbibe or store water. Having evolved in an environment relatively poor in sources of sodium, humans crave and store salt.

In addition, for most of human evolution, human ancestors inhabited environments and adopted diets relatively lacking free sugars, although typically rich and varied in other nutrients. Calories, rather than other nutrient needs, were limiting factors in the diet. As a result of both sensory perception (craving) and

The Buffalo Hunt

The following account of the traditional Blood Indian buffalo hunt was written by Mike Mountain Horse, a Blood Indian, who relied on information provided by his father and uncles about tribal life in the late nineteenth and early twentieth centuries. This hunting practice is in accord with "Optimal Foraging Theory" which posits that humans choose first to obtain animal meat for their diet.

There were two ways adopted by the Indian in despatching the buffalo. When following the first method, success depended upon numerical strength. This required the engaging of a large number of young men to participate in the hunt, which took place in the vicinity of one of the hundreds of natural "buffalo pounds" scattered throughout western Canada. These pounds were large, deep depressions in the ground at the foot of a steep bank. A runway or lane, cone-shaped, was constructed first, with large boulders on the flat at the top, in line with the depression at the bottom of the hill. These large rocks were placed at certain distances apart; behind each boulder a warrior concealed himself, armed with a robe. Mounted men previously detailed by the chief drove in a large herd of buffalo. As soon as the herd approached the first two boulders farthest from the bank, a member of the mounted warriors covered himself and his mount with a large buffalo hide and immediately galloped his horse to the head of the herd, for the purpose of decoying them through the lane of boulders. As the herd passed each boulder, the warriors crouching behind these huge rocks jumped to their feet and began shouting and yelling, accompanying this by waving their robes vigorously and extending their efforts by assisting the mounted men in driving the buffalo towards their doom, which was accomplished when they fell off the bank into the pound. Some of the animals were killed outright from the effects of the fall while others suffered broken legs and other injuries. The uninjured buffalo went round and round the inside of the pound while the warriors stood on the edge and shot them down with their arrows.

In this hazardous manner the primitive Indian acquired his supply of fresh meat which was the chief item on his menu.

Source: Mountain Horse, Mike. (1979) *My People, the Bloods*. Calgary; Canada: Glenbow-Alberta Institute; Blood Tribal Council, pp. 85–87.

what was once real need, human dietary choices and food-getting strategies have largely been driven by the search for calories. At the same time human bodies crave and monitor their intake of few other resources, making nutrient quality of food a secondary concern.

The need to obtain sufficient calories for ever-increasing populations from ever-diminishing exploitable areas resulted in the need for human beings to colonize habitats that were less and less favorable, including colder and drier regions and secondary niches among richer environments. Eventually, however, that strategy ran up against increasing circumscription by natural barriers and the competition of other populations. Population growth combined with circumscription (complicated by natural and cultural modification of existing environments) resulted in a long series of steps in which people increasingly modified their environment to provide increased calories in limited space, often at the expense of other nutrients.

Even before the evolution of modern human beings, refuse and fecal dumps surrounding habitations tended to bring favored plant (and animal) species into proximity of proto-human groups. The smallest and simplest human groups used fire to open landscapes for new growth of preferred vegetable foods and an increase in animal prey populations. Fires started by people may have been responsible for far-reaching conversion of once more-forested environments to open savanna. Human hunters may also have been responsible in whole or in part (along with post-Pleistocene epoch climate changes) for eliminating large game that had theretofore provided major contributions to human diets. Hunter-gatherers are also known to have undertaken a series of less-drastic environmental modifications, such as reseeding exploited resources, fertilizing and protecting them from competition (i.e., weeding), and even irrigating specific locations on a small scale.

The process of economic evolution has been described as the "intensification" of resource exploitation: increasing investment in preparation and modification of natural environments to permit more food to be gathered and ultimately grown on each unit of land but resulting also in the ultimate use of foods that are less and less desirable, a decline in food variety, and therefore a decline in the availability of other nutrients. The intensification took two forms, largely in sequence.

Broad-Spectrum Revolution

First, early hunter-gatherers, relying on large game (for perhaps 40 percent of their diets) and select vegetable resources, gradually broadened the spectrum of resources that they were willing to eat (the so-called broad-spectrum revolution); people ate a variety of more-plentiful but low-priority food that was harder to get and less desirable in terms of the concentration and variety of nutrients it offered. This broadening spectrum of exploitation probably added little to dietary quality because the foods were often of lower quality than those they replaced; and it probably resulted in a decline in the reliability of resources because resources once reserved for emergencies became staples instead.

Second, people increasingly focused on the intensive exploitation, ultimate domestication (farming), and storage of resources, typically cereals and root crops selected for their abilities to provide the most calories per unit of land, not for their palatability or their quality as foods. Farmed foods are commonly of lower quality than foraged ones, and storage itself tends to reduce the availability of vitamins.

Farming techniques involve concentration of one species in a particular region, the increased modification of land to support the increased density of the particular crop, the dispersal of efficiently produced crops to new regions, and the displacement of indigenous wild plants. Farming and associated storage and sedentism (a settled lifestyle) are often thought to increase the reliability of food supplies through human control. However, increased concentration of individual species, the extension of those species beyond their normal ranges, and the necessity of remaining sedentary through the growth, harvest, and storage cycle, even in the event of poor harvests, may actually have made food supplies less reliable.

The sequence, although increasing efficiency in terms of calories produced per unit of land, seems to have resulted in the declining efficiency of labor (calories produced per hour of work). Estimates of relative efficiency come from an area of study called "optimal foraging theory" (OFT). OFT argues that resources can be ranked in terms of caloric production per unit of labor. OFT also argues that hunter-gatherers should and generally do follow the sequence of ranking, taking high-ranked resources (i.e., calorie efficient in terms of labor) before taking those of lower rank and turning to the latter only as high-rank resources are depleted. (For a variety of reasons, individual groups may not always follow these rankings; but it is quite clear that on average changing worldwide patterns of human consumption in the last twenty thousand or more years conform to the predictions quite nicely.) People are seeing a sequence of declining labor efficiency through time.

Large game (according to many studies in different parts of the world) is by far the most efficiently exploited wild resource as long as it is available. Small game, fish (unless caught with large nets or weirs), shellfish, and nuts associated with a broadening spectrum of resource use are of lower rank. Small-seeded plants such as grasses (including the ancestors of the major modern staples such as wheat and barley) are among the lowest-ranked—least labor-efficient—resources. Moreover, domestication adds little if any efficiency to their exploitation.

Large-game hunting generally appears to have been more efficient than most prehistoric modes of farming. The implication is that the farming of such crops resulted not from the invention of farming techniques but from the declining availability of preferred resources.

The history of agriculture can, to a large extent, be visualized as an interaction between population density, technology, and increased intensity of farming, including the use of marginal lands, the increasing frequency of cropping on land already farmed, and the accumulation of new tools and techniques. In its most extensive forms (slash and burn), agriculture involves a ratio of as many as twenty-five or more years of fallow for each year of crop harvest (a 25–30:1 ratio), and therefore works only where population densities are low. The crop is produced largely by burning forest and planting in the ashes. The extended fallow period provides for significant regrowth of secondary if not primary forest before trees are burned again and seeds planted with no further fertilization, the only necessary tool being a digging stick. A smaller fallow crop ratio, for example, 10–15:1, supporting somewhat larger populations, permits natural recycling to produce only brush that provides less ash when burned, presents more difficult clearing problems, and requires hoeing and supplementary fertilization. A third type of farming involving ratios of only 3–4:1 permits only grasses to regrow, so that burning provides little fertilizer and does little to clear dense grass roots. Plowing and additional fertilizing become necessary. More-intensive systems associated with high population densities involve cropping three years in four (a 1:3 ratio), requiring extensive tilling or plowing and significant fertilizing. Multicropping (planting several crops per year without fallow) typically relies on irrigation water to support and fertilize plants.

Damage from Agriculture

The degree to which this sequence of declining fallow/ crop ratios represents a historical sequence, as opposed to mere use of different environmental potentials, is debated. What is clear is that significant agriculture involves massive inputs of labor well in advance of any rewards for that labor.

Extensive systems of agriculture can damage land if population density forces people into fallow/crop ratios that the soil cannot tolerate, especially if people do not understand the increasing inputs involved. It is also clear that irrigation has, over long periods of time, resulted in the elimination of farming and sometimes of *all* plant growth in some areas because of the build-up of salt in soil from evaporation. Increasing exploitation of fossil fuels and chemical fertilizers or the expansion of irrigation systems beyond the capacity of freshwater supplies may do the same in the long run.

The processes of agricultural intensification were once theorized largely as a series of inventions (hoe, plow) permitting more sophisticated and more efficient use of resources. The alternate theory suggests that the behavioral-ecological succession probably resulted from increasing demand, motivating the development of technology to increase supply, rather than the other way around. The question of the primacy of population growth or technological innovation as the major force for change depends on resolution of a disputed question: What was the relative efficiency of long-fallow and short-fallow agriculture, and hence would the succession have been desirable?

What is clear, however, is that the intensification first of hunting and gathering and then of farming appears to have resulted in a decline in the quality of human nutrition. This decline can be documented in several ways: by the known ecology and nutritional value of certain foods, by observations of the diets of various populations, by medical examination of living individuals, and by paleopathology (observation of the comparative frequency of certain pathologies in human skeletons from different times). Modern hunter-gatherer diets, largely deprived of large game, still match affluent Western diets in consumption of meat protein and far exceed modern Third World diets in meat consumption. Modern hunter-gatherers are generally far better nourished in other respects (vitamins, minerals) than contemporary small-scale farmers and modern Third World populations. Compared to modern hunter-gatherers, farmers—particularly peasants in the modern Third World—widely display increased signs of poor nutrition as a consequence of overdependence on various cereals and root crops associated with declining dietary variety because all of the major crops provide incomplete nutrition. Kwashiorkor (malnutrition) and marasmus (chronic undernourishment), as well as vitamin deficiencies, occur far more frequently among farmers than among remnant hunter-gatherers in the modern world. (Because their diets are lean, hunter-gatherers also avoid the problems of overconsumption of fats, calories, and salt that plague modern affluent populations and result in conditions such as obesity, diabetes, and high blood pressure, all unheard of among "primitives.")

The problem is compounded by an increasing load of parasites accompanying sedentism, storage, domestication of animals, and increased population density of both animals and people. For example, hookworm, a clearly density- and sedentism-dependent parasite, is a major cause of blood and iron loss; and tapeworms associated with animal domesticates also rob the body of nutrients. Domestic animals are also blamed for the appearance of most of the major modern plagues such as tuberculosis and many others that can cause major drains on nutrition.

Iron Deficiencies

The skeletons of prehistoric hunter-gatherers do show occasional signs of iron deficiency and some vitamin deficiencies, but subsequent populations almost always show significant declines in nutritional status. The overall (although irregular) tendency in human evolution displayed by skeletons since the emergence of *Homo sapiens* has been for stature to *decline* during the broad-spectrum revolution and the adoption in farming and during much of the rest of history until the last 150 years or so. In fact, the shortest populations in human history have lived in the last few centuries and in the modern world. Signs of iron deficiency and other dietary deficiencies increase dramatically with the origins of agriculture. Signs of increasing in-utero and juvenile malnutrition include delayed juvenile growth and juvenile osteoporosis.

Signs of infection, including periostitis, osteitis, and osteomyelitis as well as specific infections such as yaws/syphilis and tuberculosis, also increase through time. Specific episodes of stress recorded in teeth show an increasing frequency with farming, which is consistent with a decline, not an improvement, in the reliability of food supplies.

The evolution of state-level societies (usually called "civilizations"—a vague reference to "progress"—but, in fact, better defined by cities, specialists, class stratification, extensive trade, limited or exclusive ownership of land or other major resources, and government control by force) poses additional nutritional problems. In fact, the poor of civilized societies display a higher level of undernutrition or malnutrition than do earlier or less-complex societies. Trade associated with civilizations has resulted in the dissemination of staple crops from their centers of origin around the world (corn, wheat, barley, potatoes, and others) to the benefit of recipient populations. On the other hand, trade and transport of food have often resulted in taking nutrients from areas where they are needed. They have also resulted in processing, reducing bulk and weight in transport but also reducing the content of all nutrients except calories. Moreover, trade itself can be fragile for natural or political reasons.

Areas of the world have seen their local economies distorted by colonial powers or by the need to sell foods on fickle international markets. Countries relying increasingly on specialized crops to sell in order to import food often trade quality for quantity, and they often suffer from poor exchange ratios, contributing to undernutrition and malnutrition. Some countries have seen their land converted from their own subsistence needs to the production and export of beef or other cash crops for consumption in wealthy nations.

Forced Diets

Owners of land can require farm labor or other services and by monopolizing scarce resources can set the values of exchange, usually in their favor. As recently as the twentieth century, for example, sharecroppers in the United States were forced to give labor in exchange for a provided diet consisting almost totally of American corn (maize). Corn is deficient in vitamins, niacin, and the amino acid tryptophan and has unhealthy ratios of other amino acids—and failure to supplement the diet resulted in widespread pellagra. Other dietary diseases such as scurvy, beriberi, night blindness, kwashiorkor, and marasmus have resulted from enforced diets that had few calories, lacked meat, and relied too heavily on other vitamin-deficient staple crops.

Two problems underlie almost all of the nutritional problems of civilization. First, prior to the advent of civilization, increasing population meant increasing demand for food, and the increasing population seemed quite capable of stretching technology and supply to meet its needs. With the appearance of class stratification, the poor, who may have nothing to offer, exert no demand for food (which involves not only need but also something to offer in exchange), and therefore have no effect on supply. The Malthusian (referring to the theories of the English economist Thomas Malthus) vision of the world in which technology is independent of demand and ultimately cannot keep up is a product of civilization. It results actually from a lack of demand or incentive to economic growth. Poor nations and poor individuals simply cannot buy food even if it is available (something that would have been unheard of prior to the advent of civilization).

Second, civilization involves a major change in "entitlements" or rights to food. In pre- or nonstate societies, members of a group are entitled to share available food simply as a function of being living members of a group. No one goes hungry when food is available. However, in modern stratified societies with private property, people do not automatically have a right to share—in fact, the principle of preserving property commonly takes precedence over the right to eat. Entitlement becomes far more tenuous, limited to family or small group sharing, political or religious clout, items to trade, and possession of money.

Entitlements to food have often failed for reasons totally unrelated to food supply. The causes of hunger and famine now are tied not to natural disasters but rather to failures of entitlement. It is not at all clear that civilization has reduced the risk of famine.

The world problem is not a lack of food supplies nor of various nutrients, but rather a lack of demand for food. Demand implies not only need but also ability to pay. If the poor could pay for food, people would discover that the world has plenty.

Mark Cohen

See also Development; Domestication, Animal and Plant; Evolution and Spread of Humans; Population, Human; Sugar and Sugarcane

Further Reading

Boserup, E. (1965). *The conditions of agricultural growth.* Chicago: Aldine.

Cohen, M. N. (1989). *Health and the rise of civilization.* New Haven, CT: Yale University Press.

Dreze, J., & Amartya, S. (1991). *The political economy of hunger.* Oxford, UK: Clarendon Press.

Foster, P. (1992). *The world food problem.* London: Lynne Reiner.

Fried, M. (1967). *The evolution of political society.* New York: Random House.

Goodman, A., Darna, D., & Pelto, G. (2000). *Nutritional anthropology.* London: Mayfield.

Kiple, K., & Ornelas, K. C. (2000). *The Cambridge world history of food.* Cambridge, UK: Cambridge University Press.